Beyond Educational Disadvantage

Edited by

PAUL DOWNES AND ANN LOUISE GILLIGAN

IPA
INSTITUTE OF PUBLIC
ADMINISTRATION
50 Years
CELEBRATING PUBLIC SERVICE
1957 - 2007

First published 2007
by the Institute of Public Administration
57–61 Lansdowne Road
Dublin 4

ISBN 987-1-904541-57-8

British Library cataloguing-in-publication data
A catalogue record for this book is available from the British Library

Cover design by M & J Graphics, Dublin
Typeset in Times New Roman by Carole Lynch, Sligo
Printed in Ireland by Betaprint, Dublin

Cover image by Muriel Brandt (1909–81); *Procession Day*; oil on canvas, 38 x 31 cm;
Courtesy of the Gorry Gallery, Dublin; © The Artist's Estate;
Photo © The National Gallery of Ireland

Ann Louise Gilligan:
To Katherine Zappone, whose love encourages,
empowers and enables.

Paul Downes:
In loving memory of my father, Tony Downes

Contents

Foreword

Áine Hyland

This publication, *Beyond Educational Disadvantage*, is being launched five years after the National Forum on Educational Disadvantage was held in Drumcondra in July 2002, and provides a valuable opportunity to take stock of what has been achieved during that period. In 2002 there was widespread optimism that the time was ripe and that the will existed in Ireland to 'end educational disadvantage' – hence the title of the National Forum, *Ending Disadvantage*. The Programme for Government of June 2002 had contained an explicit commitment to building an inclusive society. It promised to fund early years education and to improve class size for pupils under nine years of age. The National, Economic and Social Forum (NESF) report of March 2002 on Early School Leavers had emphasised that a whole-child approach should be taken to educational disadvantage.

By summer 2002 the National Educational Welfare Board had been set up to implement the NEW Act, 2000, and the National Anti-Poverty Strategy had been published. The government's National Development Plan 2001–2006 had been launched, the RAPID and CLAR areas had been designated and the Statutory Educational Disadvantage Committee had been set up in March 2002 under the terms of Section 32.9 of the 1998 Education Act. Since then, the Irish economic scene has moved forward significantly.

The economic situation of the country in the past few years provided an unparalleled opportunity for the State to ensure that poverty levels would be reduced and to invest in suitable and relevant education for those whom the system had traditionally failed. One might reasonably expect that by now there would be a significant and measurable reduction in the indicators of educational failure and early school leaving in Ireland. This, however, is not the case. Relative standards of literacy and numeracy in schools in disadvantaged areas have actually fallen in recent years. There are still a significant number of young people who fail to transfer from primary to second-level school. There has been no appreciable improvement in retention rates at post-primary level, with 18 per cent of the age cohort failing to sit the Leaving Certificate – essentially the same proportion as in 1993.

There is increasing criticism of the failure of government-funded educational initiatives in the area of educational disadvantage to achieve their intended outcomes – the most recent criticism is contained in the June 2006 Value for Money report of the Comptroller and Auditor General on Educational

Disadvantage Initiatives at Primary Level. The criteria currently being used by the Department of Education and Science (DES) to identify schools for inclusion in the DEIS programme, May 2005, appear to reward failure rather than success. Post-primary schools where pupils perform poorly at Junior Cert, or where pupils drop out of school early, are rewarded by being given additional resources. Schools which, against the odds, retain pupils who are at risk of early school leaving and who help and support them to achieve creditable results in the Junior Certificate and to stay on until Leaving Certificate have lost their disadvantaged status and will, in time, lose the additional resources to which disadvantaged status entitled them.

Many of the above issues are referred to in this publication. There is much new thinking throughout the book and readers will find the proposals and recommendations contained in the different articles both encouraging and helpful as we continue to believe that we can, and indeed must, move beyond educational disadvantage at this point in Irish history.

The authors of these articles are to be commended on their enthusiasm and commitment. The editors are to be especially lauded for their persistence and determination in keeping the issues of poverty and disadvantage on the national agenda. Here's hoping that the next five years will produce positive results.

Áine Hyland
Chairperson, Educational Disadvantage Committee 2002–2005, and former Professor of Education and Vice-President, University College, Cork

Introduction

Paul Downes and Ann Louise Gilligan

The topic addressed in this book has exercised the minds of educators in Ireland over the past forty years. The editors of this collection wish to acknowledge the rich contribution of those who have engaged in the debate thus far and hope to offer new insights, rooted in current theory, as well as research, policy and practice. The title of the book, *Beyond Educational Disadvantage*, provides more than a hint about the content of the text. Each contributor (in a variety of ways) has used a different lens to capture the complexity of the issue under consideration. The composite picture emerging from the complete collection is an image of the possible. In other words, while different authors provide key insights into various aspects of the educational landscape or explore similar parts of that landscape from different angles, each contributor offers a viewpoint that, if attended to, could indeed change our practice, not only in Ireland but also in the international context, into the future.

Those who have worked in education and community development in Ireland and have participated in this system are acutely aware of the stubborn and complex problem that has been designated as 'educational disadvantage'. This jaded metaphor covers a variety of issues which in sum refer to the failure of the system to ensure that each child and adult achieves his or her range of potentials. Over time, the discourse on 'disadvantage' has shifted from 'blaming' victims for their failure, or accusing their family or community as the cause of their problem, to a much more nuanced and informed understanding that an inclusive education system places an imperative on us all to engage with. We are all participants in the creation of the problem and, thus, of the solution, both as individuals, communities, and schools.

Within this book there are many references to the relationship between poverty and educational failure and, inversely, the lack of educational opportunity leading to unemployment and poverty. The face of poverty appears in many places within a school day in an area of high social and economic disadvantage. The findings from a recent piece of research by the Educational Disadvantage Centre, conducted in four primary schools designated as disadvantaged in the Blanchardstown area, indicate that, according to the pupils, 18 per cent were either *often, very often or every day too hungry to do their work in school* (Downes, Maunsell and Ivers, 2006). Friel and Conlon (2004), Combat Poverty Agency (CPA), observe that 'food insecurity and inadequate diet are central to the

xiii

experience of poverty'. Yet these issues have been largely neglected in policy debate on poverty in Ireland.

Few if any educationalists would contest the view that poverty is the foundation and key issue that must be addressed if we are indeed to end educational disadvantage in Ireland today. Yet we are living in an Ireland rife with contradictions. There is a dissonance in the discourse about Irish society at this time. On the one hand, our current economic progress is lauded as we are now one of the richest countries in Europe. On the other, the recent *EU Survey on Income and Living Conditions* (November 2006) describes deprivation in our land where one in five people are at risk of poverty because of their low income thresholds and 7 per cent (almost 300,000 people) experience consistent poverty – going without food, heating and clothing. Women parenting children on their own are in the high-risk category of both varieties of poverty. The Combat Poverty Agency in its research report *Day-in-Day-Out – Understanding the Dynamics of Child Poverty* (May 2006) shows that one in five children live in income poverty for five years or more. The impact of poverty on children's lives has multiple long-term consequences, not least of which is that deprivation corrodes educational equality.

The thesis of this book is clear: in this society of enormous affluence and privilege, ending educational inequalities can be achieved through well thought-out and funded policy interventions. There is no denying such action will require additional expenditure, however, it is worth noting that our Government's contributions to education as a percentage of our Gross National Product (GNP) has fallen over the past ten years. A report from the Organisation for Economic Cooperation and Development (OECD), *Education at a Glance* (2006), verifies that Ireland is almost at the bottom of the international league in terms of investment in education relative to the country's economic wealth.

If the Irish State chooses to make sufficient investment to end educational inequality, the investment could be used to build a more holistic system of education. The 'life-cycle approach' proposed in the new Social Partnership Agreement (*Towards 2016*, 2007) will, if fully resourced, help to deliver the education goals outlined in this book. As with all change, aspiration is not adequate, piecemeal intervention is not productive; rather, what is needed is a coherent, consistent commitment resourced and led by those who are motivated by the imperative that now is the time to vision and shape a new educational landscape and society in Ireland where all people will be within the frame. Stated otherwise – changing the status quo requires a radical systemic change that calls for the cooperation of all. This involves listening to the voices of those who have frequently been placed on the margins in the past and placing them at the centre. Part of this listening process involves a willingness on the part of the Irish State to change the mainstream and not just the supposed margins.

This book falls naturally into six themes, which, while interlinked, call for separate in-depth analysis across a range of disciplines encompassing education, psychology, philosophy, sociology and social policy, among others. The scope of the book deliberately adopts a lifelong learning focus from the cradle to the grave, and thereby examines themes from pre-school, primary and post-primary through to adult and community education. The concluding section seeks to build on previous chapters in order to promote an agenda for a holistic system-level change.

Acknowledgements

We would like to sincerely thank Julie O'Shea, Declan McDonagh and Linda Longmore of the Institute of Public Administration for their kind support with the project throughout, and to thank Ruth Bourke for her extremely helpful comments on the text, as well as the research committee of St Patrick's College, Drumcondra, for their support. We would also like to give special thanks to Valerie McLoughlin, Administrator at the Educational Disadvantage Centre, for her invaluable contribution to bringing this project to fruition. Finally, we would like to thank all those who agreed to contribute to this collection and whose work has enriched the depth and diversity of the final text.

Editors and Contributors

Dr Paul Downes is a lecturer in Educational and Developmental Psychology at St Patrick's College, Drumcondra, directing the Educational Disadvantage Centre there since 2004. He obtained his PhD, Psychology, and Law degrees from Trinity College Dublin, receiving several academic awards including being elected a TCD Scholar of Law through the Foundation Scholarship Exam. Designer of 'Familiscope' Community Based Psychological Service, Ballyfermot, he is a Member of its Board of Directors, and of the Board of Directors of Ana Liffey Drug Project. Currently he is Co-Chairperson of Quality Development of Out of School Services (QDOSS) network association and is the Irish Coordinator for the five-year EU Project 'Towards a lifelong learning society: The contribution of the education system' with twelve other countries. Author of several commissioned research reports on early school leaving, he is published in journals internationally in areas of psychology, education, law, social policy, anthropology and philosophy. Translated into Estonian and Russian, his book *Living with heroin: HIV, Identity and Social Exclusion among the Russian-speaking minorities in Estonia and Latvia* (Legal Information Centre for Human Rights, Estonia, 2003) highlighted a range of concerns subsequently reiterated in EU and international reports and contributed to his nomination and selection for inclusion in the Marquis *Who's Who in the World* (2005, 2006, 2007).

Dr Ann Louise Gilligan holds her MA from L'Institut Catholique, Paris, and her PhD from Boston College, Mass., USA. Appointed to the staff of St Patrick's College in 1976, she has worked in the area of teacher education at undergraduate and post-graduate level for the past thirty years. In 2000 she was requested by the college to establish an Educational Disadvantage Centre that she directed for the first three years. The National Forum, 'Primary Education: Ending Disadvantage', (2002) was one of the significant events during this period. As an expression of her belief that education is the key to the transformation of poverty, Ann Louise co-founded the Shanty Educational Project Ltd, a community education organisation located in Jobstown, West Tallaght, Dublin. Celebrating its twenty-first anniversary this year, An Cosán has 400 adults in year-long education and training programmes and 100 children enjoying early childhood education and care. The organisation employs thirty-six people, many of whom are trained professionals from the local community. In 2001, Ann Louise was invited to chair the National Education Welfare Board, a statutory body charged with implementing the National Education Welfare Act 2000.

Liam Bane worked as an Adult Education Organiser with Co. Dublin VEC 1980–2004. He was responsible for the development of the South County Dublin Adult Education Service including adult literacy provision and the community education programme. He also founded the journal of adult and community education in Ireland, *The Adult Learner*, in 1985 and was editor until 2004.

Vanessa Barrett, BA, BSc, MA Ed Psych., is currently employed as an educational psychologist with the CDVEC psychological service. Her research interests lie in the domains of special educational needs and psychometrics.

Ruth Bourke, BA, MEd (Adult), joined the Targeting Educational Disadvantage Project, Mary Immaculate College (MIC), Limerick, in 2004 where she facilitates two networks of representatives of Delivering Equality of Opportunity in Schools (DEIS) primary schools. Ruth's previous work experience includes coordinating adult and community education in Southill, literacy tutoring and teaching English to asylum seekers and refugees.

Anne Boyle, BA, HDE, MEd, teaches in a Traveller preschool in Galway city and is currently working towards a PhD on parental involvement in Traveller early years education at St Patrick's College Drumcondra.

Dr Audrey Bryan teaches International Development at the School of Education and Lifelong Learning, University College Dublin. She graduated from Columbia University with a PhD in Comparative and International Education, specialising in the sociology of education. Her PhD research examined the discourses of interculturalism and anti-racism as they are articulated and interpreted at national and local levels. She is a member of the Migration and Citizenship Research and Egalitarian World Initiatives, based in UCD.

Dr Deirdre Butler is a faculty member of the Education Department of St Patrick's College, Drumcondra, and a director of the Empowering Minds project. Prior to this, Deirdre worked in primary schools for nearly twenty years. Her many guises included classroom teacher, deputy head, and teacher for the Travelling community. Deirdre's doctoral work was conducted in collaboration with Media Lab Europe under the supervision of Dr Seymour Papert of the MIT Media Laboratory. Her dissertation centres on teacher learning and was entitled 'Self-determined Teacher Learning in a Digital Context: Fundamental Change in Thinking and Practice'. Her passion in life is exploring what being digital in learning can mean; she is interested in how digital technologies could revolutionise learning by challenging us to examine how we learn and to question our assumptions about 'traditional' models of schooling.

Dr Mary C. Byrne is a senior researcher at the National University of Ireland, Galway (NUIG). Following a BA in Psychology and Music (Trinity College, Dublin) and an MA in Health Promotion (NUIG), she joined the Centre for Health Promotion Studies at NUIG in 1999. Her work there included the evaluation of a community-based mental health promotion project between two rural communities on either side of the Northern Ireland border, and a review of the international evidence base on the effectiveness of community- and school-based mental health promotion as part of the global programme on health promotion effectiveness. For her doctoral research she developed and evaluated *Mind Out*, a school-based programme promoting positive mental and emotional health for 15–18 year olds. During this time she was a member of the advisory board for the International Alliance for Child and Adolescent Mental Health in Schools (INTERCAMHS). Now based in the Department of General Practice at NUIG, she is project director of the SPHERE study, a randomised controlled trial of an intervention to improve secondary prevention of heart disease in general practice. She is also the Social, Personal and Health Education lecturer on the Higher Diploma in Education at NUIG.

Mark Candon has been a primary school teacher for sixteen years. He has been principal of St Laurence O'Toole's Senior Boys CBS, North Wall, for the past six years. He graduated with a BEd from Coláiste Mhuire, Marino, in 1989 and completed an MEd at St Patrick's College, Drumcondra, in 2005.

Dr Tracey Connolly is the project manager of a major research and development project on disadvantage in Cork city entitled *Bridging the Gap,* which is based in the Department of Education, (http://bridgingthegap.ucc.ie). Dr Connolly also lectures in education at University College Cork.

Dolores Corcoran and **Thérèse Dooley** are lecturers in mathematics education in St Patrick's College, Drumcondra. Both have several years' experience of primary teaching. Dolores is currently conducting PhD research on the effect of teacher knowledge on mathematics teaching. The focus of Thérèse's doctoral research is creativity in primary school mathematics. Dolores and Thérèse are members of the International Group for the Psychology of Mathematics Education and of the British Society for Research into Learning Mathematics.

Dr Merike Darmody works in the Economic and Social Research Institute, Ireland. Her research lies mainly in the area of education. Her more recent work includes a study on social and living conditions of higher education students and a longitudinal study on students' schooling experiences in post-primary education. Merike's research interests include educational inequality, intercultural education and comparative education. Her PhD, 'Coping with Change: Comparative Perspectives on School Transition in Ireland and Estonia', is from NUI (UCD), Department of Education and Lifelong Learning.

Louise Derman-Sparks is a Professor Emeritus at Pacific Oaks College in Pasadena, California, USA. She is nationally and internationally known for her work on anti-bias education with children and adults, writing and speaking widely on these topics. She also served on the governing board of the National Association for the Education of Young Children.

Dr Philomena Donnelly is a lecturer in early childhood education in St Patrick's College, Drumcondra. Her research interests include young children's philosophical thinking, diversity in early years classes in primary school and young children's social identity.

The late **Tony Downes** was a former chair of the National Federation of Social Service Councils, of the National Adult Literacy Agency (NALA) and of the Grange-Kildonagh Social Services Council. A former Adult Education Organiser for the Blanchardstown and North West County Dublin area, he subsequently taught modules on adult education at Kimmage Manor and UCD. His MA thesis in Adult and Community Education from NUI Maynooth was entitled 'Pedagogy of the Processed'.

Gerard Farrelly is a primary school teacher in a designated disadvantaged school in Athy. His research interests include the whole area of bullying in schools, how schools develop their own policies in dealing with incidents of bullying, particularly how teachers respond to bullying situations, and the effect that bullying has on the children in their care.

Karen Fite was Dean of Pacific Oaks College for many years and is currently teaching Masters students online in the Pacific Oaks Off Campus Education programme. She is also a lawyer with considerable experience as an advocate for children and families.

Dr Marie Flynn lectures in the Sociology of Education in St Patrick's College, Drumcondra, where she also coordinates the BA Human Development Research Programme. Her research interests include equality and inclusion in schools, multiple intelligences theory and practice, families and schools.

Noreen Flynn graduated from Carysfort College of Education with a BEd in 1977. Since then she has worked as a class teacher, learning support teacher, resource teacher and is currently part of the special education support team in Mater Dei Primary School, Basin Lane, Dublin, where she is assistant principal. While resident in the US, in the late 80s, Noreen taught sixth, seventh and eighth grade mathematics and English in Guardian Angel School, Manhattan, New York. Noreen was a member of the planning group established, under the auspices of the Educational Disadvantage Centre, St Patrick's College, Drumcondra, to convene a National Forum in July 2002 on Primary Education: Ending Disadvantage. She has served for three years on the first statutory Educational Disadvantage Committee set up under the Education Act (1998). Since 1999 Noreen has been a district representative for the south inner city and West Dublin on the central executive committee of the INTO.

Colm Hefferon is a lecturer in drama at St Patrick's College, Drumcondra, Dublin. Using drama as a research method and the development of strategies for the classroom have been a recent focus, but he is also interested in performance, practice and non-verbal communication.

Thérèse Hegarty worked in a primary school in West Tallaght for twenty years, where she developed school-based approaches to children with social and emotional problems. She was one of the pioneers of the teacher counsellor pilot project. In 2000 she left to train as a family therapist and now offers family therapy to the community where she once taught. She also teaches SPHE at Froebel College, offers consultations to schools through the School Completion Project and provides training in narrative practice in education.

Ann Higgins graduated from Mary Immaculate College in 1980. She worked within the primary school sector in a designated disadvantaged school for many years. In 1985 she left teaching for a number of years and set up a school-based community project, which is a grassroots response to the learning needs of adults and young people. The primary school where she worked evolved into a learning centre offering learning opportunities and support for young people and adults within the community. This project has featured in national and international publications and is the subject of Ann's postgraduate research. Ann returned to teaching for a number of years before joining the staff of Mary Immaculate College where she works as coordinator of the Targeting Educational Disadvantage Project. Her research interests include educational disadvantage, poverty, behavioural management, parental involvement in schooling, after-school and out-of-school educational provision.

Dr Frank Howe holds a PhD in Counsellor Education from the Union Institute. Areas of special interest include child sexual abuse prevention and treatment, classroom management, economic education and entrepreneurship, and communication and systems issues. Dr Howe is a Professor in the Department of Education and teaches Classroom Management and Human Growth and Development courses in the Longwood College Teacher Preparation Programme, Virginia. He also teaches Human Growth and Development, and Individual, Group, and School Counselling in the Longwood College Masters programme in Guidance and Counselling. He is a Fulbright Senior Specialist and in Spring 2002 was awarded the first Senior Specialist Grant for Ireland.

Jo-Hanna Ivers' research for her Masters thesis under the auspices of the Educational Disadvantage Centre, St Patrick's College, Drumcondra, is in the area of 'Fear of Success among North Inner City Youth'. Her primary degree is in Psychology (DBS School of Arts), having also obtained a Diploma in Counselling (NUI Maynooth) and a Diploma in Drug and Alcohol Intervention and Social Policy (UCD). She has worked as a rehabilitation integration worker in the addiction services, with the rehabilitation team in the HSE and in a community-based rehabilitation programme.

Sylwia Kazmierczak is a speech and language therapist. Awarded a number of scholarships from Gdansk University where the Department of Speech and Language Pathology focuses on early literacy, she graduated with an MA (Honours) in 2002, specialising in speech and language therapy. Sylwia currently works as a full-time researcher in the Educational Disadvantage Centre in St Patrick's College, Drumcondra, and is a member of the Executive Committee of the Reading Association of Ireland.

John Kelly has been teaching at primary school level in a disadvantaged community for twenty-six years. He has worked with children with special needs for six years. John has a keen interest in using digital technologies to develop engaging learning experiences for his students and has been an active member of the Empowering Minds community since 2000. The dissertation he completed for his MEd in 2003 focused on the constructionist learning environment that continues to develop in his school as a result of involvement with the Empowering Minds project.

Eithne Kennedy lectures in literacy in St Patrick's College, Drumcondra. She is currently undertaking doctoral research on literacy in disadvantaged settings. Eithne's other research interests are in workshop approaches to the teaching of writing and reading; effective teachers/schools of literacy; early intervention and prevention in literacy.

Karl Kitching taught as a mainstream class and language-support teacher in Sacred Heart of Jesus School, Huntstown, Dublin, after graduating with his BEd from St Patrick's College, Drumcondra, in 2001. He graduated with an MEd from St Patrick's College, specialising in literacy for children learning English as an additional language. Karl has taught in culturally diverse schools in Massachusetts and West Belfast as part of teacher exchange programmes. He is on secondment from his school to St Patrick's College since 2005 and is currently working on a national evaluation of Relationships and Sexuality Education (RSE) at second level and is also involved in researching teachers' lives and job satisfaction using diary methods.

Dr Claire W. Lyons is a developmental psychologist at the Department of Education, Mary Immaculate College (MIC). She is the Coordinator for the Centre for Educational Disadvantage Research, the Director of Development Education at MIC and is the Senior Researcher on the Working Together Project.

Dr Catherine Maunsell is a lecturer in Psychology and Human Development in the Education Department at St Patrick's College, Drumcondra. She has previously lectured in Life-Span Development/Developmental Psychology and Statistical Analysis/Research Methods at Trinity College, Dublin. Catherine was also employed as the psychologist to the Village Project Day Assessment Service, a unique community-based initiative working with young people who were at risk of school failure. She is an active research associate of the Educational Disadvantage Centre. Her research interests include: identification of risk factors associated with early school leaving; initiatives addressing school retention; education and community-based approaches to working with youth at risk of school failure; children and youth in the juvenile justice system and, more recently, the promotion of social inclusion and active citizenship through 'second chance' adult education/lifelong learning.

Rory McDaid, (BA, Mphil, HDE), works as a language support teacher in St Gabriel's National School, Dublin. He has previously worked as a children's consultation officer with the Irish Society for the Prevention of Cruelty to Children (ISPCC) and as an equality officer with the Union of Students of Ireland. Rory is currently enrolled on a taught doctoral programme in St Patrick's College, Drumcondra. His research interests include children's rights, specifically the voice of the child, and children who speak minority languages.

Anne McGough is a lecturer in the special education department, St Patrick's College, Drumcondra. She lectures in language teaching and learning for children with special needs and in early intervention. She is also involved in developing curriculum for the *Early Start* intervention programme and in providing continuing professional development to *Early Start* personnel. Her research interests include educational disadvantage, language acquisition and pedagogy, early years education and early intervention. Her current research focus is on exploring language pedagogy in an inclusive early intervention setting.

Denise McSweeney, MEd, currently works as a primary teacher. She was a project support worker on the Targeting Educational Disadvantage Project and the Working Together Project.

Dr Mark Morgan is head of the education department at St Patrick's College, Drumcondra, Dublin. He is a former primary school principal and obtained his postgraduate degrees in social psychology at the London School of Economics after which he did post-doctoral research at Stanford University, California. His research has mainly been in the areas of substance use, evaluation of prevention programmes and educational disadvantage. He is an editor and founding member of the European Schools Project on Alcohol and Other Drugs (ESPAD). His most recent research is concerned with teachers' lives and job satisfaction.

Dympna Mulkerrins is a primary school teacher and currently holds the position of Home School Community Liaison Coordinator in a boys' and a girls' primary school in North Dublin. Dympna serves on the education committee of the INTO and is a member of the newly formed Teaching Council.

Yvonne Mullan was a primary school teacher for twenty-two years. She has worked as an educational psychologist in the National Educational Psychological Service (NEPS) for the last five years.

Áine Murphy graduated from Coláiste Mhuire, Marino, in 2003 and teaches sixth class in St Anne's Primary School, Fettercairn, Tallaght, in Dublin. Áine is responsible for the Peer Mediation Programme, in its second year in St Anne's. She is thoroughly enjoying her involvement in the programme and can see the benefits it has for the whole school climate. Áine is currently undertaking a Masters in Education, specialising in educational disadvantage in St Patrick's College.

Paula Murphy is a lecturer in education (drama) in St Patrick's College, Drumcondra, Dublin, where she works on undergraduate, post-graduate and in-service programmes. She previously worked as a primary school teacher and as education officer for TEAM Educational Theatre. She is co-author of the recently published *Discovering Drama: Theory and Practice for the Primary School* (2006, Dublin: Gill & Macmillan) and has presented at a variety of national and international conferences. She is currently the secretary of the Association of Drama in Education in Ireland (ADEI).

Dr Maeve O'Brien currently teaches sociology on the BA and MA in Human Development and on the Inequality and Educational Disadvantage strand of the Doctorate in Education programme at St Patrick's College. Her research interests include issues of gender inequality and emotional care work and their relation to the field of education.

Fiona O'Connor, MPhil, works as a researcher in education and in language learning and is currently attached to the Curriculum Development Unit in Mary Immaculate College, Limerick.

Dr Toni Owens graduated with an MA in Communication and Cultural Studies from Dublin City University, after which she was commissioned by the National Association for Adult Education in Ireland (AONTAS) to conduct a qualitative study of barriers to male participation in education. The Department of Education and Science (DES) funded this project and the research report, *Men on the Move: An Exploration of Barriers to Male Participation in Education and Training Initiatives in Ireland*, was published by AONTAS in 2000. In 2001 Toni became Government of Ireland Scholar when the Irish Research Council for the Humanities and Social Sciences awarded her a three-year scholarship to conduct her PhD at St Patrick's College, Drumcondra. Toni's qualitative doctoral study entitled an 'Exploration of the Links between Male Identity and the Development of the Field of Men's Community Education in Ireland' was completed in 2004 and she was awarded her doctorate in 2005. During her studies, Toni conducted an evaluation of the impact of programmes funded by the Education Equality Initiative on men's development in the Ballymun area (2003).

Susan Quinn is a primary school teacher and has been working in a designated educationally disadvantaged school in Dublin for over five years. She completed her MEd in St Patrick's College, Drumcondra, in 2005. Her interests include psychology (BA in Psychology from UCD), educational disadvantage and education in the developing world. She is currently on leave of absence and is working in a teacher training college in Ethiopia.

Cathríona Ryan is a researcher with the Educational Disadvantage Centre (EDC) in St Patrick's College, Drumcondra. A graduate of the college with honours in human development and music, her MA thesis in education with the EDC, in conjunction with Ballyfermot Local Drugs Task Force, examines the experiences of children with Attention Deficit Hyperactivity Disorder (ADHD) and their families in Ballyfermot.

Noëlle Spring is the Development Officer with the Katharine Howard Foundation. In addition to managing the Foundation, she has designed and managed special initiatives including demonstration programmes and research projects. Prior to that, Noêlle worked as a Projects Officer with the Combat Poverty Agency where her duties included advising government departments on policy responses to promote social inclusion. She began her career as a social worker and subsequently a community worker with the Eastern Health Board (HSE). Noêlle is currently undertaking a part-time doctorate in education in St Patrick's College. Her chosen module of study is educational disadvantage.

Joseph Travers is a lecturer in special education in St Patrick's College, Drumcondra. He was formerly a primary teacher and worked as a resource teacher for Travellers and children with special educational needs.

Liz Waters has a BA in English and History, a postgraduate diploma in Psychotherapy and is currently undertaking an MA in Pastoral Care and Leadership. She is CEO of An Cosán, one of the largest community development organisations in the country. She has worked in West Tallaght in community education and psychotherapy for the past fifteen years; she has also taught in Mountjoy and St Patrick's. Her abiding belief is that community education is a personal and communal process that is the path to the social change needed by our communities.

Dr Katherine E. Zappone is an educator and independent researcher. She is Project Leader of the Childhood Development Initiative in Tallaght West, and has directed and contributed to its research publications including: *How Are our Kids? Children and Families in Tallaght West* (2005), *Experiencing Childhood Citizenship* (2005) and *A Place for Children. Tallaght West* (2006). She lectured for a decade in Trinity College Dublin in ethics, human rights and education, and has lectured in Canada, Australia, Europe, the USA and throughout Ireland. Widely published in feminism, ethics, equality issues and education, she conducts research, consults and teaches. Her publications include: *Achieving Equality in Children's Education* and *Messages from the Children* (Educational Disadvantage Centre, St Patrick's College, 2002); *Charting the Equality Agenda: A Coherent Framework for Equality Strategies in Ireland North and South* (Equality Authority and Equality Commission, 2001); and *Re-Thinking Identity: The Challenge of Diversity* (Equality Authority and Human Rights Commission, 2003). She is co-founder of An Cosán, a large community-based organisation in West Tallaght, Dublin, committed to eradicating poverty through education. She is also a member of the Irish Human Rights Commission.

Abbreviations

AARE	Australian Association for Research in Education
ADM	Area Development Management
ALCE	Adult Literacy and Community Education
Aontas	Irish National Association of Adult Education
BAP	Blanchardstown Area Partnership
BICS	Basic Interpersonal Communication Skills
CALP	Cognitive Academic Language Proficiency
CDI	Childhood Development Initiative
CDU	Curriculum Development Unit
CDVEC	City of Dublin Vocational Educational Committee
CECDE	Centre for Early Childhood Development and Education
CERI	Centre for Educational Research and Innovation
CESCR	Convention on Economic, Social and Cultural Rights
CMRS	Conference of Major Religious Superiors
CPA	Combat Poverty Agency
CRC	Convention on the Rights of the Child
CSER	Centre for Social and Educational Research
CSO	Central Statistics Office
CSPE	Civic, Social and Political Education
DEIS	Delivering Equality of Opportunity in Schools
DES	Department of Education and Science
DfES	Department for Education and Skills
DICPSI	Dublin Inner City Primary Schools Initiative
ECE	Early Childhood Education
ECER	European Conference on Educational Research
ECHR	European Convention on Human Rights
EDC	Educational Disadvantage Centre
EEC	European Economic Community
EM	Empowering Minds
ERC	Educational Research Centre
ESRI	Economic and Social Research Institute
Eurydice	The Information Network on Education in Europe
EWO	Education Welfare Officers
FETAC	Further Education Training Awards Council
HSCL	Home School Community Liaison
HSCLI	Home School Community Liaison Initiative
IDES	Inspectorate of the Department of Education and Science
IEA	International Association for Educational Assessment
IEEE	Institute of Electrical and Electronics Engineering

IEPs	Individual Educational Plans
INTO	Irish National Teachers' Organisation
IPA	Institute of Public Administration
IRA	Irish Reading Association
JCSP	Junior Certificate Schools Programme
KCP	Kileely Community Project
LANDS	Literacy and Numeracy in Disadvantaged Schools
LYNS	Learning for Young International Students
NALA	National Adult Literacy Agency
NAPS	National Anti-Poverty Strategy
NCCA	National Council for Curriculum Assessment
NCCRI	National Consultative Committee on Racism and Interculturalism
NCE	National Commission on Education
NCIP	National Childcare Investment Programme
NCS	National Children's Strategy
NDP	National Development Plan
NEPS	National Educational Psychological Service
NESF	National Economic and Social Forum
NEWB	National Education Welfare Board
NPAR	National Action Plan Against Racism
NUI	National University of Ireland
NWCI	National Women's Council Ireland
OECD	Organisation for Economic Cooperation and Development
OFSTED	Office for Standards in Education
OMC	Office of the Minister for Children
OSI	Office of Social Inclusion
PCSP	Primary Curriculum Support Programme
PESL	Potential Early School Leavers
PIRLS	Progress in International Reading Literacy Study
PISA	Programme for International Student Assessment
PROFKNOW	Professional Knowledge in Education and Health
RAPID	Revitalising Areas by Planning, Investment and Development
SCP	School Completion Programme
SCPA	Scheme for Commissioning Psychological Assessments
SEN	Special Educational Needs
SMART	Specific, Measurable, Achievable, Relevant, Timed
SMI	Strategic Management Initiative
SNA	Special Needs Assistant
SPHE	Social, Personal and Health Education
STTC	Senior Traveller Training Centre
TES	Traveller Education Strategy

TWCDI	Tallaght West Childhood Development Initiative
UCD	University College Dublin
VEC	Vocational Education Committee
VTOS	Vocational Training Opportunities Scheme

I

Theoretical Perspectives on Educational Disadvantage

Section one seeks to clarify and develop some of the conceptual underpinnings that inform the discourse on educational disadvantage today and into the future – both nationally and internationally. Recent advances in theory, policy and practice are outlined in order to develop a coherent, conceptual framework to celebrate diversity and achieve equality in children's education. An open systems model of 'educational balance' between school, community and the wider culture is sketched to counter the deficit model of educational disadvantage. With a philosophical emphasis, an understanding of human difference is put forward as integral to advancing the equality in education agenda. New and alternative approaches to working with diversity in education – through strategies for parents and teachers – are also developed. A trenchant critique of the prevailing orthodoxy to demonstrate measurable outcomes for all educational interventions is offered as a way of cautioning against the further marginalisation of the excluded. It concludes with an examination of the nexus of care, emotions and mothers' gendered work for their children's education as key to disrupting cycles of educational inequality.

1

Tracing the Language of Educational Disadvantage

Noëlle Spring

Introduction

Many studies have focused on inequality within education, and advances in the understanding of inequality have been mainly progressed through the sociology of education. The emergence of a continuum of equality and a proposal for a radical critique from the Equality Studies Centre in University College Dublin (UCD) raises important issues and challenges for inter- and intra-disciplinary consideration. Archer (2001) recognises the development of this radical egalitarian approach and, while welcoming the need for structural change at a societal level, he also raises significant questions about how to go about this and what we do in the meantime. Part of the answer to this dilemma, in my view, might be to focus on the emerging concepts and to further the understandings of those concepts raised through the equality debates. A philosophical engagement with the sociological understandings could strengthen the underpinning principles behind measures to eradicate educational disadvantage.

Exploring inequality in the Irish Education system within my current studies has raised questions for me regarding the language associated with educational disadvantage: What do we mean by it? Is this meaning shared? What are the implications arising from the various interpretations? Tracing the conception of this understanding needs to start by looking at language itself, its nature and its influence in relation to creating and shaping reality. I propose to examine some of the theories about language itself and explore the meaning and interpretation of language through focusing on some educational disadvantage policy and practice

3

over the last few years in Ireland. This chapter does not provide an in-depth analysis of this topic but aspires to provide some focus on the language of educational disadvantage.

What is known about language?

Language is critical to human beings' existence, has been studied by philosophers since the time of Plato and Aristotle, and is much more than a mechanism of communication. The study of language through the centuries relates to other important life issues such as identity, as is demonstrated by the age-old expression, 'we speak a common language', to describe a common bond or collaboration between people. Language is also bound to idealism, ethics and moral order. In recent times interpretation and putting language theory into practice have engaged the minds of many philosophers and critical thinkers. I propose to provide a review of some of the literature that has focused on language so that we can begin to understand the concept of educational disadvantage from a language perspective. To begin with I explore the so-called deficit language associated with educational disadvantage.

The deficit language of educational disadvantage – an Irish context

In examining language in relation to educational disadvantage we need to consider the use of the prefix 'dis-' and to consider what its role is and how it affects the meaning of certain words when placed in front of them, such as disengaged, disempowered, dismembered, dismissed and disadvantaged. At a very simplistic glance it is obvious that the prefix intends to negate and/or reverse a positive activity. There have been numerous attempts to define what we mean by the term educational disadvantage, the complexity of which has been described by many within the Irish context (Boldt and Devine, 1998; Archer, 2001; Kellaghan, 2002; Zappone, 2002). It is worth noting some recent calls for further clarification of the language used.

The action plan produced by the Forum on Primary Education, *Primary Education: Ending Disadvantage* (Gilligan, 2002), raised a number of issues relating to the definition of educational disadvantage, including the absence of a broadly agreed definition, the relative position of the term, the multi-layered effect of educational disadvantage on the individual and the negative implications of applying this deficit understanding of educational disadvantage. These flawed understandings were noted for having '… brought little change over the years to the levels of disadvantage experienced by specific communities, social classes and social groupings' (p. 143). In light of these identified shortcomings the action plan called for a more '… adequate, shared and coherent understanding of educational disadvantage of children' (p. 144). This included a shift from what was seen as the deficit/compensation model to an understanding that seeks to foster equality in children's education. The plan promotes the concept of *educational equality* as a tool to shift the emphasis from disadvantage as the primary concern to seeing the solution as the focus. This analysis shifts the focus back on to the wider structural causes of inequality in our society and the equal worth of all children and all human beings. The underlying philosophy of the plan is one of respect and recognising the individuality of all children.

The final report of the Educational Disadvantage Committee (2005) acknowledges the adoption of much of its previous recommendations through the DEIS[1] initiative, and particularly, the focus on getting the school-based solutions in place, such as the implementation of the plan to address problems of literacy and numeracy, early unqualified school leaving, improving the rate of retention to the Leaving Certificate and transfer to further and higher education and training for people from disadvantaged backgrounds. However, the report proposes the adoption of a broader framework, which acknowledges that the problems of educational disadvantage cannot be solved in mainstream school-based programmes alone but are strongly affected by the wider community and society.

Initiatives and other developments addressing this deficit

These initiatives clearly show the web of development that has built up regarding educational disadvantage in Ireland and the complexity of the range of responses. They also supply evidence to back up the urgency to find greater clarity and cohesion in the understandings underpinning initiatives and responses in this area. This raises concerns about our identity and the type of society we are now living in. Recently much dialogue has involved a focus on quality of life and general well-being. This is partly as a reaction to the emphasis being placed on labour market priorities and the apparent focus on Ireland as an economy rather than a social, cultural and economic entity. It has also been pointed out that economic success alone is not enough to ensure progress in the social sphere and that it does not necessarily mean social progress (Cantillon and O'Shea, 2001). The globalisation of economic markets has also impacted on Irish society which is now experiencing a fall in migration and an increase in immigration. Within this changing context it is imperative to explore the deficit model of educational disadvantage in greater depth.

---

[1] This action plan, *Delivering Equality of Opportunity in Schools (DEIS)*, was launched by the Department of Education and Science in May 2005 (DES, 2005) and focuses on addressing the educational needs of children and young people from disadvantaged communities, from pre-school through second-level education (3–18 years).

Shortcomings of the language of educational disadvantage

In my view there is clear evidence shown by the research and initiatives designed to inform us about educational disadvantage that the language used has not helped to shift some of the intractable barriers that exist within Irish society. As all language requires interpretation in order to be deployed it is becoming more urgent to arrive at a shared definition or understanding of educational disadvantage. Indeed this will lead us on to a further stage, as suggested by the title of the report of the Educational Disadvantage Committee, *Moving Beyond Educational Disadvantage* (2005). This report also suggests that we should 're-image education' as suggested by David Hargreaves who makes the case for a radical rethinking of school organisation and the fundamental assumptions of schooling, based on personalising learning to meet the needs of all learners. He suggests that we are in transition from the nineteenth-century 'educational imaginary' to one for the twenty-first century (Hargreaves, 2005).

The language used by Hargreaves is important because it allows us to believe that we can re-invent and re-image what we are trying to do. Hargreaves (2005) goes on to give us his account of the essential elements of a re-imaged educational system and includes the principles that have emerged through much research and experience of the education system within Western societies. These elements include the uniqueness of each person with a personalised education, an acceptance of the multi-dimensional nature of intelligence, recognition of schools as being culturally heterogeneous, school being there for all pupils, education identified as lifelong for everybody and including informal as well as formal learning and unconstrained by time and place, roles as blurred and overlapping and, finally, education as user-led (both by pupils and parents).

Mediating the power of language

This connects very closely with Paul Ricoeur's view (2004) that the interpretative nature of language allows us to understand that all concepts can be reinvented and restated within a given context and time and is reinforced by Gilligan's call for *ethical imagination* (2005). Ricoeur connects action to language and this is significant in explaining the apparent intractability of lessening inequality in education. I think we can link this with the apparent goodwill and political interest in tackling this problem but a reluctance to apply the transformations that would be required to make significant improvements. There is also a reluctance to listen to those who are affected by inequality in education. The dominant view is that those of us who are deemed to be educated know what is best. I think we have a lot to learn in this regard and I hope that we see the wisdom of understanding more fully what those who are marginalised in our society have to say about their experience of the education system.

We need an alternative analysis that embraces Ricoeur's view (2004) that there is no self-image other than a mediated image. This analysis would point to the relationship between the individual and society and might bring about a broader perspective and a move towards viewing private troubles as public issues (Lynch, 2005). Ricoeur's quest for understanding how people see themselves in relation to those around them has much to teach us about relativity and gives us many clues about why those whom society thinks should be availing of all the opportunities put their way are apparently turning their backs on mainstream society. Ricoeur refers to the importance of self-esteem in a way that has much more depth than colloquially used nowadays (Kemp and Rasmussen, 1989). In my view he implies that it is no coincidence that people believe themselves to be of lesser importance than others if they are users of what seems to be a system that is determined by society's dominant forces. The use of negative labels and deficit language to describe these systems reinforces this view.

The impact of negative labelling

Language affects how we view people through the use of labelling, and the negative connotations of 'disadvantaged' are a good example of how language can be used to distance those in powerful positions from those on the margins. Archer and Weir highlight the lowering expectations of teachers regarding the achievements of children attending designated disadvantaged schools as possibly an unintended consequence of the labelling of such schools (Archer and Weir, 2005). They suggest that teachers often assume that the lower achievements of these children can be expected due to the poor economic circumstances within which they live. In the absence of adequate literature exploring this concept in the Irish context the Educational Disadvantage Committee (2005) recommends further investigation of efforts made in countries such as New Zealand and the US to raise teachers' expectations of children from lower socio-economic backgrounds.

Cody (2002) places importance on the role of passion within language and represents language as a living thing and not as a dead, non-dynamic force. This picks up on the power of language as cited by Ricoeur and offers hope to those of us who advocate the need to change the language applied. There is much recognition of the need to reconsider the assumptions that are made and there has been a call for a '… more questioning type of conversation' (Area Development Management, 2005, p. 11). This is echoed by the Educational Disadvantage Committee (2005). These calls for a new type of dialogue are extremely welcome but real advances will not materialise unless there is a commitment to re-examine the underlying meanings and to accept that inequality in education cannot be overcome without tackling broader social inequality (Combat Poverty Agency, 2001; Kellaghan, 2002; Archer, 2001; Lynch, 2005; Educational Disadvantage Committee, 2005).

Conclusion

The call for a radical shift in how we approach tackling educational disadvantage requires a fundamental restructuring of the education system. This change will not be possible or effective without overall societal restructuring. If we are genuine about our dissatisfaction with Ireland remaining a divided society then it is imperative that we make a stronger effort to change it. This effort could be greatly enhanced by raising the debate and dialogue about what kind of society we want and why we want it and could lead us to a more comprehensive explanation of the language we use and what it is that we are trying to achieve. A shift to an equality focus in relation to the rights of all citizens to equal outcomes from our educational systems will bring many challenges to our political, social and cultural systems. This shift may not be as difficult as one might expect as we have already embraced much change. Building on the '... considerable progress already made in the direction of implementing a multi-faceted, evidence-based approach to disadvantage' (Archer and Weir, 2005, p. 31) will reap due rewards. It is my contention that this work would be greatly enhanced by embracing the ethical and philosophical meanings associated with inequality and the further exploration of the language of educational disadvantage. Careful attention to the language applied could have a transformative effect on tackling inequality within education. Consequently, I am calling for a concerted effort by all of those involved with education policy to abandon the deficit language associated with disadvantage and to embrace instead the concept of equality in education.

References

Archer, P. (2001) 'Public Spending on Education, Inequality and Poverty' in Cantillon, S., Corrigan, C., Kirby, P. and O'Flynn, J. (eds) *Rich and Poor: Perspectives on tackling inequality in Ireland,* Dublin: Oak Tree Press in association with The Combat Poverty Agency

Archer, P. and Weir, S. (2005) *Addressing Disadvantage: A Review of the International Literature and of Strategy in Ireland,* Educational Disadvantage Committee, Dublin: DES

Area Development Management Limited (ADM) (2005), *Building Equality through Education: Going Forward in Partnership,* ADM Conference Report, Dublin: ADM

Baker, J., Lynch, K., Cantillon, S. and Walsh, J. (2004) *Equality, from Theory to Action*, Basingstoke: Palgrave Macmillan

Boldt, S. and Devine, B. (1998) 'Educational Disadvantage in Ireland: Literature Review and Summary Report' in Boldt, S., Devine, B., McDevitt, D. and

Morgan, M. (eds) *Educational Disadvantage and Early School Leaving,* Dublin: Combat Poverty Agency

Cantillon, S. and O'Shea, E. (2001) 'Social Expenditure, Redistribution and Participation' in Cantillon, S., Corrigan, C., Kirby, P. and O'Flynn, J. (eds) *Rich and Poor: Perspectives on tackling inequality in Ireland,* Dublin: Oak Tree Press in association with The Combat Poverty Agency

Cody, A. (2002) 'Words, You, and Me', *Inquiry,* vol. 45, no. 3, pp. 277–93

Combat Poverty Agency (2001) Foreword in Cantillon, S., Corrigan, C., Kirby, P. and O'Flynn, J. (eds) *Rich and Poor: Perspectives on tackling inequality in Ireland,* Dublin: Oak Tree Press in association with The Combat Poverty Agency

Department of Education and Science (2005) *DEIS: Delivering Equality of Opportunity in Schools – An Action Plan for Educational Inclusion,* Dublin: DES

Educational Disadvantage Committee (2005) *Moving Beyond Educational Disadvantage,* Dublin: DES

Gilligan, A. L. (2002) (ed.) *Primary Education: Ending Disadvantage. Proceedings and Action Plan of National Forum,* Dublin: Educational Disadvantage Centre, St Patrick's College

Gilligan, A. L. (2005) 'The Shape of Things to Come: A Reflective Summary of the Seamus Heaney Lecture Series, Perspectives on Equality' in Lyons, M. A. and Waldron, F. (eds) *Perspectives on Equality,* Dublin: The Liffey Press

Hargreaves, D. (2005) 'Personalising Learning' in *Learning in the 21st Century: Towards Personalisation,* Dublin: Information Society Commission

Kellaghan, T. (2002) 'Approaches to Problems of Educational Disadvantage' in Gilligan, A. L. (ed.) *Primary Education: Ending Disadvantage. Proceedings and Action Plan of National Forum,* Dublin: Educational Disadvantage Centre, St Patrick's College

Kemp, T. P. and Rasmussen, D. (eds) (1989) *The Narrative Path: The Later Works of Paul Ricoeur,* Cambridge, Mass.: MIT Press

Lynch, K. (2005) 'Equality and Education: A Framework for Theory and Action' in Lyons, M. A. and Waldron, F. (eds) *Perspectives on Equality,* Dublin: The Liffey Press

Ricoeur, P. (2004) interview with Richard Kearney in Kearney, R. (ed.) *On Paul Ricoeur: The Owl of Minerva,* Aldershot: Ashgate Publishing

Zappone, K. (2002) 'Achieving Equality in Children's Education' in Gilligan, A. L. (ed.) *Primary Education: Ending Disadvantage. Proceedings and Action Plan of National Forum,* Dublin: Educational Disadvantage Centre, St Patrick's College

2

Towards a Living System of Education

Katherine E. Zappone

Introduction

Over the past forty years in Ireland, a variety of national schemes, strategies, community-based and school-based projects have been implemented to deal with educational disadvantage. Evaluations indicate that *some* progress has been made. Responses to the schemes have been largely positive, and there are *modest* indications of impact on children's school-staying and performance (see Weir and Archer, 2004; Archer and Shortt, 2003; Weir, Mills and Ryan, 2002; Archer and Lewis, 2002; Educational Research Centre (ERC), 1998, 2000; Conaty, 2002). Evaluations of local community-based projects reveal that models of good practice *are being* designed and implemented: Area Development Management (ADM), 1999; Cullen, 2000; National Economic and Social Forum (NESF), 2002.

Several definitions of 'educational disadvantage', 'equality of opportunity in education' and, more recently, 'educational inclusion', have been framed to guide and justify the action that abounds (Kellaghan, 1999; Kellaghan et al. 1995; Educational Disadvantage Committee, 2005; Lynch, 1999 and 2005; Tormey, 2001; Conference of Major Religious Superiors (CMRS), 1992; Irish National Teachers' Organisation (INTO), 1994). These have been named as theories of 'difference', 'deficit', 'discontinuity', 'substantive equality in education', 'fair equality of opportunity', to name but a few.

In light of modest progress though intense practice, and given the diverse and often conflicting thinking, research preparations for a National Forum on Primary Education: Ending Disadvantage (Gilligan, 2002)[1] raised a fundamental question:

---

[1] Convened by the Educational Disadvantage Centre in St Patrick's College in July 2002, under the directorship of Ann Louise Gilligan

Do we need a coherent and shared way of thinking about what we are doing?

It was decided to conduct a national research project based on the assumption that *now* is the time to fashion an answer to this question.[2]

The purpose of the national research was to build a way of thinking that could direct action for achieving equality in children's education. It was envisaged that the framework would be a resource for the Forum so that participants could come to a shared understanding of practice and intended achievements. Two of the primary building blocks for this are (1) the knowledge of practitioners – parents, teachers and other professionals supporting children's learning – and (2) the 'voices' of children. A qualitative model of research was designed to elicit in a participatory and creative way practitioners' knowledge and children's voices in sixteen sites inclusive of eleven counties throughout the country. As we travelled, we became more aware of 'shared understandings of conditions for educational equality' that *are* present among practitioners. However, we also heard some contradictions in what was voiced and indications of how these contradictions could block the desire for progress common across and throughout the groups. In presenting the outcomes of our research, I offer a framework that builds on the 'shared understandings', and outline choices that need to be made to reduce the contradictory elements.[3]

Change is required – the current context

The rationale for the National Forum and this research project had to do with the urgent need for change – in our thinking and action – if we are to end disadvantage in our children's education.

Change is required because:

1 A high level of pupils still leave school early: in 1999, 13,000 left without a Leaving Certificate, 2,400 left with no qualifications, and 1,000 primary pupils did not transfer to second level (McCoy and Williams, 2004).
2 There has been a levelling off of retention rates. Since 1996 there has been little change in retention rates – now at 82 per cent for those who leave with a Leaving Certificate – and a consistent 4 per cent who leave without any qualifications (Weir and Archer, 2004).
3 There remains a striking persistence in educational inequalities by social class since 1979. Studies indicate that though all social classes have increased their participation and performance since 1979, the gap between professional and working classes of those who complete the Leaving Certificate has not been

---

[2] I designed and directed this project, with the assistance of Ann Louise Gilligan; the research team comprised myself, Neil Haran, Colm Hefferon and Paul Murphy.
[3] For the full research report, see *Achieving Equality in Children's Education* (2002), Dublin: St Patrick's College, Educational Disadvantage Centre

significantly reduced (Smyth and Hannan, 2000; Smyth, 1999). Furthermore, there is evidence of a widening gap between the social classes in entry to third-level institutions (Smyth and Hannan, 2000).

4   The International Adult Literacy Survey conducted in Ireland in 1995 and published in 1997 provided a profile of the literacy skills of adults aged 16–64. The survey showed that about 25 per cent of the Irish population, or at least 500,000 adults, were found to score at the lowest level (Level 1), performing best at tasks that required the reader to locate a simple piece of information in a text with no distracting information, and where the structure of the text assisted the task. The survey showed that early school leavers, older adults and the unemployed were most at risk of literacy difficulties (Morgan et al., 1997).

5   The gap between the rich and the poor in Irish society is getting bigger. Since 1987 the numbers of those who are living with incomes that are only 40, 50 or 60 per cent of average household incomes has been increasing. Reports indicate that Ireland's level of income inequality is one of the highest in Organisation for Economic Cooperation and Development (OECD) countries; only the UK and the US have a higher level of inequality with regard to people's overall income (OECD, 1999).

6   There is evidence to suggest that public spending on education contributes to inequality. A study carried out in 2001 outlines that expenditure on a third-level student is still over twice the expenditure on a primary student and almost 70 per cent higher than a second-level student. So, 'the state spends much more on the education of the better off young people (who tend to remain in the system) than it does on young people from poorer families (who tend to leave the system early)' (Archer, 2001, p. 226). DES figures for 2003 do not indicate any substantive improvements since Archer's study (DES Statistics Office, 2005).

Research findings

In light of the current context, then, it was an opportune time to go to the key actors in the Irish education system in order to build a way of thinking that has potential to meet these challenges for change. Let's begin with the adults.

The adults

In each of the sixteen research sites we met with a group of parents and teachers and other professionals working in the community. We designed a participatory form of inquiry for the adults, using methods associated with participatory, learning and action research (Kane and O'Reilly de Brun, 2000). Each group was presented with one question to discuss, debate and resolve: 'Reflecting on your experience and action, what is needed so that every child has an equal chance to learn and to achieve?'

It was up to each group, through facilitated conversation and decision-making, to agree on fundamental requirements for achieving equality in children's education. In effect, it was an invitation to think deeply and to arrive at shared understandings.

The voices of parents

Our sample included a cross-section of 175 parents throughout the country involved in schools and community work. Towards the end of research sessions, parents were invited to agree on requirements for equality in children's education. Analysis of these showed a number of themes that were common to groups throughout the country. We are calling these themes 'shared understandings of conditions for equality in children's education'. Table 1 presents the themes and indicates the frequency with which they emerged in groups throughout the country. These categories were not closed, rather they emerged in response to open questions.

Table 1 Shared Understandings from Parents of Conditions for Equality in Children's Education (%)

CONDITIONS FOR EQUALITY IN CHILDREN'S EDUCATION	%
Pedagogies for Equality[4]	100
Relations of Equal Respect (between parents–teachers; children–teachers; between people with different socio-economic, cultural and racial backgrounds)	81
Parental Involvement in Children's Education	56
Enough Resources	38
Early Assessment and Intervention	31
Importance of Wider Social and Economic Equality	19
Early Access to Education and Care	19
Professional Development of Teachers	19
Power-sharing between DES and Community/School	.06
A Holistic Approach (for child; for home-school-community partnership)	.06
The Importance of Care and Love	.06

The percentage indicates how many research groups out of the total number identified this as a prime condition (e.g. 100% = 16 groups).

---

[4] This category was used to interpret the ways in which professionals (and parents) spoke about teaching and learning methodologies that support equality for children in education. Research participants validated the use of this category.

Professionals supporting children's learning

In turning to the other grouping of adults, the sample included a cross-section of 197 professionals throughout the country – engaged in developing and implementing strategies to tackle educational disadvantage. What did the professionals say? Table 2 presents the themes and indicates the frequency with which they emerged in groups throughout the country.

Table 2 Shared Understandings from Professionals of Conditions for Equality in Children's Education (%)

CONDITIONS FOR EQUALITY IN CHILDREN'S EDUCATION

	%
Home Environment and Parental Involvement	71
Importance of Wider Social and Economic Equality	65
Pedagogies for Equality	65
Power Shared between DES and Community/School	59
Coordination and Integration of Services	59
Enough Resources	53
A Holistic Approach (for child, for home-school-community partnership)	53
Early Access to Education and Care	47
Professional Development of Teachers	41
Appropriate and Responsive Government Policy	24
Early Assessment and Intervention	23
School Environment, Atmosphere, Ethos	18
Primary–Secondary Links for Transfer	18

The percentage indicates how many research groups out of the total number identified this as a prime condition (e.g. 100% = 17 groups)

Keep these adult ideas in mind as we turn now to the children.

Messages from the children

In the design of this national research project, we were committed to including children in the dialogue about achieving equality *for them*. We wanted to design a model of 'hearing the voices of children' (Devine, 1999, 2001) that would enable them to critically reflect on their experiences and to apply their imagination.

We chose 'process drama' as the method of research and Colm Hefferon designed the basic episodes of the drama to elicit the views of children on how to deal with the problem of a young boy at risk of leaving school early. Colm and Neil Haran facilitated the children's involvement to create their own dramatic responses to the circumstances of Timmy, a young lad from a background of poverty who was not doing well in school, who had forged his report by putting his name on the report of a better student, and was facing the possibility of being expelled from school. The children were invited to take on the roles of Timmy's teachers, principal and friends and within these roles to resolve what needed to happen so that Timmy would perform better and stay in school.[5]

Messages and meanings

Over 230 children throughout Ireland – in urban, rural and island settings – entered and recreated Timmy's world. The following are the messages we heard.

The call for open communication between children and adults

Perhaps one of the strongest set of messages from the children – that was enacted in almost every classroom we entered – was the call for open communication between pupil and teacher, and between pupil and parent. The children imaged open, direct, care-filled communication as a core feature of re-engaging Timmy in the learning process and school life.

We heard that the children image the teacher as initiating the communication, but they also view Timmy as an active participant in opening the dialogue.

In role as teachers and principal, the children acted again and again the importance of Timmy being able to talk to his parents about school, about his troubles, about everything.

Make children see the 'value of education'

As the drama unfolded in various settings, the children spontaneously reflected on the value of education and how 'making Timmy see the value of education' could be one solution to the problem. But, what was the 'value' that they saw?

> We have to learn … or you won't get a job when you're big. [child taking role of Timmy's friend]

> We want him to go to college and get a diploma and get a great job. You're too young to leave school and you won't get a job at your age. [child taking role of Timmy's friend]

> Education is for getting a job, getting a job, getting a job.[6]

---

[5] With the assistance of Paul Murphy we produced a video, *Messages from the Children,* to provide a creative vehicle to communicate the findings.

[6] Research undertaken after the National Forum with children in Ballyfermot (designated disadvantaged area) through questionnaire and focus group methodologies indicates that children in this setting hold a view of the value of education that is wider than the functionalist interpretation that was predominant in this study, see Downes, 2004.

Children's affirmations of adults creating an equal chance for them

There were times in the dramas when the children appeared to draw on their genuine experiences of recent reforms or additions to the education process so that all children could have a more equal chance to learn and to achieve. Perhaps we could say that some of the solutions to Timmy's problems offered by the children were affirmations of adults, parents, teachers and other professionals – creating conditions for children to achieve equality in education.

> A support teacher will give him extra support – this is not a solution only a beginning. [child taking the role of teacher]
>
> I like to bring the lads out for hurling and soccer – maybe we should increase PE time. [child taking the role of teacher]

Adult power and the agency of children

Several of the dramas enacted the full complexity of issues surrounding adults' exercise of power and control in the process of recognising the agency of children – that children too are responsible for their own learning. As they took on the roles of principal and teachers, the children struggled critically and creatively – with the reasons for rules, the purpose of punishment, and the proper extent of a teacher's authority and control. Many times it appeared as if the children were accepting of authoritarian power arrangements between pupil and teacher as the only way in which order within the learning environment could be secured for all. In one role-play it was suggested that 'there were too few rules in the school for boys like Timmy', that Timmy must 'do what he is told', 'get his act together', and the teacher is advised to have 'a firm hand and a chat with him'.

There were other times, however, when the children acted themselves into a learning environment that pried space open for Timmy and his classmates to share some of the responsibility for his learning and staying in school. The rules established by teachers, for example, could be imaged as boundaries with a positive function.

Recognition, agency, boundaries, rules, punishment, adult authority, a child's self-knowledge, self-motivation; these are the issues that the children struggled to put together in imaginative worlds. We were disturbed by their apparent acceptance of an adult authoritarian exercise of power on the one hand, yet noted their intimations of children's agency on the other.

Windows to personal and systemic change

Adults often talk and write about the need for systemic change in education if all children are to have an equal chance to learn and to achieve. Changing the system is about changing the way things are normally done. Changing the system is about creating new habits of being, doing and relating. Every so often in our travels throughout the classrooms of Ireland, we heard children's voices inviting us and themselves to personal and systemic change.

> Ask the children what they want to do. Pick something they will agree on. We need change. [child in discussion after scene]

> You just have to follow your dream. If your grades are good, you can do anything. [child taking role of Timmy's friend]

> Follow your dream. We need change. Let's work together. Find more time. Say what we feel.

Research conclusions: a conceptual framework for achieving equality in children's education

The primary conclusion of the research is the outline of a conceptual framework, built on shared understandings of parents, professionals and children, which could direct change to end disadvantage. It is a framework that describes a process and a way of thinking. It is rooted in a political and ethical view that our current systems can and should change in order to achieve equality. It focuses on the child as an individual, consequently it is not acceptable to promote policies of 'equality of educational opportunity' that at best ensure that only a certain proportion of children will achieve what the system deems valuable. If the goal is to focus on the child as an individual, systems inside and outside of education will need to change.[7]

The conceptual framework outlines both a description of education as a living system, and principles to guide future action.

Description

Achieving Equality in Children's Education Requires:

A Living System that
- Supports common ways of learning
- Accommodates diverse capacities, cultures, learning paths and achievement outcomes
- Enables communal solidarity or 'sticking together'
- Reduces inequalities of resources between social groups and geographical communities

So that
- Every child's powers are released, directed and enlarged.

---

[7] The final report of the Statutory Committee on Educational Disadvantage opts for an understanding of equality that is comparable to this (EDC, 2005).

Education ought to be a system that is alive, that is organic. Such a system generates life, progress, achievement, communication and responsibility for everyone – especially the children – involved in the system. This requires, then, mechanisms, structures and procedures for communication, integration and co-ordination between all actors and agencies: not silences and secrecies or protection of territories. It perhaps originates in the children's call for open communication with adults and extends to leadership in every sphere and sector that promotes dialogue, decision-making and resolution of conflicts and reduces movement in contradictory directions. And, if we wish to achieve *equality* in the system of children's education, this necessarily leads us to link systems of health, justice, community, family and social affairs with the system of education.

Reference points for action

Our equal worth as different human beings

Education and other services designed from the perspective of living systems are necessarily built on the ethical principle of our equal worth as different human beings. The design of national educational guidelines and programmes; school plans; local development plans; the social, economic and cultural development plans of counties; curriculum and pedagogical practices; and therapeutic and social services ought to be based on a recognition of children's differences as well as the capacities and characteristics that they hold in common. Imagine if these designs began with such an assumption of difference! Any 'extra supports' would become 'integral supports'; teaching would become the act of 'discovering a pedagogy' – as Maxine Greene (1995) speaks about it – so that every child would learn from where she or he stands.

As John Dewey said, one cannot effectively lead students outward without starting from the place where they currently reside (1938).

A community approach to decision-making

This reference point for action requires the building of respectful relations between all actors and integral mechanisms for democratic dialogue so that we create effective ways of responding to the challenges of difference and inequalities in education. A significant element of equality centres on relationships of mutual respect, ways of including diverse perspectives in the decision-making process, and flexible, targeted responses to the needs at hand. This would mean that power and responsibility are shared – from the home to the classroom to the community to the state. What we do in one sphere ought not to contradict what we do in another sphere. Imagine members of the DES located in regional offices and participating with other key actors in the local educational systems to define specific needs, develop plans – according to national guidelines

– and cost the resources required for the implementation of these plans. This would spread the responsibility with the power, thereby unleashing creativity, effectiveness and efficiency in ways that only genuine democratic ownership can. Imagine if this were the milieu within which our children could learn.

Reduction of social, economic and educational inequalities

How do we think about our overarching aim? Have we all set out to compensate for the disadvantage of many of our children, or have we built our programmes and allocated our resources to reduce the inequalities between children of different social classes, cultural and ethnic membership, and children of different abilities? These two aims are not the same. Compensating for the disadvantage means policies and patterns of spending (as 'resources allow') that assist 'the poor' and 'the different' to do better in the systems that operate. It means, as we have seen, getting more children with disadvantaged backgrounds to stay in school longer, which for some of them means accessing third level. But it does not necessarily mean, as we have also seen, that the gap of educational participation and achievement between social groups gets significantly smaller. Does this gap necessarily get smaller if our policies and patterns of spending do not aim for this? I don't think so.

Education for creativity and citizenship

The last reference point for action invites us to reconsider the nature and purpose of education itself, to think again about the question: What is education for? Or, as Joseph Dunne asks, 'What's the good of education?' (Dunne, 1995). Recalling the 'Messages from the children', is our system of education simply about 'getting a job'? While this may be one of the 'goods' of education – and a significant one – do we wish to narrow the scope of the power of what we do towards this single end? While education may be a significant vehicle through which children learn skills and know-how to contribute to the productivity and prosperity of our economy – and to their own individual material well-being – is this sufficient for a society that struggles to be just and to sustain all its members? In fact I want to suggest two things:

If we hold a broader understanding of the purpose of education, namely that it aims to activate human creativity and responsible citizenship, then our educational system *will promote* the necessary skills and competencies to sustain a productive economy. Creativity is the core of flexible intelligence, work-practices, organisational development, and entrepreneurship. But it is also the core of the 'ethical imagination' as Ann Louise Gilligan speaks about it. Education towards releasing the ethical imagination enables the 'ongoing creation of art, meaning and political activity for a common life where we take responsibility for ourselves and one another' (Gilligan, 2001).

Achieving equality in children's education is not just the work of our generation. It is an ongoing process that is part of a living system, and that is linked in with other systems in our society and economy; to keep the process and systems alive, we will need our children and our pupils to learn the habits of 'responsible citizens' (Dunne, 2002). We will need our children to learn how to participate in the common life, to converse across difference, to debate with respect, to form judgments in the interest of the whole as well as the self.

The childhood development initiative in Tallaght West: a regional experiment to create a living system

One year after the National Forum and the results of this research, a group of children's service providers, parents and community residents came together to initiate plans to enhance the lives and well-being of children in the four communities of Tallaght West. In spite of spectacular national economic progress, the children of Tallaght West continue to live in one of the most marginalised and disadvantaged geographical communities of the country. The region is characterised by high unemployment, high numbers of local authority housing and difficult social issues.

It is also a place with many home-grown leaders, residents resilient amidst poverty, and professionals from the community, voluntary and state sectors working together on various independent and government-sponsored initiatives.

Notwithstanding all the effort and work that has gone on in the region over the last number of years, parents and professionals knew that the majority of children in the area were still not receiving sufficient developmental and educational support to reach their full potential – as children. Without this, they have significantly less chance than other children from more prosperous regions of becoming independent, self-respecting adults taking an active part in social and economic life (Zappone et al., 2004).

Members of the Childhood Development Initiative (CDI) began the process of creating a living system by implementing mechanisms, structures and procedures for communication, integration and coordination between all actors and agencies. They produced a ten-year strategy – 'A Place for Children. Tallaght West' – characterised as a 'living document' and holding the potential to guide the design of education, health and care services that are built on the ethical principle of our equal worth as different human beings. They produced a 'Community Vision' – an image of the horizon that they hope will sustain their work and their respect for each other over time:

> We who live and work in Tallaght West have high expectations for all children living in our communities. We want our children to love who they are and to be cherished

irrespective of social background, cultural differences and country of origin. We see every child and every family being provided with support, opportunities and choices to meet these expectations. We see the whole community owning responsibility for the quality, beauty and safety of the local environment. (*A Place for Children. Tallaght West*, 2005)

The strategy is structured around commonly supported outcomes for children. Building common support for precise child outcomes represents an innovative approach to strategy design, and a community approach to decision-making. It is a lengthy, respectful and dynamic process that is guided by the principle of the power of inclusiveness. The principle does not result, however, in a 'shopping list'. Instead, its purpose is to ensure that what is delivered is genuinely owned and sustained in the long-term by the community. Put broadly, in the next ten years they want to see measurable improvements in the outcomes of *health, safety, learning and achieving and a sense of belonging* for Tallaght West children. By 'learning and achieving' they mean not only helping more children to stay in school longer and to improve their writing and reading skills, but also that they become more reflective and creative in all aspects of learning. Their concern that the children have a greater sense of belonging to home and community includes active giving to, and receiving from, family, friends and community.

An integrated, 'joined-up' strategy, with new services and key actors willing to collaborate requires a change of systems at local level with an intention to fit 'joined-up' efforts and change systems at national level. With investment,[8] and as outcomes for children improve, this may represent a real opportunity to move towards equality of conditions.

References

Archer, P. (2001) 'Public Spending on Education, Inequality and Poverty' in Cantillon, S., Corrigan, C., Kirby, P. and O'Flynn, J. (eds) *Rich and Poor: Perspectives on tackling inequality in Ireland,* Dublin: Oak Tree Press in association with the Combat Poverty Agency

Archer, P. and Lewis M. (2002) *Further Evaluation of Early Start. Progress Report.* Dublin: Educational Research Centre

Archer, P. and Shortt, F. (2003) *Review of the Home School Community Liaison Scheme,* Dublin: Educational Research Centre

Area Development Management (ADM) (1999) *Partnerships in Education. Learning the Lessons from Local Development,* Conference Papers, Dublin, ADM

---

[8] *A Place for Children – Tallaght West* is being co-funded by the Office of the Minister for Children through its Prevention and Early Intervention Programme, and the Atlantic Philanthropies.

Childhood Development Initiative (2005) *A Place for Children. Tallaght West*, Dublin: CDI

Conaty, C. (2002) *Including All: Home, School and Community United in Education*, Dublin: Veritas

Conference of Major Religious Superiors (1992) *Education and Poverty: Eliminating Disadvantage in the Primary School Years*, Dublin: CMRS

Cullen, B. (2000) *Evaluating Integrated Responses to Educational Disadvantage*, Dublin: Combat Poverty Agency

Devine, D. (1999) 'Children: Rights and Status in Education – a Socio-Historical Analysis', *Irish Educational Studies*, vol. 18, Spring, pp. 14–29

Devine, D. (2001) 'Locating the Child's Voice in Irish Primary Education' in Cleary, A. and Nic Ghiolla Phadraig, M. (eds) *Understanding Children*, Cork: Oak Tree Press, vol. 1, pp. 145–174

Dewey, J. (1938), *Experience and Education*, New York: Collier Books

Downes, P. (2004) *Voices of Children: St Raphael's Primary School, Ballyfermot*, Ballyfermot: URBAN

Dunne, J. (1995) 'What's the good of education?' in Hogan, P. (ed.) *Partnership and the Benefits of Learning*, Dublin: ESAI

Dunne, J. (2002) 'Citizenship and Education: A Crisis of the Republic?' in Kirby, P., Cronin, M. and Gibbons, L. (eds) *Re-Inventing Ireland*, London: Pluto Press

Educational Disadvantage Committee (2005) *Moving Beyond Educational Disadvantage*, Dublin: Report to the Minister of Education and Science

Educational Research Centre (1998) *Early Start Pre-School Programme: Final Evaluation Report*, Dublin: St Patrick's College

Educational Research Centre (2000) *Breaking the Cycle Evaluation: Executive Summary*, Dublin: St Patrick's College

Gilligan, A. L. (2001) 'Imagination and Educational Disadvantage', paper presented to the Annual Conference of the Educational Studies Association of Ireland, Educational Research Centre Newsletter

Greene, M. (1995) *Releasing the Imagination: Essays on education, the arts, and social change*, San Francisco: Jossey-Bass

Irish National Teachers' Organisation (1994) *Poverty and Educational Disadvantage: Breaking the Cycle,* Dublin: INTO

Kane, E. and O'Reilly de Brun, M. (2000) *Doing Your Own Research*, London: Marion Boyers Publishers

Kellaghan, T. (1999) 'Educational Disadvantage: An Analysis', paper presented at Inspector's Conference, Killarney

Kellaghan, T., Weir, S., Ó Huallacháin, S. and Morgan, M. (1995) *Educational Disadvantage in Ireland*, Dublin: ERC, DOE, CPA

Lynch, K. (1999) *Equality in Education,* Dublin: Gill and Macmillan

Lynch, K. (2005) 'Rhetoric and Reality: Naming the Silenced Inequalities in Irish Education' in *Building Equality through Education: Going Forward in Partnership,* Dublin: Area Development Management

McCoy, S. and Williams, J. (2004) *2002/2003 Annual School Leavers Survey,* Dublin: ESRI

Morgan, M., Hickey, B., Kellaghan, T., Cronin, A. and Millar D. (1997) *Report to the Minister for Education on the National Adult Literacy Survey Results for Ireland,* Dublin: Government Publications

National Economic and Social Forum (2002) *Early School Leavers Forum Report. No. 24.* Dublin: NFSF

OECD (1999) *Economic Surveys. Ireland OECD,* Paris

OECD (2001) *Education at a Glance. 2001,* Paris

Sheil, G., Cosgrove, J., Sofroniou, N., and Kelly, A. (2001) *Ready for Life: The Literacy Achievements of Irish 15 Year Olds with Comparative International Data,* Dublin: Educational Research Centre

Smyth, E. (1999) 'Educational Inequalities among School Leavers in Ireland, 1979–1994', *Economic and Social Review,* vol. 30, July, pp. 267–84

Smyth, E. and Hannan, D. (2000) 'Education and Inequality, in *From Bust to Boom,* Dublin: IPA

Tormey, Roland (2001) 'Finding a Language to Talk (to each other): Towards a Unified Theory of Educational Disadvantage', paper presented at the Educational Studies Association of Ireland conference

Weir, S. and Archer P. (with Flanagan, R.) (2004) *A review of measures aimed at addressing educational disadvantage in Ireland. Report to the Educational Disadvantage Committee,* Dublin: Educational Research Centre

Weir, S., Mills, L. and Ryan, C. (2002) *The Breaking the Cycle Scheme in Urban (and Rural) Schools: Final Evaluation Reports,* Dublin: Educational Research Centre

Zappone, K. et al. (2004) *How are our Kids? Children and Families in Tallaght West,* Dublin: Childhood Development Initiative

3

Pedagogy of the Processed

Tony Downes and Paul Downes

Education either functions as an instrument which is used to facilitate the integration of the younger generation into the logic of the present system and bring about conformity to it, or it becomes 'the practice of freedom', the means by which men and women deal critically and creatively with reality and discover how to participate in the transformation of their world.

(Richard Shaull in foreword to *Pedagogy of the Oppressed*, Freire, 2000, p. 15)

Introduction

In today's world we are all a processed people. We are either processed into the mainstream cultural matrix of society or processed out of it to languish and struggle for survival on its margins. There are overt and covert impersonal cultural forces at work which shape our lives, values, attitudes and behaviour, over which we seem to have little or no control as individuals, communities, societies or nations. These cultural forces constitute an almost universal pedagogy which processes, schools, programmes, moulds and influences us all as we live out our lives in society. It is the combination of these forces which constitutes the pedagogy of the processed and which either inserts us into the prevailing culture or excludes us from it. There is a need to articulate and practice a counter-cultural pedagogy of the processed to help remedy an imbalance and a state of alienation within individuals and society.

Here we offer a theoretical synthesis to articulate a pedagogy of the processed which redevelops the social activist traditions of adult education to bring about living systems, to overcome alienation and to go beyond deficit models for working-class communities. Action to develop a living organic system of education involves this pedagogy not only for adult education but for lifelong learning, including at primary and post-primary levels.

Narratives expressing features of alienation – expressing a pedagogy of imbalance – have been developed by Fromm, Freire and Marcuse. More recently, in Ireland, Zappone (2002) has articulated a narrative of balance through a view of education as a 'living system'. The central metaphor of general systems theory – the living organism – emphasises the organic characteristics of balance, flexibility, openness to change, adaptability, self-organisation, cooperation, interdependence, interaction with the environment and the multi-levelled nature of reality. As such it offers an important perspective from which to consider the development of social organisms at all levels from the micro to the macro and contrasts with mechanistic models. The following key features of a living system that can be related to an organic education system include:[1]

- Organic living systems require restoration of an imbalance or alienation, are holistic and overcome fragmentation.
- Living systems are multi-levelled and need a high degree of non-equilibrium.
- Self-organising systems are utterly dynamic yet stable and involve self-renewal and self-transcendence.
- Living systems require feedback among subsystems involving change amplifiers. They are part–whole combinations at multiple levels.

Beyond a deficit model

The Irish National Forum (2002) briefly touched on two key issues – the need to go beyond a 'deficit' model for working-class communities, and the role of the education system as a 'living system'. These concepts need to be related to each other and developed in more depth. The National Forum Action Plan (Gilligan, 2002) called into question approaches that operate out of a 'deficit' model or 'lack in the individual experiencing disadvantage, their family and/or their community that has to be made up by "compensating" for this deficit' (p. 143). Moreover, the Educational Disadvantage Committee (2005) recognises that: 'The deficit model of disadvantage, which has been the basis of most policy interventions in recent decades, is now seen as outdated and inadequate' (p. 19).

Gilligan's (2005) words, cited by the Statutory Committee with respect to the need to go beyond a 'negative emphasis on difference and disadvantage' (p. 27), highlight the need for new frames of understanding:

> The language of 'educational disadvantage' is jaded and no longer holds a moral imperative or signals the scandal of the situation and the urgency of its

---

[1] See also Downes (1993)

transformation. It is essential that we find new language to describe the reality of those young people who are being failed by the present system. We need metaphors and narratives that jolt the imagination of those educating children and young people, so that images of the possible inform their practice.

Concepts such as that of a 'living system' for education can contribute to new frames of understanding. Zappone (2002) describes education as a 'living system' and treats this as a key reference point for action:

> Education ought to be a system that is alive, that is organic. Such a system generates life, progress, achievement, communication and responsibility for everyone – especially the children – involved in the system. This requires, then, mechanisms, structures and procedures for communication, integration and coordination between all actors and agencies; not silences and secrecies nor protection of territories. (p. 41)

This term is fleshed out briefly by Zappone (2002) as implying coordination, integration and communication of policies, programmes and services.

Hyland (2002) emphasises 'that the focus of change should be on school as a whole and not just on individual teachers, however challenging this might be' (pp. 90–1). Hyland's holistic and systemic approach also implies the need to further develop understanding of the school as a living system (see also Downes 2004 on the school as a mental health system). There is a proliferation of reports in Ireland examining systemic themes of partnership and integration of services for children at risk of early school leaving (e.g., Cullen 1997, 1998; Rourke 1999; Fleming and Murphy 2000). However, features of a *living* systemic approach have not been fully developed. Such features offer a conceptual framework that goes beyond deficit models for working-class communities.

Alienation as imbalance where the subject becomes an object

A key implication of perspectives on alienation from Fromm, Freire and Marcuse is that alienation occurs across all social classes. It is not simply those viewed by deficit models as 'disadvantaged' who are susceptible to alienation. In *To have or to be?* Fromm (1980) emphasises the alienated relations of all of those conditioned by a consumerist culture: 'The attitude inherent in consumerism is that of swallowing the whole world … Modern consumers may identify themselves by the formula: I am equal to what I have and what I consume' (p. 36).

A central feature of alienation is reification, in other words, that the organic is turned into the inorganic. Alienated human subjects are turned into machines through some forms of work that make them like inanimate objects. The relationship between the subject (owner) and object (owned) is 'one of deadness not aliveness' because 'it and I have become things': 'I have it because I have the force to make it mine … this is also a reverse relationship: It has me, because my sense of identity i.e. of sanity rests upon my having it (and as many things as possible)' (Fromm, 1980, pp. 77–8).

The object consumes the subject. The object takes the place of the subject and the subject becomes the object in this reverse relationship.

For Fromm, people in Western industrialised society are characterised as being culturally conditioned to a 'having mode of existence' arising from a preoccupation with the ownership, retention and acquisition of property so that personal identity becomes reduced to being what one has rather than who one is. Consequently, people are processed into a culture of almost pathological consumption manifested in a competitive greed for material possessions. In other words, people are processed by a barely hidden Western cultural pedagogy which teaches and schools us in acquisitiveness and consumption. This is ultimately dehumanising to the extent that things become more important than people.

Central to Fromm's concept of the being-mode of existence is non-alienation, an aliveness as opposed to deadness, a movement beyond the mechanical to a 'being' as opposed to 'having'. Fromm sees students in the having mode preoccupied with dutifully attending their lectures or classes, taking copiously verbatim notes for memorisation at home in order to pass their examinations:

> But the content does not become part of their own individual system of thought … each student has become the owner of a collection of statements made by somebody else … they have one aim – to hold on to what they have 'learned' either by entrusting it firmly to their memories or by carefully guarding their notes. (1980, pp. 28–9)

Freire's (1972, p. 48) 'banking' model of education drew inspiration from Fromm's distinction between a 'having' and 'being' mode of experience. Thus Freire criticised the alienation within an objectified 'having' mode of knowledge where 'education … becomes an act of depositing'. The teacher is the depositor and students the passive depositories of an 'alienated and alienating verbosity' (p. 45) and 'knowledge is a gift bestowed by those who consider themselves knowledgeable upon those whom they consider to know nothing' (p. 45). This inversion of the subject–object relation in alienation can occur in methods of teaching where the knowledge and curriculum 'has' or consumes the person, rather than being constructed around the needs and culture of the learner. A related subject–object inversion is exemplified within an authoritarian school system where the student is to be passive, inert and de-individualised.

In contrast to the 'banking' model, Freire sees the relationship of teachers and students as a dialogic partnership. This leads to a mutual identification of 'generative themes' through 'problem posing' leading to action. This action itself leads to further reflection in an ongoing process of liberation through 'conscientisation' which has as its ultimate objective the facilitation of a humanising transformation of society.

Those 'processed out' of the cultural matrix of Western industrial societies include the 'have-nots', namely, the dispossessed, those living in poverty, the unemployed, many migrant workers and ethnic and social minorities – the 'oppressed' of Freire's pedagogy – many of whom are women. Patterns of exclusion, marginalisation and 'processing out' of the mainstream of Western industrial and economic life of increasing numbers of people in Western societies are even more evident when we consider non-industrialised, 'developing' and so-called Third World countries and continents. In tandem with economic exploitation goes the despoliation of the natural environment.

Alienation: power and control

Many practitioners in industrialised democracies in the 'developed' West, however, would instinctively resist applying Freire's dichotomy between oppressors and oppressed unquestioningly to excluded groups in their midst, and justifiably so (see Jarvis 1985). In the West, political and economic control and consensus are managed more subtly and less overtly than is evident in the polarised societies of South America and 'developing' countries generally. Because of this and because the majority of people in Western societies are often unaware, uncritical of, and relatively comfortable with, society's 'oppressive' structures, Giroux (1981) cautions that: 'It would be misleading as well as dangerous to extend without qualification Freire's theory and methods to industrialised and urbanised societies of the west' (p. 139).

Freire's (1972) conception of alienation in the context of a military dictatorship in Brazil treats alienation as oppression, where dichotomous categories exist of oppressors and the oppressed. There has been much debate about the transfer of such dualistic categories of oppressor and oppressed to the context of Western culture. The level of assumed separation and power difference between those with and largely without power may not be as extreme in many Western contexts. Nevertheless, the principle of subject–object inversion in alienation still remains evident. Fromm (1957) emphasises the role of conformity in alienation where humans are 'alienated automatons', basing security on staying close to the herd, and not being different in thought, feeling or action. Conformity to reified social categories, to objectified and advertised needs, is another form of alienation. The oppressor and oppressed is the extreme relation of alienation; another form of alienated relation is that between the *processor* and the *processed*. The student is alienated through being processed into an inorganic system.

Ruling elites, almost by definition, tend to be resistant to acknowledging themselves as oppressors (especially in Western industrial democracies). Perhaps 'conscientisation', whereby they can begin to perceive themselves as a 'processing' and 'processed' people, might be less threatening and facilitate a greater openness to change. If this perception were adopted then significant implications follow, for instance, for the current curricular content at post-primary level, for initial and in-service training of teachers at primary, second and third levels. Such an agenda seems particularly appropriate for the formal system of adult mainstream university education which is still very much curriculum-more than learner-centred. Kelly (1999) criticises educational models predominantly based on education as transmission of knowledge and curriculum as content:

> The idea of education as transmission or of curriculum as content ... is simplistic and unsophisticated because it leaves out of the reckoning major dimensions of the curriculum debate. In particular, it does not encourage or help us to take account of the children who are the recipients of this content and the objectives of the process of transmission, or of the impact of that content and that process on them, and especially their right to emancipation and empowerment.[2] (p. 53)

Marcuse (1964) emphasises the role of alienation across social classes through the construction of 'false needs' by advertising. The advertised products produce a mass of stimuli that consume the consumer: 'Most of the prevailing needs to relax, to have fun, to behave and consume in accordance with the advertisements, to love and hate what others love and hate, belong to this category of false needs' (p. 5).

Marcuse's rigid dichotomy between 'true' and 'false needs' may be somewhat simplistic. However, this dichotomy is founded on the prior principle of alienation where subjective identity is constructed through objects so that for Marcuse (1964), 'The people recognize themselves in their commodities':

> ... the irresistible output of the entertainment and information industry carry with them prescribed attitudes and habits, certain intellectual and emotional reactions which bind the consumers more or less pleasantly to the products ... And as these beneficial products become available to more individuals in more social classes, the indoctrination they carry ceases to be publicity; it becomes a way of life. (p. 12)

Substance abuse, whether of alcohol or illicit drugs, is another example of a way of life across social classes where people become consumed by products; addiction is the extreme form of the substance consuming the person. Alienation as subject–object inversion goes beyond these examples of a) knowledge/curriculum, b) advertising, c) alcohol or illicit drugs, consuming the person. Another example is that of modern media images of medically underweight 'model' women as a risk factor for anorexia nervosa (see, for example, Downes, 2004a). The human body is literally consumed by the 'objective' images.

---

[2] See also Hunting, 2000, p. 245, and Downes, 2003a for a critique of curriculum as content in the context of Estonia and Latvia

Alienation expresses a somewhat negative deficit model for all social classes in Western culture. We are all alienated at least potentially, though the forms in which our subjectivity is squeezed dry into the inorganic may vary across social class. Fromm (1964) links the inorganic state of alienation to late Freudian conceptions of the life and death drive in asking the question whether the principles of life are subordinated to those of mechanisation or whether the principles of life are dominant. Education is implicated centrally in creating proper conditions for the development of the primary potentiality of the life drive through social action; social, personal and health education; health promotion; and prevention of factors bringing alienation.

Alienation: a systems theory response

It is in relation to the pivotal concept of alienation that systems theory can become relevant. Systems theory involves a positive focus and inquiry into alienation as the imbalance of a static inorganic system. Non-equilibrium within an organic system is an imbalance which contains the potential for balance as part of a flexible ongoing internal dynamic process of change. The narrative of systems theory accommodates the less extreme form of alienation within a framework of imbalance and the need to develop organic models of balance that include a high degree of non-equilibrium – and it accommodates the extreme form of alienation as overcoming imbalance by moving from a static inert inorganic system to a living organic system. An imbalance of alienation pervades a range of levels within a system and, with extreme forms of alienation, the system becomes inert and inorganic. Systems theory does not merely accommodate a conception of alienation: it requires it, because a dynamic system has an imbalance or movement from equilibrium. And the further extreme of imbalance is the alienated stasis of an inorganic system.

Within this framework, alienation's guiding principle of subject–object inversion encompasses two levels:

- oppressors and the marginalisation of the oppressed
- processors, as well as those processed into an inorganic system and those processed out of an inorganic system.

The need arises for the 'organism' to remedy its own internal imbalance or, at a more extreme level, for a static inorganic 'alienated' system to become organic.

Movement to an organic system with the school as an exemplar

Capra (1982) outlines key differences between an organism and a machine. The latter is constructed through a precise assembly plan, the former shows a high degree of internal flexibility and plasticity. A machine's activities are determined by its structure, an organism by its process. Machines function according to linear chains of cause and effect. The functioning of organisms is guided by 'cyclical patterns of information flow known as feedback loops' (Capra, 1982, pp. 288–9), i.e., a non-linear interconnectedness. Capra (1982) notes that a living, self-organising system 'means that its order in structure and function is not imposed by the environment but is established by the system itself' (p. 290).

Toffler (1980), like Capra (1982), contrasts the holism of an organic system with a Cartesian approach that breaks an entity into its constituent parts. The New Revised Primary School Curriculum (1999) is holistic in the sense that its Social, Personal and Health Education (SPHE) curriculum, integrated with other subjects, challenges the Cartesian split between emotion and reason (see also Downes, 2003). Adopting Marcuse's (1964) somewhat limited distinction between 'high' culture and 'mass' culture, it is arguable that giving a central role to emotions in the new revised curriculum imports 'mass' culture into the traditional domain of supposedly 'high' culture in the school, as emotions are a great democratiser. Emotions of love, grief, sadness, anger and joy are experienced by all. For Glasser (1969) emotions are the 'bridge to relevance' in the education system. Concern with embodied knowledge and awareness would also help overcome a Cartesian split between mind and body.

Capra (1982) highlights that organic systems are multi-levelled: 'The tendency of living systems to form multi-levelled structures whose levels differ in complexity is all pervasive throughout nature and has to be seen as a basic principle of self-organisation' (p. 303).

In contrast to the largely school-based focus of government policy in DEIS (2005), a multi-levelled focus is now being adopted by the Statutory Committee on Educational Disadvantage which 'recognises that the problem of educational disadvantage cannot be solved in mainstream school-based educational programmes alone … the committee proposes a new strategy that places the solutions to educational disadvantage within an inclusive lifelong learning framework' (p. 4). The ambience of lifelong learning extends legitimately from the individual to the group to the local community and beyond, to initial and continuing professional education and to lifelong education – from the non-formal to the formal to the informal. It is itself a multi-levelled organism comprising many suborganisms (parts). It also legitimately operates at many levels within larger social organisms, indicating its potential role as a change 'amplifier.'[3]

Capra (1982) identifies two principal dynamic phenomena of self-organisation,

---

[3] Bronfenbrenner's (1979) systems level framework in developmental psychology offers further development of a multi-levelled focus for social action to bring constructive system-level change. This focus for social action to bring constructive system-level change can examine strategies for overcoming imbalance or alienation within what he terms the micro, meso, exo and macro systems.

namely, self-renewal and self-transcendence. The former involves 'the ability of living systems continuously to renew and recycle their components while maintaining the integrity of their overall structure', while self-transcendence is 'the ability to reach out creatively beyond physical and mental boundaries in the processes of learning, development and evolution' (p. 291). An implication of systems theory not just for the relation between primary education and adult education, but for social transformation generally, is that change amplifers must be operative throughout the entire organism if they are to effect self-transcendent change. They involve an interplay between *both* bottom-up and top-down forces for change. Such an interplay is a dynamic one where one direction does not subsume the other. This contrasts with Connolly's (2003) description of the way in which the formal education system inappropriately adopts methods from community education to suit its own purposes. While seeming to value the methodology of community education, specifically to target marginalised groups, Connolly (2003) argues that the formal adult education system borrows some of the approaches to force people to attend through 'top-down, compulsory imposition on people who have very little social power' (p. 15). Furthermore, the community education sector is contained and deprived of resources, which she terms the 'glass fence'.

Capra (1982) emphasises that a living system is never static:

> A high degree of non-equilibrium is absolutely necessary for self-organisation; living systems maintain their self-organisation which allows the system to remain in a state of non-equilibrium, in which it is always at work ... living systems are open systems that continually operate far from equilibrium. (p. 291)

In other words, a static unchanging school or institutional culture is an inorganic system. Capra (1982) further notes that because they are open systems, organisms 'have to maintain a continuous exchange of energy and matter with their environment to stay alive' (p. 291): 'These self-organising systems have a high degree of stability ... [which] is utterly dynamic and must not be confused with equilibrium. It consists of maintaining the same overall structure in spite of ongoing changes and replacement of its components' (p. 292).

The feedback relationship among subsystems and the larger wholes formed by these units is another key area of focus to facilitate an organic system. So, for example, the feedback relationship between parents and schools needs systemic support through the Home School Community Liaison Teacher or someone in a similar kind of role. Similarly, feedback from teachers regarding bullying in their class as part of a whole-school approach to bullying requires a level of open communication in the school environment. A systemic focus on the need to facilitate feedback would suggest a focus on a range of pathways for feedback, so that, for example, intermediaries on the staff allocated to specific roles could coordinate the whole-school approach to bullying – so that the communicative environment would not simply rely on one path of feedback between the teacher and the principal (see also Downes, Maunsell and Ivers, 2006).

Capra (1982) also highlights the holonic features of a living system:

> At each level of complexity we encounter systems that are integrated, self-organising wholes consisting of smaller parts and, at the same time acting as parts of larger wholes ... it is a holon in Arthur Koestler's term, manifesting both the independent properties of wholes and the dependent properties of parts. Thus the pervasiveness of order in the universe takes on a new meaning: order at one systems level is the consequence of self-organisation at a larger level. (p. 303)

Capra notes that Koestler:

> emphasised that each holon has two opposite tendencies: an integrative tendency to function as part of the larger whole and a self-assertive tendency to preserve its individual autonomy ... These two tendencies are opposite but complementary. In a healthy system – an individual, a society or an ecosystem – there is a balance between integration and self-assertion. This balance is not static but consists of a dynamic interplay between the two complementary tendencies, which make the whole system flexible and open to change. (p. 27)

Acknowledgement of this whole–part relationship in self-organising systems invites a focus on the role of the teacher, not only as a representative of a whole system that processes (i.e., as the processor) but also as a part that has been processed into the system him/herself. Such processing may have been through the limitations of pre-service education (such as the need for more development of self-awareness and conflict-resolution skills)[4] as well as through other limits within the system (such as the pupil–teacher ratio, or lack of supports for teaching at-risk children). Imbalance occurs at this holonic level. Recognition of two levels of imbalance or alienation for the teacher a) as processor of a curriculum into students and b) as being the passive recipient of a role, of being processed into a role within the system, invites a restructuring of this relation in order to bring balance into the system.

Future challenges for lifelong learning

Yet a largely narrow academic preoccupation with cognitive curricula, accreditation problems, teaching methodologies, adult learning processes, institutional problems of resourcing, skill training programmes and so forth, is no longer an adequate response for a proactive system of lifelong learning. While valid, useful and even necessary to a degree, it reflects a major imbalance of focus

---

[4] See also Barnardos (2006) and Quality Development Out-of-School Services QDOSS (Downes, 2006) on this theme

within the field – a kind of technicist approach – and indicates a flight from relevance and openness to, and engagement with, the wider society. A key agenda for lifelong learning is to become focused as much on the collective as on the individual. Issues for this agenda include concern with poverty, exclusion, marginalisation, oppression and their causes – in personal but also in local, communal, societal and global systemic settings. The challenge is to enter and engage with the struggle against 'surplus suffering' in Sam Keen's (1992) phrase. This is the social action strand of adult education, which concerns itself with 'situations not (academic) subjects' as Lindemann (1926/1989) puts it and which needs to be reactivated by educators at all levels today.

Adult education is a political social phenomenon and cannot escape its embeddedness in the economic, social and political realities and challenges of its time. Community education, as recognised by the Irish White Paper on adult education (2000), particularly embodies this political component of adult education. There is a challenge to adult education practitioners and to the field in general to:

- engage proactively with the pressing issues of the world today in order to promote and support the development of a 'people-centred' world
- commit to a vision which will contradict a sense of hopelessness by holding out the possibility of hopes, dreams and aspirations leading to action for change
- activate, renew and develop adult education's long-established and respected social action traditions
- operate whenever and wherever possible as a countercultural site of critical resistance to dehumanisation and ecological degradation within the Western industrial paradigm.

These are key elements of a living, organic, systemic-level focus for adult education and other areas of education.[5]

---

[5] In contrast to Habermas' contention that systems theory basically provides a merely reductionist account of evolution as a process of increasing capacity for adaptation (Dews, 1992, p. 2)

Model of Development from 'Alienation' to Systems Theory as a Pedagogy of the Processed

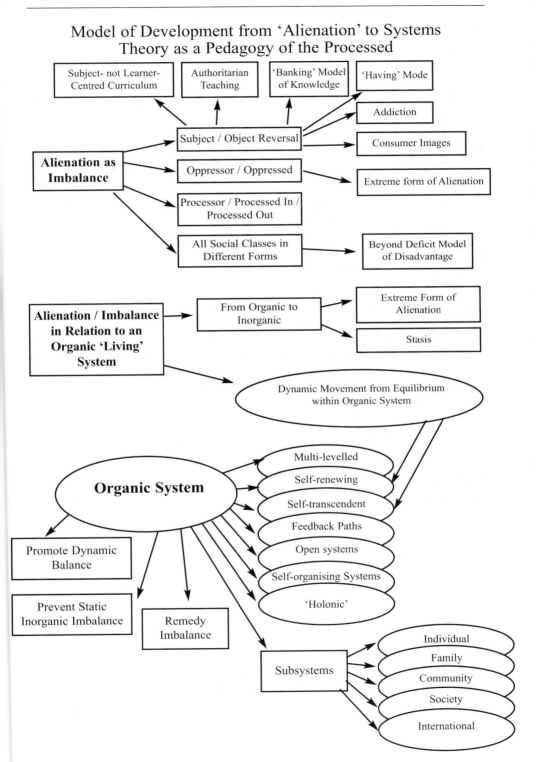

Conclusion

To conclude, the concept of alienation in critical theory challenges a view of deficit models being applied to one social class only. All social classes need to recognise their forms of alienation. Systems theory can offer a framework which views alienation as a multi-dimensional construct with regard to imbalance. Imbalance occurs, at its most extreme, within a static inorganic system. Movement from equilibrium in a dynamic living system is also a necessary imbalance for growth that is a less extreme form of alienation than the stasis of inorganic reification. Freire's binary conception of alienation between oppressor and oppressed is adapted to include alienation as also expressing a triadic dimension of processor, being processed into an inorganic system, and being processed out of an inorganic system. This leads to an integration of the concept of alienation within systems theory. This living systems focus implies a broadening of perspective from an individualist one on the deficits of the 'disadvantaged' child and his/her family to an examination of the need for promotion of balance across a range of dimensions of alienation within potentially dynamic and open living systems and subsystems of school, community and wider culture.

References

Barnardos (2006) *Make the Grade*, Dublin: Barnardos

Bronfenbrenner, U. (1979) *The Ecology of Human Development*, Cambridge, MA: Harvard University Press

Capra, F. (1982) *The Turning Point: Science, Society and the Rising Culture*, London: Fontana

Connolly, B. (2003) 'Community education: Listening to the voices', *The Adult Learner*, vol. x, pp. 9–19

Cullen, B. (1997) *Integrated services and children at risk: The integration of services for tackling early school leaving and educational disadvantage at local community levels*, Dublin: Combat Poverty Agency

Cullen, B. (1998) *Social partnership and children's services: The potential of local partnership programmes for developing children's services in Ireland*, Trinity College Dublin: Children's Research Centre

Department of Education and Science (2005) *DEIS: Delivering Equality of Opportunity in Schools – An Action Plan for Educational Inclusion*, Dublin: DES

Dews, P. (ed.) (1992) *Autonomy and solidarity: Interviews with Jurgen Habermas*, London: Verso (revised edition)

Downes, P. (2003) 'The New Curriculum of Social, Personal and Health Education in Irish Primary Schools: Self-Awareness, Introversion and the

Role of the Teacher', *Kwartalnik Padagogiczny* (Journal of Education, Poland), no. 4. vol. 190, pp. 93–112

Downes, P. (2003a) *Living with heroin: Identity, social exclusion and HIV among the Russian-speaking minorities in Estonia and Latvia*, Legal Information Centre for Human Rights, Tallinn and the Educational Disadvantage Centre, Dublin

Downes, P. (2004) *Psychological Support Services for Ballyfermot: Present and Future*, Ballyfermot: URBAN

Downes, P. (2004a) 'School promoted beauty contests in Poland and Estonia: A risk factor for anorexia and bulimia nervosa, and contrary to the UN Convention on the Elimination of all forms of discrimination against Women?' *Kwartalnik Padagogiczny* (Poland), no. 2

Downes, P. (2006) *Quality Development of Out of School Services: An Agenda for Development*, compiled by Paul Downes for the QDOSS Network: Dublin

Downes, P., Maunsell, C., and Ivers, J. (2006) *A holistic approach to early school leaving and school retention in Blanchardstown: Current issues and future steps for services and schools*, Dublin: Blanchardstown Area Partnership

Downes, T. (1993) 'Pedagogy of the processed', MA thesis, St Patrick's College, Maynooth

Educational Disadvantage Committee (2005) *Moving Beyond Educational Disadvantage 2002–2005*, Dublin: DES

Fleming, T. and Murphy, M. (2000) *Squaring the circle: An analysis of programmes in Dublin schools to prevent early school leaving*, Dublin: Dublin Employment Pact

Freire, P. (1972) *Pedagogy of the Oppressed*, London: Penguin

Freire, P. (2000) *Pedagogy of the Oppressed*, New York: Continuum

Fromm, E. (1957) *The art of loving*, London: George Allen and Unwin

Fromm, E. (1964) *The heart of man: Its Genius for Good and Evil*, New York: Harper and Row

Fromm, E. (1980) *To have or to be?* London: Cape

Gilligan, A. L. (ed.) (2002) *Primary Education: Ending Disadvantage. Proceedings and Action Plan of National Forum*, Educational Disadvantage Centre, St Patrick's College, Drumcondra

Giroux, H. A. (1981) *Ideology, culture and the process of schooling*, Lewes: The Falmer Press

Glasser, W. (1969) *Control theory in the classroom*, New York and London: Harper and Row

Habermas, J. (1990) *Philosophical Discourse of Modernity*, London: Polity Press

Hyland, Á. (2002) 'Looking to the future – Ending disadvantage?' in Gilligan, A. L. (ed.) *Primary Education: Ending Disadvantage. Proceedings and Action Plan of National Forum*, Dublin: Educational Disadvantage Centre, St Patrick's College

Jarvis, P. (1985) *The sociology of adult and continuing education*, London: Routledge

Keen, S. (1992) *Fire in the belly: On being a man*, London: Piaktus

Kelly, A. V. (1999) *The Curriculum: Theory and Practice*, London: Paul Chapman Publishing Ltd

Lindemann, E. (1926/1989) *The meaning of education*, Oklahoma: Norman

Marcuse, H. (1964) *One Dimensional Man*, Boston: Beacon Press

Rourke, S. (1999) *A learning experience: Case studies on Local Integrated Strategies to tackle educational disadvantage*, Dublin, Combat Poverty Agency

Toffler, A. (1980) *The Third Wave*, London: Pan/Collins

Zappone, K. (2002) 'Achieving equality in children's education' in Gilligan, A. L. (ed.) *Primary Education: Ending Disadvantage. Proceedings and Action Plan of National Forum*, Dublin: Educational Disadvantage Centre, St Patrick's College

4

The Dilemma of Difference

Ann Louise Gilligan

There is a growing literature on the issue of 'difference' and a deepening awareness that we must take difference seriously in our reflection and our practice. In her book *Which Equalities Matter?* Anne Phillips states, 'Difference has begun to displace inequality as the dominant concern of progressive politics' (1999, p. 20). However, there are real dilemmas about this new focus as there are various understandings about the nature of difference and how to interpret it.

In this chapter I will outline certain understandings of difference from inherited, traditional perspectives, to more liberal views and then to recent challenging insights from post-modern philosophy. I will postulate that while there is a willingness and openness within the Irish education system to accommodate to difference, as yet, we as educators have had little opportunity to examine our own presuppositions, or reflect on our inherited conceptualisations of difference. While there are a variety of interpretations of this term, some more positive than others, I will contend that to clarify our thinking could lead to more inclusive education practice.

Different understandings of difference

Many people remain mired in a very old set of oppositions endemic to Western philosophy – mind/body; intellect/emotion; reason/imagination; culture/nature; man/woman. Such dualisms translate into hierarchies that privilege and exalt one half of each dichotomy over the other. If that which is different is always less than or greater than its opposite, then such a way of thinking creates a deeply ingrained mindset that finds it difficult to embrace difference and to acknowledge otherness. Furthermore, such thinking contributes to the divisions that we experience in a rigidly bifurcated world.

There is another way of reflecting on difference and that is to make little of it, *assimilate* it into the same. Much of this thinking informs a liberal description of equality. We are all the *same*, essentially human, so our focus ought to be on that which we share in common. The liberal agenda of establishing laws and rights for the common good is informed by this kind of thinking. In the interest of *fairness* there is one set of rules, laws and regulations that apply to all. From this perspective differences are accidental, private and not essential. This focus on sameness and oneness has shaped understandings of human normativity and identity. To be free is to transcend individual and group difference and enter the great melting pot of sameness.

This whole way of thinking can have an underside, which manifests in a fear of otherness, whereby the 'other than the same' is often viewed with suspicion. When sameness is normative the expectation can grow that those who are different must leave their differences aside and pretend to be the same, especially if you are going to 'make it' in society. Many people living out of an assimilationist set of understandings are perfectly aware that there are differences between and among people but they expect that from their normative position such people ought to live their differences in private and not 'in their face'. This whole mindset allows the dominant group to ignore their differences and pretend that they are living in a neutral space.

A mirror image of assimilationist thinking is the popular notion of *complementarity*. Here again, sameness or oneness takes precedence, and the 'other than the same' is seen as part of the same, complementing the lack in the same, but clearly less than the same. To use a gender example, if the male represents *the way* to be human then the other of the human, the female, can complement his qualities to make up the whole of his essence. The expression 'his better half' is an expression of this socially constructed reality. Equally questionable but reflective of a similar mentality is the line from that popular song 'you were the wind beneath my wings'!

A further category critiques and challenges what has gone before and asks that we recognise *difference* not sameness as the norm.[1] Within this analysis of difference there is a challenge to think in a nuanced way about difference. Albeit normative, certain differences are to be celebrated, especially those related to issues of identity, while other differences, which are the result of grave injustice, are to be condemned. One of the ethical challenges in these post-modern times is to distinguish between these positions.

---

[1] This position does not dismiss the legacy of understanding on the shared nature of our common humanity. However, it suggests that current historical developments profoundly challenge our earlier presuppositions and call on us to expand our thinking to include new conceptualisations of being and becoming human that reflect radical plurality. Is there a point at which one is not yet human? Is humanity socially constructed?

Difference to be celebrated

In the first instance difference is recognised as part of the weave of the tapestry of life that ought to be celebrated. Asserting a positive sense of group difference has been a key ingredient in the emancipatory movement of various different groups. We are familiar with the Black is Beautiful movement in the US and have a growing appreciation of the special ethnicity and culture of Travellers in our own country. A further example is the Gay Pride movement which highlights homosexuality as a different sexual identity to heterosexuality, which can be recognised and celebrated. Here there is recognition of group difference, group solidarity, and a clear challenge to honour and respect such difference. This recognition and public celebration of group difference is at the heart of building a truly equitable society. As Iris Young reminds us, the promotion of equality 'among socially and culturally differentiated groups, who mutually respect one another and affirm one another in their differences', is foundational in building a participatory democracy (Young, 1990, p. 163). I would wager that a rigorous understanding of the heterogeneous nature of society would allow a new appreciation of the normativity of difference. Furthermore, it would acknowledge that all social groups must find public voice and recognition in the building of any stable society.

As we hone our thinking about difference and the importance of mutual recognition of minority group differences, it is vital that we honour the diversity within any given group. We need to avoid essentialist thinking about difference – all Travellers are not the same – there are rich Travellers who may suffer because of their ethnicity but not as a result of poverty.

This latter example illustrates that any reflection on difference calls for an analysis of the differences of *power* – it is not simply that we are different but that we share privilege and power differently. True celebration of difference should alter the power relations and challenge majority groupings to share their power and privilege in new ways. Genuine celebration of difference and diversity would alter the balance of power in any society. There is little doubt that the praxis of difference would expose privilege and challenge distortions of power.

As indicated, certain traditional understandings of difference have caused division and/or denial; during this current period we must be on our guard that growth in awareness of difference does not lead to apathy or indifference. Discourse on difference contains an ethical imperative that challenges both self-perception and understandings of the nature of human relationships. Luce Irigaray measures justice on our ability to honour and respect the absolute alterity of the other (1993, p. 6). Indeed she argues that the principle of ethics consists concretely in respect for real difference (1996, p. 52).

Hannah Arendt's counsel that we should begin by 'seeing oneself as other' could open up the reflective space to radically rethink our way of being in the world. 'The worldliness of living things means that there is no subject that is not also an object and appears as such to someone else, who guarantees its "objective" reality ... plurality is the law of the earth' (1994). Along with the challenge of seeing ourselves 'as other', there is the further challenge, namely to understand the concept of 'multiple identity', and then observe how that awareness alters our self-understanding.[2] Put simply, within each one of us there resides an intersection of differences – a lesbian woman from an ethnic minority group is such an example. 'Having multiple identities allows a person to relate to different people in different situations and contexts in different ways at different times' (Zappone, 2003, p. 15).

Difference to be condemned

A principle that all differences should be celebrated is not simply a superficial and ill thought-out position, it can serve as an undertow allowing injustices to be condoned and abuse of power to be excused rather than confronted.

I will illustrate my exploration of 'negative difference' by engaging in a brief exploration of how the education system in Ireland has tackled what is commonly but erroneously, I would contend, designated as 'educational disadvantage'.

In recent years the counterpoint to the discussion on the unchanging problem of 'educational disadvantage' has been a growing discourse on the need for a system that offers *equality* of access, opportunity, participation and outcome for all. Few would fault the idealism of such aspiration but those charged to reflect on and change the system in some lasting way would be forgiven for highlighting the ongoing failure to deliver the promise of such language. In other words, the focus on equality within the discourse on 'disadvantage' could cloak some of the fundamental problems in our system and leave them unexamined. The language of equality and access for all can distract from a radical critique of the *system* of education that should indeed aspire for the inclusion of all.[3] In light of the earlier investigation on a new conceptualisation of difference I must ask whether the *one* system, the *same* system is indeed adequate for all. Is it not correct that the language of equality of access for all to our education system starts with the presumption of the adequacy of a homogenous system to meet the needs of *all* participants? From the perspective of the 'other', is there not a presupposition that all participants are somewhat the same. There is a clear challenge to develop a discourse that recognises the right to education for all, and integral to that right resides the recognition of, and respect for, difference.

---

[2] The writings of Griffin and Braidotti (2002) and Nancy Fraser (1997) are helpful in elaborating this concept.

[3] In adopting this position my intention is not to take sides on what has become an overly dualistic debate 'whether difference or equality?', rather my aspiration is to highlight the point that mutual respect for difference must be the guiding norm for an 'equal' system of education.

Here again the issues of power and control must be addressed. The hegemony of those who control the system ought to be questioned, because the system in place best serves the offspring of those of like social, cultural and economic backgrounds. This raises an obvious question, how often do we question and highlight the fundamental differences of those who are in charge of the system – their cultural background; their economic status; their social standing; their environment and community settings? As we are aware from the literature, we frequently analyse the lives of the 'educationally disadvantaged', we recite how their failure in education is due to a complex set of factors that range from their social, economic and cultural background to their community and environmental settings. In other words, difference is reflected on negatively to account for the failure of those who experience disadvantage and who fail to meet the established educational standard. The challenge in this analysis is surely that we who live abundantly resourced lives recognise our difference, the differences of our advantage and ask whether these differences contribute to the educational failure of others in a system that we have used our power to create. Furthermore, it suggests that any efforts to change the system, to render it more inclusive should include a process of 'collective problem-solving, which depends for its legitimacy and wisdom on the expression, and criticism of, the diverse opinions of all the members of society' (Young, 2000, p. 6). A structure that deliberately attends to a representative voice across the diversity of participants should render the education system more equitable. It is hoped that the new regionalisation of the DES will seize the opportunity and embrace the challenge to develop a more democratic and representative system. It is also timely to call for a review of employment practices across the education sector, allowing those who have had little opportunity to share the power and resources of what is an almost exclusively middle-class preserve, to work professionally within the system. The Children's Aid Society has developed and funded a highly successful model of parent empowerment in community schools in areas of New York City.[4] Instead of parents being involved in their children's schooling only on the schools' terms, they have developed a parent involvement model that gives real power to the parents and encourages parent advocacy efforts. As part of this model certain parents are professionally trained (and paid) as Home School Community Liaison officers. 'The parent coordinator should have strong ties to the local community and links to the school and parents' (Dryfoss et al., 2005, p. 47). Many of these coordinators themselves attended schools in the local communities in which they now work. This model, which has now been evaluated, has proved highly successful and gives new credibility to the language of partnership with parents in their children's education.

---

[4] A full description of this model of 'Community Schools' can be found in Dryfoos, J. G. et al. (eds) (2005) *Community Schools in Action: Lessons from a Decade of Practice*, Oxford University Press.

The education system

While we can say that the formal system gives rights to all to participate, the substantive roll-out of the practice of these rights is radically different. We can highlight a number of responses, from blaming the unsuccessful to patronising the 'others' by creating criteria that so suit the privileged that those from different backgrounds need to negotiate a way to participate. Take, for example, teacher education. There is a requirement of honours in the Irish language examination, along with 440 points, in the Leaving Certificate for those who want to become primary school teachers. While few would contest the wisdom of attaining a high standard of Irish to teach in Irish schools, most who understand that equality can be achieved under conditions of difference would wonder why proficiency in the Irish language isn't a requirement at the end of the course on teacher training and not a condition of entry. As it stands, is it any wonder that there is little diversity in Colleges of Education and in the teaching profession in Ireland today?

Imaging possibility

It is important that educators search for new theoretical frameworks to understand the concept of difference and then translate these insights into transformative practice. I propose that the work of Amartya Sen and Martha Nussbaum offers such a framework in what is called the *capability approach*. While it is not possible in this article to develop fully the implications of this theory for educational practice, let me indicate some key ideas that will be explored in future work. The capability approach opens up a new and creative perspective, allowing us to examine anew that which we have falsely designated as 'educational disadvantage'. If educators focus on children's potential and their ability, rather than allowing the injustice of systemic poverty to lower their expectations and motivation, then we would initiate 'a process of expanding the real freedoms that people enjoy' (Sen, 1999, p. 3). This approach moves beyond what otherwise could be construed as a dualistic divide between negative and positive difference, placing instead an emphasis on the unique potential of each individual human being. 'At the heart of this tradition is a twofold intuition about human beings: namely that all, just by being human are of equal dignity and worth, no matter where they are situated in society, and that the primary source of this worth is a power of moral choice within them, a power that consists in the ability to plan a life in accordance with one's own evaluation of ends' (Nussbaum, 1999, p. 57). 'The capabilities approach considers people one by one' (Nussbaum, 1999, p. 34) and does not simply identify individuals with families or ignore the unique potential for a life of freedom that resides within each one, if issues of power and the just distribution of resources are addressed. All this reminds us to enquire into the need individuals have for resources and their diverse abilities to convert resources into functionings.

While it is correct that children and young people who are failed by the current education system often come from backgrounds of poverty, yet an exclusive focus on the negative differences that influence their lives can fail to acknowledge their potential and their resilience. If resourced adequately the cycle of poverty can be broken, which in turn could allow a life of well-being to be realised. Recognition of the differences in this situation calls for flexibility of the school system and a relationship of respect and expectation along with the belief that, given the right opportunity, potential will be realised and a life of well-being will be achieved. Nussbaum (1999) reminds us that most infants are born with basic capabilities. However, the development of what she calls *internal capabilities* is significantly influenced by the quality of the environment and the education afforded. Where there is resonance between an individual's internal capability and the external responding set of opportunities, it is likely that a life of freedom and fulfilment will be realised. Part of the development of this relationship is the awareness by those working within the system that many children who live with the injustice of poverty live in homes of enormous love, care and fun. Parents who have had few educational opportunities themselves often have a natural capacity to educate themselves and their own children and encourage their development in creative ways.[5]

These post-modern times place new challenges on all working within the Irish educational system to be both critically vigilant and creatively imaginative. There are many delicate balances to be held at this time. Respecting and celebrating cultural differences, different identities, the intersections of the axes of difference and the multiple identities we find even within ourselves, while at the same time expressing anger at the ongoing negative influence of poverty in this affluent land. Faced with the dilemma of difference there is an opportunity to ask some fundamental questions, such as whether there is the will to change as radically as the call for justice demands, and whether we can image and create a system of education that is open to the 'now' and is fluid and flexible enough to anticipate what 'is not yet, but still to come'.

References

Arendt, H. (1994) *Essays in Understanding 1930–1954,* New York: Harcourt Brace and Company

Dryfoo, J. G. et al. (eds) (2005) *Community Schools in Action: Lessons from a Decade of Practice,* Oxford University Press

---

[5]   Our work in West Tallaght over the past twenty years would confirm this observation; see Gilligan, A. L. and Zappone, K. (2006) *Love and Social Change, Reflecting on a Model of Community Education*, Dublin: An Cosán

Fraser, N. (1997) 'Equality, Difference and Democracy: Recent Feminist Debates in the United States' in Dean, J. (ed.) *Feminism and the New Democracy,* London: Sage

Fraser, N. (1997) *Justice Interruptus, Critical Reflections on the 'Postsocialist' Condition,* London: Routledge

Gilligan, A. L. and Zappone, K. (2006) *Love and Social Change, Reflecting on a Model of Community Education,* Dublin: An Cosán

Griffin, G. and Braidotti, R. (2002) *Thinking Differently, A Reader in European Women's Studies,* London: Zed Books

Irigaray, L. (1993) *An Ethics of Sexual Difference,* trans. by C. Burke and G. Gill, Ithaca, New York: Cornell University Press

Irigaray, L. (1996) *I Love to You,* trans. by A. Martin, New York: Routledge

Nussbaum, M. (1999) *Sex and Social Justice,* Oxford University Press

Nussbaum, M. (2000) *Women and Human Development, The Capabilities Approach,* Cambridge University Press

Phillips, A. (1999) *Which Equalities Matter?* London: Polity Press

Sen, A. (1999) *Development as Freedom,* New York: Alfred A. Knope

Young, I. (1990) *Justice and the Politics of Difference,* Princeton: Princeton University Press

Young, I. (2000) *Inclusion and Democracy*, London: Oxford University Press

Zappone, K. (2003) *Re-Thinking Identity, The Challenge of Diversity,* commissioned by the Joint Equality and Human Rights Forum

5

Disadvantage and Diversity in Early Childhood Education

Louise Derman-Sparks and Karen Fite

Those of us who work with children and families serve an increasingly diverse population. We are also challenged to provide quality care and education within a social–economic structure that disadvantages some groups of people and advantages others. We must keep learning anew what quality practice means.

Diversity, rightly considered, is a wonderful thing: it is a source of vital learning and support for children and families. On the other hand, disadvantage is a systemic blight that sabotages healthy development. However, in our experience, these two realities have become harmfully entangled in educational thought and practice in the US and elsewhere. This chapter attempts to untangle the two, an essential step in building a caring educational system and a society that truly nurtures all of its children. In addition, we also suggest elements of educational programmes that equitably treat diversity as both a strength and a disadvantage. Our comments will focus on how diversity and disadvantage issues play out in the US.

Disadvantage and advantage

The dictionary, an illuminating place to start, tells us that disadvantage is a lack of advantage, that (as a verb) it means to place at a disadvantage or to affect unfavourably, and that there are people, 'the disadvantaged', who are placed at a disadvantage, particularly with regard to social opportunities. These meanings of 'disadvantage' call for a look at another definition – that of 'advantage': the position, state, or circumstance of being ahead of another or of having the better

47

of him or her; a favourable circumstance which gives one a better position or is the result of a superior position; an increased well-being or convenience.

The meaning of advantage is the ghost that lurks within the meaning of disadvantage. How we understand the relationship between disadvantage and advantage profoundly influences our thinking about what to do about both. Disadvantage is what you get after advantage has happened, the leftovers from the table of the advantaged society. So, who gets to the table first and eats most of the meal? Who sets the table and invites the guests, and who decides where to toss the leftovers? When we identify the advantaged, we can also identify the disadvantaged.

In the US, the portrait of economic disadvantage – being poor – often has dark skin or is female or is of 'diverse' religion or language. Moreover, those who hold economic and political power get to choose the characteristics of those who get advantages and those who do not. The advantaged use the differences as the reason for not having, thus the intersection between diversity and disadvantage is constructed. In Ireland, you have had your own long struggle against those who would disadvantage you. At the same time, it is also necessary to look carefully at how the current Irish care and education systems may now be advantaging some and disadvantaging others. Whether this process is intentional or done by people unaware of creating such underlying dynamics, the outcome is equally hurtful.

Diversity and who has it

The dictionary tells us that diverse means different in character or quality; not of the same kind; unlike; and that diversity is the condition of being diverse. There is a ghost here too, an old meaning for diversity: contrary to what is agreeable, good or right. These definitions raise the question of whom do speak when we speak about diversity. In another words, who qualifies as 'diverse', as being unlike or not right?

In the US we are certainly talking about people with the darker ranges of skin colour and both citizens and immigrants whose home language, religion and cultures differ from those of the dominant white, European American societies. In Ireland you are talking about Travellers, and 'ethnic minority' asylum seekers or refugees whose way of life includes differences from the dominant Irish culture. (And, ironically, in your past, Irish culture would have been considered different from, and less than, the colonial English culture.) We are also talking about non-traditional families, including gay and lesbian families; people with physical or psychological disabilities; and girls and women because they may not adhere to the dominant norms of patriarchal culture. But, do we talk about the groups who are advantaged in our societies as being part of diversity? In the US we usually don't. People in those groups are considered to be what is 'normal' and 'right', not 'different or 'unlike'.

Thus, in another way, diversity as 'different', and disadvantage as having 'less than', get tangled.

A rationale for the disadvantaging of the diverse

In *Blaming the Victim* (Ryan, 1971) the author identified a key dynamic at the core of American society – 'justifying inequality by finding defects in the victims of inequality' (1971, p. xiii). Victim-blaming ideology operates in a four-step process. First, identify the societal problem (e.g., school failure, poverty). Second, identify those who are affected by the problem (i.e., the school dropouts, the poor) and figure out how they are different from the advantaged (i.e., the school successes, the wealthy). The third step is the critical twist: identify the *differences* in the people who are victimized by the problem as the *cause* of the problem. Then, in the fourth step, create a governmental or non-profit agency programme to correct the differences, or, in other words, to fix the victim (pp. 8–9). This solution is decided upon without any real consultation with the people who are experiencing the problem.

In contrast to victim-blaming is the work of people such as Myles Horton (1998) who did adult educational and organising work in the rural south of the US throughout most of the twentieth century, including work with many of the people who led the American Civil Rights movement of the 1960s. He relates that when he began his work, he wanted people to have the problems for which he had the solutions. He then learned that he first had to listen to what people saw as their problems and then help them figure out how they wanted to solve the problems they had identified.

Ryan argues that victim-blaming is an attempt to chart a middle course between an overtly repressive view that accepts the disadvantaging of some as necessary to maintain the proper advantaging of others, and the radical view that identifies society as the problem and seeks major systemic changes to create a more equitable society. Victim-blaming allows people to maintain their advantages while also feeling good about themselves because they are trying to help the disadvantaged. Consequently, Ryan calls it 'a brilliant ideology for justifying a perverse form of social action designed to change, not society, as one might expect, but rather society's victim' (p. 8).

And, when problems of disadvantage are not quickly solved through victim-blaming approaches, or the advantaged begin to feel the pinch of a declining economy, victim-blaming can turn into the more repressive view. In the US we are seeing a resurgence of the conviction that the privileges that affluent Americans enjoy (and that most Americans enjoy in comparison to much of the rest of the world) are simply the fruits of natural superiority and therefore deserved.

The victim-blaming perspective operates in care and education programmes under the guise of a 'cultural deprivation' argument, which posits that the family culture and language of non-dominant groups are the source of their children's problems in school and, therefore, also the cause of their subsequent low-income as adults. In the US, this cultural deprivation approach is the framework for much of the policy and programmes for 'disadvantaged' children and families. Explanations for the lack of school success range from: they don't have language (because they do not speak English, although they speak fluently at home), they don't have a concept of time, their families don't value education, the children are disrespectful because they abide by different rules of respect to adults, the children do not know how to work independently (their culture encourages them to work cooperatively with others rather than in competition). Therefore, school programmes work to teach children different ways of speaking, thinking and acting – and make clear in many ways that the children's home way of being is inferior. Here is the insidious confounding of disadvantage and diversity with tragically harmful consequences to those diverse children we want to serve. Is this happening in Ireland as well?

Ways that diversity is disadvantaged in educational practice

Polices and practices in schools disadvantage children who are 'diverse' in a variety of ways. Girls often receive subtle and not-so-subtle messages about lower expectations for their academic achievement. Teachers are much more likely to do a task for young girls rather than teach them how to do it for themselves, as the teachers of boys do. Children with various forms of disability face several obstacles to learning at their full ability. Programmes may not make adaptation for specific learning problems, because children are all expected to learn the same way and at the same speed; wheelchairs don't fit into classrooms or through doors; teachers do not know sign language; guide dogs cannot be accommodated in the school; textbooks are not available on tape.

Children in low-income families may come to school suffering the harmful effects of economic disadvantage: insufficient nutrition; toxic substances like lead in their environment affecting their health; fatigued because of overcrowding in their homes; untreated or poorly treated health problems. At school they may meet teachers who assume they will not be as intelligent or have too low self-esteem to learn, or blame parents for lack of concern and involvement when their work schedule does not allow them to attend school functions. If low-income parents do manage to come to school, they are likely to have significantly less influence than wealthy parents, or they may feel uneasy in the school setting because they carry scars from their own negative educational experiences, or they may be in a hurry because they have to get back to work or else lose income or even their job.

A child from a culturally different family may meet with an unfamiliar school culture and language, and experience the school devaluing her home culture and language. She sees no reflections of her home reality in the educational materials. She may not know the childcare centre or the school's language, rules, teaching styles, yet the school expects her to learn as if she did. She does not know the school way of being and is not allowed to use her home way of being. In these circumstances many children begin to experience a sense of 'wrongness' and lowered self-esteem, which then adds to their learning challenges.

When well-meaning childcare workers and teachers realise that the school has to intentionally teach about the school culture, too often they attempt to do so in a way that denies or erases children's home culture. When care and education programmes devalue or try to erase home-culture strengths in the name of helping children to be successful in school, they take away the tools children have to be effective, which sets them at an instant disadvantage. Under these circumstances, only a handful of children are able to catch up with their dominant culture classmates. When they do not succeed, the school and teachers are confirmed in their initial beliefs of the inferiority of the cultures and families of these children. However, this vicious circle can be interrupted.

Changing things

If we are willing to develop an early childhood care and education system in which diversity is strength and where everyone is welcome at the table, then you join a life-long journey. To get started on this journey we need to engage in several tasks.

First, we need to understand that, by definition, all children and all families exist within a cultural context, from which they derive identity, meaning, values, connection, security and strengths, as well as language and behavioural tools for interacting with people and acting in the world. Furthermore, children need to know the language and rules for success in the dominant culture. Therefore, teachers must promote bicultural and bilingual development. This means supporting the language and skills they are learning within their home culture while also teaching them how to successfully communicate and interact within the dominant culture. (Note that the suffix 'bi' means 'two': becoming bicultural is an additive, not a subtractive concept.) With the flexibility and curiosity of the young, children are eager to become bicultural and bilingual. But are we also flexible and motivated enough to learn how to do this?

Secondly, we must try to understand that non-prejudice is not based on ignoring differences, which denies children their birthrights of ethnicity, culture and identity. Rather, we must become respectfully aware, knowledgeable and at ease with the range of human diversity: colour and race, physical differences and disabilities, differences of language and culture, differences in family structure and status. We must also become comfortable and skilled in discussing human diversity with children.

Thirdly, we need to turn the spotlight on the systemic realities and dynamics of adamant disadvantage in our countries. We need to open our eyes, our minds, and our hearts to the realities of these dynamics and to understand how perfectly wonderful and intelligent children are trapped and undermined by them.

Fourth, we need to explore and understand the multiple parts of our own identity: who we are culturally and where we are advantaged or disadvantaged by our societal institutions. We need to learn how to view social reality through the lens of multiple perspectives and to make a commitment to keep working until we have built care and education systems that truly deliver equal educational services for all children.

Anti-bias educational practice

In broad strokes, sound care and education programmes would put the following three dimensions into practice for ALL children, including those from the dominant culture:

- Nurture every child's confident self and group identity. This includes knowing how to operate within their home culture and within the culture of the dominant and larger society.
- Teach all children to be able to think critically about prejudice and discrimination and to take individual and group action to challenge injustices.
- Nurture multiple perspectives, empathy and comfort, and skilled interactions with diversity.

These dimensions are the foundation of an anti-bias education approach (Derman-Sparks et al., 1989); they are also the foundation of a new early childhood initiative in Ireland, called *ÉIST*, which was developed at Pavee Point, under the leadership of Colette Murray and Annie O'Doherty. What would educational environments and practice look like if they incorporated these dimensions? The portrait I present may be ideal; it is also realisable if we begin to intentionally work towards it.

Dimension 1

The lives of all children and the strengths of their home cultures are integrated into daily practice. All educational materials depict the children's lives and backgrounds accurately. This includes Irish children from families that are poor or working class, 'non-traditional' in structure or with a parent with a disability. Staff at all levels reflect the diversity of children's backgrounds and intentionally become well-informed about the cultural practices and life realities of all the children they serve. Staff also have regular opportunities to discuss issues raised by the diversity represented by the children and to build partnerships with the children's families.

In programmes where the children come from families whose culture differs from the dominant society, teachers support bicultural and bilingual development. For children from the dominant culture, teachers promote the exploration and appreciation of differences among people in the dominant groups as well the capacity for comfortable, caring and equitable cross-cultural interaction. They may also foster bilingualism – as in fact the Irish schools are doing. The pedagogy in these schools can be adapted to support bilingualism in other languages as well.

Education informed by these practices enables children to feel strong and capable in school, so that they are free to learn. Each child can like who she or he is without needing to feel superior to anyone else. Parents can use their strengths to gain the further information and resources they need to raise their children well.

Dimension 2

Early childhood programmes can do a great deal to counter the negative impact of societal racism, classism, etc, which harm all young children's developing identity and self-esteem. Even nurturing, loving families cannot prevent this from happening by themselves. As they move into their preschool years, children's natural awareness and curiosity about differences related to gender, skin colour, hair texture, apparent physical disabilities and language begin to show the influence of messages of superiority or inferiority about themselves and others. Multiple forms of communication from the family and the larger society convey a myriad of overt and subtle messages about the significance of the various aspects of human diversity. As Dr Kenneth Clark pointed out in his pioneering *Prejudice and Your Child* (1955), the messages of bias primarily come from socially prevailing attitudes and beliefs, rather than from direct contact with people different from themselves (as is commonly believed). For example, a study of the attitudes of young children in Northern Ireland (Coulter 2002, p. 7) documented how over 80 per cent of six-year-olds held overtly sectarian views about people not in their identity/religious group. In the US, almost every four- and five-year-old has already learned incorrect and disrespectful ideas about Native Americans. We suspect the same holds true for Irish young children as regards Travellers.

However, teachers and parents can, and indeed must, guide children's development of the cognitive skills needed to identify unfair and untrue images (stereotypes). We must help children to become aware of comments (teasing, name-calling) and behaviours (exclusion, discrimination) directed at someone because of their gender, race, ethnicity, disability, class, age, weight or other such personal characteristics. Further, we must couple critical thinking with the development of empathy and multiple perspectives, so that children know that different forms of bias do hurt. But, to do this, we must first have a good idea about how our young children think and feel about various groups in our society.

Schools can also help children to learn and practice a variety of ways to act when another child acts in a biased manner towards her/him, and when one child acts in a biased manner towards another child. Learning to take action for fairness begins with the relationships among the children. Any form of bullying, rejection and name-calling based on a person's identity is never acceptable. If the teacher encourages, models and guides such behaviour, children can learn how to say no to such behaviours and engage with each other in figuring out more respectful and fair ways to handle conflicts.

Remember that these activities are not about changing the world from an adult's perspective, but rather about children making their own 'worlds' a little fairer. Use the following steps to design appropriate activism projects (Pelo and Davidson, 2000):

- Be alert to specific unfair situations and practices in the life of the classroom or immediate community that directly affect the children's lives.
- Guide children in exploring their ideas and feeling about the fairness of the situation.
- Work with children to design and implement actions that are safe and workable from your perspective

Activism projects 'nurture self-esteem and empowerment, develop empathy and appreciation for differences, facilitate critical thinking and problem solving, provide a mental model of survival for children at risk from bias, provide a model of equity and justice for privileged, dominant culture children, and contribute to community building' (Pelo and Davidson, 2000, p. 8). Here are a few examples collected by teachers and parents:

> A four-year-old tells her classmate to keep a stereotypic 'Indian warrior' figure in her cubby, because it's 'not fair' to D (their teacher who is of American Indian background). A five-year-old explains that, 'Fair is when everybody gets everything, but nobody gets everything they want. Unfair is when somebody gets left out' (Hoffman, 2004, p. 153). A six-year old tells a first grade classmate, 'You do not have to like me, but it isn't okay to not like me because my skin colour is brown.'

Dimension 3

This dimension means guiding children's development of the awareness, attitudes and skills needed to respectfully and effectively learn about differences, comfortably negotiate and adapt to differences, and identify with the common humanity that all people share. Work in the other two dimensions builds children's capacity for this dimension. Teachers regularly help children to explore and value how people, including themselves, both differ and are like each other. It is essential to balance both concepts – to help children see likeness across differences and see differences as ways of expressing a common humanity. After children have had many opportunities to learn about the differences in their own classroom and community, teachers introduce other ways of being, building on the already established valuing of how people are both the same and different from each other. With young children, the focus is on the people in their wider community and on their current life. Finally, learning about people not present in their immediate community is always accompanied by uncovering misinformation and discomforts about unfamiliar people.

Embarking on our journey

To embark on a journey of change, teachers and parents must also work on the three dimensions with regard to themselves. This means engaging in several areas of reflection and action to:

- understand your cultural background in depth and how it influences your teaching beliefs, styles, and interactions with children
- overcome the ethno-centrism that leads you to experience your cultural rules and values as the best or only way to be
- become clear about the distinction between diversity and disadvantage and ways they become tangled in care and education programmes
- uncover and eliminate previously unexamined fears, prejudices and misunderstandings, so that you can become ever more able to engage in cultural negotiation and manage cultural conflicts in the classrooms
- develop a critical analysis of the societal structures of power and privilege and the impact of these structures on care and education
- articulate a vision of the future where disadvantage based on diversity has been eliminated and where all people are welcome and equitably share – what would care and education programmes look like if you had all the resources you needed to make them work for all people?
- connect with others to build the kind of society and care and educational systems that reflect your vision.

The proclamation of the 'Provisional Government of the Irish Republic to the People of Ireland' (24 April 1916) includes the following statement: 'The Republic declares its resolve to pursue the happiness and prosperity of the whole nation and of all its parts, cherishing all the children of the nation equally.' It will be a wonderful day when this hope is truly realised.

References

Clark, K. (1955) *Prejudice and Your Child*, Boston, Massachusetts: Beacon

Coulter, C. (25 June 2002) 'Six-year-olds with sectarian ways', *The Irish Times*, Home News, p. 7

Derman-Sparks, L. and A. B. C. Task Force (1989) *Anti-bias curriculum: Tools for empowering young children*, Washington, DC: National Association for the Education of Young Children

Hoffman, E. (2004) *Magic capes, amazing powers: Transforming superhero play in the classroom*, St Paul, MN: Redleaf Press

Horton, M., with J. and H. Kohl. (1998) *The long haul: An autobiography*, New York: Teachers College Press

Murray, C. and O' Doherty, A. (2001) *'Éist': Respecting diversity in early childhood care education and training*, Dublin: Pavee Point Publications

Pelo, A. and Davidson, F. (2000) *That's not fair: A teacher's guide to activism with young children*, St Paul, MN: Redleaf Press

Ryan, W. (1971) *Blaming the Victim,* New York: Vintage

6

Why SMART Outcomes Ain't Always So Smart ...

Paul Downes

SMART (Specific, Measurable, Achievable, Relevant, Timed) outcomes are in vogue. The Statutory Committee on Educational Disadvantage in its most recent and generally very progressive report has endorsed the notion that interventions be subject to evaluation according to SMART outcomes (2005, p. 35). Archer and Shortt's (2003) evaluation of the Home School Community Liaison scheme similarly invoked SMART outcomes. Professor Áine Hyland's paper at the National Forum on Ending Disadvantage (2002) identified a move in focus from equality of access to participation to equality of outcome. She emphasised that in the previous decade a range of interventions for educational disadvantage brought 'little or no convincing evidence that measurable pupil outcomes such as examination results or literacy and numeracy levels have improved as a result of these interventions' (p. 49). Nor did outcomes for school attendance and pupil retention improve significantly.

This chapter will argue that the increasing emphasis that interventions with regard to educational disadvantage must focus on SMART outcomes needs to recognise those contexts where an outcomes-focused approach is a significantly limited approach. For example, relying predominantly on behavioural indicators[1] of outcomes may negate the importance of interventions aimed at improving the emotional state of at-risk children. It will be argued that there is a danger that the most disadvantaged children and families may become filtered out of focus

---

[1] Behavioural indicators focus solely on overt behaviour rather than internal states and motivations. Relevant overt behavioural indicators could include, for example, number of days attending school per academic year, number of times suspended from school, etc.

because it is these groups which may be most resistant to measurable gains; and programmes reliant on outcomes for funding may begin to avoid intervening where change may be slowest, even if this is where support is most needed. Focusing only on whether the intervention 'works' in playing a causal role in change, i.e., on its causal efficacy, may perpetuate the temptation to overlook other background structural problems which may be negating the positive effect of the intervention – background conditions which may include individual teacher effects or school climate effects. Attempts at isolating a one-to-one correspondence between a prior intervention and a consequent change are vulnerable to criticisms of behaviouristic reliance on one-to-one correspondences between an antecedent event (i.e., an intervention) and its consequences. A systemic more than behaviourist focus would highlight the need for interventions to be assessed with regard to their relevance to the needs of the target group and not simply to be assessed with regard to more concrete though potentially less relevant outcomes.

Any critique of a paradigm of SMART outcomes in this chapter does not seek to minimise the importance of examining gains in outcomes for literacy, numeracy, attendance, retention, or academic performance.[2] The focus of this chapter is to examine contexts where the dominion of SMART outcomes may have less relevance so that this important paradigm does not become the sole arbiter for evaluation of all interventions with regard to educational disadvantage. It is important to recognise contexts where projects still merit substantial state and private funding even if they do not fit into the Procrustean bed of SMART outcomes.

A focus on SMART outcomes needs to recognise its limitations with regard to the following issues:

- the tendency to overlook background contingent conditions for the cause to 'work'
- SMART outcomes as behavioural indicators: limitations to assumptions from behaviouristic psychology
- the need to go beyond simple causality in SMART outcomes to complex causality and a systemic focus
- an individual learner-centred focus may be in conflict with a generic outcomes focus.

---

[2] The recent setting of targets for third-level institutions with regard to access for marginalised groups by the National Office for Equity of Access to Higher Education is another example of the benefits of seeking to examine outcomes, this time at an institutional level. Such target setting can only serve to help remove the inertia among so many third-level institutions with regard to access issues. Target setting and examination of outcomes are also potentially a very useful part of Whole-School Evaluations at primary and post-primary level.

The tendency to overlook background contingent conditions for the cause to 'work'

J. S. Mill (1872) criticised a clearcut distinction between causal factors and factors perceived as having no causal role:

> It is seldom if ever between a consequent and a single antecedent that this invariable sequence subsists. It is usually between a consequent and the sum of several antecedents the concurrence of all of them being requisite to produce, that is, to be certain of being followed by the consequent. (p. 327)

Mill noted that very often one antecedent is termed the cause, the other antecedents being conditions. Intervention models that 'work' causally have hidden necessary contingent conditions, without which the more obvious causal elements could not have occurred, just as striking a billiard ball to hit another presupposes the contingent condition of gravitation. Causes necessarily operate within a background of supporting conditions that are structured sources of the cause's efficacy. It is precisely these contingent conditions that developmental psychologist Rutter (1985) argues have been frequently overlooked within psychology:

> It is commonly but wrongly assumed that a significant main effect in a multivariate analysis means that variable has an effect on its own. It does not. What it means is that there is a significant main effect for that variable, after other variables have been taken into account: that is not tantamount to an effect in the absence of all other variables. (p. 601)[3]

The impact and potential role of the other background variables supporting a significant main effect of the outcomes from an intervention needs to be given full recognition.

Rourke's (1998) evaluation of the Potential Early School Leavers (PESL) programme in Blanchardstown, Dublin, provides an example of recognition of other background intervening variables:

> There are a number of examples where individual young people were making good progress through the PESL programme and were then confronted with a trauma in

---

[3] Other areas of psychology such as, for example, cognitive science, tend to overlook or minimise the relevance of background contingent conditions. For example, Fodor's (1976) influential account of cognitive science requires purely causal explanations: 'what it [cognitive science] talks about is at most mental states that have mental causes. It may be that we are laboring in quite a small vineyard, for all that we can't now move out of its borders' (p.202). He accepts that: 'Nothing principled precludes the chance that highly valued mental states are sometimes the effects of (literally) nonrational causes' (p. 202). It is arguable however that Fodor's rigid dualism between causal mental states as 'the domain of explanatory mechanisms' (p. 202) and nonexplanatory 'nonrational' causal states is too crude and itself unprincipled as it does not give any force of relevance to the rationality of background contingent or supporting conditions for the significant main causal effect (see also Downes 2006).

their lives (family bereavement, marital breakdown, serious family illness, problems caused by alcohol or drug abuse, etc). These traumas and setbacks served to undo much of the other positive work that might have been taking place within the home, within school and within the PESL programme. (p. 14)

This is an example of the background contingent conditions becoming active to neutralise the positive effects of an intervention. The famous Whittaker Report (1985) made a similar point with regard to background contingent conditions in Irish prisons neutralising potential for rehabilitation: 'The possible rehabilitative effects of education, training, welfare and guidance are offset by the triple depressant of overcrowding, idleness and squalor which dominates most Irish prisons.'

Another possibility is that particular background contingent conditions may simply be missing and that if they were present the intervention would have causal impact. The text of Heckman's (2006) Ulysses Medal Lecture at University College Dublin recognises other intervening variables as causal factors but, arguably, does not give sufficient acknowledgement to the role of background contingent conditions as intervening variables that are key but insufficient conditions, i.e., variables beyond supposedly stand-alone causes. Heckman (2006) seeks 'true causal effect': 'We cannot know true causal effect without some further assumption because of some possible unmeasured third common cause.'[4] This is a search for what Rutter (1985), echoing J. S. Mill, criticised above as 'an effect in the absence of all other variables'.[5]

Acknowledgment of Mill's and Rutter's distinctions between cause and background contingent conditions brings a further implication. Many benefits of an intervention may not be as solid 'magic bullet' causes – the benefits may not be stand-alone causes but may be through a more fluid role serving as key supporting or contingent conditions for positive change. Yet a focus uniquely on the causal effect of an intervention with regard to outcomes will tend to exclude the benefits of an intervention as a provider of supportive or even contingent conditions for positive change.

Rourke (1998) continues:

These types of setbacks serve to emphasise the need to work on a number of different levels with young people (and their parents); and to recognise that single dimensional or one-off strategies are unlikely to be successful when dealing with young people who have serious attitudinal, behavioural or emotional problems. (p. 14)

---

[4] Heckman (2006) does acknowledge that 'correlation evidence is always suspect'. However, his account of 'some of the interpretive problems with the correlational evidence' with regard to a third intervening cause arguably does not go far enough with regard to background contingent conditions and is in danger of adopting the rigid dualism between causal explanations and supposedly 'nonrational' causes outside 'the domain of explanatory mechanisms' advocated by Fodor (1976) for cognitive science and criticised above.

[5] See also Maxwell (2004, p.6) on the 'neglect of the role of context in causal explanation'

Rourke's holistic focus acknowledges that an assumption of static stable background conditions for an intervention to have causal effect is a questionable assumption for many in the context of multiple dimensions of stressors and disadvantage. The need for stable background contingent conditions brings a danger for evaluation according to SMART outcomes in the context of people at risk of multiple disadvantages.

There is a temptation to select those with more stable background conditions in order to improve the chances of causal impact of the intervention. In other words, those who are most at risk, those with multiple disadvantages, are most likely to be filtered out of an evaluation according to SMART outcomes criteria. Those most at risk are likely to be subjected to a range of interacting background conditions which may hinder and neutralise the effect of the potentially causal dimension for change that the intervention seeks to provide (see also Rook 1984, 1992, on depressed people being more likely to drive away potential social supports). Thus, gains according to SMART outcomes may be largely a function of the selection/filtering process of potential participants in the intervention where the most marginalised become further excluded. To reiterate, SMART outcomes bring the danger that the most disadvantaged children and families may become filtered out of focus because it is these groups which may be most resistant to measurable gains; and programmes reliant on outcomes for funding may begin to avoid intervening where change may be slowest, even if this is where support is most needed.[6]

It is important to recognise that this critique of the extent of the application of the SMART outcomes framework does not reject the importance of Heckman's (2006) focus on prevention and early intervention,[7] nor his emphasis on the gains achieved in the Perry Preschool Program and the Abecedarian Program in the US contexts of Michigan and Carolina, respectively: 'The most reliable data come from experiments that provided substantial enrichment of the early environments of children living in low-income families.'

Heckman's (2006) focus is on prevention of multiple disadvantages before they arise. In other words, his outcomes focus seeks the establishment of static, stable background contingent conditions and on this assumption the causal impact of an intervention becomes likely.

It is arguable that a focus on foreground factors to the neglect of background factors such as contingent conditions is a cognitive process that reveals a Western bias with regard to thought and perception. For example, cross-cultural research on perception (see Nisbett et al., 2001 for a general account) highlights the tendency

---

[6] See also Booher-Jennings (2005) and Gillborn and Youdell (2000) on the filtering process involved in 'educational triage' in US and UK contexts, respectively, where preoccupation with test scores tended to result in a diversion of resources away from those viewed as least likely to pass and towards those on the threshold of passing the test

[7] See Downes (2004) on the need for development of a community-based psychological service focusing on prevention and early intervention in the context of Ballyfermot, Dublin

of US participants to prioritise foreground features over background dimensions. Masuda and Nisbett (2001) presented realistic animated scenes of fish and other underwater objects to Japanese and Americans and asked them to report what they had seen. The first statement by American participants usually referred to the focal fish ('there was what looked like a trout swimming to the right') whereas the first statement by Japanese participants usually referred to background elements ('there was a lake or pond'). Japanese participants made about 70 per cent more statements about background aspects of the environment. In a subsequent recognition task, Japanese performance was weakened by the showing of the focal fish with the wrong background, indicating that the perception of the object had been intimately linked with the field in which it had appeared. In contrast, American recognition of the object was unaffected by the wrong background (see also Miller, 1984, for increased causal attribution to context rather than dispositional factors for an Indian-Hindu sample compared with an American sample). The SMART outcomes focus tends to feed this cognitive bias through examining the foreground of the intervention to the relative neglect of the background contingent and supporting conditions which may or may not be present for the intervention to 'work'.

An outcomes type of focus on the foreground of a particular causal intervention may distract from the need for a more systemic change of a range of background contingent conditions such as the need for change in school climate or curriculum or teacher quality before an intervention can have significant effect. In this sense, a SMART outcomes focus may be a highly conservative one as it invites change to more malleable features of a system than to the background structural conditions of a system.[8] These background structural conditions such as school climate or curriculum, or even quality of teaching, may have greater resistance to change. Moreover, the radical nature of such change to background contingent conditions may also be more difficult to identify and describe in causal language as a precise isolated intervention for evaluation according to SMART outcomes criteria.

SMART outcomes as behavioural indicators: limitations to assumptions from behaviouristic psychology

A bias of the measurable may filter out other more relevant variables. Bronfenbrenner's (1979) concern with ecological validity in developmental psychology similarly emphasises that relevance may be lost due to selection of

---

[8] See also the Report of the Statutory Committee on Educational Disadvantage (2005) which refers to the need to 'change the mainstream, not just the margins' (p. 23). Moreover, the UN Special Rapporteur of the Commission on Human Rights (2005, 2006) on the right of everyone to the enjoyment of the highest attainable standard of physical and mental health expressly recognises the need to develop 'structural indicators' and 'process indicators', as well as 'outcome indicators'; this broader view of indicators of the right to mental health, advocated by the UN Special Rapporteur, is related to educational themes in Downes (2007) in the context of Estonia

observable features within artificial environments. A key danger with reliance on behavioural indicators such as SMART outcomes is that it filters out emotional dimensions. While many of the early behaviourists denied the existence of emotions, Skinner's (1974) behaviourism did not deny the existence of emotion but did deny its relevance and its causal relevance to behaviour.

Lee O'Sullivan's (1993) research on a school-based programme aimed at raising self-esteem and assertiveness in an adolescent population found that it was easier to find gains in the behavioural dimension of assertiveness than in the emotional dimension of self-esteem after the relatively short intervention programme. Issues of self-esteem were more long-term and enduring. A focus on behavioural indicators may tend to minimise focus on emotional gains through interventions. Emotional indicators tend to be less easily measurable, particularly with regard to questionnaire responses from marginalised groups where literacy may be a problem. Moreover, emotional indicators are less susceptible to linear assumptions of progress (see Baltes, 1989, on lifespan development as a multi-directional process of gains and losses). They may also be more vulnerable to social desirability factors of the individual responding the way (s)he thinks is sought by the evaluator and may require a longer time period for change to be manifested. Any such relegation of priority to be given to emotional development would be all the more regrettable given the centrality of emotional expression and awareness to the new revised curriculum (see also Downes, 2003) at primary level.

The problem of extracting a precise isolated antecedent (intervention) and consequent (outcome) leads to concerns with SMART outcomes as being locked within the limitations of behaviourist frameworks. Attempts at isolating a one-to-one correspondence between a prior intervention and a consequent change are vulnerable to criticisms of behaviouristic reliance on one-to-one correspondences between antecedents and consequences.[9] In the operant conditioning of Skinner's behaviourism, the 'operant' is behaviour defined by its consequences. Rachlin (1984) suggests that the pattern of determination by conditioning is more complex than a single one-to-one correspondence between a behaviour and a consequence:

> It would seem to be an important task for psychology to determine what the (overt behavioral) criteria are for the use of mental terms, how they change with circumstances, how they interact with one another. Before doing this job, it may be necessary to widen the conception of the operant, as originally advanced by Skinner, from a single discrete event (such as a lever press) to a complex pattern of events that

---

[9] Gergen (1994) also criticises behaviourist assumptions of determinism between antecedent and consequent. He highlights the role of the individual in interpreting the antecedent stimuli and thus the cognitive processes in constructing a range of possible reactions beyond a determined consequent (outcome). In other words, evaluation of (antecedent) interventions needs to factor in the individual's freedom to choose to react in a range of ways to the intervention.

may occur over days and weeks and (consequently) to alter the notion of reinforcement from contiguity between a pair of discrete events (response and reward) to more complex correlations that have meaning only over an extended period. (p. 567)

This widening of the operant to a complex pattern of events echoes Quine's (1961) critique of a discrete event falsification in science that ignored the complex systemic interaction of observations and theory. Rourke's (1998) emphasis on the need to go beyond once-off and single-dimensional interventions for prevention of early school leaving in Blanchardstown is a recognition of the need for multiple dimensions of intervention which also implies multiple dimensions of outcome. Acceptance of this holistic approach involving multiple dimensions brings a complex systemic dimension of interaction effects between these multiple dimensions. It also makes it more difficult to commit to seeking a one-to-one correspondence between a given antecedent intervention and a specific consequent outcome.

Beyond simple causality in SMART outcomes to complex causality and a systemic focus

There has been a shift of emphasis in developmental psychology away from simple causality explanations to a concern with risk and protective factors, including the interactive chain effects between a range of these factors (Rutter, 1985, 1989; Zimmerman and Maton, 1992; Cohen and Wills, 1985; Wills and Shiffman, 1985). Acknowledgement that interventions operate in complex systems challenges simple models of cause–effect. Von Bertalanffy (1967) has highlighted that at a certain threshold of complexity, namely when numerous forces are simultaneously interacting, systems' dynamics belong to a class other than causal mechanism, whether linear or circular causality. Citing Bertrand Russell who calls the law of causality 'a relic of a bygone age, surviving like the monarchy', Hardy (2001) outlines a range of challenges to traditional causality: 'While local cause-effect mechanisms may exist as component processes, enmeshed in the more complex ensemble of interactions, they are neither the sole, nor the predominant type of relations between forces in a web-system' (p. 37).

Her comments with regard to a social web are particularly relevant to interventions such as for those with regard to educational disadvantage that take place within a social web of influences:

> In a complex system such as a social web, an entity (a person or force) does not cause an effect on another one. Rather all entities in the system interact and mutually influence each other. Talking about causality in a web is irrelevant, as too many entities are inter-influencing each other, and because all those interactions not only occur simultaneously but are modifying the very forces interacting. (p. 51)

There is a need for more than single-dimensional interventions if the intervention is to be part of an integrated intervention strategy. Thus, what is generally called an outcomes focus is often merely a *unidimensional* outcome focus; and a unidimensional outcome focus is in conflict with an integrated strategy and integrated interventions focus as they are part of a complex system of interactions.

An individual learner-centred focus may be in conflict with a generic outcomes focus

One of the recommendations in the National Forum Action Plan is that 'one size does not fit all'. This arguably needs to be applied also to outcomes. In other words, outcomes need to be learner-centred, meeting the learner's individual needs through a process owned by the learner. Bronfenbrenner's (1979, p. 14) concern with individual differences in developmental psychology highlights the need to go beyond treating the individual in simplistic terms as a member of an abstract category, whether based on class, ethnicity or family structure. There is a need to start from where the learner is at and a SMART outcomes focus may invite a tendency to impose an agenda on the learner that is not necessarily shared with, and owned by, the learner, whether the learner is an adult or child.

An individual learner-centred focus may be in conflict with a generic outcomes focus. Moreover, even if the learner shares and owns the goals of the SMART outcomes, the issue of the paths to the outcome still arises. A key issue regarding the path to the outcome is the process of time, the pace of the learner's progress. The learner's pace may not fit within the limits of the SMART outcomes timeframe. Commitment to generic outcomes may be in conflict with the disparate starting points of the range of individuals involved in the particular intervention.

While at one level of description SMART outcomes may be insufficiently flexible to adapt to individual outcome needs, from another dimension SMART outcomes may be too narrowly focused on individual gains as opposed to gains in community development or family relations. Relational dimensions, including what Bronfenbrenner would term dyadic interactions (between two or more people), may be more difficult to assess through SMART outcomes than effects on the person viewed in individualistic terms.

Conclusion

A range of contexts have been identified where the dominion of SMART outcomes has less relevance. These are as follows:

The tendency to overlook background contingent conditions for the cause to 'work'

The apparent lack of causal efficacy of an intervention may not be due to a failure of the intervention itself but may be due to the presence or absence of background contingent conditions hindering the intervention from working. An outcomes type of focus on the foreground of a particular causal intervention may distract from the need for a more systemic change of a range of background contingent conditions, such as the need for change in school climate or curriculum or teacher quality, before an intervention can have significant effect. Many benefits of an intervention may not be as 'magic bullet' causes – a focus uniquely on the causal effect of an intervention with regard to outcomes will tend to exclude the benefits of an intervention as a provider of supportive or even contingent conditions for positive change. SMART outcomes provide the temptation to select those with more stable background conditions in order to improve the chances of causal impact of the intervention, thereby excluding the most disadvantaged groups from the intervention. SMART outcomes bring the danger that the most disadvantaged children and families may become filtered out of focus because it is these groups which may be most resistant to measurable gains; and programmes reliant on outcomes for funding may begin to avoid intervening where change may be slowest, even if this is where support is most needed.

SMART outcomes as behavioural indicators: limitations to assumptions from behaviouristic psychology

A focus on behavioural indicators may tend to minimise focus on emotional indicators that are less easily measurable and may require a longer time period for change to be manifested. Behaviourist assumptions of a one-to-one correspondence between an antecedent (intervention) and a consequent (outcome) have been questioned within behaviourism by Rachlin (1984). This one-to-one correspondence is oversimplified and requires acceptance of a systemic interaction between a range of antecedents and a range of consequents.

Beyond simple causality in SMART outcomes to complex causality and a systemic focus

There is a need for more than single-dimensional interventions as part of an integrated intervention strategy. What is called an outcomes focus is often a unidimensional outcome focus. A unidimensional outcome focus is in conflict with an integrated strategy and integrated interventions focus as they are part of a complex system of interactions.

An individual learner-centred focus may be in conflict with a generic outcomes focus

There is a need to start from where the learner is at and a SMART outcomes focus may invite a tendency to impose an agenda on the learner that is not necessarily shared with, and owned by, the learner. The learner's pace may not fit within the limits of the SMART outcome timeframe. Commitment to generic outcomes may be in conflict with the disparate starting points of the range of individuals involved in the particular intervention. SMART outcomes may be too narrowly focused on individual gains as opposed to gains in community development or family relations.

References

Archer, P. and Shortt, F. (2003) *Review of the Home School Community Liaison Scheme*, Dublin: Educational Research Centre

Baltes, P. B. (1989) 'The dynamics between growth and decline (Review of Emergent theories of aging)', *Contemporary Psychology*, 34, pp. 983–4

Booher-Jennings, J. (2005) 'Below the bubble: "Educational Triage" and the Texas Accountability System', *American Educational Research Journal*, 42, pp. 231–68

Bronfenbrenner, U. (1979) *The Ecology of Human Development*, Cambridge, MA: Harvard University Press

Cohen, S. and Wills, T. A. (1985) 'Stress, social support and the buffering hypothesis', *Psychological Bulletin*, 98, pp. 310–57

Downes, P. (2003) 'The New Curriculum of Social, Personal and Health Education in Irish Primary Schools: Self-Awareness, Introversion and the Role of the Teacher', *Kwartalnik Padagogiczny* (Journal of Education, Poland), no. 4. vol. 190, pp. 93–112

Downes, P. (2004) *Psychological Support Services for Ballyfermot: Present and Future*, Ballyfermot: URBAN

Downes, P. (2006) 'Newtonian space: The 'blind spot' in Newell and Simon's information processing paradigm', *Journal of Cybernetics and Human Knowing,* vol. 13, no. 3–4, pp. 27–57

Downes, P. (2007) 'Intravenous drug use and HIV in Estonia: Socio-economic integration and development of indicators regarding the right to health for its Russian-speaking population', *Liverpool Law Review*, Special Issue on Historical and Contemporary Legal Issues on HIV/AIDS, vol. 2 (forthcoming)

Educational Disadvantage Committee (2005) *Moving Beyond Educational Disadvantage 2002–2005*, Dublin: DES

Gergen, K. J. (1982/1994) *Towards transformation in social knowledge*, (2nd edn), London: Sage Publications

Gillborn, D. and Youdell, D. (2000) *Rationing education: Policy, practice, reform and equity,* Buckingham, England: Open University Press

Hardy, C. (2001) 'Self-organization, self-reference and inter-influences in multilevel webs: Beyond causality and determinism', *Journal of Cybernetics and Human Knowing,* 8, pp. 35–59

Heckman, J. (2006) *The economics of child development,* Ulysses Medal Lecture, University College Dublin, 7 June 2006

Hyland, Á. (2002) 'Looking to the future – Ending disadvantage?' in Gilligan, A. L. (ed.) *Primary Education: Ending Disadvantage. Proceedings and Action Plan of National Forum,* Dublin: Educational Disadvantage Centre, St Patrick's College

Masuda, T. and Nisbett, R. A. (2001) 'Attending holistically versus analytically: Comparing the context sensitivity of Japanese and Americans', *Journal of Personality and Social Psychology,* vol. 81, no. 5, pp. 922–34

Maxwell, J. A. (2004) 'Causal explanation, qualitative research and scientific inquiry in education', *Educational Researcher,* 33, pp. 3–11

Mill, J. S. (1872) 'A system of logic' in McRae, R. F. (ed.) *Collected Works,* vol. VII, Books I, II, III (1973) University of Toronto Press

Miller, J. G. (1984) 'Culture and the development of everyday social explanation', *Journal of Personality and Social Psychology,* 46, pp. 961–78

Nisbett, R. E., Peng, K., Choi, I. and Norenzayan, A. (2001) 'Culture and systems of thought: Holistic versus analytic cognition', *Psychological Review,* 108, pp. 291–310

O'Sullivan, L. G. (1993) 'A qualitative evaluation of a school-based programme aimed at raising self-esteem and assertiveness in an adolescent population', Masters thesis: Department of Psychology, Trinity College Dublin

Quine, W. V. O. (1961) *From a logical point of view,* (2nd edn), New York: Harper Torchbooks

Rachlin, H. (1984) 'Mental yes. Private no', *Behavioral and Brain Sciences,* 7, pp. 566–7

Rook, K. (1984) 'The negative side of social interaction', *Journal of Personality and Social Psychology,* 46, pp. 1097–118

Rook, K. (1992) 'Detrimental aspects of social relationships: Taking stock of an emerging literature' in Veiel, H. O. and Baumann, U. (eds) *The meaning and measurement of social support,* New York: Hemisphere, pp. 157–69

Rourke, S. (1998) *Blanchardstown Potential Early School Leavers Programme: Evaluation of pilot programme 1994–1997,* Dublin: Barnardos

Rutter, M. (1985) 'Resilience in the face of adversity: Protective factors and resistance to psychiatric disorder', *British Journal of Psychiatry,* 147, pp. 598–611

Rutter, M. (1989) 'Pathways from childhood to adult life', *Journal of Child Psychology and Psychiatry,* 30, pp. 23–51

Skinner, B. F. (1974) *About Behaviorism*, London: Cape

United Nations Economic and Social Council (2005) Commission on Human Rights Economic, Social and Cultural Rights, *Report of the Special Rapporteur on the right of everyone to the enjoyment of the highest attainable standard of physical and mental health* (11 February 2005)

United Nations Economic and Social Council (2006) Commission on Human Rights Economic, Social and Cultural Rights, *Report of the Special Rapporteur on the right of everyone to the enjoyment of the highest attainable standard of physical and mental health* (3 March 2006)

Von Bertanlanffy, L. (1967) *Robots, men and mind,* New York: George Braziller

Whittaker Committee (1985) *The Whittaker Report on Irish Prisons*, Dublin: Government Publications

Wills, T. A. and Shiffman, S. (1985) 'Coping and substance use: A conceptual framework' in Shiffman, S. and Wills, T. A. (eds), *Coping and substance use*, Orlando: Academic Press, pp. 3–24

Zimmerman, M. A. and Maton, K. I. (1992) 'Lifestyle and substance use among male African-American urban adolescents: A cluster analytic approach', *American Journal of Community Psychology*, 20, pp. 121–38

7

Emotions, Inequalities and Care in Education

Maeve O'Brien and Marie Flynn

Introduction

An understanding and recognition of care, and the labour it necessarily involves, is fundamental to tackling the reproduction of educational inequalities for vulnerable groups, and to disrupting the processes which privilege others, thus deepening our understandings of the significance of care and emotions in education. We explore how the emotional caring produced both inside and outside of school, and the valuing of emotional skills and intelligences support students' engagement in education.

A great deal of educational research and debate in Ireland and internationally has focused on problems of economic and cultural resources through which educational disadvantage is reproduced for particular social groups (Kellaghan, 1999; Clancy, 1995, 2001; Bernstein, 1977, 1997; Bourdieu 1984, 1986, 1999). Notwithstanding the importance of such work, this chapter draws on current radical perspectives on equality, which suggest that inequalities are also generated and experienced in the affective/emotional context (Baker et al., 2004). The significance of care and emotions in the field of education is an issue that has been marginalised in discourse and in practice, particularly as one advances through the formal educational system (Hargreaves, Earl and Ryan, 1996; O'Brien, 2004).

Drawing on radical egalitarian and feminist/critical educational discourses, and recent empirical research on emotional intelligences and caring, we provide a more holistic view of the human as vulnerable, interconnected and inescapably affected by emotional relations. Highlighting the significance of care, emotions, and their marginalisation in education is particularly urgent in the context of Ireland's 'boom economy', where the gap between rich and poor continues to grow, and finding time for caring and valuing care becomes increasingly problematic. In addition, how we define knowledge and intelligence, how we relate, how teachers are prepared to understand and prioritise/subordinate care, and how the care work and resources accessed in the home support and advantage particular groups in society, are large equality questions. It would be impossible to address each in depth here, but we do explore current discourse and research on care relations, emotional work and emotional intelligences to argue that recognising the affective context, and the care work that supports relationships, is of central importance to creating a more equal and humane educational system.

Care, emotions and their significance in education

Drawing on feminist moral philosophy, egalitarian theory, and feminist sociology of education, emotions and caring are fundamental to human well-being, an issue which should be a central concern of education. These discourses increasingly suggest that we are not detached, autonomous, rational actors in the social world. In contrast, it is argued that we are interdependent affective beings who are vulnerable and dependent at specific times in our lives (Nussbaum 1995, 2001; Kittay, 1999; Kittay and Feder, 2001). Feminist moral philosophers have problematised traditional notions of independence and autonomy, suggesting that states of dependency and interdependency are inevitable, and characteristic of what it is to be human. In terms of well-being, this necessarily implies a need for the giving and receiving of care. Involvement in the relations of giving emotional support and care is seen as a fundamental part of what it is to be a moral actor. Thus, the possibilities for well-being and development, including educational possibilities within the institutions of schooling, necessarily include a need for emotional care to be carried out and received (Bubeck, 2001; Tronto, 1989; Sevenhuijsen, 1998; Reay, 2000; O'Brien, 2005b; Griffith and Smith, 2005). Moreover, Bourdieu (1986), among others, has suggested that mothers are key players in the educational field, and that their cultural capital and habitus play a significant role in (re)producing social and class structures, or less often, managing to transform them.

As emotions are essential to particular forms of care that give meaning to life in ways that detached rational action cannot, it seems strange that emotional care has not been the subject of discourse and research on social justice, morality and educational equality until more recently. Nussbaum (1995, p. 381) argues that caring emotional relations are deeply moral, and fundamental to our development as human beings; it is the emotional capacity for empathy, for example, that assists us in caring and making moral decisions and taking moral actions where 'blunt reason' might not. Moreover, Goleman (1995) and Damasio (1994, 2004) argue that emotions and cognitive activity are connected. Emotions have a rational dimension, they are intelligent and essential to moral thinking; they are the very feelings that enable us to understand the position of another and to act to support them. Our emotional capacities are surely central to any vision of education as human development (Aristotle's *The Nichomean Ethics*).

Goleman's (1995) book on emotional intelligence underlines the importance of understanding one's own emotions and those of others as an essential part of modern living. Integral to one's emotional intelligence are 'abilities such as being able to motivate oneself, and persist in the face of frustrations; to control impulse and delay gratification; to regulate one's moods and keep distress from swamping the ability to think; to empathize and to hope' (Goleman 1995, p. 34). He argues that individuals who score highly on conventional IQ tests may not succeed in achieving their full potential if they lack emotional intelligence and that 'emotional intelligence adds far more to the qualities that make us more fully human' (Goleman 1995, p. 45). He emphasises the importance of emotional literacy for men and women and locates much of society's contemporary social ills (unemployment, depression, drug abuse) in a vacuum of emotional intelligence. Gardner's (1993) theory of multiple intelligences also highlights the importance of emotional and relationship capacities in everyday life, particularly in the workplace: 'Job success depends on many variables, such as motivation and the ability to interact well with others, which standardised intelligence tests do not explore' (Gardner, Kornhaber and Wake, 1996, pp. 83–4). Gardner's naming and recognition of intelligence in the personal domain is of particular relevance to this discussion of care, emotions and schooling. According to his theory, interpersonal intelligence is the ability to perceive and make distinctions in the moods, intentions, feelings and motivations of other people and to act accordingly. Intrapersonal intelligence is understood as the capacity that enables individuals to know their own abilities, and to perceive how to best use them.

These emotional capacities that moderate and direct our feelings, and indeed our actions, can be used for either good or ill, but clearly the denial or marginalisation of such intelligences in education is reductive and irresponsible in terms of our development (Goleman, 1995; Gardner, 1993). While the traditional association of the emotional capacities and emotions with women rather than men has contributed to the reinforcement of a patriarchal gender order in society, in education it has led to the privileging of particular modes of thought and disciplines and the marginalisation of others (Smith, 1990; Harding, 1991; Harding and Norberg, 2005). In recent times, the physical and natural sciences have enjoyed greater status as knowledge because of their so-called objective and neutral methodologies. The social sciences and in particular those that include methodologies that are taken to be subjective and not 'value- and feeling-neutral' are seen as problematic knowledge.

Radical feminist scholars across many disciplines, including feminist sociology of education, have criticised this standpoint and suggested that no knowledge is value-free. In more radical approaches to social science, knowledge is seen as a praxis for social transformation, indeed feelings and subjectivities are considered significant realities of the social world rather than an interference in the data (Harding, 1991). This clearly has significance for how we research education, and for what is regarded as knowledge, curriculum and appropriate practice. Relationships and affect will have to be taken seriously rather than factored out of the equation.

In the educational field, beyond the institution of the school, the caring efforts involved in supporting a child's schooling comprise not only the cognitive capacities but also the emotional. Emotional care is about relationship, and as such, is heteronomous and concerned with the feelings and well-being of the other; it is a disposition that places the flourishing of the other as central to one's decisions and actions (Bubeck, 2001). From an educational perspective, this is what makes emotional care morally significant and potentially socially transformative. However, if the issue of emotional care remains confined to the privatised space of individual families, the production of such care may act as a conservative force in education. Those families who possess the resources to produce care in ways that can benefit their children within the educational system will reproduce advantage for their own. However, those who are socially vulnerable and positioned more marginally in an increasingly privatised society, including the privatisation of the educational field, will have to compete to provide emotional care in ways that are not as effective due to lack of supports and resources.

Inequalities of recognition

The educational inequality that many learners face is an environment where only a limited number of intelligences are recognised and valued. Traditionally, intelligence has been seen as a single unitary capacity, measurable by an IQ test. IQ tests focus on two intelligences, the logical-mathematical and the verbal-linguistic. This conception of intelligence underpins the education system and consequently disables many learners.

For learners whose intellectual strengths lie outside the logical-mathematical and verbal-linguistic realm, the consequences are profound and disabling: they create inequality in relation to access to particular subjects, to institutions and courses of study and the capacity to participate and benefit from schooling across the levels of the system (Lynch, 1999; Baker et al., 2004). This dominant and flawed construct of intelligence shapes school organisational practices, curriculum content, teaching method, assessment modes and techniques and the hidden curriculum (Hanafin, Shevlin and Flynn, 2002). The general failure of the education system 'to provide for, let alone capitalize on, different kinds of intelligence and styles of learning resulted in clearly prejudicial practices' (Goodlad and Oakes, 1988, p. 18). These prejudices manifest themselves most visibly and cogently in the form of streaming and ability grouping practices.

School organisational policies often mean that certain types of learners are denied access to certain kinds of knowledge and teaching. At second level, those labelled as 'weak' or 'slow' and placed in lower streams as a result are often denied access to subjects that are regarded as too academic for low streams (Lynch, 1999; Smyth, 1999). Students in higher streams at second level and in higher ability groups at primary level are exposed to more critical and higher-order forms of thinking (Hallinan, 1997). Moreover, Drudy and Lynch (1993), in reviewing the research in Ireland and Britain on streaming, point out that students from lower socio-economic groupings are over-represented in the lower streams of schools. This is not to suggest that these students are less intelligent in the traditional sense but that other factors intervene and that teachers are more likely to place students from these groups in low streams. In terms of children's well-being and self-esteem, Devine's (1993) study suggests that the majority of children are aware of the differences in instruction – the same children deemed 'slow', 'weak' or 'incapable' are showing proficiency in their ability to read the hidden curriculum.

Much of the formal curriculum mediated through subject syllabi and textbooks privileges linguistic and mathematical ways of knowing. Rather than adapting the curriculum to students' needs, the predominant institutional response is to view those who have difficulty understanding the unaltered curriculum as slow or disabled (Brooks and Grennon-Brooks, 1993). Notwithstanding the inclusion of oral, aural and practical components across subject syllabi, students are assessed in most subject areas through written examinations. There are few subjects that draw on musical, spatial and kinaesthetic intelligences and fewer still that draw on intelligences in the personal realm (Hanafin, Shevlin and Flynn, 2002).

In more recent times, the plurality of intelligence has been recognised (Gardner, 1983; Ceci, 1990; Sternberg, 1990). Gardner's (1983) theory of multiple intelligences focuses on the ability to solve problems and create products that are of value in a given culture. He argues that a human intellectual competence 'must entail a set of skills of problem solving – enabling that individual to resolve genuine problems or difficulties that he or she encounters and, when appropriate, to create an effective product' (Gardner, 1983, p. 60). Such products enable an individual to show his or her intelligence in practical, not just academic ways. The products range from scientific theories to musical compositions to successful political campaigns (Gardner, 1983). Gardner (1993) argues that the naming of mathematical or linguistic skills as intelligences reflects the Western tradition, where certain cultural values dating back to Socrates are put on a pedestal: 'Logical thinking, for example, is important; rationality is important; but they are not the only virtues' (p. 12). Gardner (1983) proposes a minimum of eight separate, but interrelated intelligences: Verbal–Linguistic, Logical–Mathematical, Visual–Spatial, Bodily–Kinaesthetic, Musical, Naturalist, Interpersonal, and Intrapersonal.

In an Irish context, Drudy and Lynch (1993) highlight the importance of the personal intelligences in society and their comparative unimportance in schools: 'the personal intelligences have been ignored by students of cognition. Yet these forms of knowledge are of tremendous importance in many if not all societies' (p. 238). Irish education has tended to subordinate personal intelligences and place cognition and competition above care. Knowledge about how to develop emotionally rewarding and supportive personal relationships is not a subject for analysis in most schools (Lynch, 1999). Jobs involving liaison or contact with other people demand that one has both interpersonal and intrapersonal intelligences. This applies across a very broad range of occupations – advertising, shop assisting, medicine, public relations, social work, etc.

Such neglect of emotions and care in the educational field is a function of the low economic value placed on activities such as caring for others in the wider society. What Ungerson (1990) calls 'caring about' and 'caring for', and what Lynch has elaborated as 'love labour' (1989), are often invisible and taken for granted and not categorised or understood as work. Even care that is more visible and commodifiable is often seen as low status and rewarded with low pay (see also Lynch and McLoughlin, 1995). Noddings (1992), in her critique of liberal education, draws attention to 'the persistent undervaluing of skills, attitudes, and capacities traditionally associated with women' (p. xiii).

People learn emotional responses and responsiveness (Gilligan, 1982; Bubeck, 2001) through acculturation into society, through their parents and other family members, the mass media and the education system (Chodorow, 1999). It is crucial, therefore, that emotional literacy or intelligences in the personal domain are also recognised within education. These intelligences have traditionally been developed in the home context but they can also be fostered in formal education settings (Lynch, 1999). Some subjects such as Relationships and Sexuality Education (RSE) at second level, and the SPHE (Social, Personal, Health Education) programme at primary level, do acknowledge the importance of care and emotional relations in the field of education. However, such programmes have not been unproblematic. The time allocated to SPHE at primary level, for example, is 30 minutes per week. Lynch (1999) argues that there has never been serious consideration given to the development of the personal intelligences, except through 'ad hoc personal development courses or through some modules within the home economics programmes' (p. 277). RSE programmes have focused on sexual relationships as opposed to the 'more generic task of developing all-round personal intelligences' (p. 277).

Even within this perspective on RSE, the DES recently confirmed that approximately one in five primary schools in the Republic of Ireland is not teaching the 'Stay Safe' programme which aims to reduce the vulnerability of children to abuse. While the importance of recognising and valuing the emotions in the field of education has been underlined, the ways in which this is done are critical. More emotion is not necessarily better, as Hargreaves (2000) emphasises. He cautions against overly indulging the personal, emotional and spiritual aspects of teaching. It is particularly pertinent in relation to groups considered educationally disadvantaged because such over-indulgence can condemn poor and marginalised students 'to a warm yet "welfarist" culture, where immediate comfort that makes school a haven for children can easily occlude the long-term achievement goals and expectations that are essential if children are to make their escape permanent' (p. 812). Hargreaves suggests that care and emotions are integral to educational processes but that we must take care to unravel simplistic solutions to complex issues of educational inequalities. To suggest that school should provide emotional care for students in ways that assuage our consciences, by keeping them happy and contained, and while not tackling systematic discriminations within curricula and modes of assessment, is not real care. Recognising the significance of care and emotions is not about sidestepping the realities of poverty, racist policies, cultural misrecognition, and heterosexist and patriarchal processes within the educational system.

Inequalities in accessing and activating resources in the home context

Care has not been a central concept in debates about 'parental involvement' or 'parental resources' that support children's schooling. Traditionally, the educational discourse, including that concerned with issues of educational disadvantage, has reduced the emotional caring efforts carried out ostensibly by mothers in education to a gender-neutral rationalistic discourse of parental involvement (Smith, 1996). More recently, a body of work within feminist sociology of education has investigated and made visible parents' classed and gendered efforts to support children's education. The work of Lareau (2000); Walkerdine and Lucey (1989); Allatt (1993); David, West and Ribbens (1994); Reay (1998, 2000); Griffith and Smith (2005); O'Brien (2005, a and b) has demonstrated the significant educational care work that is produced by mothers in the context of varying social positionings, and with respect to the economic, cultural, social and emotional resources they can access.

These authors describe mothers' daily routines of performing educational work as having strong emotional components that require emotional energies and care. Although Lynch (1989) has pointed out that not all emotional work qualifies as care (indeed some emotional work may require the management of emotions for the purpose of increasing company profits, see Hochschild, 1983), the educational work described by these authors certainly comes under the rubric of 'caring about' and 'caring for' one's children. The educational care work observed in their research suggests that mothers feel required to do extensive educational work for the well-being of their children. This includes listening to children, guiding and making choices about schools and subjects, supporting children through assessments, homework support, meeting teachers, planning and organising meetings and transporting children to educational activities outside of school time. What is evident is that in order to provide this emotional care, mothers need access to resources and time, resources that are available relative to mothers' social positionings.

Moreover, this body of work suggests that mothers' caring is often shaped in specific ways and takes a very particular trajectory within the educational field. Care is performed in line with the largely middle-class codes and practices of the educational system and it becomes deeply imbricated with the capacity to access and activate dominant forms of cultural capital from within the habitus (Bourdieu, 1986). Walkerdine and Lucey's (1989) classic *Democracy in the Kitchen* suggests that middle-class mothers have greater time and energy to do educational work because they do not have to engage in paid work outside the home; work which may take energy away from time for care. In addition, the possession of cultural capital and of a middle-class habitus enables these mothers to see the home as an extended site for educational care work; where baking becomes a maths lesson, and gardening a science lesson. These authors explain that in homes where resources are tight, domestic and childcare work is seen as just that, and not as an extended site for educational care work. Thus the classed codes of care, which are to a certain extent dependent on capitals in the economic field, advantage middle-class children in ways that are not possible for those growing up in homes where educational care work is shaped by restricted access to cultural and economic capitals.

Allatt's (1993) work 'Becoming Privileged' explored routines of educational practices in middle-class families. She described how the cultural capital possessed by mothers is accessed and activated via other forms of capital that are available to them. Mothers' caring work to support children's schooling meant they used cultural resources in tandem with social and economic resources to pursue educational success and create pathways for the future 'happiness' of children. For Allatt, the possession of the classic forms of social, cultural, and economic capitals create educational advantage and reproduce privilege through the caring support work of the mother and at times the father.

Drawing on Nowotny (1981), Allatt also identified a non-traditional form of capital that is used to perform educational care work, 'emotional capital'. She described emotional capital as the skills, love, affection and willingness to spend time in caring for children, including their education. While this definition of emotional capital may be rather broad and in need of further theorizing, it does open up a space in the sociology of education to discuss the relationship between mothers' emotional work, care and capitals. Allatt's research suggested that emotional capital was a carrier for activating other capitals/resources to ensure children's educational success. This raises the problem of what has been euphemistically called educational disadvantage and its relationship to family capitals, to the availability of economic and cultural resources and, significantly, to the production of care.

Reay (1998, 2000) focuses on the problems facing mothers without dominant forms of cultural and economic capital in trying to care in the educational field. She contests Lareau's (2000) in-depth work, which argues that middle-class mothers are more intensely emotionally involved in children's schooling. Reay sees emotional involvement in education as a reality of mothers' lives regardless of social positionings and resources. She suggests that working-class mothers, and those more marginally positioned, have in fact to do greater levels of emotional work and invest greater emotional capital to support their children's education than middle-class mothers. She draws an important conclusion from her own research: that the emotional caring efforts of working-class mothers are extensive but less effective from a schooling perspective. She suggests that as working-class mothers do not generally have access to other capitals that can be used in educational care, such as knowledge of the school system, or money to buy time for activities and artefacts that create advantage in schooling, they have to put in more emotional efforts but that these are not recognised.

Reay suggests that cycles of educational inequalities are reproduced in the caring that mothers are required to provide, as mothers' own emotional capital becomes depleted through poverty, loneliness, depression and hopelessness. All mothers may wish and be willing to spend time on emotional care to support children's education (Reay, 2000; O'Brien, 2007), but without access to money, time, social support and cultural know-how, they will not be able to provide care in the ways that create educational advantage for dominant groups.

Building on Lareau's work (2000), Reay (2000) also draws our attention to how emotional investment in education can be contrary to real care. She argues that, increasingly, middle-class mothers invest emotional and other capitals so intensely that it may be at the expense of the children's emotional well-being. The ideology of success so fundamental to current educational ideas of performativity, and the drive for class security through educational activity and success, implicates some mothers in never-ending cycles of control over children's time and choices.

Hays (1996) also draws attention to the problematics for mothers of caring in today's wider cultural context. She suggests that middle-class 'expert' discourses of childrearing, and ideologies of individualism and 'homo economicus' create tensions and shape the daily routines of how mothers perform care for children, and how they understand the care they provide. The potential for mothers' emotional care to be a key force in changing social relations in society and the field of education in the current climate is thus problematic. Mothers experience the burdens and inequalities associated with caring in a society that continues to shape it through its dominant institutions, including the institutions of education. Yet, these institutions simultaneously undervalue and render this care work invisible as natural expressions of mothers' love (O'Brien, 2005a). Moreover, some of the educational literature and research in previous decades has pathologised mothers who have not carried out emotional care work in line with dominant ideologies of care, and what Hays calls the ideology of intensive mothering. This work suggests that we need to understand more fully how and why mothers as opposed to 'parents' care in the ways they do for children and their schooling. This body of research indicates that there is a need to empirically explore the relationship between mothers' care in education, the meanings they attach to it as mothers, and the resources they require in order to provide care.

Mothers' social positionings and the moral imperative

The previous sections have briefly considered the international discourse and debates in relation to the reproduction of privilege through the marginalisation of emotions and care in education and through the performance of mothers' emotional care work that supports children's schooling. The importance of emotional care to human well-being, and the need for all of us to have access to, and to experience emotional caring at particular times in our lives has also been highlighted. This section illustrates the requirements for emotional care in the Irish educational context at a time when students are undergoing significant educational change and uncertainty, the move from first to second-level schooling. Building on the work of Reay (2000) in particular, O'Brien (2007) suggests that regardless of their social positionings, and access to sets of resources, mothers experience a moral imperative to care for their children and their education. It suggests that this gendered moral imperative intensifies the inequalities that mothers experience as gendered care workers. It argues, moreover, that having to care in accordance with the expectations and norms embedded in the educational system reproduces inequalities for some groups of mothers and their children through their incapacities to access the relevant capitals.

O'Brien's (2005a) research with a theoretically selected sample of twenty-five middle-class, working-class, Traveller, immigrant, married, single and cohabiting heterosexual and lesbian women, suggests that mothers, regardless of their social positionings, feel that they 'must' and 'should' care emotionally for their children including their education. While the research does not claim that men and fathers never do this caring educational work, the evidence suggests that it is a labour traditionally allocated to mothers, and that mothers experience their identity as mothers through a moral imperative that ties them to care.

Mothers' narratives of their daily routines in caring for their children, including their education, suggest that a great deal of intensive educational caring work is done to support their children's transfer from first to second-level schooling. At transfer to second-level schooling, this work includes how to choose and get a child into a particular school, a process shaped not just by 'rational choice' but through the desire to care for the child's schooling and the resources available to mothers. Mothers do a great deal of 'donkeywork' and 'legwork' at transfer (see also David, West and Ribbens, 1994) to negotiate a choice of school, to support children through assessment tests, to secure a place in the chosen school (which was not necessarily inevitable), in doing organisational work around purchasing uniforms, equipment and books, helping with new work regimes and timetables, and transporting or arranging transport for young people. It also involves significant 'love labour' (Lynch, 1989), being available to support and encourage children and listen to their concerns. Moreover, the data indicated that emotionally caring for children at school transfer required confidence to take action and to communicate with teachers and principals where children were experiencing difficulties or needed particular resources and supports.

Contrary to discourses that have in the past pathologised mothers from working-class and marginal positions as not interested or involved enough in their children's schooling, this research suggests that *all* mothers, regardless of their social positioning, cared deeply about how this schooling transition was negotiated. Mothers performed emotional care in the educational field because they believed that education was a key to the success and happiness of their children, in the present as well as in the future. Although understandings of 'happiness' are culturally and socially relative,[1] all mothers in the sample performed educational care work towards that end. Because of their 'love' for their children and the sense of moral obligation that was deeply embedded in that 'mothers' love', not to care, and not to do the work that care involved was impossible for mothers. What was highly problematic for some mothers was that the material and social realities of their lives created significant differences in the energies required to perform care, and moreover, to do so according to the standards, norms and practices institutionalised within the second-level school system.

---

[1] See Burkitt (1997) on the social construction of emotions, their cultural and ideological bases

Mothers' educational care work is produced relative to a moral imperative located in the traditional gender order. There is an expectation that the work that supports children's schooling will be done so that children will be ready to participate in the system. It is assumed that because second-level schooling is provided for by the Irish state, economic capital does not, or should not, have a major impact on students' participation in education. Yet, in this study, for mothers on low incomes, meeting second-level school requirements necessitated greater emotional care work to manage and save money throughout the year. Money had to be carefully budgeted so there would be enough to pay for the costs of schooling, not just for books and uniforms, but also for the 'hidden costs' of extra-curricular activities and trips and events. Traveller women, immigrant and working-class mothers talked about the emotional efforts involved in materially providing for children so they 'have the right stuff' and do not feel different in school (see also Daly and Leonard, 2001).

The tensions experienced by mothers with very low incomes and from marginal positionings were different to those of the more economically comfortable middle-classes. This research suggests that economic resources have a direct impact on where students will transfer at second level, the kinds of choices that are really available to families in poor economic circumstances, and the nature of caring and level of anxieties that mothers experience in supporting children's transfer.

Mothers' capacities to perform emotional caring in accordance with the moral imperative are also shaped and constrained by access to cultural and social capitals. Those mothers who had little insider knowledge of the workings of the Irish second-level school system – Traveller mothers, immigrant mothers, and mothers from the working classes who had generally left school with minimal qualifications – were at a care disadvantage. Those who were cultural and social outsiders, for example, could not draw upon socially privileged connections and supports to get children into particular schools or to make connections with teachers and principals. Lesbian mothers with high levels of cultural capital also found themselves marginally positioned in carrying out care in the educational field. They found that school practices of including spaces for mothers and fathers on official forms discriminated against same-sex families and, moreover, that norms around parent-teacher meetings did not include the welcoming of same-sex parents.

In Bourdieu's (1984, 1986, 1996) analysis of the social production of inequality in the educational field, there is no overt recognition of the significance of the affective context or of emotional resources or capital. This has recently been addressed in the egalitarian literature on inequality and education (Baker at al., 2004). The study by O'Brien (2005a) focuses on the relationship between mothers' idiosyncratic social positionings and their access to emotional capital to do educational care work. It suggests that we need to theorise the relationship between emotional resources, educational support work, and the moral imperative that requires mothers to care for children's education. The findings of this study suggest that in order to act in accordance with the moral imperative to care, that all mothers must draw upon their emotional resources, in the form of emotional skills and supports. Although the amounts of this capital possessed by mothers may vary over time and relative to life events in the past and present, the capacity to activate emotional resources in order to care is relative to other capitals and to positionings within the social structure. While money cannot buy love, it can in various ways purchase time-out of care in order to recharge one's emotional batteries.

Furthermore, the capacity to draw on the emotional support from another, particularly from one who is in close relationship with the child, relieves mothers of carrying the entire burden of care work by themselves. All mothers struggle to carry out care in accordance with a moral imperative, but those who are without this intimate support – and who struggle with poor health, emotional grief, loss, the pain of social exclusion – find that their emotional resources are depleted daily in the ongoing invisible work of care where there is no respite. In order to 'love their children', which for them is a given, they must keep caring, and the constant demands of this unrecognised labour mean that some mothers continue to 'run on empty'.

These are inequalities in education that are hidden and difficult to measure but nonetheless a reality for many mothers. While discourses of educational disadvantage and educational inequality have theorised the problems in socio-economic and cultural relations and schooling, there needs to be a greater focus on the production of caring relations and the resources required to do this in various contexts. Unless we shift the focus and take the affective context and the reproduction of inequality in education as a central issue, we cannot properly address the reproduction of privilege or disadvantage in education and the consequences and burdens of care on women and their families.

Conclusions: recognition and resourcing of care and emotions in education

This chapter has attempted to bring together discourses and research from the fields of feminist sociology of education, sociology of knowledge, egalitarian theory and moral philosophy in order to explore the significance of caring and emotions in education, and the problems and inequalities associated with caring and recognising care. It has suggested that care as a practice and disposition is of fundamental importance to human well-being in general, and to students' capacities to participate and engage in the field of education. The reality of care and the emotional work that is carried out by mothers in the educational field suggest that mothers' care is shaped by schooling in ways that systematically privilege some and disadvantage others. Given the range of resources required to produce educational care, and how these resources are accessed from different social positionings, it is urgent that the relational work that is produced largely by mothers is valued and recognised.

If educators and policymakers are unaware of the inequalities associated with the hidden work of care that supports schooling, it will be difficult to disrupt processes and practices in education that maintain cycles of inequality in the affective context, and tackle the inequalities in educational participation and outcomes for different social groups. Research has shown that 'mothers' love' is translated into care work for their children and, moreover, that it is required to conform to codes and practices in education that are associated with dominant groups and particular sets of legitimised identities. Clearly, this indicates that those mothers occupying less dominant positions and marginalised mothers cannot expect the same return for the energies they expend on caring for children in education, and their children may not benefit from their mothers' educational care work in the ways that those from more dominant groupings can.

Notwithstanding the reality of mothers' care work in education, one of the key problems to be tackled is its invisibility and naturalisation as mothers' love. Some mothers, as has been demonstrated, have greater access to resources to do educational care work but all mothers are required to do it to support their children under a gendered moral imperative to care. Until the extensive and intensive efforts that are carried out ostensibly by mothers are recognised as a form of labour, it will be difficult for emotional caring to be valued as a significant effort that supports educational participation and that privileges those who have greater access to resources to care.

Meanwhile, it appears that the centrality of care and emotions to the processes of education and of schooling has only recently been recognised, and is still marginal to mainstream discourses. Thus, ideologies of success and performativity that are pervasive in the economic contexts increasingly inform rationalistic consumer models of education that have little to do with care, equality and the production of solidarity and a more equal society. The problem of recognising care, emotions, and personal intelligences within school contexts is urgent. In a school system dominated by narrow views of intelligence and performativity, children are systematically disadvantaged. However, there are possibilities for change; research on the cultures of schools using Multiple Intelligence (MI) theory share several characteristics. Among these is the deeply held view that all children have strengths and can learn; that care and respect among people in schools is essential.

It has been argued that schools prioritise linguistic and mathematical intelligences at the expense of other forms of intelligence. Flynn's (2000) study shows that teachers actively embraced and applied the ideas to which they were exposed during the course of an action-research project on multiple intelligences. Exposure to MI theory brought about greater levels of respect from teachers, and indeed from learners, for individuals' differing intelligence profiles. Instead of seeing some learners as 'problem' students, teachers were more willing to consider their other intelligence strengths. Teachers were more careful about the use of labels such as 'bright', 'weak' or 'poor' – terms that measure intelligence against a logical–mathematical and verbal–linguistic yardstick. Teachers questioned their own practice and this led to a consideration of how practice could change to suit the learner. A culture of care, respect and interpersonal relationships was valued above one of performativity. The biggest leap to be made for teachers in MI classrooms is 'not a methods-shift but a mind-shift' or a reconceptualisation of intelligence (Hanafin, 1999, p. 34). A reconceptualisation of intelligence is at the core of MI theory. It implies a fundamental shift in how we see intelligence, and is essentially about the recognition and valuing of all intelligences.

In spite of the fact that educational reforms aimed at creating an ethos of greater equality are frequently challenged, and that teachers in classrooms can be resistant to change in their practice, we cannot lose sight of the real potential for change. Young (1998) points out that the curriculum is not merely an external imposition on teachers and learners but is rather something with which they actively engage. Thus, not only do teachers and learners reproduce existing pedagogical and curricular patterns, but they also have the potential to affect change. The importance of attitudes that value learners, together with practices that support these attitudes, are the central tenet of MI theory-in-use.

We have argued in this chapter that recognising care and emotions is fundamental to creating egalitarian educational processes in both the context of school and home. It has been suggested that attitudes, practices and policies need to reflect the fundamental and inescapable importance of care and emotions to human development and flourishing. It appears that students' educational experiences and capacities to participate are deeply affected by the neglect of the affective context of life (Baker at al., 2004), through privileged narrow conceptions of intelligence within school, and by lack of familial resources that are required to produce care in accordance with the norms of the school system. If we are to take equality in the educational context seriously, and to tackle the systemic processes that reproduce inequality in education, it is vital that care, emotional intelligence and emotional well-being become part of public educational debate and that they are not regarded as merely frills of schooling but are understood as key issues. The emotional work and labours of care in educational contexts cannot be assumed but require understanding, recognition and resourcing.

References

Allatt, P. (1993) 'Becoming Privileged: The Role of Family Processes' in Bates, I. and Riseborough, G. (eds) *Youth and Inequality*, Buckingham: Open University Press

Aristotle, *The Nichomean Ethics* in Goleman, D. (1995) *Emotional Intelligence*, London: Bloomsbury

Baker, J., Lynch, K., Cantillon, S. and Walsh, J. (2004) *Equality, from Theory to Action*, Basingstoke: Palgrave Macmillan

Bernstein, B. (1977) 'Social Class, Language and Socialisation' in Karabel, J. and Halsey, A. H. (eds) *Power and Ideology in Education*, New York: Oxford University Press

Bernstein, B. (1997) 'Class and Pedagogies: Visible and Invisible' in Halsey, A. H., Lauder, H., Brown, P. and Wells, A. S. (eds) *Education: Culture, Economy and Society*, Oxford: Oxford University Press, pp. 59–79

Bourdieu, P. (1984) *Distinctions: A Social Critique of the Judgement of Taste*, trans. by Richard Nice, London: Routledge and Kegan Paul

Bourdieu, P. (1986) 'The Forms of Capital' in Richardson, J. (ed.) *Handbook of Theory and Research for the Sociology of Education*, New York: Greenwood

Bourdieu, P. (1996) *Elite Schools in the Field of Power*, trans. by Lauretta C. Clough, Cambridge: Polity Press

Bourdieu, P., Accardo, A., Balazs, G., Beaud, S., Bonvin, F., Bourdieu, E., Bourgois, P., Broccolichi, S., Champagne, P., Christin, R., Fageur, J. P., Garcia, S., Lenoir, R., Euvard, F., Pialoux, M., Pinto, L., Podalydes, D., Sayad, A., Soulie, C., Wacquant, L. (1999) *The Weight of the World: Social Suffering in Contemporary Society*, (trans. by P. Parkhurst Ferguson) Oxford: Blackwell

Brooks, J. and Grennon-Brooks, M. (1993) *In search of understanding: The case for constructivist classrooms,* Alexandria, Virginia: Association for Supervision and Curriculum Development

Bubeck, D. E. (2001) 'Justice and the Labour of Care' in Kittay, E. and Feder, E. (eds), *The Subject of Care: Feminist Perspectives on Dependency*, New York: Rowman and Littlefield Publishers

Burkitt, I. (1997) 'Social Relations and Emotions', *Sociology*, 31, pp. 37–56

Ceci, S. J. (1990) *On Intelligence ...more or less: A bio-ecological treatise on intellectual development*, Englewood Cliffs, NJ: Prentice Hall

Chodorow, N. (1999) *The Power of Feelings: Personal Meaning in Psychoanalysis, Gender, and Culture*, New Haven/London: Yale University Press

Clancy, P. (1995) *Access to College: Patterns of Continuity and Change*, Dublin: Higher Education Authority

Clancy, P. (2001) *College Entry in Focus: A Fourth National Study of Access to*

Higher Education, Dublin: Higher Education Authority

Daly and Leonard (2001) *Living Life on a Low Income*, Dublin: Combat Poverty Agency

Damasio, A. (1994) *Descartes Error: Emotion, Reason and the Human Brain*, New York: Putnam

Damasio, A. (2004) *Looking for Spinoza*, London: Vintage

David, M., West, A., Ribbens, J. (1994) *Mothers' Intuition? Choosing Secondary Schools*, London: The Falmer Press

Devine, D. (1993) 'A Study of Reading Ability Groups: Primary School Children's Experiences and Views', *Irish Educational Studies,* vol. 12, pp. 134–40

Drudy, S. and Lynch, K. (1993) *Schools and Society in Ireland*, Dublin: Gill & Macmillan

Flynn, M. (2000) 'Extending the Limits: The Possibility of Multiple Intelligences practices for Equality', unpublished PhD thesis, Cork: Education Department, University College, Cork

Gardner, H. (1983) *Frames of Mind: The theory of multiple intelligences*, London: Fontana Press

Gardner, H. (1993) *Multiple Intelligences: The theory in practice*, New York: Basic Books

Gardner, H., Kornhaber, M., and Wake, W. K. (1996) *Intelligence: multiple perspectives*, Fort Worth: Harcourt Brace

Gilligan, C. (1982) *In a Different Voice: Psychological Theory and Women's Development*, Cambridge, MA: Harvard University Press

Goleman, D. (1995) *Emotional Intelligence*, London: Bloomsbury

Goodlad, J. and Oakes, J. (1988) 'We must offer equal access to knowledge', *Educational Leadership,* 45, 5, pp. 16–22

Griffith, A. and Smith, D. (2005) Mothering for Schooling, New York: Routledge Falmer

Hallinan, M. (1997) *The Social Organisation of Schools: New Conceptualisations of the learning process*, New York: Plenum Press

Hanafin, J. (1999) 'Valuing Diversity: A contribution from multiple intelligences theory', paper presented to the Graduate School of Education, University of Western Australia, 12 November 1999

Hanafin, J., Shevlin, M. and Flynn, M. (2002) 'Responding to Student Diversity: lessons from the margin', *Pedagogy, Culture and Society,* vol. 10. no. 3

Harding, S. (1991) *Whose Science? Whose Knowledge*, Milton Keynes: Open University Press

Harding, S. and Norberg, K. (2005) 'Feminist Approaches to Social Science Methodologies: An Introduction', *Signs: A Journal of Women Culture and Society,* 30, pp. 2009–15

Hargreaves, A. (2000) 'Mixed Emotions: Teachers' Perceptions of their

Interactions with Students', *Teaching and Teacher Education,* 16, pp. 811–26

Hargreaves, A. and Earl, L. and Ryan J. (1996) *Schooling for Change*: *Revisiting Education for Early Adolescents*, London: Falmer Press

Hays, S. (1996) *The Cultural Contradictions of Motherhood*, New Haven: Yale University Press

Hochschild, A. (1983) *The Managed Heart: The Connection of Human Feeling*, Berkley, University of California Press

Kellaghan, T. (1999) 'Education Disadvantage: An Analysis', paper presented at Inspector's Conference, Killarney

Kittay, E. (1999) *Love's Labour: Essays on Women Equality and Dependency*, New York: Routledge

Kittay, E. and Feder, E. (2001) *The Subject of Care: Feminist Perspectives on Dependency*, New York: Rowman and Littlefield Publishers

Lareau, A. (2000) *Home Advantage, Social Class and Parental Intervention in Elementary Education*, Maryland, US: Rowman & Littlefield Publishers

Lynch, K. (1989) 'Solitary Labour: Its Nature and Marginalisation', *Sociological Review,* 37, pp. 1–14

Lynch, K. (1999) 'Equality Studies, the Academy and the Role of Research in Emancipatory Social Change', *The Economic and Social Review*, 30, 1, pp. 41–69

Lynch, K. and McLoughlin, E. (1995) 'Love Labour' in Clancy, P. et al. (eds) *Irish Society: Sociological Perspectives*, Dublin: IPA

Noddings, N. (1992) *The Challenge to Care in Schools,* New York: Teachers' College Press

Nowotny, H. (1981) 'Women in Public Life in Austria' in Epstein, C. F. and Coser, R. L. (eds) *Access to Power: Cross National Studies of Women and Elites,* London: George Allen and Unwin

Nussbaum, M. (1995) *Women, Culture and Development: A Study of Human Capabilities*, Oxford: Clarendon Press

Nussbaum, M. (2001) *Upheavals of Thought: The Intelligence of Emotions*, Cambridge: Cambridge University Press

O'Brien, M. (2004) *Making the Move: Students', Teachers' and Parents' Perceptions of Transfer from First to Second-Level Schooling*, Dublin: Marino Institute of Education

O'Brien, M. (2005a) 'Mothers' Emotional Care Work in Education: The Moral Imperative and Inequalities in Capitals', unpublished PhD thesis, University College Dublin

O'Brien, M. (2005b) 'Mothers as Educational Workers: Mothers' Emotional Work at their Children's Transfer to Second-Level Schooling', *Irish Educational Studies,* 24, pp. 223–43

O'Brien, M. (2007) 'Mothers' Emotional Care Work in Education and its Moral Imperative', *Gender and Education,* 19, 2, (March) pp. 159–78

Reay, D. (1998) *Class Work: Mothers' Involvement in their Children's Primary Schooling*, London: University of London Press

Reay, D. (2000) 'A Useful Extension of Bourdieu's Conceptual Framework?: Emotional Capital as a Way of Understanding Mothers' Involvement in their Children's Education', *Sociological Review,* 48, pp. 568–85

Sevenhuijsen, S. (1998) *Citizenship and the Ethics of Care: Feminist Considerations on Justice, Morality and Politics*, (trans. by Liz Savage) London and New York: Routledge

Smith, D. E. (1990) *The Conceptual Practices of Power: A Feminist Sociology of Knowledge*, Boston: Northern University Press

Smith, D. E. (1996) 'The Underside of Schooling: Restructuring, Privatisation and Women's Unpaid Work', *Journal for a Just and Caring Education,* 4, 1, pp. 11–29

Smyth, E. (1999) *Do Schools Differ? Academic and Personal Development among Pupils in the Second-Level Sector*, Dublin: Oak Tree Press/ESRI

Sternberg, R. J. (1990) *Metaphors of Mind: Conceptions of the nature of intelligence*, Canada: Cambridge University Press

Tronto, J. C. (1989) 'Women and Caring: What Can Feminists Learn about Morality from Caring?' in Held, V. (ed.) *Justice and Care*, Colorado: Westview Press

Ungerson, C. (1990) 'Why do Women Care?' in Finch, J. and Groves, D. (eds), *A Labour of Love: Women, Work and Caring*, London: Routledge and Kegan Paul

Walkerdine, V. and Lucey, H. (1989) *Democracy in the Kitchen: Regulating Mothers and Socialising Daughters*, London: Virago

Young, M. F. D. (1998) *The Curriculum of the Future*, London: The Falmer Press

II

Family and Community Education

Section Two takes up the challenge posed by the final report from the Statutory Committee on Educational Disadvantage, *Moving Beyond Educational Disadvantage* (2005), namely, the need to hold a broad focus at all times in order to break the cycle of poverty which is so evident in educational disadvantage. Any narrow focus on interventions with schools and children which does not at the same time address the needs of adults and communities, is simply outdated and unhelpful. Poverty is intergenerational, as a recent publication from Combat Poverty, *Day in Day out – Understanding the Dynamics of Child Poverty* (2006) highlights. Therefore, ending poverty and educational disadvantage calls for intergenerational engagement. Intensive, holistic preschool interventions – with adequate family support – are critical for children in areas marked by poverty. A 'kindergarten education' is proposed as a model to respond to the needs of children and families living in poverty, and is presented as one way of answering many of the challenges highlighted in the White Paper on Early Childhood Education, *Ready to Learn* (1999). 'Afterschool' or 'out-of-school' educational opportunities for children are an effective way to promote children's social as well as academic development, particularly through parents, teachers and community members working in partnership. Adult and community education, it is suggested, needs to be supported through an increased life-long learning needs budget, with multi-annual funding and autonomy at regional level in order to maximise its full potential to support the life-long learning needs of adults in communities marked by poverty.

The Home School Community Liaison Scheme is analysed and recommended as having the potential to support parents' participation within their children's school and education. The section concludes with two analyses of community education: men's and women's. New models within each type of community education are emerging that promote transformative change at a personal and local community level. The recognition in the new National Development Plan, *Transforming Ireland 2007–2013* (2007) that 'people of working age who are outside the labour market are particularly vulnerable to poverty or social exclusion' is accurate, along with the statement that 'community education has a particular role to play in this context' (p. 248); it must now be hoped that some of the €4.2 billion promised to the Working Age Education Programme will be readily accessible to organisations that provide adult education in communities with the greatest need.

8

Tackling Educational Disadvantage: Home and School

Noreen Flynn

The ability of a child to benefit from the education system or, on the contrary, to be disadvantaged within that system, is most likely to be established at the time of conception. The level of disadvantage experienced as a child moves through the education system is strongly influenced by the socio-economic status and the health and welfare of the family unit. While it is evident in Irish society that there is no 'quick fix' solution to inter-generational poverty and deprivation, most would agree that education is the key and schools have a huge role to play. Furthermore, to create equality of educational opportunity, children who experience deprivation in early childhood need intensive holistic early intervention, in the community, school, and home, to support the nurture/education process as they develop.

Some social issues which result from, and contribute to, educational disadvantage

It is clear that educational disadvantage stems from a combination of factors such as poverty, social deprivation and/or substance abuse. The manner in which successive governments respond systemically and systematically to these issues relates directly to the level of progress made in tackling educational disadvantage.

An examination of the prison population reveals that educational disadvantage is frequently a contributory cause of incarceration and, furthermore, while parents, especially fathers, from the most impoverished communities are imprisoned, their families suffer further deprivation. *Inclusion is Everyone's*

Business, (Nolan, 2005) indicates that levels of acute poverty in parts of Dublin remain unchanged since 1991. It also reveals that while Dublin has 12.7 per cent of the national population it produces 31.8 per cent of the national prison population, with the highest proportions coming from postal districts 1, 8, 11 and 24. The consequent devastating impact of poverty and social exclusion is highlighted in several studies of the prison population. The *Prison Adult Literacy Survey* (Morgan and Kett, 2003) identifies strong links between anti-social behaviour and educational disadvantage as manifested in the low literacy levels exhibited by the 300 prisoners surveyed. More than one in five of the prisoners scored at pre-level 1 on internationally recognised literacy tests. This level represents what was traditionally known as 'illiteracy'. Just over 50 per cent of the prison sample scored at pre-level or level 1 compared to less than 25 per cent of the general population. Morgan and Kett examined data from both national and international surveys and concluded that 'there is a considerable body of evidence showing that poor literacy skills restrict a range of life choices (particularly employment) and thus become a pre-disposing factor in criminal activities'. They recommended that 'the prevention of early school-leaving should be at the core of intervention' (*Inclusion is Everyone's Business*, 2005).

Levels of educational disadvantage, as reflected in the prison population who tend to come from areas of disadvantage, show the urgent need for multi-agency comprehensive support for these communities. The National Development Plan, 2000–2006, acknowledges that 'Spreading resources too thinly over a range of initiatives or putting in place a set of diverse programmes lacking integration and focus, will not address the real and acute needs of those suffering from social exclusion.' The findings in the Dublin City Council report seem to support this view.

The National Anti-Poverty Strategy (NAPS) Review (2001) also reflects the link between those marginalised and their educational attainment and acknowledges the key role of education in breaking the cycle of disadvantage: 'Lack of qualifications can combine with unemployment, dependence on social welfare, accommodation difficulties and health problems, and create a situation where various aspects of disadvantage become mutually reinforcing' (NAPS, 2001). This link is borne out in a study of homeless persons carried out by Seymour and Costello in 2005. They found that prisoners who were homeless on committal were even more educationally disadvantaged than the general prison sample, with almost 50 per cent having left school between the ages of seven and thirteen years in comparison to 21 per cent of the remainder of the sample.

As our society becomes more complex, those with poor standards of education have fewer opportunities for inclusion as active members of society. Investment in child and family services that pays close attention to children's developmental needs from the cradle is the only failsafe solution to breaking generational underachievement. High levels of social deprivation are shown to have a profound impact on the level of stimulation, nurture, care, and nutrition received by a child from birth. Studies emphasise the importance of the quality of that nurture/education for the child's long-term development. This presents a strong challenge for government to provide comprehensive support in the area of early-childhood education. 'The way parents care for their children, teach them skills and values, and guide them in their encounters with the world outside the home lays the foundation for children's later emotional, social and intellectual development' (Riordan, 2001).

The effects of poverty and deprivation and consequent educational disadvantage are key contributing factors for many living in communities experiencing disadvantage to become involved in drugs. Drug-taking further reduces the capacity of an individual or their children to participate in, and benefit from, the education system. Statistics from the three main maternity hospitals in Dublin show that over the last decade a significant number of children each year are born with addiction to drugs. The following table shows the number of babies admitted to the Neonatal Special Baby Care Unit of the National Maternity Hospital with symptoms of narcotic withdrawal.

Year	Number of babies
2004	21
2003	13
2002	17
2001	23
2000	10

Statistics from the Coombe Hospital for 2003 show that ninety-three women were referred to the Drug Liaison Midwifery Service. Eighty-five babies were born to drug-addicted women in that year and thirty-two babies required postnatal treatment for neonatal abstinence.

A study conducted in the Rotunda Hospital in 1999 (Milner et al.) found that during that one-year period forty-three newborn infants with neonatal abstinence syndrome were admitted to the paediatric department. These children are currently in the primary education system. Figures for 2004 show that babies were delivered to eighty-eight mothers who were on a methadone maintenance programme.

Dr Conor Farren, psychiatrist, St Patrick's Hospital, Dublin, addressing an Oireachtas Committee, stated that a conservative estimate of alcohol abuse in Ireland would be that 5 per cent of the population was alcohol-dependent and 7 per cent alcohol-abusive. Approximately 6 per cent of admissions to psychiatric hospitals in 2003 were related to alcohol problems (*Irish Times*, 3 March 2006).

Adult substance abuse manifests itself in some children who present in school with serious emotional and behavioural difficulties. These difficulties, some of which are initiated pre-birth, can be further compounded by poor nutrition and sleep patterns, lack of stimulation and poor language development in the early years. Until the care and educational needs of all children are met early in their lives, society is simply banking severe problems for the future.

The following table highlights the inadequacy of funding currently provided for early education:

Provision for Disadvantage Schemes, 2006	
Total Budget	€649.4m
Early Education	€11.1m
Primary Education	€92.3m
Primary and Second-level Schemes	€34.4m
Further Education	€197m
Third-level Access	€242m

The effects of poor funding for early intervention, as shown in the table above, are evident in an ESRI report (2004), which shows that students from poorer backgrounds are still hugely under-represented in third-level colleges. While 90 per cent of Leaving Certificate students in some prosperous areas of south Dublin go on to third-level education, this figure drops to less than 20 per cent in some poorer areas of West Dublin. Accessing third-level education can never be a reality for the marginalised until sufficient support is provided in the early years to build a solid educational foundation from which children can develop to their full potential.

Progress to date

Over many years, all of the bodies that advise government on strategies to tackle disadvantage have been recommending a comprehensive programme of early intervention. The most recent body, the Statutory Educational Disadvantage Committee, was established in 2002, under the 1998 Education Act, to advise the Minister for Education and Science on policies and strategies to be adopted to identify and correct educational disadvantage. In its final report, *Moving Beyond Educational Disadvantage* (2005), it sought to advise the Minister for Education and Science on how gaps in service might be filled by going beyond schools, in conjunction with other government departments, to promote lifelong learning and in so doing to end educational disadvantage. This report set out three strategic goals:

- achieve educational equality in the broader context of achieving social inclusion
- provide inclusive opportunities for learning at all stages of the life cycle, from birth onwards
- improve the mainstream school system so that all young people aged from three to eighteen years receive an education that is appropriate to their needs.

The challenge to government now, in achieving these goals, is to implement the principles of the National Development Plan, 2007–2013, which highlights the centrality of education in breaking the cycle of intergenerational poverty. 'Any investment framework, with children as its centre, and social inclusion as its overall objective, must include education. The National Action Plan for Social Inclusion identifies education as central to addressing poverty' (NDP, 2007–2013). This commitment, if implemented, should enhance and support formal education in schools serving areas of disadvantage, and so make a real difference. However, of the €12.3 billion to be invested in child services over the lifetime of the NDP 2007–2013 €361m is allocated to DEIS and Early Education, while €1,336m is going towards the National Childcare Investment Programme (NCIP). A better balance in funding must be struck between care and education if education is to be effective in breaking the cycle of poverty.

The OECD thematic review of early childhood education and care policy in Ireland, 2002, called for specific funding for the marginalised. It recommended that all policy in early education, care and funding be integrated into one department or placed under a designated funding and policy agency (OECD, 2002). This theme of integrated holistic support is also echoed in the EDC report. Strategic planning and management of funds is essential to ensure effective delivery of a comprehensive service. A welcome development in this regard is the establishment of the Office of the Minister for Children (OMC). The purpose of the OMC is to support the Minister for Children in implementing the National Children's Strategy (2000–2010), National Childcare Investment Programme (2006–2010) and the Children Act (2001). The OMC will also maintain a general strategic oversight of bodies with responsibility for developing and delivering children's services in areas such as early childhood care and education, youth justice, child welfare and protection. With a budget of €12.3b devoted to the children programme of the NDP 2007–2013, the OMC should enhance the development of a joined-up approach to the delivery of services for children as recommended in the final report of the EDC to the Minister for Education and Science.

Outcomes of current interventions suggest that it is far less successful to attempt remediation at four years of age in the formal school setting than to provide positive intervention from birth. By ensuring that, through early support mechanisms, developmental milestones in the early years are reached, we can give children a better chance of success within the formal education system when they come to school. When parents/guardians are addicted to drugs or alcohol, children need intensive support in the early years if they are to overcome the effects of their own addiction as babies and strive to reach the normal developmental milestones.

Many agencies are developing models of good practice in this area. These involve multi-agency, early intervention at community level that is accessible, attractive and includes input from health, social and educational services. The Department of Health and Children recently published *Working for Children and Families – Exploring Good Practice* (2003); this document sets out twenty-six models of good practice currently being implemented in child and family services throughout Ireland. The following management and intervention principles of good practice can be applied to these models:

- They provide a range of services targeted at different levels of need within a framework of prevention.
- The service has clear objectives and a management and organisational culture that facilitates its achievement.
- The service has a culture of learning and development, and measures outcomes.
- The service has adequate resources, offers value for money and has a commitment to effective partnership practice.
- The service provides good staff development and support.
- The service is whole-child focused and is attractive and accessible.
- The service is integrated and works in a way that is collaborative and strengthening.
- The service is effective and responsive to need.
- The service is culturally competent.
- Staff are interested and able.

Models of good practice relevant to early childhood education

Sligo Family Support Ltd is a good model of local accessibility, integrated services and an effective response to children's developmental needs, thus laying a solid foundation for lifelong learning. It works in a collaborative way, building on the strength and abilities of the participants and applies all of the principles of good practice outlined.

The mission of the project is to educate and empower parents of children from birth to age five so that these children are enabled to reach their full potential. The core element of the approach is a Lifestart home-visitation, child-development support programme delivered to over 300 families. The family visitor introduces the developmental stages that are relevant to the child's age. This home visitation is complemented by a quality childcare service at the centre, located in the grounds of the local primary school and therefore very accessible to parents. Courses are offered that promote self-awareness and social and personal development. The main strength of Sligo Family Support Ltd is that it addresses the needs of the child in the home by working with the parent/guardian as prime educator of the child.

Services provided heretofore were delivered mainly outside the home in breakfast and homework clubs. While these services are essential as a short- and medium-term measure, they do not impact positively on the life of the child in the home. Home is the primary source of care for the child and as parents/guardians are the prime educators, it is, therefore, vital that supports empower the carer in the home, as is the case with the Sligo Family Support project.

The Family Support Service offered through the Department of Social and Family Affairs has been a most effective home intervention, fulfilling many of the criteria outlined above. A home help is assigned to assist with the basic organisation of domestic activities. A routine of preparing daily breakfast is established. Children enjoy breakfast in their own home before going to school in a happy positive frame of mind. Effective homemaking, budgeting and shopping skills are developed to ensure the provision of nutritious food for basic meals daily.

An example of current good practice in behaviour management is the Early Focus Educational Support Project currently operating in a school in Dublin's south inner city. The project seeks to target children who are potentially at risk of leaving school early. It uses the resources of the specially equipped project room and the environs of the school and wider community to provide activities and formulate situations that seek to develop the esteem and self-worth of the children that attend. The project is coordinated and facilitated by a teacher seconded from the school, who is trained as a counsellor. The success of this project has primarily been in fostering positive relationships between the project leader and the children. Emphasis is on play and activities that encourage self-expression in a creative manner. Trust has been nurtured and the children gain confidence in an environment that is predictable and where they actually get to be children. For a small amount of time each week the burden of responsibility that is often placed upon them in their home environments is removed.

The project coordinator meets with parents on both a formal and informal basis. She also works with the Home School Community Liaison Coordinator.

Among the positive outcomes teachers report are greater participation in classroom activities, improved social skills, better attendance and punctuality. The project teacher is in constant communication with the class teachers, monitoring progress and identifying needs.

The Programme for Government 2002–2007 outlines the government commitment to early childhood education as follows:

> To ensure that early-education services deliver the maximum benefit for all children, we will introduce a national early-education, training, support and certification system and expand state-funded early education places. Priority will be given to a new national system of funded early-education for children with intellectual disabilities and children in areas of concentrated disadvantage. (Department of the Taoiseach, 2002)

Despite these commitments and the indisputable international evidence of the importance of early childhood education, the only national programme currently in operation in Ireland is the Early Start Programme. Piloted in 1994 to target three- and four-year-olds, it was subsequently extended to forty schools. The 1998 evaluation of the programme showed that teachers in infant classes were highly supportive of the project, citing improved social and language skills in children who attended. However, only marginal measurable increases in literacy and numeracy through standardised testing were found. Using such narrow indicators as literacy and numeracy is insufficient to measure progress, particularly when follow-on learning support is stretched to capacity. What can be expected, given existing resources, is that these children will develop the skills, confidence and desire to stay within the system at least until Leaving Certificate. Outcomes in this regard can only be measured by a longitudinal study.

Primary teachers see the advantages of effective early childhood education. However, transition between preschool and primary school needs to be consolidated so that any special intervention in terms of speech and language, behaviour or learning disability granted in preschool will carry through with that child to primary school. We look to the DES action plan *Delivering Equality of Opportunity in Schools* (DEIS) to ensure that, in conjunction with other government departments, a seamless support service is put in place to 'ensure that the educational needs of children and young people are prioritised and effectively addressed' (DEIS, 2005).

Literacy and numeracy standards in areas of disadvantage can be increased if, in line with international best practice, a number of measures are put in place. A revised early education programme offering a full-day preschool service is essential. Primary class sizes must be reduced to 15:1 in the infant classes and 20:1 in senior classes so that work done in preschool can be reinforced and built upon. Provision of an adequate supply of learning-support teachers to intervene at the earliest signs of literacy or numeracy difficulties is essential. Programmes such as *Reading Recovery*, which is proving very successful, must be extended to all designated disadvantaged schools. Early access to speech therapy and to psychological and psychiatric support at the same level as if it were paid for as a private service is vital if we are to give meaning to equality of educational opportunity. Expansion of the National Educational Psychological Service (NEPS) and the establishment of a panel of clinical psychologists are urgently required to support the growing number of children exhibiting emotional and behavioural problems.

All such programmes and interventions can only be effective if children attend school regularly. The Education Welfare Act (2000) provided for the establishment of a National Education Welfare Board (NEWB) to promote school attendance. The NEWB attendance report for 2004–2005 (O'Briain, 2006) shows strong links between levels of disadvantage and levels of non-attendance, with one in five pupils in the most disadvantaged primary schools absent twenty days or more compared to one in sixteen in schools least disadvantaged. Indications are that once a pattern of frequent absence is established, it continues throughout the child's school life, creating a cumulative deficit in learning. It has proven much more difficult and less cost-effective to make up that deficit in later life. The success of NEWB in improving school attendance is central to the effectiveness of all educational provision. While funding for NEWB has increased to €8.2m in 2006, no new Education Welfare Officers have been appointed since 2004 because of a government embargo on employment. Supports must be put in place to improve the attendance of children absent sixty to one hundred days a year. In a 1997 study in Mountjoy Prison, O'Mahony found that in a random sample of one in five prisoners, 63 per cent had played truant regularly while in school, which he concluded added significantly to their low levels of attainment.

Teaching a child how to read, write and do sums, without developing positive behaviour patterns, a social conscience and a desire to play an active positive role in society, will do little to change the new low our society is experiencing in terms of violent crime, robbery and assault, which leaves many people living in fear, particularly the elderly.

The Teacher Counsellor/Support Teacher scheme established in 1996 in twenty-seven designated disadvantaged schools focuses specifically on behaviour management. An INTO evaluation in 1997 revealed that the response of principal teachers to the scheme was overwhelmingly positive. The self-esteem of children with behavioural problems was perceived to have improved, suspensions were reduced significantly and school attendance was up (INTO, 2000). It is vital that this scheme is extended and developed as a model of good practice as part of *Delivering Equality of Opportunity in Schools* (DEIS).

Towards the future

In the 2004 INTO policy document on educational disadvantage entitled *Tackle Disadvantage Now!* John Carr, INTO General Secretary, strongly emphasises the INTO view that 'early intervention and structured intensive supports throughout primary education are the key priorities in tackling educational disadvantage. This philosophy should be fully embedded in the education system, to ensure that education policy is based on a firm sense of social justice.' The DES has the opportunity to pilot such a comprehensive holistic educational service in the newly built complex in Cherry Orchard, Dublin. Costing €11m, the state-of-the-art building includes special facilities for preschool children, for children outside of school hours and children with special needs, together with full primary school facilities.

The success of this project will depend largely on the level of cooperation between the various government departments in planning and funding the project adequately. Establishment of an effective management structure is essential to ensure that the project is run efficiently in accordance with the principles of good practice outlined. If resourced, this complex has the potential to be the flagship model for ending educational disadvantage.

The factors contributing to poverty and educational disadvantage are abundantly clear. The impact of social deprivation is brought to us daily in the media. We have entered a new period of prosperity as a nation where there is no financial barrier to delivering on policies to alleviate poverty and educational disadvantage for the most disenfranchised in our society. In 2004, the average investment in education per student at primary level was €5,000. The average cost of one year in prison was €85,000. The fundamental issue in tackling disadvantage is how we prioritise as a society. Radical decisions must be made regarding the funding of the early education and the growth and development of children who do not receive the same support as their advantaged peers. This is a poverty issue and in this time of economic boom there should be no further delay in providing cohesive supports, as outlined in this article, to end the human suffering and powerlessness of educational disadvantage. If the OMC delivers real state intervention, we could be looking at a period in Irish society that will frame a different kind of future for those currently marginalised by poverty and educational disadvantage.

References

Coombe Hospital (2003) *Annual Clinical Report*, Dublin: Coombe Hospital

Department of Education and Science (2005) *DEIS: Delivering Equality of Opportunity in Schools – An Action Plan for Educational Inclusion*, Dublin: DES

Department of Education and Science (2005) *Report of the Educational Disadvantage Committee, Moving Beyond Educational Disadvantage*, Dublin: DES

Department of Education and Science (2006) *Provision for Disadvantaged Schemes*, Dublin: DES

Department of Health and Children (2003) *Working for Children and Families – Exploring Good Practice*, Galway: Western Health Board, Child and Family Research and Policy Unit /National University of Ireland

Department of the Taoiseach (2002) *An Agreed Programme for Government between Fianna Fáil and the Progressive Democrats*, Dublin: Department of the Taoiseach

Economic and Social Research Institute (2004) *A Review of Entry to Higher Education*, Dublin. ESRI

Government of Ireland (1999) *Ireland: National Development Plan, 2000–2006*, Dublin: Government Publications

Government of Ireland (2006) *Ireland: National Development Plan, 2007–2013*, Dublin: Government Publications

Irish National Teachers' Organisation (2000) *A Fair Start*, Dublin: INTO

Irish National Teachers' Organisation (2004) *Tackle Disadvantage Now!* Dublin: INTO

Irish Prison Service (2005) *Annual Report 2004*, Dublin: Irish Prison Service

Milner, M., Beckett, M., Coghlan, D., McNally, M., Clarke, T. A., Lambert, I., McDermott, C. (1999) 'Neonatal Abstinence Syndrome', Irish Medical Journal, vol. 92 no. 1

Morgan, M. and Kett, M. (2003) *The Prison Adult Literacy Survey*, Dublin: Irish Prison Service

National Anti-Poverty Strategy (2001) *Review of the National Anti-Poverty Strategy; Framework Document*, Dublin: Goodbody Economic Consultants

Nolan, A. (2005) *Inclusion is Everyone's Business*, Dublin: Social Inclusion Unit, Dublin City Council

O'Briain, E. (2006) *Mori Ireland. Analysis of School Attendance Data at Primary and Post-Primary Levels for 2004/2005*, Dublin: National Education Welfare Board

O'Mahony, P. (1997) *Mountjoy Prisoners: A Sociological Study and Criminological Profile*, Dublin: Government Publications

Organisation for Economic Cooperation and Development (2002) *Thematic Review of Early Childhood Education and Care Policy in Ireland*, Paris: OECD

Riordan, S. (2001) *Supporting Parenting: A Study of Parents' Support Needs*, Dublin: Institute of Technology for the Families Research Programme, Department of Social and Family Affairs, Centre for Social and Educational Research

Seymour, M. and Costello, L. (2005) *A Study of the Number, Profile and Progression Routes of Homeless Persons before the Courts and in Custody*, Dublin: Centre for Social and Educational Research, Dublin Institute of Technology and the Department of Justice and Law Reform

9

Early Childhood Education: Absent from the Irish System

Philomena Donnelly

Economic, social and educational factors have made early childhood education and care a priority for the Irish government in recent years. The 2002 census revealed that there were 384,712 children under the age of six years in the Republic. The most recent figures indicate that 37,900 children are in childcare on a daily basis. To date, 771,000 women are part of the workforce, representing a significant social and cultural change in Irish life. Recent reports by the OECD (Government of Ireland, 2004) and the National, Economic and Social Forum (NESF) (2005) recommend radical change in where and how our children are educated and cared for from birth to the age of six. Yet, with all of the recent reports and initiatives in the area of early years there have been no proposals for a national state-run kindergarten system of education for Irish children. Ireland has much to learn from mainland European countries where organised education systems for young children have existed going back to the early eighteenth century. Education is a human right and a social duty. To fulfil one's social duty of becoming educated, a citizen needs the state to provide the necessary schooling systems. This is nowhere more striking than in areas weighted with poverty. The possibility of participating as citizens on an equal basis is denied to many children because there is no system of kindergarten education. Quality education at an early age can be the deciding factor between a life of possibilities and a denial of these possibilities. International research has consistently shown that investment in the yearly years has a long-term positive effect for the individuals concerned and for the society of which they are part. The evidence is particularly striking for children with a higher risk of poverty and disadvantage. The outcomes demonstrate that children participating in quality early years education are more likely to remain longer in the schooling system and to participate in mainstream society and are less likely to be involved in criminal activity (Heckman, et al., 2004; Schweinhart, 1993). There is also a financial benefit to society, with the NESF calculating that the present cost–benefit ratio for universal preschool in Ireland would be €7.08 for every €1.25 spent (2005, p. 127). To date, early years education and intervention programmes to end disadvantage in education have been patchy and somewhat disappointing in outcomes.

There is a need for a thorough change in attitude, conception and financing of education for Irish children between three and five years of age. There are many immediate issues surrounding this, such as childcare, afterschool services, etc., but while being related and relevant, there is a need to tackle the provision of a comprehensive, universal system of kindergarten education. I am using the term 'kindergarten' to differentiate a distinct strand within the education system and not to be confused with demands for childcare and crèche facilitates. Kindergarten (children's garden) is understood in this context as a distinct but complementary level within the education continuum to cater for the educational needs of children from three to five years of age. The neglect of kindergarten education is not an accidental event in Irish history but rather a conscious decision by conservative forces during the establishment of the Republic to keep what was regarded as 'the traditional family' in place. After reflecting on the history of the absent strand in Irish education, suggestions for the future education of children between the ages of three to five years are offered.

Women and children: a single entity?

In the past the role of women in Irish society was controlled by family life – contraception was banned, married women were barred from working in the civil service and the teaching profession, and women as individuals had few, if any, rights. This patriarchal social system was further entrenched in the 1937 Irish constitution where women were primarily viewed as mothers. Article 41 reads:

1.1   The State recognises the Family as the natural primary and fundamental unit group of Society, and as a moral institution possessing inalienable and imprescriptible rights, antecedent and superior to all positive law.

2.1   In particular, the State recognises that by her life within the home, woman gives to the State a support without which the common good cannot be achieved.

Interestingly, in the index at the end of the 1937 constitution, 'Women' is referenced by '*see* family; sex'. Women having too many children led to poverty, as families on meagre means tried to feed and clothe large numbers of offspring. More recent research warns of the same problem facing modern parents:

households with children face a disproportionate danger of falling into the poverty trap (Nolan, 2000). Children in the past were, in general, viewed as extensions of women and as such without rights or needs as a group. It was as though umbilical cords were never cut. Alongside this, control of education (primary and secondary schooling) was conceded to the churches by the state after consistent pressure from the churches. This situation still remains largely intact today. The state abdicates its duty and responsibility in the field of education. Governments collect taxes from citizens for redistribution and cede their power of management of schools to churches. Kindergarten education became and remains a casualty of such structures. To provide kindergarten schooling would have been viewed by many in positions of power as 'interference' in family life. Universal kindergarten education is still not available to Irish children in 2007.

The history of the absent strand of Irish education

Ireland, it is often claimed, has a long history of academic learning going back to the monastic tradition of the Middle Ages. This is true, but the opportunities for learning were largely for young men, so this tradition was exclusive and limited. In 1824, an official commission reported that there were 11,000 primary schools in Ireland catering for half a million children and with about 12,000 teachers. Lord Stanley, Chief Secretary for Ireland, established the national education system in 1831. This was conceived as an interdenominational system, but after much and insistent pressure from the churches, both Protestant and Catholic, the system evolved into a denominational one by the mid-nineteenth century. Young children, some as young as three years of age, were catered for within the primary education system as there was no minimum age for starting school; (for more on the history of Irish education, see Coolahan, 1981). In 1884, the enrolment of three-year-olds was declared illegal, yet in 1933 official records show that there were 7,300 three-year-olds in education. However, this is not to be confused with the provision of kindergarten education. Such children were participating in a primary school system of education. Attempts are sometimes made to suggest that the participation of three-year-olds in primary schools was in some way compensating for the lack of kindergarten schools but this is to miss the point. It certainly shows a failure to understand the educational needs of three-year-olds. The difference between early childhood education and primary education is as great as that between primary and secondary education or indeed between secondary and third-level education. Of course they collectively form a continuum but their strength is in their differing roles and approaches to teaching and learning.

The Revised Programme for National Schools (1900) was a significant development in that for the first time the importance of what was referred to as 'infant' education was emphasised. Schools were encouraged to be pleasant places for children. The term 'infant education' remains in vogue today as can be witnessed by the National Council for Curriculum Assessment (NCCA) reference to the first two years of primary school as infant education in the Primary Curriculum (1999). The term implies very young children and creates difficulties both in terms of what we understand by the word 'infant' and the conception of what is happening in schools for these children. The OECD in its report (2004) expressed concern at the lack of debate in Ireland on the education and care of young children. In many ways, the debate has begun but use of language can hinder or assist such a debate and the continuing use of the term 'infant' rather than 'early years' is a reflection of the confusion surrounding the whole area. 'Infants' implies children under a year and there is a major difference in ability and needs between a ten-month-old child and a three- or four-year-old child. Our failure to differentiate in language may be symptomatic of our failure to differentiate between, and plan for, the varying needs of children under six.

Early childhood education existed in France from the 1780s with the setting up of Jean-Frederic Oberlin's village centres in Alsace. Oberlin organised play-based instruction for children less than six years of age. The Enlightenment in Europe and the work of Jean Jacques Rousseau helped to bring the issue of educating children into general debate. In 1816 in Britain, Robert Owen established schools in New Lanark for children, where singing, dancing and open-air play was encouraged. Children between the ages of three and ten years were catered for. The three-to-five age group was given a distinct space for themselves, acknowledging their particular needs. This initiative by Owen was an integral part of his vision of establishing a new society based on radical and humane ideas. Not all in Europe were as enthusiastic about the education of young children, with the Prussian government banning kindergartens in 1851 because they were viewed as part of a socialist and atheistical plot. Education for young children took root in Europe but not with the ideas of Owen and Oberlin. Rather the need for future workers and the perceived necessity of moral instruction led to children being educated in large work-house type schools. The arrival of Friedrich Froebel in Germany put an end to any attempt to prevent the growth of kindergarten education in Germany. He was very opposed to the instruction method used in many schools and his approach was very play-based, encouraging children to develop at their own rate. Froebel's ideas on the learning and teaching of young children spread throughout Europe and are still studied and implemented today. The health of young children was also seen as significant, and Maria Montessori, an Italian doctor, introduced another radical approach to the education of young children. England had the dedicated work of the McMillan sisters, Margaret and Rachel, and in Ireland, Dr Kathleen Lynn established St Ultan's Children's Hospital in 1919.

State and church: mistrust and power

However, Ireland, like Prussia, had forces within it that were very opposed to any systematic change for children in either their health or education. In 1948, a progressive Minister for Health in a coalition government, Dr Noel Browne, introduced a Health Bill in which he proposed a universal health scheme for mothers and children. This led to a bitter dispute and debate in which the Catholic bishops became directly involved. In a letter to the then Taoiseach, John A. Costello, the Catholic bishops pronounced:

> The hierarchy cannot approve of any scheme which, in its general tendency, must foster undue control by the state in a sphere so delicate and so intimately concerned with morals as that which deals with gynaecology or obstetrics and with the relations between doctor and patient. (Kennedy, 2002, p. 200)

Anything that appeared different from Catholic social teaching was actively opposed by the church and this explains why it was so determined to control education. As mentioned previously, women and children, particularly young children, were viewed as one item. The interesting aspect of the mother and child dilemma was that even in areas where the church was not in direct control, it still influenced government decisions. This could only have happened with the agreement of the political parties. Governments and the state bowed to the power of the church and were complacent in handing over control of education to the direct power of the churches. A patriarchal, authoritarian model of family life was seen as the ideal during the years after independence and, as such, there was little hope of initiating or developing models of early childhood education that were being practiced in other European countries. It was not only Ireland's economy that stagnated in the decades after the establishment of the Republic but progress in social, educational and individual lifestyles. Donogh O'Malley, Minister for Education, finally broke this restrictive practice in education in the 1960s. He introduced a Bill establishing free second-level schooling in 1967. It was a revolutionary move and broke a stranglehold on the thinking at the time. Tom Garvin, in *Preventing the Future: Why was Ireland so poor for so long?* (2004), suggests that the idea of a generally educated and secular society ceased to be something to be feared and despised. Education became something to achieve and of which to be proud. Significantly, it offered to many the opportunity for betterment. With education came possibilities and the unfolding of potential.

Women and children as citizens

Yet, in all of these major new developments, early childhood remained the 'Cinderella' of the education system. The founding of St Ultan's Children's Hospital by Dr Kathleen Lynn and Madeleine French-Mullen in 1919 was a major effort to assist the health of children from poor and destitute families. The largest demand on many families was to keep their young children alive. Kindergarten education, if it was ever referred to, was a mere fantasy. But change did come in the role and status of women in the later decades of the twentieth century. Equal pay for women was introduced in 1974 and the Employment Equality Act came into operation in 1977, outlawing discrimination on grounds of gender or marital status in recruitment, training or provision for promotion. The Maternity Act (1981) provided for maternity leave and the right to return to work for pregnant employees. Divorce was introduced in Ireland in 1995. Because of the coupling of women with children in Irish social structures, the liberation of women has had a knock-on effect on the role and status of children. There is now a Minister for Children, a National Children's Office, a Dáil na nÓg and a Children's Ombudsman. The new body overseeing the care and education of children before primary school is centrally located in the Department of Health and Children. A new Early Years Education Policy Unit has been established in the DES to oversee the development of policies and provision for early years education. This new unit is co-located with the office of the Minister for Children. There was a need to regulate the responsibility for young children because up until 2006, seven different government departments shared the task. The OECD report (2004) recommended bringing education and care policy under one ministry or designated agency. However, having all of the care and education of young children in one government department may not be the best solution, and revisiting the White Paper on early childhood education, *Ready to Learn* (1999) may be timely. In the recommendations it is suggested that the Department of Health and Children should be the lead department for children from birth to three, and the Department of Education the lead department for children from three to six. I think this recommendation should be revived with a view to having the Minister for Education primarily responsible for the Early Years Education Policy Unit. Coordination with the Ministry for Health and Children would, of course, be essential. Interestingly, another of the OECD recommendations is to develop a publicly funded morning education service for all children of three years of age.

Here, I am directly concerned with the education of children from three to five. I acknowledge that there are many important, related issues pertaining to the care of children before the age of three and outside school time but I am consciously focusing on our non-existent system of kindergarten education. There are many well-run playgroups, playschools, Montessori preschools and Naíonraí within the Republic but my focus is on the role of the state. Offering grants for private providers to establish preschools is ad hoc and again an evasion by government of its responsibilities for education. For example, the following chart gives a good idea of where Ireland is in comparison to our European neighbours:

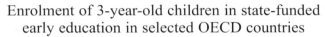

Enrolment of 3-year-old children in state-funded early education in selected OECD countries

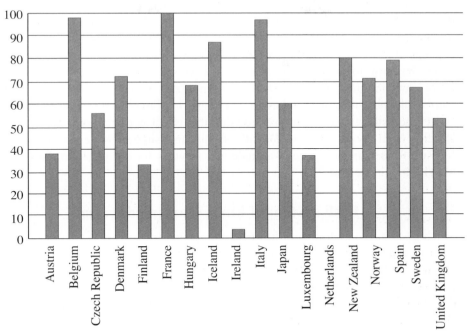

Source: OECD (2002), *Education at a Glance*, Paris

Note: Many 3-year-olds attend some form of sessional education in Ireland. However, as these sessions are organised on a private basis and are unsupported by state funding, ministry statisticians do not include them in figures supplied to the OECD and other international organisations.

The significance of this chart is not just that it shows Ireland's abysmal contribution to early education but also that it highlights how embarrassingly out-of-step Ireland is with most other democratic states. It is a damning indictment of the Irish Republic. A recent report by the Economic and Social Research Institute (ESRI) commissioned by Combat Poverty found that half of the state's one million children are affected by poverty at some stage during their childhood. Helen Johnston of Combat Poverty names the provision of preschool education as one of the solutions to eradicating this Irish disease (*Irish Times*, 30 May 2006). International research has consistently shown that quality early years education has a direct and long-term impact on the social and educational lives of children, particularly for children from areas designated as disadvantaged (Schweinhart et al., 1993; Gurainick, 1998; Roinick and Grunewald, 2003).

Importantly, those who receive such education are more likely to remain in school longer than if they had not participated in early years education. This has a cyclical effect, as the ESRI report points out, on the children of these children such that the level of education of a child's parents was found to be a critical factor in determining a child's risk of poverty. For example, France, where the concept of early years education first evolved with Jean Fredric Oberlin in the 1780s, has now, in its écoles maternelles, a universal state-funded system of early years education that has shown the long-term effects of such provision. Children who attend the écoles maternelles remain longer in primary and secondary school and French studies have demonstrated that this effect is particularly marked for children from poorer families (David, 1993). I now suggest some possible ways forward for a radical change in attitude and services for our three- to five-year-old children in Ireland.

An Irish system of kindergarten education

Much good and ongoing work has been completed in terms of a framework for early learning by the NCCA and quality indicators for practice by the Centre for Early Childhood Development and Education (Duignan and Walsh, 2004). All of this work gives a firm structure and provides underlying principles on which to establish a universal national system of education for three- to five-year-olds under the auspices of the DES. Such a system would be independent of the present primary school system but could possibly parallel it given the local nature of most primary schools. Present providers would be encouraged and facilitated to integrate and become part of the new system. There are many community-based preschools run on very meagre funds functioning throughout the country. The DES directly funds an inner-city preschool in Dublin and preschools for children from the Travelling community. They all should be encouraged to become integrated into the new system, offering an inclusive service for all children. Intervention projects for children living in poverty and children with particular educational needs, such as the *Early Start Programme*, would be an attribute of the new structure. A number of rudiments need to be instituted to make such a system a reality.

Women and children: cutting the umbilical cord

Women and children need to be de-coupled in Irish society. I am not in any way denying the importance of family life and the unique and primary role of parents. However, recent drives for childcare facilities are a result of women remaining in the paid workforce. What I am suggesting is that, irrespective of what mothers and indeed fathers are doing with their lives, kindergarten education should be available as an option for every parent for their child. By making it available, children will be accepted as a particular group within society, not just an appendix to another grouping within that same society. One of the hindrances to the evolution of kindergarten education in Ireland has been that children's roles were an extension of the role of mothers who were largely disempowered from participation in Irish life. Parents should, of course, be facilitated and encouraged to participate in their child's education and any quality kindergarten system needs to reflect this.

The role of the state

All of the churches in Ireland have overseen an undemocratic, elitist education system for many decades. I am not going to speculate here on the outcome of religious control of schooling in Ireland, good or otherwise. Rather, I want to demand that the state stops shying away from its responsibilities and, in initiating a new system within the present education system, becomes the direct provider. It is to the state that citizens pay taxes. For too long, the churches have been an interpreter between the state and its citizens. In a democracy and in an increasingly multi-cultural country, conceding control of entire systems of education to undemocratic bodies is unacceptable. The increasingly elitist system, particularly at second-level education, is furthering the divide in Irish society between the poor and the un-poor.

Funding

The funding of a universal kindergarten education system would be costly, and the government needs to plan and budget for such an expense. Again, the table from the OECD report (2004) is very telling and explains how the added expense to the Exchequer would merely be bringing Ireland into line with other European countries.

The Irish government needs to allocate the necessary funds for the new education system. It should not be sourced from within the present DES budget, rather the DES needs a larger allocation of central funds. It is worth reiterating that money spent on a quality early education system can be a key step in preventing disadvantage further on in a child's schooling.

Primary schooling would begin at six, the present senior infant class. Kindergarten education cannot be adequately provided for within the primary system. Having four- and five-year-old children studying an eleven-subject curriculum in classes of thirty is not educationally sound. Primary schools serve a different function. There are also reforms needed for six-year-olds within the primary system but they are not the focus of this particular argument.

Expenditure on educational institutions as a percentage of GDP (2001) in selected OECD countries

Country	Pre-primary (3 years plus)	Primary/ Post-primary	Third-level
Austria	0.5	3.9	1.2
Denmark	0.8	4.3	1.8
Germany	0.6	3.6	1.0
Ireland	<0.2	3.1	1.3
France	0.7	4.2	1.1
Poland	0.4	4.0	1.1
Portugal	0.3	4.2	1.1
United Kingdom	0.5	3.9	1.0
United States	0.5	4.1	2.7
Country mean	0.4	3.8	1.3

Source: OECD, *Education at a Glance,* 2004

Qualifications

Teachers in the kindergarten system would be qualified to degree level, either with a BA in Early Childhood Education (ECE) or a BEd and paid on a salary scale similar to that of primary teachers. Classroom assistants would be qualified and paid by the DES. Colleges and institutions will need to introduce new degree courses along with present ones specifically aimed at kindergarten teaching. The school buildings should be purpose-built with the kindergarten child in mind.

Conclusion

The history of early childhood education in Ireland is a history of neglect. I repeat, there is a need for the state to establish and operate a comprehensive system of education for children between the ages of three and five in Ireland. It has to be located in the DES, alongside the other strands of the education system. Only then will the Irish education system be complete. There are many good reasons for implementing such a policy. It would benefit society in general and prove to be a good financial investment by governments, but, most importantly, it would offer to all children and, in particular, to children living in poverty, the opportunity to fulfil their potential and participate in civil society. Kindergarten schooling is primarily an educational issue but it also contributes to developing an equal and democratic state. Kindergarten is a vital part of the common good.

References

Bunreacht na hÉireann (Constitution of Ireland) (1937) Dublin: Government Publications

Coolahan, J. (1981) *Irish Education: History and Structure*, Dublin: IPA

David, P. (1993) *Education Provision for our Youngest Children: European Perspectives*, London: Paul Chapman

Duignan, M. and Walsh, T. (2004) *Talkimg About Quality: Report of a Consultation Process on Quality in Early Childhood and Care and Education*, Dublin: CECDE

Garvin, T. (2004) *Preventing the Future: Why was Ireland so poor for so long?* Dublin: Gill & Macmillan

Government of Ireland (1999) *Primary School Curriculum*, Dublin: Government Publications

Government of Ireland (1999) *Ready to Learn: White Paper on Early Childhood Education*, Dublin: Government Publications

Government of Ireland (2004) *OECD Thematic Review of Early Childhood Education and Care Policy in Ireland*, Dublin: Government Publications

Gurainick, M. J. (ed.) (1998) *The effectiveness of early intervention*, Baltimore: P. H. Brooks

Heckman, J. J. and Masterov, D. V. (2004) 'The Productivity Argument for investing in Young Children', Invest in Kids Working Group, Committee for Economic Development, Working Paper No. 5

Kennedy, F. (2001) *Cottage to Crèche: Family Change in Ireland*, Dublin: IPA

National Economic and Social Forum (2005) *Report 31. Early Childhood Care and Education*, Dublin: NESF

Nolan, B. (2000) *Child Poverty in Ireland*, Dublin: Combat Poverty Agency and Oak Tree Press

Organisation for Economic Cooperation and Development (2002), *Education at a Glance*, Paris: OECD

Organisation for Economic Cooperation and Development (2004), *Education at a Glance*, Paris: OECD

Roinick, A. and Grunewald, R. (2003) *Early Childhood Development: Economic Development with a High Public Return*, Minneapolis, MN: Federal Reserve Bank of Minneapolis

Schweinhart, L. J., Barnes, H. V. and Weikart, D. P. (1993) *Significant benefits: The High/Scope Perry Preschool study through age 27*, monographs of the High/Scope Educational Research Foundation 10, Ypsilanti, MI: High/Scope Press

10

My Kids, Your Kids, Our Kids!

Ann Higgins

Introduction

In the mid-1980s, Kileely Community Project (KCP) evolved as a school-based grass-roots response to the challenge to make learning accessible to both adults and young people. In this chapter I profile the evolution of the project and share some of the research findings from my recent study which sought to uncover the impact of the project on people's lives and the life of the school. Drawing inspiration from Bronfenbrenner's ecological model (1979), I acknowledge the impact of home and school environments on the learner and propose a rationale for developing proactive partnership between these two worlds.

Context

The 1980s was an era of high unemployment, early school leaving and emigration. During that period, KCP evolved within the walls of a designated disadvantaged primary school on the north side of Limerick city. The evolution and development of the project were based on a number of basic assumptions. Firstly, that educational opportunity can enhance life chances for adults and children, secondly, that together, home and school can strategically affect change by working in partnership, and finally, that the school can facilitate the delivery of educational opportunities for the community.

Of course there were obstacles! Firstly, we had no money for staffing, equipment or resources. However, our vision and commitment led us through this period as we ran jumble sales in the school to raise money and sought funding from various agencies. Secondly, there was no tradition of adult education in the area and, at times, adult learners needed to be convinced that they were both entitled to, and capable of, participating in further education. Also, using a primary school building as a community-learning base meant changing the basic function of the building.

The project grew through a process of dialogue. Freire defines dialogue as 'an encounter among men who name the world … it is an act of creation' (Freire, 1972, pp. 61–2) and identifies five characteristics of true dialogue, namely, love, humility, faith, hope, and critical thinking. In the process of conducting my research I interviewed over fifty individuals involved in the symbiotic relationship between the formal learning sector of the school and the informal learning sector of KCP.

I come to this study as a former pupil, teacher and principal of the school in which KCP is located and as a founder member and director of Kileely Community Project (KCP). In 1985, having taught in the school for a number of years, and while on career break, I developed and delivered the initial adult education programme, 'Parents and Children Learning Together', based on the core belief that parental involvement in education and parental skill-building were legitimate ways of supporting children's learning. Since KCP pre-dated the Home School Community Liaison (HSCL) scheme, there was little culture of primary schools addressing adult education needs. Critically, while we had no financial resources we did have the goodwill of the principal and the school staff. Subsequently, a range of adult education classes were delivered within the school, sometimes drawing tutors from within the local community, and later from Limerick City Vocational Education Committee (VEC).

Six local women, along with myself, established a committee that oversaw the developments of the project. We organised morning and evening adult education guest speakers, women's holidays, family and women's day trips and social events. This core group of women was central to the development and sustainability of the project.

So, what are the factors that made returning to education attractive and attainable to adults? My research uncovered a number of key factors. Firstly, friendship and solidarity among the learners themselves were identified as factors that both encouraged and sustained involvement in KCP. Secondly, in relation to the tutors, appropriate pedagogy, which valued the prior knowledge and experience of learners, as well as learner-led course content, were identified as key to ensuring that KCP met identified needs. Furthermore, the ethos of the school ensured a welcoming, nurturing environment where all learners were valued.

Within a few months, the parents who had attended the initial classes to build their skills in supporting their own children's learning volunteered to run an afterschool programme with me. And so the '3 o'clock school' was born. Based in the school, it provided academic, social and creative learning opportunities within a unique learning environment where parents worked with tutors to provide enriching learning opportunities for children. Saturday morning art classes provided children with opportunities to develop their artistic skills within the context of a stimulating learning environment.

We were concerned that young lone mothers were not accessing our adult education classes and this led to the establishment of the SPACE initiative. This provided 'space' to these young women to build solidarity, reflect on their current situation and explore further learning opportunities. As a result of this intervention, several of the young women returned to do the Leaving Certificate and to further training. A crèche was made possible through a FÁS community employment scheme in the school. The establishment of a preschool that addressed the learning needs of young children and facilitated parental involvement in education followed this innovation. The diagram below profiles the activities of the project.

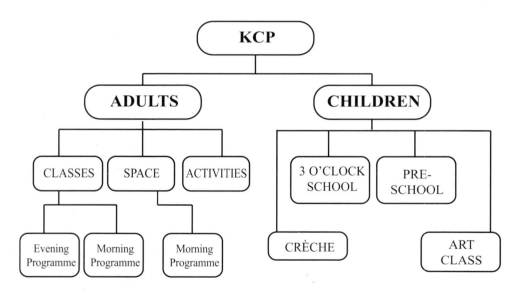

Ecological framework

Bronfenbrenner's ecological model provides a roadmap which guides us through the maze of systems which impact on the child's development. Extending beyond immediate experienced individual worlds, e.g. home and school (microsystem), to the interconnections between these worlds (mesosystem), the strategic importance of the quality of interconnections is recognised in how they impact on the child's learning, as Bronfenbrenner states: 'A child's ability to learn to read in the primary grades may depend no less on how he is taught than on the existence and nature of ties between the school and the home' (Bronfenbrenner, 1979, p. 3).

His model facilitates entry into the complex world of the learner, and forges an understanding of how home and school individually, and through their interconnections, impact positively or negatively on the learner's ability to access learning.

My kids: home context

The first and possibly the most influential environment the child experiences is the family home. According to Ryan, 'The influence of the family on a child's learning begins long before the child goes to school and extends well beyond the scope of the school' (Ryan, 2000, p. 176). Simply stated, 'Common sense tells us that children learn a great deal in the family – for good or for ill – and that parents play a significant part as educators of their own children from birth onwards (Macbeth and Ravn, 1994, p. 2).

Epstein acknowledges the significance of the role played by the family in building life skills and the resilience needed to interact effectively with the world. She believes that the child emerges from the family home with a variety of skills, attitudes and expectations reflecting their prior experience, nurtured during those early years. 'However configured, however constrained, families come with their children to school. Even when they do not come in person, families come in their children's minds and hearts and hopes and dreams. They come with their children's problems and promise' (Epstein, 2001, p. 4).

Many factors impact on the effectiveness of the home to nurture the attitudes and skills that equip the child to access learning effectively both within and outside the home environment. Research indicates that parental interaction with children plays a huge role in the child's subsequent capacity to succeed within the system, as Coleman states: 'It is not whom the parents are that matters, but what they do (with respect to schooling)' (Coleman, 1998, p. 144).

Other home-based factors which can impact on the effectiveness of the home include demographics, social and cultural capital, belief systems, and poverty. However, while negative factors such as poverty and lack of parental educational achievement may place families in a weaker position in terms of resources and insider knowledge, it must not be assumed that these families have lower aspirations or hopes for their children's attainment. As one mother who had left school at the age of eleven, to work as a domestic in a middle-class house, stated: 'I had to work hard … scrubbing out bins and all for her … I swore my three children wouldn't do that … I always valued education, and I said my children will not go through what I went through.'

Within a national context, Ryan's research into the '8–15 Early School-

Leaver's Initiative' confirms parents' high aspirations for their children: 'Parents invariably wished their children to remain in and complete school, even if they themselves had left school early' (Ryan, 2004, p. 80).

In my own research I uncovered a very high value for education and a clear understanding that educational attainment is a route out of poverty. This is the voice of a woman who raised her children by cleaning houses and other low-paid work; she is very clear on the difference that a good education can make to quality of life: '... without the education you couldn't get the jobs to pay you a decent wage and all you had is shite jobs, the shite jobs that paid you nothing and you worked twice as hard.'

Lynch cites lack of resources as a major impediment to maximising outcomes from the educational system for families living on low incomes: 'The principle problem that working-class people have in relation to education is that they lack adequate income to maximise the advantages that the system could offer ...' (Lynch, 1999, p. 57).

KCP sought to build the capacity of the home to support children's learning through a number of interrelated activities. Firstly, the programme was designed for, and delivered to, parents to build their skills in relation to supporting their children's learning. Secondly, the establishment of the '3 o'clock school', where parents and children interacted in a rich learning environment, brought benefits to children and parents: 'It made me feel good as a person 'cos I was able to help a younger child.' Its impact was acknowledged by both the parents and children: '... you can see it now in their lives today they are so well-adjusted' (voice of parent); '3 o'clock kept all of us together ... growing up like ... knowing each other a lot better and staying friends for a lot longer and put us in ... a right path later on in life (former '3 o'clock school' participant). Thirdly, it addressed parents' own skill base in areas such as literacy, communication, cookery and many other areas that they themselves identified.

My kids and your kids: school context

While it is true that families are diverse organisms, it is equally true that schools differ. The underlying school ethos dictates whether the school operates an inclusive policy, welcoming parents and forging and valuing true partnerships, or whether it functions more in isolation from parents and community

Traditionally, the school was a place where parents (My Kids) dropped off their kids and teachers taught them (Your Kids). When KCP was established it changed the function of the school. On a practical level the school building was open morning, noon and night. But the school itself changed since it became host to a diverse learning community. The presence of adult learners, many of them parents of children in the school, built on the already positive links between home and school. Parents and teachers saw each other more frequently and had easy access to each other. The project grew in a shared space, the kitchen, a converted cloakroom which functioned as a staffroom, an adult education room, and the base for the 3 o'clock school. As one research participant observed: 'It's not even like a school, it's more like a large house where everybody is on a first-name basis; everybody is treated equally; everybody is treated with respect; everybody's opinion matters.'

Having established that the research participants felt a strong affinity with the school, I sought to understand what it was that made them feel welcome, empowered and at ease in this setting. My research uncovered a strong respectful relationship between parents and teachers. This is how one parent, also an adult learner, described her interaction with a member of the school staff: 'When X speaks to me she doesn't speak to me like she is more experienced than I am or that she is superior to me; she speaks to me like I am an equal.'

The school atmosphere was described as safe, warm and welcoming; more like a home than an institution. As one participant graphically described it: 'It is a glowing school – like a Christmas tree … there is a glow about it … you are always welcome.'

The school was seen as a community resource, available and accessible to adults and children. The use of first names between teachers, tutors, ancillary school staff, parents and children; shared problem-solving; and a sense of teacher availability to discuss issues with attention to confidentiality, all contributed to building and sustaining proactive relationships between home and school. In the words of one participant:

> … it was, let's do it all together; it wasn't me and you; and so it became more like an extended home rather than a school; it's not … this building is not an institution, it's a home from home for a lot of the kids … it's a larger community for anybody that's living here; they can drop in, say hello, come to a class, meet friends and at the end of the day they treat teachers as part of an extended friendship if you like …

Our kids: partnership

The rationale for working in partnership lies in the increased potential for positive outcomes for schools, children, families and communities. Epstein contends that working in partnership can bring benefits to all stakeholders. For schools it can enable improvements in 'school programmes and school climate'; for families it can 'increase parents' skills and leadership'; and from a community perspective it can 'connect people' (Epstein, 2001, p. 403). The Organisation for Economic Cooperation and Development (OECD) publication, *Parents as Partners in Schooling*, acknowledges that 'Children, parents, teachers and the community can all achieve more if they cooperate with each other' (OECD, 1997, p. 57). Furthermore, long-term societal benefits are identified, extending beyond immediate results to making a strategic difference to young people playing their full role in society, and to adults embracing opportunities for life-long learning: '... if the young are to be educated to play their full role in society, and if their parents are to be given a chance to continue learning, partnership is the only way forward' (OECD, 1997, p. 57).

The Irish National Teachers' Organisation (INTO) is unequivocal in its recommendations to teachers to work collaboratively. It contends that if responsibilities reside solely with teachers, then they could be held responsible for educational failure if and when it does occur (INTO, 1997, p. 111)

However, barriers to partnership exist within the school and home. Schools can be very bureaucratic, where 'parents and teachers interact in a formal and ritualistic way, preventing them from having the kinds of informal interactions necessary for building trusting relationships' (Wescott Dodd and Konzal, 2002, p. 24). Schools operating from a 'medical model' (Haynes and Ben-Avie, 1996, p. 50), an approach which locates blame for underachievement solely outside the school context, opt to work in isolation and will not nurture collaborative actions, rather they will preserve their own environment. Barriers to partnership also exist at parental/family level. The OECD report *Parents as Partners in Schooling* testifies to the potential of parents to damage relationships: 'Over-critical parents can damage relationships by forcing teachers onto the defensive, making them unwilling to be open and reflective about their practice' (OECD, 1997, p. 53).

Power is central to any discussion of partnership. Lareau defines partnership as: '... a relationship between equals where power and control is evenly distributed' (Lareau, 2000, p. 35).

Ultimately, the underlying power to harness and develop partnership rests with schools. Individual teachers and schools have the opportunity to develop proactive partnerships with individual parents, the parent body and community. Dryfoo and McGuire acknowledge the growing pains associated with the changing status of relationships, and the effort involved in the process: 'It takes a great deal of effort to share decision-making and let go of turf issues' (Dryfoo, Maguire, 2002, p. 115).

KCP forged partnerships on many levels, and none of these could have developed without the goodwill of the school. It facilitated partnership-building between the formal school and wider community by making the school available for adult and child learning opportunities. Partnership was forged between the school and KCP as they consciously worked collaboratively to provide a holistic integrated service to learners; it was forged between parents and teachers as they shared common space within the school and had the opportunity for informal contact.

Outcomes: was it worth the effort?

I could not have predicted the intensity of feelings and depth of reflection I was to encounter in carrying out this study. I learned that the project had a profound impact on the lives of individuals. Adult learners identified the impact in terms of personal skill development, a boost to self-confidence and self-esteem, a social outlet, increased efficacy in relation to supporting their children's learning, and an increased sense of belonging to the community and identity with the school as a centre for learning. Interestingly, many adults saw involvement in the project as a means to contribute to their community and to build solidarity and social infrastructure. Young women who had been involved in the SPACE project spoke passionately of the impact the project had made on their lives. They said it built their confidence, developed skills, supported them in returning to learning, and offered them an opportunity to have fun with their children, reflect on their lives and develop friendships within a safe non-judgemental nurturing environment. Former 3 o'clock school participants valued greatly the opportunity to learn within a safe, fun, nurturing context where parents were integral to the learning environment. They spoke of the impact on their lives in terms of skill-development, nutrition, the opportunity to build friendships that would sustain them through their teenage years, and the value of positive adult–child relationships in which their opinions were valued. KCP also had a profound effect on my life; it enriched my life beyond measure as it pushed out the boundaries of my understanding of the role of the teacher and the school.

KCP offered opportunities for intergenerational learning. Family members shared a common experience – that of being involved in different aspects of the same project. This common experience forged relationships within the family and sustainability within the project. KCP impacted on the family context by increasing the skill-level of adults within the home, and providing learning opportunities for adults and children together. Some families had three generations involved in various aspects of the project.

The consensus was that the process of developing the project had impacted very positively on the school. Teachers valued the contribution the 3 o'clock school made to children's learning. They acknowledged the benefits of the extended use of the school, and, above all, valued the positive, appreciative relationship that it nurtured between families, community and the school. The presence of a diverse, mutually supportive learning community enriched the life of the school.

A final word …

While KCP has a number of elements in common with later DES initiatives, it also has some unique attributes. Firstly, the activities of KCP grew holistically in response to local need. Neither the programme nor the process was imposed from outside. The sustainability of the project was made possible through local people taking ownership and responsibility for its development. The school was open and willing to adjust to new challenges as it provided a home for both formal and informal learning opportunities for children and adults. The school and KCP have a symbiotic relationship in that they support each other through a partnership of respect and collaboration.

I believe our success and sustainability were achieved through dialogue, reflection, respectful relationships, shared problem-solving, effective identification of learning needs, adaptability of the school to respond to diverse learning needs and the courage to take risks to make learning more accessible to all.

I have no doubt that in the process of collaboration and partnership the children became Our Kids.

References

Bronfenbrenner, U. (1979) *The Ecology of Human Development*, Cambridge, MA: Harvard University Press

Coleman, P. (1998) *Parent, Student and Teacher Collaboration: The Power of Three*, London: Sage

Dryfoo, J. and Maguire, S. (2002) *Inside Full – Service Community Schools*, California: Corwin Press

Epstein, J. (2001) *School, Family, and Community Partnerships, Preparing Educators and Improving Schools*, Boulder, Colorado: Westview Press

Freire, P. (1972) *Pedagogy of the Oppressed*, London: Penguin

Haynes, N. M. and Ben-Avie, M. (1996) 'Parents as Full Partners in Education' in Booth, A. and Dunne, J. F. (eds) *Family-School Links: How Do They Affect Educational Outcomes?* New Jersey: Lawrence Erlbaum Associates

Irish National Teachers' Organisation (1997) *Parental Involvement, Possibilities for Partnership*, Dublin: INTO

Lareau, A. (2000) *Home Advantage, Social Class and Parental Intervention in Elementary Education*, Maryland, US: Rowman & Littlefield Publishers

Lynch, K. (1999) *Equality in Education*, Dublin: Gill & Macmillan

Macbeth, A. and Ravn B. (eds) (1994) *Expectations about Parents in Education, European* Perspectives, Glasgow: University of Glasgow

Organisation for Economic Cooperation and Development (1997) *Parents as Partners in Schooling*, Paris: OECD

Ryan, C. (2004) 'A partnership of care: an evaluation of a Department of Education and Science initiative to combat early school leaving – the 8 to 15 Early School Leavers Initiative' in Deegan, J., Devine, D. and Lodge, A. (eds) *Primary Voices: Equality, Diversity and Childhood in Irish Primary Schools*,

Dublin: Institute of Public Administration

Ryan, S. (2000) 'Developing Reciprocal Support among Families, Communities and Schools, The Irish Experience', in Canavan, J., Dolan, P. and Pinkerton, J. (eds) *Family Support: Direction from Diversity*, London: Jessica Kingsley

Wescott Dodd, A. and Konzal, J. L. (2002) *How Communities Build Stronger Schools*, New York: Palmgrave Macmillan

11

A Seagull's View – Adult and Community Education

Liam Bane

The Statutory Committee on Educational Disadvantage (2005) recognises that: 'The adult and community education sector has been very active in pushing the boundaries and in promoting systemic change. It appears that some of the fundamental principles of good adult and community education practice are beginning to influence mainstream educational thinking about the future' (p. 17). And, most significantly, it also recognises that 'the problem of educational disadvantage cannot be solved in mainstream school-based educational programmes alone', and is proposing: '… a new strategy that places the solutions to educational disadvantage within an inclusive lifelong learning framework' (p. 4).

Noting that this framework involves commitment to active citizenship, personal fulfilment and social inclusion, as well as employment-related aspects, the Statutory Committee continues:

> In the context of lifelong learning, solutions to educational disadvantage must begin at pre-birth stage and continue throughout the life cycle: through early childhood, primary, second-level, further, higher, adult and continuing education. Interventions must span the entire spectrum of formal, non-formal and informal learning, from 'cradle to the grave'. This demands a radical rethinking and re-evaluation of what learning has come to mean and cannot be done without systematic and long-term planning, and change in teacher education, work patterns and certification methods. (p. 20)

This chapter adopts a narrative style to trace aspects of the history of the development of the adult and community education sector, with a particular emphasis on the role of the Vocational Education Committees (VECs) in relation to this sector, including a perspective on current and future challenges.

Old seagulls are wisest or so the mythology has it. One such seagull, perched atop a new and awesome high-rise in the city, contemplates the changes that he has observed during what has been an inordinately long life for a bird – a long life of life-long learning – and when he thinks about it so alliteratively, he is 'beaksmacked' at the changes that have overtaken the island in so short a time.

Take, for instance, one of his favourite vantage points – the shrine that is Croke Park, Dublin. He has always loved this place because down the years he was privileged to watch as rural Ireland – De Valera's children of the soil – came to town to do battle, but also to enjoy themselves and celebrate and to forget, though for too short a time, the humdrum routine existence that was the norm in 1950s Ireland. Even here there were salutary reminders – the ball was thrown in by the Archbishop of the 'OneHolyCatholicandApostolicChurch' to start the match – but once the game was on and the tribe came together, huddled in wind and rain or, occasionally, glorious sunshine, they were involved totally – critical, vocal, elated, ecstatic, devastated.

And now as the seagull perches atop this new theatre of dreams, this state-of-the-art stadium of light, he realises that he can now climb higher – 'nearer my sky to thee' – and he realises too that higher is not always better. Here in the new shrine of the corporate boxes – no place this for the rough tweeded children of the soil – he has scaled new heights. Yes, he cannot but be impressed; but from the highest seats it's difficult to follow the game. He has lost perspective and he thinks that he would probably be better off watching the contest on the old black and white television. 'Don't it always seem to go that you don't know what you've got 'till it's gone' sang Joni Mitchell in the Big Yellow Taxi that came to take away her old man.

The year 1979–1980 was not a great one to launch a new enterprise. Of course, this is in hindsight and, as the old and, of course, wise professor used to say, 'if only one had hindsight beforehand …' This was the year when the decision was taken to appoint Adult Education Organisers (AEOs), the first full-time permanent adult education officers attached to VECs. Presumably the objective was to make a start on the development of a comprehensive adult education system. If so, then no one ever explained how this was to be done without funding and without resources. And of course, as the 1980s wore on, the situation worsened and the prospects of any level of acceptable resourcing diminished. In this time of high unemployment, it was a better time for seagulls than for humans. As our Chief Executive Officer of the time put it, 'Count your blessings – at least you have a job.'

Yes, we had a job but what was it? One thing we were afforded in this situation was time to think and with that time for thinking came the realisation that nobody really had any clear idea of what a full-time post in adult education entailed. Adult education was unknown territory. All we had were assumptions that it must be to do with evening classes which were held in second-level schools when and where there was time and space and that adults really only learned at night.

And then, suddenly, it seemed, hosts of adults were learning by day and this stemmed from the most revolutionary movement in Irish education in that decade – voluntary workers made the groundbreaking decision that if no one was going to do it for them, they had to do it themselves. Acronyms sprung up all over the place, such as KLEAR, DATE, RAVE, TACT,[1] and several groups, mostly in Dublin, did their own research and, with the support of AEOs, set up programmes that were a direct response to meeting the learning needs of adults who had been consulted and who were involved in the administration of the programmes at all levels. They had no resources, they had no funds – not even a fund of goodwill – they just did it. They ran an impressively broad range of learning programmes for adults and they even provided their own crèches.

It is interesting now to look at the programmes on offer in those early days, many of which were programmes of self-discovery, personal development, self-awareness, assertiveness and confidence-building. At this distance these may seem unnecessarily introverted and focused on the self but the underlying concept was sound: 'Let us look at ourselves first, let's see if we can improve the situation there and then let's use our new found skills to build better families, better communities.' Nobody actually used the words but there was the sense of 'building a better world'.

The Adult Literacy and Community Education Fund

The introduction of the Adult Literacy and Community Education (ALCE) fund in 1985 was a significant milestone in according adult education a status and recognition which had previously been lacking. The importance of this funding was not in the amount of money allocated – one million Irish pounds among thirty-eight VECs – but in the fact that it was a response to an identified need. The money was specifically allocated to facilitate the development of education programmes in areas of greatest need – the term 'disadvantaged' was in vogue at the time. This relatively small amount seemed a princely sum, and to those accustomed to famine, the crumbs were welcome. The ALCE fund proved crucial in two areas. Firstly, it provided a minimal security for Adult Literacy schemes, which were struggling to survive and almost entirely dependent on voluntary effort. It was also the first time that a government, while still refusing to acknowledge the extent of the problem, did at least indicate that there were adults who had literacy difficulties. It must be said that official minds were focused by the 'astounding' results of the OECD-sponsored International Literacy Survey,

---

[1] Kilbarrack Local Education for Adult Renewal; Dundrum Adult Training and Education; Rathfarnham Adults Venture into Education; Tallaght Adult Community Training

which revealed that 25 per cent of adults had literacy difficulties at Level 1. The percentage of adults at the lowest level was higher in Ireland than anywhere else, with the exception of Poland. Furthermore, 17 per cent of the sixteen to twenty-five age group were experiencing difficulties at Level 1.[2] Importantly, these findings lent credibility to the claims made by those involved in adult literacy provision about the extent of the problem. Secondly, on a practical level, the ALCE fund enabled adult education organisers to set about developing some kind of coherent adult and community education service.

Community education programmes, too, were accorded an element of security and continuity – although, of course, at the time no guarantees were given that the fund would be ongoing. Those in charge obviously felt that it was important to maintain the stress levels of those working in the field, lest they lose the run of themselves; hence the element of uncertainty in this particular area of education! There were, and indeed still are, problems to be addressed in relation to accommodation, staffing and resourcing, but it was refreshing, in those early days of groups of adult learners coming together in community centres, halls and prefabs, to sit with a tutor and debate, discuss and, above all, support one another. From early on, those magnificent part-time tutors had grasped the importance of developing self-confidence and fostering a sense of self-worth as they set about repairing the damage inflicted by previous experiences of 'education'. Mutual respect was the keystone.[3]

Vocational Training Opportunities Scheme (VTOS)

The other hugely significant development in the late 1980s was the introduction of the Vocational Training Opportunities Scheme (VTOS). The introduction of this scheme marked a hugely significant shift in establishment thinking. In the midst of an employment crisis, when it became patently obvious that those on the dole could not make themselves available for jobs, especially for jobs that did not exist, this scheme was an acknowledgment that education did indeed have a part to play. The scheme was reasonably well-funded and it gave rise to a number of highly innovative programmes for unemployed adults around the country. It was

---

[2] *International Adult Literacy Survey: Results for Ireland* (1997) Dublin: Government Publications

[3] Other key groups beyond the scope of this article include the National Adult Literacy Agency (NALA) and Aontas, the Irish National Association of Adult Education. NALA has for some time been one of the major coordinating, training and campaigning bodies for adult literacy work in Ireland. As well as getting learners involved in all aspects of adult education, it aims to develop training programmes that include high-quality literacy teaching. It also represents all participants in adult literacy before the government and the public. NALA trains literacy workers, works with students, promotes cooperation between literacy workers throughout Ireland, provides a referral and information service, and provides teaching and training materials. Aontas is a voluntary membership organisation which aims to promote a learning society through the provision of a quality and comprehensive system of adult learning and education that is accessible to and inclusive of all.

not just that it spared adults the indignity of queuing at the local exchange, although that was a welcome relief too. It was more that it afforded them the opportunity of taking a fresh look at their lives, of moving in new directions, of tackling new subjects and new disciplines, and of giving them relief from boredom and despair. This was a programme about restoring lost lives and human dignity, and participants have often spoken of the importance of this intervention in their lives (see Keogh and Downes, 1998).

Some of these VTOS students moved on to third-level institutions but found it a very unsatisfactory experience, which in itself is a comment on the important differences between the learning environment they had left and the one in which they found themselves. It is also a statement about the failure of adult and community education practitioners to influence other sectors of education by making available to them the expertise and innovative approaches which are a standard feature of adult learning provision.

The failure to communicate

There is now more funding available, which represents an increase in resources for the VECs. However, there is still a need for stable, long-term and assured funding for adult and community education against a background of clear evaluation criteria. Systems and empires *have* been built, relatively speaking at any rate. So what did we, the AEOs, leave behind? What was the legacy? Was it all as important as we thought it was then? How much change did we effect and if we did, how meaningful was it? Did we ever, for instance, make that quantum leap from the personal to the political?

We were so convinced that what we had was precious, innovative and groundbreaking – as indeed much of it was – that we largely kept it to ourselves. To put it simply, we were conscious of the need to de-school society but we did not broadcast the message. We did not really engage in the discourse; we did not seek out the wider marketplace; we did not propagate the message that there is another way. This is not to say that what we had on offer would have been any more acceptable to the mass of established institutions, but the evidence would suggest that, outside our own area of operation, very little impact was made on areas crying out for significant change.

Undoubtedly, one of the reasons for this failure to communicate and engage with other sectors was due to the 'embattled' mentality of those striving to put an adult learning service in place. And this was not just a state of mind, as it was too often made quite clear to those in this particular sector that they were not welcome. The manner, for instance, in which some school authorities felt free to discourage and obstruct part-time tutors, volunteer workers and even adult learners, was extraordinary.

From my seagull's perspective, there were two areas of education and learning where new ground was broken, where new methodologies were tested and improvements effected and that was in primary and adult education. There was, and is, no evidence that new approaches and methods have made any impact at second level (see, for example, Banks, 1994; Kelly, 1999 and O'Donnabháin, 1998, on the need for a broader, learner-centred curriculum) and even less in what is now broadly termed, further education. Old habits die hard, old assertions such as 'we have the best education system in the world' are sustained by repetition; and old ideologies remain firmly in place – worship if you will at the altar of the master of all knowledge. We must have teachers and we must have students and both must know their place. We didn't even succeed in changing the seating arrangements!

Now would be a good time to take a hard look at all aspects of our second-level provision in a world that is changing so dramatically; it is of no use to persist with a system that cannot cope with the more serious challenges. Now is the time to examine second-level objectives, education methodologies, teacher approaches and training, and student needs; and to look hard at a system that, in the end, is concerned with getting a good Leaving Certificate, and where success is, above all, a testimony to a good memory and programmed responses. It's time to bring together a team of people from different sectors – people like social welfare officers, probation officers, adult education officers, education welfare officers, community activists, parents, adult learners, business people, artists, writers, journalists, education researchers and, of course, teachers and students. If things are going badly wrong in the schools, then there are underlying causes – 'And we note our place with bookmarkers that measure what we've lost ...' (Simon and Garfunkel, 'The Dangling Conversation').

Back to the seagull watching all of this from a new, bigger, better and higher observation post. Yes, the situation has changed drastically in adult and community education: there is more funding available; some of the more pressing issues like adult literacy are being tackled, though Morgan and Kett's (2003) survey on the literacy difficulties of young prisoners in Irish prisons highlights the need for increased investment for those most at risk; there is improved accommodation for adult literacy classes; there are new posts and there are more full-time posts, although allocated according to carefully worded contracts lest they might have to be withdrawn at short notice (who knows when the Celtic Tiger will run out of steam, but guess what branch of education will be the first to suffer?); there is professionalisation, but also the danger that this may become an end in itself, as if by simply replacing part-time workers and volunteers with paid full-time workers the service will improve; there are reviews and assessments and estimates; and there are quality frameworks, strategic planning, and meetings. Slowly but inexorably, a hierarchy is taking shape and taking control.

The White Paper on adult education, *Learning for Life* (2000) promised much but has, as yet, delivered little. Symptomatic is the thinking about the establishment of the National Adult Education Council. The White Paper presented an opportunity to put in place a body that was genuinely representative and that could have been an organic development. Unfortunately, however, it now seems that the council will be established in the way that all such councils are established: those at the top will make the decision about the kind of council that is best for the rest, the kind of powers (limited company, for example) that it will have and, most importantly, what agencies and bodies will be consulted on what needs to be done. The council is unlikely to include those who succeeded in putting together a highly effective programme of adult learning with minimum resources.

It would have been interesting, if not exciting and progressive, for the White Paper to have recommended the establishment of an independent body to oversee the development of adult and community education in this state. The Action Plan of the National Forum on Primary Education (Gilligan, 2002) speaks of regional educational structures with real decision-making powers to ensure local accountability and a community approach to decision-making. This would include devolved budgets in contrast to the current more administrative regional educational structures. The regional educational structures proposed by the Forum Action Plan sound like the ideal template for an adult education council that would be representative, autonomous, flexible and inclusive. The recommendation from the monitoring committee goes on to state:

> This type of devolved governance would enable flexibility of response on a geographic basis and the delivery of educational services in the most effective way. It would enable the development of an organisational ethos that is informed by a concern to achieve equal educational outcomes for all learners based on their individual choices.[4]

May adult education have some of this please! A vibrant, innovative group concerned with developing and implementing programmes which are not just somebody's 'good idea' but which have been developed in conjunction with those involved might restore some of the dynamism that has been stifled and buried under a ton of paper.

Now here is a seagull thought. It may well be that the more pressing question for adult educators is not how much we have succeeded in influencing the system but how much the system has invaded the territory and imposed its stranglehold, bureaucratic restrictions and stifling regulations, perhaps causing adult education

---

[4] Document submitted in 2005 to the DES and Minister for Education and Science from 'Partnership in Action', the monitoring group established to implement and prioritise the recommendations contained in the Action Plan of the National Forum on Primary Education: Ending Disadvantage.

to lose much of its spontaneity, flexibility and even limited autonomy (although it might have been autonomy in the sense that no one really cared about what was going on out there!) And let's be realistic too. We were in a situation that was notoriously starved of cash and resources. We were in a situation where we could not meet the pressing education concerns of our constituents. We were in a situation that could lead to anger and frustrations because of the inability to deliver. We did need an injection of funding; we did need some kind of structure to impose order and to help towards establishing an organised, comprehensive service. I suppose we lived in hope that this would happen some day, and deep down we always knew that if and when more funding did come for the VECs, it would come at a price.

Different perspectives

Looking at it now from the seagull perspective in Croke Park, where once was a fairly miserable, isolated little hut, there has arisen a relatively imposing edifice. Except that I am not sure that this edifice is all of a piece or that it conforms to any kind of planning. But the more the edifice grows, the greater the danger of losing contact with the ground floor, which is where we came in. The edifice is in the hands of the bureaucrats and the corporate boxes are in place.

Yes, do be wary of the Greeks bearing gifts. In our gratitude for the largesse and the recognition, let us at least be aware of what might be left behind. The rising tide of progress does not lift all boats; it swamps the little boats that have been set adrift. For all the progress that has been achieved, for all the new infrastructure that has been put in place, there are basic problems that remain unresolved. Are adult learners involved in the process? Is the decision-making process any different from that of schools and colleges? Have part-time tutors a say any more? If the answer to these questions is yes, then that is good.

The most crucial aspect of the adult learning process is the engagement of the tutor with the learner. It is a matter that has merited much attention in adult literacy schemes and programmes and, indeed, where much expertise has been acquired over the years. The tutor is a key person. Fairly hefty sums of money have been expended on research projects, on ambitious workshops and conferences, on developing strategic plans – I think I see a time coming when the person presenting for interview will be armed not just with a curriculum vitae but with a strategic plan. All of these have their place in the scheme of things, but should it not have been a priority to address the situation of key people in the system – the tutors – who, over the years, have carried the burden and whose commitment and energy have been exemplary? Their situation has improved marginally, thanks mainly to legislation about the rights of part-time workers emanating from Europe, but it is not good enough. The basic securities to which they are entitled have long been absent and it is imperative that the new affluent society now recognises a glaring injustice and puts in place a strategic plan to redress it.

So now the old seagull with a reputation for wisdom that comes with age perches on top of the latest, greatest and highest rise of them all. As he contemplates the eternal verities, he is now joined by a smart young bird. The old seagull knows from the neat designer feather suit that this youngster belongs to the New Order and is a young Master of the Universe. The youngster is admiring the cranes (machines that is) and is in awe of the progress this town has seen. 'Yes, provided that it is progress,' mutters the old one enigmatically. 'Ah, so you are not impressed by the progress then', responds the youngster. 'I am indeed impressed and it is wonderful to behold. However, new is not in itself progressive. Rather than make the assumption we must always ask the pertinent questions.' The youngster shakes himself and flies away. The old one can't be sure, but he thinks that the parting remark is 'Grumpy old bird!'

This piece is based on the Tony Downes inaugural lecture which was delivered at Blanchardstown Library on 10 March 2005.

References

Banks, J. A. (1994) *An Introduction to Multicultural Education*, Boston: Allyn & Bacon

Department of Education and Science (2000) *Learning for Life*, White Paper on Adult Education, Dublin: DES

Gilligan, A. L. (ed.) (2002) *Primary Education: Ending Disadvantage. Proceedings and Action Plan of National Forum*, Dublin: Educational Disadvantage Centre, St Patrick's College, Drumcondra

Kelly, A. V. (1999) *The Curriculum: Theory and Practice*, London: Paul Chapman Publishing Ltd

Keogh, H. and Downes, T. (eds) (1998) *VTOS spells success*, Dublin: DES

Morgan, M. and Kett, M. (2003) *The Prison Adult Literacy Survey*, Dublin: Irish Prison Service

O'Donnabháin, D. (1998) 'The work-related curriculum' in Trant, A., O'Donnabháin, D., Lawton, D. and O'Connor, J. (eds) *The Future of the Curriculum*, Dublin: City of Dublin VEC, Curriculum Development Unit

Statutory Committee on Educational Disadvantage (2005) *Moving Beyond Educational Disadvantage*, Dublin: DES

12

The Transformational Potential of the Home School Community Liaison Scheme

Dympna Mulkerrins

Transformation, partnership and HSCL

The Home School Community Liaison (HSCL) scheme was established in Ireland in 1990 as an initiative to alleviate the effects of educational disadvantage. The HSCL scheme is based on the Freirean approach to community development which proclaimed a genuine trust in people's creative power, believing that through real dialogue the oppressed could be empowered to transform their reality; in short, transformation is achieved through self-discovery. This perspective took cognisance of the fact that, in practice, true dialogue is required for democratic, empowering transformation at every level of society (Freire, 1972; Giroux, 1993).

The radical and central focus of HSCL was intended to ensure that parents have a voice in the exercise of power in the school. The interaction of schools with homes and communities involved a move away from the preservation of the traditional status quo, from 'the protective cocoon' (Giddens, 1991). However, as 'transformation is only relevant if it is carried out with the people, not for them' (Freire, 1970, p. 43), parents were to be at the heart of a new way forward within the HSCL perspective. Patriarchal models of leadership and hierarchy would undoubtedly be challenged by such empowerment of parents towards 'power with' and 'power together'. It could be expected that such change would be resisted in schools, particularly if it involved close liaisons with people who, in the past, were considered 'recipients' rather than 'partners'.

The implementation of such radical change at school level through HSCL was to be led 'top down' by the Department of Education and Science (DES) and 'engineered bottom up' (Burkan, 1996, p. 190) by local HSCL coordinators. The HSCL coordinator, a teacher, would be central to this process, having a facilitative and transformative role in the dialogue between the parents and the school. The coordinator is the 'key lynchpin' of the HSCL programme and the 'key facilitator' in bonding the home, school and community (Coolahan, 2002, cited in Conaty, 2002 p. 11).

Traditionally, marginalised parents or, indeed, schools did not see parents as having a role in their children's learning; they tended to view school as a place apart, placing the teacher in the mode of expert. Parents viewed themselves, and were constructed as, consumers who are in receipt of a service provided for them by schools (Clegg and Billington, 1997, p. 100).

Partnership in the establishment and reviews of HSCL

There is no evidence that the DES consulted with marginalised parents or community groups prior to the establishment of the scheme in 1990. The non-inclusion of representatives from working-class communities in any aspect of the design, organisation, planning, management or development of the HSCL scheme since its inception suggests that only inherent middle-class values may filter through in practice on the ground. This resulted in the scheme being managed by professionals in the DES. Therefore, it could be argued that partnership was, and still is, being imposed on the 'unsuspecting partners' in HSCL. Consequently, as an initiative intended to improve the lot of those who are educationally marginalised and oppressed, HSCL could be perceived as merely serving the interests of the middle classes and those in power positions.

The most recent review of HSCL by Archer and Shortt of the Educational Research Centre (ERC, 2003) did not include parents and community representatives. That those who are currently considered partners in the daily practice of the scheme within school communities were not consulted in 2003 could be seen as contravening the ideals of partnership as espoused by HSCL. Bypassing the unsuspecting partners and not recognising parents and community personnel as key stakeholders in the scheme could invalidate the findings to some degree. The parameters of the ERC review (2003) included an analysis of all documentation and the findings of external evaluations of the scheme to date. It also incorporated the results of a survey of HSCL coordinators and principals and of interviews with a number of key personnel (Archer and Shortt, 2003, p. 3). 'Key personnel' is an unqualified term in this report. Parents and community representatives, by their exclusion, were not considered 'key' personnel. In the spirit of research for transformation and emancipation, their exclusion is disappointing and worrying, particularly since the recommendations that emerged from that review are currently becoming the basis of HSCL policy and practice with a changing focus.

Partnership with parents in the reviews of HSCL

A recurrent concern for teachers in all three DES evaluations/reviews (Ryan, 1995; Ryan, 1999; and Archer and Shortt, 2003) and in Conaty (2002) was the non-involvement of marginalised parents in their children's education. Parents termed as 'uninvolved' were those with socio-economic or literacy problems, with troublesome children or children who are frequently absent from school. Are we to assume, therefore, that a parent in any one of those categories can be automatically labelled 'uninvolved'? The demographic characteristics highlighted in the 2003 review categorised uninvolved mothers as those needing help, thus distinguishing them from the other categories of mothers. Are we also to assume that the other categories that are involved consequently don't need help? This perspective and categorisation of some working-class mothers have been strongly criticized. Tizard et al. (1983), O'Brien (1987) and O'Neill (1992) found that working-class parents, rather than choosing to be uninvolved may be reluctant to visit the school because they do not feel confident in dealing with teachers. However, such perspectives are neither included in the HSCL evaluations nor the 2003 review. Furthermore, the use of the term 'uninvolved' may be insensitive and raises other issues pertaining to definitions of 'involved' and 'uninvolved'.

Parents' understandings of the purposes and functions of the HSCL scheme

In order to evaluate parents' perspectives on their understandings of the transformative impact of the role of the HSCL, a study was undertaken in eight different schools with a small (and thus limited) sample of ten parents coming from a background of socio-economic disadvantage. Parents' understandings of the purposes of the HSCL scheme in general focused on the coordinator. Three of the parents felt that the scheme had a mediation function: the coordinator was assigned to bridge the divide between the parents and the teachers and this led to a more equitable balance of power between teachers and parents. As a result, schools had become more open and welcoming places. In the words of two parents:

> I think the liaison person ... (ensures) that the parents and the teachers might have an equal say in how things are decided. Our schools were never open; before we didn't actually come in at all' (Focus Group 1 Parent – FG1 Parent).

It is definitely more relaxed to be in the school since there is a liaison person (Focus Group 1 Parent – FG1 Parent).

Other parents felt that the coordinator's work was to introduce and develop the idea of parents as primary educators. This suggests that parents acknowledged and understood their pivotal role in their children's learning. They were aware that the coordinator supported teachers also. One parent welcomed the DES decision to accommodate parents and teachers working together in classrooms: 'The liaison scheme is there to get parents involved in their children's education. The Department of Education want(s) us to work with teachers in the classrooms and it's brilliant' (FG1 Parent).

Parents further attributed the establishment of HSCL to DES awareness that in the past, schooling was an unpleasant and negative experience for many children. All of the parents agreed with this sentiment: 'I think HSCL was set up because the Department of Education realised that (school) wasn't working; children hated school, they stayed at home and dropped out early. With HSCL school is more relaxed' (FG1 Parent).

One parent acknowledged that there was now some respect and recognition for individual children's learning needs. This made school life happier for both children and parents. This comment reflected the feeling of the group: 'I think HSCL was set up because schools needed to open up and relax a bit and they've got to help and praise each child for each child's best efforts rather than picking up on their weak points' (FG1 Parent).

In welcoming this development, parents felt that exposure of inequalities and injustices can be attributed to the transparent approach espoused by the HSCL scheme.

The impact of HSCL on parental empowerment

All parents agreed that HSCL practices have dispelled many fears around schooling, thus facilitating the enhancement of parents' confidence and self-esteem. Teachers in the past scarcely provided information, much less invited parents to ask questions: 'Yeah, the liaison scheme gives you the confidence to ask questions and how to approach teachers and the principal. It gives us confidence big time' (FG1 Parent).

Therefore, the HSCL coordinator's work is seen as facilitating parental empowerment. This involves developing relationships with and between parents and teachers. All agreed with these comments:

The liaison person makes the arrangements; like this morning we had English for fun. We were working with small groups of children on stories and discussion' (FG1 Parent).

She organises courses as well as the crèche to look after the small children. She always looks after the needs of the parents to help them get more involved (FG1 Parent).

The personal support given to individual parents by the coordinator was appreciated. However, the group acknowledged that their newly acquired sense of recognition might only be recognised by the parents themselves. Nevertheless, it is significant for them. They feel empowered now because they know that they can engage, to some degree, as partners in schools (O'Brien, 1987). One parent said that she is not as afraid anymore to challenge difficult or inequitable situations. In creating space for parents, this group felt that the coordinator's work focused on parent development. One parent spoke of the coordinator as an advocate for parents:

Principals wouldn't have the time to see you; the liaison person is always approachable and relaxes you to meet the teachers or school psychologist. This never happened before home/school, and parents were left in the dark about everything except when there was trouble (FG1 Parent).

This confirms the perceived need for rich cultural capital in order to engage with personnel in educational institutions (Bourdieu, 1986).

The impact of HSCL in the community

The coordinator's role in reaching outside the school and linking with other agencies in the community is viewed as beneficial:

I know that you link in with the District Nurse, the Vincent de Paul and the North Eastern Task Force as well as others. And, of course, all of that group meet at the local committee, with the principals, a group of parents and the home/school people. It's good because everyone is listened to there. We deal with different things there like bullying, homework. (FG1 Parent)

This comment suggests that the same gap existed between parents and community agencies as existed between parents and the school.

Home visitation is part of the remit of HSCL and is seen as crucial in developing bonds of trust between home and school. However, these parents did not regard it as positively as other reviews or evaluations of the HSCL scheme did. Four participants in this study believed that home visitation had negative connotations. One parent said that its purpose was to repair difficulties between parent/child/teacher: 'I would say that if you see a problem with a child or if you thought there was something wrong that you would go to that home and try to keep close to the parents' (FG1 Parent).

This observation could illustrate how the HSCL person is perceived as acting on behalf of the school on occasions. It must be noted that the principles of HSCL recommend that home visitation is crucial for the development of 'bonds of trust' with marginalised parents. These parents seemingly removed themselves from the category of homes that may be visited by HSCL perhaps because it carried a stigma of trouble with school or because they are more integrated into the school through HSCL participation.

The impact of parent/teacher collaboration in decision-making

Three of the parents participated in a parent/teacher policy group: this meant that their voice was heard, that their views were listened to and taken on board and that they felt included in the school's decision-making. This was a valuable experience for these parents. They saw the HSCL coordinator as being neutrally positioned to facilitate the parent/teacher dialogue and to maintain a balance between the voices and views of parents and teachers. One parent spoke positively of the meaningful parent/teacher dialogue towards school decision-making:

> I sat with a group of teachers and other parents and we gave our input on what we thought should be in the homework policy; we didn't always agree with the teachers but through working it out we ended up coming up with a consensus. (FG1 Parent)

This comment fascinated the other parents who did not participate in policymaking. If such parent/teacher dialogue became integral to the relationship between the school and its community, the new balance reached might lead to transformational change in the balance of power. However, it must be noted that the majority of these parents had not experienced involvement in any parent/teacher dialogue or school decision-making as it was not widely integrated into the operation of the school. When asked about their understanding of policy, one parent asked 'Was that about keeping the rooms tidy?' (FG1 Parent). This typifies how parents were traditionally expected to be of service in schools and they tacitly accepted this role.

The impact of HSCL on schooling practices and power relations

Parents felt that as a result of HSCL practices, schools were more open places. However, the lack of recognition afforded to parents by schools was highlighted: one parent stated that the school sought to exercise its power over them. Many of these parents felt afraid and intimidated: 'I get scared still; I get sick when I know principals or teachers are talking down at me, dismissing me' (FG1 Parent).

Communication with teachers was important for these parents and three of them spoke of difficulties in developing comfortable and meaningful relationships with some teachers. They acknowledged the necessity of the coordinator's support before approaching principals, teachers or other professionals. This was a typical comment: 'You can talk to some teachers, but some teachers don't have the rapport needed to talk to parents' (FG1 Parent).

It was felt that teachers regarded parents as being of inferior status and not worth consulting or including as an equal in their children's education. Five of the parents had experience of teachers presenting themselves with a superior attitude. They spoke of persistent unequal practices and attitudes. This sentiment was the general consensus: 'It makes us feel inferior when schools talk down to us because we feel they still believe that they are superior to us' (FG1 Parent).

One parent stated that the coordinator supported parents in communicating effectively with teachers. Dismissive treatment by teachers may partly explain why parents worry if they do not get support for 'how to talk to teachers properly' (FG1 Parent) (Bourdieu, 1986; Reay, 1998). The parents acknowledged that some teachers seem to have inhibitions interacting with them. Nevertheless, these comments suggest that parents wanted to be involved and to enjoy honest communication with teachers about their children's schooling:

> Maybe (teachers) don't know how it would help a 'sticky situation' when the child is in trouble to discuss everything with the parents. (FG1 Parent)

> Or maybe they think we couldn't help sort the problem and that they have to sort out everything because they are teachers; some teachers are good at that and that's great, but a lot are not. (FG1 Parent)

It appears, therefore, that parents believe that transformation towards meaningful partnership is a slow process and that this pace is exacerbated because of teachers' perception of working-class parents as inferior.

Parents in this study said that they did want to be involved in their children's schooling (O'Brien, 1987; O'Neill, 1992). Through the facilitation of parental involvement, the HSCL scheme is positioned to pave the way for some devolution of power. Some parents acknowledged that there are teachers who include parents as equals. However, one parent recognised the positional power of the teacher and instead of accepting it, criticised its use. This comment suggests awareness that all is still not right: 'There are good teachers. But just because they're teachers doesn't mean they know everything or that they're right all the time. Our involvement depends on the teacher and the principal' (FG1 Parent).

This suggests that parents recognised their own capacity for communication in the education of their children. However, there are obstacles created in achieving this by the institutional power of the school. It can be argued that parents are willing to take responsibility for their role in the process of their children's schooling. However, it seems inequitable to them that they must always await respectful invitations from schools for this participation (Reay, 1998).

'Service' as opposed to 'partnership'

One parent, who had contributed consistent service to the school, spoke of the school's lack of sincerity with respect to the goals of HSCL. This concerned her because teachers or principals did not give recognition to parents as co-educators of their children. Parents in general felt that this lack of sincerity translated into schools having only a superficial regard for the views and/or involvement of parents. This comment conjured the group's sense of disappointment: 'As parents I don't think we are being taken seriously really. I believe that principals and teachers have to open up and take on board the parents' input ... We are being heard but rarely are we listened to' (FG3 Parent).

Therefore, these parents believe that schools are still in control. One parent said that, in general, teachers are not approachable and that often they only communicate negative information. Another parent told of her experience that only recently and by default did she discover that her child was attending learning support for the previous two years:

> I asked the principal why I wasn't told that my child was getting help for his reading. The home/school liaison had told me to approach the principal about it and the principal said 'Isn't she only the home school liaison teacher? Why didn't you come to me?' (FG1 Parent)

Parent/teacher/community relations

On the positive side, parents identified a sense of solidarity with teachers arising from HSCL inclusive practices. This has resulted from active parental participation in classes. Positive home/school relationships were formed in this way.

Community links were seen as being important by parents in building a level of mutual support for their children's education outside the school:

> I think it has done a lot of good. I mean we would never have known each other ... only for the liaison, and aren't we all making up the community and that sort of makes you proud of your community and we get to know each other's children. (FG1 Parent)

These classes for adults have contributed to breaking down isolation for individuals. They appreciated the friendships they made through active school involvement, acknowledging that structures for this development were facilitated by the HSCL coordinator. This dynamic has uplifted the community:

Those night classes in Irish and Maths, they're good fun and all the parents (are) getting to know each other. They're advertised at mass and there is a buzz in the community about them. As someone said we'd be left at the gate without HSCL. (FG1 Parent)

Parents attribute these positive developments to HSCL practices.

The impact of HSCL on the child

The focus of HSCL is the welfare and education of children. One parent suggested that children would be the ultimate beneficiaries of parents' development and empowerment through sharing experiences and participating in classes. This reiterates that HSCL empowers parents to be the primary educators of their children: 'There again your confidence is helped; we learn from the classes, we learn from each other and then we're better able to help our children at home' (FG1 Parent). These parents are thus more confident because they have a voice in their role as co-educators of their children.

The ongoing impact of HSCL practice

Parents responded emotionally when asked if withdrawing the HSCL scheme from schools would make any difference. Participants felt that their fears and intimidation prior to the HSCL scheme might return. This was a typical comment: 'I would be afraid that all those awful arguments outside classroom doors between the parents and the teachers would start up again' (FG1 Parent).

It is acknowledged that some parents' lack of participation is due to negative school experiences, which shattered their confidence. One parent commented on the shifts towards equality that can happen because of parental participation and her regret that more parents are not involved (Ryan, 1995): 'Maybe they're still afraid of getting embarrassed. I still have unhappy memories of my own school days. I was afraid to get involved here till I decided to go along and give it a bash and I have no regrets' (FG1 Parent).

It is clear, therefore, that parents see the positive potential in building relationships with teachers through the HSCL scheme. They are aware, though, that there are many constraints to the further development of these relationships.

Conclusions and recommendations

The discussion with this small sample of parents revealed that they valued the HSCL scheme and its attendant benefits, which accrued to themselves as co-educators, to teachers and to their children's education. Among the benefits of HSCL frequently mentioned were a more open and welcoming school environment; a reduction in the fear and intimidation compared with the pre-HSCL era; the positive impact on their own self-confidence; a reduction in their sense of disempowerment when dealing with teachers; and the sense of community which had developed through the HSCL programmes.

For a minority, parental involvement with teachers in policy formation, and participation in the HSCL local committee with principals and community bodies was empowering. For the majority, however, decisions taken at school-level left them feeling uninvolved, under-represented and powerless. In general, lack of consultation was an issue for parents, all of whom felt that their voice did not really impinge upon the operation of the school or the educational process.

Parental involvement with their children's class teachers was sometimes helpful, open and easy but it was equally spoken of as inadequate, difficult, excluding and frightening. The coordinator was seen as a mediator trying to improve relationships. Parents experienced a sense of empowerment and recognition in communicating with the school, in becoming involved with their own children's learning and dealing with the wider school community.

The wisdom of applying key performance indicators to HSCL as recommended in the recent review (2003) is questionable. By concluding that the objectives of HSCL were not adequate in terms of the guidelines of the Strategic Management Initiative (SMI) (Archer and Shortt, 2003), many aspects of the HSCL scheme, which are based on process and on the development of trusting relationships, could be discarded. HSCL is based on preventative rather than curative measures. Its perspective remains that there is no quick-fix solution to remedying deep-seated problems but 'the enlightened, patient and sustained approach, which registers more in the hearts and personalities of those touched by the scheme than in media headlines' (Coolahan, 2002, cited in Conaty, 2002, p. 9).

It is arguable that any future review of the HSCL scheme must include the voice of parents and community groups as well as children, and be conducted according to wider criteria than SMART (Specific, Measurable, Achievable, Relevant, Timed) outcomes.

References

Archer, P. and Shortt, F. (2003) *Review of the Home School Community Liaison Scheme*, Dublin: Educational Research Centre

Bourdieu, P. (1986) 'The Forms of Capitals' in Richardson, J. (ed*.) Handbook of Theory and Research for the Sociology of Education,* New York: Greenwood

Burkan, W. (1996) *Wide Angle Vision*, New York: John Wiley and Sons Inc.

Clegg, D. and Billington, S. (1997) *Leading Primary Schools: The Pleasure, Pain and Principles of being a Primary Head-Teacher*, Buckingham/Philadelphia: Pitman Publishing

Conaty, C. (2002) *Including All: Home, School and Community United in Education*, Dublin: Veritas

Department of Education and Science (1999) *Primary School Curriculum*, Dublin: DES

Freire, P. (1970) *Cultural Action for Freedom*, New York: Penguin Books

Freire, P. (1972) *Pedagogy of the Oppressed*, New York: The Continuum Publishing Company

Giddens, A. (1991) *Modernity and Self-Identity; Self and Society in the Late Modern Age*, California: Stanford University Press

Giroux, H. A. (1993) *Border Crossings: Cultural Workers and the Politics of Education*, New York and London: Routledge

O'Brien, M. (1987) 'Home School Relations in Inner-City Dublin', MA thesis: Education Department, University College Dublin

O'Neill, C. (1992) *Telling It Like It Is*, Dublin: Combat Poverty Agency

Reay, D. (1998) *Class Work: Mothers' Involvement in their Children's Primary Schooling*, London: University of London Press

Ryan, S. (1995) *The Home School Community Liaison (HSCL) Scheme: Summary Evaluation Report*, Dublin: Educational Research Centre

Ryan, S. (1999) *Home School Community Liaison Scheme (HSCL) Summary Evaluation Report*, (revised), Dublin: Educational Research Centre

Tizard, B., Hughes, M., Carmichael, H. and Pinkerton, G. (1983) 'Language and Social Class. Is Verbal Deprivation a Myth?' in Woodhead, M. and McGrath, A. (eds) *Family, School and Society*, London: Hodder and Stoughton

13

The Development of Men's Community Education in Ireland

Toni Owens

While women's community education groups have been operant since the 1970s, the 1990s witnessed a new phenomenon in Irish society – the emergence of men's groups in disadvantaged communities – and issues discussed here are based on findings from two qualitative studies of community-based men's groups (Owens, 2000, 2004). Building on findings from *Men on the Move* (2000), and working collaboratively with practitioners and participants in men's groups, *An Exploration of the Links between Male Identity and the Development of the Field of Men's Community Education in Ireland* (2004) proposed a conceptual framework that might work towards supporting the development of this nascent form of education for men.

The overall framework proposed comprises a radical consciousness-raising model for practitioners working with men's groups,[1] operative within a wider support structure involving government and the academy. This chapter focuses on aspects of the model proposed for practitioners, and how they might activate the consciousness-raising experience within men's groups as a meaningful and transformative process for marginalised men. This 'live'[2] model is illustrated in Appendices 1 and 2.

While the consciousness-raising approach has been adopted in a number of contexts, the realities to be explored, analysed, challenged and transformed are unique to each 'thematic universe' or context in which the experience is activated.

---

[1] Drawing on the philosophical and pedagogical approaches of Freire (1973)
[2] The model is 'live' in that it illustrates consciousness-raising as a pedagogical strategy applied in response to particular themes relevant to a particular context at a particular moment in time.

While Freire has been sometimes critiqued by feminist scholarship for his 'gender blindness', the value of his pedagogical strategy lies in its adaptability – it is proposed here not just as a mechanism for challenging structural inequalities, as Freire employed it, but also as a mechanism for raising men's awareness of themselves as gendered beings.

This 'live' model aims to equip men with analytical tools to critically reflect on their lives within a framework of personal experience and academic theories on issues of concern to them. The thematic universe informing this particular model comprises themes arising from the findings of collaborative work with men's groups and themes raised in recent public debate on masculinity and gender relations in Irish society. This thematic universe is located within a social structure that has, from the 1970s onward, been undergoing rapid change, with ongoing implications for ways in which gender roles and relations are understood and enacted.

As a means of making the 'live' model self-explanatory, I discuss this thematic universe within a framework of cultural change, which gave rise to themes of concern to men, and of academic theory that men might draw upon in developing informed strategies for change.

Marginalised men's experiences of themselves as men

The majority of participants in the *Men on the Move* (2000) study came from the least privileged strata of society, with poor educational credentials and living in disadvantaged areas. The findings suggest that the greatest barriers to marginalised men's participation in education are located deep within the self and are linked to the question of male identity, to the question of what it means to be a man in a rapidly changing world. The phraseology these men used to articulate their experiences of themselves resulted in this author's coinage of 'Taboo Zone Oppression' as the most apt term for conceptualising these interior barriers to participation, not just in education, but also in wider social spheres.

'Taboo Zone Oppression' could be described as loyalty to a deeply internalised rigid definition of masculinity, which no longer matches today's world, and allegiance to which forecloses the possibility of negotiating alternative ways of being. Findings suggest that this circumscribed way of being can be understood as the cumulative effect of negative life experiences that erode belief in the self and diminish the capacity for creativity in the authorship of one's identity. Such experiences include low ranking or failure in the 'points race',[3] whereby individuals internalise their accorded value and worth; and because

---

[3] The 'points race' refers to the marking system for the Leaving Certificate, the final State examination at second level in Ireland; the number of points awarded determines the pathways available to pupils for further education, training and employment opportunities.

educational credentials influence life-choices, the uncredentialised are often doomed to a life of uncertainty in the labour market and a concomitant sense of powerlessness. 'Taboo Zone Oppression' is characterised by a struggle to reconcile the dominant version of masculinity as powerful and the breadwinner with the reality of powerlessness and unemployment, while loss of belief in the self diminishes the capacity to envision and negotiate alternative ways of being. In addressing the core issue of male identity, men's groups hold potential as a site for challenging 'Taboo Zone Oppression' through facilitating marginalised men to enter into critical dialogue and negotiate alternative understandings of masculinity, alternative ways to value themselves as men. It is noteworthy that isolation and suicide emerged as key concerns for the study participants, the majority of whom had been acquainted with at least one, but often several, men who had taken their own lives. Thus the importance of breaking male isolation as a key potential of men's groups cannot be overstated.

Masculinity in crisis?

In the late 1990s, the term 'masculinity in crisis' gained currency in gender discourse, and in a qualitative study of homeless men in Dublin, Cleary et al. (2004) set out to explore the relationship, if any, between the notion of a crisis in masculinity and men's real-life experiences of marginalisation, concluding that, 'despite challenge and confusion amongst men, there is no general crisis of masculinity'. However, these researchers suggest:

> In today's society, plural rather than unitary identities are to the fore and those who can accumulate identity-enhancing resources have a better chance of maintaining psychological equilibrium. Conversely those who accumulate risks in an uncertain sociological environment will be vulnerable. Some categories of men, mainly young, working-class men, have found these social and economic transformations difficult because they are confined by their gender and worldview. (p. 130)

The finding that some men have difficulty redefining themselves in today's world 'because they are confined by their gender and worldview' resonates with the suggestion of the debilitating impact of 'Taboo Zone Oppression' on some men's capacity for creativity in constructing and reconstructing identity. Importantly, these researchers highlight the relationship between social class and the negotiation of gender identity; and the consciousness-raising strategy proposed here aims to equip marginalised men to challenge systems and structures that oppress them, both socio-economic and psychological.

The impact of cultural change on inherited understandings of masculinity

Any attempt, however brief, to analyse the impact of cultural change on inherited understandings of gender identity in Ireland must take the definition of gender enshrined in *Bunreacht na hÉireann* (1937) as its starting point.[4] As Connell (1995) points out, any attempts to understand or explain male identity must take cognisance of masculinity as a political and relational concept:

> ... it is gender relations that constitute a coherent object of knowledge for science ... Masculinities are configurations of practice structured by gender relations. They are inherently historical; and their making and remaking is a political process affecting the balance of interests in society and the direction of social change. (Connell, 1995, p. 44)

Applying Connell's analytical framework, values and ideas about gender roles and relations expressed in *Bunreacht na hÉireann*, and the way those ideas are interpreted by legislatures, have implications for shaping the 'configurations of practice' that give structure and meaning to the everyday lives of men and women. Laws that derive from the state's interpretation of the Constitution impact on the lives of individuals, the balance of interests, and the direction of social change in Ireland.

Bunreacht na hÉireann portrays gender as clearly demarcated roles, based on the concept of 'natural differences', framing woman as belonging to the private sphere and man as belonging to the public sphere.[5] Up to the 1970s, this ideological construction of gender was endorsed by successive legislatures which, in assigning value to these roles, vested power and privilege in men and withheld social and economic rights from women.[6] For instance, the law compelling women, upon marriage, to leave their jobs in the public sector, often referred to as the 'marriage ban', bestowed on men superior status in the workplace and home. In the workplace, it endorsed the concept of man's 'entitlement' to work; while in the home, as sole provider, it endorsed his personal authority over his dependents. By its legislative practices, the state institutionalised an ideology of gender as an unequal, hierarchal relation: femininity was constructed as full-time dedication to motherhood, economic dependency and absence from public life; masculinity was constructed as entitlement to the breadwinner role, to public power and private authority; and fatherhood, it may be noted, is unmentioned in the constitution.

---

[4] The Irish Constitution (1937) – forging a national identity for a recently independent state

[5] See, for example, references to 'differences of capacity, physical and moral, and of social function' to 'woman's life within the home' and to 'mother's duties in the home' in Articles 40.1 and 41.2, Bunreacht na hÉireann (1937)

[6] See Scannell (1988) for a full discussion of the wide range of rights denied to women in Irish society during this period

Connell borrows the concept of hegemony for his analysis of masculinity and gender relations;[7] hegemony refers to 'the cultural dynamic by which a group claims and sustains a leading position in social life' (1995, p. 77). Upon winning hegemony then, the accepted ideal of masculinity and femininity becomes the context within which individual men and women make sense of themselves, their relation to each other, and to the world. But hegemonic victory is never complete or stable:

> Masculinities are created in specific historical circumstances. They are liable to be contested, reconstructed or displaced. The forces producing change include contradictions within gender relations, as well as the interplay of gender with other social forces. (Connell, 2000, p. 219)

The 1960s witnessed Ireland's shift from a farming to an industrial economy, bringing structural change that by 1970 had begun to produce contradictions within the social order. The hegemonic version of gender identity came under increasing challenge throughout the 1970s and 1980s.

It could be said that four key factors contributed to the challenges posed to traditional definitions of gender from the 1970s onward: women's increasing participation in an expanding urban workforce;[8] the women's movement; the populace's increasing access to television; and Ireland's entry into the European Community.

Throughout the 1970s and 1980s, the hegemonic version of gender as an unequal relation was vigorously defended in the power arena. Despite a profoundly changed socio-economic reality, 'imaginative tactics were employed by legislators, trade unions and employers to deny or delay women's social and economic rights'; and those concessions that were gradually granted had to be 'forced on representatives by either the courts, the women's movement or the European Community (EC)' (Scannell, 1988, pp. 132–3).[9] If industrialisation and membership of the EC produced contradiction and posed challenges to the

---

[7] Connell borrows this concept from Italian Marxist theorist Antonio Gramsci's conceptual framework for analysis of class relations. The notion of 'ideology as struggle' is central to this perspective which postulates that groups with power dominate not only the production and distribution of resources, but also of ideas and meanings; the social order is organised in their interest and the ideological system derives from it, working to justify and naturalise the constructed reality.

[8] Women's participation in the workforce increased from 1 in 13 in 1971 to 1 in 5 by 1984 (Breen et al., 1990, p. 117).

[9] In the public sphere, for example, the marriage ban was lifted and women were granted rights to equal pay, pregnancy leave and equal social welfare allowances. In the private sphere, for example, the Family Home Protection Act (1976), Family Law Protection of Spouses and Children Act (1981) and Family Planning Acts (1979, 1986) gradually rendered women less dependent on the goodwill of their husbands to provide for them and their children and granted women more control over their lives, and greater opportunity to define themselves, if they so wished, beyond the role of motherhood.

dominant ideology of gender, the women's movement and emergence of women's voices in the public sphere through the medium of television, played a further role in challenging ideas about gender roles and identities. Indeed, the weekly chat show, the *Late Late Show*, became a key forum for exchanging new ideas and challenging dominant ideologies right up to the 1990s. Given women's increasing participation in the workforce and range of rights denied them, it is not surprising that public debate on gender should focus on women's role and status in society. It is regrettable, however, that concomitant changing meanings of masculinity did not become a topic of debate in the public sphere or academia during the 1970s and 1980s.[10]

The 1990s witnessed the commencement of Ireland's journey from an industrial to a knowledge-based society within a wider global order, bringing further socio-economic, legislative and technological changes to bear on the structure and form of work and family life. 'Between 1991 and 2001, overall employment grew by seventy-nine per cent for women as opposed to thirty-four per cent for males' (Coughlan, 2002, p. 4). By the end of the decade, not just the gender composition of the workforce, but the very nature of work had changed utterly as skills for the information age superseded the skills of industrial labour; and 'by 1996 fathers were the exclusive breadwinner in only half of all families with dependent children' (Ferguson, 2001, p. 124). Recent decades have also witnessed increasing secularisation of society, and with it, profound diversification in family forms and norms: 'by 1996, eighteen per cent of all families with children under fifteen were headed by lone-parents'[11] (Ferguson 2001, p. 124).

The absence of public debate and academic inquiry into the impact of such change on men's lives over the past three decades limits insight into degrees of 'fit' between men's internalised understandings of masculinity and changing social realities; yet some insights may now be gained through views expressed by participants in the recent public debate that has come to be known as 'the *Exploring Masculinities* controversy'.

The exploring masculinities controversy

Exploring Masculinities (2000) was authorised by the Department of Education and Science when the legislative framework of the EU placed increasing emphasis on the concept of equality and when further legislative reform in Ireland

---

[10] Even to date in Ireland, academics, in particular male academics, have paid little attention to the study of masculinity. This dearth of scholarship may be evidenced in a lecture series (2002–2004) entitled *Boys, Men and Masculinities* co-hosted by the Centre for Gender and Women's Studies at Trinity College Dublin and the Gender Equality Unit of the Department of Education and Science at which male academics from USA, UK, Australia, Canada and South Africa presented papers, with no representation from Ireland.

[11] Of whom eighty-seven per cent were women and thirteen per cent were men

gave way to the Education Act (1998), Employment Equality Act (1998) and Equal Status Act (2000). While the legal framework enshrines the principle of equality for all, outlawing discrimination on grounds of sex, race, religion, disability, age or sexual orientation, a number of research endeavours conducted in the 1990s highlighted a gap between principle and practice in Irish society and pointed to the need for ideational change to underpin and endorse legislative reform[12] (*Exploring Masculinities*, p. v).

Themes addressed in *Exploring Masculinities* include: new life choices arising from changing gender roles; the value of unpaid as well as paid work; relationships between men and women, and between men; health; sexuality; violence; racism; and sport. The programme aims, in particular, to raise critical awareness of power dynamics and inequalities between and among the sexes, to promote understanding of and respect for diversity, and to facilitate adolescent boys in critically reflecting upon changing meanings of masculinity as they negotiate their future roles in society (*Exploring Masculinities,* pp. v–x).

The introduction of this optional programme evoked heated negative responses in the public domain. However, as Mac an Ghaill et al. (2002) note, the *Exploring Masculinities* controversy was characterised by the conflation of issues specifically pertaining to education with broader social issues predominantly concerning gender meanings and representations. These researchers also note that the controversy was characterised by sustained media attention rather than comprehensive public debate, and this media attention 'was sustained by a small number of contributors among which specific individuals were over-represented' (p. iv). This chapter is primarily concerned with issues raised pertaining to gender meanings and representations; noting that, in this respect, the most vociferous opposition to the programme came from a men's rights perspective, which provides insight into this societal grouping's perceptions of masculinity and gender relations. Mac an Ghaill et al. (2002) summarise key issues and concerns raised in the debate: 'concerns about the gendered representation of domestic violence; about young male suicide and male vulnerability; about state policy and legislation on equality-related matters; about the treatment of men and fathers by society and by the courts in particular; about the erosion of traditional Judeo-Christian religious values, specifically in respect of sexual identity/orientation, and diversity of family forms; and beliefs about a singular feminism responsible for many social ills' (p. 143)

Concerns raised in public debate overlap with themes and issues raised in men's groups, and these, along with themes identified by practitioners, inform the consciousness-raising model illustrated in Appendices 1 and 2. This model draws

---

[12] See, in particular, findings on second-level schoolboys' perceptions of masculinity and gender relations from Lynch's studies (1999), identifying high levels of homophobia, sexism, racial prejudice and discrimination in male youth culture (*Exploring Masculinities*, p. vii; Lynch, 1999)

on pro-feminist scholarship as a framework for analysis of two identifiable strands in the international men's movement: men's rights and pro-feminism. This chapter now briefly considers men's movements and masculinity politics at the international level.

Men's movements and masculinity politics at international level

Men's movements in the international arena have their roots in men's responses to second-wave feminism from the 1970s onward.[13] Initially, feminists' calls for an end to sexism were supported by some men, mostly university students, who formed consciousness-raising groups to raise awareness of gender injustice and engaged in activism to bring about change at individual, community and institutional levels. Early male liberationists held that traditional sex-roles, whilst oppressive to women, also oppress men – the male sex-role pressurises men to be competitive and successful and forbids emotional expression – thus men should support the women's liberation movement in its struggle to eradicate sexist practices. However, if initially united by their empathy with feminist ideas, individual men's groups soon developed differing views of feminism and differing interpretations of gender and power relations. By 1997 Clatterbaugh had identified eight 'perspectives' within the men's movement: conservative, socialist, gay male, men of colour, evangelical, mythopoetic, men's rights, and pro-feminist (the latter two being of particular concern to this discussion). While each perspective constitutes an aggregate in which there are many voices and viewpoints, Clatterbaugh highlights the significance for society of these competing perspectives on masculinity and gender relations: 'These perspectives on men are political; they offer an agenda for society as a whole. And each perspective is continually contentious in its discussion of other perspectives' (Clatterbaugh, 1997, p. 1)[14]

The men's rights perspective

Tracking the emergence of the men's rights perspective, Messner (1997) points to 'slippage in the discourse' from the early men's liberationist language of equal oppression faced by men and women to an 'angry antifeminist language of male victimisation' (although men's rights, as for all perspectives within the movement, comprises a broad range of viewpoints). Men's rights groups point to men's shorter lifespan, health problems, and divorce and custody rulings as evidence of men's

---

[13] The international arena here refers to America, the UK and Australia.

[14] For a flavour of discussion and analyses of masculinity politics in the international arena see, for example, Clatterbaugh (1997) and Messner (1997) USA; Buchbinder (1994) and Flood (1997) Australia; Tolson (1977) and Haywood and Mac an Ghaill (2003) UK.

oppression; claiming that men are now the 'true victims' of sexism. In short, the men's rights perspective campaigns for legislative reform, arguing that, whether pertaining to the workplace or home, state policy and practice are overprotective of women's interests, resulting in discrimination against men (Messner, 1997; Doyle, 1995; Pease, 2000; Haywood and Mac an Ghaill, 2003).

The pro-feminist perspective

The pro-feminist perspective predominantly comprises male academics who theorise that the patriarchal order is a socially constructed system of unequal power relations, not just between men and women, but also *between men*. In short, pro-feminists hold that the patriarchal order privileges men as a group over women as a group; the cost of such privilege lies in the negative impact that acquisition of traditional masculinity has on men's emotional and relational capacities; and men do not benefit equally from the 'patriarchal dividend', some are marginalised by virtue of their sexual orientation, class or ethnicity. Pro-feminist interdisciplinary scholarship analyses processes and practices by which these unequal power relations are created and sustained, identifying homophobia and sexism as key organising principles in the enactment of traditional masculinity and the reproduction of inequalities in the gender order (see, for example, Kimmel, 1994, 1996; Ferguson, 1997, 1998; Connell, 1987, 1995).

Kimmel (1994) theorises the acquisition of traditional masculinity as a 'flight from the feminine' – the project of acquiring status as a 'real man' through proving to the 'evaluative eyes' of male peers that one is not a 'sissy', thus making masculinity a 'homosocial enactment' whereby homophobia can be understood not just as fear of homosexual identity per se, but fear of being *perceived* as homosexual. Homophobia, Kimmel argues, is the constant fear 'that other men will unmask us, reveal to us and the world that we do not measure up, that we are not real men' (1994, p. 131). Homophobia could thus be explained as a controlling dynamic within male culture that sustains and reinforces hegemony for stereotypical masculinity and subordinates homosexual identity; and the internalised denigration of the feminine accompanying acquisition of hegemonic masculinity works to ideologically justify sexist practices that sustain women's subordinated position in the gender order. But aspiring to the dominant model of masculinity as 'strong' and 'successful' has a negative impact on the development of men's emotional and relational capacities: American academic and family therapist Terence Real holds that, in acquiring traditional male identity, boys learn to deny and negate their inner world, 'to replace inherent self-worth with performance-based esteem' as they come to measure and value themselves by their success in the public domain, a process he calls the 'passive trauma' of traditional masculinity (discussed in Ferguson, 1998, pp. 210–15).

The emergence of men's groups in Irish society

While men's groups have been emerging in disadvantaged communities since the early 1990s, no nationwide survey has been conducted recording their number, geographical location, sources of funding or the purposes they aim to serve; and only a handful of research reports have been published documenting the workings of individual men's groups.[15] Although not specifically focusing on men's groups per se, findings from four recent research reports highlight the need for support structures for marginalised men to renegotiate their roles in the face of rapid socio-economic change.[16] Professor Harry Ferguson, formerly of University College Cork and University College Dublin and currently at the University of the West of England has written from a pro-feminist perspective and hosted workshops and conferences as fora for discussion and analysis of the male role; he has also strongly advocated the idea of men's groups as a potential site for challenging traditional understandings of masculinity and gender relations:

> The development of a so-called 'men's movement' is proving important as one response to the need for men to engage together in critical dialogue about our lives and roles, find support and take responsibility for a positive (re)construction of masculinity and gender relations. (Ferguson, 1997, p. 4)

However, in the same year, Cousins' (1997) review of men's groups in receipt of funding[17] for personal development work since 1994 deemed such groups to be only 'of limited success'. Cousins suggested that debate and analysis on women's position in Irish society, which had been ongoing since the 1960s, provided the basis for a conceptual framework to underpin the work of women's community groups from the 1980s onward; by contrast, he noted, 'such a conceptual framework is lacking in the case of men' (p. 39). Arguably, lack of precedent and absence of comprehensive debate and analysis of men's changing role continue to hinder development of men's groups 'as a site for men to engage in critical dialogue and take responsibility for a positive (re)construction of masculinity and gender relations' (Ferguson, 1997, p. 4)

> We don't know how men's groups will evolve ... can't even guarantee it will actually happen ... but if it does it will be completely different to the way women's groups evolved. We haven't worked out a philosophy yet ... so it's about trying to define a practice ... a philosophy or belief (practitioner quoted in Owens, 2004, p. 208)

This chapter is offered as a first step in 'defining a practice' for men's groups in Ireland. In principle, consciousness-raising as a pedagogical strategy aims to equip participants with analytical tools to critically reflect on their lives within a

---

[15] Cousins (1997); Kellegher and Kelleher (1999); Owens (2000); Drury Research (2003)
[16] Corridan (2002); King et al. (2002); Stakelum and Boland (2002); Cleary et al. (2004)
[17] From the then Department of Social, Community and Family Affairs

framework of personal experience and academic theories on issues of concern to them, as a means of enabling them to challenge and transform oppressive realities.

It is hoped that this chapter's discussion of the thematic universe informing the proposed consciousness-raising model, the cultural changes that gave rise to this thematic universe, and the academic theories that could provide a framework for analysis of these themes, will render its 'live' illustration of consciousness-raising intelligible to the reader (see appendices 1 and 2). It is further hoped that for readers who may be involved with men's groups in Ireland, this thematic universe and analytical framework offer a starting point for engaging men in a process that might enable them to develop informed strategies for challenging and transforming systems and structures that marginalise and oppress them.

Appendix 1 The Consciousness-Raising Model Applied in Response to Themes Related to the External World of Gender Relations

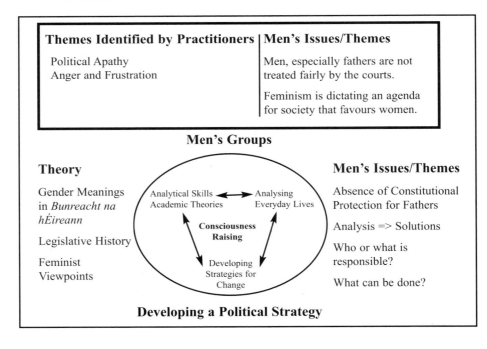

Themes Identified by Practitioners	Men's Issues/Themes
Political Apathy Anger and Frustration	Men, especially fathers are not treated fairly by the courts.
	Feminism is dictating an agenda for society that favours women.

Men's Groups

Theory

Gender Meanings
in *Bunreacht na
hÉireann*

Legislative History

Feminist
Viewpoints

Analytical Skills ⟷ Analysing
Academic Theories   Everyday Lives

**Consciousness
Raising**

Developing
Strategies for
Change

Men's Issues/Themes

Absence of Constitutional
Protection for Fathers

Analysis => Solutions

Who or what is
responsible?

What can be done?

Developing a Political Strategy

Appendix 2 The Consciousness-Raising Model Applied in Response to Themes Related to the Internal World of Constructing Male Identity

Themes Identified by Practitioners	Men's Issues/Themes
A Sense of Failure as Men	Loss of Traditional Framework for Defining Oneself as a Man
Homophobia	
Mental Health Problems	Male Isolation, Depression and Suicide

Men's Groups

Men's issues/Themes

Theory

Evaluative Eyes + Passive Trauma => Traditional Model of Masculinity

Role of Homophobia in Reproducing Inequalities in Gender Order

Analytical Skills ⟷ Analysing
Academic Theories   Everyday Lives

Consciousness Raising

Developing Strategies for Change

Developing a Political Strategy

Need to Reconstruct Meanings of Masculinity

Analysis => Solutions

By what processes and practises is a hegemonic model of gender constructed and reproduced?

What can be done to challenge the dominant model of gender?

References

Breen, R. et al. (1990) *Understanding Contemporary Ireland: State, Class and Development in the Republic of Ireland*, Dublin: Gill & Macmillan

Buchbinder, D. (1994) *Masculinities and Identities*, Carlton, Victoria: Melbourne University Press

Bunreacht na hÉireann (Constitution of Ireland) (1937) Dublin: Government Publications

Clatterbaugh, K. (1997) *Contemporary Perspectives on Masculinity: Men, Women and Politics in Modern Society* (2nd edn) Boulder, Colorado: Westview Press

Cleary, A., Corbett, M., Galvin, M., Wall, J. (2004) *Young Men on the Margins*, Dublin: Katharine Howard Foundation

Connell, R. W. (1987) *Gender and Power: Society, the Person, and Sexual Politics*, Cambridge: Polity Press

Connell, R. W. (1995) *Masculinities*, Cambridge: Polity Press

Connell, R. W. (2000) *The Men and The Boys*, Cambridge: Polity Press

Corridan, M. (2002) *Moving from the Margins: A Study of Male Participation in Adult Literacy Education*, Dublin: Dublin Adult Learning Centre

Coughlan, A. (2002) *Women in Management in Irish Business*, Dublin: Irish Business and Employers' Confederation

Cousins, M. (1997) *Review of Scheme of Grants to Locally-Based Men's Groups*, Dublin: Department of Social, Community and Family Affairs

Department of Education and Science (2000) *Exploring Masculinities: A Programme in Personal and Social Development for Transition Year and Senior Cycle Boys and Young Men*, Dublin: DES

Doyle, J. A. (1995) *The Male Experience* (3rd edn) Dubuque: William C. Brown Communications Inc.

Drury Research (2003) *Evaluation of the Education Equality Initiative*, Dublin: DES

Ferguson, H. (1997) 'Understanding Men and Masculinities', paper delivered to Men and Intimacy Conference, Carlow: St Catherine's Community Services Centre

Ferguson, H. (1998) 'State Services and Supports for Fathers' in McKeown, K. et al. (eds) *Changing Fathers?: Fatherhood and Family Life in Modern Ireland*, Cork: The Collins Press

Ferguson, H. (2001) 'Men and Masculinities in Late-modern Ireland' in Pease, B. and Pringle, K. (eds) *A Mans World? Changing Men's Practices in a Globalized World*, London: Zed Books Ltd

Flood, M. (1997) 'Men's Movements' http://www.xyonline.net

Freire, P. (1973) *Pedagogy of the Oppressed*, Middlesex: Penguin Books

Haywood, C. and Mac an Ghaill, M. (2003) *Men and Masculinities: Theory, Research and Social Practice*, Buckingham: Open University Press

Kelleher, P. and Kelleher, C. (1999) *A Review of the Social Impact of Locally-Based Community and Family Support Groups*, Dublin: Department of Social, Community and Family Affairs

Kimmel, M. S. (1994) 'Masculinity as Homophobia: Fear, Shame, and Silence in the Construction of Gender Identity' in Brod, H. and Kaufman, M. (eds) *Theorizing Masculinities*, London: Sage Publications Ltd

Kimmel, M. S. (1996) 'Try Supporting Feminism!' in Lloyd, T. and Wood, T. (eds) *What Next For Men?* London: Working With Men

King, P., O'Driscoll, S., Holden, S. (2002) *Gender and Learning: A study of learning styles of women and men and their implications for further education and training*, Dublin: AONTAS

Lynch, K. (1999) *Equality in Education*, Dublin: Gill & Macmillan

Mac an Ghaill, M. et al. (2002) *Review of 'Exploring Masculinities': Final Report*, Dublin: National Council for Curriculum and Assessment

Messner, M. A. (1997) *Politics of Masculinities: Men in Movements*, Thousand Oaks, California: Sage Publications Inc.

Owens, T. (2000) *Men on the Move: A Study of Barriers to Male Participation in Education and Training Initiatives*, Dublin: AONTAS

Owens, T. (2004) *An Exploration of the Links between Male Identity and Development of the Field of Men's Community Education in Ireland*, Dublin: St Patrick's College Library, Drumcondra

Pease, B. (2000) *Recreating Men: Postmodern Masculinity Politics*, London: Sage Publications Ltd

Scannell, Y. (1988) 'The Constitution and the Role of Women' in Farrell, B. (ed.) *De Valera's Constitution and Ours*, Dublin: Gill & Macmillan Ltd

Stakelum, A. and Boland, J (2002) *Men Talking: A Study of Men's Health in the North Eastern Health Board*, Kells, Co. Meath: North Eastern Health Board

Tolson, A. (1977) *The Limits of Masculinity*, London: Tavistock Publications Ltd

14

Community Education: A View from the Margins

Liz Waters

There is no power for change greater than a community discovering what it cares about.

(Wheatley, 2002, p. 14)

Community education is a dynamic, organic education process. At the Shanty Educational Project (Ltd) ('the Shanty') we have developed a unique model of community education that is responsive to the needs of one particular community. Its rootedness in the community gives this particular model shape, relevance and meaning. Community is the soil, the ground in which our vision roots, grows and flowers. While located within one particular community living with the injustice of poverty, the model offers an opportunity for reflection and analysis that is transferable to other communities living with economic and social disadvantage.

In this chapter I outline the vital importance of community education in the development and transformation of communities that live daily with the injustice of poverty. I will focus on the unique model that has been developed in the Shanty, locating it within the historical development of community education in Ireland. I will identify how this model both anticipated and exemplifies many of the recommendations of the White Paper on adult education (DES, 2000) and other policy position papers. I will consider the unique pedagogy of the model and examine its impact on the development of individuals and their community, while also highlighting some key challenges facing the sector.

The history of community education

The provision of adult education was initially led by the Vocational Education Committee (VEC) sector during the 1970s. This was a new and exciting development and offered significant new learning opportunities to many adults. However, because the education offered took place within the formal school system it was unable to meet the needs of marginalised adults, many of whom had been let down by the education system. Other shortcomings included the fact that the VECs were unable to meet the needs of those wishing to access courses during the day rather than at night and were also unable to offer specific supports in the areas of literacy or childcare. It was the emergence of the literacy movement in the early 1980s that highlighted many of the shortcomings in adult education. Literacy provision did not feature as an aspect of centralised policy. The genesis of the literacy movement lay in the momentum that came from concerned individuals and community groups who wanted to provide help to adults with reading and writing problems:

> There was a process of discovery emerging from groups of largely non-professional volunteers who devised methods and approaches for the delivery of literacy tuition which depended on the ultimate test – 'Is it helping students learn what they consider relevant to their lives?'[1]

Community education entered a new stage of development with the emergence of women's education groups in the 1980s. Women discovered the power of liberation in the freedom to question, explore and imagine new and different possibilities for themselves and their communities. Women began to analyse their societies. They highlighted the effects of poverty and disadvantage on women and identified the barriers many women faced in returning to employment or education. The emergence and success of this grass-roots movement were significant influences on the development of community education in Ireland. Key innovative principles guided the pedagogical process:

- An understanding of the importance of the learning space as a welcoming and beautiful environment where women can give voice to their identity
- A method and practice of education which seeks to reverse the reversals within patriarchal society and name women's experience as 'knowledge'
- A curriculum which is co-intended by the participants and facilitators alike and which has no pretensions about its neutrality
- A content that calls for a rigorous critique of women's exclusion both in the texts and events of history and a heightened awareness of women's oppression in the present time
- A constant weaving of critique with creative action for transformation.[2]

---

[1] A history of the National Adult Literacy Agency and the literacy movement in Ireland, NALA Website
[2] NWCI, 2000

Changing understandings of adult and community education, insights from the literacy movement and the critique of patriarchal models of education contributed to the development of the Shanty Educational Project (Gilligan and Zappone, 2006). The Shanty grew from a single home-based course started in 1986 to a large community education organisation employing over forty people in Tallaght West. The Shanty played a key role in crystallising women's community education in Ireland and joined with many other groups in calling for recognition of women's community education as deserving a state-supported role within the education system.

Learning for life: White Paper on Adult Education

While community education in Ireland has a relatively short history and tradition, it has nonetheless been recognised as a potent force for combating educational disadvantage, promoting social inclusion and advocating for social change. The importance of community and adult education was finally acknowledged in the government's White Paper on Adult Education, *Learning for Life*, which identified 'the community-based sector' as 'amongst the most dynamic, creative and relevant components of Adult Education provision in Ireland' (2000, p. 12). Chapter five of the White Paper focuses on community education and recognises its significance in three particular areas: 'pioneering new approaches to education; starting with the wisdom and experience of the participants; and reaching large numbers of participants in areas of disadvantage' (2000, p. 112).

The White Paper makes specific reference to the collective social purpose and inherently political agenda of community education and identifies how it can promote 'critical reflection, challenge existing structures, and promote empowerment' 'so that participants are enabled to influence the social contexts in which they live' (2000, p. 113). *Learning for Life* envisaged a key role for the community education sector in particular – as a provider in its own right that needs to be resourced, as an important voice in policy development, innovation and review, and as a key agent in successfully meeting the needs of communities and groups which are most marginalised.

Many of the insights and recommendations of the White Paper were anticipated in the model of community education that developed at the Shanty. Each of the key characteristics of community education outlined in the White Paper has been part of our model since the mid-1980s. The Shanty has had particular success in attracting and retaining participants who otherwise would be unlikely to engage in lifelong learning. While the White Paper is a most welcome policy development and is important in its acknowledgement of the sector, the failure to follow through and resource the sector adequately is disappointing.

The Shanty – a model of community education in Tallaght West today

The context

The Shanty model of education developed in response to the economic and social needs of one particular community. There are over 21,000 people living in Tallaght West, one-third of whom are under the age of fifteen (Census, 2002). Approximately one-third of these households are headed by lone parents, with one in ten people over fifteen years of age unemployed (twice the national average) (CDI, 2004).

The level of educational achievement continues to be low (Gamma analysis of Census, 2002):

- Twenty-seven per cent ceased education with no formal education or had completed primary education.
- Thirty-four per cent ceased education under the age of sixteen.
- Twenty-eight per cent ceased education at upper second level.
- Ten per cent of the population have a third-level qualification.

Families face daily challenges in the area of anti-social behaviour. Drugs, heroin in particular, pose an enormous problem in some areas. There is very limited access to childcare, which in turn interferes with employment or educational opportunities.

Research clearly indicates that those living in poverty constitute the majority of those not benefiting fully from education in Ireland. A central objective of the National Anti-Poverty Strategy (NAPS) is to ensure that all those who have already left school have an opportunity to address any lack of educational and related qualifications that militate against their ability to participate fully in society, the economy and employment.

For most adults living in Tallaght West, their experience of school and education was deeply unhappy. They left school feeling damaged, with poor self-esteem and low confidence and, as a result, were unable to reach their potential. They were excluded from participation in social and economic progress and distanced from civil society. Such oppression is internalised, and intergenerational patterns of behaviour emerge. Cycles of educational disadvantage were created and nurtured. Today more than ever, education is a 'fast track' out of poverty. In the era of the Celtic Tiger, educational achievement is what determines an individual's access to participation in the social, economic and cultural life of our society.

Most of the 400 women and men who take courses at the Shanty are early school leavers who demonstrate great courage in returning to education. They face internal struggles in terms of self-esteem, ability and entitlement, and also external struggles around family commitments, childcare, transport, finance, time and energy. Our model supports each individual to access education and employment and to participate in shaping the social, economic and cultural life of the community of Tallaght West.

The pedagogy

> It is impossible to teach without the courage to love, without the courage to try a thousand times before giving in. In short it is impossible to teach without a forged, invented and well thought out capacity to love. (Freire, 1998)

Freire was convinced that the development of a truly transformative educational process could not be achieved 'in the absence of a profound love for the world and for people'. In *Pedagogy of the Oppressed* he wrote: 'Love is an act of courage, not fear ... a commitment to others ... to the cause of liberation' (1970, p. 78). Such a proposition is a disturbing challenge to those of us working in the area of community education. The Shanty model of education is based on an understanding of education as the key to transformation and an understanding of love as the basis for social change. Such a radical imagining demands constant listening, dialogue, reflection and analysis.

Some elements of our practice which might be described as a pedagogy of love are explored below: our ethos, our relational person-centred approach, our culture of respect and acceptance, our commitment to social change and our living flexible curriculum. These are all structured to meet the needs of our participants and embody key values and principles. The space that love holds open is qualitatively different to any other space. Therefore the ethos we have developed is central to our practice. The Shanty Education and Training Centre is a place of aesthetic beauty, welcoming and hospitality. We have key supports in place for participants on our courses, in the areas of childcare, transport, study skills and ICT. There is also a large counselling service, which over 20 per cent of our participants access.

Relational

We have a relational, person-centred approach, which recognises that learning is an experience that takes place within the totality of our being. All the elements and intelligences of the person – physical, mental, emotional and spiritual – are given attention. There is a deep respect and openness to the struggles and possibilities that each person experiences.

Education facilitators

Each class has an education facilitator. Although it is the duty of the tutor to implement an all-inclusive curriculum, the role of the education facilitator is to support participants. The education facilitator supports the learning by attending to the group process and the personal development issues of individual participants.

Cooperative

Participants are encouraged to create with their tutor and education facilitator a cooperative community of learners that is different to the normal highly competitive educational environment. We are all learners together, bringing a diversity of gifts which inform and deepen the educational process. The participants' own experience, wisdom and learning are deeply valued and respected. We try to ensure that underlying the variety of curricula there is a common thread of empowerment, and that participants are first and foremost supported and challenged to develop their confidence, voice and self-awareness. We also highlight the spiritual dimension of reality. This involves an openness to the individual and communal search for the transcendent meaning in our lives. We create opportunities for all participants to nurture and develop the spiritual elements of their being – however one names that.

Focus

Community education has a clear focus on the local and the wider human community. It supports all those across the globe who are working for a better world. We believe that personal growth and development are interwoven with communal and social change and that both are essential aspects of reshaping a more just and equitable world. As individuals move successfully through their own educational journey they are supported to reflect and analyse their external reality and its impact on their lives and to take action to bring about change. Love enables us 'to dream what ought to be' (McGuckian, M., cited in Gilligan and Zappone, 2006, p. 29) at personal, political and spiritual levels.

The curriculum

We have developed a curriculum that spans the education spectrum and brings the possibility of educational progression and achievement to the heart of the community. It is flexible and responsive to the changing needs of a community, many members of which were failed by the formal school system. We have a strong commitment to ongoing curriculum development which has resulted in the development and implementation of a diverse range of programmes. In 2004, the Educational Disadvantage Committee, in its submission to the Minister for Education and Science, recognised the community sector's success in attracting the hardest-to-reach adults. It drew attention to respect for the individual learner's needs and circumstances and the provision of programmes which allow for the non-linear and often fragmented way that adults take up learning opportunities.

Such thinking is already integral to the model of the Shanty. Progression is rarely a linear process. Participants begin and finish their journey in the Shanty as best suits their individual needs. The courses are structured around a four-stage cycle that reflects this reality. Participants are involved in identifying their own learning needs and in the development and evaluation of all courses.

Components of a life-long learning model

Foundation courses

Our starting point is courses on Personal Development and Basic Education. These courses allow participants to proceed in a carefully planned progression route to mainstream education, training or employment. Participants can start with personal development, drama, health or basic English courses. Participants can then move through a series of externally accredited courses, securing Further Education Training Awards Council (FETAC) accreditation, and diplomas or degrees accredited by the National University of Ireland (NUI).

Community leadership and professional training for community work

Another set of courses responds to the development needs of the local community in the areas of community development, active citizenship and the promotion of a multi-cultural community. These courses have been developed at the bequest of local community groups and allow a process of empowerment, supporting people to shape the ongoing development of their community. Courses for the Drugs Task Force, the local resident's association, men's courses for community engagement and a two-year leadership programme for young female lone parents are examples of such courses.

Third-level qualification courses

At the Shanty there have always been courses to support people to access higher education. Some third-level courses are available in the Shanty, for example an NUI Diploma in Community Drugs Work and a BSc in Counselling and Psychotherapy. These courses help participants to realise that third-level education is as accessible to them as to any other member of society, again an area recognised by the Educational Disadvantage Committee. There is also a set of courses in relation to access to third level – advanced writing courses and preparation for college courses.

Education towards employment

In a community that continues to struggle with issues related to poverty and unemployment, it is vital that a set of courses is offered in relation to training for employment. Our Open Learning Centre, which is also an ECDL-accredited centre, runs ICT courses and supports access to distance learning programmes. The primary policy objective, as articulated in the government's action plan *New Connections* (Department of the Taoiseach, 2002), is to raise the level of access to, and participation in, the information society by increasing the numbers using information and communication technologies. We also offer a wide range of childcare training options which support access to employment as well as responding to the clearly identified need for childcare places within the community.

Impact of this model of community education

The effectiveness of the unique model of education developed at the Shanty can be seen in its outcomes, namely its potential for transformation both at individual and community levels. In 2004, the Shanty Educational Project commissioned an independent external evaluation of our services and outcomes. The evaluator called the report *A Beacon of Light* (Krizan, 2004), an interesting metaphor that highlights both the perception and experience of the local community. Krizan highlighted a number of things that distinguished the centre from other similar centres: its ethos, person-centred approach and flexible curriculum. He concluded that the services provided contribute significantly to the empowerment of women and men in Tallaght West and to the process of social change within that community.

Education and empowerment impact

Women who are participating, or who have participated in courses highlighted numerous reasons why the Shanty was a special place, and for those who studied elsewhere there was no comparison. 'I thought I was worth nothing, but now I know that is not true. I know how much I am worth. They made me see I can do anything I want' (Krizan, 2004, p. 14).

Participants noted the high level of support given during the classes. They spoke of the personal support offered by tutors, education facilitators and other staff. Some mentioned that unlike in other schools, no one would ever fall through the cracks. Other women mentioned the nurturing, holistic approach of the Shanty. From the moment they arrived to the moment they left participants claimed they were treated with respect and understanding. 'The level of support was amazing. I had never got that anywhere else. They wanted you to do more than just pass, they wanted you to excel'(Krizan, 2004, p. 34).

Many participants progress on to employment or further education. The participant quoted below was an early school-leaver, who left school at the age of fifteen but came back to education in the Shanty. She is not at all unusual.

I took up some courses that were available at the Shanty, media studies and creative writing. The next course that was on offer was a two-year NUI Certificate in Women's Studies and I decided to enrol for that. During the course our tutor recommended that some of us go on and do a BA. So I gave it some thought and did the BA and that was that! And then I did the Higher Diploma in Community Adult Education and it all started in the Shanty. (Krizan, 2004, p. 34)

Many more stories testify to the journey of transformation that so many of our people have experienced through their contact with our educational centre.

Personal and social change impact

However, personal transformation is not the only outcome of our work. The close collaboration between the centre and the community is focused on supporting the community to participate in, and initiate, social change.

In befriending life,
We do not make things happen
According to our own design.
We uncover something that is already happening
In us and around us and
Create conditions that enable it
                    Rachel Naomi Remen (cited in Wheatley, 2002)

Ten years ago, at the height of the heroin crisis in Dublin, the Shanty offered a number of courses to support local efforts to address the issue of heroin addiction in the local community. Courses in Addiction Studies, Counselling Skills, Group Facilitation Skills and Community Development were offered and all of these courses were well attended.

Rehabilitation programmes for those addicted to heroin, and family support services had been put in place. Voluntary community workers were giving invaluable service to their communities in this area, creating with, but often before, statutory services, a solid infrastructure to deal with drug issues. The volunteers had gained priceless wisdom and experience at the coal face and were best placed to operate, maintain and develop these services. They sought our support in developing training that would make them eligible for employment as it became available in the area of community drugs work. The Shanty Education and Training Centre developed a two-year NUI Diploma in Community Drugs Work with University College Dublin, funded by the Local Drugs Task Force.

Social change is critical if we are to create a more equal society. Community education has an important role to play in that process. As educators at the Shanty we continually create opportunities for reflection on crucial issues relevant to the community and explore ways of supporting the community to make its voice heard. Currently, the Shanty is developing a community leadership and development programme in response to leadership needs that have been identified. This will start at higher certificate level and culminate in an honours degree and will be delivered in the Shanty in partnership with a third-level institute. Together, educators and community reflect and respond to a range of policy issues, bring relevant issues to the attention of politicians and policymakers, call the political process to account and find diverse ways of responding to issues on the ground.

Challenges for community education today

A key challenge facing the sector remains the lack of sustainable mainstream core funding. Community education remains the poor relation in terms of resources and support from the state. In the White Paper, the government promised an increase of funding, supports and personnel as part of an overall framework for Adult/Community Education. In 2003, the ESRI's mid-term review of the National Development Plan (NDP) recommended increased resources for the achievement of the life-long learning agenda (ESRI, 2003). In 2004, the Educational Disadvantage Committee submitted its action-plan document, prioritising areas for action within the community education sector and clearly stating that 'in order for community education to develop its full potential it must be allocated specific programme funding which is specifically ring-fenced for it' (EDC, 2004, p.7). Unfortunately, since then the government has directed very little of the education budget towards community education. The Shanty is funded by seven different government departments through a variety of programmes; it receives grants from diverse philanthropic organisations, corporations and private companies; and 30 per cent of its annual budget is raised through voluntary fundraising activities.

A second challenge for the sector is the development of a truly inclusive model of community education. Community education developed from the women's education movement and as such could be described as a feminist model of education. Most of the innovative and groundbreaking principles and practices are transferable. Ways of welcoming men, older people, members of new communities and the Travelling community must be created. In the Shanty, we are actively involved in the development of such a model.[2] The Shanty always offered educational courses to men; however, moving to our purpose-built centre at the heart of Tallaght West afforded the opportunity to expand our educational programme for men. We offer single-gender education programmes particularly at basic education level and a leadership training course in community development and community education. Participants are then supported to access a range of co-educational programmes (Corridan, 2002). This approach is in line

---

[2] An Cosán (2006) *Strategic Plan 2006–2008*, Dublin: An Cosán

with the recommendations outlined in the study *Gender and Learning* (King et al., 2002). We focus on developing intercultural educational programmes to support members of new communities, allowing them to access and to contribute to educational development. Together, women and men from Tallaght West are forging a community of solidarity, support and passion to develop and practise a radical form of education that can change the world.

Community education is a relatively new development in the education process. I hope I have made a case outlining its significance as a transformative process for individuals and communities. I believe it can support individuals on their unique paths of personal development and educational achievement. I believe it is a process that challenges inequalities in society, imagines new ways of being in the world and calls forth a new and radically different understanding of community.

A Living Curriculum

Don't establish the
boundaries
first,
the squares, triangles,
boxes
of preconceived
possibility
and then pour
life into them, trimming
off left-over edges,
ending potential:
A. R. Ammons

References

Ammons, A. R. (1965) *Tape for the Turn of the Year*, New York: W. W. Norton Co.

An Cosán (2006) *Strategic Plan 2006–2008,* Dublin: An Cosán

Childhood Development Initiative, Tallaght West (2004) *How are Our Kids?*, Dublin: CDI

Corridan, M. (2002) *Moving from the Margins: A Study of Male Participation in Adult Literacy Education,* Dublin: Dublin Adult Learning Centre

Darder, A. (2002) *Reinventing Paulo Freire: A Pedagogy of Love*, Colorado: Westview

Department of Education and Science (2000), *Learning for Life*, White Paper on Adult Education, Dublin: DES

Department of the Taoiseach (2002) *New Connections: A strategy to realise the potential of the information society*, Dublin: Government Publications

Economic and Social Research Institute (2003) *The Mid-Term Evaluation of the National Development Plan and Community Support Framework for Ireland 2000 to 2006: Final Report to the Department of Finance*, Dublin: ERSI

Educational Disadvantage Committee (2004) *Priority Areas for Action within the Adult and Community Education Sector*, Dublin: DES

European Commission (2000) *Memorandum on Lifelong Learning*, Brussels: European Commission

Freire, P. (1970) *Pedagogy of the Oppressed*, London: Penguin

Freire, P. (1998) *Teachers as Cultural Workers: Letters to Those Who Dare to Teach*, Colorado: Westview Press

Gilligan, A. L. and Zappone, K. (2006) *Love and Social Change, Reflecting on a Model of Community Education*, Dublin: An Cosán

King, P. et al. (2002) *Gender and Learning: A study of learning styles of women and men and their implications for further education and training,* Dublin: Aontas

Krizan, V. (2004) *A Beacon of Light*, Dublin: An Cosán

National Women's Council Ireland (2000) *Knowledge is Power – Women and Education*, Millennium Project, Dublin: NWCI

Wheatley, M. J. (2002) *Finding Our Way*, San Francisco: Berrett-Koehler

III

Literacy and Numeracy

This section focuses on themes central to government policy prioritised in the *Delivering Equality of Opportunity in Schools* (DEIS) report (2005), namely, approaches to improving literacy and numeracy. It must be welcomed that a family literacy programme is being put in place under the DEIS action plan. As stated in the new National Action Plan for Social Inclusion 2007–2016, 'Lack of adequate literacy can be a significant barrier to self-esteem, employment and more generally to achieving social inclusion' (p. 44). There is a clear need to further develop teachers' self-efficacy with regard to literacy instruction at primary level. Key themes examined in this section include pupil motivation to read, common weaknesses in early literacy instruction, examples of a model that teachers can use for older classes (from first to sixth class), and implications for practice from a review of international research on good practice in literacy teaching. With regard to numeracy instruction, there is also an obvious need to disseminate models of intervention that constitute good practice.

Chapters in this section have direct relevance for professional development regarding literacy teaching. The literacy skill of decoding is emphasised in a promising programme called Phonographix, based on the simple insight that letters are pictures of sounds – an insight that filters a lot of arguably less necessary information like letter names and rules. Giving increased attention to pupil motivation in relation to reading in designated disadvantaged schools invites examination of connections between reading taking place in the home culture of the pupils, including magazines and newspapers, and pupils reading in school. There is a need to highlight the practices and philosophies of successful schools internationally that have managed to narrow the gap in reading achievement between children living with disadvantage and children in the wider population. Moreover, a neglected part of teacher self-efficacy in literacy instruction is to clarify what is *not* good practice.

As with literacy, there is a real need for mathematics education to take account of children's cultural backgrounds and contexts so that the problem-solving processes in mathematics are meaningful and relevant to the children. It is suggested that this vision needs to extend beyond so-called 'realistic' problems to immersion in aspects of the local environment, including parks and playgrounds, media and health education. This section examines mathematics programmes designed for children in junior infants and regarded as highly suitable in contexts of disadvantage.

15

'Only Brainy and Boring People Read'

Susan Quinn

One definition of reading literacy is 'understanding, using and reflecting on written texts, in order to achieve one's goals, to develop one's knowledge and potential and to participate in society' (OECD, 1999, p. 20). Unfortunately, studies have found that pupils from disadvantaged backgrounds have lower literacy standards (Cosgrove et al., 2000; Eivers, Shiel and Shortt, 2004). While literacy is a concern for all teachers, it may be a greater concern among teachers working in designated disadvantaged schools. Motivation and attitude have often been cited as determining factors in pupils' success or lack of success in reading (McKenna, 1994). For this reason I chose to study motivation and attitudes to reading as a means of raising standards.

The school in which I conducted this action research is part of the *Giving Children an Even Break* initiative. During this study I was teaching a fifth class of only ten pupils. Of the ten pupils in my class, four had special educational needs (Peter, Lindsey, Gary and Kelly),[1] as assessed by an educational psychologist. Two others, (Daniel and Alex) had been assessed as needing to attend learning support.

I set aside an hour and a quarter each day for reading. The period began with a fifteen-minute read-aloud session. This was followed by a fifteen-minute direct instruction literacy lesson. There were then thirty to forty-five minutes of independent reading. Running parallel with this were the guided reading groups. In the guided reading groups, pupils were grouped according to reading ability. Each group read a 'real' book suitable for its ability level. I gave assistance and instruction to each group a minimum of every second day. After this the pupils took a few minutes to record their reading in their journals. It is worth noting that

---

[1] All pupils' names have been changed to preserve their anonymity.

I supplemented the class library with a wide variety of texts and graded most of them. Extra time was given over to reading as recommended by the research (Shanahan, 2001). I had high expectations for all pupils (Pressley, 2002) and often spoke about reading to raise pupils' awareness of many aspects of it. Reading became my priority and this was expressed to the pupils in word and deed.

In order to assess any changes in attitudes towards reading, motivation to read and reading achievement, three individual interviews with each of the ten pupils were carried out before, during and after the intervention. Some of the findings from these are presented here and are supported by reference to my teacher's journal and pupils' journals. The findings show the changes, or lack of changes in the pupils' motivation to read and attitude toward reading.

Attributions for reading success and failure

It has been found that people attribute their success and failure to luck, ability, effort or difficulty of task (Dweck, 1986). These attributions are closely related to motivation. Attributing success or failure to luck, difficulty of the task and ability lead to low motivation as they are out of the person's control. Attributing success or failure to effort leads to the greatest motivation as this is within the person's control and can overcome difficulties. Pupils who refer to the role of work or practice in reading are attributing success to effort.

Read more!

In the first interview, only Jane referred to her own effort in learning to read: 'By the teacher putting words on the copy and saying them. Learning them every night. Looking, saying, covering, writing.' When asked what advice they would give other pupils to improve their reading, only three of the children made any reference to making an effort.

In the final interview many pupils responded that they read often, and read increasingly difficult books when learning to read. They recognised the effort on their part. Much of the advice for others focused on effort. Seven pupils advised others to read often and carefully, using the skills they knew. Jane's advice is focused on the changes that have taken place in our reading class and are therefore relevant to her own reading experience: 'First do your homework every night, your reading work. Then learn words off it, and then, em, ask the teacher to read books to you and do reading groups. Then do easy, medium and hard (guided reading groups).'

In terms of illiteracy, the pupils' understanding of the role of effort seemed clearer by the second interview. Nikita said that not everyone would learn: 'People who don't want to read don't read', and went on to say that that was why they didn't learn. Alex was the most aware that some people could not read; he was also aware of the possible causes and effects:

> My Auntie, when she was given books an' all but sometimes she left it. When the teacher'd say silent reading time, she'd get a book but she'd just colour. Now when she gets a note or anything, she has to ask me Ma to read it.

The reading programme emphasised time and effort in reading. It was clear that a lot more time was dedicated to reading, and pupils were fully engaged during independent reading. These children have clearly taken practice or effort on board as a way of improving reading.

Feelings about reading

> When you have hard books then you can't read it, that feels bad.

In the first interview, the pupils presented reasonably positive attitudes to reading. Three pupils referred to enjoying reading books in a series, gaining information from reading or improving their reading skills. Peter said he felt 'good' about reading but went on to say, 'When you have hard books then you can't read it; that feels bad.' Because of past experiences of failure, many of the weaker readers had developed a more negative attitude towards reading (Mathewson, 1994). Caren and Steven, two of the strongest but least motivated pupils, made a distinction between academic and recreational reading. Caren said that she found reading 'all right, I'd rather read magazines and papers than them' (pointing to Oxford Reading Tree books). I bought magazines for the class library and Caren's reading journal shows that during the intervention time she read nine magazines. Some of these were read at home but most were read during independent reading time. It was good to see this link being made between home and school reading. I observed changes during independent reading and remarked on these in my journal.

> Nikita and Caren brought in magazines for independent reading. I am pleased on so many levels. They clearly see that independent reading is a fun time and that all reading is 'good' reading. They are bringing their home reading into school, blending them. They planned this, it's not a coincidence; they obviously discussed what they would like to read today. (Teacher's Journal, 21/02)

By the final interview, five pupils said that they liked reading and felt good about it because they were improving at it, because it was helping them to learn and do their work, and because they could use it to avoid boredom. Their feelings seem to be stronger and they were clearer about specific reasons for liking reading. The increased success at reading may well have resulted in many of the pupils developing more positive feelings about it.

Normative beliefs about reading

My ma reads magazines, she wouldn't read the paper. My da reads the paper.

McKenna, Kear and Ellsworth (1995) state that the normative beliefs that people hold about reading affect their attitudes. These normative beliefs relate to the value placed on reading by the culture to which a person belongs. It is worth noting that I did not directly examine the normative beliefs of the pupils' culture. What is really being discussed is their perception of those beliefs – it is their perception that will alter their attitudes.

In the first interview, all the pupils were able to name people they knew who read – usually immediate family members, mostly parents. These I assumed to be the most influential role models. In general, they were not very specific about what texts people read, or why and how often. Three pupils said that their fathers read; six said that their mothers read. Most of the pupils said that their mothers read magazines. A number also said that their older brothers and sisters read. These were often informational texts for brothers and magazines for sisters.

In the second interview, pupils were asked what kinds of people read. Most of the pupils listed some careers that involved reading. Many of these were professional careers and few members of the pupils' community worked in them. Steven said that accountants, lawyers and engineers read for their jobs. He first felt that artists and footballers would not need to read, and that these were the careers he would like. When I challenged him about this he acknowledged that a footballer would need to read a contract. Alex gave the following account of reading behaviour in his home when he explained why he believed women read more than men:

> 'Cos me Da just sits there and won't read, says 'I'm bored' but he has books in the bedroom. Me Ma just says if she's bored she'll pick up a book or a magazine. She sent me round to the shops for a woman's magazine; I was scarlet, I was.

In the third interview, the pupils were able to give much more information about people they knew who read. They could name the books and magazines that family members had read, as well as what part of the paper they read. They often referred to why people read, for example to get information or for fun. All of the pupils said that their mothers read, again a lot of this was magazine reading. Three of them said that their fathers read. This was often newspapers and informational books. Daniel exemplified how aware the group had become of other people's reading:

R: Tell me about the people you know who read?
D: Me Ma, me Da, me sister, me brother, me and me nanny.
R: What kind of things do they read?
D: Hard books, me nanny reads all Good Sunday and all Old Town.

R: Are they stories? What about your Dad?

D: Me Da'd read all about the bombings and me Ma reads P.S. I Love you and all.

Most of the pupils referred to members of their community who read. Alex gave some examples of people who read: 'They could be a professor or they could be just a police officer, they need to know how to read for say a test, if they couldn't read they wouldn't be a cop.' Steven said, 'only brainy people and boring people read'. When I asked who would read magazines and newspapers, he said 'normal people'.

It is unlikely that the reading behaviour of the pupils' families changed during this research. Therefore the increase in information about reading behaviour would appear to be due to an increased awareness of this reading. By the final interview they had widened the variety of jobs in which they thought people needed to read, and this included more jobs that people from their community would hold. If pupils see reading as valuable to members of their culture they will see that they will use reading in the future. This would make them more motivated to read. Children are influenced by the reading behaviour of their families and significant others. As it is not usually within the remit or power of the school to change the reading behaviour of families and communities, this increased awareness is very important.

Pupils' interests, text choices and time spent reading

If it was about football or about dogs.

Pupils' interests are closely related to their behavioural intentions towards reading. For example, if they are interested in informational texts then they would choose these to read or be more engaged when reading them.

In the first interview, only two good readers gave a list of genres, others named only one or two at the most. Six of the pupils said that they enjoyed informational books. This interest in informational texts is a surprising find, given that they did not give gathering information as a reason to read. I noticed that the weaker readers all seemed to prefer informational texts. This may have to do with the way in which they are able to draw information from the pictures. Pupils do not appear to be embarrassed reading simple informational texts in the way they would be reading fiction at the same level. This may be because they are deemed to be educational, regardless of difficulty. Alternatively, they may not have mentioned information gathering as a purpose of reading because they do not see it as having value. Informational texts, such as magazines and newspapers, may not be deemed as valuable as books in society.

By the final interview, the pupils reported more specific interests. For some, this seemed almost as though their interests had narrowed, but I feel that what had happened was that they had refined them and knew exactly what they liked to read. In this way they had developed meta-awareness around their interests. I feel that the extra time spent reading books of their own choice led them to develop real interests. Another factor may be that they were listening to books being read aloud which they may not have chosen themselves. In this way they were being exposed to new genres, which may have affected their interests. The grading of texts may also have played a role as pupils had a clear guideline for difficulty. They could, therefore, concentrate on getting a book that interested them. Most pupils could name at least one fictional book they had read. These were generally from the class library and of appropriate difficulty. Many of the pupils expressed an interest in reading books from a series, which could be an extra motivating force for them. I reflected on these changes in my journal:

> Went to the library and it went really well. They were all eager, asked me all week to go. They seemed to know exactly what they wanted and where to find it. I am ridiculously excited to hear them ask me or the librarians for books by a certain author.

Self-selection is an integral part of the reading programme and therefore how pupils choose books is important – 'I go over to the library and I pick a good book off me own shelf.' Pupils use a variety of methods to choose books. If these lead to successful choices, i.e. books they are engaged in, they will have more positive experiences of reading. This in turn may improve their attitudes and motivation towards reading (Mathewson, 1994).

No method

> Just pick a book.

In the first interview, two of the children indicated that they did not have a method for choosing books, or if they had a method were not aware of it or able to articulate it. Lindsey said that she would 'just pick a book' and seemed baffled by my questioning. I was aware of this problem and wrote about it in my journal:

> I've been watching them choose books. The grading seems to have helped. I've told some of the weaker readers to take a couple to keep them going. Lindsey literally grabs the first few to hand and sits down.

In the third interview only Lindsey was still unsure. She referred to pictures, which may have been related to her difficulty with reading text.

Difficulty

> Is it easy, hard or just right?

As part of the programme I had been speaking a lot about choosing 'just right' books on the basis of difficulty. It was mentioned by three of the pupils. Daniel said: 'Look at it and say "is this hard or easy?" if it's hard you put it back. If it's hard and easy you take it and read a few pages to see.'

By the third interview, most of the pupils used the difficulty of the text as one way to choose. Kelly said: 'First get a book or a magazine, look through it and see the words and see if I can read them, if I can't I just leave it. I go by my colour.' Many of the pupils in the middle-ability group were supporting their decisions with the grading system. Naturally stronger readers were not as concerned about difficulty because fewer books in the library would be too challenging for them.

Interest

> If it was about football or about dogs, if it was a good book, a good story.

Only two of the children spoke of choosing a book on the basis of personal interest in the first interview. A few mentioned seeing if it was good but did not specify what it was that would interest them.

In the third interview, the strong readers generally said that they would look to see if the book was good but did not mention specific interests. Only Steven gave a specific interest. I observed that most pupils do have specific interests and that the good readers in particular choose books to match these.

Clues

> Look at the front, read the back. If it looks good by the pictures.

In the first interview, only three of the children referred to using the conventions of the books as clues. Gary said, 'Look at the front, read the back. If it looks good by the pictures.'

By the final interview, a significantly greater number of the pupils used clues to get more information that would help them decide what to read. Six pupils said they would use clues to choose books. I found their responses very positive as many of them used a combination of methods. Jane gave a very detailed account: 'Em, read the back and read the first page. See am I able to read it, does it look interesting, is there hard words in it and, em, what kind of book is it about.' Many of them also referred to looking for positive aspects, which indicated that they wanted to enjoy the experience. 'When you read the back of the book it gives you information. And you might read the first page of it and go, oh yeah, this looks good or funny.'

I felt there was an improvement in the pupils' awareness of the methods they used. They were more likely to combine a number of methods by the third interview. During the reading programme they had to make frequent book choices. They chose books from the class library, the school library, the public library and bookshops. This practice and the feedback from the reading experience may have made them much better at choosing books.

Time spent reading

Time spent reading has been positively associated with reading achievement (Eivers, Shiel and Shortt, 2004). Information about the time spent reading may give us information about pupils' attitudes as it reflects their attitudes to leisure or recreational reading. Frequent recreational reading indicates a positive attitude to reading. Many of the children seemed eager to impress; however, we have only their word to go on, as it is not something I could directly observe.

In the first interview, only two pupils, weak readers, said that they did not do much reading at home, only reading their homework. Two more said they read infrequently. Many of the remaining pupils referred to reading magazines and newspapers at home rather than books. As these are also the most common texts read by their families, this is not surprising. It highlights the importance of showing them the link between magazine reading and school reading.

In the final interview, only Lindsey seemed to be just reading homework at home. Peter and Steven said they read 'a bit' and 'a little bit'. The others said they read regularly, either daily or every second day. All were able to answer more specific questions about where and when they did their reading.

Implications

It is vital that the DES fund the purchasing of high quality literature for schools. The curriculum itself states that 'The importance of the classroom library in enriching the child's reading experience cannot be overemphasised' (NCCA, 1999, p. 53). It would also be extremely helpful if there were a list of graded Irish/British books. There are many graded lists available but they contain mainly American books and few of the books in my school were included. A graded list would make it easier for pupils to choose books for independent reading and also guide teachers in what books to use for guided reading. This would greatly ease teachers' trepidation at moving away from relying solely on basal readers.

The time allocated for English teaching in the curriculum is not enough to implement this programme. The same amount of time is given to English in all schools. I feel that schools with high levels of educational disadvantage require more time for the teaching of English if they are to get all pupils to a high standard. Writing and oral language were not part of this study, but of course time is also needed for these strands.

Very often, teachers in designated disadvantaged schools have a large number of pupils with special educational needs or who score below the tenth percentile. As a result of this, much of the attention paid to reading is in terms of raising the achievement of the weakest readers. This is of course extremely important and those pupils should not be neglected. However, the strongest readers in these schools are often not achieving as well as their peers nationally. This programme is one method of raising the reading achievement of the pupils they deem to be their 'good readers' as well as those of the weak readers.

Often research on the reading behaviour of children and adolescents focuses on 'book' reading. For many readers books may not be the text of choice. This may be particularly true among educationally disadvantaged students. Pupils in this study reported that their families read magazines and newspapers rather than books. This type of literacy may not be fully acknowledged by some researchers. An example of this is studies that look at the number of books in the home as an indicator of literacy. Educators who do not recognise its existence or its value may also ignore this type of reading. In order to motivate students we must first meet them where they are. If they are more comfortable with magazine and newspaper reading then we need to find ways to integrate this into the classroom and not dismiss it.

References

Cosgrove, J., Kellaghan, T., Forde, P. and Morgan, M. (2000) *The 1998 National Assessment of English Reading*, Dublin: Educational Research Centre

Dweck, C. S. (1986) 'Motivational Processes Affecting Learning', *American Psychologist*, vol. 41, no. 10, pp. 1040–8

Eivers, E., Shiel, G. and Shortt, F. (2004) *Reading Literacy in Disadvantaged Primary Schools*, Dublin: Educational Research Centre

Mathewson, G. C. (1994) 'Model of an Attitude Influence Upon Reading and Learning to Read' in Ruddell, R. B., Ruddell, M. R and Singer, H. (eds), *Theoretical Models and Processes of Reading* (4th edn), Newark, DE: International Reading Association, pp. 1131–61

McKenna, M. C. (1994) 'Towards a Model of Reading Attitude Acquisition', in Cramer, E. H. and Castle, M. (eds) *Fostering the Life-long Love of Reading: The Affective Domain in Reading Education*, Newark, DE: International Reading Association, pp. 18–40

McKenna, M. C., Kear, D. J. and Ellsworth, R. A. (1995) 'Children's Attitudes Towards Reading: A National Survey' in *Reading Research Quarterly,* vol. 30, no. 4, pp. 934–55

National Council for Curriculum and Assessment (1999) *Primary School Curriculum, English (Teachers Guidelines)*, Dublin: Government Publications

Organisation for Economic Cooperation and Development (1999) *Education Policy Analysis*, Paris: OECD

Oxford Reading Tree (1991) Oxford University Press

Pressley, M. (2002) *Reading Instruction that Works: The Case for Balanced Teaching* (2nd edn) New York: Guildford

Shanahan, T. (2001) 'Improving Reading Education for Low-income Children' in Shiel, G. and Ní Dhálaigh U. (eds), *Reading Matters: A Fresh Start*, Dublin: Reading Association of Ireland/National Reading Initiative, pp. 157–65

16

Preventing Potential Weaknesses in Early Literacy Instruction

Sylwia Kazmierczak

This chapter explores some concerns about the literacy instruction delivered in Irish infant classes. There has been a tremendous amount of research and papers studying 'effective literacy instruction'. The issue is how much this research work has been absorbed in practice, in the process of teaching. That is why this chapter takes the opposite approach and, instead of studying 'effective literacy instruction', outlines typical weaknesses in teaching literacy, embedded in a theoretical context. This concurs with Saussure (Holdcroft, 1991) and other structuralists who hold that we can engage in defining something only through examining its opposite. Consequently, here we look at what is *not* good practice in literacy teaching at sound, word and text level.

The role of the teacher during the first years of schooling, when many of the linguistic skills are still developing and the foundation of literacy is being built, is enormous and cannot be overemphasised. The teaching/learning reciprocal relationship has been acknowledged and raised frequently. The professional knowledge of teachers and the quality of teaching significantly influence the way students attain literacy. Literacy instruction has been an area of particular concern since the early 90s, and it has been emphasised that the dependence of literacy standard upon literacy instruction is higher for disadvantaged pupils (McGough, 2002; Hall, 2003).

Although a recent survey on literacy claims that the reading standard of fifth-class children is relatively high (Eivers et al., 2006), literacy standards in Irish designated disadvantaged schools are disturbing, particularly among male children. Forty-three per cent of children in designated disadvantaged schools had reading scores that fell below the twentieth percentile (IDES, 2005a). Perhaps this is partly related to the way in which literacy is being taught.

The vast majority of teachers in designated disadvantaged schools agreed that their pre-service training did not prepare them sufficiently to teach literacy (IDES, 2005a, p. 32). At the same time, newly graduated teachers said that they felt least professionally prepared to teach infant classes (IDES, 2005b). In their survey, Eivers et al. (2006) recommended that children in designated disadvantaged schools should be given a greater amount of literacy instruction. This is, however, only feasible with teachers who are confident about incorporating literacy instruction into the whole process of teaching and into various areas of the curriculum.

Hall (2003) has reviewed research into 'effective literacy teaching' and concludes that effective teaching is based on a combination of method, culture, philosophy and teacher development (p. 322). The following is concerned with the method of teaching literacy and it relates to the early years of schooling when formal literacy instruction starts.

Sound level

Phonics is about how spelling conventions relate to the sounds of spoken language. This definition focuses on the relationship of spoken and written language. It is important to remember that phonics is not equal to 'teaching the sounds' and that it does not relate to sounds other than the sounds of spoken language.

Typical weaknesses relating to phonics instruction include teaching phonics as a separate activity, in isolation from meaningful text.[1] In such a de-contextualised approach, phonics instruction might be wrongly directed in the early junior infant classes to children who have not yet attempted to read. Teaching of separate sounds and separate letters without context would be a greatly simplified version of phonics and would reduce phonics to a single-sound/single-letter relationship. This could even lead to a separation of those two levels (of spoken and written language) and create a situation in which children would be 'sensitised' to isolated sounds.

Therefore, the following example would not constitute good phonics practice. When children are required to repetitiously pronounce isolated phonemes,[2] which are often related to the sounds of non-linguistic nature, such as the sound of a snake (phoneme 's') or the roaring sound (phoneme 'r'). For example:

---

[1] The term 'text' refers here and throughout this chapter to the substance of something spoken or written and is understood as a meaningful whole: meaningful sentences in written language and meaningful utterances in spoken language.

[2] A phoneme is the smallest sound unit of speech.

T: What sound does this letter make? Does anybody have a puppy at home? Ok, everybody say rrr (…)

Child 1: Rrreeerrreeerrreee

Child 2: Rhhh, riiiii, rhhhh

T: Do you know what sound 'h' makes? When you are tired after running in the hall (…)

T: You get your egg and you crack it over a saucepan. Everybody: eeeee (…)

T: Now let's just say all of them again. From the beginning: aaa, bbb, ccc (…)

Another typical practice is introducing literacy instruction through singing songs with characters that represent each letter of the alphabet and the sound this letter 'makes in words'. Many children in the early junior infant classes are not phonemically aware, that is, they do not have the knowledge that speech could be separable into phonemes. They often do not even have phonological awareness, which is the knowledge that speech is generally separable into sounds. Thus, although the singing of these songs could perhaps be useful in a supportive role, it neither exhausts phonics instruction nor does it constitute an introduction to phonics. Most importantly, it does not constitute an introduction to the whole process of literacy learning. Operating at a phonemic level can start when children are able to consciously reflect on such abstract units; they develop this ability while attempting to read. The majority of young children are phonemically unaware until they are exposed to written language (Burt, et al., 1999).

It is essential that phonics instruction is not used to introduce literacy instruction. Learning meaningless sounds or letter-sound correspondences without understanding the purpose of such knowledge is nonsensical, particularly for young children. Such tasks are also very difficult for them and much more abstract than actually learning the correspondences between the whole printed word and its spoken versions (Harris and Coltheart, 1986, p. 85). Learning abstract letter-sound correspondences may be even more difficult for children who, prior to starting school, have had limited opportunities to become familiar with written language and the notion of reading. Every time a child acquires a new word, his/her lexicon is restructured and 'sensitivity' to sounds is enhanced (e.g. the new word 'bet' needs to be distinguished from the known word 'bat'). Thus, an ability to reflect on speech sounds is in some ways a consequence of vocabulary acquisition. It may be that some children of parents experiencing educational disadvantage have a poorer vocabulary repertoire and are thus somewhat 'less prepared' for early work with single phonemes (single sounds).

Children learn grapheme-phoneme[3] correspondences to help them to decode unfamiliar words and thus they can learn these correspondences only with

---

[3] A grapheme is a written representation of a phoneme; it consists of a letter or a cluster of two, three or four letters pronounced as one sound (e.g. 'sh' in 'shine', 'ough' in 'though', 'th' in 'the' or 'd' in 'dad').

meaningful words. Only in this way can they understand that the same phonemes can be represented differently in words, e.g. 'o' is represented differently (and in fact it could be pronounced differently) in 'go', 'coat' and 'though'.

Another weakness is teaching phonics inconsistently and in a way that does not consider the complexity of the English language and the local accent. This would most likely (but not only) occur in the de-contextualised teaching of phonics. Phonics should be taught only as required, with meaningful words, when a real phoneme-grapheme relationship can be explained to children.

The following examples would not constitute good practice in phonics:[4] when children suggest 'know' or 'knock' as examples of words starting with 'n' and are told that they are incorrect instead of being presented with further explanation; or, similarly, when children suggest the words 'shoes' and 'fuse' as examples of words with 'oo' and are simply told that they are incorrect instead of being provided with further explanation.

The teacher should instead write all the words on the board and explain the relationship between the spoken and written versions in each of them (e.g. phoneme 'u' can be represented as 'oe' in 'shoes', 'u' in 'fuse' and 'oo' in 'took'). The teacher should also explain that, indeed, 'knock' starts with 'n' when pronounced but that this 'n' is represented differently in writing 'kn' and that there are other similar words, e.g. 'knight' and 'knife'.

Children need to be instructed on the purpose of every activity, and so, when expected to provide examples of words starting with 'n' they need to be instructed whether this 'n' relates to the phonetic (spoken) or orthographic[5] (written) level. Lack of such explanation, combined with dismissal of suggestions such as 'know' and 'knock', introduce confusion at both spoken and written level. The child asked to come up with examples of words starting with 'n' might operate on a phonetic level and the appropriateness of his/her examples should not be judged against orthographic rules unless further explanation is provided.

Pupils who are provided with an isolated phonics rule that 'oo' in written language is pronounced as 'u' or sometimes prolonged 'u', might come up with various examples for a word with 'oo'. Because many words in the English language simply do not conform to phonics rules, some of these examples might contain the grapheme 'oo' in conventional spelling but some might not. The latter might contain other graphemes such as 'oe' in 'shoes', 'u' in 'fuse' or even 'ou' in 'wound' – this list would vary according to the speaker's accent. For speakers with conservative[6] Dublin accents the following pairs often rhyme: 'stood' and

---

[4] The examples relate to the very common practice of providing examples of words containing particular phonemes or graphemes or starting with particular phonemes or graphemes. There are, however, some concerns over whether to introduce such practice. This section uses these examples to illustrate a broader problem of inconsistency in phonics instruction that might also occur during other activities.

[5] Orthographic relates to written words and means spelled conventionally.

[6] See Wells, 1982

'stud', 'took' and 'tuck', 'look' and 'luck', 'blood' and 'bud' (Wells, 1982, p. 422); or they might suggest 'mug' as an example of a word with the grapheme 'oo' because they relate the grapheme 'oo' to the phoneme 'u', and 'mug', for them, resembles (rhymes with) the pronunciation of 'took'. Phonics instruction needs to be sensitive to local accents and teachers need to be aware that the reason children might 'misunderstand' some areas of phonics instruction might be because of their accents. Simply telling children that they are incorrect is likely to confuse them. It is a necessity for every teacher to operate confidently on a phonological level of words and to be able to deliver an appropriate explanation. The English language phonological system is a complex one, with up to forty-four phonemes[7] represented by different graphemes; it also has many homophones[8] and their number might vary with accent. This basic linguistic knowledge, together with a sensitivity to local accent and an awareness of the limitations and complexity of phonics, are crucial elements in teaching phonics.

Word level

As mentioned, before paying attention to grapheme-phoneme correspondences children need to comprehend what letters and sounds are, and so they need to be taught that the spoken language consists of sounds and that these sounds can have written representations, in the form of letters. The knowledge (insight) that speech can be segmented into smaller units (words, syllables, sounds) combined with the ability to perform this segmentation is broadly called phonological awareness.

Metalinguistic skills[9] are very strong predictors of literacy level but it is as yet unexplored whether prior metalinguistic skills facilitate learning to read or whether ability to read and language development in general enhance metalinguistic skills (Chaney, 2000). As this relationship is most likely reciprocal, phonological awareness training, inclusive of phoneme-level tasks, should not be neglected. Phonological awareness training helps to develop the ability to think about language structure and so contributes to metalinguistic awareness. It is also crucial that good phonological training is distinguished from phonological training that does not constitute good practice.

Typical weaknesses relating to phonological level involve lack of sufficient or planned phonological awareness training, especially prior to phonics instruction.

---

[7] Linguists disagree on the number of phonemes in the English language; their estimates range from thirty-seven to forty-nine phonemes in British Received Pronunciation.

[8] Homophones are words pronounced alike but differing in meaning, such as 'two' and 'too', 'cold' and 'called', 'write' and 'right'.

[9] Metalinguistic skills are skills that allow one to reflect on language, e.g. to differentiate between real and nonsense words (cake and keke), correct (I like the cake) and 'incorrect' sentences (The like cake I), and to segment language into units (words, syllables, phonemes), etc.

Children cannot be presented with phonics instruction in the later stages of literacy acquisition before they actually comprehend the notion of a phoneme (as a unit of spoken language) and a letter/grapheme (as a written representation of a phoneme). Research suggests that rudimentary phonemic awareness (e.g. an ability to identify phonemes in speech) facilitates the learning of letter-sound relationships, while letter-sound knowledge does not facilitate rudimentary phoneme awareness (Foy and Mann, 2006). Random teaching of phonological awareness and teaching phonological awareness without any particular order are typical weaknesses in early literacy instruction.

Thus, the following example would not constitute good practice: when children are required to provide words starting with particular sounds before they can comprehend that speech can be conceived as a string of sounds. For example:

> T: Think of a word beginning with p.
> Child: House
> T: Does house start with p/No/Is it 'pouse'?
> Child: (confusion)

Instead, children should learn to 'notice/hear' the phonemes *in words,* through focusing their attention on the sound level (and not the meaning level) of speech. This can be 'practiced' through, for example, categorising words that start with the same sounds (e.g. I will say words that start with the sound 'p' and you will repeat them/If I say a word that does not start with 'p' you are not to say anything: peacock, panda, elephant, etc.).[10]

Another weakness is testing instead of teaching phonological awareness. Children need to participate in various sound and word games that involve segmentation and blending, because the process of manipulation can be mastered only by apprenticeship. The fun of clapping and tapping, etc., make these activities enjoyable.

Thus, the following example would not constitute good practice. When children who have not yet acquired phonemic awareness skills[11] are required to work independently and colour in their workbook pictures depicting objects that start or do not start with a particular sound, such as when children are instructed to colour in pictures of things starting with 's' and are given worksheets with pictures of the sun, stairs, stars, moon, spoon, plate, etc.

Children at the early stages of phonological awareness acquisition in the early months of junior infant classes learn by participation. Participation in the process of manipulation of the units of spoken language is the only way to learn. Children

---

[10] Another task in teaching phonemic awareness (the ability to 'hear' phonemes) is a rhyme recognition task (e.g. Does 'like' rhyme with 'bike'). It is worth noting that both tasks use a top-down approach (from words into phonemes) not a bottom-up approach (from phonemes into words).

[11] Phonemic awareness requires a conscious reflection on the smallest speech units (phonemes). It requires an understanding that speech can be conceived as a string of these smallest sounds.

who are acquiring phonological awareness skills cannot work with workbooks. Activities in workbooks require them to apply the knowledge that they have not yet acquired and to work independently; they do not teach children that language is made up of separable units. Exercises in workbooks 'test' children's phonological awareness and often do so by starting at the last and most difficult stage: the phoneme level. Additionally, awareness of the sound structure of language cannot be learnt from silent pictures: 'It is a matter of serious concern that in many classrooms there is an overdependence on workbook activities' (IDES, 2005c, p. 23).

Text level

Much has been said about the interrelationship between literacy and oral language. Preparing a rich linguistic foundation is of tremendous importance in infant classes. Children need to participate in many class discussions, conversations and oral imaginative stories because these require a great deal of cognitive skills (e.g. sequencing, reasoning, planning, etc.) and linguistic processing. Children also need to hear stories frequently.

Typical weaknesses relating to textual level include lack of interaction, particularly during story time,[12] and talking, which may be perceived as interruption. Learning occurs through the process of interaction and it is essential that pupils are allowed, and encouraged to, participate in classroom dialogue. Murphy (1999) examined classroom language in Irish senior infant classes and found that children talked for only 35 per cent of the time, out of which 13 per cent was devoted to whole-class repetitions and only 2 per cent to dialogue.

During story time, children should be encouraged to interact with a story through non-directive language (e.g. Have you ever seen a pig like that? Look at that – what could it be? Does anybody have any idea, etc.). For socio-economically disadvantaged children, a child-initiated model was found to be more beneficial than a directive one (See Bryant and Maxwell, 1996, for a review).

Ideally, children would work not only on the content of stories but also on the structure of the story which would require them to sequence events and retell the story in turns. The processes of synthesising (composing parts into a whole) and analysing (decomposing a whole into parts) stories contribute to the development of metalinguistic skills.

Carefully selected stories provide rich material for teaching children various contextual clues and comprehension strategies (e.g. activating prior knowledge,

---

[12] The English curriculum recommends a range of methodologies through which oral language development can be facilitated in infant and junior classes. Undertaking story-based activities, along with participation in meaningful conversations and imaginative play, is one of them (IDES, 2005c, p. 14).

predicting, reasoning, looking at the pictures, etc.). It is of tremendous importance that children participate in analysing (Why did she go there?); synthesising (What would happen if?); categorising (What other animals might she meet in the forest?) and assimilating (Where was she at the beginning?).

Other typical weaknesses relating to textual level involve a lack of, or insufficient, teaching of comprehension strategies and replacing the teaching of comprehension with the testing of comprehension. For example, when children are asked mostly random questions that require short and often one-word answers such as, 'Can you remember the names of those three boys?' or 'What did I just read about during story time?'. Such an approach reduces questioning to a means of disciplining unfocused pupils instead of involving children in constructing the meaning.

Instead, teachers should pose questions that guide children in the comprehension process and help them to become metacognitive readers[13] (e.g. What is going to happen when daddy comes? Why are we going to read some more? Do we know now what happens when daddy comes?). Questions for which answers require only memory skills, such as the ones cited, do not scaffold children's learning. In fact, they are likely to discourage children's curiosity about a story. They 'test' the children's concentration abilities instead of providing them with various comprehension strategies. Young children's comprehension skills develop gradually and a teacher's good questioning method could become a significant contributor in this development. Creating support in the development of comprehension skills includes posing open-ended questions that require text level answers (e.g. explanation, description, reason) and the use of cognitive processes.

To conclude, the best practice in early literacy instruction is to expose young children to an abundance of meaningful language, in the form of both stories and oral discussions, instead of drilling them in single skills. However, training in the manipulation of language components is as important as a holistic language approach since the cause and effect of literacy and metalinguistic skills is not clear (Chaney, 2000). Children learn best by interaction and participation and so every instruction that relates to separable units of language needs to be embedded in context.

Phonics instruction should not be overemphasised and de-contextualised in early infant classes and should not be used to introduce literacy instruction since good phonics instruction cannot be delivered outside the context of written language. Equally, however, phonological awareness training should not be neglected in infant classes, but it is crucial that knowledge acquisition is not confused with knowledge application in this area. This important distinction between teaching and testing should also be made in the teaching of

---

[13] A metacognitive reader is aware of his/her own thinking process and decision-making (e.g. In order to understand this situation I need to know where that witch came from. In order to find out about that I am going to go back to the beginning because that was where it was written about.)

comprehension strategies. Teachers' phonological knowledge needs to be quite extensive so they can teach consistently and sensitively, taking local accents into account and incorporating phonological and phonics instruction with confidence in every situation. Children need to receive explanations and not simply be told that they are incorrect every time they provide an answer from outside a range of conventional answers.

References

Bryant, D. and Maxwell, K. (1996) 'The effectiveness of early intervention for disadvantaged children' in Guralnick, M. (ed.) *The effectiveness of early intervention: Second generation research*, Baltimore: Paul H. Brookes, pp. 3–26

Burt, L., Holm, A., and Dodd, B. (1999) 'Phonological awareness skills of 4-year-old British children: An assessment and developmental data', *International Journal of Language and Communication Disorders*, 34, pp. 311–35

Chaney, C. (2000) 'The social class does not predict reading success but language and metalinguistic skills do' in Perkins, M. and Howard, S. (eds) *New directions in language development and disorders*, New York: Kluwer/Plenum, pp. 271–9

Eivers, E., Shiel, G., Perkins, R. and Cosgrove, J. (2006) *Succeeding in Reading? Reading standards in Irish primary schools*, Dublin: Educational Research Centre

Foy, J. and Mann, V. (2006) 'Changes in letter-sound knowledge are associated with development of phonological awareness in pre-school children', *Journal of Research in Reading*, 29, 2, pp. 143–61

Hall, K. (2003) 'Effective literacy teaching in the early years of school: A review of evidence' in Hall, N., Larson, J. and Marsh, J. (eds) *Handbook of early childhood literacy*, London: Sage, pp. 315–26

Harris, M. and Coltheart, M. (1986) *Language processing in children and adults: An introduction*, London: Routledge and Kegan Paul

Holdcroft, D. (1991) *Saussure: Signs, system, and arbitrariness*, New York: Cambridge University Press

Inspectorate of the Department of Education and Science (2005a) *Literacy and numeracy in disadvantaged schools: Challenges for teachers and learners*, Dublin: IDES

Inspectorate of the Department of Education and Science (2005b) *Beginning to teach. Newly qualified teachers in Irish primary schools*, Dublin: IDES

Inspectorate of the Department of Education and Science (2005c) *An evaluation of primary school implementation in Primary Schools: English, Mathematics and Visual Arts*, Dublin: IDES

McGough, A. (2002) 'Addressing Disadvantage: The Role of Teaching' in Gilligan, A. L. (ed.) *Primary Education: Ending Disadvantage. Proceedings and Action Plan of National Forum*, Dublin: Educational Disadvantage Centre, St Patrick's College, pp. 73–89

Murphy, B. (1999) 'Social Interaction and Language Use in Irish Infant Classrooms in the Context of the Revised Irish Primary School Curriculum', *Literacy*, 38, 3, pp. 149–55

Wells, J. C. (1982) *Accents of English*, New York: Cambridge University Press

17

Raising Literacy Levels Locally

Yvonne Mullan

Over the past three decades successive Irish governments have demonstrated a commitment to tackling the problems of school failure by allocating additional resources and implementing several initiatives in schools in areas of socio-economic deprivation. These initiatives and resources continue to aim to promote equality of access, participation and benefit for all children in accordance with their needs and abilities (Government of Ireland, 1995). This chapter examines the aspiration 'equality of benefit for all', with particular regard to the essential life-skill of literacy (NCE, 1993).

There is much research evidence that points to the detrimental effects of low literacy levels on the life chances of individuals, with the effects of poor literacy skills persisting into adulthood. Low literacy levels have been associated with early school leaving, low-paid employment and unemployment (Morgan et al., 1997). Concerns have been expressed in economic terms of these effects of low literacy levels, particularly in the context of the emerging knowledge society. Other negative effects of low literacy levels include social alienation and continuing disadvantage, and therefore, addressing educational disadvantage is also viewed as a social inclusion measure. Targets have been set in an attempt to raise literacy standards, one of which is the National Anti-Poverty Strategy (2001) target to halve the proportion of pupils with serious literacy difficulties in designated disadvantaged schools by the year 2006. However, some research (Eivers, Shiel and Shortt, 2004) describes this target as extremely ambitious and cites the absence of school-level targets as one of the key difficulties.

This chapter describes how, in one school, an improvement in literacy levels was achieved when relevant in-career development was provided for teachers. Two main sources were used. The first was an interview with the principal teacher of the school and the second came from the observations of the author, a psychologist working with the National Educational Psychological Service in the school, over a period of four years. The interest of the author in the school's methodology for teaching literacy was initially aroused by an observation that children with specific learning disabilities and children with mild/borderline general learning disabilities were reading and spelling at chronological age level.

Interventions and professional development

Research by Eivers, Shiel and Shortt (2004) confirmed what many Irish studies (Archer and O'Flaherty, 1991; Cosgrove et al., 2002) had found before: children attending schools in areas designated as disadvantaged have significantly lower average reading achievement scores than their counterparts in schools in non-designated areas or in standardisation samples. At this stage it is useful to differentiate between the 80 per cent (Warnock, 1978) or the approximately 72 per cent (Eivers, Shiel and Shortt, 2004) of children who pick up literacy skills naturally in the classroom and the children who have difficulty becoming literate.

To date educational disadvantage initiatives have not had a significant impact on the literacy levels of pupils in designated schools (Eivers, Shiel and Shortt, 2004). The *Early Start Programme* (DES, 1994) is reported to have had positive effects on social and emotional maturity but its effects on literacy and mathematics achievement to date have been mixed (Kelly and Kellaghan, 1999). The reduction of class sizes in the *Breaking the Cycle* scheme (DES, 1996) and the *Giving Children an Even Break* programme (DES, 2001) have not resulted in significant improvement in pupils' reading achievements (Weir, Mills and Ryan, 2002). Sheil, Morgan and Larney (1998) found that the Learning Support Service has not made a significant difference to the literacy skills of children in disadvantaged schools. The question remains therefore, why, despite increases in resources applied across a range of initiatives in disadvantaged schools, is there little evidence of any improvement in average literacy standards? The answer to the question may be that specialist skills are required to teach children who have difficulty with literacy and that, to date, only one Irish disadvantage initiative has included regular quality professional development in the teaching of literacy to children who have difficulty becoming literate. This intervention is *Reading Recovery* (Clay, 1993). Critics of *Reading Recovery* point to the cost of its implementation – a teacher implementing *Reading Recovery* deals with at most twelve students a year (Pressley, 2002). However, although research evidence is scarce, the programme seems to have had the effect of helping to bring children's literacy levels up to class norms in schools in non-designated areas in Monaghan (Ní Thresaigh, 2004). The test will be to see if the programme will have a positive effect on the literacy levels of pupils in designated disadvantaged schools.

In their study Eivers, Shiel and Shortt (2004) found that persons who did not have a basic teaching qualification taught 13 per cent of pupils in first class. One explanation that has been given for this situation is that schools in areas designated disadvantaged may be more stressful work places than schools in non-designated areas. While many teachers spend whole careers in the same school, Coolahan (2003) argues that teacher burnout has been more intensive in recent years and, as a result, staff turnover has increased. Another explanation may be that few teachers grew up in the local community in many socio-economically disadvantaged areas. An increased proportion of teachers from local communities coupled with increased pre-service and in-service training in the skills required for teaching in socio-economically disadvantaged areas may help to reduce teacher turnover. INTO research indicates that turnover in designated schools is in the region of 10 per cent each year (INTO, 2002) and is one of the reasons why, in some designated disadvantaged schools, teachers may not have had basic teaching qualifications in the recent past. However, it must be acknowledged that there is no longer a shortage of primary teachers. Many primary teaching jobs have large numbers of candidates and thus high teacher turnover in more disadvantaged areas may be less of a phenomenon than previously.

Most importantly, teachers who *were* fully qualified in the Eivers, Shiel and Shortt study felt that their pre-service training in relation to the teaching of reading did not fully meet their needs or the needs of pupils. Only one-third of teachers had had in-career development in reading in the school year of the study (Eivers, Shiel and Shortt, 2004). These findings are similar to those of the IEA (1990–1991) literacy study, which was carried out in thirty-two countries. Teachers in only four countries had spent less time than teachers in Ireland on the further study of reading since qualification. Irish teachers were at the very bottom in terms of frequency of attendance at in-service reading courses over the three preceding years and teachers in none of the other countries reported a lower frequency of attendance (Martin and Morgan, 1994). This finding contrasts sharply with patterns of attendance found in the literature on schools effective in reading instruction (Shanahan, 2001; Lipson et al., 2004) and with the school described in this chapter.

Literacy skill teaching

Shanahan (2001) argues that an effective school reading programme can teach most children to read no matter what the income level or education level of their parents. The principles of his model are that instruction should emphasise the four fundamental components of literacy learning: word knowledge, fluency, comprehension and writing. Shanahan recommends that at a minimum two to three hours per day should be devoted to reading and writing instruction and that there should be continuity from grade level to grade level and from primary to second-level school. This time recommendation contrasts sharply with that of the National Council for Curriculum and Assessment (NCCA, 1999) which suggests that all aspects of English should be taught in three hours per week in infant classes and in four hours per week in other classes.

Numerous reasons for literacy difficulties have been cited, including poverty and low income; language and or cognitive ability; parents' literacy difficulties; lack of access to books and libraries; immigration; frequent changes of school; English as a second language; cultural differences; bereavement; trauma; terminal illness; or siblings with serious illness (Ott, 2001). While schools may not be in a position to influence some of the causes mentioned above, recent developments in literacy research have shown that children can be helped to overcome some of them.

A constant characteristic of poor readers is that they have difficulties decoding words, with this factor more than any other accounting for low comprehension (Ehrlich, Kurtz-Costes and Loridant, 1993). There has long been a debate as to how children should be taught to recognise words as part of reading instruction (Chall, 1967). In recent years there has been more support for code-emphasis approaches, e.g. phonics, over meaning-emphasis approaches, such as language experience (Pressley, 2002). Decoding involves knowing letter-sound associations, learning how to use them, mapping individual sounds represented by letters or groups of letters of a word and blending the sounds (Pressley, 2002). Conducting many trials of successfully sounding out a word increases the connections between the letter patterns defining the word and the word in memory (Adams, 1990; Ehri, 1992). By reading repeatedly there is also a strengthening of the connections between the visual stimulus and the conceptual understanding in long-term memory, so that eventually even the briefest exposure to a word elicits its concept. When words can be read by sight and recurring letter chunks can be processed as wholes, automatic reading takes place, allowing attention to be directed to comprehension (Laberge and Samuels 1974).

In a review of the literature on different phonic programmes, Stahl, Duffy-Hester and Stahl (1998) found that there were only small differences between programmes. They developed conclusions about what excellent phonics programmes should do. Programmes should:

- be based on the alphabetic principle (letters in words represent specific sounds)
- develop phonological awareness
- develop automatic recognition of the form of each letter
- involve a great deal of practice
- not teach rules (as they are always so many exceptions).

All of Stahl's (1998) recommendations were encompassed in the programme chosen by the school at the centre of this report, a programme called

Phonographix. Phonographix[1] was developed in the US by the McGuiness family (1998) and is based on the simple insight that letters are pictures of sounds. It cuts away a lot of unnecessary information like letter names and rules. Phonographix has been found not only to be a powerful remedial device, but also a preventative classroom technique. Evaluations of the programme reveal it to be one of the most effective remedial programmes available, bringing previously failed readers to chronological age in only twelve sessions (Orton Dyslexia Society, 1996). The programme has been widely adopted in England and is cited as having the largest ratio gain for reading of all interventions reviewed in a recent inspectorate report on reading interventions (DfES, 2003).

Case study school

The school was built in the early 1970s as a flat-roofed, two-storey building with two playgrounds and several grassy areas. It is situated in the heart of a community just across from a recent development of corporation townhouses on one side and high-rise flats on the other. Current enrolment in the school is 206 pupils. The school is mixed from junior infants to first class and single sex, girls only, from second class to sixth class. The profile of the children in the school has changed in recent years. The principal teacher reported that in her opinion the children currently attending the school come from the most socio-economically disadvantaged homes. The interior of the school is attractive and stimulating and is kept in a good state of repair. The walls are adorned with the artwork of children and the work of famous artists. Along with this, there is evidence on the school walls of a celebration of different cultures within the school.

The school staff works very much as a team. They meet twice a term for long staff meetings and twice a week for short staff meetings. Twenty teachers work in the school, including the principal, the Home School Community Liaison coordinator, a shared resource teacher for Travellers, two special class teachers, two teachers of international children, two learning support teachers, one resource teacher and eleven mainstream class teachers. The general atmosphere in the school is friendly and the staffroom is used frequently before and after school as a meeting place for teachers. Extra-curricular activities are a feature of the school and include French, hip-hop and Irish dancing, swimming, counselling, Gaelic football, and creativity in the classroom. The school has an active parents' association, which supports the work of the school and promotes parental involvement in the education of their children.

Phonographix was introduced to the school by one of the learning support teachers who read about its success and witnessed its effectiveness for her own

---

[1] Phonographix is available from Surgisales Teaching Aids Ltd, 252 Harold's Cross Road, Dublin 6W. Fonics Phirst is an Irish synthetic phonics literacy programme, see www.fonicsphirst.ie.

son's literacy difficulties. She and another learning support teacher began to use Phonographix with small groups of children and were impressed by the results achieved. At this stage, neither of the teachers was trained in Phonographix. The teachers taught the programme by reading a book called *Reading Reflex* (McGuinness, 1998). They brought their successes, or rather the successes of the children to the attention of the principal teacher and in the summer of 2000 the Board of Management funded Phonographix training for the principal and four teachers. After that initial training, the principal and the trained teachers began to introduce Phonographix to senior infants and first classes in a whole-class situation and again noted positive results in children's literacy skills. Two years later, nine mainstream class teachers were trained in the school during the mid-term break. In the summer of 2003, three more teachers trained on a course that was funded by the School Completion Programme (SCP) (DES, 2002) and the Board of Management. In all, fifteen of the twenty teachers are currently trained in the Phonographix method of teaching decoding skills.

The school has well-developed procedures for assessing how pupils are progressing. Each year standardised tests, teacher appraisal and diagnostic tests are used to assess progress. Because of the large investment that has been made in Phonographix, and in order to see if literacy skills are improving, the principal and teachers have begun to closely examine test results. Figure 1 is a graph of test results for the school years 2002 and 2003. There are many possible explanations for the increase in the number of children whose reading scores fell within the average range. However, the teachers and the principal put it down to Phonographix.

Figure 1 MICRA-T scores 2002 and 2003

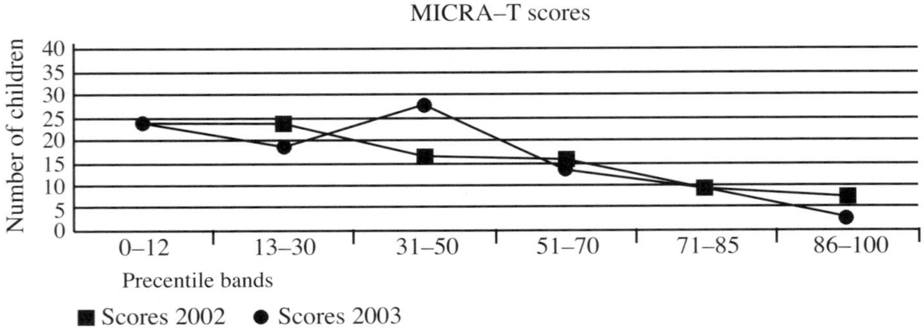

MICRA–T scores

On another test, the WORD Spelling Test, administered to eighty-seven children in March 2004, only ten children (11.5 per cent approx.) scored at or below the tenth percentile (Table 1). In the classes that had most exposure to Phonographix (first and second), fewer children scored at or below the tenth percentile.

Table 1 WORD Spelling Test scores March 2004

Class	1st	2nd	4th	6th
Number of children in class	17	21	21	23
Number of children who scored below the tenth percentile in spelling	0	2	4	4

Conclusion

The intention of this chapter has not been to promote Phonographix as an exclusive method of teaching decoding skills but rather to highlight the way in which one school managed a professional development innovation and increased literacy levels at the same time.

The success story in the school may be due in part to Phonographix, but it is clearly due to much more. It is due to the quality of leadership of the principal who believed in the importance of supporting those who support pupils, with good quality professional development. A key aim of the principal teacher over the last few years has been to improve pupils' literacy skills. It is an aim that she has often shared with her staff and it is the reason why fifteen of the twenty teachers have had literacy skill training. The success is also due to the flexibility and the autonomy exercised by the Board of Management in utilising school completion funds in an imaginative way, a way that made a tangible difference to the lives of pupils. It is due to the flexibility of staff who gave up free time to do the training and to the flexibility of the principal who was open to introducing new methods of teaching literacy into the school. It is due to the continuity between grades, which Shanahan (2001) recommends and which is now possible in the school because so many of the teachers received the same skills training. Finally, it is due to the fact that the objective to improve literacy skills was a local objective that was decided upon and implemented at school-level as opposed to a national initiative imposed on the school from outside.

Research over the years has overwhelmingly argued for more time to be spent on the teaching of literacy. Energetic, intelligent, high-quality teaching remains the best solution to the literacy difficulties of children in all schools. Increasing the amount of time spent on literacy skills is one way to improve the literacy skills of children who have difficulty becoming literate. However, increasing the amount of instructional time for literacy will of itself do little without a focus on the professional development of teachers. Decoding or word knowledge is an essential skill that children with reading difficulties need to be taught. At the same time the skill of teaching decoding is one that needs to be learned by teachers.

References

Adams, M. (1990) *Beginning to Read*, Cambridge, MA: Harvard University Press

Archer, P. and O'Flaherty, B. (1991) 'Literacy Problems Among Primary School Leavers in Dublin's Inner City', *Studies in Education*, 7, pp. 7–13

Chall, J. S. (1967) *Learning to Read: The Great Debate*, New York: McGraw Hill

Clay, M. (1993) *Reading Recovery: A Guidebook for Teachers in Training*, Portsmouth, NH: Heinemann

Coolahan, J. (2003) 'Attracting, Developing and Retaining Effective Teachers: Country Background Report for Ireland', www.oecd.org/document/31/0, 2340,en_2649_34521_1839647_1_1_1_1,00.html

Cosgrove, J., Kellaghan, T., Forde, P. and Morgan, M. (2000) *The 1998 National Assessment of English Reading*, Dublin: Educational Research Centre

Department for Education and Skills (2003) *Research Report RR380. What Works for Children with Literacy Difficulties? The Effectiveness of Intervention Schemes*, London: DfES

Department of Education (1994) *Early Start Programme*, Dublin: Government Publications

Department of Education (1996) *Breaking the Cycle*, Dublin: Government Publications

Department of Education and Science (2001) *Giving Children an Even Break by Tackling Disadvantage*, Dublin: DES

Department of Education and Science (2002) *School Completion Programme*, Dublin: DES

Ehri, L. C. (1992) 'Reconceptualising the Development of Sight Word Reading and its Relationship to Decoding' in Gough, P. B., Ehri, L. C. and Treiman, R. (eds) *Reading Acquisition*, New Jersey: Erlbaum and Associates

Ehrlich, M. F., Kurtz-Costes, B. and Loridant, S. (1993) 'Cognitive and Motivational Determinants of Reading Comprehension in Good and Poor Readers', *Journal of Reading Behaviour*, 25, pp. 365–81

Eivers, E., Shiel, G. and Shortt, F. (2004) *Reading Literacy in Disadvantaged Primary Schools*, Dublin: Educational Research Centre

Government of Ireland (1995) *White Paper on Education – Charting Our Education Future*, Dublin: Government Publications

Irish National Teachers' Organisation (2002) *Intouch*, October 2002, Dublin: INTO

Kelly, D. and Kellaghan, T. (1999) *The Literacy and Numeracy Achievements of the First Cohort Early Start Children (1994/95), When they were in Second Class*, Dublin: Educational Research Centre

Laberge, D. and Samuels, S. J. (1974) 'Toward a Theory of Automatic Information Processing in Reading', *Cognitive Psychology*, 6, pp. 293–323

Lipson, M. Y., Mosenthal, J. H., Mekkelson, J. and Russ, B. (2004) 'Building knowledge and fashioning success one school at a time', *The Reading Teacher*, 57, 6, pp. 534–45

Martin, M. O. and Morgan, M. (1994) 'Reading Literacy in Irish Schools: A Comparative Analysis', *Irish Journal of Education*, 28, pp. 3–101

McGuiness, C. (1998) *Reading Reflex: The Foolproof Method for Teaching Your Child to Read*, Middlesex: Penguin

Morgan, M., Hickey, B., Kellaghan, T., Cronin, A. and Millar D. (1997) *Report to the Minister for Education on the National Adult Literacy Survey Results for Ireland*, Dublin: Government Publications

National Anti-Poverty Strategy (2002) *Building an Inclusive Society: Review of National Anti-Poverty Strategy*, Dublin: Department of Social, Community and Family Affairs

National Commission on Education (1993) *Learning to Succeed: A Radical Look at Education Today and a Strategy for the Future*, London: Heinemann

National Council for Curriculum and Assessment (1999) *Primary School Curriculum: Introduction*, Dublin: Government Publications

Orton Dyslexia Society (1996) *Perspectives on Dyslexia*, 22, 1

Ott, P. (2001) 'Closing the Gaps in Reading Attainment: When dyslexia is successfully managed' in Shiel, G. and Uí Dhálaigh, U. (eds) *Reading Matters: A Fresh Start*, Dublin: Reading Association of Ireland

Phonographix (1998) www.readamerica.net

Pressley, M. (2002) *Reading Instruction that Works: The Case for Balanced Teaching* (2nd edn) New York: Guildford

Shanahan, T. (2001) 'Improving Reading Education for Low-income Children' in Shiel, G. and Ní Dhálaigh U. (eds), *Reading Matters: A Fresh Start*, Dublin: Reading Association of Ireland/National Reading Initiative, pp. 157–65

Shiel, G., Morgan, M. and Larney, R. (1998) *Study of Remedial Education in Irish Primary Schools: Summary Report*, Dublin: Government Publications

Stahl, S. A., Duffy-Hester, A. M., and Stahl, K. A. D. (1998) 'Everything you wanted to Know about Phonics (but Were Afraid to Ask)', *Reading Research Quarterly*, 33, pp. 338–55

Ní Threasaigh, M. (2004) cited in Education Research Centre (2004) *Reading Literacy in Disadvantaged Primary Schools*, Dublin: Educational Research Centre

Warnock, M. (1978) *Special Educational Needs. Report of the Committee of Enquiry into the Education of Handicapped Children and Young People*, London: HMSO

Weir, S., Mills, L. and Ryan, C. (2002) *The Breaking the Cycle Scheme in Urban (and Rural) Schools: Final Evaluation Reports,* Dublin: Educational Research Centre

18

Literacy in Designated Disadvantaged Schools

Eithne Kennedy

Introduction

A goal of the review of the National Anti-Poverty Strategy (2001) was to 'halve the proportion of pupils presenting with serious reading difficulties in schools designated as disadvantaged by 2006'. Despite significant government investment in these schools in terms of resources and staffing and the introduction of the revised primary school English curriculum (NCCA, 1999), this target has not been realised. The first part of this chapter provides a synthesis of the research documenting the magnitude of the achievement gap between children in disadvantaged schools and their peers in non-designated schools and situates it within the wider context of the teaching of English in schools in Ireland. The second part examines international research on the practices and philosophies of successful schools that have beaten the odds and managed to narrow the gap in reading achievement between disadvantaged children and children in the wider population. The third part examines what lessons can be learned from the international research for the Irish context and addresses current policy in relation to literacy in disadvantaged schools.

The Irish context – reading literacy in disadvantaged schools

In response to the target set by the NAPS, a large-scale survey was conducted to establish baseline data on the reading achievement of children in first, third and sixth classes in schools with designated disadvantage status (Eivers, Shiel and

Shortt, 2004). As well as the quantitative data, the survey gathered a rich range of contextual data through interviews with principals, teachers and parents.

It found that between 27 and 30 per cent of children in first, third and sixth class performed at or below the tenth percentile on a national standardised test of reading achievement. This is about three times the national norm, while only 3 per cent of children performed at the top of the scale (above the ninetieth percentile) compared to about 10 per cent nationally. Though children did make some gains between first and sixth class, the difficulties apparent in first class tended to persist as children moved up through the school. Gender differences were noted, with girls consistently outperforming boys across the class levels. While school attendance in general was good (90 per cent average), there was large variation, with some pupils' attendance rates recorded at less than 50 per cent. Other variables considered to impact negatively on performance included: unemployment, having four or more siblings, lone parenthood, poor access to educational materials, and attendance at a school with large proportions of highly disadvantaged peers.

Literacy and numeracy

The Eivers, Shiel and Shortt survey (2004) was followed by the smaller-scale Literacy and Numeracy in Disadvantaged Schools (LANDS) study that involved an in-depth exploration of the literacy and numeracy practices of twelve schools of designated disadvantage status (DES Inspectorate, 2005). While acknowledging the challenging environment in which teachers in disadvantaged schools work, and the contextual factors impinging on their work, the study focused on the quality of teaching and learning within classrooms. Observation data of actual classroom teaching was included, providing, for the first time, a picture of the reality of classroom practice in literacy instruction in schools of disadvantage.

The LANDS report confirmed the serious levels of reading difficulties highlighted in the Eivers, Shiel and Shortt survey, noting that almost half of children in the twelve surveyed schools were performing in the bottom quintile of achievement on standardised tests. In contrast to the survey, it found that achievement scores actually declined as children progressed through the school. Again, high rates of absenteeism were noted as a particular cause of concern, with between 25 and 50 per cent of children absent for more than twenty days of the school year. This correlates with attendance data from the various national reports on attendance to the National Education Welfare Board (NEWB). The most recent report, July 2006 (based on attendance for 2004–2005), found that in areas targeted by the NEWB, mean attendance rates were slightly higher than in 2003–2004. In addition, the mean percentage of pupils in the most disadvantaged primary schools absent for twenty or more days had declined from 28.7 per cent in 2003–2004 to 24.2 per cent in 2004–2005. This is good news, particularly as the 2003–2004 report found significant correlations between low achievement in literacy and poor attendance in the most disadvantaged schools.

With regard to the quality of teaching, the report highlighted significant gaps and weaknesses around the integration of assessment, planning and teaching of literacy. While teachers were using several assessment measures, there was limited analysis and use of this data to inform teaching and to differentiate instruction for the range of learning needs in the classroom. Almost 90 per cent of teachers needed guidance with the use of formative assessment to inform teaching. There was little evidence of collaboration around planning and teaching between learning support and class teachers. Significantly, the quality of classroom planning for literacy was weak in the majority of classes surveyed, with no evidence of a systematic programme for literacy in place.

Recommendations

Both the Eivers, Shiel and Shortt survey (2004) and the LANDS study (DES, 2005) made recommendations to assist schools in implementing effective strategies to address the high levels of low literacy and the gaps and weaknesses identified in teaching. Both studies recommended school-based professional development to be facilitated by the appointment of literacy coordinators to help schools develop detailed plans and set goals. Both recognised the need for highly skilled teachers in literacy and recommended that literacy coordinators be appointed to help teachers develop the necessary skills and understanding in relation to the cyclical nature of planning, teaching and assessment. Of particular interest is the recommendation in the Eivers, Shiel and Shortt survey that the instructional time allocated to literacy should increase to ninety minutes daily. This represents a significant increase in time allocation, currently only four hours weekly, in contrast to many countries which prioritise literacy instruction for up to two hours daily.

National assessments of reading

Other sources of information on the teaching of literacy in Ireland include national assessments of reading and evaluations of the implementation of the English curriculum, 1999. These reports provide insights into literacy achievement and the status of curriculum implementation in English on a national scale. It is worth noting that while the non-disadvantaged schools are not grappling with the challenging conditions associated with disadvantaged schools, they too are having difficulties implementing the English curriculum, 1999.

National assessments in three reading domains – narrative, prose and documents – take place at five-year intervals, allowing for trends in literacy achievement to be recorded and used for policy development. In addition, the assessments collect data on the views of pupils, teachers, principals, learning support teachers and, more recently, the Inspectorate. These national assessments indicate that reading standards have not changed in Ireland since 1980 and that a significant minority of children are performing poorly (Cosgrove et al., 2000; Eivers et al., 2005).

As noted in the survey of disadvantaged schools, gender differences are apparent, with girls outperforming boys on all three domains of reading. This finding is in line with international trends, as the results of the Progress in International Reading Literacy Study (Mullis et al., 2003) indicate that this is also the case in each of the thirty-five participating countries, though Ireland did not participate in this study. As Ireland has not taken part in international literacy surveys at primary level since 1991, it is difficult to say how well Irish students would perform relative to their peers in other countries. However, since Ireland performed at or about the same level as Sweden in the Programme for International Student Assessment (PISA) (Ireland sixth, Sweden seventh), and Sweden was the highest scoring country in PIRLS (2001), it is not unrealistic to expect that Ireland would perform reasonably well if assessed. In 2004, the overall pupil–teacher ratio was 19:1 compared to 27:1 in 1998, yet principals cited large class sizes as a main impediment to teaching reading. Again, like the Eivers, Shiel and Shortt survey, differentiation of classroom teaching for both higher and lower achieving children was considered problematic. Teachers were perceived by more than half of the inspectors to have a limited knowledge of methods of teaching English and one-third indicated that teachers had a poor understanding of the 1999 English curriculum. These findings can be considered alongside the evaluation of the English curriculum (DESI, 2005), which, though published in 2005, only reflects three years of curriculum implementation.

An evaluation of curriculum implementation in primary schools

This evaluation (DESI, 2005) involved twenty-six schools and fifty-nine classroom settings and included data derived from semi-structured interviews, observations of literacy teaching and the examination of school policy documents in English. The report acknowledges that 'significant progress has been achieved in the implementation of the English curriculum in three-quarters of schools'. The biggest areas of identified need were the development of appropriate, detailed, whole-school plans, coordination between the learning support and classroom teacher programmes and the use of a range of assessment policies and tools linked to instruction; up to 60 per cent of schools required guidance with these aspects. Linked to assessment is the concept of differentiation of literacy teaching to cater for the needs of pupils; this was required by 40 per cent of teachers. The teaching of writing using the process approach outlined in the curriculum was identified as being weak in more than half of the schools. Other gaps and weaknesses in instruction for one-third of teachers included the teaching of skills in a meaningful context, the development of higher order thinking skills, the critique of texts and the emotional and imaginative development of the child. Up to one-quarter of teachers were identified as having trouble with the teaching of reading in general.

The surveys and reports of disadvantaged schools, the national assessments of reading and the curriculum evaluations indicate that across school settings teachers are having difficulty teaching literacy. Together they present compelling evidence of the need for change in literacy instruction in all of our schools, not just those designated as disadvantaged.

The international context

There have been a number of attempts to close the achievement gap between children living in poverty and children who are more privileged. There is now a wide body of research providing converging and convincing evidence that the socio-economic status of the school does not necessarily determine the children's learning outcomes; rather there are a number of school-level and individual teacher variables that contribute to success.

Effective schools

The commitment and focus of a stable staff with a shared vision of goals have been found to be significant factors in highly successful schools, along with a large block of uninterrupted time for literacy teaching (Shanahan 2001; Lipson et al., 2004). In addition, the following six factors emerged as critical in increasing reading achievement across five large-scale studies in the US between 1997 and 1999: leadership, professional development, collaboration, systematic assessment of pupils, parental cooperation and specific instructional practices in literacy (Taylor, Pressley and Pearson, 2003).

Leadership

Not surprisingly, strong and determined leadership from within the school was deemed a critical factor. In most cases, leadership was provided either by an experienced principal or teacher with expertise in literacy who ensured it was top of the agenda school-wide. A heavy emphasis was put on unifying the school and on promoting a sense of collective responsibility, with everybody committed to working towards common goals. In practical terms, this translated into providing time on the timetable for collaboration and regular professional development and the provision of the necessary resources to effect changes in literacy instruction.

Professional development

There was a spirit of enquiry evident in the successful schools, and teachers were encouraged to take risks and experiment. This led to teachers owning the change process and contributed to the development of the school as a 'community of learners'. There was an emphasis on helping teachers to develop into reflective practitioners who understood the philosophy and rationale underpinning the methodologies they were using. Professional development was specific to the needs of the school and, most importantly, was ongoing and delivered on-site.

Collaboration

Another critical feature of schools that have beaten the odds is their success in building a sense of collegiality and professional community amongst the staff. Opportunities for staff to truly collaborate rather than just cooperate were apparent. Teachers saw themselves as inquirers, learners and investigators of how best to serve the varied learning needs of the children they taught. Discrete time was provided for teachers to develop teaching methods, plan instruction and assessment procedures and to coordinate the literacy programmes of the classroom teacher and the support teachers.

Systematic assessment of pupils

Successful schools had a balance of both formative and summative assessment procedures. Realistic targets were set for pupil achievement and regular checks were made to ensure that targets were being met. Teachers were adept at using formative assessment tools in reading and writing such as running records, portfolios and observations to plan differentiated instruction for their pupils.

Parental cooperation

Successful schools reached out to parents, establishing true partnerships with them and involving them in concrete ways in helping the school to attain the goal of higher student achievement. Parents' views and opinions were respected and encouraged. Schools used a variety of strategies to involve hard-to-reach parents and in many schools an 'open door' policy encouraged parents to drop in regularly, for example, for coffee in the morning or for lunch in informal 'snack and chat' sessions with the class teacher (Johnson, 2003).

Specific instructional practices in literacy

Successful schools had a balanced literacy framework in place school-wide, and all staff worked to implement it faithfully. There was a minimum commitment to a daily ninety minutes of instruction in literacy that in turn led to opportunities to engage deeply and meaningfully with literacy activities. The specific characteristics of successful teachers and practices are outlined in the next section.

Effective literacy teachers

A growing body of evidence suggests that expert teachers of literacy make a real difference to children's achievement in literacy. They have a variety of methodologies at their fingertips and know when and how to apply and combine them (International Reading Association, 2000). They are well versed in the theory and rationale underpinning these methods and understand the complexity and developmental nature of the literacy process. Several large-scale studies of exemplary teachers have consistently identified the following features in effective classroom instruction: balanced literacy instruction, small group instruction, higher-order thinking activities, and excellent classroom management (Knapp, 1995; Pressley et al., 2001, Taylor and Pearson, 2001).

Balanced literacy instruction

Exemplary teachers ensured that children were engaged in several kinds of reading and writing experiences: read aloud, shared reading, guided reading, independent reading, shared writing, interactive writing and writers' workshop. They integrated the teaching of reading and writing and the essential skills acknowledged as being critical for literacy development – alphabetics/phonemic awareness, phonics, word knowledge, vocabulary, fluency, comprehension (National Reading Panel, 2000) – were embedded in the reading and writing experiences provided. Significantly, classrooms were well stocked with excellent libraries (typically 500 books) containing a wide range of genres (Lipson et al., 2004).

Small group instruction

The classrooms of exemplary teachers were characterised by flexible grouping strategies. Instructional time was balanced between whole-class teaching, small-group and individual work. While teachers worked with individuals or small groups, the rest of the class worked independently and had been taught to self-monitor and direct their learning. Other characteristics included explicit modelling of word-identification, comprehension and writing strategies, followed by extensive scaffolding, coaching and independent practice.

Higher-order thinking skills

Reading was seen as a meaning-making activity rather than a word recognition task. Teachers emphasised a deep understanding of text and provided opportunities for children to critique and respond to text in authentic ways (Knapp et al., 1995). Writing was considered a tool of communication and children wrote in a variety of genres for real purposes and audiences. Lower level skills such as grammar, spelling and punctuation were taught in the context of children's writing as they demonstrated a need for them rather than through skill and drill exercises in workbooks (Pressley et al., 2001).

Excellent classroom management

Teachers taught many more skills per hour and managed the organisation of the class more effectively (Pressley et al., 2001). Instructional time was maximised by focusing 'on academically rich processing' activities rather than on the management and organisation of the classroom (Lipson et al., 2004). Children were motivated and engaged in challenging higher-order activities matched to their instructional needs. Classrooms were characterized by a warm, inviting, open atmosphere and were democratic and responsive to students on both an academic and emotional level (Taylor et al., 1995).

All of the outlined factors provide a road map of how best to proceed to transform schools with high levels of low achievement. The congruence between this international body of research and current Irish policy on disadvantage is presented in the next section.

Current Irish policy on disadvantage

Delivering Equality of Opportunity in School (DEIS) (DES, 2005) is the strategic response of the DES to gaps and weaknesses in educational provision in schools of designated disadvantage identified in the research over the past number of years. It aims to bring coherence to the various government initiatives targeting disadvantage already in place and charts an action plan for the next five years. In relation to raising literacy achievement, it draws on the recommendations of the various reports outlined (*Reading Literacy in Disadvantaged Primary Schools*, *LANDS, An Evaluation of Curriculum Implementation in Primary Schools*). While DEIS contains many essential elements necessary for real change to occur, it lacks specificity in relation to how the ideals and recommendations will actually be realised, particularly in relation to the teaching and learning of English.

Key elements of the change process

The DEIS plan recognises the need for a *whole-school approach* to effectively improve literacy standards. Schools taking part in the change process must develop three-year action plans for literacy and must set targets for achievement. To help schools achieve their goals 'a number of literacy advisers (cuiditheoirí) will be made available through the Primary Curriculum Support Programme (PCSP). It is unclear from the report exactly how many of these advisers will actually be hired, the extent of the training to be provided for them and, critically, the nature and scope of their contact time with schools. The PCSP already has a small number of cuiditheoirí available to support schools requesting help with English. However, in the LANDS study, only a small minority of teachers (up to

15 per cent) indicated that the service was useful. Unless the new cuiditheoir service is tailored to address the specific needs of schools, it may have limited impact. The good news is that much can be achieved with the right support and resources. A recent pilot project involving a partnership between St Patrick's College, Drumcondra, and a school of designated disadvantage succeeded in significantly raising literacy achievement on standardised tests of reading by implementing the best practice already outlined in this chapter.[1]

Professional development

A key component of the change process is the nature and intensity of the professional development provided. It is essential that the cuiditheoir is on-site on a regular basis to ensure continuity between whole-school planning and individual teacher planning. It is also crucial to ensure that all teachers 'own' the change process and understand the theory and rationale underpinning the desired changes. Realistic achievable targets should be agreed and a system put in place to monitor progress. Teachers will require sustained support to address the gaps and weaknesses highlighted by the research. While a high level of support is necessary, it should not erode classroom instructional time. Therefore the recommendation in the Eivers, Shiel and Shortt survey (2004) that substitution cover be put in place for classroom teachers when working with the cuiditheoir should be considered in the DEIS strategy. This kind of quality time would also facilitate collaboration in relation to planning, teaching and assessment between class and support programmes.

Time

A vital element of any change strategy is the provision of the ninety-minute block recommended by the Eivers, Shiel and Shortt survey and international research. This thorny issue is ignored by the DEIS plan. It is important to note that providing extra time will not achieve the desired outcomes unless it is accompanied by a change in the use of the time. Teachers will require support on how to structure the ninety minutes in order to make maximum use of it.

Another aspect that needs to be addressed is the way in which time is currently being used in schools. Classroom time is eroded through withdrawal of children for extra support and, in other cases, for extra-curricular activities that children may not experience given their socio-economic status, making it difficult for the class teacher to find ninety minutes daily to work with the whole class without interruption.

Another significant factor is the breadth of the current primary curriculum. Given that there are now eleven subjects to be taught in the same short school day

---

[1] This is an ongoing project being conducted in a number of schools by literacy practitioners in St Patrick's College.

it has become increasingly pressurised for teachers to find time to teach all subjects well. The early years of school provide a critical window of opportunity for the acquisition of literacy skills and thus should be the priority of every junior school. Literacy skills underpin every other subject in the curriculum and determine how well children can negotiate the demands of each one. Therefore, it would seem that a reappraisal of the breadth of the curriculum at the junior level should take place at policy level.

Class size

The DEIS plan commits to a maximum class size of 20:1 in junior classes and 24:1 in senior classes in the 150 primary schools located in the areas of highest economic disadvantage, though the thirty-two schools in the Breaking the Cycle scheme (Department of Education, 1996) will retain their ratios of 15:1 in junior classes. It must be noted that smaller class sizes have been in place in disadvantaged schools for a number of years and have not contributed to improved literacy levels, at least at national level. Like the provision of extra time noted earlier, smaller class sizes will only be effective if good use is made of formative assessment and teaching is differentiated.

Early intervention

Another key component of the DEIS plan is the extension of the early intervention programme *Reading Recovery* (Clay, 1993) to fifty more schools in phase one (2005–2006) and a further 50 in phase two (2006–2007). This is an individualised pull-out programme for children most at risk of reading failure. Children receive a half hour daily of focused fast-paced instruction in reading and writing for approximately twenty weeks. Teachers are highly trained in the complexities of literacy processes and tailor instruction to the specific needs of children as identified through formative assessment tools such as running records and analysis of writing. The extension of *Reading Recovery* in schools is to be welcomed but it should not be seen as the main method of tackling reading achievement. Because of its individualised nature and its focus on a particular age group, it will only reach a small percentage of the number of children who need integrated, intensive and expert teaching. Therefore it makes sense to focus attention on the quality of instruction at the classroom level.

Classroom instruction and learning support

International research, outlined above, supports balanced literacy instruction combined with flexible grouping strategies, a focus on higher-order thinking skills and excellent classroom management. It is important that teachers are supported in acquiring the expertise to integrate these critical components into their daily practice.

Research literature also notes that lack of congruence between classroom and support programmes makes the process of learning to read confusing and complicated. Many of the teaching routines of the *Reading Recovery* programme can be integrated into the regular classroom and have been successful in other countries (Fountas and Pinnell, 1996; Calkins, 2001). This should also be explored in the Irish context, given the level of investment in *Reading Recovery*. Of critical importance then is the cohesion of support and classroom programmes.

Parental involvement

A crucial feature of successful schools is their ability to reach out to parents in genuine ways and to involve them in their children's education. This is acknowledged in the DEIS plan which indicates a number of initiatives to improve involvement, including the extension of the successful Home School Community Liaison Scheme (HSCL); the promotion of paired reading projects; and the creation of a new collaborative family literacy project involving the Vocational Education Committee (VEC) sector, HSCL coordinators and the National Adult Literacy Agency (NALA). But beyond this the DEIS plan does not provide any other ideas on how individual schools can reach the parents who traditionally do not engage with the school. A successful intervention is the Family School Community Education Partnership, a multi-agency approach to disadvantage, coordinated by Mary Immaculate College. This programme harnesses the expertise and resources of several sectors interested in supporting schools and communities in developing the basic skills of literacy and numeracy and sporting and creative abilities. It endorses system-level change and puts supports in place to help achieve the necessary changes. Successful methods of reaching all parents should be disseminated to schools.

Pre-service and in-career development

Both the LANDS study (2005) and the Eivers, Shiel and Shortt survey (2004) found that a majority of teachers felt that their pre-service training did not adequately prepare them to teach in a disadvantaged setting and teachers were also largely critical of in-career professional development that they had attended in relation to literacy. The DEIS plan states that a key part of the action plan will be 'to work with the Colleges of Education and other course providers to ensure that a significantly increased focus be put on literacy'. A number of constraints at the pre-service level militate against the provision of the kind of experiences that would enable students to develop the depth of expertise now required to teach literacy well. These include the current time allocation for literacy, the high numbers of students on the BEd programme and the current structure of the degree. The provision of a fourth year on the BEd, as strongly recommended in the review of primary teacher education (Government of Ireland, 2002), would allow for a revision of teacher education but is not considered in the DEIS plan. It must also be acknowledged that learning to teach is a life-long pursuit and not everything can be dealt with at pre-service. It would be worth exploring with other partners in education, such as the INTO, the Teaching Council and the DES, how continuous professional development could be made a requirement for all teachers, as it is in some countries.

Conclusion

Shanahan believes that 'powerful reading instruction is longitudinal ... builds on quality, across classes, grade levels and schools' (Shanahan, 2001). Children living in areas of high economic disadvantage require expert teachers who have the skills to teach literacy with 'passion, purpose and energy' (Fullan, 2003b) from the children's very first year of schooling right through to the end of primary school and beyond if they are to become highly skilled readers and writers. Much is known about effective teachers and schools; the challenge is to ensure this message reaches schools and that those in positions of power realise their 'moral imperative' (Fullan, 2003a) to put the structures and funding in place to allow it to happen.

References

Calkins, McCormack L. (2001) *The Art of Teaching Reading*, New York: Addison Wesley

Clay, M. (1993) *Reading Recovery: A Guidebook for Teachers in Training*, Portsmouth, NH: Heinemann

Cosgrove, J., Kellaghan, T., Forde, P. and Morgan, M. (2000) *The 1998 National Assessment of English Reading*, Dublin: Educational Research Centre

Department of Education (1996) *Breaking the Cycle*, Dublin: Government Publications

Department of Education and Science (2005) *DEIS: Delivering Equality of Opportunity in Schools – An Action Plan for Educational Inclusion*, Dublin: DES

Department of Education and Science Inspectorate (2005) *An Evaluation of Curriculum Implementation in Primary Schools*, Dublin: DESI

Department of Education and Science Inspectorate (2005) *Literacy and Numeracy in Disadvantaged Schools (LANDS)*, Dublin: DESI

Eivers, E., Shiel, G. and Shortt, S. (2004) *Reading Literacy in Disadvantaged Primary Schools*, Dublin: Educational Research Centre

Eivers, E., Shiel, G., Perkins, R., and Cosgrove, J. (2005) *The 2004 National Assessment of English Reading*, Dublin: Educational Research Centre

Fountas, I. and Pinnell, G. (1996) *Guided reading: good first teaching for all children*, Portsmouth, NH: Heinemann

Fullan, M. (2003a) *Change forces with a vengeance*, London: Falmer

Fullan, M. (2003b) *The moral imperative of school leadership*, California: Corwin Press

Goodbody Economic Consultants (2001) *Review of the National Anti-Poverty Strategy*, Dublin: Goodbody Economic Consultants

Government of Ireland (2002) *Preparing teachers for the 21st century, Report of the working group on primary pre-service teacher education*, Dublin: Government of Ireland

International Reading Association Board of Directors (2000) *Excellent reading teachers: A position statement of the International Reading Association*, Delaware: International Reading Association

Johnson, J. F. (2003) 'High-performing, high-poverty urban elementary schools' in Taylor, B. M. and Pearson, P. D. (eds) *Effective Schools and Accomplished Teachers*, NJ: Erlbaum, pp. 89–114

Knapp, M. S. (ed.) (1995) *Teaching for meaning in high poverty classrooms*, New York: Teachers College Press

Lipson, M. Y., Mosenthal, J. H., Mekkelson, J. and Russ, B. (2004) 'Building knowledge and fashioning success one school at a time', *The Reading Teacher*, 57, 6, pp. 534–45

Mullis, I. S., Martin, M. O., Gonzalez, E. G. and Kennedy, A. M. (2003) *Progress in International Reading, Literacy Study 2001, International Report: I.E.A. Study in Reading Literacy Achievement in Primary School*, Chestnut Hill, MA: Boston College

National Anti-Poverty Strategy (2001) *Review of the National Anti-Poverty Strategy; Framework Document*, Dublin: Goodbody Economic Consultants

National Council of Curriculum and Assessment (1999) *Primary School Curriculum: English*, Dublin: Government Publications

National Reading Panel (2000) *Teaching children to read: An evidence-based assessment of the scientific research literature on reading and its implications for reading instruction*, summary report, retrieved July 2000 from http://www.nationalreadingpanel.org

Pressley, M., Wharton-McDonald, R., Block, C. C. and Morrow, L. M. (2001) *Learning to read: lessons from exemplary first grade classrooms*, New York: Guilford Press

Shanahan, T. (2001) 'Improving Reading Education for Low-income Children' in Shiel, G. and Ní Dhálaigh U. (eds), *Reading Matters: A Fresh Start*, Dublin: Reading Association of Ireland/National Reading Initiative, pp. 157–65

Taylor, B. and Pearson, D. (2001) 'The Ciera School Change Project: Translating research on effective reading instruction and school reform into practice in high-poverty elementary schools' in Roller, C. M. (ed.) *Learning to Teach Reading, Setting the Research Agenda*, Delaware: International Reading Association, pp. 180–9

Taylor, B. M., Pressley, M. and Pearson, D. (2003) 'Research-supported characteristics of teachers and schools that promote reading achievement' in Taylor, B. M. and Pearson, P. D (eds) *Effective Schools and Accomplished Teachers*, NJ: Erlbaum, pp. 361–73

Taylor, B., Short, R., Shearer, B. and Frye, B. (1995) 'First grade teachers provide early reading instruction in the classroom' in Allington, R. and Walmsley, S. (eds) *No Quick fix: Rethinking Literacy in America's elementary schools*, NY Teachers College: Columbia University

19

Mathematics: A Subject of
Rights and Wrongs?

Thérèse Dooley and Dolores Corcoran

> To fail children in mathematics or to let mathematics fail them is to close off an important means of access to society's resources. (Schoenfeld, 2002, p.13)

Mathematics is intrinsic to our understanding of the world. In fact, mathematics and nature itself are intertwined. Stewart (1995) devotes a book entitled *Nature's numbers: Discovering order and pattern in the universe* to examples of the mathematical characteristics of nature's patterns: the phases of the moon, the petals of flowers, the bilateral symmetry found in many animals, etc. Along with this rather mystical dimension of mathematics, it also has a utilitarian aspect. It helps one to solve practical everyday problems, e.g., financial exchanges; timetabling; measurements of length, weight and volume; data interpretation, etc. The contribution that mathematics makes to personal development is recognised in the primary mathematics curriculum:

> Mathematics education provides the child with a wide range of knowledge, skills and related activities that help him/her to develop an understanding of the physical world and social interactions. It gives the child a language and a system through which he/she may analyse, describe and explain a wide range of experiences, make predictions, and solve problems. Mathematics education fosters creative and aesthetic development, and enhances the growth of reasoning through the use of investigative techniques in a mathematical context. (Government of Ireland, 1999a, p. 2)

However, school mathematics has a function other than as a tool for explaining and interpreting the world in which we live. Success in mathematics has a significant impact on access to jobs and to college courses and, therefore, on the prospect of having a high income in adulthood. Studies around the world have shown that gender, linguistic background, ethnicity and social class impact on successful performance in mathematics. Historically, success at mathematics as a subject has been the prerogative of white middle-class males (Le Doeuff, 1979; Sayers, 1982; Burton, 1992). Furthermore, mathematics is often the focus of discussions on social justice and has been described as a *critical filter* (Sells, 1978), a *social filter* (Zevenbergen, 2001) and *a gatekeeper to social success* (Gates, 2002).

Studies conducted in Ireland on performance in mathematics show that social class is a key factor in tests of mathematical achievement. Children attending schools designated as disadvantaged underperform in such tests when compared to children in schools that are not so designated (Shiel et al., 2006). In a recent evaluation by the DES (Government of Ireland, 2005) it was found that 64 per cent of pupils tested in nine schools designated as disadvantaged achieved scores which fell below the 20 per cent ranking on standardised mathematics tests, and only 2.7 per cent of pupils were reported by schools to have scored within the top band. Moreover, the mathematical achievement of children in these schools appeared to decline as they moved through the primary school. These findings are based on written tests of mathematics that, by their nature, examine a fairly narrow set of skills. Data other than results of standardised tests were also collected. Thirty-five numeracy[1] lessons were observed in a school-based evaluation activity. The inspectors reported that practice in one-quarter of the classes observed was poor because it was characterised by teacher-dominated discussion, whole-class teaching and inadequate use of concrete materials. Nevertheless, it was noted that, in the majority of classrooms, there was appropriate pacing of lessons and engagement by pupils with concrete materials and with suitable activities. Despite this, it was found that the quality of pupils' learning was weak in most of the classes observed, i.e., 'good' practice seemed to have little effect on learning outcomes. Closing the gap between effective teaching and learning outcomes is crucial to addressing the equity issue.[2]

Moses (2001) and Schoenfeld (2002) have both conceived of mathematical literacy as an entitlement of every student in the US regardless of race or socio-economic status. Nearer home, the Programme for International Student Assessment (PISA) – in which Ireland participates – has defined the term 'mathematical literacy' as:

---

[1] Although numeracy has connotations of number work, the inspectorate defined it in terms of all strands and skills of the mathematics curriculum. The authors, however, use the term 'mathematics' throughout this chapter.

[2] For elucidation of assumptions underlying the use of the term 'equity' in mathematics education as opposed to the more familiar 'equality' see Zevenbergen, Dole and Wright, 2004, pp. 48–50

An individual's capacity to identify and understand the role that mathematics plays in the world, to make well-founded mathematical judgements and to engage in mathematics, in ways that meet the needs of that individual's current and future life as a constructive, concerned and reflective citizen (OECD, 1999).

The mathematical powers outlined here are strongly reflected in the aims and objectives of the primary mathematics curriculum (Government of Ireland, 1999a, b), which implies that every citizen is entitled to mathematics teaching that facilitates the development of mathematical literacy. In other words, every child in Ireland has the right to be exposed to 'good mathematics, taught well' (Even and Lappan, 1994, p. 129). So what is good mathematics for primary classrooms? And what constitutes good mathematics teaching in Irish terms? The possibility that various members of the educational community have differing conceptions of terms like 'equity', 'curriculum', 'mathematical achievement' and even of what it means to learn and teach mathematics well makes the accomplishment of equity and excellence in mathematics teaching more difficult. While an in-depth consideration of these issues is outside the scope of this chapter, we will present a summary position and give references so that the reader can pursue the subject in more detail. In particular we will address the following key questions:

- What is the nature of mathematics?
- How might mathematics be 'taught well'?
- What, from an equity perspective, are the implications of mathematics taught well for curriculum, assessment and teacher professional development?

What is the nature of mathematics?

In the quotation at the opening of this chapter, Schoenfeld suggests that mathematics fails children rather than that children fail at mathematics. Gates (2001, p. 7) argues passionately that this is the case:

For many pupils, mathematics is a series of challenges and hurdles, which they face with passion and determination. For many others, however, mathematics is a daily experience of continued failure and irrelevance. Mathematics fails too many children; it fails children on the margins of society, it fails children from ethnic minorities. And it fails children from social and cultural backgrounds that are different from the majority of mathematics teachers.

In order to examine what it is about mathematics that might be disaffecting children, it is necessary to explore, albeit briefly, some philosophies of the nature of mathematics.[3] The absolutist conception of mathematics has traditionally

---

[3] For a more complete treatment of this, see Ernest, 1991

dominated popular and academic thinking (Ernest, 1991). In this field of thought, mathematics is regarded as an objective, immutable body of facts to be handed down from generation to generation. It is characterised by certainty, objectivity and formalism. It is devoid of values and is often felt to be a cold, austere subject. These perceived qualities of mathematics, although presented in a seemingly negative fashion here, do attract some students who are drawn to the certainty and elegance that the subject can offer. However, a growing number of researchers suggest that such a view of the subject serves to alienate many.[4] There is an alternative philosophy of mathematics, fallibilism, in which emphasis is placed on the human side of mathematics. Proponents of this view believe that mathematics is a body of knowledge that is open to change. They maintain that mathematical ideas are not fixed but that they are modified and refined over time. They see mathematics as a cultural activity that is made up of different social practices (Ernest, 2004).

There is also a body of research which shows that teachers' conceptions of mathematics influence their teaching of the subject. Skemp (1979), who differentiated between types of mathematical understanding as 'instrumental' mathematics and 'relational' mathematics, was so acutely aware of differences in conceptions of mathematics among teachers that he claimed that there were two effectively different subjects being taught under the same name *mathematics*. Three conceptions of mathematics have been identified in teachers. First, there exists a dynamic, problem-driven view in which mathematics is seen as a process of enquiry and coming to know. Broadly, this problem-solving view is espoused by the Irish curriculum documents. Second, there is a view of mathematics as a static but unified body of knowledge, 'a crystalline realm of interconnecting structures and truths, bound together by filaments of logic and meaning' (Thompson, 1992, p. 132). This conservative, Platonist view has traditionally informed teaching of mathematics at second level. Third, there is a view of mathematics as a bag of tools, made up of an accumulation of unrelated but utilitarian facts, rules and skills. Thompson observes that it is often possible for teachers to hold conflicting views of mathematics though it is the third, instrumentalist view that is pervasive among pre-service and in-service teachers (Thompson, 1992). More than ever before, today's students need to learn to reason and communicate using mathematical ideas. The primary mathematics curriculum seeks to meet the need of Irish children to become mathematically literate members of society and it implicitly requires that children learn mathematics by being actively engaged. It can therefore be argued that the view of mathematics as being 'in the making' (Hersh and Davies, 1986) is the one most appropriate for teachers (Tymoczko, 1986).

---

[4] See Burton, 1986; Walkerdine, 1998; Lyons et al., 2003, for an exploration of gender differences in mathematical performance

How might mathematics be 'taught well'?

One of the disturbing findings of the recent report by the inspectorate was the mismatch between teaching and learning. It would seem that the use of concrete materials and suitable activities should enhance children's understanding of mathematical concepts but this was not always the case. Interestingly, improvements noted in pupils' learning were linked to growing public confidence levels and were attributed by teachers to increased focus on oral language development (Government of Ireland, 2005). A child-centred approach to the learning of mathematics with an emphasis on the use of manipulative materials was promoted in the 1971 mathematics curriculum (Department of Education, 1971) and is endorsed in the current curriculum (Government of Ireland, 1999a, b). These ideas are reflected in curricula around the world. However, use of concrete materials in and of themselves is not sufficient to ensure pupil learning or even to enhance a pupil's self-concept in mathematics. It is not that curricula throughout the world are ill-advised but rather that interaction with materials does not necessarily denote that the child is constructing his or her own meaning of the world (Cobb, Yackel and Wood, 1992). Let us illustrate with an example. Increasingly, base ten materials are used to help children understand the process of multi-digit addition. Although this is certainly preferable to a 'chalk, talk and drill' methodology, the materials are used to facilitate the child to comprehend a particular method of addition, usually of the following format:

$$
\begin{array}{r}
256 \\
+\ 78 \\
\hline
\end{array}
$$

It is possible that, arising from his or her way of working with the material or from life experience, a child might develop or use an 'invented algorithm' such as the following to calculate the solution:

$$250 + 50 + 26 + 8 \quad \text{or} \quad 260 + 70 + 4 \quad \text{or} \quad 256 + 80 - 2$$

Seldom is the child's own reasoning or sense-making of this process addressed. Priority is given to a single representation and method that is generally decided by the teacher or delineated in a school plan. What is often ignored is the 'hidden curriculum of mathematics education' (Skovsmose, 1990, p. 114). Pupils learn more than a method for solving an addition procedure in this instance. They learn that mathematics as a subject is divorced from their lives; that it comprises a set of skills that are explained, perhaps with materials, and that are repeatedly practised. They learn that it is devoid of creativity. Often, too, speed and competition become the norm in mathematics classes. Emphasis is placed on repetitive practice of 'the method' and on correct solutions. The pupil who attains full marks in weekly tests is lauded. Pupils who perform poorly in this system decide that they are 'no good at maths', a view that usually persists through adulthood and becomes part of their self-image.

A different view of mathematics holds that it is based on the human being's innate ability to problem-solve and make sense of the world and that it is constructed by a community of learners. This kind of mathematics must grow from the child's own experience and so it requires of the teacher that he/she gets to know the children he/she teaches, realises that their world may not necessarily be the world of the teacher or of the textbook but a world nonetheless worthy of respect and exploration. In this scenario, the children's background becomes the foreground for mathematics teaching and learning (Skovsmose, 2002). The teacher is no longer the authority but facilitates a truly interactive approach where pupils discuss, reflect, evaluate, listen, challenge, argue and justify (Burton, 1992). Cotton (2004, p. 37) claims that mathematics can be taught in a way that does not disenfranchise a vast number of students:

> We feel included when we participate actively in the business of learning mathematics. It is something we engage with. In an inclusive mathematics classroom we feel connected to the mathematics we are learning, we can see the point, we can see the big picture. We feel personally empowered through the mathematics we are engaged in. We feel powerful as we use the mathematics we learn to take control over our lives and learn new ways to see the world.

This shift in perspective will mean a change in pedagogy on which there are undoubtedly constraints, particularly annual standardised tests and pressure to complete published schemes of work. Nonetheless, neither teachers nor members of the wider educational community can continue to rely on external factors, such as reduced class sizes and increased financial supports to schools to alleviate the negative effects of the limited mathematics sometimes offered to pupils in schools. Rather, emphasis must be placed on the teaching-learning relationship in mathematics.

Implications

Schoenfeld (2002) points to research conducted in the US which shows that if curriculum assessment and professional development are aligned, students from socially disadvantaged districts can perform as well on meaningful tasks as those from more affluent districts. How might this be achieved? We will examine each of these dimensions in turn in an effort to address this question.

Curriculum

Mathematics education, if it is to be inclusive, must take into account children's cultural approaches and contexts. It must be made meaningful and relevant. There is a danger that this might be interpreted as signifying that certain groups should be considered differently and thus taught distinctive mathematics programmes. Research has shown that such an approach leads to a limited and limiting curriculum. On the other hand, the notion that there should be 'one curriculum for all' also serves to perpetuate inequalities. One way of overcoming inequalities is to examine how mathematics can be taught in a way that is effective for *all* students. Some common themes that have been identified in current research on mathematics education and diversity are that connections between new ideas and old ideas must be made evident *to the learner*; that problems must be embedded in a context that is meaningful for the child; and that emphasis must be placed on a child's intuitive representations and informal procedures (Carey et al., 1995). This is echoed by Malloy (1999); she suggests that pedagogy, not content, must become multi-cultural and that this can be realised by valuing the many and various ways that children make sense of mathematics. Only then can a non-threatening environment for mathematics learning be created.

A common practice in schools in areas of social disadvantage is to focus on basic skills. In the teaching and learning of these skills, reference is frequently made to money since this is considered to be directly within students' experience and of use to them. However, by limiting the mathematics taught in this way, children may be deprived of opportunities to develop mathematical skills that are central to the primary mathematics curriculum: applying and problem-solving; communicating and expressing; integrating and connecting; reasoning; implementing, understanding and recalling. The result is that access to the skills of critical reasoning is restricted to those who are already considered to be advantaged (Apple, 1995). A tradition of low expectations contributes to low standards of achievement and contravenes the right of every student to learn 'a significant core of challenging and meaningful mathematics' (North Central Regional Educational Laboratory, 2006). Central to the notion of mathematics for all is the assumption that, while an understanding of mathematics is linked to children's cultural referents, all children are capable of mastering the subject matter (Ladson-Billings, 1995).

A recent trend in textbooks and standardised tests is the inclusion of 'realistic problems'. Although well-intentioned, these problems bear little relationship to children's lives and are often sanitised and trivial. Real problems stemming from 'authentic' material are a means of empowering individuals to deal with the world in which they live. The kind of material Ernest (2001) recommends includes aspects of the local environment such as parks and playgrounds, media, 'local folk' mathematics and health education. He envisages that children would use these to engage in critique, make balanced judgements, reason and justify. Finding such material is difficult. However, teachers should be prepared to learn about the children in their care, and to provide opportunities for them to explore and quantify their environments. The identification of authentic resources could become the focus of curriculum planning days and might extend to include parent representatives in planning and target-setting for mathematics teaching and learning.

Assessment

It is well recognised that mathematics pedagogy is influenced by testing policy (Darling-Hammond, 1994; Tate and Johnson, 1999). High-stakes, standardised testing has a particularly negative impact on classroom practice – often leading to the phenomenon of 'teaching to the test'. In such tests, there is seldom scope to score children's reasoning, their evaluation of solutions or their ability to communicate findings. There is generally a focus on low-level procedural skills, a factor that has been identified as disenfranchising students from mathematics. The move towards making assessment items more 'real' for children may, ironically, do nothing more than sustain performance differences. There is a body of literature which shows that children from middle-class and professional backgrounds come to school armed with *cultural capital* required for school (Bourdieu, 1989). This gives them greater access to the language and the hidden rules of mathematics (Walkerdine, 1990; Zevenbergen, 2001). Research conducted by Cooper and Dunne (2000) shows that children from low socio-economic status (SES) backgrounds perform as well as their peers from higher SES backgrounds on decontextualised problems but that when presented with problems embedded in a context, their performance declines. They suggest that 'realistic' items are not actually meant to be treated as real-world problems. However, whereas children from higher SES backgrounds tend to pick up on the cues implicit in these items, children from lower SES backgrounds are more likely to draw 'incorrectly' on everyday experiences in their responses. In standardised tests, only a single correct answer is valued and, therefore, results of these tests can mask children's mathematical reasoning.

If assessment is to be aligned with an equitable curriculum, it needs to cover a wide range of content and thought processes and not be confined to those that are easily measured. Authentic assessment, examples of which include portfolios, projects, performance tasks, and structured teacher observation, can be a tool for change (Darling-Hammond 1994; Murphy, 1995). But if testing continues to be used as a means of limiting students' choices rather than as a diagnostic tool and a means of supporting and enhancing student learning, the observed inequalities in mathematics education will persist.[5] If one is serious about the notion of equity and improvement of standards, assessment should be aligned with the curriculum.

Teacher professional development

The students who present for primary teacher education are themselves the products of mathematics education in second-level schools that has been dominated by consideration of syllabus content and assessment (English and Oldham, 2004). This cycle of learning and teaching is a somewhat 'chicken and egg' situation. Any move towards helping students build 'the mathematical habits of mind that support increased learning' (Kaput and Blanton, 2005, p. 100) must start early. But it is difficult for teachers whose experience of school mathematics has consisted of rules and procedures to develop higher-order mathematical skills in themselves and in their pupils. The length of time required to effect meaningful changes in practices of mathematics teaching has implications for the design of continuous professional development for teachers. British research (Ofsted, 2006) confirms earlier findings (Hill and Rowe, 1998) that the single most important factor influencing student achievement in mathematics is the quality of teaching. What is required is that primary teachers need to conceptualise mathematics differently. Ma (1999), for example, has talked about a profound understanding of elementary mathematics as characteristic of Chinese elementary school teachers. Tate and Johnson (1999) maintain that an indicator of teacher quality is the extent to which teachers understand and extend their pupil's thinking and reasoning about mathematics. Observations made by inspectors relating to mathematics teaching in designated disadvantaged schools are that 'more than half the planning was weak' and 'fewer than half the teachers established linkages between strands of mathematics' (Government of Ireland, 2005, p. 49, p. 51). These comments refer to instances of the paucity of teachers' pedagogical content knowledge rather than of procedural knowledge of how to 'do' the mathematics involved. Such situations can be remedied by site-specific continuous professional development[6] which is focused on building mathematical capacity in the teachers themselves and on enhancing their teaching of mathematics through study of curriculum, effective use of teaching materials and observation of how their students learn.

Conclusion

In a recent article in the *Irish Times* entitled 'Economy could start to count the cost of our mathematical failure' (Butler, 2006), the poor performance of students in state mathematics examinations was lamented. Mathematics was identified as

---

[5] See Darling-Hammond, 1994, and Black and William, 2003, for a fuller treatment of this topic

[6] For a fuller exposition of the potential of Japanese Lesson Study to develop mathematics teaching, see Lewis, 2002; Kelly and Sloane, 2003; and Sloane, 2005.

a subject that is crucial to the growth of a knowledge base in our society. The author condemned the emphasis that is placed on procedural skills and called for a new approach to teaching mathematics. The act of teaching to develop mathematical process skills implies a huge change of classroom culture, a change of classroom organisation and, ultimately, a change of understanding of what it means to do mathematics as a pupil and as a teacher (Schifter and Bastable, 1995). Although these changes are complex, they open the gate to a mathematics that is relevant, engaging and inclusive. Good mathematics taught well has the potential to right some wrongs.

References

Apple, M. W. (1995) 'Taking power seriously: New directions in equity in mathematics education and beyond' in Secada, W.G., Fennema, E. and Adajian, L.B. (eds) *New directions for equity in mathematics education*, Cambridge: Cambridge University Press, pp. 329–48

Black, P. and William, D. (2003) 'In praise of educational research: Formative assessment,' *British Educational Research Journal*, 29, 5, pp. 623–37

Bourdieu, P. (1989) *The State Nobility: Elite Schools in the Field of Power*, Cambridge: Polity Press; first published in France (1988) as *La Noblesse d'Etat: Grand Ecoles et Esprit de Corps*

Burton, L. (1986) *Girls into maths can go*, London: Holt, Rinehart and Winston

Burton, L. (1992) 'Evaluating an "entitlement curriculum": Mathematics for all?', *The Curriculum Journal*, 3, 2, pp. 161–9

Butler, B. (9 May 2006) 'Economy could start to count the cost of our mathematical failure', *Irish Times*, p. 14

Carey, D., Fennema, E., Carpenter, T. P., and Franke, M. L. (1995) 'Equity and mathematics education' in Secada, W.G., Fennema, E. and Adajian, L. B. (eds) *New directions for equity in mathematics education*, Cambridge: Cambridge University Press, pp. 93–125

Cobb, P., Yackel, E. and Wood, T. (1992) 'A constructivist alternative to the representational view of mind in mathematics education', *Journal for Research in Mathematics Education*, 23, 1, pp. 2–33

Cooper, B. and Dunne, M. (2000) *Assessing children's mathematical knowledge: Social class, sex and problem-solving*, Buckingham: Open University Press

Cotton, T. (2004) 'Inclusion through mathematics education', *Mathematics Teaching*, 187, pp. 35–40

Darling-Hammond, L. (1994) 'Performance-based assessment and educational equity', *Harvard Educational Review*, 64, 1, pp. 5–30

Department of Education (1971) *Curaclam na Bunscoile: Primary School Curriculum, Part 1*, Dublin: Government Publications

English, J. and Oldham, E. (2004) 'Continuing professional development for mathematics teachers: Meeting needs in the Republic of Ireland', paper presented at 29th Annual Conference of the Educational Studies Association of Ireland

Ernest, P. (1991) *The Philosophy of Mathematics Education*, London: Falmer Press

Ernest, P. (2001) 'Critical mathematics education' in Gates, P. (ed.) *Issues in mathematics teaching*, London: RoutledgeFalmer, pp. 277–93

Ernest, P. (2004) 'Postmodernism and the Subject of Mathematics' in Walshaw, M. (ed.) *Mathematics Education within the Postmodern*, Greenwich, CT: Information Age Publishing

Even, R. and Lappan, G. (1994) 'Constructing meaningful understanding of mathematics content' in Aichele, D. B. and Coxford, A. F. (eds) *NCTM Yearbook on Professional Development for Teachers of Mathematics 1994*, Reston, VA: NCTM, pp. 128–43

Gates, P. (2001) 'What is an/at issue in mathematics education?' in Gates, P. (ed,) *Issues in mathematics teaching*, London: RoutledgeFalmer, pp. 7–20

Gates, P. (2002) 'Issues of equity in mathematics education: Defining the problem, seeking solutions' in Haggarty, L. (ed.) *Teaching mathematics in secondary schools: A Reader*, London: RoutledgeFalmer

Government of Ireland (1999a) *Primary School Mathematics Curriculum*, Dublin: Government Publications

Government of Ireland (1999b) *Primary School Mathematics: Teacher Guidelines*, Dublin: Government Publications

Government of Ireland (2005) *Literacy and numeracy in disadvantaged schools: Challenges for teachers and learners – An evaluation by the Inspectorate of the Department of Education and Science*, Dublin: Government Publications

Hersh, R. and Davies, P. (1986) *Descartes' dream: the world according to mathematics*, London: Penguin

Hill, P. and Rowe, K. (1998) 'Multilevel modelling in school effectiveness research', *School Effectiveness and School Improvement*, 7, pp. 1–34

Kaput, J. and Blanton, M. (2005) 'A teacher-centered approach to algebrafying elementary mathematics' in Romberg, T. and Carpenter, T. (eds) *Understanding mathematics and science matters*, New Jersey: Lawrence Erlbaum Associates, pp. 99–126

Kelly, A. and Sloane F. (2003) 'Educational Research and the Problems of Practice,' *Irish Educational Studies*, 22, 1, pp. 29–40

Ladson-Billings, G. (1995) 'Making mathematics meaningful in multicultural contexts' in Secada, W.G., Fennema, E. and Adajian, L. B. (eds) *New directions for equity in mathematics education*, Cambridge: Cambridge University Press, pp. 126–45

Le Doeuff, M. (1979) 'Operative Philosophy: Simone de Beauvoir and existentialism', *Ideology and Consciousness*, 6, pp. 47–58

Lewis, C. (2002) 'Does lesson study have a future in the United States?' *Nagoya Journal of Education and Human Development*, 1, 1, pp. 1–23

Ma, L. (1999) *Knowing and teaching elementary mathematics*, Mahwah, NJ: Earlbaum

Malloy, C. E. (1999) 'Developing mathematical reasoning in the middle grades: Recognizing diversity' in Stiff, L. V. and Curcio, F. R. (eds) *Developing Mathematical Reasoning in grades K-12: 1999 Yearbook*, Reston, VA: NCTM, pp. 13–21

Moses, R. (2001) *Radical equations: Math literacy and civil rights*, Boston: Beacon Press

Murphy, P. (1995) 'Sources of inequity: understanding students' responses to assessment', *Assessment in Education*, 2, 3, pp. 249–70

North Central Regional Educational Laboratory (2006) 'Critical issue: Ensuring equity and excellence in mathematics', www.ncrel.org/sdrs/areas/issues/content/cntareas/math/ma100.htm, last accessed 12/06/2006

Office for Standards in Education (2006) 'Evaluating mathematics provision for 14–19-year-olds', www.ofsted.gov.uk/publications, last accessed 12/06/2006

Organisation for Economic Cooperation and Development (1999) *Measuring student knowledge and skills: A new framework for assessment,* Paris: OECD

Sayers, J. (1982) *Biological politics*, London: Methuen

Schifter, D. and Bastable, V. (1995) 'From the teachers' seminar to the classroom: The relationship between doing and teaching mathematics, an example from fractions', paper presented at the American Educational Research Association, San Francisco

Schoenfeld, A. (2002) 'Making mathematics work for all children: Issues of standards, testing, and equity', *Educational Researcher,* 31, 1, pp. 13–25

Sells, L. (1978) 'Mathematics: A critical filter', *Science Teacher*, 45, pp. 28–9

Shiel, G., Surgenor, P., Close, S., and Miller, D. (2006) *The 2004 National Assessment of Mathematics Achievement*, Dublin: Educational Research Centre

Skemp, R. (1979) *Intelligence, learning and action: A foundation for theory and practice in education*, New York: John Wiley and Sons

Skovsmose, O. (1990) 'Mathematical Education and Democracy', *Educational Studies in Mathematics*, 21, pp. 109–28

Skovsmose, O. (2002) 'Students foreground and the politics of learning obstacles' in De Monteiro, M. (ed.) *Proceedings of the second international conference of ethnomatthematics*, CD-Rom, Ouro Preto, Brazil: Lyrium Comunacacao

Sloane, F. (2005) 'Japanese teachers lesson study in mathematics education as an exemplar of design research' in Close, S., Dooley, T. and Corcoran, D. (eds)

Proceedings of First National Conference on Research in Mathematics Education, Dublin: St Patrick's College

Stewart, I (1995) *Nature's numbers: Discovering order and pattern in the universe*, London: Phoenix

Tate, W. F. and Johnson, H. C. (1999) 'Mathematical reasoning and educational policy: Moving beyond the policy of dead language' in Stiff, L. V. and Curcio, F. R. (eds) *Developing Mathematical Reasoning in grades K-12: 1999 Yearbook*, Reston, VA: NCTM, pp. 221–33

Thompson, A. (1992) 'Teachers beliefs and conceptions: a synthesis of the research' in Grouws, D. A. (ed.) *Handbook of research on mathematics teaching and learning*, New York: Macmillan

Tymoczko, T. (1986) *New directions in the philosophy of mathematics*, New York: Birkhaüser

Walkerdine, V. (1990) 'Difference, Cognition and Mathematics Education', *For the Learning of Mathematics*, 10, 3, pp. 51–6

Walkerdine, V. (1998) *Counting girls out (New Edition): Girls and mathematics,* Studies in Mathematics Education Series: 8, London: Falmer Press

Zevenbergen, R. (2001) 'Language, social class and underachievement in school mathematics' in Gates, P. (ed.) *Issues in mathematics teaching*, London: RoutledgeFalmer, pp. 38–50

Zevenbergen, R., Dole, S. and Wright, R. (2004) *Teaching mathematics in primary schools*, Sydney: Allen and Unwin

20

An Early Intervention that Counts

Yvonne Mullan and Joseph Travers

Introduction

The acquisition of mathematical skills and knowledge is essential in a numerate society, and how these skills and knowledge are developed is a matter of much debate. Evidence suggesting that there can be a three-year gap in achievement levels in early numeracy by the time children go to school gives an added focus to this debate (Griffin, Case and Siegler, 1994; Wright, 1994). There are equity and social justice dimensions to this issue, in that the vast majority of children at risk of mathematical failure come from low-income families living in areas of socio-economic disadvantage. Without appropriate intervention this gap in achievement can be as much as seven years by the age of eleven (Cockcroft, 1982). Here we focus on an intervention programme that narrowed the achievement gap in one Dublin suburb in 2005.

Weir (2003) reports on the deterioration in mathematical standards in Irish urban schools involved in the *Breaking the Cycle* initiative in disadvantaged areas. The percentage of pupils scoring below the tenth percentile on a standardised mathematics assessment at the end of sixth class increased from 35.5 per cent in 1997 to 45.6 per cent in 2003. These results were actually inflated, as they did not include 7.7 per cent of pupils deemed by their teachers to be too weak in mathematics to sit the test. The inspectorate, in its evaluation of twelve disadvantaged schools, found that 73 per cent of the pupils in the final two grades of primary school had scores on standardised numeracy tests at or below the twentieth percentile (DES, 2005).

Counting in early number development

Early mathematics curricula have been heavily influenced by the ideas of Piaget. He believed that children were incapable of understanding number until they could understand one-to-one correspondence, ordering and number conservation, also called the concept of numerosity. Arithmetic ability, he believed, arose from general cognitive abilities (Piaget, 1952). This led to early number curricula stressing the activities of sorting, matching, classifying and ordering, which incidentally are the early mathematics activities in the revised 1999 Irish mathematics curriculum. In this approach, counting and learning number words are not necessary in constructing the concept of numerosity (Butterworth, 2005).

Alternative perspectives have challenged this view on two fronts. Firstly, there is evidence that 'broadly supports the idea of an innate specific capacity for acquiring arithmetic skills' as against general cognitive abilities (Butterworth, 2005, p. 3). Secondly, there is substantial evidence that counting is inextricably linked to the development of number knowledge (McLellan, 1993; Munn, 2001). Children learn how to count long before they understand the implications of their actions; and sorting, matching, classifying, and ordering, while important skills in their own right, do not on their own automatically lead to an understanding of number (Baroody, 1987).

Building on the work of Resnick (1983), who proposed that young children represented the addition process like a mental number line, on the work of Siegler (1976) on children's quantitative understandings, and on Gelman and Gallistel's (1978) principles of counting, Griffin, Case and Siegler (1994) devised a model of the organising schemata which, they propose, is central to children's understanding of early addition and subtraction. These schemata, which they term 'central conceptual structures' for conceptualising the world in terms of quantitative dimensions, are show below in Figure 1 (Griffin, Case and Siegler , 1994, p. 35).

Figure 1 'Mental Counting Line', Central Conceptual Structure

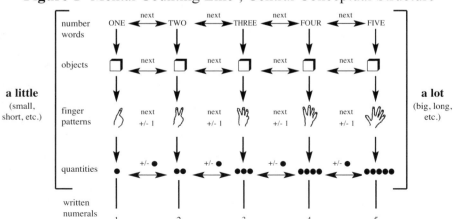

This structure describes the intuitive knowledge that appears to underlie successful learning of arithmetic in the early years of formal schooling. The top row of the structure is the *verbal labelling* line – children can recognise and generate the number words one … two … three … The second row is the *mental action line*, meant to capture the idea that children have a routine for pointing at or tagging a set of objects as they say the number words in such a way that each object is tagged only once in the process. Initially this is a sensory-motor process, which can only be applied to real objects, but it becomes a purely cognitive one, which mentally simulates the more primitive sensory motor activity (Case and Okamoto, 1996). The third and fourth rows represent the 'conceptual interpretation' through which children understand that each number label has a set size associated with it and that this set size has a certain canonical perceptual form. The children also understand that movement from one of these set sizes to the next involves the addition or subtraction of one unit. The bottom row indicates that children can recognise the written numerals from one to five. The horizontal arrows indicate transformations or rules for movement that allow children to move forwards and backwards from one item to the next in any row. The vertical arrows signify that children understand that there is a one-to-one mapping between each row and the next. The big brackets at the end indicate that the child knows that movement forward or backwards along these rows is a movement towards more or less (Griffin and Case, 1997, p. 8). This knowledge was proposed as being central to the conceptual understanding and development of early addition and subtraction skills and its absence represented the main barrier to the acquisition of these skills (Griffin, Case and Siegler, 1994).

A number knowledge test-designed to assess mastery of this knowledge revealed large differences in performance between children 'from low-income communities' (Griffin, Case and Siegler, 1994, p. 39) and middle-income children. A curriculum called Rightstart was designed to specifically teach the knowledge components underpinning central conceptual structure theory. The intervention aimed to test the theory that such knowledge was central, and bridged the conceptual gaps between children's understanding and that implied in the mental counting line structure. Thirty interactive small group games were devised, each targeting components of the structure.

The programme was used over a period of three years with small groups and whole classes of kindergarten children attending schools in Canada, Massachusetts and California. The children were all attending inner-city schools with large minority populations and were from low-income communities with school populations considered to be at risk of school failure. In an evaluation of the programme, using control groups, the gap between these groups was eliminated in four studies in the US and Canada in six separate schools. The results of the studies indicated that the Rightstart programme was effective in enabling children to acquire the conceptual knowledge that it was designed to teach. A transfer effect was seen in children's results on a money-knowledge test and a time-telling test, and positive effects of the Rightstart programme were evident one full year after the programme ended when the children were in first grade (Griffin, Case and Siegler, 1994). The evidence seems to support the authors' contention that 'it enabled children to acquire the numerical understandings specified in the central conceptual structure' (p. 48).

Number Worlds

When children come to school without the competencies implied in the central conceptual structure, it can mean that there has not been a heavy emphasis on counting and quantity in their early environments (Griffin and Case, 1997). Griffin and Case advocated that these structures should be the core focus of the early school curriculum, so that children who have not yet acquired the conceptual structures will have an opportunity to do so and children who already have them will have an opportunity to strengthen them. After Rightstart, Griffin and Case developed a more comprehensive set of programmes called Number Worlds. The Number Worlds programme was guided by feedback from teachers who taught the programme and by observation of the difficulties encountered by teachers who tried to implement underlying principals. According to Griffin and Case (1997) three salient features distinguish Number Worlds from other early years programmes: the programme teaches intuitive and explicit number knowledge that has been found to be central in later learning; it is a child-centred programme with hands-on activities that encourage children to construct their own mathematical meaning; and it introduces children to a broad range of contexts in which number is used (line, scale and dial representations of number and quantity) and to a range of linguistic terms that are used in these contexts.

Number Worlds study

The instructional principles of the Number Worlds programme were suitable for use as a mathematics intervention in an urban school designated as disadvantaged. The programme has been shown to be appropriate for children from a wide range of cultural, social and economic backgrounds. This point is particularly relevant in that in many disadvantaged schools there is a wide range of cultural backgrounds.

Given the lack of emphasis in the Irish mathematics curriculum on the importance of early counting and its link to number development we felt that a similar intervention might be beneficial for children at risk of mathematical difficulties in Irish schools.

Methodology

The effectiveness of the Number Worlds programme was evaluated using a multi-methods approach incorporating a quasi-experimental research design. During a ten-week period in the school year 2004–2005 the Number Worlds preschool programme was used in a junior infant class in a school designated as disadvantaged. The mean pre-test and post-test scores on the number knowledge test (NKT) (Griffin and Case, 1997) of the experimental group were compared with those of a matched control group in the same school and with two other control groups in a non-designated school. Analyses of data from a teacher interview, a video recording and from participant observation field notes were included in the evaluation of the Number Worlds programme.

Participants

The groups were pre-existing junior infant class groups in two schools. The Number Worlds (experimental) group and the matched control group were in the same disadvantaged school and thus were matched in terms of age, class, and community.

Both teachers were told that Number Worlds was a maths intervention for children which had been used successfully in the US and Canada to improve the number knowledge of children in areas of socio-economic disadvantage. They were both told that the programme emphasised the importance of counting in the development of number knowledge. The control and experimental groups were also matched in terms of the time allocated to maths during the school day as both abided by National Council for Curriculum and Assessment (NCCA) guidelines of thirty-five to forty minutes a day. There was a difference in teacher experience as the teacher of the control group had seven years' experience teaching junior infants and the teacher of the experimental group had not taught junior infants before.

The control group followed the revised junior infant mathematics curriculum. Counting is one of the strands of the junior infant curriculum, though not one of the early mathematics activities advocated, and therefore children in the control group would have counted but largely in a whole-class format. The children in the experimental group counted every day as a whole class and then in small groups through structured games. These sessions were followed by a short session where one child from each group had to tell the class about the game played in his or her small group. The pre-Number Worlds programme lasted for forty minutes one day per week for six weeks. The Number Worlds programme was implemented for a ten-week period.

Two further control groups, ND (non-disadvantaged) Control 1 and ND Control 2, were matched with the Number Worlds group in terms of age and class but not in terms of community as they were in a non-disadvantaged school. Like the control group, they followed the revised junior infant mathematics curriculum over the same time frame.

Differences between the number of pupils, mean ages, gender balance and numbers of international children in each of the four classes can be seen in Table 1.

Table 1 Details of class groups: Number, Mean Age, Gender Balance and Number of International Children

	Experimental	Matched Control	ND Control 1	ND Control 2
Number	21	21	20	24
Mean Age	4.92	4.87	5.04	4.86
Boys	10	9	11	11
Girls	11	12	9	13
International Pupils	9	11	0	5

Limitations of the study

One limitation of the research was the non-randomised nature of the sample while a second was the sample size. Further research into the effect of Number Worlds should be done with a larger randomised sample to allow more definitive and more advanced statistical analysis, and differences between gender and ethnic groups should also be examined. Furthermore, in the original research, the Number Worlds programme was implemented for four and five months and the teachers who implemented the programme received Number Worlds training; in the current study the teacher who implemented Number Worlds was self-instructed and the implementation period lasted for only ten weeks.

Results analysis

An analysis of variance followed by a post-hoc test (Tukey, Highly Significant Differences (HSD)) revealed the differences between the four groups before and after the Number Worlds intervention. The pre- and post-test differences had an F-value of 3.85 (p = .012) and post-test differences an F-value of 4.17 (p = .008). The difference between the pre-test mean scores of the experimental group and ND Control 1 was statistically significant. (See Table 2)

A post-hoc test (Tukey HSD) confirmed that the difference between the pre-test mean score of the experimental group and ND Control 1 was unlikely to have arisen by sampling error (p = .009). Table 3 shows the differences in group mean pre-test scores on the NKT between the experimental group and the control groups and between the matched control groups and the non-disadvantaged control groups and their significance levels.

Table 2 NKT pre- and post-test group mean raw scores and standard deviations (maximum score = 33)

	Group	Mean	Standard Deviation	N
Pre-test	Experimental	6.10	3.872	21
	Matched Control	7.33	4.778	21
	ND Control 1	10.60	5.030	20
	ND Control 2	8.58	4.042	24
	Total	8.14	4.653	86
Post-test	Experimental	11.38	3.217	21
	Matched Control	10.19	4.718	21
	ND Control 1	14.65	4.332	20
	ND Control 2	12.67	4.469	24
	Total	12.21	4.462	86

ND Control 1 and 2 are the control groups in the non-designated school.

Table 3 Differences in group mean pre-test scores on the NKT between the experimental and matched control groups

(I) GROUP	(J) GROUP	Mean Difference (I-J)	Std. Error	Sig.	95% Confidence Interval Lower Bound	95% Confidence Interval Upper Bound
Experimental	Matched Control	-1.24	1.369	.802	-4.83	2.35
	ND Control 1	*-4.50	1.386	.009	-8.14	-.87
	ND Control 2	-2.49	1.325	.246	-5.96	.99
Matched Control	Experimental	1.24	1.369	.802	-2.35	4.83
	ND Control 1	-3.27	1.386	.094	-6.90	.37
	ND Control 2	-1.25	1.325	.782	-4.73	2.23

* The mean difference is significant at the .05 level.

After the intervention, the mean post-test score of the experimental group was not significantly different from the mean score of any of the other groups. Thus, the significant difference between the experimental group and ND Control 1 had been reduced and was no longer significant. However, this was not the case with the matched control group who made less progress and whose mean post-test score was lower than that of all other groups and was significantly lower than that of ND control 1 (p = .006). Table 4 shows the differences in group mean post-test scores on the NKT between the experimental group and the control groups and between the matched control groups and the non-designated disadvantaged control groups and their significance levels.

Table 4 Differences in group mean post-test scores on the NKT between the experimental and matched control groups

(I) GROUP	(J) GROUP	Mean Difference (I-J)	Std Error	Sig.	95% Confidence Interval Lower Bound	Upper Bound
Experimental	Matched C.G.	1.19	1.306	.799	-2.23	4.61
	ND Control 1	-3.27	1.322	.072	-6.74	.20
	ND Control 2	-1.29	1.264	.740	-4.60	2.03
Matched control	Experimental	-1.19	1.306	.799	-4.61	2.23
	ND Control 1	*-4.46	1.322	.006	-7.93	-.99
	ND Control 2	-2.48	1.264	.212	-5.79	.84

* The mean difference is significant at the .05 level.

The differences between the improvement in the pre- and post-test mean scores can be seen clearly in Figures 2 and 3. At pre-test, the experimental group was weaker than all other groups. The mean score of the experimental group was 17 per cent lower than the mean score of the matched control and almost 40 per cent lower than the ND Control 1. After the Number Worlds intervention, the mean score of the experimental group had increased by 87 per cent. This contrasts with the 39 per cent improvement in the mean score of the matched control group, 38 per cent in ND Control 1 and 48 per cent in the ND Control 2. As a result, the mean score of the experimental group was higher than that of the matched control group and the significant gap between the mean scores of the experimental group and ND Control 1 had decreased from 74 per cent at pre-test score to a 29 per cent difference at post-test.

Figure 2 NKT pre- and post-test differences

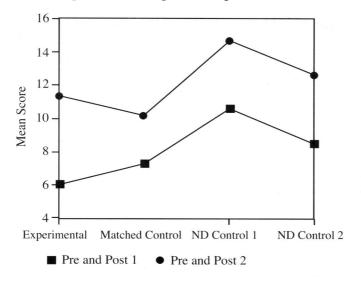

■ Pre and Post 1   ● Pre and Post 2

Figure 3 Pre- and post-test mean scores and % increase in mean score of each group

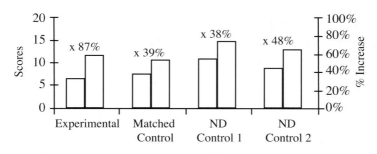

The number knowledge test results indicated that the lowest-performing pupils in the experimental group made substantially more progress than the lowest-performing pupils in the matched control group. The progress of low-attaining pupils in the experimental group and in the matched control group can be seen in Figure 4. Means and standard deviations can be seen in Table 5. The mean low score of the experimental group went from 2.33 at pre-test to 9.44 at post-test, while the mean low score of the matched control group went from 1.71 at pre-test to 5.14 at post-test.

Figure 4

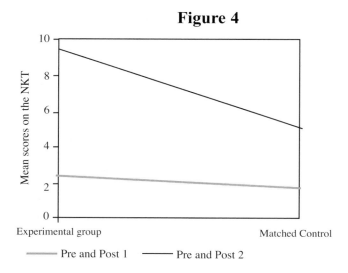

Differences in mean scores between pre- and post-test on the NKT for low-scoring students (raw score <6) in experimental

Table 5

Mean and standard deviation and number of low-attaining children, experimental and matched control groups (raw score <6) in experimental (n = 9) and matched control group (n = 7)

Group		Mean	Standard Deviation	Number of Children
Experimental	Pre-test	2.33	1.58	9
	Post-test	9.44	2.96	1
Matched Control	Pre-test	1.71	1.70	7
	Post-test	5.14	3.80	4

Discussion

There were two noteworthy outcomes from the study. The first was that the gap between the experimental group and their peers in the non-designated disadvantaged school was no longer significant (Table 4). The second was the improvement in test scores of children in the experimental group whose pre-test scores had indicated a developmental delay of up to two years (Table 5). The lowest attainers in the experimental group at pre-test made substantially greater gains than the lowest attainers in the matched control group. It is possible that these two outcomes were due to the structured and multiple opportunities for counting that were provided in the Number Worlds programme.

These opportunities for counting were made possible by a second distinctive and integral feature of the programme, small group work. Small group work was a worthwhile but a demanding feature of the programme as it was in small groups that children had opportunities to construct their own knowledge about number with help from their peers. However, when groups were not supervised adequately or professionally, some children did not engage, some became disengaged and others had difficulty playing games correctly. The demands of organising and supervising differentiated work groups are onerous. There is certainly a role for support for this activity through in-class collaboration between the class teacher and the learning support/resource teacher as well as the valuable contribution special needs assistants and parents could make in this area.

The NKT results indicated that half of the children in this study had started school with less number knowledge than the other half. This begs the question as to whether the curriculum is tailored to address this diversity. Disadvantage initiatives were impacting positively for children in the designated school, but they did not appear to significantly alter the number experiences of children in the school. If, as Griffin and Case (1997) suggest, less conceptual number knowledge is due to a lack of emphasis on counting and quantity in the early environment, then the sooner that there is such an emphasis in school, the better it will be for those who do not get the benefit of such experiences at home. Counting is not included in the Early Mathematical Activities in the mathematics primary school curriculum (DES, 1999); it is included as one of the strand units in the number strand of the junior infant curriculum. There is a professional freedom implicit in the primary school mathematics curriculum that allows teachers to meaningfully adapt and change teaching methods, content and learning experiences to meet children's needs. However, there is a dearth of information about what type of adaptation is possible or desirable. The in-service education that has accompanied the introduction of the mathematics primary school curriculum has focused on the provision of information in relation to content and methodology and there has been a lack of focus on the specific needs of children in areas designated as disadvantaged and children with learning difficulties. This need for further professional development on how to adapt the curriculum for pupils who are not ready for a particular class curriculum is recognised in *Delivering Equality of Opportunity in Schools (DEIS)* (DES, 2005) and in *Literacy and Numeracy in Disadvantaged Schools (LANDS)* (DES, 2005).

The Learning Support Guidelines (DES, 2000) specifically mention the value of implementing intensive early intervention programmes in the early primary classes 'senior infants to second class' (DES, 2000, p. 46). However, previous research findings (Griffin, Case and Siegler, 1997; Feldman, 2004) and evidence from the analyses of qualitative data in this study indicate that some children need learning support when they start school. It would seem logical to direct learning support at the foundations of learning and to help children who have difficulty with pre-number concepts rather than wait for children to develop difficulties later on in school. The caseloads of learning support teachers in disadvantaged schools tend to be dominated by children who need support for literacy (Shiel and Morgan, 1998), leaving little time for children who need learning support in mathematics. In non-disadvantaged schools, a lower incidence of serious literacy difficulties means that learning support in mathematics can be offered to a greater percentage of pupils. Thus, there is a fundamental inequality of access to learning support for pupils in disadvantaged schools in the area of mathematics. Half of the schools in the DES (2005) evaluation of literacy and numeracy, in some of the most disadvantaged areas, had no learning support in mathematics.

This research points to positive learning outcomes in the area of numeracy for children in a school in an area designated as disadvantaged following the implementation of the Number Worlds programme, an intervention based on cognitive science research. The main conclusions are that there should be early curricular intervention, more emphasis on counting in early years' mathematics and more adult support, including in-class learning support at junior infant level, especially in disadvantaged schools. The findings merit a replication of the study with a larger sample of pupils over a longer time frame.

References

Baroody, A. J. (1987) *Children's Mathematical Thinking*, New York: Teachers College Press

Butterworth, B. (2005) 'The Development of Arithmetical Abilities', *Journal of Child Psychology and Psychiatry*, vol. 46, 1, pp. 3–18

Case, R. and Okamoto, Y. (1996) (eds) 'The Role of Central Conceptual Structures in the Development of Children's Thought', *Monographs of the Society for Research in Child Development*, vol. 61, Serial 246, pp. 1–2

Cockcroft, W. H. (1982) *Mathematics Counts: Report of the Committee of Inquiry into the Teaching of Mathematics in Schools,* London: HMSO

Department of Education and Science (1999) *Primary School Curriculum, Mathematics*, Dublin: DES

Department of Education and Science (2000) *Learning Support Guidelines*, Dublin: DES

Department of Education and Science (2005) *DEIS: Delivering Equality of Opportunity in Schools – An Action Plan for Educational Inclusion*, Dublin: DES

Department of Education and Science (2005) *Literacy and Numeracy in Disadvantaged Schools*, *(LANDS),* Dublin: DES

Feldman, M. A. (ed.) (2004) *Early Intervention: The Esssential Readings*, Oxford: Blackwell

Gelman, R. and Gallistel, C. R. (1978) *The Child's Understanding of Number*, Harvard, Mass.: Harvard University Press

Griffin, S. and Case R. (1997) 'Rethinking the Primary School Curriculum: An Approach Based on Cognitive Science', *Issues in Education*, vol. 3, 1, pp. 1–49

Griffin, S., Case, R. and Siegler, R. (1994) 'Rightstart: Providing the Central Conceptual Prerequisites for First Formal Learning of Arithmetic to Students at Risk for School Failure' in McGilly, K. (ed.) *Classroom Lessons: Integrating Cognitive Theory and Classroom Practice*, Hillsdale, NJ: Erlbaum, pp. 24–49

McLellan, M. (1993) 'The Significance of Counting', *Education*, October 1993, pp. 3–13

Munn, P. (2001) 'Teaching and learning numeracy in the early years' in Askew, M. and Brown, M. (eds) *Teaching and Learning Primary Numeracy: Policy, Practice and Effectiveness*, Southwell: British Educational Research Association

Piaget, J. (1952) *The Child's Conception of Number*, London: Routledge and Kegan Paul

Resnick, L.A. (1983) 'Developmental Theory of Number Understanding' in Ginsberg, H. (ed.) *The Development of Mathematical Thinking*, New York: Academic Press

Shiel, G. and Morgan, M. (1998) *Study of Remedial Education in Irish Primary Schools*, Dublin: Educational Research Centre

Siegler, R. S. (1976) 'Three Aspects of Cognitive Development', *Cognitive Psychology*, 8, pp. 481–520

Weir, S. (2003) *The Evaluation of Breaking the Cycle: A follow-up of the Achievement of 6th Class Pupils in Urban Schools 2003: Report to the Department of Education and Science*, Dublin: Educational Research Centre

Wright, R. J. (1994) 'A Study of the Numerical Development of 5-year-olds and 6-year-olds', *Educational Studies in Mathematics*, 26, pp. 25–44

IV

Traveller and Intercultural Education

This section explores issues relating to minority groups in Irish society, including the Travelling Community and immigrant population. It is important to note that foreign nationals now represent 10 per cent of Irish society (CSO, 2007). A recent survey suggests that this group has considerably higher levels of education, with over 54 per cent having third-level qualification, which is twice the figure for Irish nationals. However, language difficulties can sometimes lead to some immigrants gaining employment in relatively low-skilled occupations. This gap between occupation and qualification must be addressed as it impacts on the lives of children in such households and can result in difficulty at school. While much focus in research on educational disadvantage tends to focus on transition points in time (primary to post-primary, preschool to primary, junior certificate to post-junior certificate), it is abundantly clear that a new focus is needed with regard to transition, namely a transition in space, involving the genuine integration of international pupils within schools in Ireland.

The Traveller Education Strategy (TES), launched in November 2006, emphasises 'inclusion in the mainstream' which 'will require building the capacity of the mainstream services to deal positively with diversity and not to be predicated on the assumption that all Traveller children and adults have learning difficulties. This will ensure that the mainstream services are accessible, relevant, welcoming and competent to include Travellers in appropriate ways.' A critique is offered of the recommendations for a Traveller education strategy 2006–2010, concentrating in particular on the topics of parents and education, as well as early childhood education. Among other issues, the question is raised as to whether the phasing out of Traveller preschools will lead to the replacement of an imperfect but valuable provision with a non-existent aspiration that could lead to the loss of expertise and experience built up in Traveller preschools. Amalgamation differs from genuine integration. An analysis is also offered of recent efforts to incorporate knowledge about Travellers in Irish society into the Irish curriculum, with a view to enhancing understanding and sensitising other students to Traveller culture. It is suggested that despite the egalitarian aim of the Civic, Social and Political Education Programme (CSPE) of encouraging students to apply positive attitudes, imagination and empathy in learning about peoples and cultures, the way in which knowledge about Travellers is constructed in CSPE textbooks can have the opposite effect of legitimising negative reactions towards Travellers and reinforcing erroneous ideas about why they are discriminated against in the first instance. It is hoped that the Social Inclusion Priority (2007) that contains a Traveller Education commitment of some €511 million over the next six years will finally allow real educational achievement for members of the Travelling community.

With regard to strategic planning for ethnic minorities, the key issue of language support to be provided by schools is examined in relation to Swedish models that could serve as examples of good practice for Ireland. This section also outlines a range of issues for strategic planning with regard to the increasing numbers of ethnic minorities, emphasising principles of community development involving consultation and decision-making processes.

References

Barrett, A., Bergin, A. and Duffy, D. (2006) 'The Labour Market Characteristics and Labour Market Impact of Immigrants in Ireland', *The Economic and Social Review*, vol. 37, no. 1, pp. 1–26

Central Statistics Office (2007) *Census 2006: Commentary*, Dublin: Government Publications, p. 25

Department of Education and Science (2006) *Recommendations for a Traveller Education Strategy 2006-2010*, Joint Working Group on Traveller Education, Dublin: DES

21

The (Mis) Representation of Travellers in the CSPE Curriculum

Audrey Bryan

This chapter focuses on that aspect of educational disadvantage concerned with 'curricular in/justice' in education, as it relates to the representation of Travellers in school textbooks designed for use with secondary school students (Connell, 1993, 1996). Curricula can be characterised as unjust in the sense that they are believed to play an important role in perpetuating social inequality along, *inter alia*, class, gender and racial–ethnic lines and in enabling dominant cultural groups to sustain their competitive advantage in education and society more generally (McEneaney and Meyer, 2000). While much of the educational disadvantage literature focuses on equalising educational access, participation, and outcomes for marginalised groups, far less attention has been devoted to the substantive content of the existing curriculum, and to how these liberal concepts of justice are mediated by the structuring of curricular knowledge (ibid.).

In recent years, the need to 'validate Traveller culture within the curriculum' has been recognised as a priority in state policies relating to Travellers (DES, 2002, p. 39). The 'Guidelines on Traveller Education for Second-level Schools' maintain that 'many subject areas in the curriculum provide opportunities to include and validate Traveller culture' and 'sensitise other students to that culture' (DES, 2002, pp. 39–40). This chapter focuses specifically on one of those subject areas believed to provide such opportunities, the Civic, Social and Political Education (CSPE) programme, which was introduced as a compulsory subject for the Junior Certificate Cycle in 1997.

An analysis of how Travellers are represented in textbooks is timely, given the increasing policy focus on intercultural education as a means of combating racism in Irish society. In 2005, the National Council for Curriculum and Assessment (NCCA), the body with statutory responsibility for developing school curricula in Ireland, published intercultural guidelines for primary schools, and an equivalent version designed for secondary schools was published in 2006. These guidelines are the culminating effort of the 'Interculturalism and the Curriculum' initiative, which was established to identify 'how the intercultural elements of the existing curricula could be maximised by teachers'. In other words, the purpose of the guidelines is to supplement and enhance existing curricular materials, without overhauling the existing curriculum (Tormey and O'Shea, 2003, p. 4). As such, it is worth examining those elements of the existing curriculum wherein Travellers are depicted.

The analysis presented below examines how Travellers are represented in CSPE textbooks currently being used throughout Irish secondary schools by those following the Junior Certificate curriculum. Many areas of the CSPE curriculum have been identified as being '… relevant to mutual understanding between Travellers and the rest of the population' (DES, 2002, p. 40). While 'the aims of the [CSPE] syllabus encourage students to apply positive attitudes, imagination and empathy in learning about peoples and cultures' (ibid), the research evidence presented below suggests that the content of CSPE texts often has the opposite effect of legitimising negative reactions towards Travellers and reinforcing erroneous ideas about why they are discriminated against in the first instance.

Methodology

These findings are based on a discourse analysis of CSPE textbooks and related materials designed for use with lower secondary school students attending school in the Irish Republic. The discourse analysis involved a multilayered process of reading, writing, interpreting, re-reading, re-writing and re-interpreting each of the texts to derive recurring patterns and themes. The general method employed was to examine various degrees of presence or absence in the texts, such as *foreground information* (those ideas that are present and emphasised), *background information* (those ideas that are explicitly mentioned but de-emphasised), *presupposed information* (that information which is present at the level of implied or suggested meaning) and *absent information* (Fairclough, 1995).

Key findings

The inclusion of information about Travellers in CSPE textbooks, like depictions of other racialised minority groups in school texts (e.g., asylum seekers and refugees), can be characterised as an 'add-on' approach, which typically begins with a brief description of who Travellers are, statistics on the number of

Travellers in Ireland, and explanations for their marginalisation within Irish society (Eyre, 1997). Whereas the add-on approach fills a void in curricula that were previously silent about diversity issues, the representation of Travellers in school texts is not without its problems. One notable feature of the discourse about Travellers is the tendency to associate Traveller oppression with the terms 'discrimination' or 'prejudice' and not 'racism', a tendency which is reflective of a broader resistance among some members of the Irish public and some policymakers and politicians to naming or identifying the treatment of Travellers as racist (Exchange House Travellers Service, 2005, www.exchangehouse.ie).

The failure to acknowledge Traveller oppression as racism may stem in part from the failure to acknowledge Travellers as a distinct ethnic group. While Travellers are 'visibly racialised' in Irish society by their nomadism, they are also marked by their (physical, though not structural) 'whiteness'. This failure to associate the marginalisation of Travellers in Irish society with racism, or to explicitly name it as such, in CSPE texts, supports a false understanding of racism as pertaining exclusively or primarily to 'people of colour', despite a host of theorisations of racism which suggest that racism pertains to the racialisation of groups of people across ethnic and cultural lines.

While CSPE texts do acknowledge that Travellers occupy a marginal position within Irish society, this recognition is rarely linked to broader political and institutional contexts. The significance of this marginalisation is further minimised by language that constructs Traveller discrimination as something which Travellers (and not the dominant settled majority) *perceive* to exist, as opposed to something which *actually* exists and which is indeed widespread in Irish society. As the following example illustrates, on those occasions where discrimination, marginalisation and the poor living circumstances Travellers experience are represented as a real feature of their existence, the explanation stops short of acknowledging a causal relationship between the racism, or 'discrimination', and the poverty, low life expectancy, etc., which Travellers experience (McVeigh, 1997).

The following quotation, which notably identifies Travellers as a 'distinct ethnic minority group within Irish society', is taken from CSPE textbook *Connected 2*:

> ... As a minority group, Travellers suffer discrimination and oppression. They are marginalised and excluded by people in the settled community. Many Travellers experience poverty in their daily lives. Many 'settled people' blame this poverty on their nomadic way of life and suggest that Traveller poverty could be solved by 'settling down and getting a job'. This *well-intentioned attitude* does not respect their different culture and way of life of the Travellers but tries to impose on them the values of the majority population. (de Búrca and Jeffers, 1999, p. 121; emphasis added)

Whereas the foregoing explanation is helpful in challenging the idea that the inequality experienced by Travellers is attributable to their nomadism, its positive potential is diminished by the characterisation of the perceived link between the poverty they experience and their 'lifestyle' as 'well-intentioned'. Rather than offering a structural explanation for Traveller poverty or anti-Traveller racism, or indeed an understanding of these experiences from the point of view of Travellers themselves, the interpretation offered is that of the dominant cultural group which is imposed on Travellers. Discrimination against Travellers is thus explained as a benevolent yet misguided 'attitude' on the part of settled people, which has the effect of excusing, to some extent, the marginalisation and oppression to which Travellers are subjected. While the representation of Travellers does allude to the fact that 'many Traveller households reside at the side of the road' or in 'temporary sites many of which are without toilets, electricity and proper washing facilities', and while it alludes to low life expectancy and low participation rates in school, it is implied that it is people in the settled community (and not state institutions) who are deemed responsible for the marginalisation and exclusion of Travellers ('They are marginalised and excluded by people in the settled community.'). The attribution of Traveller marginalisation and exclusion to the settled community constitutes a discursive strategy known as *top-down transfer*, most often attributed to political elites. Top-down transfer occurs in those instances where racism or discrimination is attributed to individuals or groups (e.g. many 'settled' people), rather than to the state or its political representatives (Van Dijk, 1997). In other words, to the extent that discrimination against Travellers is acknowledged to exist in Irish society, it is attributed to 'settled people,' obfuscating the state's role in producing these discriminatory attitudes in the first place and, indeed, producing and institutionalising the actual marginalisation and exclusion of Travellers. This strategy, which reduces racism and discrimination to the individual level, has the dual effect of deflecting attention from the systemic features of racism and prioritising ineffective and at times counterproductive 'softly-softly' approaches to anti-racism.

It would not be accurate to suggest that consideration of institutional racism (or rather institutional discrimination) is wholly absent from CSPE texts or intercultural resources. In a section on racism in Irish society, the same text, mentioned above, does acknowledge the existence of institutional racism on the part of a host of social institutions:

> Non-Irish people and Irish people belonging to minority groups have been the victims of discrimination from members of the majority population and they have also encountered discrimination by state organisations, businesses and media. (de Búrca and Jeffers, 1999, p. 125)

This narrative is highly commendable in that it is one of the few moments where racism is located beyond the realm of individualised thought in school texts and where racial discrimination on the part of 'state organisations, businesses and media' is actually acknowledged. However, the focus on institutional racism is almost instantaneously overshadowed by a story that focuses exclusively on a minimalist and individualist account of the causes and consequences of racism. As part of this section on 'racism', a 'human interest' story detailing a Ugandan woman's experiences of racism in contemporary Irish society is presented. The story opens with Jumaa Aupai describing how she had lived in Ireland in the 1980s and had found 'the Irish people friendly and welcoming' (p. 125). It then goes on to describe her perceptions of how much the country had changed when she returned there on a short holiday with her family in 1998:

> Wow! The country looked very different. Lots of new buildings, roads, shopping centres. Dublin looked a very wealthy place. I was really excited about meeting the people and showing my family the places I had grown to love. But all the changes were not good ones. My friends were glad to see us but it seemed that ordinary people on the street were not. On city streets, we were pushed. People said things like, 'Why don't you go back to where you came from?' or 'Dirty nigger' and 'lazy spongers'. In a shop, we waited to be served while 'white' people who had come in later than us were attended to. At the airport, we were questioned about where we had come from, why we were coming to Ireland and how long we would be staying. I did not notice any 'white' people being stopped. My friends explained that the number of immigrants had increased greatly in the previous years and that there was a problem with people entering the country illegally. That certainly explained the change in attitude but I still felt very sad. (de Búrca and Jeffers, 1999, p. 126)

The purpose of 'Jumaa's story' is presumably to highlight the problem of racism in Irish society, and to evoke empathy and understanding for those who are 'wrongly' subjected to it. However, it further misrepresents migrants and the phenomenon of contemporary immigration to Ireland more generally by focusing on (and indeed explaining racism as a response to) the problem of so-called 'illegal' immigration, a discursive strategy which legitimates anti-immigrant sentiment and projects the blame for racism on the victims themselves.

The notion of institutional racism also receives attention in some of the intercultural educational materials produced for schools. Contrary to the original meaning of the term, however, which stressed the historical institutionalisation of racial inequalities as well as inter-institutional linkages and their role in reproducing social inequality (Troyna and Williams, 1986, p. 54), these accounts typically reduce institutional racism to the 'unintentional' operations of a single social institution, e.g., the school (Rizvi, 1993). This reductive understanding of institutional racism, which explains it in terms of the failure of a single institution or organisation, is evident in the CSPE intercultural resource *Changing*

Perspectives (Gannon, 2002) produced jointly by the Curriculum Development Unit (CDU) of the City of Dublin Vocational Educational Committee (CDVEC) and the National Consultative Committee on Racism and Interculturalism (NCCRI).

This resource defines institutional racism as:

> The collective failure of an organisation to provide an appropriate and professional service to people, because of their colour, culture or ethnic origin. It can be seen or detected in processes, attitudes and behaviour which amount to discrimination through unwitting prejudice, ignorance, thoughtlessness and racist stereotyping which disadvantage minority ethnic people (Stephen Lawrence Inquiry 2000). (Gannon, 2002, p. 90)

Similar to the foregoing explanation of Traveller marginalisation and discrimination which associated it with a benevolent, albeit misguided 'attitude' on the part of settled people, this definition privileges 'unwitting prejudice, ignorance, thoughtlessness and racist stereotyping', as the basis for institutional racism. Other accounts of institutional racism define the state's role in perpetuating institutional racism in terms of a failure to provide adequate services to racialised minorities which has the effect of positioning social institutions as passively, rather than actively engaging in practices which have racist outcomes. The acknowledgement of such educational practices as entry criteria that do not allow for nomadic lifestyle and the indiscriminate use of non-normed standardized tests with ethnic minorities as indirectly discriminatory notwithstanding, the NCCA's intercultural guidelines also privilege a view of institutional racism as a primarily unintentional and passive phenomenon. This is achieved through examples which characterise institutional racism as a failure to act, such as 'a lack of positive action', 'a lack of systemic data' and a 'lack of workable facilities' (NCCA, 2005, p. 16). A more critical approach to institutional racism would reflect some of the most obvious and most damaging ways in which social institutions legitimate inequalities between groups designated as racially or ethnically different, such as the active promotion of 'streaming' or 'tracking' policies in schools, as well as enrolment-related policies, which actively discriminate against religious minority students. In the Irish context, for example, schools have the right to give preference in enrolment to students of the denomination of the school (Devine, 2005). As Devine points out, this right can prove problematic for those of minority or other personal belief systems, given the predominance of Roman Catholic schools in Irish society.

When the role of the state in contributing to Traveller oppression is acknowledged in school texts, it is usually Travellers' groups or 'their supporters' who utter their dissatisfaction. While this acknowledgment is preferable to accounts which fail to make any mention of structural discrimination, the representation of Travellers within such accounts is often highly negative. In *We are the World* (Cassidy and Kingston, 2004), for example, the failure of state programmes to 'meet legal obligations' for the provision of suitable Traveller accommodation is acknowledged, but only from the perspective of the Irish Traveller movement. This criticism of local authority programmes is alluded to in a reprinted newspaper article about the planned eviction of Travellers from a playing field in South Dublin. The article contains multiple references to 'illegal' and 'unauthorised' stopovers, (words which, among others like rubbish-strewn; frictions; evictions; halting site, etc., are highlighted in bold font) and a reference to Travellers as 'flouting the law' by 'camping illegally'. Collectively, these words work to frame Travellers in a very negative light. While the article does draw attention to the fact that Travellers have 'little choice' but to 'flout the law' 'as the traditional roadside sites ... have been systematically blocked off over the years', (p. 22), the fact that these arguments are made by Travellers themselves, and not by a politician or member of the settled community, for example, detracts from the legitimacy of the claim to the extent that Traveller oppression is often represented as something that is perceived by Travellers, as opposed to something that actually exists. Indeed, the legitimacy of the Travellers' argument is further minimised by the presentation of 'objective' statistics following a series of questions about the article, which describe both an 'increase in Traveller families in the state' as well as significant increases in the amount of government funding devoted to providing accommodation for Travellers:

> Almost €18 million was provided by the government for the provision of Traveller accommodation in 2001, compared with €8.25 million in 1996.

> Some 595 Traveller families have been provided with accommodation since 1995. 458 units of Traveller-specific accommodation have been **refurbished** during this period, with 470 families allocated standard local authority housing. (Cassidy and Kingston, 2002, p. 24; emphasis in original)

As mentioned above, other rhetorical strategies work to privilege a view of discrimination against Travellers as a problem which is 'in their heads' as opposed to something which really exists 'in the world' (Lichtenberg, 1998; Montgomery, 2005). In the CSPE text Impact (Barrett and Richardson, 2003), for example, a section on 'The Travelling Community' states: 'Within Irish society there are different groups that *feel* they are discriminated against ...' (p. 13; emphasis added). Referring specifically to Travellers, it then maintains: 'The Travelling community is a group within Irish society that *feels* discriminated against and that *feels* that their needs and rights are not being met (Barrett and Richardson, 2003, p. 15; emphasis added).

Similarly, *Taking Action Revised* (Quinn, Mistéal and O'Flynn, 2004) maintains that:

> The Irish Traveller Movement *believes* that discrimination is part of Travellers' everyday life. It argues that this discrimination is experienced in terms of being refused access to goods and services as well as in terms of a failure to recognise and accept Traveller culture. (Quinn, Mistéal and O'Flynn, 2004, p. 55; emphasis added)

While in both instances these comments are immediately followed by personalised accounts by Travellers describing their experiences of discrimination, the preceding emphasis on beliefs and feelings implies that this discrimination could very well all be 'in their heads'. Additionally, beyond questions like 'what do you think should be done to end this form of discrimination?' (Quinn, Mistéal and O'Flynn, 2004, p. 56), there is little to indicate that Travellers' feelings are, in fact, justified. In fact, one of the questions asks 'are there any Travellers living close to your home? If so, how *have they been accepted* by the local community?' (ibid; emphasis added). The positive framing of this question, which presupposes that Travellers have indeed been accepted by the local community, despite Traveller testimony to the contrary (in the form of getting 'dirty looks' from both staff and customers; 'not being allowed into many hotels or pubs'; doctors who refuse to take Travellers as patients; 'settled people object[ing] to halting sites being built near them'; some schools refusing to take Traveller children) further suggests that the discrimination described by representatives of the community is perceived, rather than real.

Another reprinted article from the *Irish Times* in *We are the World* describes an important legal case, which states: 'A county Galway leisure centre was found guilty of discriminating against a Traveller by refusing him entry to play in a soccer competition …' In the questions following the article, students are asked: 'Why does Mr Donovan *think* that he was discriminated against? (Cassidy and Kingston, 2004, 2004, p. 28; emphasis added). Once again, the implication is that the discrimination took place in Mr Donovan's thoughts, i.e., in his head, despite the fact that in the article itself, readers are informed that the investigating equality officer 'concluded that Mr Donovan had shown there to be an obvious case of discrimination and that the council did not succeed in proving untrue the suggestion of discrimination' (Cassidy and Kingston, 2004, p. 28).

Another section of the same text, titled 'Talking about Travellers', which takes the form of a reprinted Letter to the Editor from *The Irish Times*, adds further legitimacy to the understanding that discrimination against Travellers may be more perceived than real, or at least minimises the extent to which one might feel empathy towards 'them', by highlighting 'their' unlawful ways and the distress 'they' cause members of the settled community:

> While her [writer Teresa Judge's] feature documented the difficulties faced by the Travelling community in Donegal, it did not mention the damage inflicted on the settled community in this country every year.

There was no mention of the distress and financial hardship faced by individuals and communities following occupation and vandalism by some Travellers on property, both public and private – housing estates, sports centres and even schools. Any local councillor foolhardy enough to express even the mildest concern about this lawlessness is branded a racist …

It seems as if the rights of Travellers as a distinct ethnic minority must be maintained at all times, even if that means the rights of other citizens to peace and security are trampled into the ground. (Cassidy and Kingston, 2004, p. 29)

The foregoing account offers a confrontational 'us' versus 'them' view which pits Travellers against the settled community. The representation of Travellers as a 'lawless' group who 'inflict damage on the settled community every year', positions 'them' as a perpetual threat to the 'peace and security' which is otherwise maintained by the settled community.

In another activity in the same text, students are asked to respond to a number of questions about the 'Citizen Traveller' campaign, which was designed 'to promote the visibility and participation of Travellers within Irish society, to nurture the development of Traveller pride and self-confidence, and to give Travellers a sense of community identity that could be expressed internally and externally' (Irish Traveller Movement website, 2005). In the final question, students are asked to 'Read the last line of each picture. Write down what you know about Traveller culture and needs and the contribution Travellers *could* make to the community' (Cassidy and Kingston, 2004, p. 30). The conditionality of this statement implies that Travellers do not, at present, make any contribution to the community, thereby seriously undermining the core message of the actual campaign.

The overall intent of including letters to the editor in CSPE textbooks may be to serve as a springboard for classroom discussion. The inclusion of the question 'What is your opinion of the views expressed in this letter?' (p. 29) in relation to the aforementioned quotation from 'Talking about Travellers' suggests that its purpose is indeed to get students to formulate their own opinions about Travellers' rights. However, I maintain that the 'evidence' presented in this instance is weighted unfavourably against Travellers. While the behaviour of small groups of Travellers might rightly be deemed unacceptable (just as with any social group), a more balanced basis for classroom discussion would arguably have included the original newspaper article documenting the difficulties faced by Travellers to which the 'disappointed' and 'angry' author of the letter to the editor was responding. Instead, the section contains yet another article about an illegal Traveller encampment and illegal dumping of garbage, which cost 'up to €76,000 to clear', and which characterises 'a core group of trader Travellers' as 'irresponsible'. Articles of this nature ensure that it is the Traveller problem, and not the problems experienced by Travellers, which remain at the forefront in school texts (Fanning, 2002). Anti-Traveller hostility becomes justified within a racialised discourse which depicts them as deviant, lawless and irresponsible – a threat to the dominant community who are positioned as the 'real' victims (ibid).

Existing criticisms of the CSPE programme have tended to emphasise that the subject is only offered at Junior Certificate level and that it does not allow for a wide range of issues to be covered in any depth (e.g., Lodge and Lynch, 2004, p. 74). The evidence presented above suggests that more attention needs to be focused on the substantive content of the knowledge that students are believed to acquire about Travellers and racialised minorities in Ireland more generally. Despite recent curricular efforts to incorporate knowledge about various minority groups in Irish society with a view to enhancing understanding and appreciation for diversity, these efforts often have the effect of legitimising negative reactions towards groups designated as racially or ethnically other and reinforcing erroneous ideas about difference. In other words, while promoting knowledge, facilitating attitudinal change and developing empathy are central tenets of intercultural education, the examples provided above suggest that the nature of the knowledge being provided about racism, racialised minorities, and Travellers in particular, is perhaps more likely to reproduce, rather than contest, racist ideologies.

Existing policy documents concerned with racism and interculturalism operate according to a liberal framework of equality which stresses access, participation, and outcome. The overall aim of the National Action Plan Against Racism (NPAR), the most recent and comprehensive articulation of official thinking on Anti-Racism in Ireland, is to 'provide strategic direction to combat racism and to develop a more inclusive, intercultural society in Ireland based on a commitment to inclusion by design, not as an add-on or afterthought and based on policies that promote interaction, equality of opportunity, understanding and respect' (Department of Justice, Equality and Law Reform, 2005, p. 27). Apple (1979) and Troyna (1993) refer to concepts like equality of opportunity as 'slogan systems' which are deployed in policy rhetoric to claim legitimacy for certain reforms, while enabling policymakers to distance themselves from alternative, more radical conceptions of equality. Similarly, Lynch (2000) maintains, liberal definitions provide but one possible set of definitions and tend to ignore more fundamental problems of equality of condition. In other words, they fail to address power and resource differentials between social groups which affect their ability to avail of opportunities in the first place.

What I am advocating here is the need for more radical notions of justice and equality in education. From the point of view of curriculum – the main focus of this chapter – this amounts to the advocacy of a 'curricular justice' perspective, which seeks to dismantle curricular knowledge that is constructed by, and for, the benefit of privileged members of society and to reconfigure it so that it is reorganised from the perspective of the least advantaged and marginalised in society (Connell, 1993, 1996). Curricular justice extends far beyond 'add-on' approaches to the curriculum, which further misrepresent and marginalise minority groups. It also eschews those perspectives which encourage the 'participation' of, and 'consultation' with, minority groups, including Travellers, about their views, wherein participation thus gets reduced to the level of simply asking or 'consulting' with minority groups about their wants and needs, without them necessarily having any real influence in terms of how related policy decisions are framed or enacted. To this extent, intercultural guidelines that supplement, but do not in effect alter, the existing curriculum are unlikely to ensure that curricular justice is served. Rather, what is needed is a reconfiguration of the existing curriculum so that it is reconstituted from the point of view of those who are most marginalised within society. A radical reconstitution of curricular knowledge as it pertains to the representation of Travellers in school texts is a small, yet essential step in this process.

References

Apple, M. (1979) *Ideology and Curriculum*, Boston: Routledge

Barrett, L. and Richardson, F. (2003) *Impact! CSPE for Junior Certificate* (3rd edn) Gill & Macmillan

Cassidy, C. and Kingston, P. (2004) *We are the World*, Dublin: Mentor

Connell, R. W. (1993) *Schools and social justice*, Philadelphia: Temple University Press

Connell, R. W. (1996) *The Men and The Boys*, Cambridge: Polity Press

de Búrca, U. and Jeffers, G. (1999) *Connected 2: Civic, social and political education for second and third year*, Dublin: The Educational Company of Ireland

Department of Education and Science (2002) 'Guidelines on Traveller Education for Second-level Schools', DES

Department of Justice, Equality and Law Reform (2005) *Planning for Diversity: The National Action Plan Against Racism*, Dublin

Devine, D. (2005) 'Welcome to the Celtic Tiger? Teacher responses to immigration and ethnic diversity in Irish schools', *International Studies in the Sociology of Education*, 15, 1, pp. 49–70

Eyre, L. (1997) 'Reforming (Hetero) Sexuality Education' in Eyre, L. and Roman, L. (eds) *Dangerous Territories: Struggles for difference and equality in education*, Routledge, New York, pp. 191–204

Fairclough, N. (1995) *Critical discourse analysis*, Longman: London

Fanning, B. (2002) *Racism and Social Change in the Republic of Ireland*, Manchester: Manchester University Press

Gannon, M. (2002) *Changing perspectives: cultural values, diversity and equality in Ireland and the wider world: a resource for civic, social and political education*, CDVEC, Curriculum Development Unit

Lichtenberg, J. (1998) 'Racism in the Head, Racism in the World' in Zack, N., Shrage, L. and Sartwell, C. (eds) *Race, Class, Gender, and Sexuality: The Big Questions*, Malden, MA: Blackwell, pp. 43–8

Lodge, A. and Lynch, K. (2004) *Diversity at School*, IPA: Dublin

Lynch, K. (2000) 'Research and theory on equality in education' in Hallinan, M. (ed.) *Handbook of Sociology of Education*, New York: Kluwer, pp. 85–105

McEneaney, E. and Meyer, J. W. (2000) 'The content of the curriculum: An institutionalist perspective' in Hallinan, M. (ed.) *Handbook of the sociology of education*, New York: Kluwer Press, pp. 189–212

McVeigh, (1997) 'Theorising Sedentarism: the Roots of Anti-Nomadism' in Acton, T. (ed.) *Gypsy Politics and Traveller Identity*, University of Hertfordshire Press

Montgomery, K. (2005) 'Banal Race-thinking: Ties of blood, Canadian history textbooks and ethnic nationalism', *Paedagogica Historica*, 41, 3, pp. 313–36

National Council for Curriculum and Assessment (2005) *Intercultural education in the primary school, Guidelines for schools*, Dublin: NCCA

Quinn, R., Mistéal, S. and O'Flynn, O. (2004) *Taking Action* (revised edn) Dublin: CJ Fallon

Rizvi, F. (1993) 'Critical Introduction: Researching racism and education' in Troyna, B. (ed.) *Racism and Education: Research Perspectives*, Buckingham: Open University Press

Tormey, R. and O'Shea, M. (2003) 'Rethinking Ireland through the national curriculum' in Lasonsen, J. and Lestinen, L. (eds) *Thinking and learning for intercultural understanding, human rights and a culture of peace*, conference proceedings from UNESCO Conference on Intercultural Education, 15–18 June 2003, Jyväskylä, Finland

Troyna, B. (ed.) (1993) *Racism and Education: Research Perspectives*, Buckingham: Open University Press

Troyna, B. and Williams, J. (1986) *Racism, Education and the State: the racialisation of education policy*, Beckenham: Croom Helm Ltd

Van Dijk, T. A. (1997) 'Political Discourse and Racism: Describing Others in Western Parliaments' in Riggins, S. H. (ed.) *The Language and Politics of Exclusion: Others in Discourse*, Thousand Oaks, California: Sage, pp. 31–65

22

Traveller Parents and Early Childhood Education

Anne Boyle

Introduction

Irish schools face significant challenges in relation to the education of Traveller children. The chief inspector in the DES remarks that, 'despite the almost full participation of Travellers in primary education, the low achievement level of the majority ... is a matter for concern' (DES, 2005b, p. v). The position in respect of post-primary education is even more bleak, with the chief inspector noting that, 'the vast majority of Travellers are leaving post-primary schools early, and without qualifications.' This is despite the fact that since the 1970s resources and initiatives have been developed which target support for Traveller children in education (DES, 2005b, p. 4). The report of the Joint Working Group on Traveller Education, *Recommendations for a Traveller Education Strategy 2006–2010* (DES, 2006), proposes major changes in educational provision for Travellers which, if implemented, could significantly change the way Travellers experience education. Though the Traveller Education Strategy (TES) covers all levels of education, this chapter focuses on two areas: parents and education (DES, 2006, Chapter 4), and early childhood education (DES, 2006, Chapter 5). The focus on parents derives from a belief that many of the educational difficulties experienced by Traveller children are due to a chasm between school and home, a chasm that might be bridged through increased involvement of Traveller parents with the schools. The focus on early childhood education derives from a belief that preschool, as the child's first contact with education outside the home, is an ideal site in which to begin a process of involvement. Though the TES is a major source here, discussion is also informed by other recent publications, including the *Preschools for Travellers: National Evaluation Report* (DES, 2003), the *Survey of Traveller Education Provision in Irish Schools* (DES, 2005b) and the *Report of the High Level Group on Traveller Issues* (Department of Justice, Equality and Law Reform, 2006).

Core values

Core values underpinning the TES include a focus on the rights of the Traveller child and on the role of parents (DES, 2006, p. 9). The reference to the rights of the child represents an advance on the report *Task Force on the Travelling Community: Executive Summary* (Government of Ireland, 1995), in which children were viewed only in relation to Traveller women, as pointed out by the *Second Progress Report of the Committee to Monitor and Coordinate the Implementation of the Recommendations of the Task Force on the Travelling Community* (Government of Ireland, 2005, p. 42). In setting out its position on the rights of the child, the TES refers to the UN Convention on the Rights of the Child (1989) which compels authorities to take account of their needs and their culture in all aspects of education (DES, 2006, p. 10). The TES calls for Travellers to be included in the mainstream education system in a way that respects their culture, including nomadism. It acknowledges that this will require equipping mainstream services to deal with diversity in a way that is 'accessible, relevant, welcoming and competent to include Travellers in appropriate ways' (DES, 2006, p. 10).

Concepts of equality and inclusion are also central to the TES report. Equality is taken to comprise equality of access, participation and outcomes. This focus on outcomes is important, since increased participation by Travellers in education has not delivered satisfactory outcomes, as demonstrated in the *Survey of Traveller Education Provision in Irish Schools* (DES, 2005b). Inclusion is defined as the integration of Travellers into mainstream education provision, the sharing of accommodation and other physical resources with non-Traveller learners, and the provision of these resources on the basis of identified need. This reflects developments which have been underway for the past few years, moving away from the separate provision for Travellers which has been common in the past, and which has been a source of resentment for many (see, for example, Boyle, 2006). Inclusive provision will, it is claimed, avoid creating dependency and isolation and will promote 'interactive and interdependent engagement with the mainstream service' (DES, 2006, p. 9). Each educational setting will be required to include the 'reality, needs, aspirations, and validation of culture and life experiences of Travellers in planning the curriculum and in the day-to-day life' (DES, 2006, p. 10).

An implication of the call for inclusion and equality is that all staff development for school personnel should be informed by these principles and that all involved in education should have an understanding of anti-discrimination and interculturalism (DES, 2006, p. 11). A further implication is the recognition of diversity within the Traveller community. For example, Travellers with disabilities and their parents need to be affirmed and supported and all Travellers should be able to experience education in a way that accepts and validates their identity while recognising their particular individual needs.

Traveller parents

The benefits of parental involvement in education have been well established in educational research (see, for example, the meta-analyses by Jeynes 2004, 2005) and there is widespread agreement that parental involvement is a key element in addressing educational difficulties faced by Travellers (DES 2003, 2005a, 2005b, 2006). In relation to Traveller education, the chief inspector has said, 'the role of parents as partners in education must be developed' (2005b, p. v) and all schools contacted for the *Survey of Traveller Education Provision in Irish Schools* 'appreciated the importance of fostering involvement by parents' (2005b, p. 73).

In addressing the need for parental involvement in education, it is important to recognise the many challenges that Traveller parents face. Noting that 9 per cent of Travellers live in unauthorised sites, the TES points out that living without access to basic services and being under threat of eviction can impact in a very negative way on a Traveller child's education. The TES also notes that parents' capacity to engage with education can depend on factors such as their own educational and socio-economic background as well as, for many, 'their negative experience in school, illiteracy and the widespread experience of exclusion' (DES, 2006, p. 22). It suggests that Traveller parents cannot assume that their children will be treated fairly and respectfully in schools (DES, 2006, p. 22). The *Report of the High Level Group on Traveller Issues* (2006) also notes that factors extraneous to the education system can have a positive or negative impact on educational attainment, factors such as 'cultural issues, housing standards, health, childcare and parental employment status' (Department of Justice, Equality and Law Reform, 2006, p. 44).

The *Survey of Traveller Education Provision in Irish Schools* (DES, 2005b) reports that most Traveller parents have high expectations for their children in the education system; more than half expressed concern about the attainment levels of their children, particularly in the area of literacy and numeracy, and were disappointed that their children were falling behind the other pupils in the class (DES, 2005b, p. 52). Many of the parents reported that they themselves had missed out on education and 'this had created barriers to their own advancement and to their ability to play a full role in society' (DES, 2005b, p. 64). They were anxious that their children should benefit from a good education, and they expressed the desire to gain more information on ways to support their children in achieving their potential (DES, 2005b, p. 64). The TES mentions two DES-supported projects, in Mayo and Ennis, which respond to this desire by seeking to upskill Traveller parents to support their school-going children with homework and to interact effectively with their children's schools (DES, 2006, p. 65). The TES sets out an overall objective for Traveller parents:

> Traveller parents should benefit from a comprehensive and inclusive programme of community-based education initiatives which will empower them to understand the education system, to participate in it and to further support their children in education. (DES, 2006, p. 25)

The TES also recommends that Traveller parents should be encouraged and supported to participate in representative structures. Though desirable, representation needs to be meaningful and these structures need to be examined to see how they operate and to ensure that representatives can influence policy. Hanafin and Lynch (2002) noted from research they conducted with parents in a primary school in the disadvantaged area scheme in Ireland that the role of parent representatives is quite limited. Members of parents' councils reported that 'once they became involved in the council, they found that their role was less influential regarding policy and decision making than they had first thought' (Hanafin and Lynch, 2002, p. 42). Likewise, parents' perceptions of boards of management was that 'membership as a parent didn't involve any opportunity to influence school policy' (Hanafin and Lynch, 2002, p. 43).

Though proposals for parents in the TES are positive, one could argue that they are based on an overly benign view of the education system. Parents are rightly urged to acquire 'greater understanding of the value of education and of the education system' (DES, 2006, p. 27), but this needs to be a critical awareness and it should be complemented by a call on the education system to consider how it excludes Traveller parents. In this context, proposals for schools to facilitate dialogue with parents are welcome (DES, 2006, p. 26). The TES recommends that schools provide a positive environment for Traveller parents, who should be 'invited and encouraged to partake in all aspects of school life' (DES, 2006, p. 26).

Recognition of failings in the education system is evident in the TES report's call for the system 'to continue to evolve into an inclusive system that welcomes diversity in all its forms' (DES, 2006, p. 27). It recommends that teachers receive training and development in the areas of equality and diversity, a call which is echoed in the *Survey of Traveller Education Provision in Irish Schools* (2005b, p. 83), which claims that 'schools need support and training in relation to intercultural education'. Many schools were uncertain about how to incorporate

Traveller culture into the school curriculum and environment and reported that 'Traveller parents expressed conflicting views about presenting Traveller culture in the school setting' (2005b, p. 75). This highlights a dilemma for Traveller parents, who may feel it is easier if their children are not identified as Travellers, thus denying their identity. O'Hanlon and Holmes (2004), writing in the UK context, claim that 'for the most part, Gypsy and Traveller children who have succeeded in school and adult learning have done so mainly by denying their identity and presenting as members in the mainstream community, for fear of hostility, prejudice and rejection' (p. 31). They note that this denies positive role models to other Gypsies and Travellers in the community.

Parents are being asked to engage more fully with the education system, to consider further education for themselves and to participate more fully in the education of their children. Education providers are being asked to engage pro-actively with Traveller parents by including them as active partners in the education system (DES, 2006, p. 27).

Creating an inclusive preschool

'There is increasing recognition of the importance and value of the early years for all children's development' (DES, 2006, p. 29). The TES goes on to assert that investment in early childhood education is cost-effective in tackling educational disadvantage, as it reduces the need for spending on remedial measures later in a child's life. School principals also strongly support the need for preschool education for Traveller children (DES, 2005b, p. 56). The DES has supported Traveller preschools since the 1980s and there are currently approximately forty-five Traveller preschools throughout the country. Recommendations in the TES related to Traveller preschool education should be read in conjunction with the *Preschools for Travellers: National Evaluation Report* (2003), since the TES calls for the implementation of the recommendations of this report (DES, 2006, p. 32).

A requirement for parental involvement in preschools is evident in the evaluation report where it recommends that each preschool 'develop and implement a policy to encourage involvement by parents in the life of the preschools' and that this policy should be developed in consultation with the parents and be sensitive to 'the cultural characteristics of the Traveller community' (DES, 2003, p. 86). It states that preschools should regard consultation with parents as part of the school planning process (DES, 2003, p. 87). Also, parents should be facilitated to engage directly with the education services rather than to rely on support structures (DES, 2003, p. 70). It should be noted that in the years since the publication of the evaluation report, little effort has been made to facilitate implementation of these recommendations.

Amalgamated preschool services

While acknowledging the value of early childhood education for tackling educational disadvantage, the TES comments that due to separate provision, children attending Traveller preschools miss the opportunity to mix with their settled neighbours (DES, 2006, p. 29). It recommends that no new Traveller preschool be established and that existing Traveller-only preschools amalgamate 'with existing and future early childhood education services' (p. 32). It states that Traveller preschools should not be located on halting sites or other Traveller-specific sites, though this proposal seems redundant in light of proposals to completely phase out the Traveller preschools. It suggests that future early years provision for all children, including Traveller children, should be inclusive and resourced in all aspects and 'with appropriately trained professionals operating in suitable and good quality premises' (p. 32).

The TES seems to confuse amalgamation with integration. Why call for Traveller preschools to amalgamate with as yet non-existent services? The goal of integration could be more readily achieved by enabling Traveller preschools to implement inclusive, integrated enrolment policies. This would avoid much of the disruption likely to arise from attempts to amalgamate services with different histories, structures, staffing arrangements and funding mechanisms. The evaluation report (2003) acknowledges that one of the strengths of the Traveller preschools is their acceptance by parents and the Traveller community (DES, 2003, p. 78), an acceptance that has allowed the targeting of resources to a community that experiences severe educational disadvantage. The proposed policy of amalgamation puts at risk the parental support for preschool education, which has been built up over many years.

There are many difficulties associated with the amalgamation of services with different structures and different staffing arrangements. For example, staff in each Traveller preschool includes a teacher and a childcare worker, similar to *Early Start*, but different from most other early years provision. However, the TES introduces the term 'early learning practitioners', a terminology that tends to mask the likely problems to which amalgamation would give rise. According to the *Delivering Equality of Opportunity in Schools* (DEIS) report, the broad emphasis in current early childhood provision in disadvantaged communities is on childcare, with only a limited number of projects addressing both education and care needs simultaneously. Among the latter are the Traveller preschools (DES, 2005, p. 33). The Centre for Early Childhood Development and Education (CECDE) notes that the most commonly held nationally recognised qualification amongst early childhood care and education personnel outside the primary sector is Fetac Level 2 childcare qualification (CECDE, 2003, p. 11). Amalgamation could give rise to significant potential for conflict and confusion concerning working conditions and terms of employment for staff, and to a shift in emphasis from education to care.

The evaluation report (2003) had recommended that, where feasible, consideration should be given to siting Traveller preschools in, or adjacent to, primary schools in order to foster closer links between the Traveller community and mainstream schools, and that vacant classrooms should be used to accommodate Traveller preschools. Though the rationale for such a recommendation appears sound, it is noteworthy that it is absent from the TES recommendations concerning early years provision. Preschools on primary school premises pursuing a strong policy of parental involvement could help build trust and understanding between parents and schools.

The TES states that Traveller families with resources should have access to privately run preschool facilities (DES, 2006, p. 30). It is difficult to discern what this statement means, since equality legislation already ensures that Traveller families have the same rights as other families in this regard. Traveller preschools have always been just one option open to Traveller parents, who could choose other early years provision if they wished, including privately run facilities, and parental choice has always been stressed by the DES. This comment may imply that state-funded preschooling will not be available to Travellers with resources, which could alter the relationships built up between Traveller families and Traveller preschools over the years. Many Traveller extended families prefer that their young children be educated together. Given the historically difficult relationships between Travellers and schools, and the fact that early years education is not compulsory, it is to be hoped that Traveller children would not be denied preschool places based on resources.

This also brings to light a further issue in relation to proposals for integrated early years provision. The TES advocates 'inclusion' as one of its core values, and this is a value that runs through recent education and social policy. Nutbrown and Clough note the 'heterogeneity of meanings' of this term (2006, p. 3). Where services are not universally available, but are provided on the basis of social need, one result may be a separate service for children from disadvantaged backgrounds, while children from more advantaged backgrounds will attend separate private services. This would lead to a two-tier system in which services are segregated on the basis of the social background of the families.

Role of Travellers in early years education

The TES suggests that intercultural materials and resources should be developed in consultation with Traveller childcare workers and with children. This seems an ill thought-out and patronising proposal, in that it ignores the expertise of parents and teachers, along with other community expertise, which might be drawn upon for such work. A further issue in relation to this proposal is the assumption that there will be a Traveller childcare worker in each setting, and, indeed, that the teacher will not be a Traveller. In an integrated setting there can be no assurance that there will be a Traveller staff member, and it should be noted that within the current Traveller preschools, some of the teachers are members of the Traveller community. The TES report does call for positive action measures to increase access to professional training for Travellers for all roles in the early childhood sector, but employment in these roles cannot be guaranteed for Travellers.

Intended outcome

The TES intends that, within five years, Traveller children should have access to inclusive well-resourced and managed provision with appropriately trained professionals which will include representatives from the Traveller community in quality premises (DES, 2006, p. 34). It calls for expansion in the number of preschools 'even beyond the proposed 150 DEIS sites' (DES, 2006, p. 33). This call, going beyond its brief in relation to Traveller education, highlights the underdeveloped nature of the preschool sector and draws attention to the danger implicit in this strategy, that by seeking to replace an imperfect but valuable current provision with a more perfect but currently non-existent aspiration it could instead lead to the loss of expertise and experience built up in the Traveller preschools. The phasing out of Traveller preschools in the absence of sufficient places in high-quality accessible, integrated and inclusive settings may lead to some Traveller children not gaining access to culturally appropriate preschool places.

Conclusion

The Traveller Education Strategy (2006) seeks an end to separate Traveller provision in education, to be replaced by inclusive provision in integrated mainstream services. The core values of the report stress the role of parents and the need for partnership and inclusion in the education system. Though the goals are admirable, much work remains to be done to acknowledge Traveller culture within the education system generally, and to establish meaningful partnerships with Traveller parents. The proposals in relation to early childhood education are dependent upon major changes in the overall provision of services in this area, changes which are not currently planned or resourced.

References

Boyle, Anne (2006) 'Traveller Education in Ireland: Parental Involvement in Preschool Education', *Aesthethika: International Journal on Culture, Subjectivity and Aesthetics*, vol. 2, no. 2, May 2006

Centre for Early Childhood Development and Education (2003) CECDE submission to Education Disadvantage Committee 2003, p. 11, www.cecde.ie, accessed 1/4/06

Department of Education and Science (2003) *Preschools for Travellers: National Evaluation Report*, Dublin: DES

Department of Education and Science (2005a) *DEIS: Delivering Equality of Opportunity in Schools – An Action Plan for Educational Inclusion*, Dublin: DES

Department of Education and Science (2005b) *Survey of Traveller Education Provision in Irish Schools*, Dublin: DES

Department of Education and Science (2006) *Recommendations for a Traveller Education Strategy 2006–2010*, Joint Working Group on Traveller Education, Dublin: DES

Department of Justice, Equality and Law Reform (2006) *Report of the High Level Group on Traveller Issues*, Dublin: DJELR

Government of Ireland (1995) *Task Force on the Travelling Community: Executive Summary*, Dublin: Government Publications

Government of Ireland (2005) *Second Progress Report of the Committee to Monitor and Coordinate the Implementation of the Recommendations of the Task Force on the Travelling Community*, Dublin: Government Publications

Hanafin, J. and Lynch, A. (2002) 'Peripheral voices: parental involvement, social class and educational disadvantage' *British Journal of Sociology of Education*, vol. 23, No. 1

Jeynes, William (2004) 'Parental involvement and secondary school student educational outcomes: a meta-analysis', *The Evaluation Exchange*, vol. x, no.4, Winter

Jeynes, William (2005) 'A meta-analysis of the relation of parental involvement to urban elementary school student academic achievement', *Urban Education*, vol. 40, no. 3, pp. 237–269

Nutbrown, C. and Clough, P. (2006) *Inclusion in the Early Years*, London: Sage Publications

O'Hanlon, C. and Holmes, P. (2004) *The Education of Gypsy and Traveller Children*, Trentham Books

23

New Kids on the Block

Rory McDaid

There has been a significant rise in the number of immigrant children coming to Ireland since the start of the 1990s. The vast majority of these do not speak English as a first language (L1), and can be identified as minority language children. This category can also be extended to include children born in Ireland but who might not speak English in the home. Research from other jurisdictions illustrates that while some immigrant children outperform native children in educational attainment (Suaréz-Orozco, 2001, p. 580), these are usually children from advantaged economic, social or cultural backgrounds. Minority language children, as an identifiable group within the education system, do consistently less well than their classmates born in that country to parents also born in that country. Recent data from the Organisation for Economic Cooperation and Development (OECD, 2006) illustrates that while most immigrant children are motivated learners and have positive attitudes towards schools, they often perform at significantly lower levels than their native peers in key school subjects. However, targeted programmes have significantly reduced these differences in certain education systems detailed in the OECD report. Research shows that restricted linguistic development of both the child's own language (L1) and the majority language of their new country (L2) plays an important role in creating and compounding this disadvantage (Ramírez, 1992; McGovern, 1995).

Given the rise in the level of inward migration into Ireland and the evidence in Devine and Kenny (2002) that immigrant children in Irish primary and secondary schools possess a strong motivation to learn, it is both imperative and opportune that Irish policymakers choose to learn from international best practice on this issue and move to prevent the educational disadvantage of minority language children in Ireland that has characterised these children elsewhere.

Levels of inward migration

Immigrant children, or their families, have arrived in a number of different ways in Ireland, for instance as immigrant workers, refugees or asylum seekers. Between 1 January 1999 and 31 October 2005, the Irish government issued 110,884 new work permits to international workers (See Table 1). A further 91,226 work permits were renewed during this period. The majority of these permits were issued in five distinct sectors: service, catering, agricultural/fisheries, industry, and medical/nursing (Department of Enterprise, Trade and Employment, 2005). With regard to refugees and asylum seekers, the Irish government received applications from 67,468 people between 1992 and 31 October 2005 (Office of the Refugee Applications Commissioner, 2005).

Table 1 Work permits issued from 1 January 1999 to 31 October 2005

	New permits	Renewal	Group	Total
1999	4,328	1,653	269	6,250
2000	15,434	2,271	301	18,006
2001	29,594	6,485	357	36,436
2002	23,326	16,562	433	40,321
2003	21,965	25,039	547	47,551
2004	10,020	23,246	801	34,067
2005[1]	6,217	15,970	745	22,932

Following enlargement of the European Union (EU) to include ten accession countries on 1 May 2004, Ireland extended full working rights to people from these countries to work in Ireland without work permits. Though reports at the time that Ireland would be overrun with immigrant workers have proven unsubstantiated, Ireland has seen a significant increase in migrant workers from certain countries. The number of Personal Public Service (PPS) numbers issued to migrants from EU accession countries between May 2004 and the end of April 2006 was 206,165. Of these, 116,206 were issued to Polish nationals, 35,497 to Lithuanian nationals and 18,008 to Latvian nationals. While some of these people might have returned to their home country, or travelled to another country, there has been a clear increase in the number of migrants in Ireland from EU Member Countries. As a further example of this change, in 2004, 8,016 babies were born in the Coombe maternity hospital to women from ninety-two different countries (Donnellan, 2005).

---

[1] Data refers only to 31 October 2005.

These developments have resulted in significant demographic changes for Irish schools. Indeed, it is estimated at present that there are 20,000 minority language children in primary schools, with a further 12,000 such children in post-primary (McManus, 2007). In my school alone (in Dublin 7) there were students from thirteen different countries in the school during the year 2005–2006, and over the last two years we have had children from seventeen different countries. There are examples of primary schools in West Dublin with over 100 children from different linguistic, cultural, social and ethnic backgrounds enrolled, and further examples of schools where such children make up more than 80 per cent of the junior infant classes.

The Population and Labour Force Projections (CSO, 2004) assert that Ireland has changed from having a long-standing pattern of emigration to a new pattern of relatively strong immigration and concludes that it is very unlikely that this will be reversed to any substantial degree before 2036, the period covered by this report (CSO, 2004, p. 18). Two population projections are considered in this report. Migration Scenario 1 (M1) projects an average net inflow of 22,600 until 2036, while Migration Scenario 2 (M2) projects an average net inflow of nearly 11,000 until 2036 (CSO, 2004, p. 18). While noting that attempts at such predictions can often prove extremely erroneous, it is generally accepted that, for the foreseeable future, the migration issue in Ireland will be characterised by immigration rather than emigration.

Human rights – legislative and policy context

Ireland signed the United Nations Convention on the Rights of the Child (CRC) (UN, 1989) on 30 September 1990 and ratified it without reservation on 21 September 1992. In doing so Ireland became a State Party to the convention and made a commitment to promote and protect the rights of the child enshrined in the convention. This means in effect that all children under the age of eighteen in Ireland have the same rights, irrespective of the child's, parent's/parents' or legal caregiver's/caregivers' race; colour; sex; language; religion; political or other opinion; national, ethnic or social origin; property; disability; birth or other status (Immigrant Council of Ireland, 2003, p. 48). Article 28 of this convention enshrines the right of all children to education, while Article 2 prohibits discrimination in relation to the provision of all of the rights laid out in the convention on the basis of language. Minority language children in Ireland also have their right to education enshrined in Article 13 of the International Convention on Economic, Social and Cultural Rights (CESCR) (1966) and Article 14 of the European Convention on Human Rights (ECHR) (1950). Once again, discrimination on grounds of language in relation to the provision of this right is prohibited under Article 2.1 of the CESCR and Article 14 of the ECHR. Thus, Ireland has clear responsibilities regarding the human rights of minority language children in the country.

Ireland also has responsibilities in this area through its membership of the EU. In 1977, the then European Economic Community (EEC) issued Council Directive 77/486/EEC on the education of the children of migrant workers. Article 2 of this directive stated that Member States shall ensure that children of migrant workers are given free tuition, adapted to their specific needs, in one of the official languages of the host state. The Member State should also take such measures necessary for the training and further training of teachers who are to provide this tuition. Article 3 of this directive required Member States to take appropriate steps to promote, in coordination with normal education, the teaching of the mother tongue and culture of the country of origin of these children. Member States are to inform the Commission of the measures taken to comply with this directive.

With regard to national policy, Objective K of the National Children's Strategy (NCS) envisages that '[c]hildren will be educated and supported to value social and cultural diversity so that all children including Travellers and other marginalised groups achieve their full potential' (Department of Health and Children, 2000, p. 70). Acknowledging that the social, cultural and linguistic diversity of Ireland is now represented by over 100 nationalities, the strategy argues that such a transformation has brought significant challenges to a society which generally considered itself to be relatively homogeneous. The Education (Welfare) Act, 2000, established the school leaving age as sixteen years or the completion of three years' second-level education. As a result, all children under the age of sixteen must be engaged in full-time education.

Cummins' theoretical perspective

Cummins (2001, pp. 64–6) sets out a theory of second language development based on three dimensions of language proficiency. This theory is an extension of his original work on the distinction between everyday conversational use of a language or Basic Interpersonal Communication Skills (BICS) and the level of the language necessary to operate at a higher academic level in context-reduced situations or Cognitive Academic Language Proficiency (CALP) (Cummins, 1980), in that it also includes an understanding of the role played by discrete language skills in second language acquisition. Cummins' original work has been highly influential in areas of both policy and practice (Baker, 2001, p. 170) and has, for instance, been adopted by the inspectorate for children and learners in England, Office for Standards in Education (OFSTED, 2001, p. 5). Cummins now distinguishes between conversational fluency, which is the ability to carry on a conversation in familiar face-to-face situations, and academic language proficiency, which includes knowledge of less frequent vocabulary of the second language as well as the ability to interpret and produce increasingly complex language. According to Cummins '[d]iscrete language skills reflect specific phonological, literacy and grammatical knowledge that students acquire as a result of direct instruction and both formal and informal practice' (Cummins, 2001, p. 65). Discrete language skills range from knowledge of the letters of the alphabet acquired early in schooling to conventions about capitalisation and punctuation which are acquired at later stages.

Cummins argues that conversational fluency can be attained by a minority language child within two years, however, it might take that child between five and seven years to be able to properly manipulate their new language in decontextualised academic situations or, in other words, to achieve academic language proficiency. Based on this theory Cummins argues that prolonged bilingual programmes enhance a child's educational and cognitive development. Furthermore, he contends that literacy-related abilities are interdependent across languages such that knowledge and skills acquired in one language are potentially available in the other language (Cummins, 1992).

Cummins' argument is reinforced by the findings of Ramírez's investigation into the academic progress of several thousand Latino/Latina elementary school children in different parts of the US (Ramírez, 1992). This work identified that those students who had prolonged first language instruction were closing the academic gap between themselves and majority language speakers. It also found that while children from immersion (in L2) and quick transitional programmes were not falling further behind their majority language classmates, they were not catching up with them, as was the case with those children in the prolonged programmes. The report concludes that:

> Students who were provided with a substantial and consistent primary language development programme learned mathematics, English language, and reading skills as fast, or faster, than the norming population used in this study. As their growth in these academic skills is atypical of disadvantaged youth, it provides support for the efficacy of primary language development in facilitating the acquisition of English language skills. (Ramírez, 1992, pp. 38–39)

This theoretical perspective can be applied to two aspects of language support for minority language children in the Irish education system. The first of these is the absence of occasion for children from different linguistic backgrounds to develop their own first language within the formal education setting. The second aspect is the support for English language learning.

First language learning

International best practice in this regard can be seen in Sweden, for example, where preschool children must be given the opportunity to develop both their own first language and Swedish. In addition, children and youths in compulsory schooling have the right to receive first language instruction and also education in their own first language in other school subjects, though this does not have to be provided if there are less than five students in the language group or if a suitable teacher cannot be located. First language instruction may be offered either within the school day or outside the regular timetable. The students are entitled to a combined total of seven years of first language instruction during their school years in the public school system (Swedish National Agency for Education, 2005).

It is interesting to note that there is one very good example of how first language development is being facilitated in the Irish education system, in The Centre for European Schooling based in Dunsaughlin, Co. Meath. This centre caters for the first language needs of the children of employees in the European Union Food and Veterinary Office in Grange, Co. Meath. The main school does not open until 9.20 a.m. but the pupils eligible for support in the European school attend from 8.30 a.m. for language classes. The children are removed from class during Irish language teaching every day and attend lessons in French, Spanish, Dutch, Portuguese, Italian, Czech, Hungarian and Swedish. These children also receive English language support during this time if they require such support. In the initial stages of pupils' time in the school the language teachers may also provide a translation service for them. This operates on an in-class basis with the support of the class teacher and in effect means that the class teacher continues to teach through English while the support teacher translates and helps the pupil to adjust to the class work. The centre is funded by the DES through Meath Vocational Education Committee (VEC) and the VEC has appointed a coordinator to run the centre in conjunction with the principals of the primary and post-primary schools in question.

This facility highlights the elitism at the core of the Irish education system. One does not begrudge these children the opportunity to engage in first language development, indeed such an opportunity is to be welcomed. Nevertheless, resources such as these should be made available to all children whose first language is not English, not just the children of those people whose work is most valued by the state. It is disappointing to note that the purpose of the Language School is to attend to the needs of the children in the school whose parents work in the Food and Veterinary Office only. While it does on occasion facilitate other children who are not proficient in English, this is at the discretion of the teaching staff and is not a fundamental aspect of their job.

There are examples of community groups taking the initiative to establish schools where their own children can be taught their language and culture. In May 2005, for instance, members of the Latvian community in Ireland, supported by the Latvian embassy, founded a Latvian school with the overt purpose of preserving Latvian language and traditions. These initiatives, however, remain on the periphery of the education system and need to be properly supported and more fully incorporated.

Majority language learning

Given that English is the majority language of Ireland, it is vital for educational purposes and social and economic prospects that minority language children develop full proficiency in English. With regard to education, schooling in Ireland is conducted through English or Irish. In essence then, children who cannot speak either of these languages must learn them as a matter of urgency before they can access the curriculum or, to a great extent, participate in many other events within the school setting.

Moving out of the education system for a moment, it is alarming to note the impact that a lack of ability to converse in the dominant language of a country can have on employment, income and social networking prospects. A study by the New Zealand Department of Labour (1999) found that English language acquisition was vital to the employment success of migrants. Drawing on Winkleman and Winkleman (1998) they found that immigrants of Eastern European origin who could converse in English had an employment rate of 62.4 per cent, while those who could not converse in English had an employment rate of only 26.6 per cent. In total they found that of immigrants aged between twenty-five and fifty-four, 74.1 per cent of those who could converse in English were in employment, while only 39.1 per cent of those who could not converse in English were in employment (New Zealand Department of Labour, 1999, p. 52). With regard to income, Winkleman and Winkleman found that the gap between migrant males and otherwise similar New Zealand born males was 30 per cent, while the gap was 23 per cent for females (New Zealand Department of Labour, 1999, p. 52). The qualitative data of Ligard et al., 1998, and Ip, Wu and Inglis, 1998, illustrates the disadvantageous social implications for adult migrants who are not able to converse in the majority language of a state. This international data is supported by the findings of McGovern (1995) in relation to the marginalisation of children of Vietnamese refugees in Ireland due to, among other factors, their lack of proficiency in the English language. Given the importance of language acquisition and the compulsory nature of school for children from different linguistic backgrounds, we must question the kind of English language support schemes for students in this category in Irish schools.

Department of Education and Science (DES, 2005a) guidelines state that schools which have fourteen or more non-national pupils with significant English language deficits are entitled to an additional temporary teacher for a period of up to two years. Schools with twenty-eight or more such pupils will be entitled to two temporary teachers. Schools eligible for these teachers also receive a grant of

€634.87 to obtain necessary resources. Those schools which have between three and thirteen non-English speaking children receive grant assistance for a period of up to two years; schools with between three and eight such children received €6,348.69; and schools with between nine and thirteen such children receive €9,523.04. Schools with less than three such pupils are expected to provide for the educational provisions of those pupils from their existing resources (DES 2005b). In 2004, there were 600 teachers working in language support, 400 in primary-level schools and 200 in second-level schools. By the end of January 2007, the number of such teachers working in primary schools had more than doubled to 880.[2] In addition to this, the National Development Plan announced (January 2007) a commitment to provide a further 550 language support teachers (Government of Ireland, 2006, p. 48).

The present system is hampered by some fundamental flaws. The two most troublesome issues are the virtual cap on the number of teachers to be allocated to a school, and the time limitation placed on the availability of this support to students. With regard to teacher allocation, it is proving quite difficult for schools to receive sanction for an adequate number of language support teachers so that they can maintain a 1–14 teacher–pupil ratio.

The second, related problem is that each child is entitled to language support for a maximum of two years. While special cases can be made for extensions of this provision, such applications have a low success rate. Notwithstanding the argument made by Cummins with regard to the development of academic language proficiency, some children have not even attained conversational fluency by the end of this time period. Further difficulties arise in relation to the availability of resources for language support teachers, the temporary nature of their positions and the shortage of in-service training. The manner in which the DES has franchised out the provision of resources and training to Integrate Ireland Language and Training (Ltd) is also questionable. Surely the provision of language support is an issue worthy of consideration and development within the DES itself?

The above analysis illustrates that the Irish government is not meeting either its stated policy commitments or its responsibilities to protect the human rights of minority language children within the Irish education system. It might well be argued that upholding these rights is an extremely difficult exercise in a country that has experienced such rapid transformation since the early 1990s. Nevertheless, given the healthy state of the Irish economy at present, and the role that immigrants are playing in maintaining this situation, policymakers have a responsibility to draw on international experience and ensure that we do not repeat mistakes made elsewhere. It is from this perspective that the following recommendations are made.

---

[2] Personal correspondence with the DES, 31 January 2007

The DES should take full responsibility for meeting the needs of minority language students in the Irish education system. To this end it should establish a unit to deal specifically with this issue within its structures. This unit would deal with areas such as language and other support, resource issues and home/school/community liaison activities. Such a unit would possibly be headed up by a national coordinator as per the recommendation by Learning for Young International Students (LYNS) (2004). In addition, the DES needs to begin to collect data in this area. At present, vital data, such as the number of minority language children in the education system, remains unknown (Hanafin, 2006). Such data is a prerequisite for policy formulation in this area.

The present system of English language support for minority language children should be restructured and based on empirical data so that it properly meets the needs of students. In the first instance a proper curriculum needs to be created which includes clearly defined goals and standards and is interwoven through curricular areas at both primary and second level. Furthermore, such a systematic programme needs to be expanded into early childhood education. In addition, there should be no cap on the number of English language support teachers that can be allocated to a school. English language support teachers need to be available to individual students on the basis of their needs and this should be enshrined in legislation.

Research needs to be conducted to analyse the best method for assessing the length of time required for attaining academic language proficiency in the Irish educational context. There is also an urgent need for data on the heterogeneity of the immigrant and minority language students in the Irish education system so that additional resources can be deployed in a targeted and strategic manner for those most in need.

Other supports need to be developed to meet the needs of minority language children. The DES should consider schemes such as the provision of intercultural mediators, proficient in a variety of languages, who are available to schools and students in Italy, Luxemburg and Portugal (Eurydice, 2004, p. 39). These mediators can come to the school at the request of teachers, parents or school authorities to help with immigrant, asylum-seeking or refugee children and can communicate with the child in his or her own first language. Finance should also be made available to fund extra out-of-hours English-as-a-second-language classes for minority language children if they need them, and also for their parents, should they wish to learn English. Translation services need to be made available for schools so that they can communicate with the parents and guardians of minority language children. Finally, with regard to English language learning in schools, there is a need to develop bilingual textbooks and other resources that are specifically in line with the Irish primary curriculum (DES, 1999).

The issue of first language education should be addressed without delay. The positive educational benefits of late-exit bilingual programmes established by

Ramírez (1992) highlight the need for an imaginative approach to providing this support for all minority language children in the Irish education system.

In conclusion, it is important at this juncture for policymakers to take advantage of the opportunities provided by the linguistic diversity in Irish schools. By drawing on international best practice, and learning from empirical data, it is possible to provide the leadership and resources to meet the human rights of minority language children. It is hoped that this chapter will have provided some guidance in this regard.

References

Baker, C. (2001) *Foundations of Bilingual Education and Bilingualism* (3rd edn) Clevedon: Multilingual Matters

Central Statistics Office (2004) *Population and Labour Force Projections 2006–2036*, Dublin: CSO

Council of Europe (1950) *The European Convention on Human Rights*, Rome: Council of Europe

Cummins, J. (1980) 'The Entry and Exit Fallacy in Bilingual Education' in Baker, C. and Hornberger, N. H. (eds) *An Introductory Reader to the Writings of Jim Cummins*, Clevedon: Multilingual Matters, pp. 110–138

Cummins, J. (1992) 'Empowerment through Biliteracy' in Baker, C. and Hornberger, N. H. (eds) *An Introductory Reader to the Writings of Jim Cummins*, Clevedon: Multilingual Matters, pp. 258–84

Cummins, J. (2001) *Negotiating Identities: education for empowerment in a diverse society*, Los Angeles: California Association for Bilingual Education

Department of Education and Science (1999) *Primary School Curriculum*, Dublin: DES

Department of Education and Science (2000) *Education (Welfare) Act*, Dublin: DES

Department of Education and Science (2005b) *Education provision for non-English speaking pupils*, Dublin: DES

Department of Education and Science, (2005a) *New Guidelines will contribute to developing a school culture that is welcoming, respectful and sensitive to the needs of all children,* Dublin: DES

Department of Enterprise, Trade and Employment (2005) www.entemp.ie/labour/workpermits/statistics.htm, accessed on 19 November 2005

Department of Health and Children (2000) *The National Children's Strategy: Our Children– Their Lives*, Dublin: Government Publications

Devine, D. and Kenny, M. (2002) *Ethnicity and Schooling – A study of ethnic diversity in selected Irish primary and post-primary schools*, commissioned report, Dublin: DES

Donnellan, E. (2005) 'Record summer for babies in Coombe', *The Irish Times*, 15 September 2005, p. 3

European Economic Community (1977) Council Directive 77/486/EEC on the education of the children of migrant workers, Brussels: European Economic Community

Eurydice (2004) *Integrating Immigrant Children into Schools in Europe*, Brussels: European Commission

Government of Ireland (2006) *Towards 2016: Ten Year Framework Social Partnership Agreement 2006–2015*, Dublin: Government Publications

Hanafin, M., TD, 7 June 2006, in response to Dáil Question 367 tabled by Enda Kenny, TD

Immigrant Council of Ireland (2003) *Handbook on Immigrants' Rights and Entitlements in Ireland*, Dublin: Immigrant Council of Ireland

Ip, D., Wu, C. T. and Inglis, C. (1998) 'Settlement experiences of Taiwanese immigrants in Australia', *Asian Studies Review,* vol. 22, pp. 79–97

Learning for Young International Students (2004) Presentation to the Oireachtas Joint Committee on Education and Science, 11 March 2004, htthttp://debates.oireachtas.ie/DDebate.aspx?F=EDJ20040311.xml&Ex=All &Page=2, accessed 7 June 2006

Lidgard, J. E., Ho, Y-Y., Chen, J., Goodwin, P. and Bedford, R. (1998) 'Immigrants from Korea, Taiwan and Hong Kong in New Zealand in the mid-1990s: macro and micro perspectives', *Population Studies Centre Discussion Paper*, 29, Hamilton: University of Waikato

McGovern, F. (1995) 'The Education of Refugee Children in Ireland', *Oideas*, Summer 1995, pp. 82–93

McManus, B. (2007) Meeting of the Public Accounts Committee, 12 October, 2007, www.joanburton.ie/bblog/pbpdf/470_06.10.12PACsection.1.doc

New Zealand Department of Labour (1999) *Migrant Settlement, A Review of the Literature and it's Relevance to New Zealand*, Aukland: New Zealand Department of Labour

Office for Standards in Education (2001) *Inspecting English as an Additional Language*, London: OFSTED

Office of the Refugee Applications Commissioner (2005), http://www.orac.ie/pages/Stats/statistics.htm, accessed 19 November 2005

Organisation for Economic Cooperation and Development (2006) *Where Immigrant Students Succeed: a comparative review of performance and engagement in PISA 2003,* OECD Publications: France

Ramírez, A. G. (1992) 'Executive Summary of the Final Report: Longitudinal Study of Structured English Immersion Strategy, Early-Exit and Late Exit Transitional Bilingual Education Programs for Language-Minority Children', *Bilingual Research Journal*, vol. 16, pp. 1– 62

Suaréz-Orozco, C. (2001) 'Understanding and Serving the Children of Immigrants', *Harvard Educational Review*, vol. 71, pp. 579–89

Swedish National Agency for Education (2005) 'Education for students of non-Swedish backgrounds and recognized minorities', http://www.skolverket.se/sb/d/354/a/1256, accessed on 29 November 2005

United Nations (1966) *The International Convention on Economic, Social and Cultural Rights*, Geneva: UN

United Nations (1989) *The United Nations Convention on the Rights of the Child*, Geneva: UN

Winkelmann, L. and Winkelmann, R. (1998) 'Immigrants in New Zealand: a study of their labour market outcomes', Occasional Paper, 1998, 1, Wellington: Labour Market Policy Group, Department of Labour

V
Teachers, Teaching, Learning

This section explores the themes of teachers, teaching and learning. The pivotal role of teachers in making a difference to the lives of children at risk of early school leaving was centrally acknowledged in the National Forum in 2002. Since then a number of reports from the Educational Disadvantage Centre have emphasised the need for positive relations between teachers and students to support students to stay on at school. This section emphasises the importance of building on existing good practice through renewed focus on the centrality of the relationship of teaching to learning.

The new revised primary school curriculum (1999) represents a real opportunity to develop innovative teaching strategies across a range of subjects to engage pupils in designated disadvantaged schools. Themes explored in this section include process drama and emotional expression; Social, Personal and Health Education (SPHE); and digital learning. All of these espouse the principles of democratic, holistic and culture-relevant learning which are essential to meaningful participation and intrinsic motivation in all learning contexts. These principles resonate with the needs-led, interagency approach advocated by the Bridging the Gap Project, which works with forty-two designated disadvantaged schools in Cork, and is also discussed in this section. Dialogue is extremely important to disseminate good practice, not only across schools but also between statutory and community agencies and schools. The need for more dialogue between the National Educational Psychological Service (NEPS) and teachers and parents is also explored, together with an attempt to understand the factors and system-level supports needed to increase job satisfaction for teachers in designated disadvantaged schools.

24

Addressing Disadvantage:
What about Teaching?

Anne McGough

In this chapter I outline a particular perspective on the role of teaching in educational intervention for children at risk for reasons of socio-economic disadvantage, and suggest that attempts to address the problem of educational disadvantage in Irish primary schools have continually failed to focus on the relationship of teaching to learning or to acknowledge that any analysis of the educational difficulties experienced by children should include an examination of curriculum and of the practice of teaching, as a necessary part of that analysis. Neglect of the role of teaching is evident in the ways in which we continue to provide intervention programmes which look to schools and teachers to address children's problems of low achievement and early school leaving, but do not acknowledge that changes of emphases in relation to curriculum content, and changes in teaching approaches, may be necessary qualities of the intervention. I also examine current research perspectives on intervention and teaching, with reference to existing school-based intervention programmes in the Irish primary school system and also to a recent policy initiative in educational disadvantage.

Within Irish primary education, low levels of achievement in literacy and numeracy for children experiencing social and economic disadvantage are a continuing concern for educators and present an ongoing challenge to policy and practice aimed at addressing educational disadvantage. Recent research has again provided evidence of the high levels of literacy difficulties being experienced by children in designated disadvantaged schools, with 27 per cent of first and sixth class children and 30 per cent of third class children performing at, or below, the tenth percentile on standardised tests of English reading (Eivers, Sheil and Shortt,

2004). These outcomes are similar to those of a 1997 study in which, in a group of disadvantaged urban schools, almost one-quarter of all third class pupils and almost one-third of sixth class pupils scored below the tenth percentile in literacy and would have been eligible for intervention in the form of learning support. In that study, the distribution of scores in mathematics, for both third and sixth class levels, showed a marked under-representation of high scores and an equally marked over-representation of low scores (Weir and Eivers, 1998). In a follow-up study three years later, tests administered to the same grade levels showed a statistically significant decrease in the average literacy and numeracy levels of children in sixth class, with more than one-third of pupils scoring below the tenth percentile in reading and more than 40 per cent scoring at that level in mathematics (Weir, Mills and Ryan, 2002).

We know that low levels of achievement in the core areas of reading and mathematics in primary school will inhibit children's learning across the wider curriculum and will place them at a serious disadvantage in terms of the demands of the second-level system. We know too that this disadvantage results in early school leaving and in poor, or no, second-level qualifications. Equally, research continues to document the link between educational attainment and employment opportunity (National Economic and Social Forum, 1997, 2002). For children who are educationally disadvantaged, the negative aspects of that equation are realised in terms of a continuing cycle of school failure, unemployment and poverty.

The positive link between educational attainment and employment opportunity means that education continues to be one of the central agents for personal advancement within society. In this regard, education is potentially a force for equalising opportunity. However, this potential can only be realised when the relationship between education and equality is seen not just in terms of access to, and participation in, the education system, but in terms of opportunity for *achievement* within that system (Kellaghan et al., 1995; National Commission on Education, 1996). The concept of equality of educational opportunity has come to be defined in terms of opportunity for achievement within the school system, and the concept of educational disadvantage can be defined in direct relation to this position. From this perspective, it is relevant to consider whether our intervention strategies to date have included approaching problems of learning by examining approaches to teaching.

The DES has introduced a number of school-based intervention programmes during the last decade. The titles of the programmes, *Early Start* (1994), *Breaking the Cycle* (1996), *Giving Children an Even Break by Tackling Disadvantage* (2001), and the available documentation, show their explicit intention to intervene in children's lives in ways which will make a difference in terms of educational outcomes. Both *Breaking the Cycle* and *Giving Children an Even*

Break focus on children of primary-school age (4–12). *Early Start* offers a one-year early intervention to three-year-old children in forty schools designated as disadvantaged. The most recent initiative, DEIS: An Action Plan for Educational Inclusion (2005), is explicitly signalled as *Delivering Equality of Opportunity in Schools*. It outlines policy and provision for addressing the educational needs of young people from disadvantaged communities, aged three to eighteen years.

Factors for effectiveness in intervention

There is a large body of literature on intervention for children whose potential for achievement is at risk for reasons of socio-economic disadvantage. Within that literature, there is a consensus that children and their families need comprehensive programmes of intervention involving a range of supports that must be in place early in the children's lives and must focus on the children themselves, their families and communities. This level of intervention is described variously in the literature as a resource-based model (Trivette, Dunst and Deal, 1997), a transactional model (Sameroff and Fiese, 2000), and a developmental systems model (Guralnick, 2005), and is referred to here as a social support model. This model acts to enhance families' knowledge and awareness and to provide actual facilities that affect a child's broader experience, enhancing the quality of that experience and influencing the quality of a child's early learning. It is served by, and rests on, the collaboration of a range of agencies. It is intended to provide a web of support constituting a comprehensive programme of intervention that is sensitive to the needs of children and families at risk.

An educational intervention is included within this social support model. The defining characteristic of the educational input is that it is concerned, in a very particular way, with the nature and quality of a child's learning and with providing teaching that is carefully planned to enhance learning in ways that are appropriate and relevant to a child's needs and to the demands of the curriculum. Recent reviews of intervention research identify relevance and appropriateness as among the most pressing concerns in relation to the design and implementation of intervention programmes (Guralnick, 1997, 2002; Wolery and Bailey, 2002). The view is that we have now moved beyond a general commitment to provision of intervention programmes, to a point where our commitment must be to finding the specific programme features which provide optimum outcomes for children and their families. The consensus in the literature is that we need further knowledge of the *specifics* of programme implementation. From the *specifics* we inform practice, improve the cost-effectiveness of services, minimise false expectations, provide a research framework for evaluating innovative approaches and come to greater understanding of the mechanisms through which interventions operate (Guralnick, 1997).

Effectiveness in teaching

What we know already from the literature is that, in terms of rationale, the programme objectives must be clearly stated; in terms of curriculum, the content must be carefully organised and differentiated; and the teaching must be structured for small groups and for individual children and must be intensive, highly focused and planned specifically to meet individual, identified needs (Casto and Mastropieri, 1986; Reynolds et al., 1996; Ramey and Ramey, 1998; Guralnick, 2005). These have been identified as the features of successful intervention programmes and we have known these features for some time. The research literature now advises further research for more specific insights in these areas. The view is that the key to more effective programmes lies in the degree to which we can fine-tune the relationship between the characteristics of the child as learner, the curriculum content and delivery, and the required programme outcomes. We now need to advance our knowledge and understanding of this relationship. We need to describe what intensity might look like in a classroom or other early years setting. We need to define what is meant by relevant adaptation of curriculum and, critically, we need to identify those qualities of teacher–child interaction which make curriculum more accessible to learners and more appropriate to their learning needs, including the need to be motivated and engaged.

Changes in curricular emphasis and teaching style are often a necessary feature of educational intervention. The requirement is to provide intervention that is relevant and appropriate to children's needs. This view is supported by the literature on class size and children's achievement. While this literature is quite tentative in its interpretation of the research, there are a number of studies from which positive outcomes have been presented (Slavin et al., 1996; Campbell and Ramey, 1995) and, from this general range of studies, a number of points of consensus have emerged. These are that small classes, probably less than twenty students, in the early years of schooling, can generate substantial gains in achievement and, where studies have looked at the population in general, these gains are greater for children who are at risk of educational disadvantage. Equally, there is some evidence that these gains are maintained through the higher classes even when the favourable ratios no longer apply. In these studies, the positive relationship between reduced class size and academic achievement is attributed to changes in the nature and style of teaching, with much of the benefit depending on whether teachers adapt their methods to take advantage of the smaller numbers of learners. It is expected that the small class environment will be structured differently from that of the large class, with less time being spent on management and more time on focused teaching. In this context, the amount and quality of teacher–child interaction increases as teachers structure teaching time differently, giving more support for learning through small groups and one-to-one teaching. The recurring theme in this literature is that unless changes in children's physical environment are matched by changes in curricular emphasis and pedagogic style, reduction in class size will have little impact on learning (Ehrenberg et al., 2001; Biddle and Berliner, 2002). The cautionary note is that teachers do not necessarily change their teaching style to match class size and that changing practice requires concentrated professional development even for teachers who have opted for involvement in intervention programmes (Biddle and Berliner, 2002).

Continuity in teaching focus and style

Another point of consensus in the literature is the need for intervention to be conceptualised as a seamless provision for children aged three to eight years, with continuity in terms of curricular approaches and teaching styles. The Carolina Abecedarian Project (Campbell and Ramey, 1995) is widely reported as one of the more intensive and comprehensive intervention programmes for children at risk for reasons of socio-economic disadvantage. It combined a structured preschool intervention having specific emphasis on language and early literacy and on cognitive development, with a follow-through intervention for the early school years that included a specific home–school focus. Recent longitudinal outcomes show intervention children scoring significantly higher on individual tests of achievement in reading and mathematics at age twelve and fifteen, with fewer grade retentions and fewer special educational placements (Ramey et al., 2000; Ramey and Ramey, 2003). An important finding in these studies is that the lasting, significant effects were attributed to the preschool intervention. No significant gains were made by the children who had the school-age intervention only.

Duration and relevance

The duration of the intervention is another factor for effectiveness. Intensity has been identified as a critical feature of intervention, with intensity defined in terms of structure and content of curriculum and teaching. However, the literature also considers intensity in terms of children's length of exposure to, and records of attendance in, the intervention programme. In relation to interventions for children of pre-primary age, there are serious concerns about the efficacy of programmes that offer children a short number of hours per day and for only one year's duration (Farran, 2000).

There is a particular concern too to provide relevant early intervention and follow-through programmes for children who may be further disadvantaged and at risk of exclusion for reasons of disability or minority status. The research literature is unequivocal in stressing the importance of the early years for children with disabilities. Within the broad area of disability, children with mild general learning disability are most at risk of not getting an appropriate service. There is a high prevalence of children with this level of disability in disadvantaged communities and many of these children are identified as needing support only after a number of years in school. Yet there is evidence that children with mild learning disabilities benefit particularly from comprehensive programmes of early intervention (Garber, 1998; Campbell and Ramey, 1995).

Content and design

In this discussion on the role of teaching in addressing educational disadvantage, a number of factors for effectiveness that relate specifically to curriculum and pedagogy have been identified. These factors are:

- the provision of structured programmes of teaching and learning which are appropriate and relevant and which are planned to increase children's levels of interest, self-esteem and motivation
- fine-tuning of the teacher–learner relationship and a close match between the characteristics of the learner and the nature and content of the teaching
- recognition of the potential need for change in teaching style and emphasis in the intervention setting
- programmes of professional development and in-class support to create and to enable such change.

In addition, a number of factors for effectiveness relating to the structural features of intervention have been identified. These interact with factors relating to curriculum and pedagogy and are also critical to programme outcomes. These factors are:

- the need for comprehensive programmes of intervention that include early intervention and follow-through school-age programmes that have continuity in terms of curricular emphasis and teaching style
- the need for parent partnership and collaboration in the design and implementation of these programmes
- the need for intensity in terms of duration of the intervention programme and length of individual sessions within it.

This position on intervention requires a level of response that goes far beyond recognition of the need for programme provision. Rather, it identifies a number of imperatives relating to the nature and implementation of that provision.

Intervention in the Irish context

To date, in school-based intervention in Ireland, we have, in the main, designed programmes that rely on two key features: reduced teacher–pupil ratios and increased financial assistance to schools. These have been the two main provisions in *Breaking the Cycle* (1996) and in the new programme, *Giving Children an Even Break* (2001). In this regard, the expectation for the outcomes of the intervention could be said to rest in the most basic structural features of the programme, features which could be regarded as providing only the minimum in prerequisites for the comprehensive support systems and innovative practices required in the intervention. To date the *Giving Children an Even Break* programme has not focused on, or provided support for, curriculum and pedagogy which the discussion so far has identified as critical factors in intervention effectiveness. A further concern is that provision for children under four is not a necessary or integral part of either programme.

The *Early Start Programme* was also poorly supported in the initial stages of its implementation. When the programme was first initiated in 1994, no clearly articulated curriculum framework was offered and no coherent programme of curriculum development and teaching support was included in the programme design. In the years since then, in collaboration with *Early Start* teachers and childcare workers, draft curriculum guidelines have been developed and a model of in-class support, focusing on curriculum and pedagogy, has been designed and piloted in a number of *Early Start* centres (1998). This model has been developed to include in-class support as part of the induction of new teachers and child-care workers. Further development of this model and its full extension to the entire group of *Early Start* classes, as a model of on-going support, would be a positive development.

Recent evaluations of *Early Start* have identified the current curricular and pedagogic focus as consistent with evidence on effective practice (Lewis and Archer, 2003; Archer and Weir, 2005). However, the short daily session of two-and-a-half hours does not meet the requirements for programme duration advised in the literature and this remains a weakness in this provision. Among its strengths, *Early Start* now includes a number of key factors for effective intervention, including high levels of staff qualifications, appropriate curriculum and pedagogy, and high levels of parental involvement. An appropriate extension of the daily sessions would greatly enhance this provision.

Action Plan for Educational Inclusion, DEIS (2005)

The discussion so far has focused on a number of intervention programmes that have looked to teaching and learning to address issues of educational disadvantage in the Irish primary education system. The most recent initiative from the DES is *DEIS: Delivering Equality of Opportunity in Schools – An Action Plan for Educational Inclusion* (2005). This document outlines policy and provision for addressing the educational needs of young people from disadvantaged communities, aged three to eighteen years. Among the measures provided for in the action plan, those related to school-based supports for literacy and numeracy and those that focus on provision for three-year-olds are directly related to the discussion in this chapter.

The provisions for literacy and numeracy suggested in the document take account of the serious nature of the difficulties being experienced by children in schools and recognise the need for school-based supports which will focus directly on teaching and learning. High priority is to be given to specific planning for literacy and numeracy within schools and measures are outlined for developing staff expertise in this regard and for the provision of advisers (cuiditheoirí). These measures are in line with recommendations from research outlined in the discussion so far, and are a welcome inclusion in this action plan. The challenge to practice here will be to develop the innovative and creative approaches to teaching and learning which allow for sufficient levels of intensity in the intervention while providing appropriately stimulating and engaging learning experiences for children.

While a number of the measures planned for literacy and numeracy are welcome, the absence of an appropriate emphasis on children's oral language development is a serious concern. There is an established body of knowledge on the relationship between language and learning and, in particular, on the role of language in developing the complex modes of thought necessary for educational knowledge (Halliday, 1993; Bruner, 1996). Equally, there is a growing research emphasis on the specific link between children's oral discourse skills and achievements in literacy (Snow, Burns and Griffin, 1998; Snow, Tabors and Dickinson, 2001; Griffin et al., 2004). The interventions required by the population of children for whom DEIS is intended need to include an intensive focus on developing oral language as a basis for learning, across all areas of the curriculum. The action plan puts no emphasis on a comprehensive approach to oral language development. Rather, the one tangible provision relates to support from speech and language therapists.

Provision of therapy to children with specific speech and language difficulties is a necessary part of the web of supports which should constitute a comprehensive early intervention programme, as discussed in an earlier section of this chapter. However, language teaching and learning in the context of an intervention curriculum is a different enterprise to providing a therapeutic service. Responsibility for the language curriculum sits firmly within the remit of the school and this is the primary focus for intervention. In tandem with support for the teaching of literacy, as part of the action plan, teachers need to be supported in developing the skills to plan and to teach a language curriculum which is matched to the differentiated needs of the learners.

Provision for early intervention in DEIS

A further, major concern in DEIS is the nature of the provision outlined for three-year-old children. In the action plan, the DES only takes responsibility for providing *an educational dimension* within existing childcare services in disadvantaged communities. This plan ignores the body of existing research on effective early intervention for this population of children. The factors which contribute to effective early intervention for children at risk for reasons of socio-economic disadvantage have been outlined at length here. From a teaching and learning perspective, these factors relate to the quality of curriculum and pedagogy and they rest on an assumption of high levels of qualifications in programme providers. One of the central points in the discussion is the need to deliver on-going professional development to staff who are already starting from a high base in terms of qualifications. The lack of such supports has been regarded as a persistent problem, militating against programme effectiveness to date. The provisions for three-year-olds in DEIS present a wholly new kind of problem. Here the DES is planning to provide early intervention in settings that are unregulated in terms of staff qualifications, curriculum content and pedagogic practice.

The existing provision in the unregulated early years sector does not meet requirements for effective intervention in a range of critical areas. A recent study of provision for children with disabilities and children at risk for reasons of disadvantage, in two geographical areas in Ireland, highlighted low levels of training, absence of structured curriculum and poor knowledge of pedagogy as serious concerns in provision for children under four (McGough, Carey and Ware, 2005). The need for the provision of a range of training options so that critical conditions for quality can be met in the wider early years sector in Ireland has been documented (Donnelly, D. et al., 1998; OECD, 2004). Indeed the report of the national evaluation of preschools for Travellers (DES, 2003), which was conducted by the DES Inspectorate, recommends that the DES should ensure the provision of accredited courses leading to a recognised minimum qualification for personnel working in this preschool service. Given these circumstances, the present position taken by the DES is difficult to sustain.

It is recognised that there is a need to build partnerships between the range of departments and agencies that impinge on the lives of young children in disadvantaged areas and a need also to include and to build upon the contributions of existing early years providers. However, there is, predominantly, the acute need to provide appropriate early intervention for the cohort of three-year-old children living in the targeted areas who are, potentially, among the most vulnerable and marginalised in the school-going population. This need requires a radical and imaginative approach which could include a role for all of the relevant agencies and providers and which could mark a new milestone in provision at this point in our intervention history. Such an approach would require the will and commitment to plan and to fund the innovative, comprehensive service that is required. The existing action plan does not suggest such will or commitment. It remains to be seen whether there is still an opportunity to seek a creative way forward at the planning and implementation stage. Otherwise all of the lessons of research will have been wasted.

References

Archer, P. and Weir, S. (2005) *Addressing Disadvantage: A Review of the International Literature and of Strategy in Ireland,* Educational Disadvantage Committee, Dublin: DES

Biddle, B. J. and Berliner, D. C. (2002) 'Small class size and its effects: What does the evidence say about the effects of reducing class size?', *Educational Leadership*, 59, 5, pp. 12–22

Bruner, J. S. (1996) 'Frames for thinking: Ways for making meaning' in Olson, D. R. and Torrance, N. (eds) *Modes of thought; explorations in culture and cognition*, Cambridge: Cambridge University Press, pp. 93–105

Campbell, F. A. and Ramey, C. T. (1995) 'Cognitive and school outcomes for high-risk African American students at middle adolescence: Positive effects on early intervention', *American Educational Research Journal*, 32, pp. 743–72

Casto, G. and Mastropieri, M. A. (1986) 'The efficacy of early intervention programmes: A meta-analysis source', *Exceptional Children*, 52, 5, pp. 417–24

Department of Education and Science (2003) *Preschools for Travellers: National Evaluation Report*, Dublin: DES

Department of Education and Science (2005) *DEIS: Delivering Equality of Opportunity in Schools – An Action Plan for Educational Inclusion*, Dublin: DES

Donnelly, D. et al. (1998) *Report on the national forum for early childhood education*, Dublin: The National Forum Secretariat

Ehrenberg, R. G., Brewer, B. J., Gamoran, A. and Willms, J. D. (2001) 'Does class size matter?' *Scientific American*, November

Eivers, E., Shiel, G. and Shortt, F. (2004) *Reading Literacy in Disadvantaged Primary Schools*, Dublin: Educational Research Centre

Farran, D. C. (2000) 'Another decade of intervention for children who are low income or disabled: What do we know now?' in Shonkoff, J. P. and Meisels, S. J. (eds) *Handbook of Early Childhood Intervention* (2nd edn) Cambridge: Cambridge University Press, pp. 510–48

Garber, H. L. (1988) *The Milwaukee project: Preventing mental retardation in children at risk*, Washington DC: American Association on Mental Retardation

Griffin, T. M., Hemphill, L., Camp, L. and Palmer Wolf, D. (2004) 'Oral discourse in the preschool years and later literacy skills', *First Language*, 24, 20, pp. 123–47

Guralnick, M. (2002) 'Model service systems as research priorities in early intervention', *Journal of Early Intervention*, 25, 2, pp. 100–4

Guralnick, M. (ed.) (1997) *The effectiveness of early intervention: Second generation research*, Baltimore: Paul H. Brookes

Guralnick, M. (ed.) (2005) *The developmental systems approach to early intervention*, Baltimore: Paul H. Brookes

Halliday, M. A. K. (1993) 'Towards a language based theory of learning', *Linguistics and Education*, 5, pp. 93–116

Kellaghan, T., Weir, S., Ó Huallacháin, S. and Morgan, M. (1995) *Educational Disadvantage in Ireland*, Dublin: ERC, DOE, CPA

Lewis, M. and Archer, P. (2003) *Early start evaluation: Report on observation visits to schools*, Dublin: Educational Research Centre

McGough, A., Carey, S. and Ware, J. (2005) *Early years provision for children from birth to six years with special needs in two geographical areas in Ireland*, Dublin: research commissioned and funded by the Centre for Early Childhood Development and Education

National Commission on Education (1996) *Success against the odds: Effective schools in disadvantaged areas*, London: Routledge

National Economic and Social Forum (1997) *Early school leavers and youth unemployment*, Dublin: Government Publications

National Economic and Social Forum (2002) *Early School Leavers Forum Report. No. 24*. Dublin: NFSF

Organisation for Economic Cooperation and Development (2004) *Thematic review of early childhood education and care policy in Ireland*, Dublin: OECD

Ramey, C. T. and Ramey, S. L. (1998) 'Early intervention and early experience', *American Psychologist*, 53, 2, pp. 109–20

Ramey, C. T., Campbell, F. A., Burchinal, M., Skinner, M. L., Gardner, D. M. and Ramey, S. L. (2000) 'Persistent effects of early childhood education on high risk children and their mothers', *Applied Developmental Science*, 4, pp. 2–14

Ramey, S. and Ramey, C. (2003) 'Understanding efficacy of early educational programs: Critical design, practice, and policy issues' in Reynolds, A., Wang, M. and Walberg, H. (eds) *Early Childhood Programmes for a New Century*, Washington, DC: CWLA Press, pp. 35–70

Reynolds, A. J., Mavrogenes, D., Bezruczko, N. and Hagemann, M. (1996) 'Cognitive and family support mediators of pre-school effectiveness: A confirmation of analysis', *Child Development*, 67, 3, pp. 1119–40

Sameroff, A. J. and Fiese, B. H. (2000) 'Models of development and developmental risk' in Zeanah, C. (ed.) *Handbook of Infant Mental Health*, New York: The Guilford Press, pp. 3–19

Slavin, R., Madden, N., Dolan, L. and Wasik, B. (1996) *Every child, every school: Success for all*, Thousand Oaks, CA: Corwin Press

Snow, C. E., Burns, M. S. and Griffin, P. (eds) (1998) *Preventing reading difficulties in young children*, Washington, DC: National Academy Press

Snow, C. E., Tabors, P. O. and Dickinson, D. K. (2001) 'Language development in the preschool years' in Dickinson, D. K. and Tabors, P. O. (eds) *Beginning literacy with language*, Baltimore: Paul H. Brookes, pp. 1–25

Trivette, C. M., Dunst, C. J. and Deal, A. G. (1997) 'Resource-based approach to early intervention' in Thurman, S. K., Cornwell, J. R. and Gottwald, S. R. (eds) *Contexts of Early Intervention*, Baltimore: Brookes Publishing Co., pp. 73–93

Weir, S. and Eivers, E. (1998) *The Breaking the Cycle Evaluation*, Dublin: Educational Research Centre

Weir, S., Mills, L. and Ryan, C. (2002) *The Breaking the Cycle Scheme in Urban (and Rural) Schools: Final Evaluation Reports,* Dublin: Educational Research Centre

Wolery, M. and Bailey Jr, D. B. (2002) 'Early childhood special education research', *Journal of Early Intervention*, 25, 2, pp. 88–99

25

A Model of Drama for Educational Disadvantage

Colm Hefferon

Children are increasingly involved in research that affects their lives. This seems to be recognised by children's organisations who realise that children should have a 'voice in affairs that affect them' and that 'children's views will be given due weight in accordance with the age and maturity of the child'. The National Children's Strategy key objective is 'to support research and evaluation of new mechanisms to give children a voice'. (Tallaght West Childhood Development Initiative, 2005, p. 6)

Supporting ideas: the arts as a paradigm of research

'New paradigm' teachers such as Egon G. Guba urge us to be 'methodological trailblazers' (Gray et al., 1995). On a practical level, recent and current teachers in the Arts have found themselves exactly in that role: in the absence of appropriate methodologies they have taken it upon themselves to adapt and/or invent procedures and tools of enquiry. This can involve a creative hybridisation of existing models, which in this case integrate and exploit the particular characteristics of the spoken arts: theatre, drama and role-play, in order to make manifest the ideas and themes being explored.

Referring to the work of Sir Herbert Read, Elliot Eisner argues:

> ... that the aim of education ought to be conceived of as the preparation of artists. By the term artist neither he nor I mean necessarily painters and dancers, poets and playwrights. We mean individuals who have developed the ideas, the sensibilities, the imagination and the skills, to create work that is well proportioned, skillfully executed and imaginative, regardless of the domain in which an individual works. (Eisner, 2004, p. 4)

The method proposed in this article provides participants with a dramatic experience, its function being to use the types of thinking that dramatic artists use to explore the issues at hand in an indirect way, through the use of fiction. When Maxine Greene talks of 'releasing the imagination' (Greene, 1995), she seems to suggest that children should be free to look at situations which affect their lives in new imaginative ways. In drama, this is achieved through the safety of working in the fictional imagination. It is important to say that this imagination is not an indulgent daydream but both effective and critical. The critical imagination's power is harnessed instrumentally, allowing the cognitive and affective domains to combine holistically in a considered judgement.[1]

Structure: the graduated framework is identified

It is generally accepted that stories told through theatre and drama are historically fundamental to social bonding. For the purposes of this chapter, theatre is defined by the notion of participation, i.e. the audience as observer. In storytelling the audience participates as listener; however, drama, as defined here, involves the audience as active doer. The model works in chronological stages as follows: storytelling, theatre, drama, fictional research and factual research.

This five-stage model is an integrated hybrid method, which is imaginative, artistic, and practical. The author's drama teaching experience indicated that shy children were often quite fearless in role, whilst often appearing passive and docile in other contexts. Repeated occurrences of this nature indicated that drama could increase self-esteem and academic motivation whilst also improving a pupil's sense of responsibility and social harmony (Hefferon, 2000). The answers given in role to complex questions indicated that a child's register of language often deepened and expanded to amplify the role being played, leading to fluent use of often quite unfamiliar adult registers of vocabulary.

Drama creates a forum in which all these criteria can be valued and integrated by the questing child as artist, learner, and teacher of their own lives. This type of drama then involves imaginative and emergent thinking, multiple perspectives, and openness to alternative solutions, which may emerge as the work progresses.

The attempt here is to develop a dialectic model of drama in which participants have an artistic experience and a discussion of relevant issues, whilst the teacher, also an artist, gathers authentic data about the attitudes, values, opinions, and behaviour of a particular group of children. Everyone is a winner: not only does the teacher gain access to authentic data, but the children also discover their own artist voice and develop effective agency within and among themselves.

---

[1] A short video emphasising this point is available from the Imagination in Education Research group at http://www.ierg.net/confs/2004/video/Case_conf04.mov, retrieved 11/02/06.

Drama as research

Unlike quantitative research, which uses numbers to prove or disprove a hypothesis, qualitative research often uses a biographical story to engage the reader in issues of relevance to the subject under observation. Conclusions are based on interpretations of the subject's story. The teacher seeks to interpret and understand, rather than judge, the lives of the people with whom he or she is working. How drama as research differs from other forms of qualitative research is that the central character is typical, though fictional. The teacher's purpose is to structure the fictional story as a stimulus to receive the participants' concerns, questions, ideas, and potential solutions to the emerging problems and complications. In the emergent drama model, the participants engage with a typical though fictional person who shares some of their own qualities, culture and lifestyle. In the model under review, *Christy's Dream* (Binch, 1999) was the stimulus for the Tallaght West Childhood Development Initiative (TWCDI) research. Immediacy of identification engages participants' attention and focuses them on the task in hand. With children who experience educational disadvantage, this has particular significance as they are meeting a 'real' child from a background similar to their own, as opposed to a book or project on the issue. Through this experience of metaxis (the state of belonging completely and simultaneously to two different, autonomous worlds: the image of reality and the reality of the image), the participant is experiencing the particular in a fictional world but generalising the behaviour in his own real world.

The teacher's role in this drama model draws on Freire's principle of transformative education, with the teacher/researcher acting as guide and wise friend of the participants (Araújo-Freire and Macedo, 1998). The teacher is not imposing his or her ideas on children, but working with them to explore the issues and allow inherent meaning to emerge; allowing for contextualised, embodied knowledge leading to a holistic understanding of the issue being explored.

Using the drama conventions of storytelling, monologue, and role-play, this graduated method seeks to identify, prioritise, embody, and resolve the potential challenges and dilemmas raised by the children in relation to the fictional material (Bruner, 1990). The drama becomes a search for personal and social meaning rather than a paper chase for information. If this epistemology has value for art could it not also have value for teaching and research? After all, both are led by a question. In art, the question may be implicit, in research explicit. In the case of this type of drama, the questions are artistic and factual, fictional and real, satisfying the complementary needs of all participants in the research – the observers and the observed. In order to create a critical lens to illustrate the structure it would be useful to use an example of this method as a prototype. Here is a brief sketch of the story used.

Christy and the horse – summary

Christy dreams of owning his own horse. The one big problem is Ma; she doesn't want him to have anything to do with them. Unknown to her, Christy buys a little grey filly with dark eyes and calls her Jasmine. When Ma finds out the horse has to go. One night, Jasmine runs out on the motorway and Christy is disabled as a result of a serious accident. Christy's friends are shocked and believe that something has to happen to make the area a better place for Christy and children like him. The Minister for the Environment promises €5 million. The children have to pitch proposals to the Minister on how it should be spent.

The research model referred to below was implemented in Tallaght West with several classes of eleven-year-old children as part of the research project 'Experiencing Childhood Citizenship, Consultations with Children in Tallaght West' (TWCDI, 2005).[2] It is based on an earlier prototype used for the report to the National Forum on Disadvantage in Education, St Patrick's College (2002). Though similar in approach, the methodological emphasis of the earlier drama-as-research project, *Timmy*, was on pupil engagement with a fictional child; through this fictional lens, pupils' perceptions of the personal and systemic change needed to facilitate every child's learning and achievement were explored. The approach of this model, *Christy's Dream*, is similar, although the focus is less on personal agency and more on systemic change to Christy's neighbourhood. A significant artistic difference, however, is that in the earlier *Timmy*, participants could influence both the fictional and real outcomes, whereas involvement in *Christy's Dream* is more interpretive in emphasis, as the artistic outcomes were preset. The participants' role in *Christy's Dream* is to enact the fictional events that lead up to the climax. The dénouement in *Christy's Dream* is the pupils articulating changes that need to be made to the environment so that Christy won't feel he has to ride horses again. In *Timmy* the emphasis was personal and systemic and was made through the role of Timmy's teacher. The changes in *Christy's Dream*, though hypothetical, are systemic and made out of role; the pupils move from in-role discussion to out-of-role discussion – the bridge being the fictional character of Christy.

The five-stage developmental method is described in brief. The stages of the model are based on a hybridised and integrated framework using three anchor concepts: Robert Reasoner's five pillars of self-esteem (security, identity, belonging, purpose, personal competence); the five-stage dramatic structure of the

---

[2] Readers would benefit from having access to the actual plan used, which is available on the EDC website at http://www.spd.dcu.ie/main/academic/edc/documents/ChristyKellyandtheHorselesson plan.doc in order to clarify some of the points made. Neither model would exist without the input, facilitation, support and involvement at every stage of Neil Haran, a freelance researcher with the National Forum and later the TWCDI.

well-written play (context, rising action, complication, climax and dénouement); and the five functional roles played by the teacher in the drama-as-research method – planner, games facilitator, storyteller, drama facilitator and researcher.

Action: the chronological development of active researcher roles is reviewed

The work is divided into three chronological phases, i.e. the pre-fiction, in-fiction and post-fiction phases of the research. The roles in each phase are directly related to the dramatic and research requirements of each phase (See Figure 1 below).

Figure 1 Overview of phases, stages and roles

Phase	A Pre-fiction	B In-fiction	C Post-fiction
Role	1 Planner	1 Storyteller	1 Teacher out of role
	2 Games facilitator	2 Drama facilitator	
		3 Teacher in role	

Pre-fiction phase

Planning

The researcher/teacher chooses a story that is culturally relevant to his or her group. Issues such as the age of the main character, experiences in the story and the themes generated will reflect the learning needs of the participants and the area of research that the teacher wishes to explore.

Teacher games

The facilitator selects the focus and builds motivation through games that reflect the theme and/or create the level of energy and concentration required. The games have a number of defining characteristics:

- **Energy:** Checking the group's energy level to bring participants to the required level of concentration involves a balance of high-energy and low-energy games.
- **Focus:** Games should not put one participant in high focus, i.e. watched by others. If the teacher is a stranger it can militate against trusting relations. Whole-group games mean that no one is in focus. Gradually move the energy from physical activity to focused verbal activity.

- • **Group dynamics:** A movement from whole group to pairs is normal. Often after a few partner changes participants have voluntarily broken down their friendship groups (Poulter, 1991).

In-fiction phase

Storytelling

Teacher/researcher using storytelling. Teacher-in-role as a family member of the child character. In the story used, the role chosen was that of the grandfather who, although he took only a small role in the story, was amplified in the drama. For the teacher, aspects such as playing one's own gender and age are important. At this early contact stage, neither accent nor voice change is required, although some minor costume details would help, e.g. a jacket. At the beginning of the event, it is better that the first character the participants meet is both plausible and a type, i.e. the father, mother, teacher or nurse. In effect s/he becomes an in-role narrator, developing the context so that participants can more easily believe. The participants are brought into the story very fast.

Story reading

Having finished the introduction in role, the teacher, now out of role, reads the story up to a point of tension. There is a need to discuss and highlight main points of tension and to try to find where the main focus of interest or tension might be.

Drama facilitation

There is a need to set up the situation of a dilemma for the main character. Participants enter into role as advisers to the protagonist. Advice is offered as to how he can persuade his parent to get his desired outcome, i.e. what he wants out of the situation. This interactive theatre convention of group role-play has antecedents in sociodrama (Sternberg and Garcia, 2000), psychodrama (Pitruzzella, 2004), storytelling and process drama (Simpson and Heap, 2002). Role-play involves the participant in spontaneously taking on the attitudes, values, motives and behaviour of the role, without the attendant worry of taking on an accent, props, costume and bearing that a well-rehearsed actor might. In eschewing the external details of the role, a sophisticated, focused and pared-down approach reduces participants' fears of exposure, enriches the data and maximises time on the task. Role-play is a valuable research instrument as it provides both the motivation to engage and tools to enquire into the themes being examined. Through the emotional distance afforded by the fictional story, the participant is knowingly and simultaneously engaging with being 'me' and 'not-me'.

In this imaginative 'elsewhere', the children make truthful responses to situations that they feel are important to them. Isn't it a useful irony that children can be more themselves in role, than they can in reality? Such is the protection provided by the mask that is role-play. It is in this threshold space, provided by the belief in the fiction, that the group identifies the important issues in relation to the themes under investigation. It is through the oblique nature of the in-role dialogue that the power of the imagination to isolate and focus, finds expression. In working with children, this threshold experience has an attractive value, as it can be a crucible for lasting change.

Teacher-in-role

Participants meet the establishing character again to hear the effect of the awful event in the life of the central character and the family. S/he enlists their help. This character, as teacher-in-role, begins the process of assessing the needs of the neighbourhood and the changes needed to make life better for the character. The teacher-in-role as this trusted character begins the process of examining the assessment of the needs of the area and the change needed to make life better for the character, so that the awful events will never happen again.

Competition-in-role

The teacher, out of role, informs participants of the funding available but that its disbursement is competitive. The participants, in groups of four, must pitch for the money. The teacher goes into role as 'assistant to the funder'. The participants formally present their idea and the reasons why they should get the funding to the assistant. He will in turn try to persuade the chairman, or the Taoiseach in our case, of the merits of the proposals. The constraint on the participants is that they need the assistant to get access to the Taoiseach. The assistant can refuse any ideas he/she does not think serious by using the Taoiseach, the senior person, as a shield. His attitude to the participants can be quite demanding, as he is looking for hard facts and real reasons. After all, he has to sell the ideas to a 'reluctant chairman'. He takes away the charts to present to the Taoiseach. No decision is made as to who has won. Closure is usually a reflection on the experience in a circle; perhaps participants may wish to return to the story in dramatic form at a later date.

Collaboration or competition in role-play?

At the highest point of suspense in the drama the teacher, in role as a funder, offers the children a huge amount of money to create the change they wish to see. This device fills the need for a role-play mechanism to harness the energy of the drama, and make a competitive pitch for the change they want. The element of group competition raises participants' focus to a new level, which also increases energy.

Moreover, by placing the responsibility on the participants, teachers create a practical focus for their ideas. On charts, the participants make notes on the merits of their proposals and present these to the teacher-in-role as funder. These charts become a record of the major themes of the research and can be taken away for further study by the teacher. The value of competition seems to go against the philosophy of drama, but at this particular stage of the work it can increase commitment, engagement and focus on the emerging themes. Also, at this stage the group is moving from the protected fiction to the less protected real; they are moving into talking about themselves. Working in small groups allows the children to discuss their ideas before they make their pitch. It also adds pace and speed to the process, which at two hours in length might otherwise begin to flag. Participants are supported across that fictional bridge back to the reality of the classroom and are therefore less likely to get self-conscious or trivialise the issues.

Post-fiction phase

Teacher out-of-role

Some time later, perhaps a few days to allow for thinking time, the teacher comes back to the group and makes the transition between fiction and reality. It is here, through the post-drama engagement, that the pupils begin to realise the close link between the life of the character they have experienced in dramatic fiction and the facts of their own lives. The teacher asks participants to think about activating their ideas in their own neighbourhood. Issues of funding, responsibility and implementation are dealt with. At this stage, the teacher judges how far he/she can take this. The teacher, out of role, encourages participants to reflect on the questions 'Who will create this change? How will it be done?' Going from effect to cause, the participants research the causes of the problems they have outlined. For example, in our research, bullying of younger children by teenagers was identified as a problem, the cause being lack of amenities for teenagers, e.g. no football pitches. Finally, they identify the responsible social agencies (e.g. County Councillors who look after parks) and may lobby them with letters and request a visit to present their concerns. The participants are challenged to identify who in their community will help to bring about the necessary change. Organisation of responsibility for this is discussed and, if possible, activated. It is important that participants make some connection between the fictional characters and the reality of their lives. Their agency is affirmed so that they can see that they may act on the world and transform their lives.

Conclusion

The integration of all these stages in one event can create a holistic experience of *communitas*, to paraphrase Victor Turner, whereby, in the threshold or liminal space of the imagination, a group explores issues of change and transformation (O'Reilly, 2004, p. 76 *et seq.*). What drama creates is an offer of a vision for change and a forum for making choices. Whether a participant chooses to cross the threshold of change is dependent on contextual factors. However, the choice, once envisioned, may become a real option, because one is aware, and awareness is the beginning of a lived life. The next step, in the real world, is the personal choice of whether to engage with one's unknown but exciting future, or remain in the life that is known. Drama can do this effectively for our children, so that they make their choices, not based on what they heard at the back of a bus, but on reasoned argument, imaginative response, empathy and respect for others. What an epiphany for a child to realise that change is possible, to see that there are questions to ask, and that the right to know is a democratic imperative; to demand for themselves and their communities a clear coherence between political rhetoric and action on the ground. The stages described here are transferable to other artistic stimuli – poem, story or object – and can be used effectively with these.

References

Araújo-Freire, A. M. and Macedo, D. (1998) *The Paulo Freire Reader*, New York: Continuum Press

Binch, C. (1999) *Christy's Dream*, London: Mammoth

Bruner, J. (1990) *Acts of Meaning: Four lectures on mind and culture*, Harvard: Jerusalem-Harvard Lectures

Eisner, E. W. (2004) 'What can education learn from the arts about the practice of education?' *International Journal of Education and the Arts*, 5, 4, retrieved 13/06/06 from http://ijea.asu.edu/v5n4/

Gray, C., Douglas, A., Leake, I. and Malins, J. (1995) 'Developing a research procedures programme for artists and designers', Aberdeen: Gray's School of Art, Robert Gordon University,
http://www.rgu.ac.uk/criad/cgpapers/drpp/drpp.htm

Greene, M. (1995) *Releasing the Imagination: Essays on education, the arts, and social change*, San Francisco: Jossey-Bass

Hefferon, C. (2000) 'Process drama: its effect on self-esteem and inclusion of primary Fifth Class boys and girls', MEd thesis,
http://www.spd.dcu.ie/main/academic/edc/documents/hefferon_c_thesis.pdf.

National Forum on Primary Education (2002) *Primary Education: Ending Disadvantage, Proceedings and Action Plan of National Forum*, Dublin: St Patrick's College

O'Reilly, A. F. (2004) *Sacred Play-Soul Journeys in Irish Theatre*, Dublin: Carysfort Press

Pitruzzella, S. (2004) *Introduction to Dramatherapy: Person and Threshold*, New York: Brunner-Routledge

Poulter, C. (1991) *Playing the Game*, California, Studio City: Players Press

Reasoner, R. (1992) *Building Self-Esteem in Elementary Schools and Building Self-Esteem in Secondary Schools*, Palo Alto, CA: Consulting Psychologists Press

Simpson, A. and Heap, B. (2002) Process drama: a way of changing attitudes, Stockholm: Save the Children

Sternberg, P. and Garcia, A. (2000) *Who's in your shoes?* Westport, CT: Greenwood Publishing Company

Tallaght West Childhood Development Initiative (2005) 'Experiencing Childhood Citizenship, Consultations with Children in Tallaght West', Tallaght, Dublin: TWCDI

Turner, V. (1977) *The Ritual Process: Structure and Antistructure,* Ithaca, NY: Cornell University Press

26

Drama as Radical Pedagogy

Paula Murphy

Introduction

This chapter explores the notion of *process drama* as a site for radical change. Through a review of the theory and practice of Paulo Freire, the relationship between educational methodology and oppression or, indeed, between educational methodology and what Freire refers to as 'humanisation', will initially be examined. Freire uses the term 'humanisation' to refer to the process of 'becoming more fully human', which he proposes is the ultimate goal of education. It results from a person's perception of the world as an unfinished reality, and from his/her experience of reflection and action upon that reality (Freire, 1970, p. 26). The practice of process drama will be explored in light of this philosophy, and in light of its particular espousal of the principles of democratic and holistic learning which are essential to meaningful participation in all learning contexts.

Context

Despite the many efforts of policymakers and funders in the area of educational disadvantage in recent decades, overall achievements in crucial areas such as early school leaving, retention rates and literacy have been relatively limited (Hyland, 2002; Kellaghan, 2002). In other words, despite much ongoing evidence of the very real achievements of individual pupils and their teachers on a variety of levels, the overall correlation between social class and underachievement seems to have remained intact (National Anti-Poverty Strategy, 1997). Such findings have led to a gradual shift in emphasis in policy documents on educational disadvantage in recent years, from a focus on *access* to education (Government of Ireland, 1992), to *participation* in education (National Anti-Poverty Strategy, 1997), to *achievement* in education (The European Social Fund Programme Evaluation Unit, 1997; Government of Ireland, 2003). The ongoing struggle represented in these documents to identify the central factors which lead to increased levels of achievement in our education system, gives us a clear reminder that access to education alone does not necessarily imply meaningful engagement with it, nor indeed does it guarantee success.

The strong message emerging from much research on educational disadvantage is that while structural and financial developments are undeniably essential to change in schools serving disadvantaged areas, it is the quality of what *happens* within our educational establishments that ultimately determines whether a child feels alienated from, or inspired to continue in, the system. Such a viewpoint inevitably leads to a refocusing of our attentions on fundamental questions relating to both *what* we teach and *how* we teach it, and on supporting and developing our most crucial resource in all such endeavours, the classroom teacher. It was emphasised on several occasions during the National Forum on Educational Disadvantage that 'the quality of teaching is the single most important factor in improving pupil achievement' (Hyland, 2002, p. 54; McGough, 2002). Conaty (2002) also acknowledged the central role of the teacher in contexts of educational disadvantage in terms of highlighting the important relationship between high quality teaching and the meaningful empowerment of children. In her review of the Home School Liaison scheme in Ireland which began as a pilot project in 1990, one of her key observations was that 'teachers who can make the shift from being a teacher to an educator will inevitably move from being an expert to an agent' (Conaty, 2002, p. 158).

This return to a focus on the nature of teaching in the general discourse of educational disadvantage must also of course include a review of the nature of learning itself. In this regard John Dewey's (1938) call to start where learners are at, seems particularly pertinent in terms of our responsibility to children who can often feel alienated from the material under scrutiny in our classrooms, and indeed from the culture of school life itself. Such issues are given crucial relevance in Boldt and Devine's definition of educational disadvantage:

> Educational disadvantage may be considered to be a limited ability to derive an equitable benefit from schooling compared to one's peers by age, as a result of school demands, approaches, assessments and expectations, which do not correspond to the student's knowledge, skills, attitudes and behaviours into which (s)he has been socialised (as opposed to those with which (s)he is naturally endowed). (Boldt and Devine, 1998, p. 10)

Given that the possibility of achievement is unfeasible in the absence of meaningful participation, I would argue that this definition represents yet another call to return with renewed urgency to some of the more critical questions, which are central to all learning and particularly relevant in our fight against the mal-effects of educational disadvantage in this country – What motivates young people to learn? What motivates them to participate? What motivates them to stay in the system? What motivates them to become active citizens in a democratic society? For me, one of the most essential issues in any examination of the phenomenon of learning is the question of motivation, the question of desire.

Discovering a pedagogy

In his acknowledgement of the link between the education system and the servicing of the economy in the Irish context, Dunne (1995) also suggests a need for a review of how children are motivated to participate in our educational establishments. In a system where the need for points seems to have replaced the need to learn, the connection between learning and the world to which it refers seems to have become increasingly fractured. As a way of reconnecting children more meaningfully with the purpose of their learning, Dunne proposes a review of learning activity in terms of its essential relationship with long-established social, intellectual, artistic and work-related 'practices':

> There are important practices that, even though they contain possibilities of great virtuosity, are nonetheless available with real integrity at quite modest, even rudimentary levels of accomplishment. Examples of these are writing, reading or playing a musical instrument. It seems likely that many people have been greatly short-changed in their education, precisely because they were introduced to these activities not as practices, but rather as sites where decomposed drills, exercises, and 'micro-skills' were rehearsed as means, while a taste of the whole activity as an end was continually deferred or displaced. (Dunne, 1995, p. 74)

This notion of motivating children through rewards which are integral to the nature of an activity itself, and to its application in the world, is reminiscent of the emancipatory pedagogy of Paulo Freire. Freire argued that any educational practice that isolates learning from its relevance in the world confounds the oppression of people experiencing disadvantage (Freire, 1970). His notion of a 'problem posing' approach to education, seeks to invoke in participants a fundamental awareness that the way in which the world evolves is not inevitable and laid down by divine rule. On the contrary, it is an unfinished entity and thus within the capacity of each individual to change. Once again, a passionate concern for learning in 'life-like' contexts, demonstrated to be interrelated, is one of the central tenets of Freire's philosophy:

> Students, as they are increasingly posed with problems relating to themselves in the world and with the world, will feel increasingly challenged and obliged to respond

to that challenge. Because they apprehend the challenge as interrelated to other problems within a total context, not as a theoretical question, the resulting comprehension tends to be increasingly critical and thus constantly less alienated. Their response to the challenge evokes new challenges, followed by new understandings: and gradually the students come to regard themselves as committed. (Freire, 1970, p. 62)

Freire would argue that the other significant factor, which leads to commitment in learning, is the extent to which the participants are reliant on each other in the learning encounter. In this regard he gives much attention to the radical shift in relationship which takes place not only between the students themselves in the problem-posing approach, but perhaps more significantly between the teacher and the students. If knowledge is considered to be problematic as opposed to complete, shared as opposed to given, then the traditional relationship of authority between the perceived knower-of-all and the perceived knower-of-little is no longer possible.

While many teachers would have little argument in principle with the ideas presented thus far in this chapter, the apparent idealism of such discourse can sometimes serve to create increased pressure in what may already be a challenging classroom situation – in the short term how can I convince a disaffected child of the pleasure of a practice in the absence of any apparent immediate gains from the activity? What is the nature of the problems with which I should engage the children? How do I overcome the seemingly insurmountable reality that the school is not in itself the world upon which the children will eventually act? What impact does a shift in the nature of my relationship with the children have on the need for discipline in the classroom? It is at this point in the discussion that I wish to consider process drama in terms of the way, as an art form and as an educational methodology, it can begin to help teachers to bridge the difficult gap in which they tend to find themselves between theoretical idealism and the reality of the classroom.

Process drama: historical overview

Process drama as an artistic and pedagogical activity has its roots in both theatrical and educational circles. The refocusing of attention away from traditional sources of authority and on to the material with which participants are engaging is a phenomenon which, of course, has not only been confined to the realms of education. The theatre practices of Bertolt Brecht, Augusto Boal and Jerzy Grotowski are examples of what evolved from a serious concern, particularly in the second half of the twentieth century, with the potential of theatre to manipulate and reinforce passivity among its audiences. In their work, such directors sought to re-examine the political, artistic and pedagogical relationship that exists between the theatre and the society within which it operates, due to its unparalleled capacity to engage participants on an emotional and intellectual level simultaneously. In their practical attempts to empower audiences, they recognised that 'the difference between whether the theatre represents a vehicle for liberation or for oppression depends largely on the extent to which the audience in question is permitted to participate in and own the event' (Murphy and O'Keeffe, 2006, p. 4).

Not surprisingly, the paradigm shifts which took place in education and in the theatre had a significant impact on contemporary approaches to the teaching of drama in schools. While, traditionally, children tended to be cast in the role of either audience members or actors in the school play, the innovators of process drama desired to test the perceived boundaries within which children could own and control their dramatic experience further. In the 1980s particularly, practitioners such as Dorothy Heathcote (1984) and Gavin Bolton (1984) began to critically re-evaluate children's opportunities for not only learning *about*, but also learning *through*, drama within the context of education. In doing so they sought to develop a particular dramatic form which would move young people beyond what were often considered to be superficial engagements with theatre scripts and theatrical devices, so that they could exploit the social, artistic and educational benefits of theatre in a way that was more meaningful and relevant to their lives.

Process drama: principles and practice

Process drama, as a radical theatrical and educational medium, embodies many of the most fundamental elements of the traditional theatre play. Drawing on the artistic imagination of all its participants, it focuses on a person or group of people in a particular fictional context, who we gradually come to empathise with through a series of key episodes or moments. A human theme or philosophical question is usually explored through this fiction, which often comes into direct focus through climactic moments of high tension, decision-making or threat. However, it is the predominantly improvisational nature of process drama which represents its defining characteristic (DES, 1999) and which, I hope to demonstrate, aligns it in a particular way with the radical pedagogies discussed previously. It is also one of the fundamental characteristics which writers on the subject of drama teaching have drawn upon in recent years to assert that drama-in-education is in itself a form of radical theatre practice (Lacey and Woolland, 1992).

In general, process drama tends to emphasise social and artistic experience over performance. It allows participants to improvise with both form and content to explore fictional situations that have some thematic relevance to their lives.

Children do not follow pre-determined scripts in process drama but are rather stimulated by pretexts which are designed to provoke initial engagement and action (O'Neill, 1995).[1] The most pertinent point I wish to explore here in relation to the issue of participation is that the motivation for exploration within these fictions is based not only on the children's attraction to the imaginative context in question but, more fundamentally, on their increasing need to address unexpected tensions, threats or dilemmas which are central to the situation at hand.

Process drama and pedagogies for equality[2]

Let us now consider the above point in light of a particular, albeit brief, example. The fictional drama in question involves a group of fourth-class children who have demonstrated a particular interest in sea travel, adventure and exploration. Through a carefully constructed pretext, they are asked to get into role as a group of expert explorers who are given the important task of finding an apparently deserted island that has held an important place in the history and mythology of their people. As a result of the teacher's provocative questions relating to the preparation for such an important expedition, the children in this drama might decide that they need to engage in such context-building tasks as creating maps for the journey ahead; examining the winds and nature of sea currents on route; designing the most appropriate ship for the expedition; or writing to the king of their country to inform him of their progress. They may also wish, through image, dance or improvisation, to construct the stories about this mysterious island, which have been handed down within their culture for generations. The important point to recognise here is that as the children become more invested in the drama, their motivation for undertaking all of these artistic and cross-curricular tasks is not to gain points, their teacher's approval, or even (at least initially) the pleasure of participation. They are fundamentally engaging in all such activity because they *need* to find the island!

The motivation for engagement becomes even stronger if further tensions are skilfully inserted into the drama as it progresses. This is generally done through the teacher's intermittent introduction of new information that will serve to raise tension and disturb the status quo. One of the most effective ways that this can be done is through the convention of *teacher-in-role*. For example, in this drama the teacher might unexpectedly go into role as a sick crew member who will only survive if s/he receives expert medical assistance from the doctors at home.

---

[1] The pretexts for such explorations can be drawn from a range of sources, including folktales, paintings, objects, letters, newspaper articles, songs, and items of interest in other areas of the curriculum or popular culture.

[2] The term 'pedagogies for equality' is a term which was used to reflect one of the key recommendations of the parents, teachers and children in the national research project on educational disadvantage (Zappone, 2002).

Another possibility for provocative tension could be introduced when they reach the island itself. Here they might meet the teacher-in-role as a local tribal leader who tells them that the island has already been inhabited for many years and that it would be impossible for him to ask his people to leave their ancestral home. Such major dramatic and human tensions in a drama are usually tied in with the underlying philosophical themes that have been identified as a key focus for the work. In the first example above, the children's attention is focused on the universal task of balancing the needs and rights of the individual with the needs and rights of society. The second example raises important issues related to citizenship and democracy, such as human rights and responsibilities, interculturalism and land ownership.

One of the key aspects to note in relation to the content of this drama is that a human situation representative of the personal, social and political activity which usually takes place in the world outside the classroom has become the focus of enquiry for the world inside the classroom. It is also important to note that this has been done in a way which corresponds very powerfully to the child's natural tendency to make sense of the world through improvisation, artistic endeavour and play. Finally, the contextual quality of the activity responds in a very immediate way to the child's need for relevance in learning, while simultaneously helping him/her to develop the skills and qualities needed in order to engage with the social and political complexities of the contemporary world. In light of Boal's view that the theatre can be a rehearsal for life, he argued that 'spect-actors [as opposed to spectators] must be the protagonists of dramatic action, and these spect-actors must prepare themselves to be the protagonists of their own lives' (Boal, 1992, p. 242).

I will now briefly consider some of the further ways in which the *form* of process drama itself relates to the issue of motivation, which I have argued is one of the central concerns of Freire's philosophy, and of all teaching endeavours. I will confine the remainder of this discussion to the issues of communication, praxis (the interplay between reflection and action), and the role of the teacher, as they are realised in process drama. Process drama is a social art form. Most decisions, both artistic and otherwise, are made in the context of a group, and most challenges are framed in the context of a need to collaborate with others in order to reach a shared fictional goal (Heathcote, 1984). While individual children in our sample drama may express a variety of opinions about *how* this goal might be achieved, their ultimate aim as a group of explorers is to find the island. As a result, the child is intrinsically called upon to focus not only on his/her responsibility to the task in question, but also to the fictional and real group with whom he/she is working. This tends to be gently encouraged through the teacher's careful framing of questions in communal terms. For example – *How are we going to complete the journey in the short time available to us? What supplies will we need? What jobs do we each need to take on so that everything is ready for the time of departure?* Such an emphasis provides a healthy alternative to conventional approaches to motivation in schools that can often have the effect of encouraging the child to compete with others, or to succeed at their expense (Dunne, 1995). Of course it is also evident from this drama that there is much room for debate and disagreement within a process drama, particularly if we consider the difficult dilemmas relating to the fate of the sick crew member in this particular drama or the future ownership of the island. Indeed, it is arguably in the context of such 'dis-ease' that the most significant learning in the drama takes place, and it is precisely because of the fruitful tension between communal responsibility and individual inclination that such a richness of experience can occur.

As children employ a range of theatre conventions and elements to explore fictional situations in drama, their learning inevitably shifts from the predominantly cognitive to the artistic and experiential realms. One of the main features of dramatic activity that contributes to this holistic quality is that of working 'in role'. Children in process drama are given the unique opportunity to step into the shoes of another and in doing so begin to see, feel and reflect on the world from that perspective. The impact of such an experience is made even more significant as a result of the intermittent call on children to move out of role to reflect on the experience, and to decide on future courses of action. This constant shifting from being inside the experience to standing outside of it, which is particularly characteristic of process drama, represents a powerful embodiment of Freire's notion of 'Praxis'.[3]

Finally, let us reflect on the role of the teacher in process drama. The teacher in such an activity does not act as a director in the traditional sense, but employs the principles of the dramatist to facilitate the process from the inside. While the teacher introduces the initial pretext of the drama, it is his/her ambition that the children will gradually begin to own and take responsibility for the direction of the work, as they come to care for its characters, their worlds and their dilemmas. Of course in guiding the children into the experience; in setting up initial contextual moments which will assist them in their emotional investment; in manipulating dramatic tensions which will focus their attention on the underlying questions of the work, and in helping them to explore the capacity of the art form itself to make meaning, the teacher plays a vital facilitatory role which is not within the scope of this chapter to discuss in detail. However, what I wish to draw the reader's attention to here is the very particular way in which the traditional relationships of power in learning contexts are carefully subverted to powerful effect in process drama, through the convention of teacher-in-role.

---

[3] Freire uses the term 'praxis' to refer to the interplay between action and reflection in effective learning experiences. He argues that 'a mere perception of reality not followed by critical intervention will not lead to a transformation of objective reality – precisely because it is not a true perception' (Freire, 1970, p. 34).

Teacher-in-role involves the teacher taking on the role of one or more characters for relatively short intervals during the drama process. In our sample drama she took on the roles of the expedition leader, the tribal leader and the sick crew member. This allows her to stimulate and intrigue children in a unique manner, while also challenging them to focus on the underlying 'human' questions of the work. Children get the opportunity to interact with their teacher on a very different level during such experiences. They sometimes meet her in high-status roles, such as the head of the expedition or the tribal leader. These can be very effective in terms of initiating challenges or tasks, particularly in the early stages of the drama. However, they also get the opportunity to meet their teacher in low-status roles such as that of the sick crew member on the island expedition. Low-status roles tend to include characters who need help or who do not know how to overcome a difficult problem. Such roles, if carefully manipulated by the teacher, can move the children very effectively from functioning as *learners* to functioning as *experts*, which is one of the characteristic features of process drama activity and, in my view, one of the most fundamental goals of education.[4] Because of the teacher's apparent lack of knowledge in such situations and her expectation of their significant expertise in relation to the same, the children's self-esteem is raised during the encounter as is their capacity to work often well beyond their expected levels of ability; to work in what Vygotsky termed 'the zone of proximal development' (Heathcote and Bolton, 1995, p. 35).

The future

This chapter has sought to posit process drama as an artistic and pedagogical medium, which provides a particularly powerful site for extending the visionary and far-reaching potential of radical pedagogical theories into the reality of Irish classrooms. Its capacity to motivate children through engaging fictional contexts and challenges, which correspond to their reality, has been given particular attention. This has been done in light of the difficulties that many teachers experience in terms of helping children to participate and succeed in a system whose curriculum content and reward systems can often feel alien to their worlds. In recent times the DES has given significant support to projects that have advocated such an approach to teaching and to the arts in contexts of educational disadvantage.[5] Indeed it is often the case, as was demonstrated by Freire in Peru,

---

[4] See Dorothy Heathcote's mantle of the expert approach, which is based on this particular frame for learning and involves extensive drama processes which seek to develop children's skills and aptitudes across the whole curriculum (Heathcote and Bolton, 1995).

[5] Examples of such projects in the Dublin area alone are the Abbey Outreach Interactions project (1998–2000), the ongoing work of theatre-in-education companies such as TEAM Educational Theatre company, and the Larkin Community College project which is focusing on the potential for an arts-based approach to curriculum in secondary schools.

that it is out of such contexts that the most radical developments in educational methodology and curriculum content tend to emerge. However, I would argue that the introduction of drama to the Irish primary school curriculum in 1999 represents one of the most innovative departures for the Irish Education system in recent years, and an unprecedented opportunity for the meaningful engagement of all our children.

References

Boal, A. (1992) *Games for Actors and Non Actors* (trans. by Jackson, A.) London: Routledge

Boldt, S, and Devine, B. (1998) *Educational Disadvantage and Early School Leaving*, Dublin: Combat Poverty Agency

Bolton, G. (1984) *Drama as Education*, London: Longman

Bolton, G. (1998) *Acting in Classroom Drama*, Stoke on Trent: Trentham Books Limited

Conaty, C. (2002) *Including All: Home, School and Community United in Education*, Dublin: Veritas

Department of Education and Science (1999) *Drama, Arts Education, Teacher Guidelines*, Dublin: DES

Dewey, J. (1938) *Experience and Education*, New York: Collier Books

Dunne, J. (1995) 'What's the good of education?' in Hogan, P. (ed.) *Partnership and the Benefits of Learning*, Dublin: ESAI

European Social Fund Programme Evaluation Unit (1997) cited in Hyland, Á. (2002) 'Looking to the Future – Ending Disadvantage?', *Primary Education: Ending Disadvantage. Proceedings and Action Plan of National Forum*, Dublin: St Patrick's College

Freire, P. (1970) *Pedagogy of the Oppressed*, London: Penguin

Government of Ireland (1992) *Education for a Changing World: Green Paper on Education*, Dublin: Government Publications

Government of Ireland (2003) *National Action Plan against Poverty and Exclusion 2003–2005*, Dublin: Government Publications

Heathcote, D. (1984) 'Signs and Portents' in Johnson, L. and O'Neill, C. (eds) *Dorothy Heathcote: Collected Writings on Education and Drama*, London: Hutchinson

Heathcote, D. and Bolton, G. (1995) *Drama for Learning: Dorothy Heathcote's Mantle of the Expert Approach to Education*, Portsmouth: Heinemann

Hyland, Á. (2002) 'Looking to the future – Ending disadvantage?' in Gilligan, A. L. (ed.) *Primary Education: Ending Disadvantage. Proceedings and Action Plan of National Forum*, Dublin: Educational Disadvantage Centre, St Patrick's College

Kellaghan, T. (2002) 'Approaches to Problems of Educational Disadvantage' in Gilligan, A. L. (ed.) *Primary Education: Ending Disadvantage. Proceedings and Action Plan of National Forum*, Dublin: Educational Disadvantage Centre, St Patrick's College

Lacey S. and Wolland B. (1992) 'Educational Drama and Radical Theatre Practice', *Theatre Quarterly*, 8, pp. 81–91

McGough, A. (2002) 'Addressing Disadvantage: The Role of Teaching' in Gilligan, A. L. (ed.) *Primary Education: Ending Disadvantage. Proceedings and Action Plan of National Forum*, Dublin: Educational Disadvantage Centre, St Patrick's College

Murphy P. and O'Keeffe, M. (2006) *Discovering Drama: Theory and Practice for the Primary School*, Dublin: Gill & Macmillan

National Anti-Poverty Strategy (1997) *Sharing in Progress*, Dublin: Government Publications

O'Neill, C. (1995) *Drama Worlds: A Framework for Process Drama*, Portsmouth: Heinemann

Outreach Education Programme of the National Theatre (2000) *Interactions; The National Theatre's Educational Initiative 1998–2000*, Dublin: The National Theatre

Zappone, K. (2002) 'Achieving Equality in Children's Education' in Gilligan, A. L. (ed.) *Primary Education: Ending Disadvantage. Proceedings and Action Plan of National Forum*, Dublin: Educational Disadvantage Centre, St Patrick's College

27

The Digital Era: Empowerment or Digital Divide?

Deirdre Butler and John Kelly

> Above all, even beyond the love of knowledge, is this principle: If you love what you learn, you'll get to love yourself more. And this has to be the goal of education that each individual will come out with a sense of personal self-respect, empowerment, and love for oneself, because from that grows all other loves: for people, for knowledge, for the society in which you live. (Papert, 1990, p. 13)

As educators we have to ask the questions: what kind of future do we want to create for our students, what kind of people do we want to nurture and what values do we want to live by? A learning environment needs to be inclusive and must respect the inherent dignity of the person. Without this inclusion, the existing digital divide, which Dickard and Schneider (2002) describe as 'the gap between those individuals and communities that have, and do not have, access to (the) information technologies that are transforming our lives' (p. 1), would be further widened. As educators, we must acknowledge that learners are coming to a learning situation with a unique set of experiences, needs and interests which should inform the learning process.

It was the above principles that informed the Empowering Minds (EM) Project, which was started in Ireland during October 1998 (http://empowering minds.spd.dcu.ie). It began with a vision of a learning environment in which learners are at the centre and their experiences, needs and interests constitute the learning process, with a focus on 'learning how to learn'. (For more on the overall design of the EM project, the role of teachers within it and the unifying narrative theme of story, myth and legend, see Butler, Martin and Gleason, 2000; and Martin, Butler and Gleason, 2000.)

A critical factor in the development of this culture of thinking and learning is the exploration and innovative use of expressive computational materials informed by a constructionist philosophy. Constructionism is grounded in the idea that people learn by actively constructing new knowledge, rather than having information 'poured' into their heads. Moreover, constructionism asserts that people learn with particular effectiveness when they are engaged in constructing personally meaningful artefacts (Papert, 1991, p. 1) that can be shown to, and discussed with, others. These artefacts are 'objects to think with' (Papert, 1980, p. 12; Turkle, 1995) and a means by which others can become involved in the thinking process. If sufficient time is available and the appropriate supportive environments cultivated, learners can construct their own understandings of what it is to learn and be actively involved in the learning process. Having the support of a community could also prove to be a very powerful learning environment as 'other people are the greatest source of alternative views needed to stimulate new learning' (von Glasersfeld, 1989).

The commercially available LEGO *Mindstorms* product formed the core materials around which the EM project was developed. This robotic construction kit, launched by the LEGO Group in 1998, is based on the Programmable Brick research at the Massachusetts Institute of Technology (MIT) Media Lab (www.media.mit.edu). The programmable brick was a derivative of the LEGO/Logo work done in the mid-1980s by Seymour Papert, Mitchel Resnick, Stephen Ocko and Brian Silverman (Resnick and Ocko, 1991; Resnick, 1993). Situating the use of the materials within a story theme was central to creating a rich learning environment. This contributed to the immersive nature of the EM project as it provided a multi-disciplinary focus to the many projects that were developed.

The school from which we draw the examples in this paper became involved with the EM project in 2000 when the sample of schools was expanded to include more small rural schools and designated disadvantaged schools, as well as some single-sex schools and schools with children with special needs. The school is an all-boys' school in a disadvantaged area on Dublin's northside. Many of the children come from households experiencing poverty, long-term unemployment, drugs and alcohol abuse, and having absent parents and imprisoned family members. At present the area is undergoing a major regeneration programme at a cost of €2bn, the largest in the history of the Irish state (www.brl.ie).

The special class at this school was marginalised in terms of day-to-day activities and culture. Ostensibly, the boys in this class, aged ten to thirteen years, had 'failed' within the existing educational system. They had little experience of 'the feeling of being lovable and the feeling of being capable' (Humphreys, 1993, p. 3), the two dimensions central to self-esteem. Reasoner defines self-esteem as 'the degree to which people feel worthy, capable, significant, and effective' (1992,

p. 12). These children were generally regarded as 'very different' and not as capable as the mainstream children. Nobody liked to be part of the special class, as its members were classified as 'dummies' by the rest of the school. No wonder, then, that every child within the unit had a very poor self-image and lacked self-esteem.

Through involvement with the EM community from the year 2000 to date, a meaningful learning community has developed in the school comprising teachers, mainstream mixed-aged pupils and pupils from the special class, working collaboratively. As the teachers engaged with the computational materials, they have become learners alongside the students. The children in the special class have gained a new respect and identity in the learning community.

The learning community

In order to have a framework and a lens to analyse the children's learning, we used Jonassen, Peck and Wilson's (1999, pp. 7–11) characteristics of meaningful learning. They list five independent attributes of meaningful learning that are characteristic of constructivist-learning environments (Figure 1). Furthermore, they note that: 'learning activities that represent a combination of these characteristics result in even more meaningful learning than the individual characteristics would in isolation' (Jonassen, Peck and Wilson, 1999, p. 11).

Figure 1 Attributes of meaningful learning in a constructivist environment

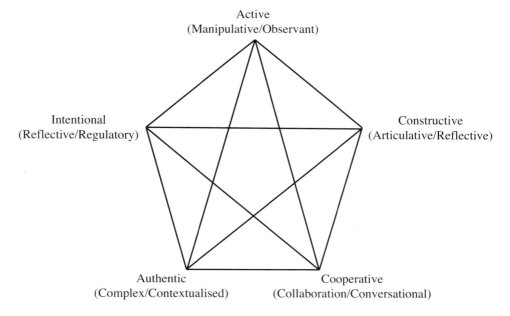

Active learning (manipulative/observant)

Active learning puts the responsibility of organising what is to be learned in the hands of the learners themselves. 'Real learning requires active learning where people are engaged by a meaningful task' (Jonassen, Peck and Wilson, 1999, p. 9). The story of David, a pupil from the special learning class, is an example of a learner who was actively engaged in meaningful learning as a result of his engagement with the *Mindstorms* materials. David, aged thirteen, had experienced many years of failure in mainstream classes and in the special class. He was disengaged with everything that was happening in school and his self-esteem was very low. He announced to the school principal and class teacher that he 'was not coming to school anymore because he was no good at anything and that he had no friends'. This incident coincided with the arrival of the *Mindstorms* materials into the school.

Living in an area that is undergoing a major regeneration project and is constantly surrounded by cranes and other building machinery, David, on his own initiative, decided to build a crane. He threw himself into finding out as much as he could about how a crane is structured and the complexities of how it works. David spent hours working on his creation, ultimately constructing an elaborate, working crane. He displayed his model around the school with great pride. This LEGO robotic crane (Figure 2) became the stimulus for numerous learning activities and the skill developments that, up until then, David could not or did not want to work on. With this boost to his self-esteem, David became more sociable and confident. Members of the learning community held him in high regard and he had achieved a new self-respect. His peers called on him regularly to assist others with LEGO robotic construction, both in his own class and in the mainstream class. David's reading also improved, as he wanted to learn all the programming words and the names of the LEGO parts. His work with cranes was personally meaningful for him and he had ownership of it. His project tapped into his sense of wonder and curiosity and brought a feeling of self-empowerment to his life.

The following January, David displayed his model at the National Young Scientist and Technologist Exhibition held at the RDS, Ballsbridge, Dublin.. When he left the primary school, David gave the class teacher a thank-you card (Figure 3). His reference to himself as 'your best LEGO maker' indicates the positive self-image that he had developed and continues to have of himself. David moved on to a second-level school but he comes back to the primary school regularly to mentor other pupils. Rather than regarding David as a 'dummy', teachers and children alike respect David, and he enjoys his new role as 'building consultant'.

Figure 2 David tests his crane construction

Figure 3 David's letter of thanks

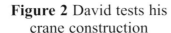

Just To Say A Very Big THANK YOU

for the Leggo
You gave me
and
me to for bringing
the R.D.S
from your best Leggo
Maker

This active learning has provided many opportunities for the special class pupils to demonstrate to the mainstream children how they have developed new talents and skills. The special class now has a new identity within the school. For example, after one building session, when Brian from the special class told the boys in fourth class about a robotics train that he had made, a classmate remarked to Paul (Brian's brother) that he was lucky to have a brother who is a 'genius at LEGO'. In contrast to how he felt in the past, Paul is now proud of his brother in the special class as he realises that his brother is indeed a 'genius at LEGO'. The children in Paul's mainstream class would not have known of Brian's ability unless they were working in the same learning environment and engaged with the same materials because he would have been tagged as just another 'dummy' from the special class.

In this disadvantaged school, parents rarely visit the school to see their children's work or to discuss their children's progress with the teachers. However, since the school's involvement with the EM project, the children are now actively creating projects that are meaningful for them. Because they are actively involved, have ownership of, and are responsible for, setting their own learning goals, they want their parents to see and share in their work. In disadvantaged areas there seems to be an ethos among some families that it is acceptable to miss school on a regular basis. Consequently, 'children are sometimes absent from school with the tacit consent of parents. Perhaps such parents do not see the value or relevance of a school programme' (INTO, 1995, p. 2). Coupled with this is also the fact that 'home life may be unstructured with no fixed routines established so that there is no responsible adult to ensure that children go to bed and get up at appropriate times ...' Such children are largely left to their own devices (INTO, 1995, p. 2) and often make the choice themselves about coming to school without parental encouragement. This situation contrasts strongly with middle-class areas where the usual pattern is that children are sent to school every day and parents make sure that they attend. For one mainstream class in the school, Thursday has become known as 'Mindstorms Robotic Day' and the attendance on this day is higher in comparison with other school days. An examination of the attendance book shows that there is an average of three boys absent each school day. On Thursdays, however, there has been full attendance on thirteen of the twenty *Mindstorms* sessions, and in the remaining seven sessions there has been only one absentee on each of the mornings. This demonstrates that the children value the *Mindstorms* work and they have made a conscious decision to come to school on these days.

Authentic learning (complex/contextualised)

'Learning is not separate from reality. Their culture affects their interactions with the materials and consequently how they learn' (Papert, 1990, p. 179).

Figure 4 Opening the power drill   **Figure 5** Gerard's first drill

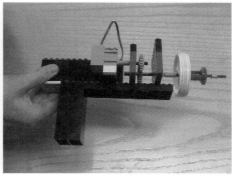

In the EM project, the world of the learner is respected and the teachers involved have designed activities that are driven by the children's interests which, they believe, make them inherently authentic. In grounding the activities in a real-world context, the learners are being engaged and stimulated to construct knowledge for themselves, in meaningful ways. The constructed models are based on the reality of the children's experiences.

Gerard and his drill project is an example of how learners in the EM community are actively determining their own goals rather than functioning passively in the classroom. Gerard is a sixth class mainstream pupil with an interest in power tools. The class teacher noticed this interest when constructing the shelving and storage units for their new robotics workshop. He helped Gerard to open the power drill (Figure 4) they were using to construct the shelving units and, after a discussion about the parts, Gerard said he would like to make a working drill, using the *Mindstorms* materials (Figure 5).

He describes his sense of achievement when he finished the model: 'It took me a while. I made a drawing and gathered the parts. I put it on the shelf in the workshop and when I made it, I felt great. I took a photo of it and I brought it up to my class.' This learning by doing is much more meaningful than rote learning or reading something from a book. Gerard was driven by his own sense of wonder, had ownership of his learning agenda and was actively constructing knowledge for himself. This pursuit of personally set learning goals concurs with the research by Jonassen, Peck and Wilson (1999, p. 118) who note, 'when students own the knowledge rather than the teacher or the textbook, they become committed to building knowledge rather than merely receiving and reprocessing it'. Gerard was motivated to do further experimentation with drills, and a second drill demonstrates a significant internalisation of gearing concepts. The photograph of this second drill shows that his thinking has become more complex as he continues to work on constructing a more complex model. He has incorporated a gear train, instead of the two idle gears of the first drill, a touch sensor and the RCX brick (Figure 6).

Figure 6 Gerard's second drill

Constructive learning (articulative/reflective)

The learners need to reflect on the activity and the thinking processes they have been through in coming to a solution so that they can engage in their own construction of knowledge. The EM project encourages multiple means of expression. The children can review and reflect on their experiences by keeping a journal where they actually write up a report which can be supplemented by using audio or video recordings as they talk about their models, thus enabling them to reflect on their progress. As Resnick and Ocko note: 'in this way, students get a sense of the way in which real designers go about their work, as part of a community of designers' (1991, p. 6). Having a digital camcorder and a computer available in the classroom have proven to be important in helping the children to engage in constructive learning. Figure 7 shows an example of a child's reflective journal.

Figure 7 Example of child's reflective journal

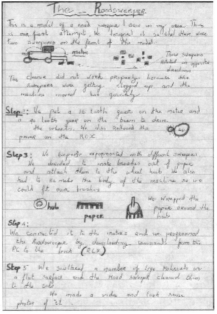

Cooperative learning (collaborative/conversational)

In terms of this attribute, there are many instances of peer-to-peer tutoring, cooperative learning, collaboration with more experienced learners, and teacher-student collaboration, while working with the *Mindstorms* materials. Sugrue (2004), who carried out an ethnographic study in the special class described in this paper, noted:

> There is evidence of prolonged engagement, tenacity and a willingness to tinker with things in pursuit of their own learning quite independently of the teacher, while recognising also that help is at hand from the teacher or a peer should the need arise, something that encourages and fosters a degree of risk-taking that would be unlikely to occur in other circumstances. (Sugrue, 2004, p. 15)

Figure 8 Shane's script

Figure 9 Scrolling text model

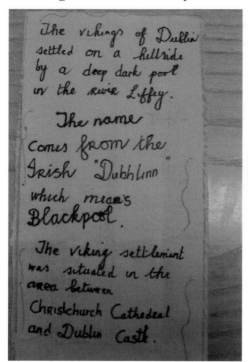

In the teacher–student collaborations, teachers are often learning alongside their students, which demonstrates that they are willing to engage in a process to work out solutions to problems together. The story of Shane's scrolling text model is a good example of this type of collaboration. Shane had won a prize for his penmanship and had received a lot of recognition for this in the school. He was a reluctant LEGO builder and did not socialise well with the other groups, preferring instead to sit on his own practising his penmanship. The class teacher mentioned to Shane that a scrolling text model for the Viking Dublin project was needed, believing that his penmanship skill might, if incorporated into a robotic model, be a good entry path into *Mindstorms* robotics for him. Shane got very excited and took up the challenge. He wrote the text on a piece of cloth (Figure 8) and making the model became a collaborative venture between Shane and the class teacher. A model was made using pulley wheels, beams, axles and LEGO bricks (Figure 9). The material was stitched around the axles.

When the motor was attached, the scroll would not turn. The class teacher did not know what to do. Shane suggested putting four forty-tooth gear wheels on the axles behind the material because he believed that the teeth would grip into the material. The designers of LEGO *Mindstorms* probably did not envision LEGO gear wheels being used in this way, but Shane did not feel constrained by standard usage. Shane manually turned the axle and the scroll rotated. He was thrilled that his own idea had worked. When the motor was attached to the scroll, it would not turn. Shane did not know that the power being transmitted from the motor was insufficient to turn the scroll. He was getting frustrated and the class teacher felt that this was an appropriate moment to 'scaffold' Shane's learning. They looked at applying gear reduction and, in the process, Shane understood that the weak but fast motor energy could be transformed into a slow but strong rotation. The class asked Shane to try to stop the motor from turning. He was unable to stop it and it was explained to him that this strong rotation was called 'torque'. They also looked at worm gears and Shane decided to use this type of gear for the model. There was a great sense of shared achievement with this scrolling text model and the collaborative experience proved to be Shane's entry point into LEGO *Mindstorms*. Shane displayed his model around the school and the teachers were amazed at his articulation and enthusiasm when he was in the class explaining how the model worked. By the end of the school year, Shane was one of the most accomplished LEGO builders in the learning community.

Intentional learning (reflective/regulatory)

Articulating an intention is essential for meaningful learning (Jonassen, Peck and Wilson, 1999) and, in the EM learning environment, learners are encouraged to articulate their learning goals, the decisions they make, the strategies they use and the answers they find. All of the children and teachers have learned the new vocabulary associated with the *Mindstorms* materials in order to communicate ideas and problem-solving strategies. The importance of listening to other children's contributions became increasingly apparent when the children realised that the teacher did not have all the answers. Papert (1993, p. 80) points out that 'student bugs become topics of conversation and, as a result, they learn an articulate and focused language to use in asking for help when it is needed'.

The following conversation was recorded during a building session when David and Dean were attempting to slow down the swivel motion on a crane. (It is worth noting that Dean attends learning support for maths.)

> David: We have to put a small wheel with a big wheel [holding up a big gear wheel]. How many spikes on this one?
> Dean: They're called teeth, it's a forty-tooth gear wheel.
> David: How do you know?
> Dean: Look, four by ten. One-quarter way round is ten. Halfway round is twenty. Three-quarters is thirty. One full turn is forty.

David: Cool!

Dean: [Holding small tooth wheel]. This is an eight-tooth gear wheel. Look, four by two. This will have to turn around five times to make the big wheel turn once.

David: So, if you put the big one first, it would turn the eight-tooth gear around five times.

David and Dean used maths to understand the physical world of gears and together reasoned out the concept of gear reduction. Powerful evidence like David and Dean's story effectively quells criticisms by others who may accuse the special class teacher of 'allowing his boys to play around with LEGO and computers all day'. When they complain that he is 'not covering the curriculum', he can now demonstrate that the very children who had 'failed' with traditional methods now actually have appropriated 'powerful ideas' that not only encompass the prescribed curriculum but also are far more challenging and complex.

As a result of the school's involvement in the EM project, there have been numerous visitors to the school. These include Mary Hanafin, the Minister for Education and Science, Kathryn Holmquist, a journalist with the *Irish Times* newspaper, and the Minister for Education from the Czech Republic. During these visits, the teachers took a back seat and the children loved the opportunity to be able to talk about the work they were doing. All of the visitors were very impressed with how articulate the children were. These experiences are powerful and significant boosts to the children's self-esteem. The teachers and visitors have exalted them and said that what you do and what you are is important.

Conclusion

Papert (1980) noted that 'through the construction of educationally powerful computational environments', an alternative learning environment to the traditional instructionist approach could be developed. In the constructionist environment that has developed over time in this disadvantaged school, a learning community has emerged which comprises teachers, mainstream mixed-aged pupils and the special class, working collaboratively. The school has moved from a situation where the special class pupils were treated as outcasts and perceived to have nothing of worth to contribute in the school, to a new scenario where they are valued and active members of the learning community.

In addition to the development of a supportive framework, other factors have contributed to the development and sustainability of the constructionist learning environment within the school. Foremost has been the development of the teachers' confidence in engaging with this type of learning by ongoing professional development workshops; the reaffirmation of the validity of teachers' work through the ongoing visits of interested teachers and dignitaries to the school to see the project; evidence of children's active engagement with learning; encouraging feedback from attendees each year at the Esat Young Scientist and Technologist Exhibition; and the new respect for the special class in the school community.

The constructionist approach of the EM project encourages teachers and pupils to explore the boundaries of the *Mindstorms* materials and to experiment with using these expressive materials in creative and innovative ways. The teachers and pupils are free to develop projects and select project themes that are personally meaningful. In the EM project, the learners' needs, interests and experiences drive activities. As a result, the learning experiences are inherently authentic as the learners are not being forced to follow pre-specified objectives and teacher-driven instructional strategies. The constructionist approach creates an environment where the students truly care about their work and, by actively constructing their own models, take ownership of their learning goals and create external representations of their knowledge construction. They have, in effect, created 'objects to think with' (Papert, 1991, p. 1) which requires them to converse and reflect on what they are doing. As the teachers engage with the materials, they too become learners alongside their students.

Implementing a constructionist approach is not easy, and developing a constructionist-learning environment takes time. It is critically important to have a supportive learning community with a diverse range of backgrounds which addresses each individual's needs, interests and experiences. Provocative, engaging, and challenging computational materials are also needed and, most importantly, there must be adequate time to allow self-directed learning to develop and changes to take place.

Developing a constructionist-learning environment requires 'buy-in' from teachers, students and the administrative staff in the school. Teachers and students are challenged to assume new roles with different beliefs and values than they have traditionally pursued. Teachers have to develop skills to support students' thinking, set challenging learning experiences, and create a learning environment which encourages students to explore and test out new ideas, set learning goals and take responsibility for attaining these goals, and, in time, become self-determined learners. These implications of adopting a constructionist approach imply risks for teachers, students and administrators, but the enthusiasm and excitement generated by the teachers and students as they construct their own understandings and engage in using the materials are more than sufficient reward for taking these risks.

References

Butler, D., Martin F. and Gleason, W. (2000) 'Empowering minds by taking control: Developing teachers' technological fluency with LEGO Mindstorms' in *Proceedings of the Society for Information Technology and Teacher Education Conference*, Charlottesville, VA, pp. 598–603

Dickard, N. and Schneider, D. (2002) 'The Digital Divide: Where we are today' http://www.edutopia.org/php/print.php?id=Art_995&template=printarticle.php

Humphreys, T. (1993) *Self-esteem – the key to your child's education*, Dublin: Gill & Macmillan

Irish National Teachers' Organisation (1995) *Promoting School Attendance*, INTO: Dublin

Jonassen, D. H., Peck K. L. and Wilson, B.G. (1999) *Learning with Technology – a Constructivist Perspective*, Columbus, Ohio: Prentice-Hall

Martin, F., Butler D. and Gleason W. (2000) 'Design, story-telling, and robots in Irish primary education' in *Proceedings of the IEEE International Conference on Systems, Man, and Cybernetics*, (Institute of Electrical and Electronics Engineering), Piscataway, NJ, pp. 730–5

Papert, S. (1980) *Mindstorms: Children, Computers and Powerful Ideas*, Brighton, England: The Harvester Press Ltd

Papert, S. (1990) 'A critique of technocentrism in thinking about the school of the future', http://www.papert.org/articles/ACritiqueofTechnocentrism.html

Papert, S. (1991) 'Situating Constructionism' in Harel, I. and Papert, S. (eds) *Constructionism*, Norwood, NJ: Ablex, pp. 1–12

Papert, S. (1993) *The Children's Machine: Rethinking School in the Age of the Computer*, New York: Basic Books

Reasoner, R. W. (1992) *Building Self-esteem in the Elementary Schools*, California: Consulting Psychologists Press

Resnick, M. (1993) 'Behavior Construction Kits' *Communications of the ACM*, vol. 36, no. 7

Resnick, M. and Ocko, S. (1991) 'LEGO/Logo: Learning through and about design' in Harel, I. and Papert, S., (eds) Constructionism, Norwood, NJ: Ablex Publishing, pp. 141–50

Sugrue, C. (2004), 'Structure and Agency in the Construction of Creative Teaching and Learning: A View from the Margins', paper presented to the Ethnography in Education group, European Conference on Educational Research (ECER), Crete, September

Turkle, S. (1995) *Life on the Screen: Identity in the Age of the Internet*, New York: Simon and Schuster

Von Glasersfeld, E. (1989) 'Introduction: Aspects of Constructivism' in Fosnot. C. T. (ed.) *Constructivism. Theory, Perspectives, and Practice,* New York: Teachers College Press, pp. 3–7

28

Strengthening the School Social Climate

Merike Darmody

Introduction

The complexity of factors that have an effect on pupils' experience of schooling and their subsequent life-chances is well documented. A corpus of literature in the area deals with family-related influences on pupils' educational outcomes (Dustman, 2004; Grolnick and Ryan, 1989; Ball, Bowe and Gewirtz, 1995; Grolnick, et al., 2000). In particular, these outcomes are adversely influenced by the economic and social marginalisation of pupils' families in disadvantaged communities (Machin, 2006). Similarly, the role of school processes and structure in reproducing inequalities (Shavit and Blossfeld, 1993) and the role of peer groups in influencing pupils' appreciation of the value of succeeding in school (Bland, 2002) have received a great deal of attention. It is not possible to discuss the confluence of factors that impact on pupils' experience at school in detail here; instead, given the importance of supportive social relationships in promoting and maintaining pupil engagement and motivation to learn at school level (see Lingard et al., 2002; Wang, Haertel and Walberg, 1993), I focus on the nature of teacher–pupil relationships in Irish schools. I also attempt to explore the quality of social interaction between teachers and ethnic minority pupils, namely, international pupils and Travellers – groups most likely to experience educational disadvantage. It is argued that the nature and quality of teacher–pupil interactions have a profound influence on the school climate, have strong implications for the future life-chances of pupils and can contribute to a continued cycle of disadvantage.

Teacher–pupil interaction

There is a general consensus in international research that the type and quality of teacher–pupil interaction have a strong effect on pupils' school engagement (Willms, 2003). Australian researchers Lingard et al. (2002) note that 'after holding pupil backgrounds constant, teacher effect upon pupil outcomes is much greater than whole school effect' (p. 108). In other words, this relationship is central in shaping pupils' experiences of schooling and combating educational disadvantage. In the Irish context, studies have shown that the quality of such interaction may influence pupils' subject choice in school, hence having an impact on their further educational pathways (Darmody and Smyth, 2005). In addition, poor school attendance and early school leaving are strongly associated with negative attitudes pupils have towards their teachers (McCoy et al., forthcoming 2007). In contrast, in an American context, Brookover et al. (1979) report that positive interaction, high expectations and encouragement from a teacher greatly enhance pupils' educational outcomes. Elsewhere, researchers have found that supportive teacher–pupil relationships help to develop a sense of school belonging – being accepted, respected, included and supported at school (Gutman and Midgley, 2000; Anderson et al., 2000). Pupils appreciate a teacher who consults them, who is fair, who makes them feel important and who treats them in an adult way (Demetriou, Goalen and Rudduck, 2000, p. 431). These authors observe that 'the qualities that matter to pupils tend to be as much about how they are *treated* as how they are *taught*' (p. 431). Exploring the experiences of pupils at risk of early leaving, researchers have found that pupils liked teachers who were friendly, firm, related well to their pupils, had a sound knowledge of their subject area, showed an interest in their lives and were willing to help them (Lingard et al., 2002; Keddie and Churchill, 2003). In the same vein, studies carried out in the Irish context highlight the importance of positive interaction between teachers and pupils in terms of raising pupils' motivation and self-esteem as well as encouraging school engagement (Boldt, 1997; Smyth, 1999; Smyth, McCoy and Darmody, 2004; Smyth et al., 2006).

Conversely, an absence of positive social relationships and contacts with teachers was seen to deny pupils the resources that 'help them develop positively' (Croninger and Lee, 2001, p. 569). Research evidence from Ireland suggests that negative experiences and attitudes are predictive of early leaving and underperformance (see Smyth, 1999). Pupils deeply resented the use of sarcasm, humiliating sanctions, shouting at them and not being given a right of reply as practiced by some teachers (Lynch and Lodge, 2002, p. 155). In addition, Smyth, McCoy and Darmody (2004) note that a significant minority of pupils in Irish second-level schools receive little, if any, praise and encouragement from their teachers and are uneasy about approaching them with their problems (see also

McCoy, et al., forthcoming 2007). This raises serious issues about the school climate and its influence on pupil outcomes, especially for some pupils. Worryingly, Smyth et al. (2006) note that the highest level of negative pupil–teacher interaction has been reported by boys in lower-stream classes in streamed schools – pupils most at risk of early school leaving and most in need of supportive relationships with teachers that could be seen as a source of social capital. In their study carried out in the US, Groninger and Lee (2001) discovered that teacher-based social capital[1] helped to reduce the number of early school leavers and proved especially effective in the case of pupils from socially disadvantaged backgrounds and those who had experienced academic difficulties in the past.

In general, teacher–pupil relations characterised by control, domination, a managerial rather than pedagogical focus, and lack of connection and mutual respect may be perceived by some pupils as constraining and may lead to disengagement and rebellion against school culture (Lingard et al., 2002; Martino and Pallotta-Chiarolli, 2003; Keddie and Churchill, 2003). In addition, research evidence shows that the quality of teacher–pupil interactions varies by social class, whereby pupils from a background characterised by unemployment and those from a Traveller background are more likely to report negative interactions with teachers (Smyth et al., 2006; Lynch and Lodge 2002). In other words, pupils who are already in a disadvantaged position are experiencing less positive interactions with their teachers. Furthermore, a negative social climate in school increases the risk of early school leaving and denies some pupils an opportunity to reach their full potential.

Diversity and social climate in schools

In Ireland, classroom diversity today reflects a demographic shift. In particular, over the last decade Ireland has seen a substantial wave of immigration, which has resulted in a more mixed pupil population in terms of race, culture and language. Teachers now face multiple and complex issues that challenge many of their educational practices and assumptions and present new demands to integrate 'various ethnic groups with a sense of belonging within schools' (Coolahan, 2000, p. 119). Apart from Traveller students, many teachers in Ireland have had no previous sustained contact with pupils from other cultures. Subsequently – as noted by a study conducted in the UK – they may find it difficult to identify pupils' learning needs and expectations:

> … to know enough about how learning might be affected by the attitudes and expectations that people bring to the learning situation, which are influenced by

---

[1] The authors define the concept by the extent to which teachers support pupils' efforts to succeed in school and by teachers' reports about whether individual pupils receive guidance from them about school or personal matters (Groninger and Lee, 2001).

social forces within both the institution and the wider community outside the classroom, and which in turn influence the ways in which people deal with each other in the classroom. (Holliday, 1994, pp. 9–10)

In this context, positive classroom relationships are becoming more difficult to establish as a growing diversity affects social interaction at school (Gay, 1993). Indeed, some research evidence indicates that social relations between teachers and minority pupils are found to be somewhat less positive (Irvine, 1990; Fine, 1991; Nieto, 1992), perhaps reflecting inadequate understanding of the culture and identity of minorities. An additional problem is the low level of English language proficiency of some international pupils and limited support available to schools to address this issue. In addition to coping with the integration of newly arrived pupils into Irish schools, a lot of effort is also needed to address the needs of indigenous Traveller pupils. While significant progress has been made in increasing participation rates and school attendance among this group, there is still significant scope for improvement, especially in the second-level sector (DES, 2005). Evidence suggests that those Traveller pupils who attend second-level schools are likely to leave within the first two years, indicating that their needs are not being met (Irish Traveller Movement, 2004). While acknowledging the importance of broader social factors in influencing the attitudes of Traveller pupils to the importance of education, schools can make a difference in supporting these pupils by fostering a positive social climate based on the quality of social interaction and equality. In order to address the issue of educational disadvantage, it is important to ensure that all pupils have equal opportunities at school.

Recent studies

This chapter draws on two studies carried out in Ireland that have explored, among other issues, the relationships between teachers and pupils. The first study[2] provides information about the position, experiences and attitudes of school leavers[3] one year after leaving second-level schools (Gorby, McCoy and Watson, 2005). The sample consisted of 3,345 students, including international pupils.[4] Among other information, the questionnaire consisted of items providing insights into pupil perceptions on the quality of social interaction in school. It included the following statements: 'My teachers didn't care about me'; 'My teachers helped

---

[2] The Annual School Leavers' Survey was carried out for the Department of Education and Science by the Economic and Social Research Institute in 2004. The survey is based on a stratified (by programme) random sample and is weighted to a population. There are some differences between the figures presented from the School Leavers' Survey (SLS) 2004 Survey in this chapter and those in the report by Gorby, McCoy and Watson, 2005. The reason for this is the exclusion of individuals over 25 years of age from the SLS report.

[3] The school leavers who left second-level schools in the 2002–2003 academic year

[4] For the purposes of this study, neither parent of an 'international pupil' is Irish.

me to do my best'; 'Teachers could not keep order in class'; 'Teachers listened to my ideas and views'; 'Teachers often gave me homework'; 'If I had a problem there was always a teacher I could talk to.'

The second set of data comes from a project that examined the transition from primary to second-level schools, carried out by the Economic and Social Research Institute (ESRI) for the National Council of Curriculum and Assessment (NCCA). As part of the project, a survey was carried out among all second-level school principals in 2002.[5] Data from the survey was used to select twelve case study schools in which school characteristics (size, gender mix, designated disadvantaged status) were related to the pattern of variation of first-year provision (See Smyth, McCoy and Darmody, 2004). In these case study schools a survey was carried out among 916 first-year pupils, including a small number of international and Traveller pupils.

Main results

Figure 1 Interaction with teachers (% within each qualification group who agree with the statements)

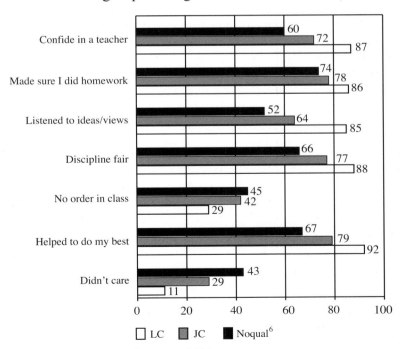

Source: Gorby, McCoy and Watson, 2005

---

[5] There was a high response rate (78%, n = 567) to the survey.

[6] Noqual = no qualifications (left before sitting for the first formal state exam)

Teacher–pupil relationships

In the first study young people were asked to indicate the main factors that influenced them to leave school. The analysis showed that 41 per cent of pupils who had left school without qualifications had done so because of 'school factors'. The participants were also asked to agree or disagree with a number of statements characterising teacher–pupil relationships. The analysis showed that the majority had experienced positive teacher–pupil relationships during their time at school (see Figure 1). An overall majority of the whole sample found that teachers had helped them to do their best (81 per cent), that they could confide in their teacher (84 per cent) and that teachers had listened to their views (81 per cent). However, 15 per cent of pupils felt that teachers did not care about them.

The proportion of pupils who reported that they had experienced negative teacher–pupil interaction was highest among early school leavers. Many of them felt alienated in school and believed that the teachers were not interested in their lives. There is some evidence that pupils showed some resistance in the class by reporting that teachers were unable to control the class. These findings suggest that pupils' experiences at school, including their interaction with their teachers, have a notable role in shaping pathways for pupils, whereby pupils who had left school early were also more likely to have experienced strained interaction with teachers, in line with Fingleton (2003).

The quality and quantity of interaction with teachers was also explored in a survey of first-year pupils in twelve case study schools. An examination of the views of these pupils reveals that an overall majority had very positive teacher–pupil relationships (see Figure 2).[7] Over 90 per cent found that teachers helped if they had a problem with schoolwork, 81 per cent thought that most of the teachers were friendly and 81 per cent liked most of their teachers. However, some pupils (31 per cent) were afraid to tell teachers if they didn't understand something, perhaps indicating that some teachers were not considered to be approachable by pupils. It could be argued that by not asking questions in class, the subject matter may remain unclear and a pupil may fall behind. Consequently, they may start to feel alienated and 'act out' (Flutter and Rudduck, 2004). Only a small minority of first-year pupils had negative experiences with their teachers: 19 per cent did not consider teachers friendly, 9 per cent felt that teachers did not help if they had a problem with schoolwork, 22 per cent could not talk to any teacher if they experienced a problem and 19 per cent did not like most of the teachers (see Figure 2). In addition, 20 per cent of pupils thought that friendlier teachers would help them to settle into the school better, indicating the importance of teacher–pupil interaction on pupils' school experiences.

---

[7] The quality of this relationship deteriorates in some cases in second year (Smyth et al., 2006).

Figure 2 Teacher–student relationship (percentage agreeing with the statements)

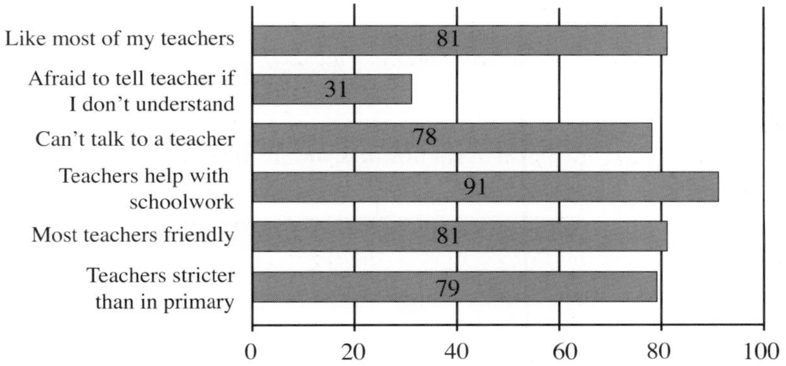

Source: Smyth, McCoy and Darmody, 2004

Overall, variation in pupils' perceptions of their relationships with teachers was not associated with the type of second-level school they attended or whether the school had designated disadvantaged status. However, male pupils in lower stream classes were more likely to report the class interactions as negative.

International pupils and Travellers

School Leavers' Survey

International research suggests that teachers' relations with minority pupils may differ from those with other pupils (See Fine, 1991; Nieto, 1992). In order to explore these issues in the Irish context the analysis presented here explores the quality of these relationships with international and Traveller pupils in second-level schools. Figure 3 presents the perceptions of international pupils.[8] It shows that there were no significant differences between their views and those of Irish nationals. An overall majority of international pupils had experienced positive relationships with their teachers. They found that teachers had been helpful, that discipline in school was fair and that teachers had listened to their views. However, international pupils were somewhat more likely to report that teachers did not care for them, although the finding is not statistically significant.

---

[8] 'International' pupils form a very diverse group, which includes English speakers and those whose mother tongue is not English. It is also worth noting that the majority of immigrants are generally found to be highly educated (Barrett, Bergin and Duffy, 2006).

Figure 3 The perceptions of international pupils
(percentage agreeing with the statements)

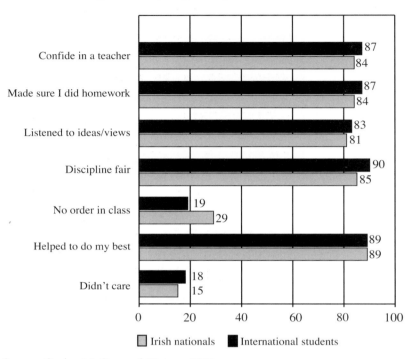

Source: Gorby, McCoy and Watson, 2005

On the other hand, Travellers, an indigenous minority, reported having had rather negative teacher–pupil relationships at school, compared to the perceptions of other pupils. Figure 4 shows that this is the case in most spheres of interaction. In particular, Traveller pupils reported that teachers in their school did not care about them and did not listen to their ideas and views. They also reported that they couldn't talk to a teacher if they experienced a problem. While these figures should be approached with caution due to small numbers in the sample, it may still indicate that this group of pupils is most marginalised and excluded in Irish schools. Worryingly, 38 per cent of them reported skipping 'a day here and there', some missing weeks at a time.[9] International pupils, on the other hand, were much less likely to miss school, with just over 50 per cent of them reporting having never skipped school.

---

[9] It is worth noting, however, that over 26 per cent of Traveller pupils reported having never missed school.

Figure 4 The perceptions of Traveller pupils (percentage agreeing with the statements)

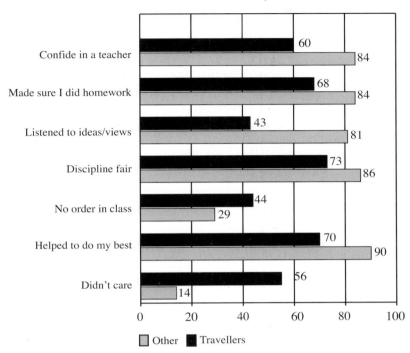

Source: Gorby, McCoy and Watson, 2005

First-year pupils: international pupils and Travellers

The sample of first-year pupils included a small proportion of pupils whose parents were not Irish nationals. The analysis of their perceptions of interaction with teachers showed that there were no notable differences between the perceptions of international and other pupils.

Most pupils found that they could talk to a teacher if experiencing a problem and considered the majority of their teachers helpful and friendly. Perhaps the greatest difference between groups of pupils was evident when exploring whether pupils were afraid to tell a teacher if they did not understand something in class. The analysis showed that Traveller pupils and especially international pupils were much more likely to feel this way. These groups of pupils were also more likely to report that there was nobody among the teachers to talk to when they experienced problems. The study of first-year pupils in second-level schools indicates that teachers should pay more attention to the nature of interaction with minority pupils. While acknowledging that there is limited time available in subject classes to address the needs of this pupil population, an unsupportive social climate in class may affect the educational outcomes of these pupils.

Conclusion

Various international studies indicate that school social climate has implications for pupils' experiences at school and their educational outcomes. A negative social climate, affecting the quality of teacher–pupil relationships, may jeopardise pupils' full personal and academic development and put them at risk of early school leaving. While the relationship between teachers and pupils in Irish second-level schools appears to be largely positive, some pupils have rather different experiences at school. A significant minority of them, mostly from the lower social class and Traveller background, reported that teachers showed little interest in them, confirming the research by Leavy (2005), Rist (1970) and Coladarci (1983). This raises serious questions about combating educational disadvantage in schools, because positive teacher–pupil relationships are particularly important in addressing the needs of at-risk pupils in terms of providing them with the social capital they may lack at home and enhancing their self-confidence, self-esteem and motivation to learn. Feeling alienated and excluded at school, pupils may start disengaging, avoiding school and leaving school prematurely, thus limiting their future life-chances in terms of access to the labour market. On a more positive note, the relationships of international pupils with their teachers seem to be largely positive, echoing Vekic (2003). Irish classroom settings have become more diverse over the years due to unprecedented immigration, and more comprehensive research is only now starting to build up (see Devine, 2002, 2005). As international pupils constitute a very diverse group, the topic of integration of these pupils into Irish primary and secondary schools merits further research.

In order to cope with the diversity of the student population, teachers need sufficient preparation at both pre- and in-service level in dealing with disadvantage and intercultural issues. Early leavers often quoted school-related issues as a reason for terminating their education. Hence, the social climate in school (including relationships between teachers and pupils) has a strong role to play in pupils' educational outcomes. I support recommendations made elsewhere which state that teacher education in Ireland – including an extended Higher Diploma (HDip) at post-primary level if necessary – should include a compulsory module on educational disadvantage, covering issues such as social change, social relationships in school (Devine, 2002; Barnardos, 2006), conflict resolution and behaviour management (Downes, 2004), in order to fully prepare teachers to cope with the multitude of classroom situations. Another compulsory module on intercultural education should address the fact that Ireland is no longer a monocultural society (Barnardos, 2006). As a growing number of pupils in Ireland live in two parallel worlds, one at school and one at home, teachers need an education that would prepare them for dealing with a diverse pupil population – including the indigenous Traveller population – and creating a positive and mutually supportive atmosphere in class. In order to address these issues it is suggested here that the duration of teacher education should be lengthened and more resources and training made available to staff in order to address the issues of disadvantage and diversity.

References

Anderson, L. W., Jacobs, J., Schramm, S. and Splittherber, F. (2000) 'School Transitions: Beginning of the End or a New Beginning?', *International Journal of Educational Research*, vol. 33, pp. 325–39

Ball, S., Bowe, R. and Gewirtz, S. (1995) 'Circuits of Schooling: a Sociological Exploration of Parental Choice of School in Social Class Contexts', *Sociological Review*, vol. 43, pp. 52–78

Barnardos (2006) *Make the Grade*, Dublin: Barnardos

Barrett, A., Bergin, A. and Duffy, D. (2006) 'The Labour Market Characteristics and Labour Market Impact of Immigrants in Ireland', *The Economic and Social Review*, vol. 37, no. 1, spring, pp. 1–26

Bland, D. (2002) 'Crossing the line. A study of peer influence on pupils from low income backgrounds in transition from school to university', paper delivered at AARE conference, http://aare.edu.au/02pap/bla02263.htm, (Australian Association for Research in Education)

Boldt, S. (1997) *Hear my Voice: a longitudinal study of the post-school experiences of early school leavers in Ireland*, Dublin: Marino Institute of Education

Brookover, W., Beady, C., Flood, P., Schweitzer, J. and Wisenbaker, J. (1979) *School Social Systems and Pupil Achievement: Schools Can Make a Difference*, New York: Praeger

Coladarci, T. (1983) 'High school dropout among Native Americans', *Journal of American Indian Education*, 23, 1, pp. 15–22

Coolahan, J. (2000) 'School Ethos and Culture within a Changing Education System' in Furlong, C. and Monahan, L. (eds) *School Culture and Ethos*, Dublin: Marino Institute of Education

Croninger, R. C. and Lee, V. E. (2001) 'Social Capital and Dropping Out of High School: Benefits to At-Risk Pupils of Teachers' Support and Guidance', *Teachers College Record*, vol. 103, no. 4, August, pp. 548–81

Croninger, R. C. and Lee, V. E. (2001) 'Social Capital and Dropping Out of High School: Benefits to At-Risk Students of Teachers' Support and Guidance',

Teachers College Record, vol. 103, no. 4, August, pp. 548–81

Darmody, M. and Smyth, E. (2005) *Gender and Subject Choice. Take-Up of Technological Subjects in Second-Level Education*, Dublin: The Liffey Press

Demetriou, H., Goalen, P. and Rudduck, J. (2000) 'Academic Performance, Transfer, Transition and Friendship: Listening to the Pupil Voice', *International Journal of Educational Research,* vol. 33. pp. 425–41

Department of Education and Science (2005), *Survey of Traveller Education Provision in Irish Schools*, Dublin: DES

Devine, D. (2005) 'Welcome to the Celtic Tiger? Teacher Responses to Immigration and Increasing Ethnic Diversity in Irish Schools', *International Studies in Sociology of Education*, vol. 15, no. 1, pp. 49–70

Devine, D. and Kenny, M. (2002) *Ethnicity and Schooling – A study of ethnic diversity in selected Irish primary and post-primary schools*, commissioned report, Dublin: DES

Downes, P. (2004) *Psychological Support Services for Ballyfermot: Present and Future*, Ballyfermot: URBAN

Dustman, C. (2004) 'Parental Background, Primary to Secondary School Transitions, and Wages, *Oxford Economic Papers*, 56, 2, pp. 209–30

Fine, M. (1991) *Framing Dropouts: Notes on the Politics of an Urban Public High School*, Albany, NY: SUNY Press

Fingleton, L. (2003) *Listen B4 I Leave: Early school leavers in the Canal Communities area and their experiences of school*, Dublin: Canal Communities Partnership Ltd

Flutter, J. and Rudduck, J. (2004) *Consulting Pupils: What's in it for schools?* London: Routledge Falmer

Gay, G. (1993) 'Building cultural bridges: A bold proposal for teacher education', *Education and Urban Society*, 25, 3, pp. 285–99

Gorby, S., McCoy, S. and Watson, D. (2005) *2004 Annual School Leavers' Survey of 2002/2003 Leavers*, Dublin: ESRI and DES

Grolnick, W. S. and Ryan, R. M. (1989) 'Parent Styles Associated with Children's Self-Regulation and Competence in School', *Journal of Educational Psychology*, vol. 81, 143–54

Grolnick, W. S., Kurowshi, C. O., Dunlap, K. G. and Hevey, C. (2000) 'Parental Resources and the Transition to Junior High', *Journal of Research on Adolescence*, vol. 10, no. 4, pp. 465–88

Gutman, L. M. and Midgley, C. (2000) 'The Role of Protective Factors in Supporting the Academic Achievement of Poor African American Pupils During the Middle School Transition', *Journal of Youth and Adolescence*, vol. 29, no. 2, pp. 223–48

Holliday, A. (1994) *Appropriate Methodology and Social Context*, Cambridge: Cambridge University Press

Irish Traveller Movement (2004) 'Irish Travellers in Education: Strategies for Equality', http://www.itmtrav.com/publications/reports.html, accessed 10/07/06

Irvine, J. J. (1990) *Black pupils and school failure: Policies, practices, and prescriptions*, Westport, CT: Greenwood Publishing Group

Keddie, A. and Churchill, R. (2003) 'Power, control and authority: Issues at the centre of boys' relationships with their teachers', *Queensland Journal of Educational Research*, 19, 1, pp. 13–27, http://education.curtin.edu.au/iier/qjer/ qjer19/keddie.html

Leavy, A. (2005) '"When I meet them I talk to them": the challenges of diversity for pre-service teacher education', *Irish Educational Studies*, vol. 14, nos 2–3, pp. 159–77

Lingard, B., Martino, W., Mills, M. and Bahr, M. (2002) *Addressing the educational needs of boys – Strategies for schools*, Canberra: Commonwealth Department of Education, Science and Training, http://www.dest.gov.au/schools/publications/2002/boyseducation/Boys_Repo rt_Final1.pdf, accessed 10/06/06

Lynch, K. and Lodge, A. (2002) *Equality and Power in Schools*, London: Routledge Falmer

Machin, S. (2006) 'Social Disadvantage and Educational Experience', OECD Social, Employment and Migration Working Paper no. 32, http://http://www.oecd.org/dataoecd/13/60/36165298.pdf, accessed 10/07/06

Martino, W. and Pallotta-Chiarolli, M. (2003) *So what's a boy? Addressing issues of masculinity and schooling*, Maidenhead: Open University Press

McCoy, S., Darmody, M., Smyth, E. and Dunne, A. (forthcoming September 2007) *Attendance and Pupils' School Experiences*, Dublin: ESRI/NEWB

McCoy, S., Smyth, E., Darmody, M. and Dunne, A. (2006) *Guidance for all? Guidance provision in Second-Level Schools*, Dublin: The Liffey Press

Nieto, S. (1992) *Affirming diversity: The socio-political context of multicultural education*, White Plains, NY: Longman

Rist, (1970) 'Pupil Social Class and Teacher Expectations: The Self-fulfilling Prophecy in Ghetto Education', *Harvard Educational Review,* vol. 40, pp. 411–51

Shavit, Y. and Blossfeld, H. P. (1993) *Persistent Barriers: Changes in Educational Opportunities in Thirteen Countries*, Boulder, Col.: Westview Press

Smyth, E. (1999) *Do Schools Differ? Academic and Personal Development among Pupils in the Second-Level Sector*, Dublin, Oak Tree Press/ESRI

Smyth, E., Dunne, A., McCoy, S. and Darmody, M. (2006) *Pathways through the junior cycle*, Dublin: The Liffey Press

Smyth, E., McCoy, S. and Darmody, M. (2004) *Moving up: the experiences of first year pupils in post-primary education*, Dublin: The Liffey Press

Vekic, K. (2003) *Unsettled Hope: Unaccompanied minors in Ireland, from understanding to response*, Dublin: Marino Institute of Education

Wang, M. C., Haertel, G. D. and Walberg, H. J. (1993) 'Toward a Knowledge Base for School Learning', *Review of Educational Research*, vol. 63, no. 3, pp. 249–94

Willms, J. D. (2003) 'Pupil engagement at school: A sense of belonging and participation', results from PISA 2000, Paris: OECD

29

Health For All

Mary C. Byrne

Introduction

In this chapter I would like to highlight the importance of matching the content and delivery of educational programmes with the social and educational needs of the particular group of young people for whom they are intended. The area of Social, Personal and Health Education (SPHE) is taken as an example, beginning with an overview of the evidence for effectiveness in this area and followed by a case study of the adaptation of one particular programme from the post-primary school setting for use with groups experiencing social and educational disadvantage.

SPHE in Ireland

In 1998, the Education Act placed an obligation on Irish schools to 'promote the … social and personal development of students and provide health education for them' (p. 13). In response, SPHE became one of the six main subject areas of the new Primary School Curriculum in 1999. This was followed in 2000–2003 by the phased introduction of SPHE at post-primary level as part of the core curriculum for junior cycle.

Although health and social education in various forms had been available in some schools prior to 1999, teachers and schools were not supported by the provision of training or resources at national level; as a result, its delivery was ad hoc and unregulated. Now, for the first time, all school-going Irish young people, irrespective of their level of social or educational disadvantage, are expected to receive regular SPHE classes up to Junior Certificate level. Furthermore, this new subject is arguably properly resourced by the provision of both in-service and pre-service teacher training at post-primary level as well as high-quality classroom materials and teacher guidelines. The very logic of SPHE is a challenge to a Cartesian-type split between reason and emotion and presupposes a democratic classroom environment at post-primary level (Downes, 2003).

Evidence for effectiveness

The introduction of SPHE as a required subject in Irish schools is a welcome investment in our young people's personal development. Internationally, there is a solid and growing empirical evidence base indicating that well-designed, well-implemented, school-based programmes can positively influence a diverse array of social, health and academic outcomes (Greenberg et al., 2003). For example, a UK review of health promotion activities in schools found that, among other things, they are particularly effective in promoting healthy eating and fitness, preventing injuries and abuse, and promoting mental health (Lister-Sharp et al., 1999). Echoing this last finding, a separate review found that curriculum-based mental health promotion programmes help young people to develop coping skills in readiness for stress situations (Tilford, Delaney and Vogels, 1997). Durlak and Wells (1997) reviewed 129 school-based programmes designed to prevent behavioural and social problems in children and young people under the age of eighteen. They found that most programmes were successful in both reducing problems (e.g. anxiety, depressive symptoms, difficult behaviour) and increasing competencies (e.g. communication skills, assertiveness, self-confidence). Pupils participating in such programmes fared better than non-participants by between 59 per cent and 82 per cent on average. Another review of 207 school-based programmes to prevent substance use found that interactive programmes (like SPHE) focusing on skills such as goal-setting, assertiveness, communication, coping and refusal skills, had a positive effect while the traditional didactic class format had minimal impact (Tobler et al., 2000; see also Morgan, 2001). The year 1996 saw the launch of the 'Blueprints for Violence Prevention' project to identify and replicate effective youth violence prevention programmes across the US (Mihalic et al., 2002). Since then, eleven 'model' programmes and nineteen 'promising' programmes have been shown to be effective in reducing pre-delinquent childhood aggression and conduct disorders, as well as adolescent violent crime, aggression, delinquency, and substance abuse. In Ireland, an evaluation of the Mind Out programme (which aims to promote positive mental and emotional health amongst fifteen- to eighteen-year-olds) demonstrated a number of positive short-term impacts, including raised levels of awareness of support services, greater compassion and understanding for a young person in distress, and more constructive action in seeking help for self and others (Byrne, Barry and Sheridan, 2004; Byrne et al., 2005). At primary level, the benefits of circle-time, a problem box, etc., have been documented with regard to issues of bullying in a designated disadvantaged school in Ballyfermot (Downes, 2004b). Other examples of the potential of SPHE to transform school climate in designated disadvantaged primary schools in Ireland include the theme of the 'Peaceful School', a primary school in the Dublin 8 area (Hegarty, 2006), and the authentic democracy programme in a primary school in Dublin's north inner city (Caffrey, 2006). The role of other pupils as providers of a social network of emotional support has been highlighted in the context of Ballyfermot schools (Downes, 2004a).

Despite these benefits, the argument is sometimes heard that SPHE is yet another demand on teachers' already impossible workload. This view is more prevalent at post-primary level, where the emphasis on academic success and achieving high grades in examination subjects means that competition for space in the curriculum can be intense. This argument is an empty one, however, as research has demonstrated a strong relationship between social and emotional learning and academic success (Zins et al., 2004). Specifically, social and emotional learning has been demonstrated to increase mastery of subject material and motivation to learn; to reduce anxiety, enhance attention, and improve study skills; and to increase commitment to school and the time devoted to schoolwork. Social and emotional learning has also been shown to improve attendance and graduation rates, as well as constructive employment, while it reduces suspensions, expulsions, and grade retention (Zins et al., 2004). Improved competencies such as the ability to set goals, manage one's emotions, solve problems effectively, communicate well and work cooperatively with others can play an important role in academic success (Elias et al., 2003); correspondingly, interventions that improve academic performance have been shown to reduce delinquency (Catalano et al., 1998). Howard Gardner's influential work (1993) on 'multiple intelligences' demonstrated that there are different – and equally valid – ways to be 'intelligent'. Success in the adult world depends both on academic/intellectual ability and interpersonal, intrapersonal, or practical intelligence. As Daniel Goleman (1996) says in his book *Emotional Intelligence*, 'it's a different way of being smart' (p. 38). The different types of intelligence are said to support each other and are intricately linked. For example, social competencies have been shown to be better predictors of performance on standardised achievement tests than children's previous academic success (Zins et al., 2004). In the US, the Collaborative for Academic, Social and Emotional Learning (CASEL) has championed the study of this interplay between academic and social-emotional intelligence in recent years. CASEL advocates the simultaneous development of intellectual and social-emotional development (IQ and EQ) in an integrated approach, rather than framing the debate as a choice between the two. Educators, researchers and policymakers are increasingly aware that social and emotional learning needs to be a part of education in order to maximise academic outcomes.

Who benefits?

The evidence is clear, then, that school-based health and social education *can* have a positive impact on young people's personal development. Many programmes of proven effectiveness are available to achieve this goal. However, a well-designed programme is not, in itself, a recipe for success for every learner: the *way* it is delivered is also of critical importance. There is a danger that such programmes will have the greatest impact on students who are already cognitively and emotionally well developed, while those most in need of this development may benefit the least (see Rook, 1984; 1992 on the risk of people with depression driving away their social supports). Programme implementers (teachers, policymakers) need to be vigilant against this pitfall and ensure that programme content and/or implementation is adapted to the needs of those who stand to gain the most.

The principles of differentiation (correctly matching the work expected from students with their developmental capacities) apply to SPHE as to any other area of the curriculum. The design of teaching and learning strategies that will meet pupils' diverse learning needs is a key feature of the professional role of the teacher (DES, 2001). Within a single class group these needs can vary over the course of a term, or even over the course of a day. Between different class groups, even of similar ages, needs and abilities can vary widely so that programmes designed for particular age groups may require adaptation if they are to be effective. A similar heterogeneity of needs and abilities also exists in designated disadvantaged schools.

Case study

The remainder of this chapter will draw on experiences with Mind Out, an Irish mental-health promotion module that was first implemented and evaluated in a school setting and later, following adaptation, with disadvantaged groups in the Traveller training and out-of-school Youthreach settings (O'Keeffe et al., 2005).

The 'Mind Out' programme

Mind Out aims to promote positive mental and emotional health for fifteen- to eighteen-year-olds through an exploration of:

- stress and coping
- sources of support (family and friends as well as support services in the community)

- emotions (anger, conflict, rejection, feeling down)
- relationships
- understandings of mental health
- the importance of supporting others.

Following consultation with teachers and students, as well as a review of international best practice in the area, a thirteen-session module was designed to run over two years in the school setting. Most of the sessions included an activity-based exercise followed by time for reflection and discussion.

Figure 1 Age and gender profile of Mind Out participants
in school setting

	Intervention (n = 521)	Control (n = 475)
Gender (%)		
Male	44.2	28.6
Female	55.8	71.4
Age		
Mean (SD)	16.2 (0.9)	16.2 (0.6)
Min.	13.8	15.0
Max.	18.9	18.8

Differential programme effects

Details of the evaluation study are reported in full elsewhere (Byrne, Barry and Sheridan, 2004; Byrne et al., 2005). Overall, the module was well received by both teachers (n = 33) and pupils (n = 521), and was found to have a number of positive effects on participating students compared with control students in other schools. However, subgroup analysis revealed that some groups benefited from the programme to a lesser extent than others. For example, several teachers felt that more 'able' students seemed to 'tune in' better and that the programme needed some adjustment in order to reach students perceived as 'weaker'. One teacher discontinued the programme after five sessions primarily for this reason. It is important to note that this age group had never experienced SPHE at primary level – including the emphasis on group work and consequent listening and turn-taking skills developed therein – and that immersion in SPHE approaches at primary level may change the findings for future students of the equivalent age range.

Boys also responded to the programme less favourably than girls, both in terms of its impact and their attitudes towards it. A similar trend amongst a different group of Irish post-primary students was reported by NicGabhainn and Kelleher (1995) in their evaluation of a more general health education programme, and, internationally, gender differences in relation to mental, emotional and social issues are well established (Emslie et al., 2002; Gallagher and Millar, 1998). One consistent finding is that adolescent girls report experiencing greater levels of stressful events than do their male counterparts (McNamara, 2000). This could be the result of more stress in their lives, or different coping strategies; whatever the reason, the trend suggests that teenage girls and boys may respond differently to mental and emotional health interventions.

This raises the question of whether programmes should be designed to target single-sex groups separately. Weare (2000) recognises that the two groups have different needs, and that this should be borne in mind when planning educational strategies for emotional competence building. Nonetheless, she sees this diversity as 'a difference in emphasis, not kind' (p. 79) and concludes that both sexes need to learn the complete range of skills required to develop emotional competence. The same point can be applied to the different learning styles and abilities present in any group of students, irrespective of gender. Elias et al. (2003) recommend that 'instruction for academic and social-emotional learning should use varied modalities and approaches to reach the diverse styles and preferences of all learners' (p. 15). The conclusion, then, is that programmes like Mind Out need to be adapted to meet the range of needs that exist both within and between groups.

Programme adaptation

Following the initial evaluation study, it was agreed that the content of the Mind Out programme might need to be reviewed in light of differential effects on some groups and perhaps modified to better meet the needs of male participants and more vulnerable students. Around the same time a proposal was put forward to implement the module in Youthreach Centres which provide programmes for young people who have left the regular school system. A decision was made to pilot an adapted version of the module with this group.

The settings

The adapted programme was implemented and evaluated in four Youthreach Centres and one Senior Traveller Training Centre (STTC) in Co. Donegal in 2004 (O'Keeffe et al., 2005). Figure 2 shows the age and gender profile of those who participated.

Figure 2 Age and gender profile of Mind Out participants in disadvantaged settings

	Youthreach Intervention (n = 17)	Youthreach Comparison (n = 23)	STTC* Intervention (n = 11)	STTC* Comparison (n = 4)
Gender (%)				
Male	64.7	43.5	0	0
Female	35.3	56.5	100	100
Age				
Mean (SD)	17.9 (2.1)	16.3 (1.5)	31.6 (7.7)	25.2 (10.6)
Min.	15	14	19	18
Max.	23	19	49	41

*STTC = Senior Traveller Training Centre

Senior Traveller Training Centres provide basic compensatory education for Travellers over the age of fifteen who have left school with either minimal or no qualifications. There is no upper age limit and parents are particularly encouraged to join the scheme because of the impact this can have on their children's subsequent participation in education. Programmes place a key emphasis on the core skills of literacy, numeracy, communications and new technology skills, while providing a range of vocational options allied with a work experience programme.

Youthreach provides educational opportunities to unemployed early school leavers aged fifteen to twenty years. It offers a programme of integrated general education, vocational training and work experience, and is structured around two distinct phases:

- foundation phase to help overcome learning difficulties, develop self-confidence and gain a range of competencies essential for further learning
- progression phase providing more specific development through a range of educational, training and work experience options.

The main objectives of Youthreach are:

- personal and social development and increased self-esteem
- second-chance education and introductory-level training
- promotion of independence, personal autonomy and a pattern of lifelong learning
- integration into further education, training opportunities and the labour market

- certification relative to ability and career options
- social inclusion.

Process of adaptation

Youthreach tutors, local Health Service Executive (HSE) personnel and university researchers worked together to modify the programme materials. On a practical level, words like 'school', 'teacher' and 'pupil' were replaced with 'centre', 'tutor' and 'trainee'. Relatively low literacy levels were also taken into account. A session on 'Dealing with Anger and Conflict' was extended to include a focus on the consequences of expressing anger. Another session on 'Group Support' was adjusted to offer a more simplified way of assessing levels of different types of support. In the school-based evaluation, boys had expressed a strong preference for the activity-oriented exercises over the more discussion-based format; teachers also felt that these structured activities were more beneficial to students who might be less cognitively and emotionally well-developed. In response, the adapted programme emphasised teaching and learning methodologies that would be particularly suited to some students within contexts of disadvantage, including a range of optional extra activity-based exercises. Class time periods in the Youthreach programme are typically longer than in post-primary schools, allowing tutors to incorporate additional activities to reinforce important learning points. Once again it is important to note that this age cohort would not have experienced SPHE at primary level and this may influence interventions with future cohorts of the equivalent age. Finally, since the student population is more transient in the Youthreach sector than in schools, explicit links between the thirteen sessions were minimised in favour of allowing each session more scope to stand alone if necessary.

Conclusion

In 1999, with the introduction of SPHE, the Irish education system took a major step towards acknowledging the role of schools in addressing the need for early intervention for social and emotional health – in effect, in educating students for life. The experience of adapting the Mind Out programme for settings of students experiencing significant levels of disadvantage contains lessons which can be applied to the delivery of SPHE at post-primary and possibly also primary level, as well as to other programmes within or beyond the health arena, and to other groups within or outside of the school sector. Diverse individuals and groups of young people will naturally have diverse needs, and programme implementers must be responsive to the particular starting-point of a group before embarking on a programme with them. Although classroom-based programmes alone will never be enough to bring about lasting positive change, they can be an important cog in the wheel of a comprehensive and coordinated systems approach, if delivered with due regard for the needs of those most vulnerable in our society who may stand to gain the most.

References

Byrne, M. C., Barry, M. M. and Sheridan, A. (2004) 'Implementation of a school-based mental health promotion programme in Ireland', *International Journal of Mental Health Promotion*, 6, 2, pp. 17–25

Byrne, M. C., Barry, M. M., NicGabhainn, S. and Newell, J. (2005) 'The development and evaluation of a mental health promotion programme for post-primary schools in Ireland' in Jensen, B. B. and Clift, S. (eds) *The health promoting school: International advances in theory, evaluation and practice*, Copenhagen: Danish University of Education Press

Caffrey, A. (2006) *Authentic Democracy Programme*, Dublin: Rutland St School

Catalano, R. F., Arthur, M. W., Hawkins, D., Berglund, L. and Olson, J. L. (1998) 'Comprehensive community- and school-based interventions to prevent antisocial behavior' in Loeber, R. and Farrington, D. P. (eds) *Serious and violent juvenile offenders: Risk factors and successful interventions*, Thousand Oaks, CA: Sage, pp. 248–270

Department of Education and Science (2001) *Social, Personal and Health Education: Junior Certificate guidelines for teachers*, Dublin: DES

Downes, P. (2003) 'The New Curriculum of Social, Personal and Health Education in Irish Primary Schools: Self-Awareness, Introversion and the Role of the Teacher', *Kwartalnik Padagogiczny* (Journal of Education, Poland), no. 4. vol. 190, pp. 93–112

Downes, P. (2004a) *Psychological Support Services for Ballyfermot: Present and Future*, Ballyfermot: URBAN

Downes, P. (2004b) *Voices from Children: St Raphael's Primary School Ballyfermot*, Ballyfermot, Dublin: URBAN

Durlak, J. A. and Wells, A. M. (1997) 'Primary prevention mental health programs for children and adolescents: A meta-analytic review', *American Journal of Community Psychology*, 25, 2, pp. 115–52

Elias, M., Zins, J. E., Graczyk, P. A. and Weissberg, R. P. (2003) 'Implementation, sustainability and scaling-up of social-emotional and academic innovations in public schools', *School Psychology Review*, 32, 3, pp. 303–19

Emslie, C., Fuhrer, R., Hunt, K., Macintyre, S., Shipley, M. and Stansfeld, S. (2002) 'Gender differences in mental health: evidence from three organisations', *Social Science and Medicine*, 54, pp. 621–4

Gallagher, M. and Millar, R. (1998) 'Gender and age differences in the concerns of adolescents in Northern Ireland', *Adolescence*, 33, 132, pp. 863–76

Gardner, H. (1993) *Frames of mind: The theory of multiple intelligences* (2nd edn) Glasgow: Fontana

Goleman, D. (1996) *Emotional Intelligence*, London: Bloomsbury

Government of Ireland (1998) *Education Act*, Dublin: Government Publications

Greenberg, M. T., Weissberg, R. P., O'Brien, M. U., Zins, J. E., Fredericks, L., Resnik, H. and Elias, M. J. (2003) 'Enhancing school-based prevention and youth development through coordinated social, emotional and academic learning', *American Psychologist*, 58, 6–7, pp. 466–74

Hegarty, T. (2006) *The Peaceful School*, in collaboration with pupils and staff of Presentation Primary, Warrenmount, Dublin 8

Lister-Sharp, D., Chapman, S., Stewart-Brown, S. and Sowden, A. (1999) 'Health promoting schools and health promotion in schools: Two systematic reviews', *Health Technology Assessment*, 3, 22, UK: NHS R&D HTA Programme

McNamara, S. (2000) *Stress in young people: What's new and what can we do?* London: Continuum

Mihalic, S., Fagan, A., Irwin, K., Ballard, D. and Elliott, D. (2002) *Blueprints for violence prevention replications: Factors for implementation success*, Boulder, Colorado: Institute of Behavioral Science, University of Colorado

Morgan, M. (2001) *Drug use prevention: Overview of research*, Dublin: National Advisory Committee on Drugs

NicGabhainn, S. and Kelleher, C. C. (1995) *Lifeskills for health promotion: The evaluation of the North-Western Health Board's health education programmes*, Galway: Centre for Health Promotion Studies, University College Galway

O'Keeffe, J., Sheridan, A., Barry, M. and Meade, K. (2005) *Evaluation of the pilot Mind Out Programme in Youthreach and Senior Traveller Training Centres*, Galway: Health Promotion Department, HSE North West and Centre for Health Promotion Studies NUI Galway

Rook, K. (1984) 'The negative side of social interaction: impact on psychological well-being', *Journal of Personality and Social Psychology*, 46, pp. 1097–108

Rook, K. (1992) 'Detrimental aspects of social relationships: Taking stock of an emerging literature' in Veiel, H. O. and Baumann, U. (eds) *The meaning and measurement of social support*, New York: Hemisphere, pp. 157–69

Tilford, S., Delaney, F. and Vogels, M. (1997) *Effectiveness of mental health promotion interventions: A review*, London: Health Education Authority

Tobler, N. S., Roona, M. R., Ochshorn, P., Marshall, D. G., Streke, A. V. and Stackpole, K. M. (2000) 'School-based adolescent drug prevention programs: 1998 meta-analysis', *Journal of Primary Prevention*, 20, pp. 275–337

Weare, K. (2000) *Promoting mental, emotional and social health: A whole school approach*, London: Routledge

Zins, J. E., Weissberg, R. P., Wang, M. and Walberg, H. J. (2004) *Building academic success on social and emotional learning: What does the research say?* New York: Teachers College Press, Columbia University

Acknowledgements

Anne Sheridan of the Health Promotion Department, HSE North West, was a significant partner in the design and evaluation of the school-based Mind Out programme, and played a lead role in the adaptation of programme materials and their implementation and evaluation in the Youthreach and SSTC settings. Thanks also to Margaret Barry, Kathryn Meade, Jo O'Keeffe and Sandra Buchanan.

30

Future Steps for NEPS?

Cathríona Ryan and Paul Downes

The National Educational Psychological Service (NEPS), which was established on 1 September 1999, was the first national psychological service after more than thirty years of discussions. In 1999, NEPS set out a number of objectives and policies to be achieved over a five-year period, including its aim to have 200 full-time psychologists working in primary schools, i.e., one psychologist per 5,000 pupils. NEPS has now been in service for over seven years. It has increased the number of psychologists from 43 on establishment to 121 in February 2006 (Hanafin, 2006), with a government commitment to bring the total number to 158 in 2007 (Hanafin, 2007). The service provides one psychologist per 6,000–7,000 pupils and has set up regional structures throughout Ireland. This chapter will examine a small sample of both rural and urban disadvantaged primary schools' perceptions of a selection of NEPS objectives and policies.

Funded by the Department of Education and Science (DES), NEPS specialises in working with both primary and post-primary schools. Its mission is to support the personal, social and educational development of all children through the application of psychological theory and practice in education, having particular regard for children with special educational needs (NEPS, 2003, p. 1). It also has a broader role, for example, in 'engaging with teachers, either individually or in small groups, as a partner in a shared endeavour, the psychologist can work cooperatively in identifying issues and in developing strategies and programmes' (NEPS, 1998, p. 46). Furthermore, it aims to provide a vital element of the government's developing policy on special needs education and social inclusion (1998, p. 40). Each NEPS psychologist is assigned to a group of schools. Their work is officially divided between 65 per cent casework and 35 per cent support and development work.

Apart from a chapter in the 2002 Annual Report of the Comptroller and Auditor General, there has not yet been a systematic external evaluation of NEPS, though Irish National Teachers' Organisation reports have raised a range of issues. For example, in an INTO/DES meeting, the INTO emphasised the need 'for appropriate support from the NEPS service (on educational disadvantage) and highlighted that because of a lack of NEPS services, there were long delays in accessing appropriate assessments ... [and the need] to provide a faster response for children who are demonstrating serious emotional and behavioural difficulties' (INTO, 2006, p. 10). The INTO has reported that 'the appointment of 142 psychologists, the setting up of regional structures and the development of a coherent model of services have all been achievements which the service can be proud of' (INTO, 2004a, p. 1). However, this report also highlighted 'that not every school in the country has access to the services of a NEPS psychologist ... INTO is also concerned that the creation of NEPS has led to a withdrawal of psychological services by Health Boards' (INTO, 2004a, p. 2). The INTO criticised the NEPS verification of assessments through the Scheme for Commissioning Psychological Assessments (SCPA) and claimed that it 'has seen little systemic or preventative work in schools' (INTO, 2004a, p. 2). It also raised concerns about 'the lack of a clinical psychological service to schools from NEPS' (2004a, p. 3). The INTO stressed that the weighting system has been 'slow to respond, overly bureaucratic and hugely demanding of time for all concerned' (INTO, 2004b, p. 2).

In an attempt to solicit feedback from school principals in Ballymun, Ryan (2004) found that there was a 'lack of impact of NEPS in Ballymun' (p. 13). Key themes which emerged in his research in Ballymun include: a lack of assessments being carried out, the need for easier access to assessments at junior level and the need for NEPS to carry out the prioritised school assessments. He points out that two-thirds of the assessments the school needed were considered 'insufficient' to meet the 'typical needs'. Attempts to solicit feedback from teachers and principals regarding NEPS have also been made in all primary schools in Ballyfermot (Downes, 2004). Key themes which emerged include: the need for assessments to include practical recommendations of how to work with the child rather than 'just summarise what we already know', the need for more culturally appropriate methods of assessment for Travellers and the lack of direct engagement in family-level work or with groups of parents due to time constraints. Feedback from designated disadvantaged schools in Blanchardstown (Downes, Maunsell and Ivers, 2006) included recognition that the 'individual psychologist is very good but overworked', that the 'service provided is excellent, but availability is very inadequate', as well as the views that the service is 'not adequate at all', and that 'not enough assessments [are] being done and more follow-up [is] needed'.

Apart from this, there has been very little research into the work carried out by NEPS. It was very difficult to analyse the progress made by NEPS from its internal reports. *Responding to Critical Incidents, Report on NEPS 1999–2001 – Working Together to Make a Difference for Children* (2001) is the only report that made some attempt at evaluating the work done by NEPS since its establishment. There is arguably a need for more transparency of information.

School psychologists in the US spend most of their time performing assessments to determine special educational eligibility (Gutkin and Conoley 1990; Short and Talley 1997). Like school psychological services in the US (see Reeder et al., 1997), NEPS does not wish to confine its role to assessment. Reeder et al.'s review of the US literature in this context observes that the time required to provide such assessments, in conjunction with prevailing funding mechanisms, effectively preclude efforts to intervene in a broader fashion.

The following preliminary discussion involves a small sample from both rural and urban designated disadvantaged schools of teachers' and principals' views of NEPS regarding a selection of NEPS objectives and policies that NEPS seeks to provide to primary schools. A qualitative research methodology was employed using questionnaires and interviews (March–December 2005). The sample of client users was chosen on the basis of two of Miles and Huberman's (1994) sampling approaches:

Maximum variation

This was achieved by documenting principals', teachers', and resource teachers' views of NEPS in a rural and urban designated disadvantaged school setting. It also accommodated a variety across schools in the length of time they had been involved with NEPS.

Criterion

All participants met the same criterion of working in a designated disadvantaged primary school. The number of participants within the school depended on the criterion of their availability.

It is not being claimed that the views of these schools are necessarily representative of other designated disadvantaged schools throughout Ireland, as it was not a random sample (Table 1).

Twenty-two teachers/school principals participated in total. Interviews were conducted with the principals of each school and with a class teacher of one rural and one urban school. Ten questionnaires were given to each school, except one urban school. The questions asked were the same in both questionnaire and interview. Typical responses as well as the individual perspectives of teachers and principals will be outlined below. The following themes, containing the substance of the responses, will be focused on:

- involvement of NEPS in assessments
- work carried out by the NEPS active panel of psychologists
- assessments for pupils with emotional and behavioural difficulties
- collaboration of NEPS with teachers, and understanding the methods and systems used in a classroom
- NEPS support for the school as a system
- collaboration of NEPS with parents and its support for parents[1]

Table 1 Type of designated disadvantaged school, experience of NEPS, number of participants

Type of Designated Disadvantaged Primary School	Rural school No. 1	Rural school No. 2	Urban school No. 3	Urban school No. 4	Urban school No. 5
Time NEPS have been working in the school	3rd year working with	Since the scheme started	5th/6th year working with	4th year working with	$1/2$ day a year since the scheme started
Number of people from each school participating in the research					
Principal	1	1	1	1	1
Teacher	4	3	5	1	–
Resource teacher	2	–	2		–

Involvement of NEPS in assessments

The NEPS method of allocating special educational resources sees an assessment as a 'gateway' to the procurement of teaching resources, placing a priority on assessments (INTO, 2004a, p. 2). Eight respondents suggested that assessments carried out have been successful, with answers such as 'have had some success in the past' and 'they have been very successful because these children are now getting the extra hours they require'. Some participants reported that assessments have provided children with the help they required: 'assessments have generally been successful and helpful in devising Individual Education Plans'. Another response was that 'assessments are only of benefit if they provide insights into

---

[1] Other key themes that emerged which are beyond the scope of this chapter include: the need for Individual Educational Plans (IEPs) for international pupils and for IEPs to be more specific, practical and simplified; and concerns regarding the weighting system for schools and with the use by NEPS of a three-stage approach to assessments.

learning styles and difficulties and this varies widely, some reports are very effective'.

Ten respondents were of the view that there was scope for improvement regarding assessments: 'needs still not being addressed', 'I don't believe in assessments anyway. I only get them for resources. They focus on the disability of a child and not on the child'. Another response stated:

> ... their results are only partially helpful to us in so far as granting the child access to a special class. I don't find their assessments particularly helpful and we always give the psychologist a very detailed report to ensure that the child's needs are met. I found two assessments to be unsuccessful. Two children in the school have had assessments done over two years ago and now I applied for them to get exemptions from Irish because they are too weak to keep up. But because it's over two years since they were assessed, it's not valid any more and they have to be re-assessed before they can leave [primary] school to grant them the exemption [from Irish in secondary school].

The issue of early intervention was also raised with regard to assessment, as well as the need for greater cultural understanding of the children:

> I only get NEPS to assess the pupils in the more senior part of the school. We know the kids. We are able to screen them in such a way that a psychologist doesn't because they are not familiar with our pupils.

> The tests don't pick up on special needs of children until the age of eight. Children with special needs before the age of six don't get any attention from NEPS. We are slow to get a child assessed before the age of six because it will come back that the child is fine. The tests don't pick up on a lack of verbal skills. Pupils don't get the service until between seven and eight and it's too late. The whole psychological service is not good enough. Over a decade ago, psychologists were asked to come into schools and this is still not happening ... I don't have time to fight for a better NEPS service ... The service we have doesn't allow the psychologist to get to know the kids or provide psychological support. If you're middle-class you don't know how to deal with the life the poor deal with.

Another response raised the need for more practical recommendations based on the assessments, including improved continuity over time: 'follow-up is poor ... not enough time in the school ... unrealistic recommendations'. The need for more resources for NEPS is evident:

> ... they are not an independent professional body. They work within resources. They don't identify needs and then work to have these needs met. They convey the belief that the service they provide to 3,000 children is satisfactory. Our school has NEPS services for two days a year or one psychological assessment.

NEPS active panel of psychologists

Thirty-one per cent of both rural and urban responses claimed to be unaware of the existence of such a service. Two out of twenty-two answers gave positive feedback about the panel. The first reported that:

> ... when we got assessments done from the NEPS panel, we found that they seemed keener to get work done. Our NEPS psychologist can only assess two pupils a day, however, she assessed six.[2] She did more for the school in one visit than my psychologist did all year.

The second response suggested that the panel was 'probably good in crisis situations'. One response did not mention having difficulty accessing the panel: 'In the past we raised funds and hired a private psychologist approved by NEPS.' However, the remaining responses indicated difficulties in accessing the panel because the psychologists do not work full time: 'Yes, three years ago I found it very hard to get a psychologist because some on the list will only work on Fridays and others were too busy.' Others stated, 'Yes but it's so difficult to get a psychologist off that list. A lot of them are only working part-time'; 'NEPS inform schools that they have an active panel of psychologists to give assessments to schools. However, there are only two psychologists on it with kits for assessments. This is a joke and needs to change.' Another complained that 'Schools have had very poor service from these psychologists – there is very little follow up and hardly no opportunity to check any of the recommendations.'

The need for a broadening of the scope of NEPS to work with pupils with emotional and behavioural difficulties

In the NEPS *Report of the Planning Group* (1998, p. 77), it is stated that the cases considered to be appropriate to be referred to psychologists will include pupils thought to have emotional and/or behavioural disorders. Some responses claimed that 'similar attention is given' to children with behavioural difficulties and children with learning disabilities. However, 73 per cent of responses suggested that children with learning difficulties are given much more attention and NEPS gives 'nowhere near the same attention' to behavioural problems; 'they haven't been given the same attention. Teachers are left coping with behavioural disorders, more or less, on their own.' This concern was raised in a number of other responses:

> I once asked the psychologist to deal with a bullying issue in the school. She said that she would but it would take from her time doing assessments so I ended up doing it myself.

---

[2]   A strong argument can be made that six assessments per day is too many and too rushed. However, there is a need for increased transparency of communication from NEPS to schools as to the rationale for taking more time to do assessments.

> There are at least ten pupils with behavioural problems in my class. I said it to the principal and he said that there isn't a lot we can do.

As one principal remarked, 'NEPS is not interested in behavioural problems. We need clinical psychologists for this kind of advice.'

Two responses suggested the need for more emphasis on dealing with behavioural difficulties in NEPS psychologists' training:

> There is a gap, including kids with behavioural difficulties. These are kids living in crisis situations. They provide strategies as a guide. It doesn't work.

> NEPS psychologists are not qualified to actually diagnose behavioural disorders. Their focus is on cognitive rather than emotional problems. I think their training should be extended to include both clinical and educational difficulties. Teachers have to deal with the whole child. NEPS psychologists need to take the same approach. A lot of children's behaviour in school is influenced by the behaviours they encounter in the home. NEPS psychologists need to take these factors into account. If a child is finally linked with a child guidance clinic they cannot avail of speech and language therapy at the same time. This needs to be addressed. A teacher in our school who has done a counselling course is currently working as a support teacher dealing specifically with behavioural issues.

The general view was that NEPS needs to spend more time on emotional and behavioural difficulties:

> Teachers don't know what they are supposed to provide. NEPS mainly provide assessments. We need assessments done. However, I would like to see the educational psychologist come in and engage with the children in therapy groups.

> I have found that some of the recommendations that our psychologist has made regarding behavioural problems have not been adequate. They need to spend more time helping us with behavioural management.

The collaboration of NEPS with teachers and understanding of the methods and systems used in a classroom

According to the *Report on the National Education Convention* (1994), NEPS aspires to work in 'close collaboration with teachers' (p. 67). Twenty-one out of twenty-two responses suggested that teachers seek an improved experience of this collaboration, while one response made no comment. Typical answers suggested that NEPS does not have enough time with teachers:

> It is very hard for her to work in partnership with teachers when she is only working part-time and has twenty schools to cover.

> You cannot collaborate visiting a school three times a year. Problems/issues need to be addressed and cannot be glossed over.

> I have to say I've got no help from NEPS. I think unless you're a class teacher at the time of assessment you won't ever meet a member of NEPS.

Other answers claimed that such collaboration is not practical under present circumstances – 'idealistic view – not practical support when all things are considered' – and that NEPS does not take the whole-class situation into account: 'feel that they don't take whole-class situation into account ... not practical support', 'very idealistic view ... I found their recommendations unrealistic ... They refuse to see the whole class when planning for an individual child.'

In the 1998 *Report of the Planning Group*, it was recommended that NEPS 'should have an understanding of the methods and systems which are pedagogically appropriate and are capable of being implemented by teachers' (p. 48). Two responses suggested that NEPS does have a sufficient and practical understanding: 'Teachers have found that in general suggestions are practical'; 'Many of the NEPS personnel I have worked with have had a primary teaching background and are very much in touch with the classroom. However, some recommendations could have been more appropriately addressed as there is only a limited amount any teacher can receive.'

Six responses stated that there was 'not enough' understanding of pedagogically appropriate methods and systems by NEPS psychologists working with the sample schools. Other responses were:

> Not at all. We had one staff meeting with a NEPS psychologist for forty minutes this year and I can't even remember it! I'm told that some of my pupils are on IEPs and that's it. In my class the best pupils score 5/10 in any subject and it's so frustrating that we have a service that could do so much but does so little to help.

> They are respectful of teachers but I don't know if they understand the system very well because we only use them for assessments.

> My teachers' commitment to the children is unbelievable. A psychologist doesn't see this.

As another teacher remarked: 'some ideas are given when a child is observed, but it's not always suitable'. Concern was expressed that some NEPS psychologists are 'not taking whole-class situations into account', while another teacher suggested 'why don't they visit our classroom and observe workings?'. The need for increased communication with schools was directly expressed in the following response:

> NEPS psychologists need to take off their departmental hats and communicate with us. They don't communicate with us by saying 'I'll see you next year'. NEPS doesn't give dignity to the needs of children. The structure isn't there to work collaboratively. What is our official relationship with NEPS? We don't know our rights and

responsibilities. How do I go about resolving disputes with a NEPS psychologist? Do we have to meet NEPS? Could they overturn the policy of a school? I don't know what our legal status is with NEPS. There is no system in place to make complaints. I have never been invited to make recommendations although I'd love to.

NEPS support of the school as a system through whole-school approaches to a range of issues: lack of time as a key issue

In the NEPS Statement of Strategy (2004, p. 11), it states that NEPS will support schools, provide advice and devise policies and practice in the development of whole-school approaches to such issues as disability, specific learning difficulties, behavioural management, bullying and responses to critical incidents. A typical view was that if NEPS supports the school, it will provide less assessments: 'NEPS will support any of these areas but at the expense of responding to the needs of individual children who are failing the system.' The issue of NEPS not spending enough time in schools seemed to be a common response:

> It doesn't. NEPS will say that it does so much but when it comes down to it we have to prioritise everything we want done. I would love to complain NEPS to the TD but I can't because NEPS will then have to write to the Minister explaining why we are unhappy with the service and the time taken to write to the Minister is then deducted from the time spent in my school and I can't afford to lose one of the three days NEPS spends in the school.

Most answers suggested that NEPS does not have enough time to support the school as a system:

> I haven't experienced any support in this area.

> Their theory and vision is good. A lot of what she has to say though is good theoretically but what can we do if we don't have the resources. They just don't have enough time. The NEPS psychologists are frustrated with their own system. It must be frustrating for NEPS psychologists to find that they are so stretched and can't get much done. Once I rang her and she said 'I can give you two hours but I'm very busy out in Castleknock.' I have a lot of anger with half a day a year. If we have a respect for communities, a lot of psychological problems would disappear.

The collaboration of NEPS with parents and its support for parents: issues for discussion

In the Irish context, the need to involve parents more actively in their children's education was recognised in the National Programme of Special Measures for Schools in Disadvantaged Areas (1984) and the Report of the Irish Department of

Education Working Party on the Primary School Curriculum and the Disadvantaged Child (1985) (see also Burke 1992). The Irish White Paper on Education, *Charting our Education Future* (1995), further affirmed the crucial role of parents 'in forming the child's learning environment' and pointed to the need for positive attitudes to education and the need to encourage self-esteem. Against this backdrop, in 1998, the *Report of the Planning Group* recommended that NEPS 'should ensure that parents are directly involved in and consulted about any individual interventions regarding their child' so that their knowledge of their child's needs could be clearly understood and enhanced.

Some respondents in the survey said that NEPS does ensure that parents are directly involved: 'most of the time'. However, the interaction NEPS had with parents seemed to vary. One answer claimed that NEPS 'meets parents before assessments and goes through in detail what is going to be done. I haven't had any complaints from parents anyway', while another claimed, 'The psychologist we have here meets the parents after assessment but she doesn't meet them before.' In contrast, another stated that 'The NEPS Educational Psychologists do meet families before and after assessments and explain everything in detail.' However, many answers suggested that NEPS interaction with parents is minimal. Six of these responses specifically mentioned that it is left up to teachers to involve parents: 'Parents are certainly involved but teachers do most of the work with parents' and 'In my experience we, as teachers, have had to speak to and explain the assessments to parents. There have been no follow-up programmes with parents.' Another stated: 'NEPS have little impact in our school on improving parents' knowledge of their children's needs.'

The 1998 report also emphasises that NEPS should consult and support parents so that their confidence in their own ability to help their child is increased. Only two answers reported that NEPS support parents: 'Parents have never complained about the psychological work done here' and 'An educational psychologist we had in the past, who came in through the NEPS panel, did not cooperate with teachers or parents. However, the NEPS educational psychologists do meet families before and after assessments and explain everything in detail.' However, the majority of responses from both rural and urban schools suggested that this occurs rarely or not at all: 'not very much'; 'very formalised around the assessment and not much after'; 'almost non-existent'; 'they have never worked with parents here'. One principal mentioned the need for improved support from NEPS regarding children of ethnic minorities: 'They don't support parents at all. Parents, especially with non-national children, need support but they don't get any.'

Preliminary conclusions

This preliminary dialogue with a limited sample of teachers and school principals regarding their perceptions of NEPS raises a number of questions and issues that invite further consideration. The question arises regarding the need for a systematic external review of NEPS, which would consult principals, teachers and parents and would focus, in particular, on designated disadvantaged schools. Dialogue with schools in this small sample also highlighted the need for:

- more solution-focused recommendations for working with children who have been assessed
- more consistent strategies to accommodate the centrality of parental involvement with NEPS psychologists, including sustained follow-up programmes
- where possible, the development of assessment tools for children from junior classes
- increased time to be allocated for psychologists working in designated disadvantaged schools
- a more holistic approach to intervention that does not separate children's emotional needs from their learning needs, an approach that develops teachers' behaviour management strategies.

The new revised curriculum requires primary teachers to go beyond the traditional Cartesian split between reason and emotion and to integrate the child's emotional development with his or her learning (Downes, 2004). This adds to the anomaly of the Cartesian structure underlying the bifurcation within psychology between educational and clinical psychologists, as expressed through the view that 'NEPS is not interested in behavioural problems'.

It is also arguable that more practical solution-focused strategies following assessments – and communication between NEPS and schools – would be facilitated by an increased proportion of psychologists coming from a primary school background. There are clear advantages regarding the independence of assessments in having NEPS psychologists who are external to the school staff. Nevertheless, an argument can be made that perhaps another level within a future NEPS could marry external psychologists with the resource of a psychologist being attached to a cluster of schools, as in, for example, the Home School Community Liaison Scheme (HSCL). As one principal stated: 'It would be ideal if they were spread out between four out of five schools and be shared at a local level with parents and teachers.' Such an extra level to NEPS would go a long way to meet most of the concerns raised above.

References

Annual Report of the Comptroller and Auditor General (2002) (No. 8 of 1993)

Burke, A. (1992) *Teaching: Retrospect and prospect*, Dublin: St Patrick's College, Drumcondra

Department of Education (1984) *National Programme for Schools in Disadvantaged Areas*, Dublin: Government Publications

Department of Education (1985) *Report of the Irish Department of Education Working Party on the Primary School Curriculum and the Disadvantaged Child*, Dublin: Government Publications

Department of Education and Science (1995) *Charting our Education Future*, Irish White Paper on Education, Dublin: DES

Downes, P. (2004) *Psychological Support Services for Ballyfermot: Present and Future*, Ballyfermot: URBAN

Downes, P., Maunsell, C. and Ivers, J. (2006) *A holistic approach to early school leaving and school retention in Blanchardstown: Current issues and future steps for services and schools*, Dublin: Blanchardstown Area Partnership

Gutkin, T. B. and Conoley, J. C. (1990) 'Reconceptualising school psychology from a service delivery perspective: Implications for practice, training and research', *Journal of School Psychology*, 28, pp. 203–23

Hanafin, M. (2006) 'Psychological Service', http://193.178.1.238/xml/29/DAL20060215A.PDF, 15 February

Hanafin, M. (2007) 'Minister announces extra psychologists', *The Irish Times*, 4 January

Irish National Teachers' Organisation (2004a) *Submission to the National Educational Psychological Service Strategic Review*, Dublin: INTO

Irish National Teachers' Organisation (2004b) *Consultative Conference on Special Education*, Dublin: INTO

Irish National Teachers' Organisation (2006) *In Touch*, May, Dublin: INTO

Miles, M. and Huberman, A. (1994) *Qualitative Data Analysis* (2nd edn) Thousand Oaks: Sage

National Education Convention Secretariat (1994) *Report on the National Education Convention*, Convention Secretariat, Dublin: Government of Ireland

National Educational Psychological Service (1998) *Report of the Planning Group*, Dublin: NEPS

National Educational Psychological Service (2001) *Responding to Critical Incidents, Report on NEPS 1999–2001 – Working Together to Make a Difference for Children*, Dublin: NEPS

National Educational Psychological Service (2003) *The NEPS Model of Service – Working Together to Make a Difference for Children*, Dublin: NEPS

National Educational Psychological Service (2004) *The NEPS Customer Quality Service Statement and the National Educational Psychological Service Agency Statement of Strategy 2001–2004 – Working Together to Make a Difference for Children*, Dublin: NEPS

Reeder, G. D., Maccow, G. C., Shaw, S. R., Swerdlik, M. E., Horton, C. B. and Foster, P. (1997) 'School psychologists and full-service schools: Partnerships with medical, mental health and social services', *School Psychology Review*, 26, pp. 603–21

Ryan, G. (2004) *Get it Right First Time. An Education Strategy for Ballymun*, Dublin: Ballymun Local Area Partnership

Short, R. J. and Talley, R. C. (1997) 'Rethinking psychology and the schools: Implications of recent national policy', *American Psychologist*, 52, pp. 234–40

31

The Job Satisfaction of Beginning Teachers

Mark Morgan and Karl Kitching

A relatively high number of beginning primary teachers start their careers in schools that are designated disadvantaged (Morgan and O'Leary, 2004). However, in Ireland, as in many countries, these same teachers gravitate towards other schools, either at the end of their probation period or a short time later. At the same time, the number of vacancies in schools serving disadvantaged communities has increased due to new positions being created involving resource and learning support teachers (Linnane, 2005). These trends result in two consequences. One is that there is a constant turnover of teachers in schools serving disadvantaged communities, resulting in lack of continuity that can affect planning and cohesion. The other, and perhaps more important, result is that at times of teacher shortage, disadvantaged schools are among the first to experience difficulties in recruiting teachers, resulting in the need to hire un-trained personnel. These are major issues for the system as we attempt to address educational disadvantage in a comprehensive way (DES, 2005).

To consider the issue of job satisfaction from the perspective of teachers serving in designated disadvantaged schools we draw on data sources that have generated the study of 'Teachers' Lives', a collaborative project of the Colleges of Education Research Consortium (CERC). Specifically, one of our databases is a survey of beginning teachers in primary school and another is based on diaries kept by beginning teachers (one to five years after qualification), which focused on daily incidents that made them feel good and/or bad about their work as teachers. Finally, our work is also informed by a focus group discussion with teachers currently teaching in designated schools.

General ideas informing job satisfaction:
the international context

Surveys of practising teachers and of factors motivating people to enter teaching generally reveal a positive picture of motives and intrinsic job satisfaction (Spear, Gould and Lee, 2000). On the other hand, evidence from both the UK and US indicate that the retention of teachers is a major problem, particularly in the case of beginning teachers. The evidence from the US is that up to 40 per cent of beginning teachers leave before they complete five years' teaching (Ingersoll, 2001), and the figure for the UK is broadly similar.

The educational context that results in such a dramatic loss from teaching is influenced by a number of features which are shared among countries in the Western world and some of which are specific to particular countries. Among those factors that are common to many countries are those that make higher demands on teachers in more curricular areas. These greater demands on teachers (sometimes referred to as 'intensification') have their origin in the growing complexity of the knowledge society. Another major influence on the intensification of teachers' work is the expectation that schools will deal with a variety of social issues that traditionally might have been expected to be dealt with by families only. The problem with these social issues is that they multiply over the years as society changes. For example, while many issues arise as a result of the interaction of many varied societal structures as opposed to education alone, schools are expected to have programmes to prevent child abuse, bullying, drug and alcohol misuse, obesity and youth suicide.

One way of considering the history of teaching in recent years is in terms of a decline in teachers' professionalism. While there is no single marker of what constitutes professionalism, some degree of autonomy over what is taught and how it is taught may be regarded as a major constituent. A major European project focusing on teachers' and nurses' professional lives and knowledge – the Professional Knowledge in Education and Health (PROFKNOW) project – has demonstrated that teachers throughout Europe see themselves as more accountable, more regulated and needing to provide fuller documentation than was the case when they began their careers (Sugrue, Dupont and Morgan, 2006).

There is substantial evidence that changes in the nature of teaching (particularly intensification and accountability) play a major role in job dissatisfaction among newly qualified teachers and have led to an exodus from teaching in many countries. For example, in a study in the US involving interviews with teachers who had either quit or moved schools, perceptions of success with students were a major influence as was the existence of support structures that allow for personal growth and collegial interaction (Johnson and Birkeland, 2003). In other words, we can think of job satisfaction as a mediating variable originating in working conditions and resulting in teachers quitting or moving on to a different school. For these reasons, a fuller understanding of the processes underlying job satisfaction and dissatisfaction can help develop appropriate interventions.

Guiding ideas on job satisfaction

A number of general principles regarding job satisfaction are especially pertinent; these are relevant to experiences of satisfaction in several domains of people's lives but are especially applicable to the situation in which beginning teachers find themselves and to how they judge the extent to which they have a fulfilling career. The first of these concerns expectations; an event is judged as satisfying in relation to what is expected. If the outcome exceeds or matches the expectation, then satisfaction is experienced. If, however, an outcome is less than what is expected, then disappointment and dissatisfaction results. This can explain why the same people can experience exactly the same result and yet have very different reactions.

Another relevant factor that influences satisfaction is comparison with others. Someone may be happy with outcomes until they realise that others with whom they compare themselves have done relatively better. A corollary of this is what is called the 'Big Fish Small Pond' phenomenon: people are more satisfied with themselves and their rewards in situations where the reference group against whom they compare themselves is not very large and has a modest average level of achievement.

The way we judge is not simple, as is clear from these ideas regarding comparisons and expectations. But there are other complicating factors arising from the different ways in which people judge success and which in turn derive from the domain in which they have staked their feelings of self-worth. We can easily accept that success in teaching is a critical experience for a beginning teacher. There are, however, very different ways in which teachers judge themselves to be successful. For someone who has an orientation towards affirmation by others, praise of a principal or senior colleague may be the most salient, while for others the intrinsic rewards brought about by children's engagement in learning tasks may be the most rewarding kind of experience.

A final important principle relating to job satisfaction centres on the nature of the events that cause people to 'feel good' or experience satisfaction. The interactions that bring about such outcomes are not necessarily inherently pleasant; indeed they may be normally considered stressful. However, because the events result in a teacher solving a problem or at least alleviating distress, they will be experienced as satisfying rather than stressful. Thus, while an encounter with a child who is distressed or anxious may be inherently difficult, if a teacher can be helpful, they are likely to feel enhanced. As will become clear in our discussion of the diary studies, the key issue is what a teacher can do, rather than the event itself.

Job satisfaction of beginning teachers in disadvantaged schools

A study by Morgan and O'Leary (2004) sought to explore some of the determinants of teacher satisfaction among beginning teachers based on a survey of 468 former students of St Patrick's College who had spent between six and eighteen months in the classroom. The teachers responded to a structured questionnaire dealing with (among other topics) their background characteristics, satisfaction with work, perceptions of self-efficacy in teaching, perceived support and their perception of their capacity to teach the various subjects on the curriculum.

Measures of satisfaction with teaching focused on a number of broad areas:

*   global satisfaction
*   salary and conditions
*   relationships with colleagues, the inspectorate and parents
*   features of professional development and teaching.

For each of these areas, the respondents were asked to indicate on a five-point Likert-type scale how satisfied they were with the feature in question. The items measuring job satisfaction have satisfactory internal reliability and can therefore be taken as a scale.

It is interesting to note that job satisfaction did not relate to gender, course (BEd vs Postgraduate Diploma) or experience (whether the teacher had one year's experience or had just graduated). Overall, these factors did not emerge as important. While female teachers had, on average, marginally higher levels of satisfaction than male teachers, the differences were not statistically significant. Those who graduated a year earlier had an almost identical satisfaction score than those who graduated one year later. It is also of interest to note that academic performance either in the Leaving Certificate or in the degree course did not correlate with job satisfaction.

In Table 1 we show the correlations between two factors that were of particular importance for the job satisfaction of teachers who had just graduated and for those who had graduated one year earlier. The first of these is perceived efficacy. Self-efficacy is different from self-confidence or self-esteem in that it refers to the specific judgement of what a person can do in particular circumstances. The various aspects of teachers' self-efficacy have been shown to be powerful predictors of classroom performance and children's learning. The research in this area has shown that teacher efficacy is linked with readiness to try instructional experimentation, a desire to find better ways of teaching, willingness to work with students who are experiencing difficulties, as well as student achievement gains and affective development (Bandura, 1997; Pajares, 1996).

Table 1 The link between job satisfaction and self-efficacy and support in school*

	Graduated in current year	Graduated one year earlier
Self-efficacy: broad areas of teaching	.41**	.25**
Self-efficacy: helping students with difficulties	.37**	.28**
Self-efficacy: creating a positive classroom climate	.38**	.15**
Self-efficacy: working with disadvantaged children	.29**	.18**
Self-efficacy: persistence	.31**	.17**
Perceived support	.50**	.62**

* * adapted from Morgan and O'Leary, 2004
** $p<.01$

In our study a number of measures of teacher efficacy were utilised, including efficacy in creating an atmosphere conducive to learning, efficacy in helping students with learning difficulties and efficacy in working with children from disadvantaged backgrounds. In each case the correlation with job satisfaction was substantial and significant.

The other major factor that was associated with job satisfaction was extent of support that beginning teachers experienced; included were colleagues (from same and other schools) as well as principal and inspector. It is of particular interest to note that support from their peers was experienced more frequently than support from other sources. As in the case for self-efficacy, the link with job satisfaction was significant, $r = .50$ ($p<.001$).

Micro-study of teachers' lives

The final area of research that we deal with is one on which we have spent a considerable time and effort over the last two years. The emphasis in this research has been the identification of the ordinary everyday incidents that occur routinely in the classroom and which make teachers either feel good or bad about their work as teachers. In order to identify these incidents with some precision, we asked teachers to keep diaries and to complete them at the end of the week. An example of a completed diary for a week is shown in Figure 1 (below).

Figure 1 Example of one week's diary entries

F/2-3/Inf.

Description of event(s)	Rating (please number each event)
I made a suggestion in relation to the management of children on the yard during a school planning day. The suggestion was discussed and welcomed.	7
Pupil with a mild G.L.D. who has been making very slow progress did some very good work.	8
Children really enjoyed a new game in P.E.	5

13/05/03

Description of event(s)	Rating (please number each event)
During a school planning day the strategies for dealing with misbehaviour were being discussed. The use of "extra work" was being advocated strongly by many staff members as a viable sanction. This highlighted for me how different my colleagues philosophies and attitudes are to my own.	6
Correcting workbooks - feel that the workbook is (educationally) a waste of valuable time, for me and the children.	9
Heard the reading of two of my weakest children one after another - I am worried that I am not meeting their needs and feel my time is so streched I don't know where I can fit in more work with them.	8

A number of points emerge clearly from the diary entries. Firstly, it is evident that while the incidents themselves are relatively minor in nature, they have a triggering impact on the feelings of the teachers, resulting sometimes in significant emotions or at least good/bad feelings. It is the personal significance of the incidents to the teacher concerned that matters rather than the event itself. Thus, while it is the case that an overheard or casual remark by a colleague is not of itself a major incident, the consequences for the train of thought can be dramatic.

Secondly, the fact that positive things happen does not preclude negative events. When teachers report a list of good events for the week, they are equally likely to report negative events. Furthermore, they experience negative events just as strongly, even when they are apparently having a good week. This emerged in a statistical analysis, which showed that the correlation between the intensity of positive and negative events approached zero. In other words, negative and positive events co-occur in most days in a teacher's life, and the occurrence of one kind does not preclude the full experience of the other.

Thirdly, the indications are that positive events have a different origin in classroom events than is the case with negative events. Table 2 shows the origin of positive and negative events reported by teachers; here it is immediately obvious that events causing positive experiences are not a mirror image of those causing dissatisfaction. For example, student engagement, student achievement and student well-being are mentioned largely in the context of positive events. On the other hand, student behaviour and interactions with students' homes are most frequently mentioned in relation to occasions giving rise to dissatisfaction.

Table 2 Sources of positive and negative feelings of teachers
(N = 254 events)

	Category	Times mentioned	Satisfaction	Dissatisfaction
A	Student engagement	53	46	7
B	Student behaviour	49	17	32
C	Student achievement	35	28	7
D	Teaching/planning/management	29	13	16
E	Home interactions and influence	21	5	16
F	Interactions with colleagues	18	12	6
G	Student personal well-being	13	12	1
H	Miscellaneous	36	20	16

Table entries are numbers of events described in teachers' diaries

Fourthly, the incidents described in the teachers' diaries relating to satisfaction in particular are extremely important in the sense that they influence the likelihood that teachers will remain in their jobs. With this in mind, we measured commitment to 'teaching' as a career as well as teachers' belief that they would remain in the particular school in which they were working. The teachers indicated the strength of their commitment (scale 1–10) at the end of each of the five weeks. What was interesting was that there was a much stronger relationship between positive events and commitment to remain in teaching than was the case with negative events. In other words, the presence or absence of satisfying events was more important than dissatisfying events. The case for the greater significance of positive events may be strengthened by our finding that negative events do not prevent positive events from happening.

These findings have important implications for an understanding of the reasons why teachers stay or move on. Until now, the emphasis has been on the stresses, difficulties and problems that teachers experience, with a view to helping them cope with such difficulties. The diary work suggests that it is much better to start with positive events and try to build on these, since the findings show that it is not the presence of negative experiences but rather the *absence of positive ones* that is critical to a teacher's commitment to remain in a school.

Focus group interview in a disadvantaged setting

A largely exploratory focus group interview was held with five teachers (four female and one male) in a designated disadvantaged school setting, which reflected on some of the themes considered here. Those interviewed were between their second and fifth year of teaching, and were teaching between the second and sixth class primary grades. The school was founded in the 1950s in an inner-city location. The school serves a varied student population, ranging from those who come from very disadvantaged backgrounds to those whose home environment has high levels of resources. Pupil behaviour is viewed as one of the major issues consistently facing the school as a whole. Pupil behaviour was considered by the group participants to be influenced positively by a Discipline for Learning policy, which had been in place for the previous three years. Major curricular concerns in the school are the literacy and numeracy achievement of pupils, as standardised tests scores reveal low levels of literacy and numeracy achievement across the school.

The young staff, the collegial atmosphere, the close relationship the teachers have with the children, relationships with parents, the strong support and leadership the principal provides and the overall challenge inherent in teaching in a designated disadvantaged school were all cited as factors that made those in the group remain in the school and were named as factors that contributed to their 'global' satisfaction. Indeed, job satisfaction for this group was often viewed more in global terms, or in reference to the overall year's work, rather than in terms of positive daily events. It was suggested in the group that the absence of negative events is one way of deriving satisfaction in a designated disadvantaged school on a day-to-day basis. When asked whether they expected to experience satisfaction on a daily basis, one teacher remarked:

> T2: I don't think on a daily basis. But, em, like maybe at the end of the year, when you do see that one of the guys have gotten on well, or have even lasted the year or grasped something that you really thought they had no hope of it. That really will make you happy and you're delighted that has happened, and that you hope in some way that you have contributed to it.

It was recognised that negative events impact on the teacher on a more day-to-day basis:

> T4: I suppose (dissatisfying events occur) more on a day-to-day basis, whereas if you look back on the long-term, you know, it kind of wouldn't affect you that way. You know it's more the day-to-day things that grind you down at the end of the day.

This is not to say that satisfaction should be viewed in negative terms, or that overtly satisfying events could not be experienced on a daily basis. As was found in the diary study, the group referred to small achievements the pupils make, or seeing the pupils enjoy learning or sport as sources of daily encouragement for themselves as teachers. Combining our findings on the importance of the presence or absence of positive events over negative ones for commitment to teaching in the diary study with these exploratory comments may lead us to speculate that it is the overall, global satisfaction one derives from teaching in a designated disadvantaged school that should be focused on in efforts to keep teachers committed to working in such schools.

As referred to already, relationships within the school (teacher–pupil, teacher–teacher, etc.) were viewed as part and parcel of the enjoyment these teachers derived from teaching in what they saw as the more informal disadvantaged setting. The collegial and social atmosphere amongst the staff was highly regarded:

> T5: The staff I suppose (is another appealing factor about the school) because I generally, and I think it's the same for most disadvantaged schools, it's quite a young staff and, because the job can be so difficult at times when we go up and take our breaks we really have a break … The staff make this job a million times easier.

One participant argued that the 'energy of youth' might not be regarded as an explanation for the high number of younger teachers in designated disadvantaged schools, given that there are a few members of staff who have been teaching almost thirty years in the same school. The group felt that individual personality traits play a major role in teachers' ability to cope with teaching in a disadvantaged setting. The ability not to take events 'too seriously' and to avoid over-attributing negative events to personal failure and becoming highly anxious about negative events may be valuable. These ideas are particularly important in considering how individual personality traits impact on one's perceptions of self-efficacy, job satisfaction and subsequent commitment to teaching. The following comments from the focus group are of interest in this regard:

> T5: I think you wouldn't survive long in here if you took everything personally … if you had a messy day and you didn't get everything done and you go home feeling dreadful, you couldn't come back.

> T2: Sometimes it's hard not to though as well, not to take it personally or not to feel you should have managed the day better.

> T4: If you get through your first year here and you've got the type of personality that you don't get stressed and take it home with you then you're gonna make it really … There've been people that have worked in this school and they've been completely stressed to the hilt at the end of the year and they've always left at the end of the year … because if you most days step back from it … sometimes you have to abandon it and go with the flow.

One teacher suggested that in designated disadvantaged schools one has to let go of control over one's own satisfaction to a certain extent, as satisfaction or lack thereof can depend to some extent on the children's circumstances or demeanour each day. She described the following situation as an example:

> T5: One parent opened the door one morning and threw the lunch at them (a child in her class), you know, and you're supposed to have a good day with that kid, you know … If you're a person that likes being in control of your own day, that could be very frustrating.

Teacher education

Murphy (2005) suggests that teachers feel unprepared for teaching in designated disadvantaged schools and recommends that more time be allocated to teaching practice in disadvantaged settings, as well as greater teacher induction and mentoring in disadvantaged areas. Certainly there is scope to build on the existing initiatives at pre-service level. For example, St Patrick's College Educational Disadvantage Centre currently runs several electives for final-year BEd students which provide students with the opportunity to reflect on, and experience, teaching in an area of educational disadvantage, and to relate to disadvantaged communities, examine Irish policy in relation to educational disadvantage and/or develop literacy for struggling readers and writers and for pupils of diverse backgrounds.

Induction programmes for newly qualified teachers have a major role to play. In a review of the international research and its implications for the Irish situation, Murphy and Killeavey (forthcoming) concluded that teachers who had experienced induction were more committed to staying in the profession and more capable of moving beyond initial concerns with classroom management problems to dealing with instructional and curricular issues.

Significantly, a pilot induction project has been under way in St Patrick's College for the last four years, and is scheduled for expansion. The initial evaluation of the induction project has shown it to be extremely successful (Murphy and Killeavy, forthcoming). The project was successful in helping new teachers in relation to planning, classroom management, catering for different abilities and discipline (areas of major concern initially). The findings on induction have important implications for the system as a whole and for the experiences of teachers in designated disadvantaged schools in particular. As noted above, a disproportionate number of beginning teachers start their careers in designated disadvantaged schools. It is therefore crucial that the pilot programme be expanded to include all of such schools.

References

Bandura, A. (1997) *Self-efficacy: the Exercise of Control*, New York: Freeman

Department of Education and Science (2005) *DEIS: Delivering Equality of Opportunity in Schools – An Action Plan for Educational Inclusion*, Dublin: DES

Ingersoll, R. (2001) 'Teacher turnover and teacher shortage: An organisational analysis', *American Educational Research Journal*, 38, pp. 499–534

Johnson, S. M. and Birkeland, S. E. (2003) 'Pursuing a sense of success: New teachers explain their career decisions', *American Educational Research Journal*, 40, pp. 581–617

Linnane, T. (2005) 'Teacher turnover levels and related issues in the disadvantaged areas scheme (2001–2005)', unpublished MEd thesis, Dublin: St Patrick's College, Drumcondra

Morgan, M. and O'Leary, M. (2004) 'A study of factors associated with job satisfaction of beginning teachers', *Irish Journal of Education*, 35, pp. 73–86

Murphy, M. (2005) '"No Country for Old Men": A critical analysis of migration, retention and motivation of teachers in schools designated as disadvantaged', unpublished MEd thesis, Dublin: St Patrick's College, Drumcondra

Murphy, R., and Killeavy, M. (forthcoming) *National pilot project on teacher induction: Final report*, Dublin: DES

Pajares, F (1996) 'Self-efficacy beliefs in academic settings', *Review of Educational Research*, 66, pp. 543–78

Spear, M., Gould, K. and Lee, B. (2000) *Who would be a teacher? A review of factors motivating and demotivating prospective and practising teachers*, Slough: NFER

Sugrue, C., Dupont, M. and Morgan, M. (2006) 'Accountability, Regulation and Trust in the Professional Lives of Teachers', paper read at DCU Humanities Conference, 11–12 May 2006

32

Bridging the Gap

Tracey Connolly

If you are planning for a year, sow rice;
if you are planning for a decade, plant trees;
if you are planning for a lifetime, educate people.
                                        Chinese Proverb

Educational disadvantage in Ireland is well-documented and research acknowledges that it is debilitating for the individual who experiences it and that it has a negative impact on society. Educational disadvantage can become apparent at school through low attainment, satisfaction and self-esteem; lack of participation; truancy; school refusal; dropout; behaviour problems; and delinquency (Evans, 1995). At school level, children who become educationally disadvantaged may experience difficulties in numeracy and learning to read and write. The gap between their achievement and that of their peers from advantaged backgrounds increases as the children progress in their schooling. According to UNICEF (2002), this gap between children of the same age can be the equivalent of many years' schooling. UNICEF (2002) views these consequences as follows:

> Looking back, such disadvantage at school can be strongly linked to disadvantage at home. Looking forward, it may be predicted that disadvantage is likely to perpetrate itself through educational under-achievement and a greater likelihood of economic marginalisation and social exclusion.

Disadvantaged children are more likely to drop out of school, often without formal qualifications. Hence, early school leaving is a consequence of educational disadvantage, and, in general, the cycle of educational disadvantage repeats itself, whereby an individual has the same poor employment prospects as their parents. The literature shows that early school leaving is linked to unemployment as, in general, 'the ratio of unemployed people who have not completed upper secondary education to the total youth population is 1.5 times higher on average than for upper secondary graduates' (OECD, 2003). In 2004, the unemployment rate of early school leavers was a considerable 21.8 per cent (CSO, 2005).

Aims of *Bridging the Gap*

Bridging the Gap commenced in September 2001 and works with forty-two disadvantaged schools in Cork city. Based in the Education Department, University College Cork (UCC), the project aims to 'bridge the gap' between the educational experiences, opportunities and achievements of pupils in schools in the disadvantaged areas of Cork city with their peers in more advantaged areas. In essence, it seeks to bring about an enhancement of the educational experiences of the young people involved.

From the outset, *Bridging the Gap* aimed to be participatory – it has a bottom-up approach and project activities are needs-led. *Bridging the Gap* is emancipatory as it aims to support pupils from disadvantaged backgrounds to:

- stay in full-time education for as long as possible
- achieve their full potential at school
- have a positive and rewarding experience of schooling
- develop the necessary skills and motivation to be lifelong learners.

Bridging the Gap aims to complement national and local initiatives in schools to enhance school-based work. School communities are supported by the project to enable them to achieve their goals. Statutory and voluntary agencies are invited to contribute their expertise and experience, working together through an inter-agency approach towards a common strategy.

The expected outcomes of *Bridging the Gap* are:

- a coherent and comprehensive strategy for changing the attitudes and behaviours of learners, families, schools and other institutions
- a measurable improvement in the educational experience of learners from disadvantaged backgrounds
- improved motivation for success among learners, families, teachers, school management and others
- a model that can be replicated elsewhere in the educational system to produce quality improvement.

Each annual internal evaluation has indicated that these outcomes are emerging and growing from year to year.

Framework of *Bridging the Gap*

The *Bridging the Gap* framework took much inspiration from the Berkeley Pledge, which was one of the models of good practice researched prior to the commencement of the project. The Berkeley Pledge was based in the University of California, Berkeley, and worked with local deprived communities by supporting pupils in schools (Hersch Gabelko, 2000). Being a university-based project, the Berkeley Pledge drew on the expertise within the university to support schools, and was a model that was transferable to the UCC context. An important element of *Bridging the Gap* has become the development of a model of university–community collaboration. Its framework has the following five operational strands, which work in tandem:

- professional development
- research
- school-level initiatives
- networks
- dissemination.

Professional development

Bridging the Gap invests in enhancing the quality of teaching by running regular professional development events. As a university-based project, *Bridging the Gap* is in a position to draw on a wide range of expertise to provide professional development for principals and teachers.

Research

Through *Bridging the Gap* major empirical research is undertaken. All schools are involved in data gathering and the purpose is to provide a baseline measure against which the impact of the project can be monitored. Research on educational disadvantage is often primarily focused on the causes and consequences rather than tracking what works well on the ground. *Bridging the Gap* promotes the use of child-centred research, and schools carry out child-centred research (particularly through focus groups) to identify pupils' needs. Arising from this research schools set goals for the interventions they plan to undertake. The evaluation of outcomes has, in many schools, employed child-centred research through the use of brief questionnaires. In a number of schools, pupils self-evaluate their own progress by creating graphs to monitor their development; they generally use test results to create these graphs. The pupils use the graphs to set their own goals for the next tests and discuss how they can achieve their goals. Many schools have carried out longitudinal child-centred research whereby the impact of a *Bridging the Gap* initiative, such as a reading or music project, on a cohort of pupils has been tracked over a number of years. All schools engaged in child-centred research have claimed that it has been most useful in identifying issues and seeking solutions on a needs-led basis.

Through research by schools, *Bridging the Gap* aims for a sense of ownership, both of the data and the solutions. It also adopts an innovative approach to research by making data gathering a focus for action-learning by groups of teachers and principals. While all activities within *Bridging the Gap* have an implicit research dimension, school-based projects are particularly structured to set targets and monitor results in a formal way.

School-level initiatives

Bridging the Gap provides financial support for targeted interventions at school level, which are termed as school-based projects. These projects are needs-led, as schools set their own project goals and identify their target area and group. As already outlined, some schools use child-centred research to identify issues, set goals and evaluate outcomes. In essence, the whole school sets these goals and, as part of the whole-school community, parents are consulted to advise on setting project goals. Parents provide feedback on the impact of interventions and this is sought by most schools on a monthly basis as part of the monitoring of the project that feeds into the end-of-year evaluation. The consultation with parents forms a vital link between school and home so that continuity of project work is made possible. In each school the interventions through *Bridging the Gap* have been greatly complemented by the work of the Home School Liaison Coordinator with regard to engaging parents. Many projects funded by *Bridging the Gap* actively involve parents as facilitators on projects such as paired reading, maths for fun, and music and drama projects. Schools undertaking projects which involve parents as facilitators claim that parental involvement makes a difference in improving pupils' motivation and aspirations.

Schools monitor and document the development of the school-based projects and write the final evaluation at the end of the school year. Each school starts with a goal, devises small steps to achieve the goal and identifies what is successful and how it can be measured within each step. In essence, these projects take an active research approach as they involve planning, acting, observing and reflecting, while the projects also incorporate the elements of being emancipatory and participatory, key features of action research.

Networks

Bridging the Gap is conscious that teaching can sometimes be an isolating profession. Often teachers can find it difficult to become aware of teaching practices that can improve the experiences of learners from disadvantaged backgrounds. With this in mind, *Bridging the Gap* set up networks of teachers, principals and others on topics of interest identified in collaboration.

Dissemination

Bridging the Gap aims to disseminate good practice emerging from the project in relation to addressing educational disadvantage. The media used include a website (http://bridgingthegap.ucc.ie) and an annual internal evaluation. In addition to this, the project has received much publicity within the national and local press and within the university.

From the outset *Bridging the Gap* sought to be different from other local and national initiatives on educational disadvantage in terms of its aim to link the university with disadvantaged communities and to engender a partnership within schools especially around data gathering and collaborative reflection.

Evaluation of *Bridging the Gap*

According to Scriven (cited in Worthen and Sanders, 1987), evaluation plays many roles in education, even though it has a single goal, which is 'to determine the worst or merit of whatever is being evaluated'. Brophy, Grotelueschen and Gooler (cited in Worthen and Sanders, 1987), outlined three major reasons for conducting evaluations:

- planning procedures, programmes, and/or products
- improving existing procedures, programmes, and/or products
- justifying (or not justifying) existing procedures, programmes, and /or products.

For *Bridging the Gap*, the annual internal evaluation serves to give the project direction in analysing the project activities and outcomes while also providing recommendations for the future direction of the project. The internal evaluation of *Bridging the Gap* is an integrated part of the action plan, and internal evaluation runs concurrently with project activities.

The internal evaluation process corresponds to the Tylerian Evaluation Approach. Tyler conceived of evaluation as the process of determining the extent to which the educational objectives of a school programme or curriculum are actually being attained. His approach to evaluation followed these steps:

- establish broad goals or objectives
- define objectives in behavioural terms
- define situations in which achievement of objectives can be shown
- develop or select measurement techniques
- collect performance data

- compare performance data with behaviourally stated objectives.

(cited in Worthen and Sanders, 1987)

Discrepancies between performance and objectives would lead to modifications intended to correct the deficiency, and the evaluation cycle would be repeated. Tyler's belief was that educators primarily needed to discuss the importance and meaning of general goals of education.

Within *Bridging the Gap*, goal-setting is the cornerstone of evaluation so that progress can be systematically recorded. Each school sets its own goals using SMART (Specific, Measurable, Attainable, Realistic, Timed) targets. Projects are monitored by schools and evaluation is made by comparing progress and outcomes with the goals set. This documentation helps to build motivation for success and makes this success visible as well as feeding into the overall internal evaluation of the project.

Metfessel and Michael's eight steps in the evaluation process, heavily influenced by Tyler, are as follows:

- involve the total school community as facilitators of programme evaluation
- formulate cohesive models of goals and specific objectives
- translate specific objectives into a communicable form applicable to facilitating learning in the school environment
- select or construct instruments to furnish measures allowing inferences about programme effectiveness
- carry out periodic observations using content-valid tests, scales, and other behaviour methods
- analyse data using appropriate statistical methods
- interpret the data using standards of desired levels of performances over all measures
- develop recommendations for the further implementation, modification, and revision of broad goals and specific objectives.

(cited in Worthen and Sanders, 1987)

Bridging the Gap's evaluation relates best to this model, as whole schools are involved. Essentially, the evaluation is a collaborative exercise, engaging participants in setting goals and in monitoring the achievement of these goals while encouraging reflection. This approach is both holistic and systematic. In this way, the focus is clearly on results, and evaluation positively supports participants in achieving their desired goals.

One of the primary contributions of Metfessel and Michael was in expanding the educational evaluator's vision of alternative instruments that might be used to collect evaluation data. *Bridging the Gap* promotes the use of various instruments to measure projects, and, to date, schools have used statistics, rubrics (scoring tools that list the criteria for a piece of work and articulate gradations of quality for each criterion), interviews, focus groups, and audio and visual recordings as instruments for evaluation.

Developments within *Bridging the Gap*

Each year schools put forward proposals for initiatives to address aspects of educational disadvantage in their school community. The initiatives are wide-ranging and include literacy projects, music, drama, visual arts programmes and whole-staff development training. Many schools showcase the work of pupils for a community audience through performances and award ceremonies.

The integration of literacy and the arts has been an important development within schools. For example, a digital story-telling project was undertaken, whereby the pupils wrote their own stories, drew pictures depicting the stories and performed the stories with their pictures as a digitised background; this culminated in the production of a DVD. This project integrated literacy – writing and oral language – with the arts – visual and performance arts. Another example of the integration of literacy and the arts was a 'Kidz Opera' that was written and performed by pupils as part of the celebration of Cork City Capital of Culture 2005, which again integrated literacy and the arts.

Teachers participate in a range of focused professional development activities and share learning, expertise and experience with other teachers. A wide range of professional developments have taken place, including using multiple intelligences, literacy through the arts, active learning, multi-culturalism and interculturalism, IT in the classroom, exploring science at primary level, linguistic differences and educational disadvantage, coping with bullying, reading for enjoyment, strategies to improve literacy, and leadership in schools. These events are in addition to twice-yearly sessions on school-based project planning and monitoring.

Many teachers have embarked on extended research projects within their schools. A number of teachers have been supported by *Bridging the Gap* to undertake postgraduate research in the following areas: a case study on early school leaving and the response to early school leaving, specific speech and language disorders, project management and education, and a study of community music.

Each year a number of principals in *Bridging the Gap* schools receive scholarships to attend the Project Zero Summer Institute at the Harvard Graduate School of Education. The Summer Institute is concerned with professional development in the areas of Multiple Intelligences and Teaching for Understanding.

Following the Summer Institute the principals have identified how ideas from Project Zero can best serve their schools. A number of principals have increased their schools' involvement in the arts due to the Summer Institute. A significant outcome of the principals' attendance at the Summer Institute is the networking that takes place as they share how attendance at the Institute made a difference to their practice and their school.

Significant progress has been made in gaining support for the project from staff in a wide range of departments in UCC. The link with university departments enabled the project to facilitate further networks and to provide professional development for teachers. Schools benefited considerably from collaborating with university staff, as expertise was shared through the professional development and school-based project strands. Each year groups of pupils from the Gaelscoileanna involved in *Bridging the Gap* visit Ionad na Gaeilge Labhartha, which is a UCC centre responsible for the promotion of Irish on campus. *Bridging the Gap*, with the help of UCC staff, facilitates visits by parents to UCC. These visits heighten awareness of the educational opportunities available. University students are becoming more involved in the project; for example, music students have organised a concert for primary school pupils on the university campus.

Each year *Bridging the Gap* hosts a showcasing event at UCC where 1,500 pupils participating in the school-based projects have an opportunity to demonstrate their work, mainly in the performing and visual arts.

Over the years, schools have started to show that significant improvements have been achieved in relation to the targets that they set themselves. Such improvements were highlighted through pupils' improved attitudes, performance and motivation, as well as in the more focused approach to educational inclusion that has been adopted by participating schools. A number of schools began to develop and apply rubrics to measure the performance of pupils in targeted areas of achievement.

The whole-school approach has become more evident in schools. The majority of school evaluation reports showed that the number of teachers and pupils participating in the project had increased over previous years. It also became evident that schools had become very familiar with the model of focused goal-setting and monitoring of results that is promoted within the project. Numerous schools highlighted that this approach had enabled them to identify the learning needs of their whole school community, including parents, pupils, principals and staff.

Bridging the Gap has fostered important links with the Home School Community Liaison (HSCL) programme and parents, particularly through funding Maths for Fun projects. Clusters of HSCL coordinators formed networks in the Maths for Fun project, which involved parents working in the classroom alongside teachers and pupils.

More networks develop each year as neighbouring schools collaborate on joint projects in a number of cases, with very positive results. Schools continue to disseminate the work of the project in their own communities. They were involved in numerous city concerts, and one school produced a prize-winning project in the Esat Young Scientist of the Year exhibition. Another developed monthly food fairs and there were many art exhibitions and displays of pupils' work. As a result, the project became widely known throughout Cork city and among the education community at national level.

The internal evaluation of *Bridging the Gap* sees the main strength of the project as its unique approach in giving schools ownership and freedom to choose projects rather than imposing projects on them. There are numerous initiatives in Ireland designed to support pupils from disadvantaged backgrounds, and to address the problems of underachievement, failure and early school leaving. Often they are limited in their scope and impact, chiefly because they have not attempted to change the culture of the school or to take a whole-school approach to setting educational inclusion goals and monitoring outcomes. Some are centrally devised and controlled and therefore afford limited opportunities to the principals and staff to design their own unique response to the special problems in their schools.

Educational disadvantage has many causes, which generally arise out of poverty, family and community issues. Consequently, tackling educational disadvantage needs to be holistic in its approach. As circumstances vary, tackling educational disadvantage should be needs-led. *Bridging the Gap* takes such an approach as it works on the basis of being participatory in all of its activities. In addition to this, schools are responsible for spending project funding as they see fit, which creates greater ownership than imposing rigid criteria as is done in many initiatives on educational disadvantage. In this regard, *Bridging the Gap* recognises expertise within schools rather than seeing expertise as being external only.

Goal-setting and self-evaluation within schools are unique aspects of *Bridging the Gap*, unlike some initiatives on educational disadvantage which tend to put little emphasis on documenting goals, progress and outcomes. Through *Bridging the Gap*, collective goals are set by schools, which entail teamwork and leadership from within. Simple measurement techniques are used so that there is early analysis as results are tracked, and efforts can be adjusted as necessary. Consequently, success can be achieved quickly, which can increase confidence and expand the vision of what is possible. This approach allows for innovation and risk-taking which ties in with whole-school development planning.

Bridging the Gap places celebration of participation and achievement high in all of its project activities. In particular, it applauds the achievement of goals set by schools.

The fact that *Bridging the Gap* involves a small community of schools is a unique aspect, as there are greater opportunities to forge relationships than in a larger community. This enables networking to proceed with relative ease. It also provides opportunities to share examples of good practice for dissemination within the project and greater collaboration within schools and between schools.

Bridging the Gap aims to ensure that project activities will ultimately become mainstreamed within the operation of schools. To this end *Bridging the Gap* involves the whole staff in its activities. One teacher in a small group is often responsible for the development of other initiatives on educational disadvantage. This approach generally means that other teachers have little awareness or understanding about these projects. The whole-school approach, especially the involvement of all teachers in the setting of goals and the monitoring of outcomes, has been a key feature of *Bridging the Gap* from the outset. As the project progresses, it is clear that this aspect plays a pivotal role in consolidating its impact, and, ultimately, it is hoped to contribute to the sustainability of the project.

The linking of the university with schools, particularly primary schools, is a unique aspect of *Bridging the Gap*. Writing in the *Irish Times* (June 2003), Dr Garrett Fitzgerald, Chancellor of the National University of Ireland, stated:

> *Bridging the Gap* draws on the skills available among both staff and students at the university, in this way introducing primary school pupils to its facilities and grounds; an arrangement that makes the idea of going to third-level much less intimidating for children from disadvantaged areas.

In September 2003, UCC became the *Sunday Times* University of the Year; *Bridging the Gap* was commended by the newspaper for its work in 'bringing educational opportunities to the students in disadvantaged areas of Cork city'.

Indeed, much of the success of *Bridging the Gap* is due to the support of UCC staff and students in sharing their expertise. Some schools and staff members have said that the linking of the university with the project and the schools enables learning for all to take place, fostering a learning organisation within the university and schools. As schools benefit from the learning provided by the university, the university learns from the school communities.

Future development

Bridging the Gap has come a long way since its foundation in 2001. The project framework, its reflection on progress, and the annual evaluation by schools have enabled the project to move forward steadily. The main successes of the project have been in strengthening the active learning partnership between schools, parents, the community and the university. The research aspect of *Bridging the Gap* has shown improvement in the quality of school research by systematically gathering and analysing data to measure the impact of school activities, while the collaboration within schools in conducting action research has highlighted the effectiveness of the action research approach within the project in promoting educational inclusion.

For the future, *Bridging the Gap* plans to work further with principals to identify and enhance the leadership qualities and practices that promote high achievement and educational inclusion in schools. By strengthening the networks within *Bridging the Gap*, greater integration of schools and their local communities may be achieved. *Bridging the Gap* plans to further the link between the university and the schools and communities within it, thereby creating a learning organisation and further integrating it within the community mission of the university. The main challenge that lies ahead is to look back over its lifetime since 2001 and seek to answer these key questions:

- How have schools changed as a result of participating?
- Has it produced sustainable benefits in schools and communities?
- How can the learning be transferred to other classrooms, other communities, other universities and other regions?

References

Central Statistics Office (2005) *2004 Annual Report*, Dublin: CSO

Evans, P. (1995) 'Children and Youth at Risk' in *Our Children at Risk*, CERI, Paris: OECD

Hersch Gabelko, N. (ed.) (2000) *Towards a Collective Wisdom: Forging Successful Educational Partnerships*, Berkeley: University of California

Organisation for Economic Cooperation and Development (2003) *Education at a Glance*, OECD Indicators, Paris: OECD

United Nations Children's Fund (2002) *A League Table of Educational Disadvantage in Rich Nations*, New York: UNICEF

Worthen, B. and Sanders, J. (1987) *Educational Evaluation: Alternative Approaches and Practical Guidelines*, New York: Longman

33

Models of Intervention for
Challenging Behaviour

*Claire W. Lyons, Ann Higgins, Fiona O'Connor, Frank
J. Howe, Ruth Bourke and Denise McSweeney*

Introduction

There are few topics within education that receive as much attention or that cause as much concern for adults as children's behaviour that is seen as problematic. Here we consider how to make sense of challenging behaviour; we look at three different models of working with children whose behaviour is challenging. While each of the models makes different assumptions about the ways in which to modify behaviour, each is compatible with an understanding of behaviour in which it is seen as a child's attempt to meet his/her needs within a particular context. The findings from our own questionnaires and interviews with children and teachers in an Irish primary school inform our findings, and the school in question was part of the *Working Together Project* at Mary Immaculate College, Limerick. The project team worked with this school and with two others to construct an effective response to challenging behaviour.

Each of the schools that participated in the *Working Together Project* is located in an urban, disadvantaged setting. Of the three, one is a large co-educational school, with approximately 500 pupils and thirty-four teaching staff, one is a boys' school with approximately 115 pupils and fifteen teaching staff and one is co-educational up to first class and girls only thereafter, with approximately 216 pupils and twenty-three teaching staff. The project used a combination of quantitative and qualitative methods to explore behavioural issues with children, teachers and parents.

In order to get a broad picture of behaviour across the schools we constructed a teacher and a child questionnaire. The children's questionnaire was administered to children in third to sixth class. A group of children was selected from senior infants and fourth class on the basis of a behaviour checklist completed by teachers. The children were chosen to reflect a range of behaviours from those whose behaviour was considered non-problematic, to those whose behaviour was considered average, and finally to those whose behaviour was considered problematic. Permission to interview these children was sought from their parents and they participated in one-to-one interviews and in focus groups in which they were asked about their own and their classmates' behaviour and their teachers' responses to behaviour. They were also asked about their views of school in general. The teachers and parents of the children were also interviewed. Teachers were asked about different aspects of school policy as well as their attitudes to education. They were also asked about their approaches to behaviour. The parents were asked about the importance of education, their own experiences of education and how their children's experiences were different from their own. They were also asked what role education played in their children's lives.

The data presented here is drawn from the interviews and questionnaires conducted in the co-educational school in the first year of the project. A total of seventeen children were interviewed: six six-year-olds, three girls and three boys; eleven ten-year-olds, six girls and five boys. The children selected came from four different classes and each of their teachers was interviewed. Eight parents of the selected children were interviewed, seven of whom were female. Other teaching and ancillary staff, namely two learning resource teachers and two special needs assistants working in the children's classes, were also interviewed. A member of the project team also observed each child twice in class and once at break time.

Understanding behaviour

In general, there are three perspectives on challenging behaviour:

- can be defined objectively by listing or describing behaviours that are considered disruptive and undesirable, for example, shouting could be seen as an unacceptable behaviour;
- can be seen as contextual or relative, for example, shouting in class is unacceptable but shouting in the yard is not; we may even be lenient about shouting in the class if a child shouts up the answer to a question;
- can be seen as a response to environmental and individual needs while recognising the objective undesirability of some behaviours, for example, we recognise that John hits out at others when he loses his patience; at the

same time we work to eliminate this behaviour because hurting others is not acceptable.

It is this last perspective that is favoured by the *Working Together Project*. In order to understand why let's look at each approach in turn.

Identifying behaviours that are problematic

Descriptions of challenging behaviour can concentrate on specific behaviours. Within this framework, certain behaviours can be defined as challenging per se (Cameron, 1998). At the extreme end of such categorisation is the diagnosis of behaviour that is indicative of a conduct disorder (American Psychiatric Association, 1994; World Health Organisation, 1992). The assessment of conduct disorder involves measuring the presence or absence of certain behaviours across a range of contexts (Merrell, 1999).

There is evidence to suggest that the rate of behavioural and emotional difficulties is greater amongst children from lower socio-economic groups, who live in areas of social disadvantage, particularly those who live in poverty (Cooper, 2005, p. 75; DES, 2006; Schneiders et al., 2003). In other words, the risk of emotional and behavioural difficulties is greater amongst such children. Studies of school behaviour also suggest that challenging classroom behaviour is more common in designated disadvantaged settings (Furlong, 1985; Holman and Coghill, 1987; INTO, 2002; Martin, 1997, p.32). Furthermore, there is evidence to suggest that while most challenging behaviour tends to be minor in nature, regardless of the social setting, teachers in designated disadvantaged schools are more likely to report experiencing seriously challenging or aggressive behaviour (DES, 2006; Lynch, 1999, pp. 125–6; McSweeney, 2004).

While classifications of conduct disorder recognise the contextual and environmental contributions to the problem, the description of such behaviour as a 'disorder' (Jones, 2003, refers to it as the 'medical model') tends to locate the difficulties in the individual child. A number of physical and biological factors within the child are thought to contribute to behavioural difficulties (Carr, 1999; Jones and Charlton, 1996; Prior et al., 2001).

An insight into practitioners' definition of problem behaviour can be gained by looking at the kinds of behaviours identified as problematic by teachers. Most studies ask teachers to list behaviours that they consider challenging or to identify challenging behaviours from a list (Lynch, 1999; INTO, 2002), thereby implying that classroom behaviours can be objectively identified as challenging without reference to the context in which they take place.

The behaviours described as problematic by teachers tend to involve challenges to the teacher's authority and aggression towards others. Some challenges to the teacher's authority are not serious when they occur at a low frequency or in isolation. In our current study, inattentiveness was not seen as a serious misbehaviour, although disruption of classroom activities was. In line with previous research (INTO, 2002), the most serious challenging behaviours involved physical and verbal aggression and refusal to cooperate with teachers' direction.

Control seems to play a central role in our current definitions of problem behaviour, a fact that is reflected in the data from the children's interviews in our study. When asked to describe naughty or 'bold' behaviours, the children frequently mentioned talking out of turn, being out of one's seat, disrupting class activities and messing or playing. Aggression also featured in their discussion, with hitting, fighting and teasing being frequently given as examples of misbehaviour.

The importance of control and 'doing what you are told' in perceptions of what is challenging is underlined by the fact that few studies of teachers' views recognise that withdrawn behaviour that is not disruptive can also be considered a problem or challenging. In the current study, teachers were divided on the seriousness of withdrawn behaviours. While most teachers rated these behaviours as minor, a significant minority considered them to be serious.

In the definitions discussed so far, challenging behaviour is defined with reference to what is considered 'normal' for children of a particular age. Yet the basis of such normality is not always clear. While the children in our study could give examples of misbehaviour they were somewhat confused when asked to describe good behaviour. They frequently responded 'What do you mean like?' when asked to describe good behaviour in interviews and then fell back on 'being good' and doing work: 'Q: And ... what does being good mean?; A. Like behaving inside school and listening to the teacher and don't complain.'

There appears to be a general assumption that we all know what it is to be well-behaved or 'good' and that this needs little explication. As Kutnick and Manson (1998, p. 167) comment:

> Children who deviate from the expected norms of behaviour within the social system in which they participate (in the main, the school classroom) are the subjects of study ... Within the literature, scant attention is paid to what constitutes normalcy, either in terms of its description or its development; it is taken for granted.

Challenging behaviour as contextual

The term 'challenging behaviour' is preferred in some quarters because it emphasises the challenge of the behaviour to the system, rather than locating that behaviour within the individual (Psychological Society of Ireland, 1998). Such an approach recognises that behaviour is considered a problem if it does not fit the social situation in which the individual is located.

The suggestion has been made that ethnic and social-class differences in the rate of behavioural problems are due to a 'clash of cultures' between home and school (Furlong, 1985; Gilbourn, 1993, Runnymede Trust, 1996, both cited in Cameron, 1998; Hargreaves, 1987; Martin, 1997). In our study, teachers saw standards and expectations at home as key to pupil misbehaviour. Teachers felt that, in many cases, social standards at home contradict those at school:

> Q. So when, where and how would you say that children learn social skills?
> A. Well, they learn certain skills in school. But I think that the skills they learn in school are only applied in school because outside of school, at home, in a lot of cases, anything goes.

Parents agreed with teachers that children's behaviour is different at home than it is at school: 'A. At school there's a lot more discipline and they're a totally different child when they're at school.'

However, the teachers' assertions that parental values are essentially different from those of the school were not substantiated in the parents' interviews. The parents interviewed all expressed the view that learning to get along with others was part of learning at school. This fits with Gorman-Smith, Tolan and Henry's (1999) research in the US which questions the assumption that the problems of poor urban communities are a consequence of the social values held by members of those communities. They argue that the best evidence suggests that such problems have arisen from long-term changes in the economic and social environment, which have had a detrimental impact on the lives of parents and children. Of course, teachers in our study said that it is a minority of parents who are unsupportive, but their perception of this minority appeared to dominate their discourse about the causes of challenging behaviour.

When we move beyond the opinions of adults to consider children's explanations for challenging behaviour we find a greater emphasis on relationships between teachers and children and relationships between peers (Miller, Ferguson and Byrne, 2000; Wise and Upton, 1998). Factors in the teacher–pupil relationship that are considered important include fairness, consistency, positive attitude and methods of control.

Peer-related causes of challenging behaviour included being picked on by other children on the way to school, not getting along with peers and not liking to share with others. One common reason for fighting amongst older children was 'slagging' or teasing. Although a certain amount of 'slagging' is acceptable, it can go too far. For example, when asked to suggest a possible reason why boys in a picture were fighting, one child suggested that it was because 'they're always slagging each other and they slag each other too much'. Teachers recognised the importance of peer factors in misbehaviour, but the children gave them more prominence in their responses to the questionnaire.

Children also identified boredom as a factor in misbehaviour, particularly in their interviews. In response to a picture of a boy throwing a paper aeroplane the children gave responses such as the following:

> Q. Is there any other reason that people would do that in class? Why don't people just sit and listen and do their work in class?
> A. 'Cos they're bored … they just make loads of work and your arms are tired.

Children recognised that such behaviours might be fun for the perpetrator. They also suggested that some children 'like being bold'.

These children's observations echo the findings of sociological studies that suggest that students who do not accept the school's set of standards and expectations create their own subcultures and adaptations (Haralambos and Holborn, 1991; Willis, 1977; Woods, 1979). Coie and Jacobs (2000), for example, suggest that in neighbourhoods where anti-social and aggressive behaviour is the norm, the anti-social youth is not a rejected outsider, rather he is a popular, functioning member of his social group. Carving out and maintaining an identity can involve thwarting the rules and expectations of the school through overt rule-breaking and also through behaviour that is annoying to teachers but cannot be clearly identified as rule-breaking.

The following extract shows children's awareness that rule-breaking can form part of the child's presentation of self to peers: 'Q. Why do you think they break the rules?; A. 'Cos they think they're tough inside the school. They get jealous and stuff they think they're tougher than other people. They say stuff they don't really mean.'

An integrated approach: challenging behaviour as a response to environmental and individual needs

Contextual explorations of challenging behaviour are illuminating in terms of our understanding of the function and nature of behaviour. They show us that even seemingly dysfunctional behaviour can be functional for the individual. Furthermore, they highlight the manner in which the social structure of the school is exclusionary to the extent that some groups define themselves in opposition to it. On their own, however, such explanations do not account for the full range of challenging behaviours. Nor do they explain the range of responses to the school context. On the other hand, explanations that look at the behaviour as located in the individual do not allow for the significant environmental and contextual elements of challenging behaviour. The issue is summed up by Jones (2003, p. 152):

> On the positive side, the anti-medical discourse indeed drew attention to the importance of classroom relationships and communication patterns vis-à-vis hostility in the classroom. At worst, however, it promoted the sentiment that teachers who

claim that a pupil 'has' a problem ought to question their own expectations. Such sentiments deny school realities as some teachers and EPs experience them: namely that some pupils 'are' troubled, not merely troublesome ... (author's emphasis)

A full understanding of challenging behaviour requires an integration of both approaches. What is in question is behaviour-in-context. Each individual responds to his/her environment within the scope of his/her capacities. That environment can be enabling or disabling. Living in a socially disadvantaged context increases children's risk of emotional and behavioural difficulties (Cameron, 1998; Dodge, Pettit and Bates, 1994; Gardner, Sonuga-Barke and Sayal, 1999; Gorman-Smith, Tolan and Henry, 1999; Mills and Rubin, 1998; Riding and Craig, 1998; Snyder and Stoolmiller, 2002). It may also increase the risk that some of their behaviours will be defined as challenging by teachers. Nonetheless, *there is a need to challenge sweeping assumptions that children from a socially disadvantaged background will be more challenging than children from more advantaged backgrounds.*

The individual shapes his/her environment and in turn is shaped by it. Thus the concept of behaviour-in-context is reciprocal. For example, children have a need for autonomy or some sort of control. Their current educational situation may not provide them with a suitable outlet for satisfaction of that need. They may, for example, have difficulty conforming to expected standards due to low levels of attention or ability. They may, therefore, exert control in a subversive way. Through challenging behaviour, the child can, in effect, control an entire class. The adult's response may be to strengthen existing controls to teach the child a lesson by being stricter. This in turn presents a further challenge to the child and so behaviour worsens.

The approach to the understanding of challenging behaviour being promoted here can be summarised under the following key principles:

- Every individual has needs and their behaviour is functional to them in some way, even though that functionality may not always be apparent to others. Children are active in trying to meet their needs.
- The manner in which needs are met can sometimes be objectively unacceptable, specifically where it involves causing harm to others. Such unacceptable behaviour can be displayed by adults as well as by children. To understand behaviour does not always mean to condone it.
- Children's temperaments and capacities differ, e.g., their attention span. The differing needs of children defy precise classification and can change over time. Children's capacities can be determined more or less by biological and environmental factors.
- Our education system has constraints built into it, e.g., that education takes place within a certain time span, in a certain place. Within these 'hardwired' constraints of the system, there are also expectations, beliefs

and values that define our reactions to behaviour. Some of these constraints are implicit. In many school settings, for example, children are expected to obey rules that are set and enforced by adults and to meet learning outcomes and engage in learning activities that are set by adults. These expectations, beliefs and values are not always those of the child or his/her home. The current constraints of the educational system limit its capacity to meet the needs of individual children.

- Notwithstanding the differing needs and interactional styles of children, their developmental needs include the need for guidance in accommodating their behaviour to better interact with those around them so that they can achieve the maximum benefit from the educational setting. Children's access to such guidance will vary depending on the capabilities of the adults around them.

- Educational practice is built on relationships, between children, and between children and teachers. Each individual comes to that relationship with a history of experience and a set of values and beliefs. The behaviour of the child both influences and is influenced by the behaviour of others. Just like children, teachers vary in their capacity to accommodate the needs of others.

Models of intervention

Essential to any model of behaviour management is the provision of an engaging learning environment. We also need to be very clear about what our behavioural expectations are. Ideally, children and teachers should engage in discussion around the kinds of behaviour that are accepted in their classroom and school. Teachers and children should also be very clear about what happens when behavioural expectations are met and when they are not met. The behaviour of some children may continue to be challenging, even within such a behaviour management context. In these cases, teachers need to appropriately employ one or more models of intervention. This intervention is drawn from the teacher's theoretical base, i.e. the teacher's own well thought-out understanding of where, when and how children acquire and refine pro-social behaviour, and therefore stems from our previous discussion of the nature of challenging behaviour.

There are three overriding approaches to developing an individual model for intervention. These include models constructed with an internal focus, models constructed with an interactive focus, and those constructed with an external focus.

Internal focus

Models constructed with an internal focus are essentially therapeutic in nature. The assumption is that pro-social behaviour is natural to human beings and that each child develops through an inner unfolding of potential for positive growth. Appropriate nurturing and encouragement, coupled with reflective guidance through a student-driven problem-solving process, will help students make appropriate choices and behave in pro-social ways. One example of models with an internal focus is *Teacher Effectiveness Training* (Gordon, 1989). The steps in an intervention using this approach are as follows: Select one behaviour to address. Find three or four uninterrupted minutes to talk with the child. Give the problem back to the child using an 'I' message.

The goal of the 'I' message is to present the child with the problem of his/her own making. Once the child accepts the problem as his/her own, the teacher can offer support and encouragement, through the problem-solving process. There are three components to the 'I' message: Describe the child's behaviour. Describe the effect of the behaviour. Describe the teacher's feeling in relation to the behaviour. For example, 'Sorcha, when you talk loudly in class the other children get distracted and it slows our work down. I get frustrated when that happens.'

Get the child to define the problem

This step involves waiting until the child gives his or her perception of the problem. This may involve several sessions but the teacher resists the temptation to define the problem for the child.

Generate solutions

In this step the teacher encourages the child to come up with solutions to the problem, again, resisting the urge to suggest solutions.

Evaluate alternatives

The teacher and child then evaluate possible solutions to the problem. How will they work?

Implement

A solution is chosen and the teacher and child agree to implement it.

Evaluate

The teacher and child meet again to evaluate how successful the solution has been.

Interactive focus

Models constructed with an interactive focus are essentially educational in nature. The assumption is that pro-social behaviour is nurtured in human beings through an interactive process of recognising and meeting internal wants and needs, while attending to, and negotiating with, the environment in which each individual functions. Appropriate attention to these internal and external factors enables caring adults to foster pro-social behaviour in children. One example of the models with an interactive focus is *Reality Therapy* (Glasser, 1998). The steps in an intervention using this approach are as follows: Select one behaviour to address. Find three or four uninterrupted minutes to talk with the child. Get involved – show the child that you care. The teacher voices his/her concern for the child.

Identify the problem (impose reality if necessary)

It is in this step that this model differs from the internal focus model. The teacher identifies the challenging behaviour. If the child denies that such behaviour is taking place, the teacher calmly describes incidents of that behaviour.

Get the child to define the problem

In this step the teacher asks the child to talk about the challenging behaviour.

Evaluate present behaviour

The teacher asks the child to consider how his/her present behaviour is meeting her needs and the consequences of that behaviour. What consequences would the child like to avoid?

Generate alternatives

Once again, the child is asked to generate alternatives. If the child is unrealistic about alternatives the teacher will gently point out the consequences of his/her suggestions.

Evaluate and select an alternative. Obtain a commitment to try an alternative.

Implement

A solution is chosen and the teacher and child agree to implement it.

Evaluate

The teacher and child meet again to evaluate how successful the solution has been.

External focus

Models constructed with an external focus are essentially controlling in nature. The assumption is that pro-social behaviour is fostered in human beings by appropriately structuring the consequences of behaviour. According to this view, children develop in response to external conditions. If these conditions are appropriately structured, pro-social behaviour will result. It is important to note that external approaches do not necessarily deny that behaviour has internal causes but they do suggest that the way to modify behaviour is to restructure external consequences. One example of the models with an external focus is *Behaviour Modification* (Herbert, 1987). Behavioural contracts are commonly used in this approach. The steps involved in drawing up a behavioural contract are as follows: Select one behaviour to address. Establish a baseline through careful observation. Write a contract using the K.I.S.S. (Keep It Simple and Specific) method. Explain the contract to the child. Implement the contract. Evaluate the behaviour.

As with the previous interventions, the teacher and child meet to discuss the success of the contract.

The following is an example of a behavioural contract:

Contract for Improved Behaviour

It is important for Kevin to speak respectfully in class so that he and others can learn and can complete their work. This contract is an agreement between Kevin Lynch and Ms Dunn to help him remember and follow this rule.

During class time, Kevin will earn one (1) point for each ten (10) consecutive minutes he speaks and acts respectfully. If, at the end of the day all his work for the day is complete, his points will be doubled.

Ms Dunn will keep track of time and will use the '**Let's focus**' signal to help remind Kevin to follow this agreement. Each day at 10:00 a.m., 1:00 p.m., and 2:30 p.m., Ms Dunn will tell Kevin his current point total.

Each day Kevin will be allowed to exchange his earned points for time to listen to music during breaktime and at the end of the day. Each point will earn one (1) minute during this time.

At the end of two weeks Kevin Lynch and Ms Dunn will meet again to evaluate the success of this agreement.

I agree to the above conditions:

_____   _____

Name – Kevin Lynch   Date

_____   _____

Name – Ms Dunn   Date

Conclusions

The intervention literature is clear that an adequate response to challenging behaviour requires a careful analysis of the behaviour and the context in which it takes place (Miller, 2003). Thus, Cooper (1996, p. 150) argues that '*all* common

Emotional and Behavioural Difficulties (EBD) possess a psychosocial element, which implies that all problems are amenable (to differing degrees) to environmental influences …' (author's emphasis). Such an analysis requires us to examine our expectations and their basis and legitimacy. Equally, the child's perspectives, responses, and behavioural choices need to be explored so that their influence on their context can be clarified and possibly changed. The models of intervention outlined here challenge the teacher to really listen and pay attention to the children in their care and to engage in the long-term problem-solving that is at the heart of successful coping with challenging behaviour.

References

American Psychiatric Association (1994) *Diagnostic and Statistical Manual of the Mental Disorders* (4th edn) Washington, DC: American Psychiatric Association

Cameron, R. J. (1998) 'School discipline in the United Kingdom: Promoting classroom behaviour which encourages effective teaching and learning', *School Psychology Review,* vol. 27, no. 1, pp. 33–44

Carr, A. (1999) *The Handbook of Child and Adolescent Clinical Psychology: a contextual Approach*, London: Routledge

Coie, J. D. and Jacobs, M. R. (2000) 'The roles of social context in the prevention of context disorder' in Craig, W. (ed.) *Childhood Social Development: The Essential Readings*, Oxford: Basil Blackwell

Cooper, P. (1996) 'Giving it a name: the value of descriptive categories in educational approaches to emotional and behavioural difficulties', *Support for Learning*, vol. 11, no. 4, pp. 146–150

Cooper, P. (2005) 'Social, emotional and behavioural difficulties, social class and educational attainment: Which are the chickens and which are the eggs?', *Emotional and Behavioural Difficulties*, 10, 2, pp. 75–7

Department of Education and Science (2006), *School Matters: The Report of the Task Force on Child Behaviour in Second Level Schools*, Dublin: DES

Dodge, K., Pettit, G. S. and Bates, J. E. (1994) 'Socialization mediators of the relation between socio-economic status and child conduct problems', *Child Development*, 65, pp. 649–65

Furlong, V. J. (1985) *The Deviant Pupil: Sociological Perspectives*, Milton Keynes: Open University Press

Gardner, F. E. M., Sonuga-Blake, E. J. S. and Sayal, K. (1999), 'Parents anticipating misbehaviour: An observational study of strategies parents use to prevent conflict with behaviour problem children', *Journal of Child Psychology and Psychiatry*, 48, 8, pp. 1185–96

Glasser, W. (1998) *Choice Theory in the Classroom*, New York: Harper Collins

Gordon, T. (1989), *Teaching Children Self-Discipline at Home and at School*, New York: Times Books

Gorman-Smith, D., Tolan, P. H. and Henry, D. (1999) 'The relation of community and family to risk among urban-poor adolescents', in Cohen, P., Robins, L. and Slomkowski, C. (eds) *Where and When: Influence of Historical Time and Place on Aspects of Psychopathology*, Hillside, N.J.: Lawrence Erlbaum Associates, pp. 349–67

Haralambos, M. and Holborn, M. (1991) *Sociology: Themes and Perspectives* (3rd edn) London: Collins Educational

Hargreaves, D. H. (1987) 'The Two Curricula of Schooling', in Cohen, L. and Cohen, A. (eds) *A Sourcebook for Teachers*, London: Harper and Row, pp. 108–17

Herbert, M. (1987) *Behavioural Treatment of Children with Problems: A Practice Manual*, London: Academic Press

Holman, P. G. and Coghill, N. F. (1987) *Disruptive Behaviour in Schools: Causes, Treatment and Prevention*, Kent: Chartwell-Brent

Irish National Teachers' Organisation (2002) *Discipline in the Primary School*, Dublin: INTO

Jones, K. and Charlton, T. (eds) (1996) *Overcoming learning and behaviour difficulties: Partnership with pupils*, London: Routledge

Jones, R. A. (2003) 'The construction of emotional and behavioural difficulties', *Educational Psychology in Practice,* vol. 19, no. 2, pp. 147–57

Kutnick, P. and Manson, I. (1998) 'Social life in the primary school: towards a relational concept of social skills for use in the classroom' in Campbell, A. and Muncer, S. (eds) *The Social Child*, Hove, East Sussex, UK: Psychology Press

Lynch, L. (1999) 'Discipline in the Primary School: An Examination of Misbehaviour in Disadvantaged and Non-Disadvantaged Schools', unpublished MEd thesis, Dublin: Education Department, University College Dublin

Martin, M. (1997), *Report to the Minister for Education Niamh Bhreathnach, T.D. on Discipline in Schools*, Dublin: Government Publications

McSweeney, D. (2004) *Aggression and Peer Rejection among 5th Class Children in Limerick City*, unpublished thesis (MEd), Limerick: Mary Immaculate College

Merrell, K. (1999) *Behavioural, social and emotional assessment of children and adolescents*, Mahwah, NJ: Lawrence Erlbaum Associates

Miller, A. (2003), *Teachers, Parents and Classroom Behaviour: A Psychological Approach*, England: Open University Press

Miller, A., Ferguson, E. and Byrne, I. (2000) 'Pupils' causal attributions for difficult classroom behaviour', *British Journal of Educational Psychology*, vol. 70, pp. 85–96

Mills, R. S. L. and Rubin, K. H. (1998) 'Are behavioural and psychological control both differentially associated with childhood aggression and social withdrawal?', *Canadian Journal of Behavioural Science*, 30, 2, pp. 132–6

Prior, M., Smart, D., Sanson, A. and Oberklaid, F. (2001) 'Longitudinal predictors of behavioural adjustment in pre-adolescent children', *Australian and New Zealand Journal of Psychiatry*, vol. 35, pp. 297–307

Psychological Society of Ireland (1998) *Responding to behaviour that challenges*, Dublin: PSI

Riding, R. and Craig, O. (1998), 'Cognitive style and problem behaviour in boys referred to residential special schools', *Educational Studies*, 24, 2, pp. 205–22

Runnymede Trust (1996) *This is where I live: stresses and pressures in Brixton*, London: Runnymede Trust

Schneiders, J., Drukker, M., Van der Ende, J., Verhulst, F. C., Van Os, J. and Nicolson, N. A. (2003), 'Neighbourhood socioeconomic disadvantage and behavioural problems from late childhood into early adolescence', *Journal of Epidemiology and Community Health*, 57, 9, pp. 699–703

Snyder, J. and Stoolmiller, M. (2002), 'Reinforcement and coercion mechanisms in the development of antisocial behaviour: the family', in Reid, J. B., Patterson, G. R. and Snyder, J., (eds) *Antisocial Behaviour in Children and Adolescents*, Washington D.C.: American Psychological Association, pp. 65–100

Willis, P. E. (1977) *Learning to Labour*, Hants., England: Saxon House

Wise, S. and Upton, G. (1998) 'The perceptions of pupils with emotional and behavioural difficulties of their mainstream schooling', *Emotional and Behavioural Difficulties*, vol. 3, no. 3, pp. 3–11

Woods, P. (1979) *The divided school*, London: Routledge and Kegan Paul

World Health Organisation (1992) *The ICD-10 Classification of Mental and Behavioural Disorders*, Geneva: WHO

VI

Children's Voices

It becomes ever clearer that achieving equality in education is rooted in our capacity as adults to attend to the life of each child and young person who is currently participating in the system in Ireland today. Policies and their implementation, programmes and their evaluations will not achieve desired outcomes, however well-intentioned or well-funded, without a clear reference to the lives and voices of young people today. The UN Convention on the Rights of the Child (1989) is a key driver of policy in this respect and it inspires the title of section six: 'Children's Voices'.

The chapters in this section draw on the insights of the users of our school system to further research on how children and young people themselves can influence change for their futures. They examine students' perceptions of being treated fairly in school and, for example, the willingness of pupils and students to ask a teacher a question in class regarding an academic issue. Young people are asked about their anticipated transition from primary to secondary school and anxieties are revealed that deserve a listening response from those in leadership positions within the system. The complex issue of bullying is examined and new methods for empowering young people to take control of their own lives and to develop fresh narratives for their personal and social identity are proposed. A moving account of 'peer mediation' reminds us that childhood is a special way to be human and that adults can learn so much from children's insights into conflict resolution and forgiveness.

34

The Jolt between Primary and Post-Primary

Paul Downes, Catherine Maunsell and Jo-Hanna Ivers

The UN Convention on the Rights of the Child, ratified by Ireland, espouses the child-centred principle that children and young people have a right to be consulted and to have their voices heard in matters related to their own welfare. The National Conjoint Child Health Committee report (Denyer et al., 2000, p. 30) also emphasised the importance of direct consultation with young people. A key objective with regard to drug prevention in the National Drugs Strategy 2001–2008 is: 'To equip young people and other vulnerable groups with the skills and supports necessary to make informed choices about their health, personal lives and social development' (p. 109). Expression of this strategy within post-primary schools presupposes a basically democratic school culture, as does implementation of the Social, Personal and Health Education (SPHE) curriculum at primary and post-primary levels (Downes 2003a). At a local level, the Blanchardstown Area Partnership Strategic implementation plan (2004–2006) commits to 'supporting and promoting the right and capacity of all groups to fully participate in society by appropriate provisions for consultation and involvement in decision-making and by provision of necessary supports to enable their organisation'. The child-centred principles underlying this research logically flow from this concern with participation and consultation.

Based on research drawn from questionnaire responses from sixth-class pupils and first-year students across a number of designated disadvantaged schools in Blanchardstown, Dublin, we focus on two key issues, namely, pupil and student perceptions of being treated fairly in school, and willingness of pupils and students to ask a teacher a question in class regarding an academic issue. These two issues pertain to a range of other themes, also examined.

The need for positive pupil/student–teacher relations in order to minimise risk of early school dropout is directly relevant to questions of perceptions of being treated fairly in school and of willingness to ask a teacher a question in class.

In the US context, Doll (1996) highlights the role of school psychologists in creating 'emotionally healthy environments within which students can learn most effectively, including essential characteristics of the physical environment, peer social systems and adult-student relationships' (p. 38). US adolescents cite a sense of isolation and lack of personally meaningful relationships at school as equal contributors to academic failure and to their decisions to drop out of school (Institute for Education and Transformation, 1992; Wehlage and Rutter, 1986). Meier (1992) cites personalised, caring relationships with teachers as a prerequisite for high-school level reform. Using primarily populations deemed to be 'at risk', research in the US has shown that students' sense of belonging influences acceptance of educational values, motivation and commitment to school (Goodenow and Grady, 1992; Wehlage et al., 1989). The perception of school as a personally supportive community is critical to school completion and satisfaction (Fine, 1986; Kagan, 1990).

In the Irish context, Smyth (1999) argues that a positive interaction between teachers and students raises students' motivation and self-esteem, while negative experiences and attitudes are predictive of early leaving and academic underperformance (see also The National Educational Psychological Service report, 2004, on the relevance of a supportive and caring ethos in the school through SPHE programmes for planning for critical incidents). Other research in a range of areas associated with socio-economic disadvantage in Dublin also emphasises the role of teacher–student interaction as a risk factor of alienation from the school system and as a protective factor to motivate at-risk students to stay on at school. Quinlan (1998) observed that one of the interviewed teachers in Blanchardstown referred to the alienation of young people from an authoritarian educational system. Teacher-student relations was also a pervasive theme in Fingleton's (2003) interviews with eleven early school-leavers in the Canal Communities Area of Dublin. These interviews highlight their alienation from the school system as well as the desire of many for further paths to education, though not through traditional routes. Forkan (2005) touches on the theme of teacher–student relations in the conclusion of his report in Blanchardstown: 'treat all young people with respect, as this will be reciprocated'. Casby's (1997) interviews with early school leavers in Ballyfermot also noted that: 'More attention must be paid to the process by which a young person comes to leave school early. Early school leavers attribute most significance to factors related to school: relationships with teachers, suspensions and difficulties with curricula' (p. 6).

This view, that teachers need to develop their skills in promoting mental health in schools and in using a strengths-based approach to intervention, has been emphasised in two reports in Ballyfermot, Dublin (Downes, 2004a, 2004b), with a focus on the need to support teachers with regard to issues such as conflict resolution, behaviour management and self-awareness. Rourke's (1995, p. 21) evaluation of the Prevention of Early School Leaving (PESL) programme (now called 'Oasis') in Blanchardstown also highlighted the importance of a role for afterschool projects in developing the quality of interaction between teachers and young people, as well as parents:

> The PESL programme can only be truly effective if it also impacts on the quality of interaction between the parents/teachers and the young people. Hence the importance of involving parents and engaging the active support of teachers. Unless this happens the programme is unlikely to achieve more than providing the young people with some diversion and alternative activities for a couple of hours each week.

Rourke's (1995) evaluation also touched on the theme of fear of failure through highlighting the positive effects of a prevention of early school-leaving programme in Blanchardstown with regard to the benefit of helping students overcome fear of failure or being ridiculed. Fear of failure is another key theme related to issues of pupil/student perceptions of being treated fairly in school and willingness to engage in asking questions in class. Nolan, Duffy and Regan (2003) refer to the danger of 'fatalism' at a community level within Corduff, Blanchardstown, that 'nothing can be done'. Fear of failure is an example of fatalism at the level of the student's experience of school (see also international research on fatalism and risk behaviour, Kalichmann et al., 2000; Downes, 2003b). Fatalism refers to individual's beliefs in their ability to control their fate (Goodwin et al., 2003). Fatalism proved to be a strong indicator of the ability to establish close relationships, according to research in Central and Eastern Europe (Goodwin, 1998; Goodwin et al., 1999). Furthermore, fatalism may be associated with risk-taking behaviour such as intravenous drug use.

A focus on a supportive classroom environment to minimise a fear of failure would emphasise developing the strengths of the student (see also McKeown, Haase and Pratschke, 2001, on a strengths-based approach). A plethora of educational theorists and educational psychologists recognise the danger of labelling students as failures (e.g. Glasser, 1969; Warnock, 1977; Handy and Aitken, 1990; Casby, 1997; Kellaghan et al., 1995; MacDevitt, 1998; Kelly, 1999) with the consequent knock-on effect of early school dropout. In the words of Kellaghan et al., 1995: 'A first influence [on early school dropout] is school failure. While there may be occasions when young people who are doing well may leave school, the vast majority will have had a history of doing badly' (p. 92).

Rosenberg (1965) describes self-esteem as feeling that you are 'good enough'. Self-esteem is positively associated with school achievement (Purkey, 1970; Brookover, Thomas and Paterson, 1964; Hay, Ashman and van Kraayenoord, 1997).

A democratic school and classroom climate invite a constructivist approach to learning, where pupils and students begin to own the goals of their learning and can relate them to their life experience. This kind of learning, with echoes of a Freirean emphasis on the student–teacher relation as one of dialogue and mutual learning, invites a certain level of initiative and autonomy for the learner. Lack of autonomy is well recognised in Western cultures as damaging student motivation. For example, teachers who are autonomy-supportive, in contrast to controlling, catalyse in their students greater intrinsic motivation, curiosity and desire for challenge (Deci, Nezlek and Sheinman, 1981; Flink, Boggiano and Barrett, 1990; Ryan and Grolnick, 1986; Deci and Ryan, 1992; Ryan and Stiller, 1991), and students taught with a more controlling approach not only lose initiative but learn less effectively, especially when learning requires conceptual, creative processing (Amabile, 1986; Grolnick and Ryan, 1987; Glasser, 1986).

Young people's direct input into the consultation process was obtained through questionnaires given to all sixth classes in Revitalising Areas by Planning, Investment and Development (RAPID) area primary schools (230 responses) and all first-year classes in RAPID area secondary schools (162 responses). This focus on sixth class and first year was cognisant of the difficulties of transition from primary to post-primary raised in a range of research in Ireland (for example, O'Brien, 2004).

Fear of failure: sharp increase in students who would not tell teachers about problem with schoolwork in secondary compared to primary

The responses to the question 'If you had a problem with your schoolwork would you tell your teachers(s) about it? Why/Why not?' were as follows:

Primary: sixth class

YES	NO	MAYBE	N/A
210	18	1	1

Secondary: first year

YES	NO	MAYBE	N/A
122	27	8	6

While a large majority of post-primary students, approximately 75 per cent do feel comfortable in raising a problem with their schoolwork with their teachers, it must be acknowledged that a sizeable minority, over 20 per cent, do *not* or are not sure if they do. It is of concern that there is a sharp increase in first-year compared to sixth-class responses in those students who are *not* willing or are *not* sure if they would tell a teacher about an academic problem – from 8 per cent at primary level to more than 20 per cent at second level. Similarly, there is a sharp decrease in first-year compared to sixth-class responses in those students who *are* willing to tell a teacher about an academic problem – from approximately 91 per cent at primary level to 75 per cent at second level. These differences between primary and second level are statistically significant ones.

The effect of this sharp change in communication is evident after one term at secondary school. Concern must be raised as to whether a climate of fear of asking questions to seek academic help may increase in students after more than one term at secondary school. The following accounts are given by this sizeable minority of students, as to why they would not tell their teachers about a problem with schoolwork:

'No. The teachers would think I'm not paying attention and would think I'm stupid' 13F
'No because I wouldn't feel comfortable' 13F
'No because you would be called dumb' 13M
'No because I would feel stupid' 13F
'No because I'm too shy' 12M
'No because they'll think I'm stupid' 13M
'No because other people could think you're stupid' 13F
'No because they'd think you're stupid' 13F
'No because they'd probably try and get me moved down' 13F
'No because they will get me in trouble' 13M
'It depends if they're in a good mood or not' 12F
'No because they will row in my face' 12M
'No they don't give two shits they would just say do it we done it before that's what wrecks my head' (no age, gender indicated)
'No because they tell you to just do it' 13M
'I probably would but I don't know if they would help me' 13F
'Yes but they don't do nothing' 14M
'Sometimes they might not help you' 12F
'No I tell my dad or my mum' 15M
'No because I would feel more comfortable telling my ma or da' 13F
'No because the teacher is not my parent' 13F
'No I'd ask my mam to help me with it' 12F
'Yes because they're supposed to teach us how to do it but I'd probably just tell me ma' 13F

Sharp increase in students who perceive that they are not treated fairly in secondary school compared to primary school

The responses to the question: 'Are you treated fairly by teachers in school? Why/Why not?' were as follows:

Primary: sixth class

YES	NO	YES BUT	DON'T KNOW/NO ANSWER
170	36	21	3

Secondary: first year

YES	NO	YES BUT	DON'T KNOW/NO ANSWER
90	41	21	10

Approximately 74 per cent of pupils at primary level (sixth class) stated that they were treated fairly by teachers in school. Approximately 55 per cent of students at second level (first year) stated that they were treated fairly by teachers in school. Approximately 15 per cent of pupils at primary level (sixth class) stated that they were *not* treated fairly by teachers in school. Approximately 25 per cent of students at second level (first year) stated that they were *not* treated fairly by teachers in school. It is worth noting that these differences between sixth-class primary and first-year secondary are statistically significant, i.e., there is a statistically significant increase in perception of being treated unfairly by teachers in secondary school compared to primary school.

Conclusion

As far back as 1988, child-centred reforms in education were advocated by IFAPLAN, the German research institute with responsibility for coordinating projects in the (then) European Community, concerning transition from school to work. Its report concluded:

> These changes have meant a new climate in secondary education. In the schools, the effect has been a push towards putting the student more at the centre of the teaching/learning process. The challenge is to stimulate re-thinking of the use of the school and its resources in terms of what it can do for her/him, instead of how young people can be fitted into what the school-system, or individual subject-teacher, have traditionally offered.

In O'Donnabháin's (1998) words:

> As the IFAPLAN working document reported, it was no longer possible for schools to insist on young people fitting into whatever the school decided. Disgruntled young

people react in one of two ways – they either rebel openly and cause major discipline problems or they simply drop out and grow up as a part of the deviant section of the society. Thus many educational initiatives attempt to put the young persons at the centre and allow the learning environment to grow around them so that they can develop a sense of active citizenship (pp. 46–7).

The Combat Poverty Agency policy submission (2003) set a target to reduce the proportion of early school leavers nationally to 10 per cent by 2005. Its annual report (2004) notes that the targets in the National Anti-Poverty Strategy (NAPS) and National Action Plan against Poverty and Social Exclusion to reduce early school leavers by 85 per cent by 2003 and by 90 per cent by 2006 is 'unlikely' to be met, 'although programmes are being put in place to support this objective'. However, it is evident that it is not simply a matter of providing add-on supports to the mainstream school, such as the development of afterschool projects and psychological supports at an individual level for the pupil or student – change also needs to occur at the level of the school climate itself at post-primary level, based on the sample of responses in this current study. The report of the Statutory Committee on Educational Disadvantage (2005) refers to the need to 'change the mainstream, not just the margins' (p. 23).

The issue of perceptions of being treated fairly or otherwise in school needs to move beyond an individualised focus on the individual teacher or student to a systems-level analysis (see also Hyland, 2002, on the need to focus on change within schools rather than individual teachers). It is a systems-level problem and improvement of this problem requires a systems-level intervention, for example, at a national level with regard to teachers working on their conflict resolution strategies and awareness of educational disadvantage at pre-service and in-service levels (see also Barnardos, 2006, and the €318m to be invested in professional development of teachers and curriculum reform under the new National Development Plan 2007–2013; Flynn, 2007). Moreover, it is highly unlikely that this problem of a 'jolt in school climate' from primary to post-primary is unique to Blanchardstown. The focus needs to move beyond attributing 'blame' to teachers or students to examining the systems-level problem and supporting improvements at a systemic level that will lead to an increase in skills to facilitate better communication and cooperation between teachers and students at second level in particular.

Another systemic-level issue is the possibility that the new revised curriculum at primary level helps foster a more emotionally supportive school climate; for example, through circle time in Social, Personal and Health Education (SPHE), and emotional expression through drama – and this creates a greater contrast of transition, an increased 'clash of school cultures' than previously, between primary level and post-primary level, which is still more subject-centred and less constructivist in its teaching methods. A strategy of continuity between local primary and secondary schools also needs to focus on a continuity of implementation of SPHE. Pupil needs and expectations within a supportive climate at primary level need to be sustained at second level to minimise the 'culture shock' of acclimatisation to second level. The openness of the primary school environment may create expectations in pupils of an emotionally communicative and supportive environment at second level that could lead to a heightened sense of disillusionment if this atmosphere is not sustained across the transition to second level. There is a real onus on primary and second-level schools to work together to sustain continuity in approaches to SPHE and the broader school climate in practice, as well as through provision of social and emotional supports.

References

Amabile, T. M. (1996) *Creativity in context*, New York: Westview Press

Barnardos (2006) *Make the Grade*, Dublin: Barnardos

Blanchardstown Area Partnership (2004) *Strategic implementation plan 2004–2006*, Dublin: BAP

Brookover, W., Thomas, S., and Paterson, A. (1964) 'Self-concept of ability and school achievement', *Sociology of Education*, 37, pp. 271–8

Casby, A. (1997) *Making connections: Access to education in Ballyfermot*, Ballyfermot Partnership Co. Ltd

Combat Poverty Agency (2003) *Working towards a poverty free society. Policy submission to National Action Plan against Poverty and Social Exclusion 2003–2005*, Dublin: CPA

Deci, E. L. and Ryan, R. M. (1992) 'The initiation and regulation of intrinsically motivated learning and achievement' in Boggiano, A. K. and Pittman, T. S. (eds) *Achievement and Motivation: A social-developmental perspective*, New York: Cambridge University Press, pp. 9–36

Deci, E. L., Nezlek, J. and Sheinman, L. (1981) 'Characteristics of the rewarder and intrinsic motivation of the rewardee', *Journal of Personality and Social Psychology*, 40, pp. 1–10

Denyer, S. et al. (eds) (2000) *Get connected: Developing an adolescent friendly health service*, Dublin: National Conjoint Child Health Committee

Doll, B. (1996) 'Prevalence of psychiatric disorders in children and youth: An agenda for advocacy by school psychology', *School Psychology Quarterly*, 11, pp. 20–47

Downes, P. (2003a) 'The New Curriculum of Social, Personal and Health Education in Irish Primary Schools: Self-Awareness, Introversion and the Role of the Teacher', *Kwartalnik Padagogiczny* (Journal of Education, Poland), no. 4. vol. 190, pp. 93–112

Downes, P. (2003b) *Living with heroin: Identity, social exclusion and HIV among the Russian-speaking minorities in Estonia and Latvia*, Legal Information Centre for Human Rights, Tallinn and the Educational Disadvantage Centre, Dublin

Downes, P. (2004a) *Psychological Support Services for Ballyfermot: Present and Future*, Ballyfermot: URBAN

Downes, P. (2004b) *Voices from Children: St Raphael's Primary School Ballyfermot*, Ballyfermot: URBAN

Educational Disadvantage Committee (2003) 'A more integrated and effective delivery of school-based educational inclusion measures', submission to the Minister for Education and Science

Educational Disadvantage Committee (2005) *Moving beyond educational disadvantage 2002–2005*, Dublin: DES

Fine, M. (1986) 'Why urban adolescents drop into and out of public high school', *Teachers College Record*, 87, pp. 393–409

Fingleton, L. (2003) *Listen B4 I Leave: Early school leavers in the Canal Communities area and their experiences of school*, Dublin: Canal Communities Partnership Ltd

Flink, C., Boggiano, A. K., and Barrett, M. (1990) 'Controlling teaching strategies: Undermining children's self-determination and performance', *Journal of Personality and Social Psychology*, 59, pp. 916–24

Flynn, S. (2007) 'Modernisation of Primary, Second-level Schools Planned', *The Irish Times*, 24 January, p. 8

Forkan, C. (2005) *Joint Education Development Initiative (J.E.D.I): An audit of issues relating to early school leavers in the Greater Blanchardstown Area*, Dublin: Fingal County Council

Glasser, W. (1969) *Schools without failure*, New York and London: Harper and Row

Glasser, W. (1986) *Control theory in the classroom*, New York: Harper and Row

Goodenow, C. and Grady, K. E. (1992) 'The relationship of school belonging and friends' values to academic motivation among urban adolescent students', *Journal of Experimental Education*, 62, pp. 60–71

Goodwin, R. (1998) 'Invited programme overview. Personal relationships and social change: The 'realpolitik' of cross-cultural research in transient cultures', *Journal of Social and Personal Relationships,* 15, pp. 227–47

Goodwin, R., Kozlova, A., Kwiatkowska, A., Luu, L. A. N., Nizharadze, G., Realo, A., Kulvet, A. and Rammer, A. (2003) 'Social Representations of HIV/AIDS in Central and Eastern Europe', *Social Science and Medicine*, 56, pp. 1373–84

Goodwin, R., Nizharadze, G., Nguyen Luu, L. A., Kosa, E. and Emelyanova, T. (1999) 'Glasnost and the art of conversation: A multi-level analysis of disclosure across three cultures', *Journal of Cross-Cultural Psychology*, 30, pp. 78–90

Grolnick, W. S. and Ryan, R. M. (1987) 'Autonomy in children's learning: An experimental and individual difference investigation', *Journal of Personality and Social Psychology*, 52, pp. 890–8

Handy, C. and Aitken, R. (1990) *Understanding schools as organizations*, London: Penguin Books

Hay, I., Ashman, A. and van Kraayenoord, C. (1997) 'Investigating the influence of achievement on self-concept using an intra-class design and a comparison of PASS and the SDQ-1 self-concept tests', *British Journal of Educational Psychology*, 67, pp. 311–21

Hyland. A. (2002) 'Looking to the future – Ending disadvantage?' in Gilligan, A. L. (ed.) *Primary Education: Ending Disadvantage. Proceedings and Action Plan of National Forum*, Dublin: Educational Disadvantage Centre, St Patrick's College

IFAPLAN (1988) *Transition education for the 90s: The experience of the European Community's Action Programme*, Brussels: IFAPLAN

Institute for Education and Transformation (1992) *Voices from the inside: A report on schooling from inside the classroom – Part I: Naming the problem*, Claremont, CA: Claremont Graduate School

Kagan, D. M. (1990) 'How schools alienate students at risk: A model for examining proximal classroom variables', *Educational Psychologist*, 25, pp. 105–25

Kalichman, S. C., Kelly, J. A., Sikkema, K. J., Koslov, A. P., Shaboltas, A. and Granskaya, J. (2000) 'The emerging AIDS crisis in Russia: Review of enabling factors and prevention needs', *International Journal of STD and AIDS*, 11, pp. 71–5

Kellaghan, T., Weir, S., Ó Huallacháin, S. and Morgan, M. (1995) *Educational Disadvantage in Ireland*, Dublin: ERC, DOE, CPA

Kelly, A. V. (1999) *The Curriculum: Theory and Practice*, London: Paul Chapman Publishing Ltd

MacDevitt, D. (1998) 'Measures to combat early school-leaving in EU countries' in Boldt, S., Devine, B., MacDevitt, D. and Morgan, M. (eds) *Educational Disadvantage and Early School Leaving*, Dublin: Combat Poverty Agency

McKeown, K., Haase, T. and Pratschke, J. (2001) *Springboard promoting family well-being: Through family support services*, Dublin: Department of Health and Children

Meier, D. (1992) 'Reinventing teaching', *Teachers College Record*, 93, pp. 594–609

National Drugs Strategy 2001–2008 (2001) *Building on experience*, Dublin: Department of Tourism, Sport and Recreation

National Educational Psychological Service (2004) *Responding to critical incidents: Advice and information pack for schools*, Dublin: NEPS

Nolan, A., Duffy, V. and Regan, C. (2003) *A new dawn: Corduff Community Survey*, Dublin: CPA

O'Brien, M. (2004) *Making the Move: Students', Teachers' and Parents' Perspectives of Transfer from First to Second-Level Schooling*, Dublin: Marino Institute of Education

O'Donnabháin, D. (1998) 'The work-related curriculum' in Trant, A., O'Donnabháin, D., Lawton, D. and O'Connor, J. (eds) *The Future of the Curriculum*, Dublin: City of Dublin VEC, Curriculum Development Unit

Purkey, W. (1970) 'Self-perceptions of pupils in an experimental elementary school', *Elementary School Journal*, 71, pp. 166–71

Quinlan, C. M. (1998) *Early school leaving in Blanchardstown*, Dublin: BAP

Rosenberg, M. (1965) *Society and the adolescent self-image*, Princeton: Princeton University Press

Rourke, S. (1995) *Programme for potential early school leavers: Interim evaluation report*, Dublin: Barnardos and the Blanchardstown Youth Service

Ryan, R. M. and Grolnick, W. S. (1986) 'Origins and pawns in the classroom: Self-report and projective assessments of individual differences in children's perceptions', *Journal of Personality and Social Psychology*, 50, pp. 550–8

Ryan, R. M. and Stiller, J. (1991) 'The social contexts of internalization: Parent and teacher influences on autonomy, motivation and learning' in Maehr, M. L. and Pintrich, P. L. (eds) *Advances in motivation and achievement*, vol. 7, Greenwich, CT: JAI Press, pp. 115–49

Smyth, E. (1999) *Do Schools Differ? Academic and Personal Development among Pupils in the Second-Level Sector*, Dublin: Oak Tree Press/ESRI

Warnock, M. (1977) *Schools of thought*, London: Faber

Wehlage, G. G. and Rutter, R. A. (1986) 'Dropping out: How much do schools contribute to the problem?', *Teachers College Record*, 87, pp. 374–92

Wehlage, G. G., Rutter, R. A., Smith, G. A., Lesko, N. and Fernandez, R. R. (1989) *Reducing the risk: Schools as communities of support*, New York: The Falmer Press

35

Primary to Post-Primary: Perceptions of Pupils with Special Educational Needs

Catherine Maunsell, Vanessa Barrett and Mark Candon

Introduction

In this chapter we look at the findings of a qualitative study which sought to gain an insight into the primary school experience of a sample of sixth-class pupils with special educational needs (SEN) and their perceptions of second-level schools in light of their impending transfer. The participants, five girls and three boys, were drawn from two single-sex primary schools in inner-city Dublin. Both schools had designated disadvantage status. The aims of the study were to establish the students' feelings about primary school and ascertain their hopes and fears around the transfer to second-level education. Two parents were also interviewed in relation to their child's transition from primary to second-level schooling.

Review of the literature

In Ireland, young adolescents typically make the transition from primary school to post-primary school between the ages of eleven and thirteen years. In contrast to many other transitions in life, this particular transition is compulsory for most pupils and takes place at a time when young people are experiencing many other changes in relation to the onset of adolescence. This time of transition evokes a wide range of emotions and concerns for young adolescents and their parents. Among the worries of students about to embark on post-primary education is coping with a longer school day, more teachers, a new school building, a larger peer group and higher academic expectations (Hardy, Bukowski and Sippola, 2002). Students who do not make a successful transition to secondary school are at risk of leaving school early.

Research shows that there are a number of vulnerable groups who are at a greater risk of encountering difficulties during the transition from primary school to secondary school (Ainley, Foreman and Sheret, 1991). One such vulnerable group is students with special educational needs, particularly exacerbated in the context of socio-economic disadvantage. Indeed, planning for the transition of young people with special educational needs is a crucial but often overlooked element of social inclusion (Dee, 2006). Research indicates that these students are often alienated academically and socially to a greater degree than their mainstream counterparts during the transition phase. To contextualise their difficulties we first turn our attention to the transition challenges experienced by all students.

Transition to second-level schools: challenges experienced by students generally

The transition to second-level schooling is marked by several changes in educational expectations and practices. At primary level, students are taught in self-contained classrooms with a familiar set of peers and usually just one teacher. At second-level, students must learn to cope with more teachers, more classroom changes, more subjects and a greater number of peers. Added to this are increased academic demands and more impersonal student–teacher relationships. According to Hardy, Bukowski and Sippola (2002), second-level schools are characterised by a greater emphasis on control of pupil behaviour by teachers, a practice that fails to meet early adolescents' developmental needs for autonomy and self-management (Eccles et al., 1993). All of this occurs at a time when students are experiencing a host of changes associated with the onset of puberty. They have been the senior students at primary school and move on to be the youngest students in the post-primary school. Many aspects of this transition from primary to second-level education can cause anxiety for the prospective first-year student. O'Brien (2003, 2004) has pointed to the lack of attention paid in Ireland to students' transitions from first- to second-level schooling. She pointed out that this transition is an emotional time for pupils and identified the need for greater communication between primary and post-primary schools. O'Brien also focused on the negative effects of streaming on pupils in first year, the decrease in the quality of student–teacher relationships in first year and the importance of friendships in mediating the stressful effects of transition.

Research by Naughton (1997) points out that the transition of students from primary to second-level in Ireland is especially problematic because of the historical separateness of the two sectors and the resulting lack of communication between them. His research found that student transition anxieties centred on academic performance, rules and regulations and successful social integration. Sixty per cent of the pupils interviewed claimed to know a lot about their intended second-level school, while 40 per cent said that they knew only a little. Only 17 per cent of the students said that their primary school or secondary school were the main source of information. This shows that there is plenty of opportunity for myths about secondary school to propagate in such an informal transference of information. Naughton's research points to the need for schools to be more active in passing on pertinent school-related information to prospective students. According to research by Measor and Woods (1984) it is not enough that schools pass on information relating to the official culture of the school, e.g. rules, timetabling, etc., but also information relating to the unofficial culture of the school, e.g. policy for dealing with bullying, homework, etc.

A restructuring of pedagogical and assessment practices at second-level was recommended by Naughton (1997) in order to lessen the experience of discontinuity for the first-year student. According to Eccles et al. (1993) there are higher standards in judging students' competence at second-level. It was found that first-year students generally received lower marks in secondary school house exams than they had received in primary school. No corresponding decline, however, was found when these students were administered standardised achievement tests. Such changes in grading practices can dent the self-esteem of first-year students. It is evident from this research that greater links between first- and second-level schools are required to promote dialogue between teachers on the nature and purpose of their educational endeavours and to transfer information about students that is necessary for successful educational planning.

School transition: further challenges for students with special educational needs

For students with special educational needs (SEN), within the broad context of multiple disadvantage, the transition from primary to second-level education is even more complicated. Students with SEN often have their educational needs provided for within a special class or through withdrawal at primary level. The class teacher would have been aware of the particular student's difficulties as well as the learning support staff in the school. The student's peers are also likely to have adapted to the student's difficulties. However, on transition to post-primary school, transfer of information about the student's special educational needs may be scant or incomplete. In some cases the student's difficulties may not be brought to light until later in the student's educational career. When information on the student's SEN is transferred to the post-primary school, it may not be made available to all subject teachers. The student with SEN will, like other students, be forging a new identity for himself/herself and may be afraid of unfavourable social comparisons with other children if they draw attention to their difficulties, and, as a result, many students with SEN do not access the support they need at post-primary level.

The social experience of students with special educational needs is also a cause for concern and has implications for transition planning. Research on children with SEN integrated in mainstream schools shows that students with SEN form fewer friendships than mainstream children and are teased more often (Martlew and Hodson, 1991). It was also found that when choosing friends, mainstream children preferred to make friends and communicate with other mainstream peers rather than children with SEN (Martlew and Hodson, 1991). This research pointed out that being alone at playtime or not having many friends is a risk factor for being a victim of bullying. Further research by Smith and Sharpe (1994) found that students with SEN in mainstream schools were more likely to be bullied than their mainstream counterparts. In Ireland, O'Moore and colleagues (Mitchell and O'Moore, 1987; O'Moore and Hillery, 1989) found that the incidence of being bullied was twice as high among those children attending remedial and full-time special classes than mainstream classes.

A legislative basis ensuring that students with SEN are supported by their schools to make an effective transition from primary to post-primary school is laid out in the Education for Persons with Special Education Needs Act (2004), where it is stated that a school's education plan should include 'where appropriate, the special educational and related support services to be provided to the child to enable the child to effectively make the transition from primary school education to post-primary school education' (Sect. 9, subsec. 2, paragraph (g)).

This is further highlighted in the Dublin Inner City Primary Schools Initiative (DICPSI) report, *A Plan for Dublin Inner City Primary Schools*, which states:

> The majority of pupils in forty-one primary schools located in or around Dublin city centre come from the most educationally disadvantaged communities in the country. Up to twenty per cent qualify for Special Needs, and an even larger number qualify for Learning Support. Seventy to eighty per cent are below the national average in reading and mathematics. A substantial number display poor attendance, a disinterest in education, inappropriate behaviour and low self-esteem. Many drop out of the system at an early age. (DICPSI, 2003, p. 4)

In light of such findings this study sought to look at the attitudes to school of sixth-class pupils with special educational needs, in one inner-city community, as they come to the end of their primary schooling and prepare for transfer to second level.

Method

Participants

The participants in the study were sixth-class students from two small single-sex primary schools in inner-city Dublin. Both schools had designated disadvantage status. Eight students took part, three boys and five girls. The sample interviewed in this study was selected on the basis of Miles and Huberman's (1994) 'criterion' sampling approach. Thus, each of the eight students met the criterion of having identified special educational needs. The purposive non-probability sampling approach was employed due to the small scale and time limitations of this qualitative study.

Parental consent was obtained for participation in this study. Two parents also took part in this study.

Design of the study

A qualitative design was used for the purposes of this study in order to ascertain the pupils' and parents' perceptions about the transition from primary to post-primary schooling. The data presented herein was collated in the school year 2003–2004. This study was part of a broader quantitative study on transition from primary school to post-primary school (Candon, 2004).

Two semi-structured interview schedules were developed for use in this study. The first schedule was drawn up to interview students, the second to interview parents. The interview schedules concentrated on the following areas: experience of primary school; perceptions about secondary school; perceptions of social experiences at secondary school; perceptions of academic experiences at secondary school; perceptions of disciplinary procedures at primary and secondary school; accessing support at primary and secondary school; perceptions of learning support at primary and secondary school; preparation for transition from primary to secondary school.

Procedure

Once consent was obtained from parents, the pupils were interviewed individually in their school. Parents were also interviewed individually in the school setting. The information from these sources was then collated and is outlined in the next section.

Results

Experience of primary school

The students were generally positive about their experience in primary school. All three boys interviewed indicated that they liked their class a lot. Three of the five girls stated that they liked it a lot, while two said that they liked it a little. Aspects of school experience such as outings, sports, subjects and their teacher were mentioned by the students as adding to their positive experience of primary school. When asked what they would miss about primary school, seven out of the eight students said that they would miss their teacher. Five students said that they would miss particular sports and subjects. Another four students said that they would miss going on outings as a class. One student said that he would miss the level of work at primary school 'because it's easy here and it'll be much harder in secondary'.

Perceptions about secondary school

When asked what they were looking forward to most about secondary school, five students mentioned doing new subjects, especially those of a practical nature. Five students said they were looking forward to meeting new teachers. Making new friends was something that four of the students were looking forward to. Just one student was positive about moving around classes during the school day. When asked what their biggest fears were about going to secondary school, the two most frequent answers were 'harder work' and 'bullying'. Other fears included doing tests, having new teachers and going from a single-sex school to a mixed school. Three of the students interviewed said that they decided to go to a certain secondary school because their friends were going there. One student said that his principal recommended the school, one student cited his parents as making the decision and one student said she made the decision herself based on the sporting reputation of a secondary school. One parent said that she had decided on a school for her son because it had a reputation for having 'little bullying there'.

Visiting the secondary school prior to the start of the new school year was seen as positive by six out of the eight students. Two parents also felt that it would be a good idea for their children to go and visit the school before they started in September. Three students said that they had no information on their prospective secondary school. Two students said that they had received information from family/friends attending the secondary school.

Perceptions of social experiences at secondary school

Fears about bullying were expressed by seven of the eight students. For parents, bullying was also a major concern. One parent felt that it would be a good idea to keep first years on their own at break-times to avoid bullying. A total of six students felt that first years get picked on more because they are the youngest in the school. It was felt by the majority of students that it was good to know other first years before starting. For some this was seen as a deterrent to bullying; 'if you didn't know anyone you might get pushed around'.[1] Both parents felt that it was good for their children to know other first years: 'It's good to have a bit of support.'

Two students expressed fears about the difficulty of making new friends: 'it's hard to make new friends, hard to talk to new people'. However, three students were looking forward to making new friends at secondary school. When asked how the secondary school could help her child settle in and make friends, one parent stated that they should 'try and make it more like primary at first and change it gradually ... be welcoming and mind them more ... get them used to the rules and the timetable'.

Perceptions of academic experiences at secondary school

In terms of academic experience, five of the students felt that they would like having a greater number of teachers. However, three students said that they would prefer to have just one teacher: 'I like to stick to one teacher, it's good to get to know a teacher and them to know you.' This was also supported by one of the parents who stated that 'He likes having one teacher ... he might find it difficult having lots of different teachers.' A second parent felt that 'they might get mixed up between the teachers and keeping track of all the homework they get in the different classes can be hard'.

All of the students felt that they would have a greater amount of work to do at secondary school, with three students identifying that this was a worry for them. Six students felt that the work at secondary school would have a greater degree of difficulty: '... it'll be much harder at secondary'. Having to do more tests and homework were also identified as academic worries by the students.

Perceptions of disciplinary procedures at primary and secondary school

Six students were happy with the rules at primary school, while two students were very happy with the rules at primary school. When asked if they thought they would be happy with the rules at secondary school, three said they thought they would be happy with them, while five said they didn't know. One of the two parents felt that the discipline procedures would be much harsher at secondary school.

Accessing support at primary and secondary school

Seven out of eight students said that they would go to a teacher if they needed academic help at primary school. One student said that he would go to the principal. When asked who they thought they would go to if they needed help at secondary school, six students said they would go to a teacher. One student said he would go to the principal. One student said she would go to an older student

---

[1] Data was not collated on whether the pupils had older siblings currently attending secondary school.

and ask them what to do: 'it's good to be able to talk to older students, it's easier to ask them questions than teachers'. One parent felt that it would be a good idea to have a liaison officer working between the primary and secondary schools. It was felt that this person could help prepare sixth-class students for the transition. Another parent felt that there should be more communication between primary and secondary teachers in order to transfer information about individual students and their learning styles.

Perceptions of learning support at primary and secondary school

When asked how happy they were with their learning at primary school, four students said they were 'happy' and four students said that they were 'very happy'. All eight of the students were positive about the learning support that they received at primary school. When asked what kind of learning support they would prefer at secondary school, all three boys and two girls said that they would prefer to be taken out of class individually for help: 'It's easier to concentrate when you're on your own, other people distract you.' The other three girls said that they would prefer in-class assistance: 'I'd prefer to get help in the class because I might be teased if I was taken out.' Two of the students stated that they were worried about their learning at secondary school. One student said that she would like extra help before she started in secondary school so that she would be better prepared.

One parent felt that his son would prefer to be taken out of class for extra help, as 'it's less embarrassing when he is on his own for the work'. The other parent felt it would be better for her son to be in an integrated special class where everyone is getting extra help as 'it would be embarrassing to be taken out of class or to have a teacher in the classroom teaching just him'.

Preparation for the transition from primary school to secondary school

The students came up with a number of suggestions in relation to how the primary and secondary schools could better prepare them for the transition. Four students felt that it would be a good idea to meet the secondary school teachers before starting. Meeting other first-year students before starting was thought to be a good idea. One student suggested that the schools organise some games to facilitate new friendships. Three students said it would be a good idea to find out more about the secondary school, to have a look around and find out about the kind of work they do. Two students felt that they should do more work at primary school to better prepare them for secondary school.

Conclusion

Overall, the results suggested that the students were generally positive about their experience of primary school. All of the students interviewed said that they liked their class and seven out of eight students said that they would miss their teacher when they left. These results point out the centrality of the student–teacher relationship at this stage in the students' academic career. Galton and Wilcocks (1983) found that for students about to embark on post-primary education, changing teacher was of more importance than changing schools.

The students had positive perceptions of post-primary school in relation to a number of areas. In academic terms, many of the students were looking forward to doing new subjects, especially those of a practical nature such as woodwork and home economics. The majority of students were looking forward to having new teachers and making new friends. However, for a minority of students, having new teachers and making new friends were a cause for anxiety rather than excitement. Other anxieties voiced by the students and their parents included fears about academic work, homework and tests. Many of the students felt that as well as having a greater amount of academic work to get through, the work would also be more difficult. A number of the students felt that they were not ready academically for the move to post-primary education and asserted that they needed to do more work at primary level to prepare them for the move. One student was particularly worried about doing tests at post-primary school as he had heard that they were very difficult. This student's first experience of doing tests at post-primary level is likely to be an entrance examination or transition test. These tests are often pitched at a standard beyond the average student's ability and as such are completely inaccessible to students with special needs, especially those with a general learning difficulty. Naughton (2003) points out that these entrance examinations are often unrelated to the sixth-class programme in both standard and content, that they take place in pressurised conditions and measure a narrow range of abilities. This initial experience of assessment in conjunction with other differences in assessment procedures at post-primary level can only serve to alienate the student with special educational needs.

Anxieties about bullying were prioritised by the majority of students and their parents. It was felt that being victimised was a particular problem for first-year students. Forming friendships was seen by many as a protective factor against being bullied. As bullying is a reality in all schools and the research shows that students with special needs are at an even greater risk of being bullied (Mitchell and O'Moore, 1987), it is essential that schools put in place programmes to promote friendship and reduce bullying behaviour.

Coping with timetables, extra teachers, homework and moving around classes were anxieties for a number of the students. Children with general learning difficulties can often have poor organisational skills, making it difficult for them to cope with the huge organisational changes in their school day at post-primary school. Naughton (2003) discusses the possibility of transferring some primary-school practices into post-primary school for a period in first year, e.g. mixed-ability teaching, a small group of teachers responsible for all subject areas, arranging a 'homebase' for first-years, etc. A notable development in this regard is the Junior Certificate Schools Programme (JCSP), an alternative approach to the Junior Certificate which aims to keep 'at-risk' students in school longer, as well as providing a more appropriate curriculum for the weaker student. JCSP classes generally aim to have a smaller number of teachers involved with each class and, where possible, the students stay in one classroom (with the exception of practical classes). Naughton (2003) also points out the possible benefit of making some organisational changes at sixth class to prepare students for the transition, e.g. introducing timetables, involving more teachers in delivering the programme, etc.

Transition support programmes are important for all young people moving from primary to post-primary schooling. However, they are essential for more vulnerable groups such as students with special educational needs. The parents and students in this study identified the need for communication and coordination between primary and post-primary schools in order to prepare students for the transition. The majority of students said that they would like to visit their post-primary school prior to starting there to familiarise themselves with the building. A number of pupils suggested that the post-primary teachers could visit them in their primary school. This would also provide the post-primary teachers with an opportunity to get valuable information on the individual students, an idea that was advocated by one of the parents in the study. A further suggestion from pupils was for the designation of a student liaison officer who would work for both the primary school and post-primary school. This person could help prepare students in sixth class for the transition and would be a familiar person to support them once they reach post-primary school, thus adding an element of personnel continuity to the young person's overall school experience. Other themes arising included involving students in a mentoring programme at secondary school and enhancing the level of partnership with parents during the process of transition.

References

Ainley, J., Foreman, J. and Sheret, M. (1991) 'High School Factors that Influence Students to Remain in School', *The Journal of Educational Research,* vol. 85, no. 2, pp. 69–80

Candon, M. (2004) 'Pupils' Perceptions of the Transition from Primary to Secondary School: A Quantitative Analysis', unpublished MEd paper, Dublin: St Patrick's College

Dee, L. (2006) *Improving transition planning for young people with special educational needs*, Maidenhead: Open University Press/McGrawHill Education

Dublin Inner City Primary Schools Initiative (DICPSI) (2003) *A Plan for Dublin*

Inner City Primary Schools, unpublished report, Dublin Inner City Partnership and the Integrated Services Process

Eccles, J. S., Midgley, C., Wigfield, A., Miller-Buchanan, C., Reuman, D., Flanagan, C. and Mac Iver, D. (1993) 'Development During Adolescence: The Impact of Stage-Environment Fit on Young Adolescents' Experience in Schools and in Families', *American Psychologist*, vol. 48, no. 2, pp. 90–101

Galton, M. and Wilcocks , J. (1983) 'Changing teachers and changing schools' in Galton, M. and Wilcocks, J. (eds) *Moving from the primary classroom*, London: Routledge and Kegan Paul

Hardy, C. L., Bukowski, W. M. and Sippola, L. K. (2002) 'Stability and Change in Peer Relationships During the Transition to Middle-Level School', *Journal of Early Adolescence*, vol. 22, no.2, pp. 117–42

Martlew, M. and Hodson, J. (1991) 'Children with mild learning difficulties in an integrated and in a special school: Comparisons of behaviour, teasing and teachers' attitudes', *British Journal of Educational Psychology*, 61, pp. 355–72

Measor, L. and Woods, P. (1984) *Changing Schools: pupil perspectives on transfer to a comprehensive*, Milton Keynes: Open University Press

Miles, M. B. and Huberman, A. M. (1994) *Qualitative data analysis* (2nd edn) Thousand Oaks, CA: Sage Publications

Mitchell, J. and O'Moore, A. M. (1987) 'The identification of the problem of bullying in relation to other behavioural problems in the primary school', unpublished manuscript, Dublin: Trinity College

Naughton, P. (1997) 'Time for Change: A Study of Primary to Second-Level Schooling Transition, *Irish Educational Studies*, vol. 17, pp. 312–26

Naughton, P. (2003) 'Primary to Second-Level Transition Programmes: Rationale, Principles and a Framework', *Oideas*, 50, pp. 40–65

O'Brien, M. (2003) 'Girls and Transition to Second-Level Schooling in Ireland: "moving on" and "moving out"', *Gender and Education*, vol. 15, 3, pp. 249–68

O'Brien, M. (2004) *Making the Move: Students', Teachers' and Parents' Perspectives of Transfer from First to Second-Level Schooling*, Dublin: Marino Institute of Education

O'Moore, A. M. and Hillery, B. (1989) 'Bullying in Dublin Schools', *The Irish Journal of Psychology*, vol. 10, no. 3, pp. 426–41

Smith, P. K. and Sharpe, S. (eds) (1994) *School Bullying: Insights and Perspectives*, London, Routledge

Acknowledgement

This study was supported, in part, through funding received from St Patrick's College Research Committee.

36

Bullying and Social Context: Challenges for Schools

Gerard Farrelly

Introduction

The complexity of bullying in school poses difficulties for teachers, principals and other staff members in knowing how to deal with it, how to intervene and how to establish methods for preventing it from occurring and recurring. Rigby (2002, p. 14) suggests it is a 'massive and enduring social problem', one that is not necessarily confined to schools. Evidence suggests that bullying is present among adults in the workplace, prisons and the armed forces (Ananiadou and Smith, 2002; Rigby, 2002; Byrne, 2004). Media attention has been drawn to the phenomenon because of persistent headlines detailing incidents of chronic bullying in schools which allegedly have resulted in young people taking their own lives, including in Ireland (O'Regan, 2004; Stone, 2004; Lucey, 2002) and in the UK (Brooks, 2003). This link to suicide and suicidal ideation is supported by research (Carney, 2000; Rigby and Slee, 1999, Morita et al., 1999).

This chapter addresses the issue of bullying from the perspective of Irish schools that are identified by the Irish government as being 'disadvantaged', and how labels which are applied to pupils can influence the way bullying behaviour is tackled. Cross-cultural comparisons are also made with other studies from around the world that have addressed the issue of bullying.

Social class and the prevalence of bullying

Studies by Lane (1989) and Whitney and Smith (1993) in the UK and O'Moore, Kirkham and Smith (1997) in Ireland, all indicate lower social class to be a significant factor in bullying behaviour, although Smith (1997) in Sheffield found that bullying was only 10 per cent higher in lower social classes. In the UK and Ireland, social class and quality of housing serve as a measure of social disadvantage.

In their nationwide study of bullying in Irish schools, O'Moore, Kirkham and Smith (1997) requested that information on the social class of pupils be provided. The school principals were asked to submit percentages of pupils within each social class grouping according to parental occupation. Results indicated that bullying behaviour was more prevalent in schools where there was a higher concentration of pupils from lower socio-economic groupings. However, this was not the case for pupils being bullied. O'Moore, Kirkham and Smith (1997) found there were no significant differences in the proportion of pupils who were bullied in primary or post-primary schools that were designated disadvantaged by the Irish government. Nevertheless, significantly more pupils in designated disadvantaged primary and post-primary schools reported bullying others. This latter result confirms the same findings from other studies (Stephenson and Smith, 1989; Whitney and Smith, 1993). In some disadvantaged working-class areas, bullying may be open and more verbal and physical in nature, but in schools deemed to be in 'middle-class' areas, bullying may be more subtle in origin, with exclusion perhaps being more common. However, Downes (2004), in the context of Ballyfermot schools in Dublin, found that principals tended to underestimate the level of bullying and that bullying was a key concern of pupils across schools and influenced the non-school attendance of a notable minority.

The research above points to a greater onus placed on teachers who work in disadvantaged areas to identify bullying behaviour and take positive action. The research also indicates the need for schools to adopt a whole-school approach, where written policies provide guidelines for teachers to follow. This would allow for consistent responses to be made to bullying incidents. Sandler (cited in O'Moore, Kirkham and Smith, 1997, p. 165) suggests that in disadvantaged areas there is an increased likelihood that some children will resort to aggressive and impulsive means to solve interpersonal problems. This may be due to poor social support within the family and community that adversely affects self-esteem, sense of security and feelings of mastery over situations. Some pupils and parents may need support in developing their linguistic expression of feelings. Downes (2004b) has also highlighted the key role of a class teacher in changing a climate of bullying in her class in Ballyfermot, through use of strategies such as a problem box (into which pupils anonymously place their written descriptions of problems) and a focus on the different contexts where bullying may be taking place, e.g., the yard, after school, between classes.

In a study of Maltese primary school children, Borg (1999) found no correlation between a father's socio-economic status and bullying behaviour. He also found that children who bully and those who are bullied can belong to any social background, and there was no connection in relation to whether a bully or victim's mother was working or not. The differences between results in Malta and Ireland and the UK may highlight a fundamental social difference between different cultures which impacts on bullying behaviour, with a distinct demarcation of social class being more common in the UK and Ireland than possibly in other countries such as Malta.

In a study of the role that peer support plays in helping victims of bullying, Cowie and Olafsson (2000) interviewed teachers in a disadvantaged school in inner-city London, and recorded interesting teacher attitudes towards bullying and intervention strategies. The principal expressed a commitment to a whole-school policy and peer support, but he and his staff felt that the bullying situation was out of their control. He indicated how difficult it was to protect children during break times when bullying occurred, with pupils regularly beaten, threatened, humiliated and robbed. He believed this was due to a large campus with few staff. The principal perceived that the victims were shy, introverted, and lacking confidence and the ability to cope and manage, making them easy prey. He claimed that the pupils were unmotivated to ease their own suffering. The bullying itself was, according to the principal, caused by the disadvantaged homes the children came from, with a drab existence and lack of stimulation. He felt that they had to deal with aggressive and disruptive pupils who had been expelled from other schools. A teacher who was responsible for implementing peer support felt that no supervision had been given to the intervention strategy because of other school pressures. The consequence of this was an increase in bullying episodes and a hardening of attitudes, with few sanctions against the bullies (Cowie and Olafsson, 2000). However, if teachers focus predominantly on blaming factors such as home background they are less likely to intervene.

Background factors and personalities of children involved in bullying behaviour

Rather than teachers focusing on the individual characteristics of the perpetrator or victims of bullying and laying blame with them, it is more important to focus on the context in which the behaviour occurs. As Rivers and Soutter (1996) argue, while most pupils may at times be bullies or victims, bullying is not a personality trait but a response to circumstance. To distinguish between the typologies of bullies and victims is, according to Cullingford and Morrison (1995), misleading because many children act as both victim and bully. It may be that bullying is a strategy to overcome victimisation and peer rejection, an alternative way of gaining status. However, throughout the literature on bullying, theorists have described in great depth the traits and background factors which affect a child's propensity for bullying behaviour as victim or bully, and teachers/school staff also frequently refer to the background of a child as affecting their behaviour. This chapter emphasises systems theory in relation to the school, family and community.

Labelling

In applying Capra's (1982) systems theory there is a continual interplay and mutual influence between the outer world and our human inner world. Consequently, teachers' response to bullying may be influenced by their home background and upbringing. It is determined by past experience, expectations, our purposes, and the 'individual symbolic interpretation of our perceptual experience' (Capra, 1982, p. 321). Teachers ascribe labels to students such as 'bully' and 'victim', but these labels can be undesirable (Smith, 1991). Using the term 'victim' tends to further victimise and the term 'bully' may label the pupil permanently. It is more appropriate to focus on the behaviour of the child committing the bullying act or the reaction of the child who is a victim of this behaviour – rather than labelling these children as 'bully' or 'victim'.

The labels teachers ascribe to certain behaviour and more so to the individuals concerned can have a negative impact on children involved in bullying incidents. Lane (1989), who examined background factors, personality traits and academic school progress in relation to bullying in a mixed secondary school (100) and a girls' secondary school (120), found a correlation between the labelling of pupils as 'difficult' and bullying behaviour. The behaviour of individuals labelled as difficult was often also identified as bullying by a person in a position of power such as a teacher or principal, and the incidents occurred within a social context such as break time in the school playground. The behaviour was not necessarily bullying but it was deemed such, and once the label 'bully' was applied it remained. Lane (1989) also found that those labelled as bullies experienced greater health problems and poor relationships with peers. Children labelled as 'bullies' also came from large families and were from a lower social class. This latter finding supports those of Whitney and Smith (1993) in their comprehensive UK study and O'Moore, Kirkham and Smith (1997) in their Irish study, which identified a greater tendency for children from families in lower socio-economic groups to be involved in bullying. This does not necessarily mean it will always be the case that children who bully once will always bully, nor does it mean children from big families or a lower social class will bully others. Teachers have to be aware of how the background of children can be a contributory factor in children bullying others, and understand how the application of labels to a child can have negative consequences. If teachers adopt an attitude whereby they label individual children as 'bullies,' they may automatically assume that all aggressive behavioural incidents involving a particular child warrant the label of bullying.

A key problem of dealing with bullying in schools arises because there is little agreement about what constitutes bullying behaviour and how it is defined (Rigby, Smith and Pepler, 2004). In Ireland, the accepted definition of bullying as stated by the Department of Education (1993) is: 'Bullying is repeated aggression, verbal, psychological or physical, conducted by an individual or group against others.'

Child protection

It is unclear what percentage of teachers in Ireland know that preventing bullying behaviour forms an integral part of the national guidelines for protecting children, and whether teachers have a positive or negative attitude towards protecting children from bullying. The National Guidelines for the Protection and Welfare of Children (Department of Health and Children, 1999) stipulate that school management boards should have an anti-bullying policy in place and that teachers have to be aware of the policy and the procedural guidelines to deal with bullying. In the event of what the document terms 'serious bullying' and 'potentially abusive' behaviour (Department of Health and Children, 1999, p. 107), the school is encouraged to contact the relevant health board. This is supported by a definition of bullying which stresses a degree of intentionality and repetition. The responsibility for dealing with bullying remains with the school authorities, with due consideration to the guidelines on bullying behaviour (Department of Education, 1993).

In considering the role of the teacher in protecting children, teachers' perception may be that this relates solely to issues of child protection and abuse, which includes sexual, physical, and emotional abuse and neglect by adults. There may also be a lack of consideration of the physical and emotional abuse carried out in bullying behaviour. Webb and Vulliamy (2001) in the UK found that teachers who were exposed to the traumatic abusive situations which children in their care had experienced, complained of considerable feelings of stress and anxiety in dealing with them, and teachers were encouraged not to become emotionally involved. However, teachers who are not empathic towards victims of bullying will often view the behaviour with less seriousness than someone who is empathic (Craig, Henderson and Murphy, 2000). There is a need for teachers to fully realise that in an abusive bullying situation there is a risk of suicide or serious long-term emotional and psychological damage (Roland, 2002).

Prevalence of bullying in Ireland compared to other nations

In comparing Ireland (O'Moore, Kirkham and Smith, 1997) to other nations, it is clear that bullying is prevalent in other countries, such as Malta (Borg, 1999), with 60.5 per cent of the sample identified as self-declared victims (see Table 1 for further figures). This compares to 22.9 per cent of the sample of primary school pupils in Ireland (O'Moore, Kirkham and Smith, 1997) who admitted being bullied in a self-report questionnaire. These studies used the same type of questionnaire with very different results. However, it may be that Irish children are more reluctant to admit to being bullied or teachers intervene consistently, while Maltese children may be more open and ready to admit to it because of a heightened awareness within schools in the country.

Table 1 Cross-cultural comparison of the prevalence of bullying in Ireland, England, Malta and Northern Ireland

Research	Country	Sample	Methodology	Findings
Witney and Smith (1993)	England	2,623 primary pupils (1,271 boys, 1,352 girls) (8–11 years); 4,135 secondary pupils (2,152 boys, 1,983 girls (11–16 years)	Self-report questionnaire (Olweus definition and questionnaire)	27% primary pupils are bullied sometimes (10% once a week or more); 10% secondary pupils are bullied sometimes (4% once a week or more); 12% primary pupils bullied others sometimes (4% once a week or more); 6% secondary pupils bullied others sometimes (1% once a week or more)
O'Moore, Kirkham and Smith (1997)	Republic of Ireland	9,599 primary pupils (4,485 girls, 5,114 boys) (8–12 years); 10,873 secondary pupils, (6,663 girls, 4, 210 boys) (11–18 years)	Self-report questionnaire (Olweus definition and questionnaire)	18.5% (1,777) primary pupils bullied occasionally (5% (480) bullied once a week or more); 10.8% (1,172) secondary pupils bullied occasionally (1.9% (207) bullied once a week or more); higher incidence of victimization amongst boys in both primary and secondary; 26.3% (2,524) primary pupils had bullied others; 14.8% (1,606) secondary pupils bullied others

Research	Country	Sample	Methodology	Findings
Borg (1999)	Malta	6,282 pupils (9–14 years)	Self-report questionnaire (Olweus definition and questionnaire)	Rate of serious bullying for once a week and several times a week is high; 1 in 3 pupils involved as victim or perpetrator; 60.5% self-declared victims; 48.9% self-declared bullies.
Collins, McAleavy and Adamson (2004)	Northern Ireland	1,079 primary pupils (year 6); 1,353 post-primary pupils (year 9)	Self-report questionnaire (Olweus definition and questionnaire)	40% primary pupils bullied to some degree (4% several times a week); 30% post-primary pupils bullied (3% several times a week); 25% primary bullied others; 28% post-primary bullied others

Interesting insights do emerge when Ireland is compared to England (Whitney and Smith, 1993) and Northern Ireland (Collins, McAleavy and Adamson, 2004) (see Table 1). Results from England indicate that a high percentage of pupils are bullied, 27 per cent of 2,623 primary pupils, while in Northern Ireland, 40 per cent of 1,079 pupils admitted being bullied. This latter result could indicate not simply a higher prevalence of bullying in Northern Ireland but also that the school culture there may be more vigilant and aware regarding bullying – being more open to the possibility because of the history of sectarian violence within the community. Table 2 highlights the data from studies that are quantitative, using self-report questionnaires regarding the extent of bullying in various countries. If bullying is so prevalent at an international level then it requires teachers to have the self-efficacy to intervene.

Table 2 Cross-cultural comparison of the prevalence of bullying

Research	Country	Sample	Methodology	Findings
Olweus (1993)	Norway	140, 000 pupils (8–16 years)	Self-report questionnaire (Olweus definition and questionnaire)	9% reported being bullied; 7% reported bullying others now and then or more often

Research	Country	Sample	Methodology	Findings
Kalliotis (2000)	Greece	117 pupils (68 girls, 49 boys) (11–12 years)	'Life in School' self-report questionnaire (Arora and Thompson, 1987)	Combined percentage results were available for this study with each of the five schools involved in the study reporting 30% of pupils having been bullied at some time in the school year. Girls reported less incidence of being bullied.
Wolke et al. (2001)	Germany England	3,449 English pupils (6–8 years); 1,538 German pupils (8 years)	Structured interview (Olweus definition and questionnaire)	24% of English pupils became victims every week with 8% of German pupils; 2.5%–4.5% English boys engaged every week in bullying, with 7.5% German boys; no differences found between girls
Nazuboka (2003)	Zambia England	522 English pupils (270 boys, 252 girls); 248 Zambian pupils (143 boys, 105 girls) (7–19 years)	'Life in School' self-report questionnaire (Arora and Thompson, 1987)	English pupils reported proportionally more incidents of bullying than Zambian pupils. Behaviour more predominant among boys than girls in both countries, significantly more so among English pupils.

Criticisms of methodologies

It is difficult to make valid comparisons especially as any understanding of bullying and measure of bully and victim problems reported in research depends on the definition used, as well as the instrument employed to measure it (Kalliotis, 2000). Besag (1989) infers that data from one country cannot be freely generalised to another. The use of different definitions, even the semantics of the word bullying, together with sample selection and data collection procedures employed at international research level, make bullying more complicated and difficult for multi-national comparisons. The reliance on the Olweus self-report questionnaire brings reliability into question, with translation of the questionnaire into different languages being required, which would include a definition of bullying. The definition used in these questionnaires will differ according to the country where the study is undertaken.

When analysis is made of the many empirical studies conducted it is evident that there are wide-ranging methodological differences (see Tables 1 and 2). Kalliotis (2000), in his study of 117 Greek eleven- and twelve-year-olds, argued that the 'Life in School' questionnaire, as adapted from Arora and Thompson (1987), concentrated mainly on physical rather than psychological aggression. However, reference was not made to verbal or social bullying behaviour in the questionnaire and results refer mainly to physically hitting, hurting another, threat and extortion. No mention is made of name-calling or exclusion. Other studies referred to in Tables 1 and 2 include reference to the self-report questionnaire that has been adapted from Olweus (1993).

In the comparative studies of Nabuzoka (2000), (England and Zambia), and Wolke et al. (2001) (Germany and England), larger samples of pupils were used in the element of the study completed with English pupils. This indicates that the studies may be unreliable, thereby reducing the validity of each study. Nabuzoka (2003) also uses the 'Life in School' questionnaire, and mentions that indigenous definitions of bullying may be different in Zambia compared to England. Also, different behaviours may constitute bullying in Zambia. This highlights definitions as a major issue in cross-cultural referencing. It would be helpful to interview teachers in the aforementioned countries to see if their attitudes affect their self-efficacy in dealing with the problem.

Methodologies to date

To date, research on bullying has been limited by a focus on the characteristics of individual bullies and victims and an over-reliance on questionnaire methodologies. Questionnaires do provide assessments of the prevalence of bullying problems, characteristics of the bully and/or victim, and the type and location of bullying episodes, and follow-up interviews will extract peers' attitudes. The anonymous nature of the questionnaire recognises the importance of the subjective experience in defining bully or victim status. However, as Craig, Henderson and Murphy (2000) observe from their Canadian study, questionnaires are limited by the children's ability to report and their inability to identify the complex multi-level processes underlying bully–victim interactions. Bullying has to be examined from within the social context in which it occurs. Rigby (2002) perceives that respondents give socially desirable responses to questionnaires, making results inaccurate. Interviews in relation to bullying are rare as a methodology (Cullingford and Morrison, 1995; Torrance, 2000). In conducting a qualitative study, the data produced is 'thick description', which allows for meaning to emerge. This allows key areas to be identified that will inform practice and hopefully lead to greater teacher self-efficacy in dealing with bullying.

In conclusion, the following issues need to be highlighted regarding teacher self-efficacy for intervening in bullying:

- If teachers focus predominantly on blaming factors such as home background they are less likely to intervene.
- A systemic focus invites examination of change to the school environment that supports and tolerates bullying.
- There is a need to go beyond labelling of children as 'bullies'.
- There is a need for more clarity of definition of bullying, including events that may not simply be repeated incidents.
- Teachers need to view bullying as a child-protection issue.

References

Ananiadou, K. and Smith, P. (2002) 'Legal Requirements and Nationally Circulated Materials Against School Bullying in European Countries', *Criminal Justice*, vol. 2, pp. 471–91

Arora, C. and Thompson, D. (1987) 'Defining Bullying for a Secondary School', *Education and Child Psychology*, vol. 4, pp. 110–120

Besag, V. (1989) *Bullies and Victims in Schools*, Buckingham and Philadelphia: Open University Press

Borg, M. (1999) 'The Extent and Nature of Bullying Among Primary and Secondary Schoolchildren', *Educational Research*, vol. 41, pp. 137–53

Brooks, L. (2003) 'Death of a schoolboy', *The Guardian*, 25 September

Byrne, T. (2004) 'Bullying in the workplace' in Byrne, T., Maguire, K. and Byrne, B. (eds) *Bullying in the Workplace, Home and School: Questions and Answers*, Dublin: Blackhall, pp. 1–65

Capra, F. (1982) *The Turning Point: Science, Society and the Rising Culture*, London: Fontana

Carney, J. (2000) 'Bullied to Death: Perceptions of Peer Abuse and Suicidal Behaviour During Adolescence', *School Psychology International*, vol. 21, pp. 44–54

Collins, K., McAleavy, G. and Adamson, G. (2004) 'Bullying in Schools: A Northern Ireland Study', *Educational Research*, vol. 46, pp. 55–71

Cowie, H. and Olafsson, R. (2000) 'The Role of Peer Support in Helping the Victims of Bullying in a School with High Levels of Aggression', *School Psychology International*, vol. 21, pp. 79–95

Craig, W., Henderson, K. and Murphy, J. (2000) 'Prospective Teachers' Attitudes Toward Bullying and Victimization', *School Psychology International*, vol. 21, pp. 5–22

Cullingford, C. and Morrison, J. (1995) 'Bullying as a Formative Influence: The Relationship Between the Experience of School and Criminality', *British Education Research Journal*, vol. 21, pp. 547–60

Department of Education (1993) *Guidelines on Countering Bullying Behaviour in Primary and Post Primary Schools*, Dublin: Government Publications

Department of Health and Children (1999) *Children First: National Guidelines for the Protection and Welfare of Children*, Dublin: Government Publications

Downes, P. (2004a) *Psychological Support Services for Ballyfermot: Present and Future*, Ballyfermot: URBAN

Downes, P. (2004b) *Voices from Children: St Raphael's Primary School, Ballyfermot*, Ballyfermot: URBAN

Kalliotis, P. (2000) 'Bullying as a Special Case of Aggression: Procedures for Cross-Cultural Assessment', *School Psychology International*, vol. 27, pp. 47–64

Lane, D. (1989) 'Violent histories: bullying and criminality' in Tattum, D. and Lane, D. (eds) *Bullying in Schools*, pp. 95–105

Lucey, A. (2002) 'Bullying "a key factor in high suicide rate"', *Irish Independent*, 29 November

Morita, Y., Soeda, H., Soeda, K. and Taki, M. (1999) 'Japan', in Smith, P. K., Morita, Y., Junger-Tas, J., Olweus, D., Catalano, R. and Slee, P. (eds) *The Nature of School Bullying: A Cross-National Perspective*, London: Routledge

Nabuzoka, D. (2003) 'Experiences of Bullying Related Behaviours by English and Zambian Pupils: A Comparative Study', *Educational Research*, vol. 45, pp. 95–109

O'Moore, A., Kirkham, C. and Smith, M. (1997) 'Bullying Behaviour in Irish Schools: A Nationwide Study', *The Irish Journal of Psychology*, vol. 18, pp. 141–69

O'Regan, E. (2004) 'Suffering in silence: Fifty per cent of bullying victims are suicidal', *Irish Independent*, 15 September

Olweus, D. (1993) *Bullying at School: What We Know and What We Can Do*, Oxford: Blackwell

Rigby, K. (2002) *New Perspectives on Bullying*, London: Kingsley

Rigby, K. and Slee, P. (1999) 'Suicidal Ideation Among Adolescent School Children, Involvement in Bully-Victim Problems, and Perceived Social Support', *Suicide and Life Threatening Behaviour*, vol. 29, pp. 119–130

Rigby, K., Smith, P. and Pepler, D. (2004) 'Working to prevent school bullying: key issues' in Smith, P., Pepler, D. and Rigby, K. (eds) *Bullying in Schools: How successful can Interventions be?*, Cambridge and New York: Cambridge University Press, pp. 1–13

Rivers, I. and Soutter, A. (1996) 'Bullying and the Steiner School Ethos: A Case Study Analysis of a Group Centred Educational Philosophy', *School Psychology International*, vol. 17, pp. 359–77

Roland, E. (2002) 'Bullying, Depressive Symptoms and Suicidal Thoughts', *Educational Research*, vol. 44, pp. 55–67

Smith, P. (1991) 'The Silent Nightmare: Bullying and Victimisation in School Peer Groups', *The Psychologist*, vol. 14, pp. 243–8

Smith, P. K. (1997) 'Bullying in Schools: the UK Experience and the Sheffield Anti-Bullying Project', *Irish Journal of Psychology*, 18, 2, pp. 191–201

Stephenson and Smith, (1989) 'Bullying in the junior school' in Tattum, D. and Lane, D. (eds) *Bullying in Schools*, Stoke-on-Trent: Trentham Books, pp. 45–59

Stone, A. (2004) 'Suicide teen's letter reveals taunts and jeers from bullies', *Irish Independent*, 29 September

Torrance, D. (2000) 'Qualitative Studies into Bullying Within Special Schools', *British Journal of Special Education,* vol. 27, pp. 16–21

Webb, R. and Vulliamy, G. (2001) 'The Primary Teacher's Role in Child Protection', *British Educational Research Journal*, vol. 27, 59–77

Whitney, I. and Smith, P. (1993) 'A Survey of the Nature and Extent of Bullying in Junior/Middle and Secondary Schools', *Educational Research*, vol. 35, pp. 3–25

Wolke, D., Woods, S., Stanford, K. and Schulz, H. (2001) 'Bullying and Victimization of Primary Schoolchildren in England and Germany: Prevalence and School Factors', *British Journal of Psychology*, vol. 92, pp. 673–96

37

Towards a Narrative Practice: Conversations in a City Centre School

Thérèse Hegarty

White and Epston's 1990 book, *Narrative Means to Therapeutic Ends*, resonates with the work I have been developing with troubled children, a work I had been unable to theorise but felt quite passionate about. The authors gave me a language with which to articulate what I had been doing and instigated a learning curve that continues to this day. Working with an inner-city school between 2003 and 2006 and employed by the School Completion Project, I was accountable to the dream of supporting children to stay in school as long and as happily as possible. Two days each month were spent working alongside students, teachers and parents; this is one account of some of my efforts that, it is hoped, will convey a brief insight into the narrative ideas that inspire my work.

We make sense of our lives through stories, but our lives are made up of many stories. My life as a teacher, a mother, a gardener or as a music lover are all true but neither one is the whole truth. As our identity develops in a social context, one story often comes to dominate our identity. White claims that 'persons experience problems, for which they frequently seek therapy, when the narratives in which they are 'storying' their experience, and/or in which they are having their experience 'storied' by others do not sufficiently represent their lived experience, and that, in these circumstances, there will be significant aspects of their lived experience that contradict these dominant narratives' (2000, p. 14). Children, whose reputation in school does not sufficiently represent their lived experience, very rarely ask for therapy, but often act out or withdraw. A problem-saturated

---

Note: I agreed not to name any teacher or student in this article apart from the principals. All names have therefore been altered to protect confidentiality.

story can then begin to dominate the conversations that take place about them in the school community:

> Deficit descriptions are often taken on board in a totalising way, as if they touched the very essence of the person. Teachers, parents, and children themselves start to assume that a person is, for example, an addictive personality in their very essence, a school refuser by nature, a behaviourally disordered being-to-the-core, an unintelligent person for all time and in all contexts. Thought of in this way, deficit descriptions have a stabilising effect on people. Like photographic fixing chemicals, they make images of personhood permanent. Despite educational and therapeutic efforts to the contrary, deficit descriptions often work to fix a particular understanding of a person. In this way they work against change. (Winslade and Monk, 1999, p. 60)

In Narrative Practice we work to externalise problems. The person is not the problem. The problem is the problem. It is an approach which 'encourages persons to objectify and, at times, to personify the problems they experience as oppressive' (White and Epston, 1990, p. 38) This practice 'decreases unproductive conflict … undermines the sense of failure … paves the way for persons to cooperate with each other ... and opens up possibilities for persons to take action to retrieve their lives and relationships from the problem and its influence' (p. 39). There is a whole richness of experience outside the dominant story. Externalisation maps the effect of the problem on the person's life and the effect of the person on the life of the problem. In doing this, space opens up for 'unique outcomes', which fall outside the plot of the dominant story. We invite persons to be an audience to their own neglected stories. This enhances the stories and their sense of personal agency. By ascribing meaning to these initiatives, a counter-story can be excavated and a new preferred identity can emerge.

Narrative practice involves viewing persons as experts on their own lives. We do not try to change behaviour. Instead we try to understand experience. 'Experience is not equivalent to the more familiar concept of behaviour. The latter implies an outside observer describing someone else's actions, as if one were an audience to an event; it also implies a standardised routine that one simply goes through. An experience is more personal, as it refers to an active self, to a human being who not only engages in, but also shapes, an action. We can have an experience but we cannot have behaviour: we describe the behaviour of others but we characterise our own experience. It is not customary to say "let me tell you about my behaviour"; rather we tell about experiences, which include actions and feelings, but also reflections about those actions and feelings. The distinguishing criterion is that the communication of experience tends to be "self-referential"' (Bruner, 1986, p. 5).

Narrative practice also concerns itself with the documents that describe persons. The written word has great validity in the Western world and for this reason narrative practice uses letters and certificates to make permanent new meanings and understandings that support persons' preferred stories.

The children are not the problem; the FEUD is the problem

One of the first challenges put to me was to conduct an anger management programme with fifth class students. My immediate response was to refuse, but to seek another way to intervene, as offering students an anger management programme might contribute to a definition of these children in which anger dominated. I asked to meet with the two teachers involved and their description of the problem was quite different. They described an ongoing feud between the two classes that resulted in the yard being a bit of a battleground on a daily basis.

I then met each class separately and through Circle Time explored with them what sort of actions supported them to get on with each other and what sort of actions undermined that 'getting on'. I asked them to assess how well they got on together. Each class reported that they got on well within the classroom but could not get on with the other class. Neither class expressed a preference for this state of affairs continuing. Before my second visit I wrote a curious letter to each class asking for their cooperation to work together:

Dear Maura and girls,

It was lovely to meet you on Friday and hear your ideas about what helps people get on and what spoils people getting on. I learned a lot from listening to you. I'm enclosing the list we made together and I think it is full of ideas.

Do you ever watch the news? Have you seen the trouble that is going on in Israel and Palestine at the moment? When I was reading over your list I began to wonder what would happen there, if people made a choice to live by your helpful list and to try not to live by your unhelpful list. What do you think would happen? If you get a chance to look at the news and think about this question, I think your ideas would be very interesting.

I think you know that I also talked to Ms Swann's class. They also came up with an interesting list that you will find out about tomorrow.

I also asked them on a scale of 1–10 how well they get on in the classroom together and their score was really high like yours. If both groups can get a high score in the classroom do you think we could work together for all the 35 girls to get a high score together as a big group? The good news is that they too are willing to work at it.

I'm dying to find out what will happen when two groups who want to solve a problem work together on it. In the meantime you might take a few minutes to fill in the attached sheet. This is to make sure that no good ideas get lost along the way.

Best wishes

Thérèse

On the sheet I asked for their ideas and I asked them to draw a time in the past when they got on well with someone from the other class. I wanted their expertise and I wanted positive stories from the past to be brought out of hiding. Before meeting together I asked to speak with Pauline. She seemed to have a lot of power in the group. Others seemed to ask her through eye contact whether they should cooperate with me. I told Pauline I could not solve this problem without her help and I truly believed this to be the case. I was astounded by her response. 'Me! You want to ask me! Nobody here listens to me. I'm only known for fighting.' I asked if she would prefer to be known for something else. Again she was definite. 'There is no way you can change what people think of me. You only have to look at what is written down in the yard book. I bet that will go to the secondary school too.' I persisted and asked her if she could help me solve the battle of the yard. She then gave me the whole history of the problem, which had begun outside the school eighteen months previously. Not only did she tell me who the other key players in my proposed peace process were but she went to the other class and brought them to me. Because I saw the feud as the problem, rather than the girls, they were able to unite against it. Half an hour later when I met with the classes together, paired them randomly with someone from the opposite class and asked them to compare the lists we had made the first day, Pauline and another girl were conducting mini-negotiations under my feet. By the end of this session everyone was united against the feud and started to brainstorm tiny initiatives each of them could take to undermine its influence. Nobody was being blamed and the problem was clearly the problem.

On my third visit I took the classes to the yard and asked them to collect signatures from each other according to certain criteria. Children who had never spoken found themselves discussing sport, fashion and pop music and found much in common. They concluded that the battle zone had turned into a peace line. They ceremoniously shook hands. I then asked them to write the story of what had happened. I wanted to 'thicken the description' (Geertz, 1983) of the initiatives they had taken, the meaning of these initiatives and the hopes and dreams with which these initiatives were in keeping. 'The endurance of new stories, as well as their elaboration, can also be enhanced by recruiting an "external' audience"' (White and Epston, 1990, p. 17). Using language taken directly from the children's own writings, I composed a certificate for them, which was given publicly at an event involving their parents. In this way the new story began to become embedded in a wider social domain. Who needed anger management now? The feud never developed again.

Watermill Primary School

Escape from Fighting Certificate

This is to certify that

_____

belongs to a group of 35 girls who have turned their back on fighting and have chosen to cooperate, forgive and work together. They have made this choice in preparation for taking on the task of being the 6th class leaders in Watermill Primary School.

They have given up fighting and chosen friendship. They have become allies not enemies. They have found that they are happier as a result. Any school who has a battle zone in the yard should think of contacting the Watermill girls for advice on how to turn a battle zone into a peace line!

_____

Thérèse Hegarty

The peaceful school project

When Thérèse came to our school she started working with all of the different classes. When she came to my class we did Circle Time and we talked about our feelings, and by the time Thérèse would leave at the end of the day everyone would be happy and all our problems were gone. She helped many different children in many ways.

Thérèse brings us to our own special place and it is called the quiet room. The quiet room is a place where you can relax and tell about your feelings. In the quiet room there are beanbags, cuddly teddies, pillows, blankets and all sorts of flashing lights. No matter what, she would help you with your feelings. If you were sad she would make you happy and if you were happy then Thérèse would be happy.

But the two things I like most was that Thérèse had the most wonderful stories and the two stories I liked most were *A Wibble called Bipley* and *The Frog who Longed for the Moon to Smile*, and the other thing that I liked was that me and some of my friends made a fantastic film about our feelings. Even though Thérèse is gone there will still be a part of her in the school and in every student she worked with.

Daisy Braitway, Sixth class

I asked Daisy to write an account of our work together because I wanted the children to have a voice. To that voice I now want to add my version of the same story. There continued to be a concern with fighting, name-calling, and arguing in the school as a whole, a concern that is echoed in almost every school I have been involved with in recent years. That concern and the resulting frustration, discouragement and tiredness, which teachers experience, can give us a clue to what we really long for. We can enquire into what is absent but implicit. Describing this process in therapy, White explains: 'That which is absent but implicit that these enquiries bring forth can include hopes that things would be different in one's life, "promises" of better things to come, "dreams" of a life lived more fully, "anticipation" of arriving at a particular destination in life, "visions" of new possibilities, "wishes" to be elsewhere, to be in other territories of life and so on. Once identified, these can be richly described' (2000, p. 38).

I believe that these dreams, hopes and visions can be explored with children and the resulting conversations can begin to change the discourses in the school. I believe that in planning a Social, Personal and Health Education (SPHE) programme, teachers need to take seriously their own dreams, visions and hopes for children's relationships with themselves, each other and the wider world and create opportunities for children to taste these dreams. For that reason we began a whole-school SPHE programme exploring peace. When Daisy talks about problems being gone at the end of the day, I understand her to be describing an experience where blaming practices were replaced by externalising problems and where children's experience was heard and respected. Children were encouraged to be aware of, and to value, their feelings, even the uncomfortable ones, as a tool to self-understanding, but to choose actions which expressed those feelings in respectful ways. When Daisy talks about feelings, these were no trivial things, as the level of fear, grief and responsibility in her own life over these years had been very significant.

The previous principal of the school had a big dream of peace. She was concerned that in this fast, urban, noisy environment it was difficult for children to experience peace. She set up a small multi-sensory room. Her successor took it a step further and with a generous grant from Allied Irish Banks, converted a full-size classroom into a multi-sensory room. Now, exploring peace was easy and the children valued it highly.

> When I go down to the quiet room I feel so relaxed. The sound of the bubbles is great and if you were angry you could go down and sit down and take a few deep breaths and relax. It is soooooooooo – good. I wish my bedroom was like that. The lights make me feel comfy. When I feel tired and I go down I don't be tired anymore!

> The quiet room is all about letting your feelings out of your mind, to relax and come down and let your anger out of your body, listen to the soft music and relax, tuck a teddy in your arms. There is no place like the quiet room. I just enjoy it every time I go.

All the colours are lovely … and the kids don't mess 'cos they like it so much.

I think the multi-sensory room is a great place to go when you are angry or just need to chill out … It's a very peaceful place. I wish there was one in my house. I say my Ma would like it very much.

Fifth class students

In the quiet room experiences can be shared and stories can be created. Visualisations can be enjoyed, therapeutic stories can be read and classical music can be enjoyed as we curl up with teddies or even sleep. I believe it is a unique experience that will never leave the children and will inform a search for rest and peace throughout their lives.

The care team

A care team has been in operation in this school for three years. Its principal aim is to look out for needy children who may be having difficulty coping with school life. This year I have participated in this team, as there is a boy (Ryan) in my class with severe behavioural problems. The home circumstances of this child are also extremely difficult. The care team meetings were attended by Ryan's Special Needs Assistant (SNA), two support teachers and the principal.

Through these meetings I became aware of Ryan's family background, which helped me understand the root of his problems. The meetings provided the members with the opportunity to express our concerns about Ryan. My initial role, as class teacher, was to discuss his behaviour in the classroom and on the yard. The group then considered strategies to best deal with his disruptive behaviour. The group provided a back-up support to what was happening in the classroom. The advice of a clinical psychologist was also sought. She observed in the classroom and joined in with the care team meetings. We discussed development to date and planned further interventions to deal with Ryan's challenging behaviour.

The greatest challenge in this case was dealing with Ryan's parents. The care team provided great support in this area. Collectively we spoke to his parents, explaining the problems we were having with their son and discussed possible ways to coordinate our efforts at school with their efforts at home. Members of the team referred Ryan's parents to relevant local services that could help them.

I think the phrase 'a problem shared is a problems halved' is appropriate to refer to when describing these meetings. To have a team of professionals to discuss problems, plan improvements and evaluate developments meant that there was more than one teacher dealing with a difficult situation. It also meant that there was cohesion between the parties concerned. Consequently, decisions could be made quickly and effectively. This was of enormous benefit to the child.

Class Teacher

Care teams or pastoral care teams are common now and each school develops its own structure. We decided to meet once a fortnight at a fixed time for about eighty minutes. The time was written into the timetable of all non-classroom teachers so that they could be available either to attend or to supervise for the most important participant, the class teacher. At each meeting we shared our answers to four questions:

- What do we appreciate about this child at the moment?
- What concerns do we have?
- Listening to each other, what plans might we put in place?
- When we will review our progress?

We have tackled problems rather than children through this process and, with the benefit of the presence of several teachers, have made very appropriate referrals. We have been joined by parents, family support workers, the Education Welfare Officer and psychologists. Sometimes we simply found ourselves acknowledging that we were in fact doing all we could. We often found ourselves in awe of the strength and resilience of children. Perhaps the greatest success was an amelioration of teacher isolation.

As my time comes to an end in the school, the teachers have reached a conclusion that we are more effective when we include parents in the care-team meetings. A narrative approach would include not only parents but also the children themselves and centre their understandings in all the conversations. I could have pushed this idea and often struggled with this dilemma, but I can sit more comfortably with having followed the best thinking of the staff, allowing them to reach their own conclusions.

From 'worst class in the school' to 'learning the adults'

We done all sorts of things with Thérèse, like in second we done a sand box and we called it the 'mean free zone'. We played games about cooperation and feelings. In third class we played games as well and cooperation, like making squares out of shapes. We learned how many hats there is for thinking. The colours were yellow, black, white, blue, red, and green. We learned other classes as well and we learned adults. We built towers and we did drama and learned cooperation songs. I thought it was very good fun.

When we were in second class we had to work on bullying. The activity was a sandbox and we had to pick a teddy and tell the problem. Also in second class we had to work on cooperation because we weren't very good at sharing.

In second class we did the sand box and we were trying to get the bullying out and we did it!

By second class this group had gotten themselves quite a bad reputation. They were difficult to manage. Competitions for negative attention were common. Telling tales was endemic. I decided to ask them if they thought there was a problem and how they would name it. Their names were 'bullying' and 'meanness'. But I had a problem. How would I get their attention for long enough to explore the problems when their listening skills were so poor? To try to get a focus and to explore the problem in a distanced way I brought in a sand box and a box of small animals. Each child chose one animal and in the sand we created a story about 'the animal school with a serious bullying problem'. To my great relief all twenty-seven of them listened as the story built up. We brainstormed all the feelings in the school as a result of this bullying problem. We asked about the influence of the problems on the teacher and the parent animals. By the end nobody was on the side of bullying. At a later session we brainstormed tiny initiatives that each animal might take to reduce the effect of the problem. Everyone had an idea and the tiny initiatives added up to something a little bigger. Some hope emerged that bullying and meanness could give way to stories of inclusion, care and sharing. Choices seemed possible.

It was in third class that the real change began. Their new teacher made a commitment to notice and affirm everything positive she saw. It was exhausting, but by November she was beginning to see change. My role was simply to augment this by creating positive experiences and opportunities to articulate what was positive. I began with four months of cooperative tasks, games, artwork, and construction. To succeed they had to pull together and they discovered that they could. On one occasion when a child scribbled on everyone else's work they all expressed their disappointment without naming or blaming her. She later stopped me on the corridor and did some spontaneous self-evaluation.

I felt that the group needed to be able to argue and discuss from different positions so I took them through Edward de Bono's thinking skills programme and once they had six ways to think, we set about applying these skills to decision-making. Finally, we demonstrated our skills to another class and to a group of teachers, who reflected back that they had learned something valuable themselves. It was essential to me that this new identity as a class was given a wider audience so that the counter-story about cooperation and thinking well could spread through the school community.

Final hopes

'Discourse can be thought of as circulating through and finding expression in, many conversations, ultimately shaping the thinking of who participates in these conversations. Eventually this thinking finds expression in the decisions that shape the organisations of the school community. If we can make changes that are transformative enough to dominant discourses, the effects of counselling can be felt in the structuring of the life in the school. For counsellors, working to change the discourse around specific problem issues is perhaps more manageable than operating directly on organisational structures and systems' (Winslade and Monk, 1999, p. 97).

It seems appropriate for me to leave now. The care team will continue and all the classes visit the quiet room regularly. I believe I have modelled how problems can help us plan a focused Social, Personal and Health Education (SPHE) programme. I hope that I have contributed to a practice which understands problems as stories, among many stories, which can take many possible directions, and that problems will not succeed in dominating the identity of any child or any group in the future.

References

Bruner, E. (1986) 'Experience and its Expressions' in Turner, V. and Bruner, E. (eds) *The Anthropology of Experience*, Champaign, Illinois: University of Illinois Press, Chapter 1

De Bono, E. (1992) *Six Thinking Hats for Schools*, Victoria, Australia: Hawker Brownlow Education

Geertz, C. (1983) *Local Knowledge: Further essays in interpretive anthropology*, New York: Basic Books

Sunderland, M. (2000) A Wibble called Bipley [and a few Honks], Brackely, UK: Speechmark

Sunderland, M. (2000) The Frog who Longed for the Moon to Smile, Chesterfield, UK: Winslow

White, M. (2000) *Reflections on Narrative Practice*, Adelaide, Australia: Dulwich Centre Publications

White, M. and Epston D. (1990) *Narrative Means to Therapeutic Ends*, New York: Norton

Winslade, J. and Monk, G. (1999) *Narrative Counselling in Schools: Powerful and Brief*, Thousand Oaks, CA: Corwin Press

38

Peer Mediation: the Power and Importance of Children's Voices

Áine Murphy

This chapter looks at how the peer mediation process reflects the principles of various theorists, in particular Paulo Freire. The author, however, acknowledges that although Freire's views remain hugely influential, they are inevitably restricted by the passing of time, and therefore must be supported by the work of more contemporary educationalists, particularly Devine and Zappone. The peer mediation process has been set up on a pilot basis in a school in West Tallaght in an attempt to encourage children to understand and manage the conflicting situations they encounter in their own lives. The school in question is a vertical school (infants through sixth class) of mixed gender and is situated in an area of designated disadvantage.

The primary focus of peer mediation is to build children's problem-solving and communicative skills and develop in them a deeper respect for others. It is hoped that some improvements in behaviour would materialise as a result. The programme offers children the opportunity to take an active part in decision-making about issues that interest and concern them. It enables children to provide a mediation service for minor conflicts among their peers.

Peer mediation in an education context is seen as an alternative means of dealing with conflict. It is unlike the conventional arbitration or judicial processes in that the responsibility is given solely to the children. It involves a third party intervening in a dispute; this third party is a peer of the disputants rather than a higher authority. Farrell (2005) applauds this process for having the potential to 'develop children's sense of their own worth and that of others, their capacity to manage their emotions, their ability to learn, and the social and personal skills that they will need as adults including confidence and ability to manage conflict' (2005, p. 9).

Peer mediation is based on a fundamental respect for all. The school ethos must be one that values each individual child. The school must provide a context 'in which the seeds sown could flourish' (Farrell, 2005, p. 16). According to Farrell, 'teamwork' and 'collaboration' are desired from the staff if the programme is to be effective. Conflict is an inevitable aspect of human relationships. Peer mediation is a programme that aims to enable children to deal with conflicting situations in their own lives. A situation where unresolved conflict exists is the antithesis of a good learning atmosphere. In dealing with such problems an understanding of pupils' behaviour is necessary. Teachers must understand that children have 'reasons for their behaviour' and that 'the behaviour is the problem and not the child' (Farrell, 2005, p. 9). The school needs to take ownership over its programme from the beginning and must adapt it to suit its own needs.

The conventional approach of 'behaviour management' has proven ineffective. The child acts in a certain way, the teacher reacts in the way the child expects and as a result the child is given confirmation of her self-image, and therefore the behaviour has accomplished its goal. Peer mediation can assist in building the child's confidence and self-esteem, enabling a better understanding of emotions and conflict, developing communicative and problem-solving skills and perhaps even improving the child's behaviour.

Training involves a series of seven workshops – six successive weekly half-day workshops and one final all-day workshop. During the series of seven workshops, the pupils are introduced to the various steps involved in the mediation process, as well as the set of ground rules which include *no interrupting* and *no name-calling*. These rules are designed to encourage cooperation and boost self-esteem. The children explore conflicting situations through role-play, group work, discussion and reflection.

An entire class group participates in the training (usually fifth class). Unfortunately, not all children are required as mediators the following year; the mediators are selected deliberately. Where possible, a child with good literacy skills is paired with a child with good communicative skills to create a balanced team. They must apply formally for the position and undergo an interview before being selected. The process is treated very seriously. They must be willing to go *on patrol* at yard-times and keep a record of children who are in need of mediation.

Mediation is totally voluntary. Nobody is forced to attend. Each session involves the interaction of four children – two mediators and two disputants. The role of the mediators is to help the disputants to identify the problems and achieve the solutions. In response to what the disputants tell them, the mediators fill out two worksheets. The first worksheet is *Problems and Feelings* and the second is *Brainstorming, Give and Take and The Final Agreement*.

The steps are quite consistent in each session. Firstly, the mediators welcome and introduce the disputants and revise the ground rules. They then offer both disputants the opportunity to share their story with the group and the mediators repeat the story and ask for clarification. Next, the main problems are written down. The mediators now give the disputants the opportunity to speak with the mediators privately (it is often found that the children speak more openly in the absence of the other disputant). Then the possible solutions are written up and the disputants discuss which they are willing to agree on. Finally, the four children sign 'the final agreement'.

Farrell (2005, p. 1) reminds us that 'relationships are at the core of teaching'. Teacher–pupil relationships must be based on a mutual respect. Pupils no longer respect teachers simply because of their position – the element of fear left with corporal punishment. Nowadays this respect must be earned. The Victorian perspective that children should be seen and not heard is disrespectful of the child. Children are entitled to have their voices heard. Farrell asserts that 'children are not waiting to become human beings. They already are' (2005, p. 3), and ought to be respected as such. Adults need to recognise that the behaviour is the problem, not the child, and that every child 'irrespective of behaviour, is deserving only of total respect' (Farrell, 2005, p. 4). Farrell's 2005 report is extremely positive. The comments made by the teachers, children and principal of the school in question are very encouraging and all involved have indicated that the programme has been constructive, not only for the children but the school as a whole. One such comment reads:

> Already there is informal mediation going on in the yard and to see that is just fantastic. You'd see them asking those in a fight to tell their stories and say how they are feeling, and then that often seems to be enough for those who have been fighting and they go off happy! And that's often all that children need – to be listened to and to vent and then it's all over. (Farrell, 2005, p. 12)

Peer mediation offers a promising alternative to conventional approaches to dealing with errant behaviour. The programme can be perceived as a balance between the Freirean concepts of freedom and authority. Both freedom and authority are mutually conscious of their own limitations. Authority recognises our ability to adapt and change through the process of intercession, while freedom respects the need for boundaries to our will. Freire's internal authority (autonomy) is examined next to an authority of modern culture (technical training). Freire's concept of freedom has two elements: adaptation and change, and dialogue. Adaptation and change will be juxtaposed with Zappone's concept of education as a Living System under the heading 'Change', and dialogue will be juxtaposed with Devine's notion of Adult Discourse under the heading 'Communication'.

Change

Change is a significant element of our lives. Our contemporary epoch has been, and continues to be, a time of constant change. We must be open to change if we are to thrive in the world. Freire echoes constructivist thought in underlining the fact that we humans are active in the world and must come to understand change and its rationale. It is through our active involvement in the world that our future is constructed. 'The future does not make us; we make ourselves in the struggle to make it' (Freire, 2004, p. 34). Freire believes in the liberating value of education. He states that the task of the educator is to enable the children to take ownership over their own learning. Education must facilitate experimentation and questioning. A child must be actively engaged if learning is to emerge. Education, therefore, must be concerned with adaptation and change.

Zappone examines the system and describes the ultimate education system as 'A Living System', one that is constantly changing, that 'accommodates capacities, cultures, learning paths and achievement outcomes' (2002, p. 82). Only by achieving this 'Living System' can equality in children's education be achieved. In her opinion education ought to be a system that is 'alive' and 'organic' (2002, p. 83), generating life and equality for all children from all backgrounds. According to Devine, if children are to be considered 'active social beings' (Devine, 2003, p. 111), a system that is stationary cannot adapt to the changing needs of the child. (2003, p. 111); according to Zappone, a flexible system is required if we wish to release, direct, activate and enlarge the powers of *every* child from *every* social community, 'our current systems can and should be changed in order to achieve equality' (2002, p. 81). This new model system would aim to promote 'dialogue, decision-making, resolution of conflicts and reduction of moving in contradictory directions' (2002, p. 83). In making significant systemic changes we need to establish a coordinated, integrated multi-systems approach across schools, boards, communities, regions, professions and departments.

Communication

In highlighting the importance of dialogue, Freire states, 'it is through communication that human life can hold meaning' (2004, p. 58). Dialogue, according to Freire, involves the interaction of two people. 'Reflection' and 'Action' are the two essential elements of Freire's dialogue. It is the interaction between the two that fosters the process of dialogue. Reflection for Freire requires thinking through 'the what of things, their what for, how, in whose favour and against what or whom they are' as they are discovered (2004, p. 86), because it is only by 'acting in the world that we make ourselves' (2004, p. 72).

Devine has developed her own viewpoints while echoing the work of other theorists such as Foucault and Giddens. Devine, like Freire, recognises and appreciates the magnitude of dialogue. She also recognises the negative role our language can play on children and conveys this through an analysis of adult discourse on children in Ireland. Our language does indeed reflect reality, but it also constructs realities because the use of language impacts on our actions. It is, after all, through the power of dialogue that we become accustomed to norms of behaviour. Devine cites Foucault in stating that 'power is exercised not through physical coercion and punishment but through the promotion of discourses which define and normalise our behaviour and identities in line with certain ideals' (2003, p. 112). She describes how children are normalised to live and act in a certain way through adult discourse. Teachers and other adults enforce power in schools through the use of judgements. She examines how adults exercise the power they have over children through adult discourse in determining what the children should learn, how they should learn it and how they should behave. In doing so, certain standards are established and these standards become the norm. Children have often been regarded as 'other' and adults as 'norm'. Devine continues: 'Children were defined as in a state of incompleteness, to be formed and reformed in terms of the adult ideal' (2003, p. 112). The development of the Revised Primary Curriculum is an example of adult discourse on children. The need for active and constructive learning was acknowledged and the children were considered active agents in their own education, however, they were not consulted at any stage in the compilation of the curriculum. As Devine states, this paradox indicates a 'particular power relation between adults and children, itself governed by discourses relating to the nature of children and childhood' (2001, p. 146). This omission by the DES highlights the fact that there is a significant disparity between theory, policy and practice.

Economic discourse – an authority of modern culture

Education that is entirely established by those in authority is reduced to 'technical training rather than educating' (Freire, 2004, p. 1). As everything is predetermined, the only thing we need to do is adapt ourselves to suit the process. Freire sees this type of education as 'pure professional teacher training', where the goal is the transference of technical skills to ensure productivity for industry (Freire, 2004, p. 84). Questioning and analysing are discouraged. The emphasis is placed on the product rather than the process.

Devine (2003, p. 117) examined Foucault's analysis of this economic discourse that 'permeates through the emphasis that is placed on schooling as a preparation of children for their future adult working lives'. Like Freire, Devine maintains that the purpose of our modern-day education system is to prepare the future generation for the 'maximisation of children's productivity to the ultimate benefit of the economy' (2003, p. 118), rather than actually enhancing their lives as children. Devine has found much evidence of this economic discourse in teachers' and children's views of school. Teachers were overly concerned with issues such as timetabling and preparation for entry into secondary school, while children, even at a very young age, recognised the main purpose of education as a means of getting a good job in the future. Institutionalisation is evident here. Children are conditioned into thinking in a certain way. Devine states that children have a universal understanding of the ideal pupil, 'as one who is obedient, works hard, is restrained and self-controlled' (2003, p. 119) and it is this model that they compare themselves to.

We cannot lose sight of the fact that education must always incorporate the needs of future adults to some extent. An ideal education system would embrace and celebrate childhood as an entire life stage in its own right and, in doing so, prepare children for adult life. This does not solely refer to the economy of the future. Social skills need to be developed from a young age if tomorrow's world is to be successful. Children need to learn to communicate effectively as communication is not an intrinsic skill. Children need to be trained for a democratic future. This aspect of education is particularly relevant to children coming from areas of designated disadvantage. Because of the socio-economic and domestic problems that often accompany some children from such areas, emotional or behavioural problems tend to be more pronounced and so, inevitably, more disputes ensue. The problems lie with their inability to cope with the conflicting situations they face. These coping and decision-making skills should be instilled in the children from a young age. Devine states that we fail our children when we fail to do so, 'to exclude children from decision-making in matters of concern to them is ... to detract from developing within them the critical skills with which all citizens living in a democratic pluralistic society should be equipped' (2001, p. 171).

Unemployment and early school leaving is seen by Freire as a 'fatality at the end of the century' (2004, p. 33). Children from disadvantaged areas often fall victim to the conventional education system in this way. For these children, the system neither enhances their lives as children nor trains or prepares them for the workforce. Instead, it appears to delay them from entry to the workforce. The National Economic and Social Forum Report on Early School Leavers shows us that 'approximately 13,000 children leave school annually before the completion of the Leaving Certificate' (NESF Report No. 24, 2002). Freire would see this as a result of our adaptation to society and failure to change it.

An internal authority

In combining and balancing one's own beliefs and ideas with those of others, an internal authority will emerge. Freire considers the development of an internal authority to be a crucial part of freedom and authority. A learner can only develop autonomy through experiencing freedom. It is only through interaction that the learner recognises herself/himself as actually being part of the world. According to Devine 'children are central actors within schools, yet they are frequently presumed not to have the capacity to reflect critically and constructively on their experience' (2001, p. 170). Children need to be given independence and freedom, but also support, in enabling them to construct their own knowledge and opinions in a way that is inherently rational to them. Shor speaks of the inherent element of curiosity in humans while discussing the need for the development of learner autonomy through adequate teacher support. He describes how education can either embrace or repress child inquisitiveness, depending on the approach of the teacher, 'if the students' task is to memorise rules and existing knowledge, without questioning the subject matter or the learning process, their potential for critical thought and action will be restricted' (1992, p. 12). Children are not merely empty vessels waiting to be filled with information by the superior, more knowledgeable adults. They are individuals with independent thoughts and ideas. Like adults, they combine the views of others with their own views and internalise them.

Peer mediation can be credited with representing the Freirean dynamic of freedom and authority rather than merely engaging the child in technical training. Freire maintains that both freedom *and* authority are desired if children are to be empowered to develop a true understanding of conflict resolution. Within peer mediation the children are 'active social beings' (Devine, 2003, p. 111) who intervene in the process to bring about change in behaviour and attitudes. The school culture must be prepared to accept these changes, as they will filter throughout the whole school. In peer mediation the children are being given the opportunity to make lasting changes by being permitted to (a) develop opinions, (b) voice their opinions, and (c) influence the younger more impressionable school members to do likewise.

Communication through dialogue is a hugely influential force and its power must not be underestimated. Meaningful communication can break down all sorts of barriers – from political or religious to minor home or schoolyard arguments. It is our inability or perhaps our unwillingness to communicate that becomes the central problem. Peer mediation attempts to create a safe environment where meaningful dialogue can occur. An important factor in the success of peer mediation is the skill of dialogue. For Freire, reflection and action are the two key elements of dialogue. Both reflection and action are central to the peer mediation process. Children's involvement in this process, in which they are given a voice, is a significant step in attempting to reduce the dominance of the adult discourse where 'significant steps have been made to incorporate the hidden voices into educational policy making' (Devine, 2001, p. 146).

The process of the peer mediation programme is more important than the product. The peer mediation initiative aims to enhance the coping skills of the children in training more than the disputants whose conflicts are being solved. The programme must not be seen as something that the children do, but rather as a process that has the potential to change school culture through the active intervention of the children. Undoubtedly Freire would be approving of the manner in which the mediators and disputants engage in discussion in an attempt to understand each other and unearth their own solutions. Group work, discussion, reflection and brainstorming are all central to the process. Through dialogue the children are developing an internal authority by incorporating the needs and attitudes of others with their own.

Devine believes that children are controlled within a 'disciplinary framework in which they are required to monitor their behaviour in line with a series of rules and regulations' (2001, p. 162). Peer mediation, though it involves a certain amount of adult guidance, allows children to regain their voice and some measure of autonomy. The pupils are not being given a freedom without limits; there are very definite rules that both the disputants and mediators abide by, but it is the children themselves who determine these rules. The teacher empowers the pupils with a freedom with responsibility. If peer mediation is adopted as a whole-school approach to conflict resolution, children will see and value it as part of their education. Conflict is an inevitable part of every relationship; we cannot shield our children from it and we are obligated to equip our children with skills to deal with conflict.

Change is of the essence in all our lives. It is only by actively engaging with the world and with others that we become capable of understanding and changing our world. In giving all children a voice in a 'living' education system (Zappone, 2002, p. 82), Devine asserts that we are gearing them towards the development of 'democratic participation' which will assist in incorporating 'concepts of equality, difference and respect into their world view' (2001, p. 172). If we are to be active in our world, we must engage in dialogue. Dialogue is concerned with the interdependency of reflection and action. While these are the two essential elements of Freire's dialogue, they are also the two essential elements of Devine's discourse which recognises that language *reflects* actuality but that it also impacts on our *actions*. Technical training is concerned with skills being forced on the learner as a result of economic discourse, rather than adapted to suit the needs of the individual. Freire's internal authority encompasses the wants and needs of the individual with those of others.

Children are not waiting to become human; they already are human. The work of these theorists suggests that the peer mediation process is one that recognises the power and importance of children's voices. Through peer mediation, children are given freedom to share in decision-making and take more responsibility for their own autonomy. More importantly, however, the children are given a fundamental respect. The principles of peer mediation could be extended beyond conflict resolution and throughout the curriculum in an attempt to achieve lasting change whereby Freire's freedom and authority could interrelate. The following poem highlights the need for mediation in our lives. It demonstrates how bad feeling can grow to be rage when neglected and underlines the consequences of ignoring it rather than confronting it.

A Poison Tree

I was angry with my friends:
I told my wrath, my wrath did end.
I was angry with my foe:
I told it not, my wrath did grow.
And I water'd it in fears,
Night and morning with my tears;
And I sunned it with smiles,
And with soft deceitful wiles.
And it grew both day and night,
Till it bore an apple bright,
And my foe behind it shine,
And he knew that it was mine.
And into my garden stole
When the night had veil'd the pole:
In the morning glad I see
My foe outstretch'd beneath the tree.

By William Blake
(Heaney and Hughes, eds, 1982, p. 161)

References

Department of Education and Science (1999) *Revised Primary Curriculum*, Dublin: DES

Department of Education and Science (2002) *NESF Report on Early School Leavers: Forum Report No. 24*, Dublin: DES

Devine, D. (2001) 'Locating the Child's Voice in Irish Primary Education' in Cleary, A. and Nic Ghiolla Phadraig, M. (eds) *Understanding Children*, Cork:

Oak Tree Press, vol. 1, pp. 145–174

Devine, D. (2003) *Children, Power and Schooling: How childhood is structured in the Primary School*, Stoke on Trent: Trentham Books

Farrell, S. (2005) *Peer Mediation in Schools: An Update Report on a Pilot Project*, Dublin: Mediation Bureau

Freire, P. (2004) *Pedagogy of the Indignation,* Colorado: Paradigm Publishers

Heaney, S. and Hughes, T. (eds) (1982) *The Rattle Bag*, London: Faber and Faber

Shor, I. (1992) *Empowering Education, Critical Thinking for Social Change*, Chicago: University of Chicago Press

Zappone, K. (2002) 'Achieving Equality in Children's Education' in Gilligan, A. L. (ed.) *Primary Education: Ending Disadvantage. Proceedings and Action Plan of National Forum*, Dublin: Educational Disadvantage Centre, St Patrick's College

VII

Beyond Educational Disadvantage

39

Some Conclusions

Paul Downes and Ann Louise Gilligan

The rich variety of views presented in this book is a clear indication that no one perspective, no single insight will end educational disadvantage in Ireland today. This is indeed a complex issue and one that regretfully has a long, embedded history and tradition. Yet there is an optimism here indicating that what is socially constructed can be changed. The healthy state of our economy places an imperative on all adult citizens to work tirelessly for an education system that not only allows all children and young people to achieve their range of potentials but also provides life-long opportunities to achieve that goal.

Investment in education at every generational level in a family and community is vital if those who live with the injustice of poverty are to receive the opportunity and the conditions to break this cycle.[1] Given the extent of intergenerational poverty in Ireland at this time, the level of financial commitment required would suggest that we need to revisit the percentage of Gross National Product assigned to education from the national budget and raise it by 1 per cent. The education of the electorate to this revision of tax revenue expenditure would arguably not be difficult, especially as, historically, there has always been a deep appreciation of the value and importance of education in our country.

In this concluding chapter we wish to highlight, develop and revisit some of the policy recommendations that have been made throughout the book. Furthermore, some of the key themes that have emerged from the chapters will be signalled. While there is a certain commonality in the way these themes are addressed, there is also a diversity that will hopefully encourage healthy debate. It also needs to be stated that the value of an edited collection such as this enables

---

[1] See Flynn, Chapter 8

a much-needed interdisciplinary dialogue to take place that can inform future engagement with theory, policy and practice. Finally, our recommendations will be rooted in the models of good practice that are suggested and the emerging challenges that flow from the insights of many of the contributions.

Key themes

The opening section of the book clusters a set of chapters that seek to clarify the key concepts that underpin any policy formulation in relation to what has been called 'educational disadvantage'. Reading this section leaves one in no doubt as to whether the very term 'educational disadvantage' is still an appropriate metaphor for what we aspire to create, namely, a life-long organic education system that encourages everyone in our society to achieve their full range of potentials. The challenge to stretch towards formulations that respectfully name the positive and create an understanding of educational inclusion for all is something that we cannot afford to neglect. Designations must also include the voice and response of the designated. Those named as 'educationally disadvantaged', 'marginalised', 'excluded' must be asked if these terms are acceptable to them.[2] Those students and parents who participate in a school that is 'designated disadvantaged' need to be informed about how the system speaks of their school and their response to this categorisation needs to be listened to. This may lead to the removal of the label 'designated disadvantaged' from schools. The sole purpose of this label is to secure positive discrimination for extra supports and funding, yet those supports and funding could still be provided without the use of this arguably destructive label. Other ways of describing the schools could be as 'Zone A, Zone B, Zone C' schools for priority funding or simply priority investment schools, etc.

The theme of diversity and difference emerges from a number of articles as an urgent topic for those engaged in policy formulation to address in an ongoing way. Again, the initial challenge is to clarify our thinking and ensure a set of common understandings among educationalists. Diversity in education is a mark of our age and, with over one million involved in education from early childhood to later adulthood and over forty-thousand employed, there is a need for policy formulations that will allow the implementation of a system that is truly inclusive of diversity and radically committed to eradicate negative difference.[3] While the Equality Authority and Equality Tribunals have raised awareness in relation to the amount of legislation now governing this area, those working in the education system need to be brought to a full understanding of that legislation (see also Lodge and Lynch, 2004). Connecting issues of poverty and ethnic diversity, the

---

[2] See Spring, Chapter 1
[3] See Derman-Sparks and Fite, Chapter 5; Gilligan, Chapter 4

Report of the High Level Group on Traveller Issues (2006) notes that factors extraneous to the education system can have a positive or negative impact on educational attainment, factors such as 'cultural issues, housing standards, health, childcare and parental employment status'. It is clear that for many Traveller parents, 'their negative experience in school, illiteracy and the widespread experience of exclusion' (DES, 2006, p. 22) lowers their expectations that their children will be treated fairly or with respect (p. 22). The challenge rests with those working in schools and those charged to create an inclusive system to prove such presumptions wrong.

While the National Forum on Educational Disadvantage, *Primary Education: Ending Disadvantage* (2002), highlighted a very positive debate about the need for a 'living system' of education, it is interesting that this book returns to that theme on a number of occasions. It becomes ever clearer that we need a continuous and self-renewing dynamic system of education[4] that is generously resourced and attentive to the ongoing need for learning that should mark any human life. In recent years there has been a consistent statement from policymakers and government that we need greater integration of the various initiatives that are already funded to create equality of educational provision before any new funding can be released. This call for integration, coupled with a government embargo on the appointment of new staff, has created some confusion. Integration must be led by a dynamic, joined-up system of education which requires clear protocols between and among different agencies and partners as well as examples of joined-up government at inter- and intra-departmental levels, so that a top-down leadership can facilitate and inspire bottom-up practice as part of a multi-levelled organic system.[5] Without this dual commitment, people on the ground interpret the reduction of staffing levels and the blocking of funding as postponement measures that have little to do with a strong commitment to a living, dynamic system of education. Leadership towards the integration of an education system that would focus on the unique, individual needs of each child would also involve addressing the issues of professional jealously and territorialism.

The *Bridging the Gap* project in Cork[6] emphasises the importance of schools setting goals as part of a whole-school approach to working on issues and themes. Key themes for whole-school evaluations of the future could include the extent to which good practice of process drama,[7] narrative,[8] activity-based approaches to SPHE,[9] peer mediation approaches to bullying,[10] teacher self-efficacy in relation

---

[4]   See Zappone, Chapter 2; Downes and Downes, Chapter 3
[5]   Ibid.
[6]   See Connolly, Chapter 32
[7]   See Hefferon, Chapter 25; Murphy, Chapter 26
[8]   See Hegarty, Chapter 37
[9]   See Byrne, Chapter 29
[10] See Murphy, Chapter 38; Hegarty, Chapter 37

to bullying,[11] school and community-based strategies for parental involvement,[12] learner-centred approaches to ICT,[13] transition strategies,[14] as well as best practice in literacy and mathematics are *inter alia* implemented. Key conclusions on some of these and other themes that emerged in this volume are discussed below, as well as other recommendations implied in the discussion.

Literacy

While the government report *DEIS: Delivering Equality of Opportunity in Schools* (2005) contains many essential elements necessary for real change to occur, it lacks specificity in relation to how the ideals and recommendations will actually be realised, particularly in relation to the teaching and learning of English.[15] The DEIS plan recognises the need for a whole-school approach to effectively improve literacy standards. Schools taking part in the change process must develop three-year action plans for literacy and must set targets for achievement. To help schools achieve their goals – to improve teacher self-efficacy in literacy instruction – a number of literacy advisers (*cuiditheoirí*) will be made available through the Primary Curriculum Support Programme (PCSP). It is unclear from the report exactly how many of these advisers will actually be hired, the extent of the training to be provided for them and, critically, the nature and scope of their contact time with schools.[16] The PCSP already has a small number of *cuiditheoirí* available to support schools requesting help with English. However, in the *Literacy and Numeracy in Disadvantaged Schools (LANDS)* study (DES, 2005), only a small minority of teachers (up to 15 per cent) indicated that the service was useful. Unless the new *cuiditheoir* service is tailored to address the specific needs of schools, it may have limited impact.

Schools with high levels of educational disadvantage require more time for the teaching of English if they are to get all pupils to a high standard. It is essential that the *cuiditheoir* is on-site on a regular basis to ensure continuity between whole-school planning and individual teacher planning. It is also crucial to ensure that all teachers 'own' the change process and understand the theory and rationale underpinning the desired changes.[17] Realistic achievable targets should be agreed and a system put in place to monitor progress. Teachers will require sustained support to address the gaps and weaknesses highlighted by the research. While a high level of support is necessary, it should not erode classroom instructional

---

[11] See Farrelly, Chapter 36
[12] See Mulkerrins, Chapter 12; Higgins, Chapter 10; Owens, Chapter 13; Waters, Chapter 14
[13] See Butler and Kelly, Chapter 27
[14] See Downes, Maunsell and Ivers, Chapter 34; Maunsell, Barrett and Candon, Chapter 35
[15] See Kennedy, Chapter 18
[16] Ibid.
[17] Ibid.

time. Therefore, the recommendation in the Eivers, Shiel and Shortt study (2004) that substitution cover be put in place for classroom teachers when working with the *cuiditheoir* should be considered in the DEIS strategy. This kind of quality time would also facilitate collaboration in relation to planning, teaching and assessment between class and support programmes.

Another key component of the DEIS plan is the extension of the early intervention programme *Reading Recovery* (Marie Clay) to fifty more schools in phase one (2005–2006) and a further fifty in phase two (2006–2007). It is an individualised pull-out programme for children most at risk of reading failure. Children receive a daily half-hour of focused, fast-paced instruction in reading and writing for approximately twenty weeks. Teachers are highly trained in the complexities of literacy processes and tailor instruction to the specific needs of children as identified through formative assessment tools such as running records and analysis of writing. The extension of *Reading Recovery* in schools is to be welcomed but it should not be seen as the main method of tackling reading achievement.[18] Because of its individualised nature and its focus on a particular age group, it will only reach a small percentage of the number of children who need integrated, intensive and expert teaching. Therefore, it makes sense to focus attention on the quality of instruction at the classroom level. Many of the teaching routines of the *Reading Recovery* programme can be integrated into the regular classroom and have been successful in other countries. This should also be explored in the Irish context, given the level of investment in *Reading Recovery*. Of critical importance then is the cohesion of support and classroom programmes.

A crucial feature of successful schools is their ability to reach out to parents in genuine ways and to involve them in their children's education. This is acknowledged in the DEIS plan which indicates a number of initiatives to improve involvement, including the extension of the successful Home School Community Liaison Scheme (HSCL), the promotion of paired reading projects and the creation of a new collaborative family literacy project involving the VEC sector, HSCL coordinators and the National Adult Literacy Agency. But beyond this, the DEIS plan does not provide any other ideas on how individual schools can reach the parents who traditionally do not engage with schools.[19] Successful methods of reaching all parents should be disseminated to schools.

It is vital that the DES fund the purchase of high quality literature for schools. It would also be extremely helpful if there were a list of graded Irish/British books.[20] There are many graded lists available but they contain mainly American books. A graded list relevant to Irish working-class culture would make it easier for pupils to choose books for independent reading and also inform teachers

---

[18] Ibid.
[19] Ibid.
[20] See Quinn, Chapter 15

regarding what books to use for guided reading. This would greatly ease teachers' reluctance to move away from relying overwhelmingly on basal readers.

Teachers in designated disadvantaged schools often have a large number of pupils with special educational needs or scoring below the tenth percentile. As a result of this, much of the attention paid to reading is in terms of raising the achievement of the weakest readers. This is of course extremely important and those pupils should not be neglected. However, the strongest readers in these schools are often not achieving as well as their peers nationally. Approaches focusing on pupil motivation to read and relating this to continuity with aspects of the home or extended family culture need to be developed in classes to raise the reading achievement of the pupils they deem to be their 'good readers' as well as that of the weak readers.[21]

Research on the reading behaviour of children and adolescents often focuses on 'book' reading. For many readers, books may not be the text of choice as their families read magazines and newspapers rather than books.[22] Some educators may not recognise the existence or value of this type of reading. In order to motivate students we must first meet them where they are. If they are more comfortable with magazine and newspaper reading then ways are needed to integrate this into the classroom.

Phonographix, based on the simple insight that letters are pictures of sounds, has been found not only to be a powerful remedial device, but also a preventative classroom technique. Decoding or word-knowledge is an essential skill that children with reading difficulties need to be taught. By the same token, the skill of teaching decoding is one that needs to be learned by teachers. There is a need for dissemination of the Phonographix approach to schools.[23]

Phonics instruction should not be overemphasised and decontextualised in early infant classes. Phonological awareness training cannot be neglected in infant classes but it is crucial that knowledge acquisition is not merged with knowledge application in this area. This important distinction between teaching and testing needs to be made also when it comes to the teaching of comprehension strategies. Teachers' phonological knowledge needs to be quite extensive so they can teach consistently and sensitively to local accents and incorporate phonological and phonics instruction with confidence in every situation.[24]

The recommendation of the NCCA (1999) suggests that all aspects of English should be taught in three hours per week in infant classes and in four hours per week for other classes. The recommendation in the Eivers, Shiel and Shortt survey (2004) is that the instructional time allocation for literacy should increase

---

[21] Ibid.
[22] Ibid.
[23] See Mullan, Chapter 17
[24] See Kazmierczak, Chapter 16

to ninety minutes daily. This represents a significant increase in time which is currently only four hours weekly, in contrast to many countries internationally which prioritise literacy instruction for up to two hours daily.

A vital element of any change strategy is the provision of the ninety-minute block recommended by the Eivers, Shiel and Shortt survey and international research. This issue is ignored by the DEIS plan.[25] It is important to note that providing extra time will not achieve the desired outcomes unless it is accompanied by a change in the use of the time. Teachers will require support on how to structure the ninety minutes in order to make maximum use of it. Increasing the amount of instructional time for literacy will, of itself, do little without a focus on the professional development of teachers. Literacy skills underpin every other subject in the curriculum and determine how well children can negotiate the demands of each one. Given the broad curriculum at primary level, there is a need for increased focus on how other curriculum subjects can be integrated with good practice regarding literacy teaching. It is essential that teachers' self-efficacy is developed, incorporating literacy instruction into the whole process of teaching and into various areas of the curriculum. More emphasis on, and support for, integration of literacy and the arts, such as has been developed in the *Bridging the Gap* project in Cork,[26] would be an extremely important development within schools (see also Barnardos, 2006, on the need for priority to be given to community arts and literacy).

Mathematics

Neither teachers nor members of the wider educational community can continue to rely on external factors, such as reduced class sizes and increased financial supports to schools, to alleviate the negative effects of the limited mathematics sometimes offered to pupils in schools. Rather, emphasis must be placed on the teaching–learning relationship in mathematics.[27]

Mathematics education, if it is to be inclusive, must take into account children's cultural approaches and contexts. It must be made meaningful and relevant. There is a danger that this might be interpreted as signifying that certain groups should be considered differently and thus taught distinctive mathematics programmes. Research has shown that such an approach leads to a limited and limiting curriculum. On the other hand, the notion that there should be 'one curriculum for all' also serves to perpetuate inequalities. One way of overcoming inequalities is to examine how mathematics can be taught in a way that is effective for all students. Some common themes that have been identified in

---

[25] See Kennedy, Chapter 18
[26] See Connolly, Chapter 32
[27] See Dooley and Corcoran, Chapter 19

current research on mathematics education and diversity are that connections between new ideas and old ideas must be made evident to the learner, that problems must be embedded in a context that is meaningful for the child and that emphasis must be placed on a child's intuitive representations and informal procedures.[28] Pedagogy, not content, must become multi-cultural and this can be realised by valuing the many and various ways that children make sense of mathematics. Only then can a non-threatening environment for learning mathematics be created.

A common practice in schools in areas of social disadvantage is to focus on basic skills. In the teaching and learning of these skills, reference is frequently made to money since this is considered to be directly within students' experience and of use to them. However, by limiting the mathematics taught in this way, children are being deprived of opportunities to develop mathematical skills that are central to the primary mathematics curriculum: applying and problem-solving; communicating and expressing; integrating and connecting; reasoning; implementing, understanding and recalling. The result is that access to the skills of critical reasoning is restricted to those who are already considered to be advantaged.[29]

Use of concrete materials in and of themselves is not sufficient to ensure pupil learning or even to enhance a pupil's self-concept in mathematics. It is not that the curricula throughout the world are ill-advised but rather that interaction with materials does not necessarily denote that the child is constructing his or her own meaning of the world. Often, too, speed and competition become the norm of mathematics classes. Emphasis is placed on repetitive practice of the 'method' and on correct solutions.

A recent trend in textbooks and standardised tests is the inclusion of 'realistic problems'. Although well-intentioned, these problems often bear little relationship to children's lives. Real problems stemming from 'authentic' material are a means of empowering individuals to deal with the world in which they live. The kind of material recommended includes aspects of the local environment such as parks and playgrounds, media, 'local folk' mathematics and health education. The identification of authentic resources could become the focus of curriculum planning days and might extend to include parent representatives in planning and target setting for mathematics teaching and learning.[30]

High-stakes standardised testing has a particularly negative impact on classroom practice – often leading to the phenomenon of 'teaching to the test'. In such tests, there is seldom scope to score children's reasoning, their evaluation of solutions or their ability to communicate findings. There is generally a focus on

---

[28] Ibid.

[29] Ibid.

[30] Ibid.

low-level procedural skills, a factor that has been identified as disenfranchising students from mathematics. Research conducted by Cooper and Dunne (2000) shows that children from low socio-economic status (SES) backgrounds perform as well as their peers from higher SES backgrounds on decontextualised problems but that, when presented with problems embedded in a context, their performance declines. They suggest that 'realistic' items are not actually meant to be treated as real-world problems. However, whereas children from higher SES backgrounds tend to pick up on the cues implicit in these items, children from lower SES backgrounds are more likely to draw 'incorrectly' on everyday experiences in their responses. In standardised tests, only a single correct answer is valued and, therefore, the results of these tests can mask children's mathematical reasoning.[31]

There is a need to work on teachers' pedagogical content knowledge rather than on their procedural knowledge of how to 'do' the mathematics involved. This can be addressed (as with literacy) by site-specific continuous professional development that focuses on building teachers' mathematical capacity and enhancing their teaching of mathematics through study of the curriculum and an emphasis on the effective use of teaching materials and observation of how their students learn.

The Number Worlds programme has been shown to be appropriate for children from a wide range of cultural, social and economic backgrounds, with promising examples of gains in the context of a Dublin designated disadvantaged school. It is recommended that this programme be disseminated to more schools.[32] Three salient features distinguish Number Worlds from other early years programmes: the programme teaches intuitive and explicit number knowledge that has been found to be central in later learning; it is child-centred, with hands-on activities that encourage children to construct their own mathematical meaning; and it introduces children to a broad range of contexts in which number is used (line, scale and dial representations of number and quantity) and to a range of linguistic terms that are used in these contexts.

Counting is not included in the early mathematical activities in the mathematics primary school curriculum (DES, 1999). Counting is included as one of the strand units in the number strand of the junior infant curriculum. There is a professional freedom implicit in the primary school mathematics curriculum that allows teachers to meaningfully adapt and change teaching methods, content and learning experiences to meet children's needs. However, there is a dearth of information about what type of adaptation is possible or desirable. The in-service education that has accompanied the introduction of the mathematics primary school curriculum has focused on the provision of information in relation to content and methodology and there has been a lack of

---

[31] Ibid.
[32] See Mullan and Travers, Chapter 20

focus on the specific needs of children in areas designated as disadvantaged and children with learning difficulties. This need for further professional development on how to adapt the curriculum for pupils who are not ready for a particular class curriculum is recognised in the recent DEIS (DES, 2005) and LANDS reports (DES, 2005). There is need for an early curricular intervention, more emphasis on counting in early years mathematics and more adult support, including in-class learning support at junior infant level, especially in designated disadvantaged schools.[33]

It is logical to direct learning support at the foundations of learning and to help children who have difficulty with pre-number concepts rather than wait for children to develop difficulties later on in school. The caseloads of learning support teachers in designated disadvantaged schools tend to be dominated by children who need support for literacy, leaving little time for children who need learning support in mathematics. In non-designated disadvantaged schools, a lower incidence of serious literacy difficulties means that learning support in mathematics can be offered to a greater percentage of pupils. Thus, there is a fundamental inequality of access to learning support for pupils in designated disadvantaged schools in the area of mathematics.[34]

Early childhood education

There is a real need for the state to establish and operate a comprehensive system of education for children between the ages of three to five in Ireland. It has to be located in the DES, alongside the other strands of the education system.[35] Irish state investment in early years education is dramatically out-of-step with most other democratic states. The new ten-year social partnership framework agreement commits to the 'creation of 50,000 new childcare places, including 10,000 preschool and 5,000 afterschool places, as part of the €2.65b National Childcare Strategy 2006–2010'. Moreover, 'development of a national childcare training strategy' 'will aim to provide 17,000 childcare training places during 2006–2010, and include quality and training provisions of the National Childcare Investment Programme (NCIP)'.

The absence of an appropriate emphasis on children's oral language development is a serious concern with regard to the DEIS government strategy. The action plan puts no emphasis on a comprehensive approach to oral language development.[36] Rather, the one tangible provision relates to support from speech and language therapists. In tandem with support for the teaching of literacy, as part of the action plan, teachers need to be supported in developing the skills to

---

[33] Ibid.
[34] Ibid.
[35] See Donnelly, Chapter 9
[36] See McGough, Chapter 24

plan and to teach a language curriculum which is matched to the differentiated needs of the learners.[37]

A major concern in DEIS is the nature of the provision outlined for three-year-old children. In the action plan, DES is taking responsibility for providing an educational dimension within existing childcare services in disadvantaged communities. From a teaching and learning perspective, effective early intervention relates to the quality of curriculum and pedagogy and rests on an assumption of high levels of qualifications in programme providers. One of the central points in the discussion is the need to deliver on-going professional development to staff who are already starting from a high base in terms of qualifications. The lack of such supports has been regarded as a persistent problem, militating against programme effectiveness to date. The provisions for three-year-olds in DEIS present a wholly new kind of problem. Here the DES is planning to provide early intervention in settings that are unregulated in terms of staff qualifications, curriculum content and pedagogic practice.[38]

The existing provision in the unregulated early years sector does not meet requirements for effective intervention in a range of critical areas. The need for the provision of a range of training options so that critical conditions for quality can be met in the wider early years sector in Ireland is well documented. Indeed the *Preschools for Travellers: National Evaluation Report* (2003), which was conducted by the Department Inspectorate, recommends that the DES should ensure the provision of accredited courses leading to a recognised minimum qualification for personnel working in this preschool service.

In collaboration with *Early Start* teachers and childcare workers, draft curriculum guidelines have been developed and a model of in-class support focusing on curriculum and pedagogy has been designed and piloted in a number of *Early Start* centres (ERC, 1998). This model has been developed to include in-class support as part of induction for new teachers and child-care workers. Further development of this model and its full extension to the entire group of early start classes, as a model of on-going support, is recommended.[39] The need for parent partnership and collaboration in the design and implementation of programmes is essential.

Traveller education

In setting out its position on the rights of the child, the *Recommendations for a Traveller Education Strategy 2006–2010* (DES, 2006) refers to the UN Convention on the Rights of the Child (1989) which compels authorities to take account of 'their needs and their culture in all aspects of education'. The DES intends that, within five years, Traveller children should have access to inclusive,

[37] Ibid.
[38] Ibid.
[39] Ibid.

well-resourced and well-managed provision, with appropriately trained professionals, which will include representatives from the Traveller community, in quality premises. It calls for expansion in the number of preschools even beyond the proposed 150 DEIS sites. There is a danger implicit in this strategy: that by seeking to replace an imperfect but valuable current provision with an improved but currently non-existent aspiration it could instead lead to the loss of expertise and experience built up in the Traveller preschools.[40] The phasing out of Traveller preschools in the absence of sufficient places in high-quality accessible, integrated and inclusive settings may lead to some Traveller children not gaining access to culturally appropriate preschool places. The goal of integration could be more readily achieved by enabling Traveller preschools to implement inclusive, integrated enrolment policies. This would avoid much of the disruption likely to arise from attempts to amalgamate services with different histories, structures, staffing arrangements and funding mechanisms. The proposed policy of amalgamation puts at risk the parental support for preschool education that has been built up over many years.[41] The goal of the new Social Partnership Agreement 2006–2010 to create 10,000 preschool places will need to encompass not only high levels of planning in any proposed amalgamation, but also high levels of consultation with the current Traveller preschools and Travellers at a range of local levels, to ensure amalgamation is not simply assimilation.

The DES proposal that intercultural materials and resources should be developed in consultation with Traveller childcare workers and with children also needs to include the expertise of parents and teachers, along with other community expertise which might be drawn on for such work. Existing criticisms of the Civic, Social and Political Education (CSPE) programme have tended to emphasise that the subject is only offered at Junior Certificate level and that it does not allow for a wide range of issues to be covered in any depth. More attention needs to be focused on the substantive content of the knowledge that students are believed to acquire about Travellers and racial minorities in Ireland more generally. Despite recent curricular efforts to incorporate knowledge about various minority groups in Irish society with a view to enhancing understanding and appreciation for diversity, these efforts have often had the effect of legitimising negative reactions towards groups designated as racially or ethnically 'other' and reinforcing erroneous ideas about difference.[42]

Curricular justice extends far beyond 'add-on' approaches to the curriculum, which may further misrepresent and marginalise minority groups. It also eschews those perspectives which encourage the 'participation' of, and 'consultation' with, minority groups, including Travellers, about their views, wherein participation

---

[40] See Boyle, Chapter 22
[41] Ibid.
[42] See Bryan, Chapter 21

thus gets reduced to the level of simply asking or 'consulting' about their wants and needs, without them necessarily having any real influence on how related policy decisions are framed or enacted. A reconfiguration of the existing CPSE curriculum is needed so that it is reconstituted from the point of view of those who are most marginalised within society.[43]

Adult and community education

There are clear indications here that the separations that marked and marred education in the past are now being questioned and eroded. A clear example is the breaking down of the image of the school as a 'gated' premises in the local community. Parents tell stories of a time when they were locked out in the rain waiting for their children to be released to them while they stood outside the railings. However, the development of adult community education, the work of the Home School Community Liaison (HSCL) teachers, and the opening up of the school for afterschool activities, have all allowed many in local communities to see the school as theirs in a new way. Opening up the asset of a school building to the whole community in which it is located enables a new set of partnerships to be established. The growth and implementation of a model of 'community school' will call for an effective infrastructure, strong leadership and developed organisational skill on behalf of all those responsible for the different activities that take place at different times, from afterschool, to evening educational activities, to weekend use. This model has been developed in a number of places in the US and has been evaluated as contributing to educational inclusion in areas of poverty.

One of the key actions recommended by the Statutory Committee on Educational Disadvantage (2005) is to 'make the school a focal point of community education'. The Home School Community Liaison (HSCL) scheme plays a key role in bringing this to fruition. Benefits of the HSCL include the possibility of a more open and welcoming school environment, a reduction in the fear and intimidation of parents with histories of alienation from the school system compared with the pre-HSCL era, the positive impact on parents' self-confidence, a reduction in their sense of disempowerment when dealing with teachers, and the sense of community which can develop through the HSCL programmes. The potential of parental involvement with teachers in policy formation and participation in the HSCL local committee with principals and community bodies needs further exploration to be consistently achieved.[44] The emphasis on culturally relevant reading[45] and also mathematics materials[46] throughout this volume also offers scope for increased parental involvement.

---

[43] Ibid.
[44] See Mulkerrins, Chapter 12
[45] See Quinn, Chapter 15
[46] See Dooley and Corcoran, Chapter 19

It is essential that any future review of the HSCL scheme must include the voice of parents and community groups as well as children[47], and be conducted according to wider criteria than SMART (Specific, Measurable, Achievable, Relevant, Timed) outcomes.[48] Strategic planning is also needed so that the HSCL role can be outside school hours and can also be filled in future by parents from the community. It is timely to call for a review of employment practices across the education sector, allowing those who have had little opportunity to share the power and resources to work professionally within a system that is almost exclusively a middle-class preserve. The Children's Aid Society has developed and funded a highly successful model of parent empowerment in community schools in areas of New York City. Instead of parents being involved in their children's schooling only on the school's terms, the society has developed a parent involvement model that gives real power to parents and encourages parent advocacy efforts. As part of this model certain parents are professionally trained and paid as HSCL officers. Many of these coordinators themselves attended schools in the local communities in which they now work and this model of good practice regarding genuine partnership with parents needs to be incorporated within the Irish education system.

The action plan of the National Forum on Primary Education recommends the establishment of regional educational structures with real decision-making powers to ensure local accountability and a community approach to decision-making. This would include devolved budgets and be population-based. The current regional educational structures are more administrative than policy-making. It is essential to the integrity of local community development strategies that the National Adult Education Council includes representatives from grass-roots community-based projects. The White Paper on Adult Education (DES, 2000) presented an opportunity to put in place a body which was genuinely representative and which could have been an organic development.[49] The regional educational structures proposed by the National Forum action plan could, if implemented in full, serve as a template for an adult education council which would be representative, autonomous, flexible and inclusive. There is a clear need for an independent body to oversee and strategically support the development of adult and community education in this state.[50]

The need for continuity has emerged from a range of other areas including early childhood education and issues of transition from primary to post-primary. Continuity is also a key issue regarding funding for adult and community education as well as career development for staff working in this area. There is a

---

[47] See Mulkerrins, Chapter 12
[48] See Mulkerrins, Chapter 12; Downes, Chapter 6
[49] See Bane, Chapter 11
[50] Ibid.

need for stable, long-term, assured funding for adult and community education,[51] including women's community education,[52] against a background of clear though sufficiently broad evaluation criteria.[53]

The National Educational Welfare Board

A clear example of an opportunity to create a new practice of integration of services and to articulate protocols for service delivery to parents, children and young people of school-going age has arisen under the National Educational Welfare Act (2000). Under this legislation the National Educational Welfare Board (NEWB) (2002) was established to ensure that every child's right to receive an education is realised. Regular school attendance is a fundamental stepping stone towards securing educational qualifications and this in turn influences a young person's ability to access further education or training, where appropriate. The NEWB is the single national statutory agency with responsibility for implementing this legislation. In 2005, the first independent evidence emerged to show that the new legislation does in fact work. School attendance improves by 4 per cent in the areas where educational welfare officers are based. As an independent statutory agency, the NEWB must take leadership to put in place agreed protocols for an integrated service delivery in this whole area. Such leadership must recognise and affirm models of best practice among different practitioners in relation to school attendance, whether these are school or community-based practices. It is also necessary that the leadership of the NEWB and its responsibility in this whole area are recognised and that it is adequately funded.

While the NEWB has a responsibility to deliver a national service under the legislation, the Board is aware, and the data proves it correct, that those from lower economic backgrounds are more likely to miss school. There is ample evidence to demonstrate that school absenteeism leads to school dropout and often to a life of poor employment possibilities. The data collected by the NEWB, from the annual school returns, indicates that 84,000 children under the age of sixteen are absent from school for more than twenty days per year and close to 30,000 miss up to forty days. Given these statistics, it is now possible to accurately calculate the staffing needs of the Board if it is to meet its national responsibilities under legislation. The NEWB requires a staff of over 300, while at present there are only 94 employees, 83 of whom are involved in service delivery. Any commitment at policy level to tackle educational inequality requires full funding and legislation aimed at ensuring that all young people are assisted to attend school and realise their right to an education.

---

[51] Ibid.
[52] See Waters, Chapter 14
[53] See Downes, Chapter 6

The call by the DES for the integration of services is to be welcomed, and its challenge to articulate protocols that inform how different agencies can best serve children who are most in need of assistance, is to be affirmed. However, those directly involved have a sense that the emphasis on integration and the requirement for protocols have led to an unnecessary postponement of the appointment of much-needed staff. While the development of interagency cooperation is now an integral part of service delivery in local areas, the reality is that greater integration and clarification of protocols across services are highlighting the need for more, not less, staff. There is also a need for strong leadership to clarify who has ultimate responsibility for different service areas.

The premise that working together and communicating across services will allow the rationalisation of staff serving the most vulnerable in our society is false. For example, it is common knowledge that the NEWB has been blocked from appointing any new Education Welfare Officers (EWOs) for the past two years and has had to hand back part of its 2005 budget to DES because of an embargo on the appointment of staff and its need to ensure that all those working within educational disadvantage initiatives are cooperating in their work on school attendance. However, although protocols are now in place and interagency work respected, the latest annual returns from schools to the NEWB reveal that there is an urgent need to fully resource the work of the NEWB and to put in place the staff required to address, at a national level, the ongoing issue of non-attendance in Irish schools. Over 10 per cent of primary pupils and up to 20 per cent of post-primary students miss more than the legal limit of school days each year. Due to understaffing, seventy-three EWOs share a case load of 6,000 young people who have chronic difficulties in relation to school attendance.

It is interesting to note that the Rochford Report commissioned by the NEWB in 2002 to estimate staffing needs, recommends that if the national average of school absenteeism was 10 per cent at primary and 20 per cent at post-primary, then a staff of 360 would be required if the Board was to fulfil its legal requirement under the New Act (2000). The annual data collected and analysed by the NEWB makes the point clearly: this service urgently requires more staff. Children and young people who have difficulties with school attendance now and who are living their lives in the Ireland of 2007 will find no solace or consolation in the acceptance that this and other vital services in education will be funded incrementally and gradually. It is now and only now that their right to education can be fully delivered.

NEPS

The latest Social Partnership agreement, the ten-year framework agreement for 2006–2015, states that 'to help further address absenteeism, early school leaving, behavioural problems and special needs, an additional one hundred posts in total will be provided for the NEWB and The National Educational Psychological Service (NEPS) by 2009'. As well as more investment in the NEPS service so that psychologists have time to meet the goals of the NEPS policy documents, there is a clear need for more dialogue between NEPS and schools, together with families, as part of a future external review of NEPS. There is also a need for further consideration of the following issues:

- more solution-focused recommendations from NEPS for working with children who have been assessed
- more consistent strategies to accommodate the centrality of parental involvement with NEPS psychologists, including sustained follow-up programmes
- development of assessment tools for children from junior classes
- increased time to be allocated for psychologists to designated disadvantaged schools
- a more holistic approach to intervention that does not separate children's emotional needs from their learning needs, an approach that develops teachers' behaviour management strategies.[54]

Though there are clear advantages regarding the independence of assessments in having NEPS psychologists as external to the school staff, another level within a future NEPS could marry external psychologists with the resource of a psychologist attached to a cluster of schools, as in, for example, the HSCL scheme. Such an extra level to NEPS is suggested in order to meet most of these concerns.[55]

Transition and teacher–student relationships

The issue of a 'jolt in climate' between primary and post-primary through perceptions of being treated fairly or otherwise in school needs to move beyond a focus on the individual teacher or student, to a systems-level analysis.[56] It is a systems-level problem and so improvement requires a systems-level type of intervention at a national level with regard to teachers working on their conflict resolution strategies and their awareness of educational disadvantage at pre-service and in-service levels (Barnardos, 2006). Early school leavers often quote school-related issues as a reason for terminating their education. Hence, the social climate in schools, including relationships between teachers and students, has a strong role to play in students' educational outcomes.[57] The focus needs to move

---

[54] See Ryan and Downes, Chapter 30
[55] Ibid.
[56] See Downes, Maunsell and Ivers, Chapter 34
[57] See Darmody, Chapter 28

beyond attributing 'blame' to teachers or students to an examination of the systems-level problem and to the support of improvements at a systemic level, thus increasing skills to facilitate better communication and cooperation between second-level teachers and students in particular.[58]

Another systemic level issue is that the new revised curriculum at primary level helps to foster a more emotionally supportive school climate, for example, through circle time in Social, Personal and Health Education (SPHE), and emotional expression through drama – thus creating an increased 'clash of school cultures' between primary and post-primary level, which is still more subject-centred and less constructivist in its teaching methods.[59] A strategy between local primary and secondary schools needs to focus on continuity in the approach to SPHE. Pupil needs and expectations within a supportive climate at primary level need to be sustained at second level to minimise the culture 'shock' of acclimatisation. The openness of the primary-school environment may create expectations in pupils of an emotionally communicative and supportive environment at second level that in turn could lead to a heightened sense of disillusionment if this atmosphere is not sustained across the transition. There is a real onus on primary and secondary schools to work together to sustain continuity in approaches to SPHE and the broader school climate in practice, as well as through provision of social and emotional supports.

Transition, continuity and afterschool project supports

Continuity in afterschool clubs from primary to post-primary also needs recognition. The Educational Disadvantage Committee (2003) has recommended that school plans address 'key areas' such as extracurricular programmes and connection to youth service provision within the local area as well as transition from primary to post-primary. These two elements need to be firmly connected to each other so that a plan exists for continuity between extracurricular activities at primary and second level. This point has recently been reiterated in the document *Quality Development of Out of School Services: An Agenda for Development* (Downes, 2006) on behalf of the recently established QDOSS network.[60]

A feature of afterschool projects such as the Oasis project in Blanchardstown, Dublin, (see also Barnardos, 2006) is continuity between primary and postprimary students. It is arguable that going to the same afterschool project –

---

[58] See Downes, Maunsell and Ivers, Chapter 34; Darmody, Chapter 28; Lyons et al., Chapter 33
[59] See Downes, Maunsell and Ivers, Chapter 34
[60] QDOSS (Quality Development of Out of School Services) is a network to promote out-of-school services and includes the following member organisations: Barnardos; Border Counties Childcare Committee; Children's Research Centre, Trinity College Dublin; Educational Disadvantage Centre, St Patrick's College, Drumcondra; Foróige; Limerick Childcare Committee; Targeting Educational Disadvantage Project, Mary Immaculate College, Limerick; Youth Work Ireland.

which has links to both primary and secondary school – is even more important if the student is attending a different school from his/her peers and from those he/she was with in primary school.[61] For purposes of continuity of supports, as well as recognising that many significant life events happen for young people outside school and the school term, it is important that services are also available throughout the summer.

Emotional support and a mental-health strategy for education in contexts of socio-economic disadvantage

An important aspect of drug prevention programmes in the National Drugs Strategy 2001–2008 is to 'seek to strengthen resilience amongst young people in or out of school by fostering positive stable relationships with family or key community figures especially in the early years …' (p. 98). While afterschool projects have an important role to play regarding provision of social and emotional support, it is important to recognise the need for a further level of therapeutic intervention for children and youth experiencing a range of deep-rooted emotional problems. It is a remarkable contrast that Estonia, for example, has a counsellor in every secondary school, while the Irish secondary-school system does not have enough qualified counselling psychologists to serve as a key emotional support for adolescents at a crucial and vulnerable time in their lives. Afterschool projects cannot replace the need for multi-disciplinary teams offering psychological support for those most at risk, whether provision of that support is based in the school, community or both locations (see also Downes, 2004, for development of 'Familiscope', a multi-disciplinary team in the context of Ballyfermot, Dublin). Levels of suicide, binge drinking and substance abuse among the Irish teenage population are well documented and await a truly systemic response by the Irish state, such as the provision of school and community-based therapeutic support for teenagers. Such support is necessary across all social classes and essential in areas with high levels of social problems associated with socio-economic disadvantage.

Implementation of the SPHE curriculum needs to be viewed as one key dimension to a mental-health strategy for education in contexts of disadvantage. However, it is by no means the sole pillar of such a strategy. Other key pillars include implementation of systemic supports for the speech and language development of children, including professional development for teachers within areas of literacy, as well as family-level systemic supports in relation to the language development of their children. This is a mental-health issue, as limited linguistic capacity for expression detrimentally impacts upon social skills and emotional expression, as well as conflict-resolution skills. Other key pillars to a

---

[61] See Downes, Maunsell and Ivers, Chapter 34

mental-health strategy for education in contexts of disadvantage include state investment in services that provide early intervention for emotional support where the school can be one important site for referrals to therapeutic services in the community. For this to occur there needs to be close engagement and genuine collaboration between schools and community-based mental health and therapeutic services for young people – services particularly needed in socio-economically disadvantaged areas. Collaborative interaction between multi-disciplinary community-based mental health and therapeutic services and schools should develop in an integrated and coherent fashion following agreed protocols. This collaboration is pivotal to a mental-health strategy in education and would facilitate provision of support from community-based services to schools – especially secondary schools – in developing a positive, emotionally supportive school climate which is a key protective factor against early school leaving.

Transition and children with special needs in designated disadvantaged schools

Children with general learning difficulties can often have poor organisational skills, making it difficult for them to cope with the huge organisational changes in their school day at post-primary school. Coping with timetables, extra teachers, homework and moving around classes can make some students anxious. There is a need to examine the possibility of consistently transferring some primary-school practices into post-primary school for a period in first year, for example, mixed-ability teaching, a small group of teachers responsible for all subject areas, arranging a 'homebase' for first-years, etc.[62] This could also extend to visits from post-primary teachers to the primary school, especially for those children with special needs. This would also provide a post-primary teacher with the opportunity to get valuable information on individual students. Another recommendation is the appointment of a student liaison officer who would work for both the primary school and post-primary school and with this target group in particular. This person could help to prepare students in sixth class for the transition and would be a familiar person to support them once they reach post-primary school, thus adding an element of personnel continuity to the young person's overall school experience.[63]

Bullying

The dissemination of a range of good practice taking place across schools in Ireland with regard to bullying also needs to include a focus on dissemination

---

[62] See Maunsell, Barrett and Candon, Chapter 35
[63] Ibid.

within the school of beneficial preventative and intervention strategies. The peer mediation[64] and narrative[65] approaches highlighted in this volume also have much to offer. The following issues also need to be highlighted regarding teacher self-efficacy for intervening in bullying:[66]

- If teachers solely blame factors such as home background they are unlikely to intervene.
- A systemic focus invites examination of change to the school environment supporting and tolerating bullying.
- There is a need to go beyond labelling of children as 'bullies'.
- There is a need for more clarity in defining bullying, which includes events that may not simply be repeated incidents.
- Teachers need to view bullying as a child protection issue.

Pre-service teacher education

The need for school climate supports to minimise staff turnover in designated disadvantaged schools[67] was a point emphasised by the Monitoring Committee for the National Forum in its submission of priority recommendations from the Forum Action Plan to the Minister for Education and Science in 2005. It goes without saying that there is a clear need for pre-service training at both primary and second level to ensure that student teachers emerge with a sense of self-efficacy in teaching in designated disadvantaged areas. As already seen with regard to literacy[68] and numeracy[69] teaching, this requires site-specific work in designated disadvantaged schools. Some Colleges of Education already provide this for all students and this needs to be extended, not just at all Colleges of Education, but, most importantly, through the training provided for post-primary teachers at Higher Diploma (HDip) level (see also Barnardos, 2006). Teacher education in Ireland must include a compulsory module on educational disadvantage, as well as conflict resolution and behaviour management[70] in order to help teachers to fully prepare to cope with the multitude of classroom situations. The logic of this position may also require the extension of the duration of the HDip at post-primary level to accommodate the increasing complexity of the relational, cultural and methodological aspects of teaching in today's society. The National Forum recommended a compulsory teaching practice module in a designated disadvantaged school. The logic behind this

---

[64] See Murphy, Chapter 38
[65] See Hegarty, Chapter 37
[66] See Farrelly, Chapter 36
[67] See Morgan and Kitching, Chapter 31
[68] See Kennedy, Chapter 18
[69] See Dooley and Corcoran, Chapter 19
[70] See Downes, Maunsell and Ivers, Chapter 34; Lyons et al., Chapter 33

recommendation is the need for site-specific work in designated disadvantaged schools, whether as part of project-based small group work with children or as whole-class teaching experience. The principle of continuity emphasised throughout this conclusion across a range of themes also applies to pre-service level regarding practical experience on-site in a designated disadvantaged school setting – at both primary and post-primary levels.

An increased proportion of teachers from local communities coupled with increased pre-service and in-service training in the skills required for teaching in socio-economically disadvantaged areas are key factors in reducing teacher turnover. A pivotal issue is that of access to third-level generally and to the teaching profession for students from lower socio-economic backgrounds. There is a clear need for more teachers to be facilitated to emerge from the local community in many socio-economically disadvantaged areas. The benefits to pupils and students of local role models and the likelihood of less 'culture gaps' in communication between teachers and students cannot be overestimated. Currently there is a requirement of honours in the Irish language examination, along with 440 points in the Leaving Certificate for those who want to become primary school teachers. It is recommended that proficiency in the Irish language be a requirement at the end of the teacher training course and not a condition of entry.

Need for more strategic planning from local services for communities with high levels of international students

There is a clear need for a state strategy for engagement with the representatives of ethnic minorities in community affairs, including developing community leaders who represent the voices of their ethnic groups. Building on good practice already in existence at local levels, this needs to eventually result in representatives from local ethnic minorities (including more Travellers) attending accredited leader training. A logical extension of such training is outreach programmes targeting representatives from ethnic minority communities. Community leaders from a range of ethnic minority groups need to be facilitated in developing and participating in community-wide fora to articulate and resource the changing needs of their groups and encourage dialogue with other groups.

The need to involve parents more actively in their children's education is long recognised in the Irish context. The importance of parental involvement needs to be reiterated with regard to ethnic minority parents. There is a need to integrate the adult education and lifelong learning needs of ethnic minorities with the educational needs of their children; this integration will help facilitate increased parental involvement in their children's education. Such a strategy requires the active collaboration with ethnic minorities in the planning of short, medium and long-term interventions targeting the needs of adults and children.

Local services must be resourced to commit dedicated staff to liaise with targeted ethnic minority groups in areas with high levels of an immigrant population. This targeting would not be limited to programmes solely designed for ethnic minorities (e.g., English language programmes) but also for programmes that have a wider client group. This targeting would recognise that different ethnic groups may have different needs, while also recognising that members of the same ethnic group may also have very different needs. In other words, it is obvious that ethnic minorities (including refugees, asylum seekers) are not to be treated as a homogenous group.

Many local services need to set targets regarding employment of a significant proportion of staff who are from a range of ethnic minorities living in their area. There is a need for the employment of researchers from a range of local ethnic minority groups to interview ethnic minorities with little English in their native language in order to document their perceptions of their learning needs, emotional stresses, difficulties in acclimatisation to school and living in the local community, supports/strengths in acclimatisation to school and living in the local community, and employment needs. This research would examine the different needs of parents, youth, and secondary and primary students across the different ethnic groups. It would also serve as a key point of contact between local agencies and ethnic groups to help further facilitate and accelerate a process of developing community leaders from within these different groups.

All schools need to be assisted in developing procedures and fora for representative groups of a range of local ethnic minorities to be engaged in dialogue with the school regarding how best to meet their children's needs. School Completion Programme (SCP) committee members need to become more inclusive of representatives from sizeable local ethnic minority groups. The good practice of mentoring between Irish and international students, as well as with students from the Travelling community, which takes place in some schools, should be adopted at a systemic level. All of this is in addition to the key issue of providing adequate language support teachers for children in schools, with Sweden providing a model of good practice in this regard.

It is arguable that more strategic thinking is needed at a national level with regard to improving 'continuity' within the classroom, as part of a strategy for integrating international students as well as pupils with other needs. In other words, removing children from the classroom on a regular basis throughout the day can bring a disruption to the whole-class dynamic, to individual learning as well as monitoring of this learning.

A strategy needs to be further developed in conjunction with the Colleges of Education and institutions running HDip courses in secondary teaching to increase access of representatives from ethnic minorities to the teaching profession and to all local schools. In order to cope with the diversity of pupil population in class, teachers need sufficient preparation at both pre- and in-service level in dealing with disadvantage and intercultural issues (see also Barnardos, 2006).

There is a need for discourse surrounding ethnic minorities to recognise not only a view of integration that is broader than mere assimilation into Irish culture, but also to acknowledge the need for development of an understanding of minority rights in Irish culture. It is to be hoped that this broader discourse will also include recognition by the Irish state that the indigenous ethnic minority of Irish Travellers is a legal minority under international law.

A rights-based approach to disadvantage in education: educational disadvantage as a mental-health issue

While the UN Convention on the Rights of the Child gives vital momentum to a rights-based approach for children in Ireland, another important dimension of a rights-based approach should be given fuller recognition, especially in the context of educational disadvantage. This other pivotal dimension is the right of everyone to the enjoyment of the highest attainable standard of physical and mental health. This right is given legal foundation by a range of international instruments, including Article 25 (1) of the Universal Declaration of Human Rights (UDHR); Article 12 of the International Covenant on Economic, Social and Cultural Rights (ICESCR); Article 24 of the Convention on the Rights of the Child (CRC); Article 12 of the Convention on the Elimination of All Forms of Discrimination against Women (CEDAW), as well as the right to non-discrimination as reflected in Article 5 (e) (iv) of the International Convention on the Elimination of All Forms of Racial Discrimination (ICERD). The UN Special Rapporteur (2006) notes that the right to health, which most significantly includes mental health, is subject to progressive realisation and this requires development of indicators and benchmarks.

This amounts to a reiteration of the position of the Special Rapporteur in his 2005 report where he noted that progressive realisation means that 'all States are expected to be doing better in five years time than they are doing today and what is legally required of a developed state is of a higher standard than what is legally required of a less-developed country'.

The Special Rapporteur (2006) emphasises the importance of focusing on 'disadvantaged' individuals and communities in relation to the right to health:

> In general terms a human rights-based approach requires that special attention be given to disadvantaged individuals and communities; it requires the active and informed participation of individuals and communities in policy decisions that affect them; and it requires effective, transparent and accessible monitoring and

accountability mechanisms. The combined effect of these – and other features of a human rights-based approach – is to empower disadvantaged individuals and communities.

A key theme highlighted by the Special Rapporteur (2005, 2006) is the importance of community participation in health policymaking as 'vital' to the fulfilment of the right to health (see also Downes, 2007).

The UN Special Rapporteur is explicit on this point of access and participation of ethnic minority, disadvantaged and local groups as key issues regarding fulfilment of indicators of the right to health under the ICESCR:

> It must be accessible to all, not just the wealthy, but also those living in poverty; not just majority ethnic groups, but minorities and indigenous peoples, too … The health system has to be accessible to all disadvantaged individuals and communities. Further, it must be responsive to both national and local priorities … Inclusive, informed and active community participation is a vital element of the right to health.

The right to mental health offers a new legal and conceptual framework to understanding children's educational needs from a health-based perspective (see also Downes, 2006, on the need to bridge health and education needs in out-of-school services). It is well recognised that unemployment causes and reflects an increased likelihood of physical and mental health problems (e.g. Luft, 1978; Brenner, 1973; Berg and Hughes, 1979) and that self-esteem is positively associated with school achievement (Purkey, 1970; Brookover, Thomas and Paterson, 1964; Hay, Ashman and van Kraayenoord, 1997). Significantly, there is some evidence to suggest that early school leaving is itself a key factor detrimental to mental health. For example, Morgan (1998) cites Kaplan, Damphousse and Kaplan's (1994) North American study of 4,141 young people tested in seventh grade and once again as young adults which found a significant damaging effect of dropping out of high school on mental-health functioning as measured by a ten-item self-derogation scale, a nine-item anxiety scale, a six-item depression scale and a six-item scale designed to measure coping. This effect was also evident when controls were applied for psychological mental health as measured at seventh grade. Moreover, the significant damaging effect of dropping out of school was also evident even when controls were applied for gender, father's occupational status, and ethnic background. Significantly, the Irish National Drugs Strategy 2001–2008 links the issue of early school leaving and substance abuse. It is arguable that rates of early school leaving are relevant benchmarks with regard to the progressive realisation of the right of everyone to the enjoyment of the highest attainable standard of physical and mental health (Downes, 2007).

One concern with the National School Completion Programme is that the local flexibility and discretion does not give expression to rights-based services; they are more ad hoc interventions than systematic, timed and developmentally progressive interventions (see also Downes, Maunsell and Ivers, 2006, for other criticisms of ad hoc dimensions to School Completion Programmes in the context of Blanchardstown, Dublin, namely, with regard to referral structures which were not reaching the large majority of those pupils and students most alienated from the school system). Even if school completion programmes adopt a focus on structural, process and outcome indicators to evaluate progress regarding early school leaving, it is arguable that school completion programme committees are an intermediate phase to this process of development of interventions that are seen as best practice for contexts of educational disadvantage – and which will become key ingredients of a rights-based approach to the progressive implementation of services to improve young people's mental health. This rights-based approach has to combine the UN Convention on the Rights of the Child with the right of everyone to the enjoyment of the highest attainable standard of physical and mental health.

The publication of this book is timely as it coincides with the issuing of a number of government commitments to tackle poverty and social exclusion in our society into the future.[71] The government recognises that the multifaceted nature of poverty requires a coordinated multipolicy response. To this end it appointed the Office of Social Inclusion (OSI) to take responsibility for coordinating a single annual report indicating the achievements in implementing the various measures outlined.

Substantial investments are promised in a number of areas of educational need. Under DEIS, extra resources are committed to combat the effects of poverty in primary and secondary schools within areas designated as disadvantaged. Further resources are committed to Traveller education, and to improving literacy and numeracy in the whole population. For the first time the NEWB's work in implementing the National Educational Welfare Act (2000) is mentioned, and extra resources are promised for its work on tackling absenteeism. Also welcome are the expansion of the NEPS and an adequate resourcing in the area of special needs. Substantial monetary commitments to adult and community education are forecast.

All of these areas are addressed in this book; different authors cite how under-funding has frequently undermined their efforts in these very areas. This has been particularly difficult for educators and those they serve, especially as in recent years Ireland has achieved its greatest economic growth in the history of the state. The new emphasis in government publications of setting clear targets and allocating specified funds to achieving different goals, along with measuring

---

[71] The Partnership Agreement: Towards 2016; The National Development Plan: 2007–2013: Transforming Ireland; The National Plan for Social Inclusion: 2007–2013; The National Report on Strategies for Social Protection and Social Inclusion: EU 2007.

success, is to be welcomed. It can be anticipated that the Social Inclusion Unit of the DES will feed into the single annual report of the Office of Social Inclusion. This means that the Department will indicate each year how the different monies promised are being spent, how targets are being met, and how outcomes are being achieved. Those working on the ground will welcome such investment and transparency.

With strengthened resolve – working together – we will move 'beyond educational disadvantage'.

References

Barnardos (2006) *Make the Grade*, Dublin: Barnardos

Berg, I. and Hughes, M. (1979) 'Economic Consequences and the Entangling Web of Pathologies: An Esquisse' in Ferman, L. A. and Gordus, J. P. (eds) *Mental Health and the Economy*, Kalmazoo, Mich: W. E. Upjohn Institute for Employment Research, pp. 15–62

Brenner, M. H. (1973) *Mental Illness and the Economy*, Cambridge, Mass.: Harvard University Press

Brookover, W., Thomas, S. and Paterson, A. (1964) 'Self-concept of ability and school achievement', *Sociology of Education*, 37, pp. 271–8

Cooper, B. and Dunne, M. (2000) *Assessing Children's Mathematical Knowledge: Social class, sex and problem solving*, Buckinghamshire: Open University Press

Department of Education and Science (2000) *Learning for Life*, White Paper on Adult Education, Dublin: DES

Department of Education and Science (2003) *Preschools for Travellers: National Evaluation Report*, Dublin: DES

Department of Education and Science (2005) *DEIS: Delivering Equality of Opportunity in Schools – An Action Plan for Educational Inclusion*, Dublin: DES

Department of Education and Science (2006) *Recommendations for a Traveller Education Strategy 2006–2010*, Joint Working Group on Traveller Education, Dublin: DES

Department of Education and Science Inspectorate (2005) *Literacy and Numeracy in Disadvantaged Schools (LANDS)*, Dublin: DES

Department of Justice, Equality and Law Reform (2006) *Report of the High Level Group on Traveller Issues*, Dublin: DJELR

Downes, P. (2004) *Psychological Support Services for Ballyfermot: Present and Future*, Ballyfermot: URBAN

Downes, P. (2006) *Quality Development of Out of School Services: An Agenda for Development*, Dublin: QDOSS

Downes, P. (2007, forthcoming) 'Intravenous drug use and HIV in Estonia: Socio-economic integration and development of indicators regarding the right to health for its Russian-speaking population', *Liverpool Law Review*, Special Issue on Historical and Contemporary Legal Issues on HIV/AIDS, vol. 2

Downes, P., Maunsell, C and Ivers, J. (2006) *A holistic approach to early school leaving and school retention in Blanchardstown: Current issues and future steps for services and schools*, Dublin: Blanchardstown Area Partnership

Educational Disadvantage Committee (2003) 'A more integrated and effective delivery of school-based educational inclusion measures', submission to the Minister for Education and Science

Educational Disadvantage Committee (2005) *Moving Beyond Educational Disadvantage 2002–2005*, Dublin: DES

Educational Research Centre (1998) *Early Start Preschool Programme: Final Evaluation Report to the Department of Education and Science*, Dublin: ERC

Eivers, E., Shiel, G. and Shortt, F. (2004) *Reading Literacy in Disadvantaged Primary Schools*, Dublin: Educational Research Centre

Hay, I., Ashman, A. and van Kraayenoord, C. (1997) 'Investigating the influence of achievement on self-concept using an intra-class design and a comparison of PASS and the SDQ-1 self-concept tests', *British Journal of Educational Psychology*, 67, pp. 311–21

Kaplan, D. D., Damphousse, J. R. and Kaplan, H. B. (1994) 'Mental health implications of not graduating from high school', *Journal of Experimental Education*, 62, pp. 105–123

Lodge, A. and Lynch, K. (2004) *Diversity at School*, IPA: Dublin

Luft, H. S. (1978) *Poverty and health: Economic causes and consequences of health problems*, Cambridge, Mass.: Ballinger Publishing Co.

Morgan, M. (1998) 'Early school leaving interventions: International comparisons' in *Educational Disadvantage and Early School Leaving*, Dublin: Combat Poverty Agency

National Council for Curriculum and Assessment (1999) *Primary School Curriculum*, Dublin NCCA

National Drugs Strategy 2001–2008 (2001) *Building on Experience*, Dublin: Department of Tourism, Sport and Recreation

Piaget, J. (1952) *The Child's Conception of Number*, London: Routledge and Kegan Paul

Purkey, W. (1970) 'Self-perceptions of pupils in an experimental elementary school', *Elementary School Journal*, 71, pp. 166–71

Statutory Committee on Educational Disadvantage (2005) *Moving Beyond Educational Disadvantage*, Dublin: DES

United Nations Economic and Social Council (2005) *Report submitted by the Special Rapporteur on the right of everyone to the highest attainable standard of physical and mental health*, Paul Hunt, Mission to Romania, Commission on Human Rights, Economic, Social and Cultural Rights (21 February 2005) United Nations Economic and Social Council (2006) Commission on Human Rights Economic, Social and Cultural Rights, *Report of the Special Rapporteur on the right of everyone to the enjoyment of the highest attainable standard of physical and mental health* (3 March 2006)

Index

The suffix 'f' following a page locater indicates a figure, 'n' indicates a footnote and 't' a table.